# RESEARCH HANDBOOK ON DIGITAL STRATEGY

T0317559

# Research Handbook on Digital Strategy

*Edited by*

Carmelo Cennamo

*Professor of Strategy and Entrepreneurship, Copenhagen Business School, Denmark and Affiliate Professor of Digital Transformation, SDA Bocconi School of Management, Italy*

Giovanni Battista Dagnino

*Chair of Management and Professor of Digital Strategy, University of Rome LUMSA, Italy*

Feng Zhu

*Professor of Business Administration, Harvard Business School, USA*

**EE** Edward **Elgar**
PUBLISHING

Cheltenham, UK • Northampton, MA, USA

Published by
Edward Elgar Publishing Limited
The Lypiatts
15 Lansdown Road
Cheltenham
Glos GL50 2JA
UK

Edward Elgar Publishing, Inc.
William Pratt House
9 Dewey Court
Northampton
Massachusetts 01060
USA

Paperback edition 2024

A catalogue record for this book
is available from the British Library

Library of Congress Control Number: 2023933750

This book is available electronically in the **Elgar**online
Business subject collection
http://dx.doi.org/10.4337/9781800378902

ISBN 978 1 80037 889 6 (cased)
ISBN 978 1 80037 890 2 (eBook)
ISBN 978 1 0353 4446 8 (paperback)

Printed and bound by CPI Group (UK) Ltd, Croydon, CR0 4YY

# Contents

# Contributors

**Aleksi Aaltonen**, Temple University, USA

**Sungu Ahn**, Bayes Business School, UK

**Cristina Alaimo**, LUISS University, Italy

**Paolo Aversa**, Bayes Business School, UK

**Charles Baden-Fuller**, Bayes Business School, UK

**Yongjian Bao**, University of Lethbridge, Canada

**Kevin J. Boudreau**, Northeastern University, USA

**Francesco Burelli**, INSEAD, France

**Francesca Cabiddu**, University of Cagliari, Italy

**Carmelo Cennamo**, Copenhagen Business School, Denmark, and SDA Bocconi, Italy

**Panos Constantinides**, Manchester University, UK

**Ioanna Constantiou**, Copenhagen Business School, Denmark

**Giovanni Battista Dagnino**, University of Rome LUMSA, Italy

**Alberto Di Minin**, Sant'Anna School of Advanced Studies, Pisa, Italy

**Giulio Ferrigno**, Catholic University of the Sacred Heart, Milan, Italy

**Igor Filatotchev**, King's Business School London, UK

**Nathan Furr**, INSEAD, France

**Oksana Gerwe**, Brunel Business School, UK

**Werner H. Hoffmann**, WU Vienna, Austria

**Thomas Huber**, ESSEC Business School, France

**Francesca Hueller**, Bayes Business School, UK

**Lars Bo Jeppesen**, Copenhagen Business School, Denmark

**Kimmo Karhu**, Aalto University, Finland

**Niloofar Kazemargi**, LUISS University, Italy

**Pantelis Koutroumpis**, Oxford University, UK

**Thomas Kude**, ESSEC Business School, France

**Guglielmo La Bruna**, University of Rome LUMSA, Italy

**Gianvito Lanzolla**, Bayes Business School, UK

**Aija Leiponen**, Cornell University, USA

**Jan Lepoutre**, ESSEC Business School, France

**Feng Li**, Bayes Business School, UK

**Anoop Madhok**, York University, Canada

**Julien Malaurent**, ESSEC Business School, France

**Milan Miric**, Marshall Business School, University Southern California, USA

**Ludovica Moi**, University of Cagliari, Italy

**Ramya K. Murthy**, York University, Canada

**Oleksiy Osiyevskyy**, University of Calgary, Canada

**Per Egil Pedersen**, University of South-Eastern Norway, Norway

**Danilo Pesce**, Politechnic of Turin, UK

**Andrea Prencipe**, LUISS University, Italy

**Yanina Rashkova**, University of Cagliari, Italy

**Richard Reinsberg**, University of South-Eastern Norway, Norway

**Georg Reischauer**, WU Vienna, Austria

**Paavo Ritala**, LUT School of Business and Management, LUT University, Finland

**Andrew Shipilov**, INSEAD, France

**Sophia Shtepa**, University of Calgary, Canada

**Rosario Silva**, IE Business School, Spain

**Birgit A.A. Solem**, University of South-Eastern Norway, Norway

**Paolo Spagnoletti**, LUISS University, Italy

**Llewellyn D.W. Thomas**, IESE Business School, Spain

**Christopher Tucci**, Imperial College Business School, UK

**Stephan von Delft**, University of Glasgow, UK

**Yang Zhao**, Aston University, UK

**Feng Zhu**, Harvard Business School, USA

# Introduction: digital strategy – linear evolution or paradigm shift?

*Carmelo Cennamo, Giovanni Battista Dagnino and Feng Zhu*

Digital has become a pervasive aspect of the economy, with digital transformation occurring in an ever-increasing number of sectors, to the point that the digital-based economy will soon become the new normal (Adner et al., 2019; Cennamo et al., 2020; Dagnino & Resciniti, 2021). Concepts such as big data, artificial intelligence (AI), blockchain, platforms, or digital ecosystems, to name a few of the recent emerging trends that digital has brought along, have entered the business vocabulary, captivated the attention of scholars and practitioners alike, and are now at the center of every company's strategic thinking. It is no wonder that in recent years we have witnessed the rising excitement and the growing enthusiasm, at times even the frenzy, about these new phenomena, on the grounds of the pressing demands on managers to deal with the new reality and on academics to understand these phenomena.

Enthusiasts and advocates of the digital revolution would submit that digital transformation changes everything, from product design to how value is built and captured in the market. In some cases, particularly when a product's value is derived from connecting it with and integrating it into other products that form an integral part of ecosystems or when it is delivered through platform marketplaces (Cusumano et al., 2019a), the product's relevant market and the logic of competition themselves change drastically. So does the required strategy to effectively create and capture value in this new context (Adner & Lieberman, 2021; Cennamo, 2021). Accordingly, existing strategy frameworks developed for traditional markets are not applicable to the new digital context. Digital strategy thus involves a sufficiently substantive break with the economics and the competitive and cooperative logics (see Cennamo, 2021; Cozzolino et al., 2021) that have characterized the (traditional) economy so far, to represent a paradigm shift. Thus, it requires formulating the new (departing) assumptions, logics, and mechanisms of this new digital strategy research field. As Volberda et al. (2021) put it: "with these advances in digital technology, the very nature of strategy is changing".

Others might argue that there is "nothing new under the sun" about digital strategy. It is just "dressing up" the competitive context in which firms operate, but operating effectively in such a context and gaining competitive advantage would "not require a radically new approach to business. It requires building on the proven principles of effective strategy" (Porter, 2001, p. 64). In this sense, digital strategy represents just a *linear* evolution along the existing knowledge paradigm(s) of the strategy field.

To help shed light on how digital strategy relates to or differs from traditional strategy, we embarked on this *Handbook* project. We believe that with the rapid intensification and the inescapable consolidation of the key issues of the digital transformation of organizations, markets, and sectors, the time has come to produce a wide-ranging book about current research on digital strategy. Simultaneously, the inception of the digital age, with all its multiple remarkable fallouts, contributes to making the received body of strategy theories and tools (Andrews, 1971; Porter, 1985) progressively less adequate. It also makes it increasingly less enlightening to interpret the expanded and fast-changing digitally grounded realities in a helpful manner. For this reason, we feel the urgent need to take stock of the advancements made in the last three to four years to develop novel and extended knowledge that is in turn capable of explaining the new digital realities by leveraging existing strategy theories and tools and cultivating new ones. As such, our endeavor turns into a wonderful opportunity to encapsulate in one comprehensive volume the state of the art of a rapidly emerging research field and ruminate on its most important current and future developments.

In this chapter, we start by explaining the reasons why the current digital age has triggered the inception of novel business settings and organizations that are extremely different from those that have previously characterized the industrial age (Birkinshaw, 2018). Second, we define what digital strategy is and explain how it matters to competition. Third, we highlight a few themes from this book's chapters that illustrate how digital strategy is different from traditional strategy. Finally, we outline the structure of this *Handbook*.

## WHAT IS NEW IN THE DIGITAL AGE?

We know that we live in the digital age. Although the term is frequently used, there is little or no real consensus on its ultimate meaning. Therefore, we ask, what is the digital age? How can we define it? The digital age is a period in history that is clearly epitomized by the advent and affirmation of the electronic processing and sharing of data at a magnitude and speed that in no way we have seen before. The digital age is enabled by the emergence and adoption of four key technologies (Menz et al., 2021): computer hardware, software applications, internet and mobile communications, and AI, especially when tied to machine learning and deep learning.

The relentless adoption of these technologies, which in the last couple of years has been vastly accelerated by the global outbreak of COVID-19 and its related lockdowns in several regions of the world, has led to a massive shift in how we, as individuals, interact with one another and live our everyday life (Autio et al., 2021). In fact, the combined effects of these four key technologies have driven an unexpected dramatic compression in the cost of producing, searching, amassing, storing, analyzing, and sharing data. This condition occurs, at least for a good portion, because the use of the forceful technologies indicated above makes the fixed costs of producing, storing, and using data exponentially lower than they were in the past. Concurrently, the marginal costs of sharing data become infinitesimally low. This condition, which can be described as the one stemming from replicator dynamics or economies,[1] transcends even what Shapiro and Varian (1999) call the "economic principles of information". Shapiro and Varian suggest that, while the fixed costs of producing data may be high, the costs of using them may be much smaller. The marginal costs of sharing information may be low and declining (Menz et al., 2021). Accordingly, in the digital age, firms and organizations of all kinds face an extremely strong incentive to increase their market shares, especially by means of developing and exploiting network effects (Afuah, 2013; Boudreau et al., 2021; Katz & Shapiro, 1994) and big data effects.

One of the major effects of big data on businesses is that their dependence on the internet will increase; so will the amount of the data generated by the rapid development and evolution of technology. Big data enable firms and organizations to make smarter and faster decisions. Big data analytics also allow businesses to improve their operations and efficiency, explore other new waves of big data use opportunities, and eventually exploit new sources of competitive advantage, including superior learning about the business environment and customer needs, as well as the ability to act faster on it and seize opportunities through new complementarities (Alaimo & Aaltonen; Aversa & Hueller; Ritala & Karhu; Kazemargi et al.; Thomas et al., all in this volume).

These new possibilities of developing and exploiting network effects and data-driven learning and organizing bear the potential to generate new ways of creating and capturing value, and of stretching and redefining the traditional boundaries of the (single) firm that are leaning toward more decentralized models of value creation (albeit generally tightly coordinated under the governance of a hub firm), such as digital platforms (Cennamo, 2021) and ecosystems (Adner, 2017; Jacobides et al., 2018).

Digitally born (or sometimes digitally transformed) firms usually reach an efficient scale and size that are comparatively and impressively much larger vis-à-vis industrial-age firms operating in a traditional physical infrastructure. For instance, the China-based firm Alibaba has spawned a massive shift from wholesale to consumer markets, as well as in financial services by operating its gigantic financial arm, called the Ant Group. For this reason, the traditional way of strategizing and the extant strategy tools appear today as increasingly *not* exhibiting a great fit to the new environments of the digital age as they are inexorably misaligned with the fast-changing new needs and requirements. By activating strong network effects and data-learning effects, the digitally driven, low-variable cost structures of digital firms and organizations, platforms (Cennamo, 2021), and ecosystems (Adner, 2017; Jacobides et al., 2018) become capable of driving a change in the nature of competition and, consequently, in the cooperative and competitive logics and strategies that firms employ to gain an edge over competitors. In turn, this requires dramatic changes in the received paraphernalia of strategic thinking, theories and approaches, methods, and tools (see Leiblein & Reuer, 2020). In a nutshell, we need new methods, tools, and conceptualizations to interpret properly and understand better the moving target of the digital world. This is a more polarized view vis-à-vis the pre-pandemic one of Adner et al. (2019, p. 254), who earlier deemed that while digitalization "does not require us to abandon the basic conceptualizations of the economic phenomena we are familiar with" (i.e., transaction cost, bounded rationality, and industry analysis), it is concurrently essential to acknowledge the necessity of forging "new additional tools and conceptualizations".

## WHAT IS DIGITAL STRATEGY? WHY IS IT IMPORTANT?

Grappling with the concept of digital strategy while the underlying field of inquiry is in its genesis and scattered around different topics and foci is all but easy. The diversity of perspectives, levels of analysis, and objects of focus (Durand et al., 2017) is also evident in the contributions to this *Handbook*. These range from the consideration of specific digital technologies (e.g., platforms, ecosystems, business models, coopetition, AI, cloud computing, digital competition, digital convergence, open-source governance, open innovation, big data analytics) and their properties and effects to the strategic challenges and new set of tradeoffs that companies face while dealing with these technologies and digital more generally, as well as how those affect their performance.

Examining these perspectives from this angle, compared with traditional strategy (Grant, 2010; Rumelt et al., 1994), the concept of digital strategy appears multifaceted and multilevel.

It encompasses the different aspects of a firm's capacity to create as well as capture value *by means of* digital tools and/or *in* digitally enabled operating contexts (Acemoglu et al., 2020). However, and somewhat unique compared with traditional strategy, digital strategy is also about the context itself; that is, the deliberate strategic choices implemented by a (set of) firm(s) to change the structure of the economic relationships in which it is (they are) embedded in a way that serves its (their) own strategic objectives and helps it (them) shape and control the customer journey to a greater extent. Instead of taking the market and the industry as the given context defining the battlefield, with the strategy being about the choices to win in such a context, digital strategy is also, and especially so, about the strategic choices to redesign the market space and rewire the linkages along the value chain that entirely redefine the market and industry boundaries. In other words, digital strategy entails *changing the competition game* and how value is created in the first place. In this sense, digital strategy is inherently disruptive (Adner & Lieberman 2021; Cennamo et al., 2022) since it is unremittingly devoted to changing the rules of the game, whether in relation to how value is created or how it is captured within the new economic structure. Firms operating in digital markets need to continuously search for new technological, organizational, and strategic solutions to face these new intensified competitive dynamics (Dagnino et al., 2021). In fact, the burgeoning literature on platform and ecosystem strategy is all about how digital platforms and their associated ecosystems change the rules of the game and how firms can leverage them to redesign and redefine the competitive space (Cusumano et al., 2019b). In this sense, digital strategy is increasingly a "science of design", whose primary study's object is the design of new architectures of value that redefine the ways that value is created, delivered, and captured (Cennamo et al., 2022). In this regard, digital strategy is foundationally multilevel (e.g., Cennamo et al., 2020; Dąbrowska et al., 2022), involving the design of digital technologies and related processes (micro-level); the organizational boundaries and value-creation/value-capture mechanisms leveraging those technologies (macro-level); and the enlarged system of value, the value architecture, spanning multiple organizations, markets, and sectors that digital technologies empower (meso-level).

If we would, prima facie, attempt to capture this multifaceted and multilevel concept in a definition, we could define digital strategy as the design of a firm's operating model using digital technologies to transform its business model (i.e., how it creates and captures value) and/or the architecture of the value in which the firm is embedded.

The adoption of digital strategy has changed the nature of competition, thereby affecting in depth the fundamental way in which firms compete in digital markets (Cennamo, 2021; Cennamo et al., 2020). As maintained by Cennamo (2021), "with value shifting increasingly from a standalone product to platform systems, product market boundaries are no longer relevant for defining the type and intensity of competition and identifying relevant competitors. [...] the competitive advantage of a firm increasingly depends on platform competition" (p. 266). Platform competition is relevant because it shifts emphasis from product competition and value capture in well-defined product markets to competition between alternative market(place)s spanning multiple product markets and ways to create greater value (consumption benefits) for the customer, often by linking one's own offering value to somebody else's product offerings.

In this way, far from leveraging traditional static competitive models rooted in the industrial organization economics-based structure-conduct-performance paradigm (Bain, 1956; Mason, 1957; Porter, 1981), the new digital competition may reward competitive dynamic moves and countermoves (Giachetti & Dagnino, 2014; 2021), first-mover advantages (Lieberman

& Montgomery, 1998), and preemptive strategies (Wind, 1997) in markets that are able to reach one or more tipping points (Gladwell, 2002). However, and despite the initial mantra and winner-take-all characterizing these dynamics, we also witness changes of leadership and the emergence of new winners along with the incumbent Big Tech initial dominators of the digital landscape (the ascent of TikTok on the social media landscape being an iconic example), suggesting a far more dynamic domain than how it has been so far characterized by new conceptual models (Cennamo et al., 2022; Hanelt et al., 2021). We still have a long way to go to capture the intricacies of these dynamics.

## HOW IS DIGITAL STRATEGY DIFFERENT FROM TRADITIONAL STRATEGY?

Adner et al. (2019, p. 254) characterize the transition from traditional strategy to digital strategy as a shift from the "quantitative advances" that historically epitomized the digitally grounded advances (such as those of Moore's law and Metcalfe's law) "to a set of qualitative changes" that they essentially identify in three key processes of digital transformation (i.e., representation, connectivity, and aggregation). These "qualitative changes" are reflected well in the contributions to this volume. The chapters in this *Handbook* collectively illustrate many differences between digital strategy and traditional strategy. Rather than reiterating their main findings, we highlight a few key themes:

**Digital Strategy Affects Not Only the Scale of the Firm But Also Its Scope Choices**

Corporate strategy has been central to the strategy field from its inception (Andrews, 1971), dealing with diverse decisions at the corporate level on the optimal scale and scope of the business, including diversification, vertical integration, make-or-buy decisions, mergers and acquisitions, and strategic alliances. Digital challenges many of the underlying assumptions in extant research. For instance, regarding scope choices, what is related or unrelated is no longer a matter of product-level synergies, often presumed from belonging to the same or similar product markets and sectors. Complementarities at the digital technology level that support those products or related digital capabilities that can be redeployed in yet distinct markets and domains affect the scope of a firm in totally different ways. Moreover, the multiple affordances that digital technologies provide allow the organization to not only optimize its scale and operations but also expand into new areas of business and even explore new business models (Lanzolla et al., 2018). Digital offers new opportunities to expand the set of business models' archetypes; it also presents firms with new challenges to revisit, upgrade, or entirely redesign their business model(s) to remain competitive in the digital environment (D'Aveni, 2013). Contributions to this volume highlight these aspects.

In Chapter 1, Aversa and Hueller explore how digital diversification changes the traditional cost–benefit drivers in traditional diversification and how the relation between relatedness and performance shifts from a classic inverted U-shape curve in traditional diversification to an S-shaped curve in digital diversification, which increasingly favors less related diversification. They distinguish between supply-side versus demand-side and product versus business model digital diversification. They also discuss how mapping a company's digital diversification strategy across these two key dimensions helps in understanding the overall strategic stance of the company in the competitive landscape.

In Chapter 7, Murthy and Madhok discuss how the scope choices around the digital platform helps the platform provider manage uncertainties in value co-creation by attracting the right set of complementors and fostering a predictable set of complements. They conceptualize platform scope as encompassing three elements: platform technology, sponsor, and market scope. They maintain that platform scope choices signal value co-creation opportunities, define complementors' access to shared resources for co-creation, shape the platform provider's latitude to govern the ecosystem, and define the market identity of the platform ecosystem. Therefore, compared with traditional corporate scope decisions that focus on the optimal internal system configuration, platform scope choices relate largely to the external system of value encompassing third-party firms in the attempt to design and control an interfirm organizational form that will allow the corporation to influence such a value system and thus create complementarities from which it can benefit.

In Chapter 8, Shipilov, Furr, and Burelli focus specifically on the different types of interfirm structures, proposing three archetypes of ecosystems: centralized, adaptive, and decentralized. Building on insights from the graph theory, they propose a new tool, the ecosystem canvas, to help design the ecosystem by exploring various possible configurations and business models. This tool helps managers understand how ecosystems differ from other mechanisms through which the firm manages its interdependencies with the external environment. Central to the ecosystem design is the customer journey, understood as a sequence of activities, transactions, and experiences that the ecosystem as a whole (as opposed to a sole firm's offerings) will deliver to its customers. Thus, in contrast to the traditional business model design that focuses only on a firm's core offerings, the ecosystem canvas is believed to help in developing the configuration of the activities that go beyond a firm's boundaries and involve other firms' complementary offerings and business models.

In Chapter 2, Moi, Rashkova, and Cabiddu emphasize the importance of strategic agility for organizations to innovate their digital business models across three intertwining dimensions – the business model's content, structure, and governance – to adapt to changing market conditions. This contention seems pretty well aligned with Ritala et al. (2021), who encouraged the building of digitally agile firms and organizations.

In Chapter 3, von Delft and Zhao consider the creation of new digital business models along the continuum between two polar modes: innovation (introducing new activities, and/or linking activities in novel ways, and/or creating new ways of governing activities) and imitation (borrowing certain ingredients from another business model). They define a digital business model as "the architecture of the value creation, delivery, and capture mechanisms of a firm, embodied in or enabled by digital technologies" and discuss different types of strategies to craft digital business models that fall within the innovation–imitation spectrum.

In Chapter 5, Ahn and Baden-Fuller focus on some key forces that influenced the framing of business model choices of the fourteen most important firms in the global messenger industry from 1998 to 2018. They are particularly interested in why a subset of firms, which were late entrants to the business, adopted a different business model approach that successfully challenged the leading US firms in their domestic markets. In their analysis, the authors show how cognitive motivations played a key role, challenging the idea that optimal business model templates and configurations fit into specific digital domains. The authors propose that managers and their cognitive ability can still play a major role in designing alternative value configurations and in challenging incumbents by "changing the rules of the game" through new business models.

In Chapter 4, Lanzolla, Pesce, and Tucci take a step back in the process and focus on the different types of digitization and the interactions among the digitized units. Their conceptual development reveals how digitization of physical objects is a matter of degree and may range from full to partial digitization. This choice will likely depend on contextual factors at the firm level (the intended strategic objective) and at the level of the external environment and can rest on different logics driving value.

In Chapter 6, Boudreau, Jeppesen, and Miric consider the unique business model of "freemium" (offering both free and paid versions), which is a common approach that firms use to sell digital goods. Rather than representing mere product marketing tactics, they argue that freemium choices affect the whole organization as these involve complex product design decisions (i.e., what features are included with which products), as well as organizational design decisions (i.e., the cost structure of a business, separate versus joint management of free and pay customers, etc.). Accordingly, freemium strategies might not be viable options for all and might not lead to the expected benefits, even in the cases where freemium is a good option, *ex ante*. This might be because of what the authors call the "freemium death spiral", a pattern that may emerge when both the focal firm and its main competitors switch to freemium strategies; equilibrium can emerge where all firms observe lower revenues than what would otherwise occur.

**Data: The New Core, Valuable Asset (Together with Analytics)**

Firms traditionally leverage key assets they control internally (in the hierarchy) or indirectly via strategic contracting and alliances to build products and services and deliver the related value propositions to customers, as well as to capture greater value from their offerings.

In a broad sense, the term "assets" is used in strategy research to refer to both physical resources and the required knowledge and capabilities to use them (Amit & Schoemaker, 1993). Thus, a firm's human resources and technologies are conceived as core assets that it can leverage to gain competitive advantage. Competition in products is often influenced and won via competition in the underlying factor markets for those core assets (Markman et al., 2009). Strategy scholars distinguish between core and complementary assets; for instance, Teece (1986, p. 288) defines core assets as those directly relating to the core product or service, whereas complementary assets are those supporting the value delivery of the core assets in the marketplace (e.g., marketing or after-sales support). They still refer to people or technologies types of assets, related to production processes upstream (e.g., Kapoor & Furr, 2015) or distribution channels downstream (e.g., Roy & Cohen, 2017) in the firm's value chain. However, with the advent of digital, what is complementary in a traditional value chain may become the core building block in the new, redesigned value architecture market for instance, due to digital platforms leveraging the flow of data between firms and end users to structure new interactions (Alaimo et al., 2020; Cennamo et al., 2022). Data also become increasingly important to upend a firm's ability to create and deliver value to its customers and enhance its competitive positioning in the evolving competitive landscape (e.g., Krakowski et al., 2022; Zhu & Liu, 2018). A dataset thus becomes a new critical asset that firms can use as a key input resource *and* medium to build value (see, for example, Alaimo & Aaltonen, this volume). Different contributions to this volume provide information on these aspects and highlight the key strategic levers, as well as tradeoffs, that firms face when building and managing this new class of asset.

In Chapter 13, Alaimo and Aaltonen challenge the emerging common view that perceives a larger volume of data, the so-called big data, as offering advantages to firms mainly because of their scale and scope. They argue that data are not just resources to be harvested and fed into business processes. In fact, as they advance, data do not exist as resources; businesses are the ones that turn data into strategic assets through their internal data production or as part of larger ecosystems structuring the entire data value chain. They view data as "carriers of potential meaning". Accordingly, data become valuable only when the organization meets certain technological and organizational conditions to act on the data's meaning and realize the potential value that this hints at. A dataset is both a resource that organizations use for strategizing and the medium through which they create value. This dual aspect of data has implications for how firms design their strategies to produce, use, and leverage data to create (and capture) value. For instance, the way that data are collected and produced becomes a new domain of strategic thinking and design, one that can be even more important than the focal strategy itself because data production is often tightly coupled with the kind of prediction and evaluation exercise needed to formulate and assess one's strategy validity. The authors present three characteristics of digital data production – heterogeneous, fast, and unbundled – and discuss the implications for strategizing in the context of two illustrative cases.

In Chapter 14, Thomas, Leiponen, and Koutroumpis consider the strategic challenges of building competitive advantage in the data economy and, in particular, the tension between value creation and appropriation in commercializing data products. They define data products as collections of data that are tradable. They also argue that value creation from data products depends on not only data quality but also, and more importantly, complementary data. In contrast, value capture depends on the ability to exclude others from using the data product and the complementary data. From an economic standpoint, they thus consider data as an intermediate input into a process of transformation. They discuss the data characteristics enhancing value creation and the business model implications for properly managing the tensions between creating value from data products and excluding others from appropriating such value.

In Chapter 15, Ritala and Karhu also conceptualize the value proceeding from data to the extent that "data complementarities" can be attained; that is, when data are combined and aggregated into actionable and meaningful goods, objects, and artifacts. They focus on the recombinatorial characteristic of data as the foundational element of data complementarities and consider how and at which level (e.g., internal to the firm versus interfirm) data recombination occurs and affects a firm's ability to capture value. They offer a multilevel model describing how value is captured from four types of data complementarity: internal (hierarchy), relational (bilateral contractual relationship), supermodular (platform ecosystem), and unbounded (data markets).

In Chapter 16, Kazemargi, Spagnoletti, Constantinides, and Prencipe focus on data control as a critical element of digital strategy in digital ecosystem contexts and examine how actors coordinate data control activities to co-create value. They define data control as the control over the data access, storage, and processing activities of different actors in relation to the digital strategies of each actor. Drawing on the case of the cloud-based GAIA-X ecosystem, they show that coordination starts by resolving data control bottlenecks in multilateral agreements before engaging in innovative activities that lead to value co-creation. They identify three domains of coordination to resolve data control bottlenecks: rules and policies, data security, and service platforms. Once coordination over these domains unfolds, the actors in the ecosystem can properly engage to more effectively co-specialize their resources and capabilities, and unlock value creation and innovation opportunities from cooperation. Data control coordination thus acts as a precursor to generating complementarities among ecosystem actors, a finding that bears important implications for data strategies, especially in the context of digital ecosystems.

## Digital Strategy Pushes Organizations to Focus on Resources Outside the Firms' Direct Control

Firms have always tried to influence the external environment in ways that would benefit their products and business processes. Traditionally, firms have used internal resources and assets under their own control to achieve their strategic objectives (see, for example, Jacobides et al., 2006, on how firms leverage internal assets to influence the industry architecture) or work on open innovation (e.g., Chesbrough et al., 2014; Masucci et al., 2020), showing how firms can share part of their internal assets with external firms to build complementary value and deliver more innovation. As firms now increasingly transform themselves into platform and ecosystem hubs or participate in ecosystems orchestrated by others, central to any organization's strategy design becomes the issue of how to connect to, orchestrate, and leverage resources within the ecosystem that reside outside a firm's direct control (Adner et al., 2019; Cennamo et al., 2020). Different contributions to this volume discuss distinct aspects of this strategic challenge, including the implications for how firms design competitive and cooperative strategies, how they create value in platform business models, and how they govern firm relationships with an ever-expanding set of loosely connected yet interdependent firms.

In Chapter 9, Gerwe and Silva discuss the peer-to-peer platform business as a new business model and strategic approach to source, direct, and control value co-created by platform end users. They categorize peer-to-peer platforms along three salient dimensions: the type of asset underlying the transaction, the mode of transaction, and whether monetary compensation to the peer-provider exists or not. They also discuss the key strategic choices for leveraging this business model, mainly in relation to attracting, matching to, and retaining users in the platform.

In Chapter 10, Reinsberg, Solem, and Pedersen discuss the different strategic logics for value creation of digital platform businesses, with a specific focus on transaction platforms; that is, those facilitating transactional exchanges between or among two or more groups of customers.

They present four fundamental value logics and explain how these are specific to platform business models compared with traditional pipeline business models. The common feature of all types of value logics is that the platform value increases with the size, scope, or quality of the resources residing outside the platform firm's direct control, but the digital platform somehow helps in coordination by structuring interactions with the (end and business) users controlling those resources.

In Chapter 11, Constantiou discusses the role of user-engagement strategies in social media platforms for value creation. A platform's user base is by now considered a critical external resource for creating and capturing value in digital, platform-mediated markets. However, Constantiou argues that effective platform management strategies must go beyond attracting new users and ensure that current users remain active and engaged with the platform in the long term. She conceptualizes user engagement as one's emotional, cognitive, and behavioral investment in a brand or a technology. In the specific case of social media platforms, user engagement manifests in users interacting and sharing content readily and voluntarily with others, as well as cognitively and emotionally bonding with the platform. Accordingly, user engagement goes beyond marketing tactics and involves the design of the core platform technology, for instance, regarding which technology features to introduce and how to structure and govern interactions among users. User-engagement strategies also have implications for how firms decide to compete. User engagement can be leveraged, for instance, to create hidden switching costs – that is, to increase user retention and lock the user into the platform services – or to build platform differentiation and escape winner-take-all dynamics with rival social media platforms.

In Chapter 12, Huber, Kude, Lepoutre, and Malaurent consider the broader spectrum of user interactions with the platform, as well as the range of social actions that business users, as a collective, might engage in to challenge some of the governance practices imposed by the platform owner and create a counterweight to the latter's relational power by joining forces and forming a movement. They distinguish among six types of collective actions and study how they become connected and evolve over time. Focusing on Apple's iOS ecosystem, they illustrate how a movement of third-party developers, who were initially disconnected and isolated, emerged and organized between the summer of 2016 and the summer of 2021, forcing Apple into changing some of its App Store rules. It also managed to influence regulatory initiatives in the European Union and the US.

In Chapter 17, Filatotchev and Lanzolla focus on the internal corporate governance system (i.e., the system governing a firm's internal relationships) to assess its validity in the era of digital transformation. While corporate governance has traditionally been based on a *closed-system* framework focused on aligning the interests of managers (agents) and shareholders (principals), the authors consider an *open-system* approach to governance as more effective in dealing with increased interdependencies among external stakeholders, firms, and resources ensuing from digital technology diffusion and use. They advance the concept of open-source governance to signal the shift to more shared, participatory governance of the corporation that relies more on strategic rather than financial controls in the firm's governance mechanism. They maintain that strategic controls deploy more informal systems of communication between managers and stakeholders and allow risk-management systems to include broader risks of de-legitimization. In this type of governance, reputational and trust considerations, rather than the market for corporate control, underpin external governance pressures on managers. Overall, open-source governance shifts the emphasis from the internally narrow focus of the agency perspective to the development of a system of interactions between the firm and its ecosystem.

In Chapter 18, Shtepa, Bao, and Osiyevskyy assess the microfoundational impact of information technologies, such as AI algorithms (e.g., machine learning) and big data, on the managerial decision-making process, thereby stressing their capability to enable automated and augmented rationality. Actually, according to the authors, AI systems lessen the managerial bounded rationality problem by moving from the satisfying mode to the optimizing mode in managerial decision making. Subsequently, they analyze the effect of AI in four specific domains of decision making: determination, design, deliberation, and discovery. The authors advance a microfoundational framework to examine the strategic impact of AI on organizational business models and the sources of competitive advantage.

In Chapter 19, Dagnino and La Bruna examine the strategic use of big data analytics by firms to grasp their applications in business practice and relevant effects on performance. They first illustrate the four main types of advanced analytics (AAs; i.e., descriptive analytics, predictive analytics, prescriptive analytics, and automated analytics) and the key factors driving the performance effects of AAs: Some sectors benefit more than others from using AAs. The information intensity of each sector influences AA effects on firm performance. Large firms are usually those that have more direct access to AA advantages vis-à-vis small and medium-sized enterprises (SMEs). They feature the main characteristics of the application of AAs in four relevant economic sectors (finance and insurance, manufacturing, healthcare, and logistics and supply chain) and discuss the strategic advantages and disadvantages stemming from the firms' adoption of AAs.

In Chapter 20, Reischauer and Hoffmann consider some of the implications of increased dependence on external resources for how firms design their cooperative and competitive strategies, particularly for how they handle coopetition – the simultaneous engagement in cooperation and competition with firms, ecosystems, or platforms. They introduce the concept of digital coopetition, which they define as the simultaneous and technologically embedded competition and cooperation among firms to create and capture value for one another. Digital coopetition thus differs from traditional coopetition in that firms' value creation and value capture are fundamentally embedded in digital technologies. This brings forth new opportunities for collaboration, but at the same time it also creates strong incentives for opportunistic efforts to leverage control over data, customer relationships, or both in order to gain advantage over the coopetitor. They lay out the firm-level conditions that give rise to digital coopetition and discuss the key aspects departing from traditional coopetition. For instance, in the digital context, coopetition occurs through standardized modes as opposed to bilateral contracting. This has implications in terms of the nature of the interplay, as well as the tensions, and how to manage them, which the authors discuss at the end of the chapter.

In Chapter 21, Ferrigno and Di Minin review previous studies on open innovation to shed light on its three constructs that, in their view, firms need to take into account when they design, develop, and implement digital strategies. These three items are purposeful knowledge exchange, business model alignment, and the strategic management of intellectual property. Using a qualitative design analysis, they explore the three constructs directly in several firms that opened up their innovation processes by developing digital technologies: King of App, GoOpti, and Cynny. From the analysis of the three cases, Ferrigno and Di Minin extract five managerial implications that need to be adopted for an effective open-innovation approach and digital strategy design.

Finally, in Chapter 22, Li tackles the notion of digital strategy and digital technology adoption to propose a framework in order to understand the reasons why every company is currently in need of having its own digital strategy. Li also detects the key implications for incumbents and digital-native firms competing in the digital age. Li's proposed framework is rooted in two key alterations in the environment: the changing nature of the economy and the rapid development of digital technologies. These changes in combination are able to redefine the rules of the game, forcing companies to reevaluate and regenerate their strategies and business models by exploiting their digital capabilities. According to Li, business leaders' main challenge does not lie in generating new ideas but in effectively managing the crucial transition to the adoption of new technologies, strategies, business models, and organizational designs as well.

## WHAT IS NEXT IN DIGITAL STRATEGY?

What is next in digital strategy? This is essentially a question we pose for future research. Unfortunately, we do not have access to the fortune teller's legendary crystal ball; hence, we can hardly predict how the field will evolve. But, on the ground of the current trends, we may share few guesses. The next stride we envisage for developing digital strategy is to have it engaged in the rising "sustainability challenge". This means that digital strategy may be called on to develop corporate sustainability, sustainable business models and sustainable development (Ritala et al., 2021). For instance, the application of digital technologies may serve to deal with grand challenges such as climate change (George et al., 2021) and digital platforms might support the nurturing of circular economy business models through an efficient use of resources (Ciulli et al., 2020).

Another stride we envisage is for management scholars to engage increasingly with the "competition and social policy challenges" that digital technology involves. For all the enthusiasm of current strategy scholarly research to document the value-creation capacity (and related strategies) of digital technologies and their associated new organizational structures such as platforms, ecosystems, and decentralized governance, the field has largely eschewed from dealing with the sort of puzzling questions that antitrust busters, policy makers, and society at large are posing in relation to the potential distortions on competition and even society's democratic dynamics that excessive monopolistic power of Big Tech can produce. For instance, there is emerging research highlighting possible "market failures" taking place in ecosystems in idiosyncratic forms, including "cooperation failures" – lowered incentives to invest in quality and cooperate due to value-capture problems (e.g., Miller & Toh, 2022; Panico & Cennamo, 2022); "access failures" – exploitation of data aggregation and control to dictate excessive terms of participation (Kramer et al., 2019; Parker et al. 2021); and "self-preferencing" – promotion of a platform's own services at the expense of those equally (or more) valuable of complementors (Sokol & Zhu, 2021; Zhu & Liu, 2018).

Some of the fundamental questions in business, such as how value jointly produced is split among firms, what is a fair distribution of economic value among firms, and when does competition turn into an unfair game, take on new shape and relevance in the digital economy context. To fully develop the new digital strategy paradigm, strategy scholars would need to address these questions, else the risk for the field might be of developing theories and frameworks that are foundationally vitiated in terms of their exploitative nature, and hence be of little relevance if not harmful in their practical application.

## STRUCTURE OF THIS *HANDBOOK*

This volume is structured as follows. In Part I, the *what* question of digital strategy is explored, considering digital strategy as fundamentally about the design choice of an effective digital business model. The chapters focus on the different aspects of digitization (e.g., Chapter 4), what parts of the business model change as a result of digitization and what are the enabling factors (Chapters 2, 3, and 5), and which new strategies at the corporate level (e.g., digital diversification – Chapter 1) or the product level (e.g., freemium strategies – Chapter 6) are implemented and how they differ compared with the analog reality.

Parts II and III deal with the *how* question of digital strategy. Part II focuses on the design of the digital organizational architectures and their inner logics of functioning, with the chapters emphasizing decisions about digital platform boundaries (Chapter 7), the design of ecosystems (Chapter 8), the value logics of these new organizing modes (Chapters 9, 10, and 11), as well as new tensions and governance forms (Chapter 12).

Part III focuses more specifically on how value is created and captured through data strategies. It explores how digital data empower the strategy-making and implementation process to unlock new value-creation opportunities (Chapter 13), how firms capture value from data (Chapters 14 and 15), and how data can be used as means of structuring and coordinating interfirm relationships (Chapter 16).

Finally, Part IV tackles the *why* question of digital strategy, pointing to the challenges that managers face when dealing with digital, which challenge the same essence of the firm and recast the question of its role in the business environment. Chapter 17 focuses on the challenges of the extant corporate governance system and offers an alternative open-source model to cope with the new demands of the digital era. Other chapters inspect the impact on management practices of specific digital technologies and processes (Chapters 18, 19, 20, and 21).The concluding chapter (22) poses some foundational and provocative questions about the impacts of digital strategy that managers should ask before embarking on crafting specific strategies.

## NOTE

1. In the digital age, many items (i.e., products or services) are free of charge in the sense that their cost is so low or proximate to zero as to come unnoticed. This trend is possibly destined to continue in a way that will cover more products. As such, it is concurrently likely to have profound consequences for the nature of work and society.

## REFERENCES

Acemoglu, D., Lelarge, C., and Restrepo, P. (2020). *Competing with Robots: Firm-Level Evidence from France*. NBER Working Papers. Cambridge, MA: National Bureau of Economic Research.

Adner, R. (2017). Ecosystem as structure: an actionable construct for strategy. *Journal of Management*, 43: 39–58.

Adner, R., & Lieberman, M. (2021). Disruption through complements. *Strategy Science*, 6(1): 91–109.

Adner, R., Puranam, P., & Zhu, F. (2019). What is different about digital strategy? From quantitative to qualitative change. *Strategy Science*, 4: 253–61.

Afuah, A. (2013). Are network effects really all about size? The role of structure and conduct. *Strategic Management Journal*, 34(3): 257–73.

Alaimo, C., Kallinikos, J., & Valderrama, E. (2020). Platforms as service ecosystems: lessons from social media. *Journal of Information Technology*, 35: 25–48.

Amit, R., & Schoemaker, P.J. (1993). Strategic assets and organizational rent. *Strategic Management Journal*, 14(1): 33–46.

Andrews, K.R. (1971). *Concept of Corporate Strategy*. Homewood, IL: Dow Jones-Irwin.

Autio, E., Mudambi, R., & Yoo, Y. (2021). Digitalization and globalization in a turbulent world: centrifugal and centripetal forces. *Global Strategy Journal*, 11: 3–16.

Bain, J.S., Jr. (1956). *Barriers to New Competition: Their Character and Consequences in Manufacturing Industries*. Cambridge, MA: Harvard University Press.

Birkinshaw, J. (2018). How is technological change affecting the nature of the corporation? *Journal of the British Academy*, 6: 185–214.

Boudreau, K.J., Jeppesen, L.B., & Miric, M. (2021). Competing on freemium: digital competition with network effects. *Strategic Management Journal*, early view. https://onlinelibrary.wiley.com/doi/abs/10.1002/smj.3366#:~:text=Research%20Summary&text=We%20find%20that%20stronger%20network,advantage%20of%20leaders%20over%20followers.

Cennamo, C. (2021). Competing in digital markets: a platform-based perspective. *Academy of Management Perspectives*, 35(2): 265–91.

Cennamo, C., Dagnino, G.B., Di Minin, A., & Lanzolla, G. (2020). Managing digital transformation: scope of transformation and modalities of value co-generation and delivery. *California Management Review*, 62(4): 5–16.

Cennamo, C., Diaferia, L., Gaur, A., & Salviotti, G. (2022). Assessing incumbents' risk of digital platform disruption. *MIS Quarterly Executive*, 21(1): 55–74.

Chesbrough, H., Kim, S., & Agogino, A. (2014). Chez Panisse: Building an open innovation ecosystem. *California Management Review*, 56(4): 144–71.

Ciulli, F., Kolk, A., & Boe-Lillegraven, S. (2020). Circularity brokers: digital platform organizations and waste recovery in food supply chains. *Journal of Business Ethics*, 167: 299–331.

Cozzolino, A., Corbo, L., & Aversa, P. (2021). Digital platform-based ecosystems: the evolution of collaboration and competition between incumbent producers and entrant platforms. *Journal of Business Research*, 126: 385–400.

Cusumano, M.A., Gawer, A., & Yoffie, D.B. (2019a). *The Business of Platforms: Strategy in the Age of Digital Competition, Innovation, and Power*. New York, NY: Harper Business.

Cusumano, M.A., Gawer, A., & Yoffie, D.B. (2019b). How digital platforms have become double-edged swords. *MIT-Sloan Management Review*. https://sloanreview.mit.edu/article/how-digital-platforms-have-become-double-edged-swords.

D'Aveni, R.A. (2013). 3-D printing will change the world. *Harvard Business Review*, 91: 34–5.

Dąbrowska, J., Almpanopoulou, A., Brem, A., Chesbrough, H., Cucino, V., Minin, A. Di, Giones, F., Hakala, H., Marullo, C., Mention, A.-L., Mortara, L., Nørskov, S., Nylund, P.A., Oddo, C.M., Radziwon, A., & Ritala, P. (2022). Digital transformation, for better or worse: a critical multi-level research agenda. *R&D Management*, 52(5): 930–54.

Dagnino, G.B., Picone, P.M., & Ferrigno, G. (2021). Temporary competitive advantage: an investigation into the core of the literature and challenges for future research. *International Journal of Management Reviews*, 23(1): 85–115.

Dagnino, G.B., & Resciniti, R. (2021). Introduction to the Special Issue: the age of digital internationalization: strategic capabilities, cultural distance and customer value. *Journal of Management and Governance*, 25(4): 967–81.

Durand, R., Grant, R.M., & Madsen, T.L. (2017). The expanding domain of strategic management research and the quest for integration. *Strategic Management Journal*, 38: 4–16.

George, G., Merrill, R.K., & Schillebeeckx, S.J. (2021). Digital sustainability and entrepreneurship: how digital innovations are helping tackle climate change and sustainable development. *Entrepreneurship Theory Practice*, 45(5): 999–1027.

Giachetti, C., & Dagnino, G.B. (2014). Detecting the relationship between competitive intensity and firm product line length: evidence from the worldwide mobile phone industry. *Strategic Management Journal*, 35(9): 1398–1409.

Giachetti, C., & Dagnino, G.B. (2021). Competitive dynamics in strategic management. *Oxford Research Encyclopedia of Business and Management*. Oxford: Oxford University Press. https://oxfordre.com/business/view/10.1093/acrefore/9780190224851.001.0001/acrefore-9780190224851-e-16.

Gladwell, M. (2002). *The Tipping Point: How Little Things Can Make a Big Difference*. Boston, MA: Back Bay Books.

Grant, R.M. (2010). *Contemporary Strategy Analysis: Concepts, Techniques and Applications*, 7th ed. New York, NY: Wiley.

Hanelt, A., Bohnsack, R., Marz, D., & Antunes Marante, C. (2021). A systematic review of the literature on digital transformation: insights and implications for strategy and organizational change. *Journal of Management Studies*, 58: 1159–97.

Jacobides, M.G., Cennamo, C., & Gawer, A. (2018). Towards a theory of ecosystems. *Strategic Management Journal*, 39: 2255–76.

Jacobides, M.G., Knudsen, T., & Augier, M. (2006). Benefiting from innovation: value creation, value appropriation and the role of industry architectures. *Research Policy*, 35: 1200–221.

Kapoor, R., & Furr, N.R. (2015). Complementarities and competition: unpacking the drivers of entrants' technology choices in the solar photovoltaic industry. *Strategic Management Journal*, 36(3): 416–36.

Katz, M.L., & Shapiro, C. (1994). Systems competition and network effects. *Journal of Economic Perspectives*, 8: 93–115.

Krakowski, S., Luger, J., & Raisch, S. (2022). Artificial intelligence and the changing sources of competitive advantage. *Strategic Management Journal*. DOI: 10.1002/smj.3387.

Kramer, J., Schnurr, D., & Wohlfarth, M. (2019). Winners, losers, and Facebook: the role of social logins in the online advertising ecosystem. *Management Science*, 65(4): 1678–99.

Lanzolla, G., Lorenz, A., Miron-Spektor, E., Schilling, M., Solinas, G., & Tucci, C. (2018). Digital transformation: what is new if anything. *Academy of Management Discoveries*, 4: 378–87.

Leiblein, M.J., & Reuer, J.J. (2020). Foundations and futures of strategic management. *Strategic Management Review*, 1: 1–33.

Lieberman, M.B., & Montgomery, D.B. (1998). First-mover (dis)advantages: retrospective and link with the resource-based view. *Strategic Management Journal*, 19: 1111–25.

Markman, G.D., Gianiodis, P.T., & Buchholtz, A.K. (2009). Factor-market rivalry. *Academy of Management Review*, 34: 423–41.

Mason, E.S. (1957). *Economic Concentration and the Monopoly Problem*. Cambridge, MA: Harvard University Press.

Masucci, M., Brusoni, S., & Cennamo, C. (2020). Removing bottlenecks in business ecosystems: the strategic role of outbound open innovation. *Research Policy*, 49(1): 103823.

Menz, M., Kunisch, S., Birkinshaw, J., Collis, D.J., Foss, N.J, Hoskisson, R.E., & Prescott, J.E. (2021). Corporate strategy and the theory of the firm in the digital age. *Journal of Management Studies*, 58(7): 1695–1720.

Miller, C., & Toh, P.K. (2022). Complementary components and returns from coordination within ecosystems via standard setting. *Strategic Management Journal*, 43: 627–62.

Panico, C., & Cennamo, C. (2022). User preferences and strategic interactions in platform ecosystems. *Strategic Management Journal*, 43: 507–29.

Parker, G., Petropoulos, G., & Van Alstyne, M. (2021). Platform mergers and antitrust: special issue on regulating platforms and ecosystems. *Industrial and Corporate Change*, in press.

Porter, M. (1981). The contributions of industrial organization to strategic management. *Academy of Management Review*, 6: 609–20.

Porter, M.E. (1985). *Competitive Advantage: Creating and Sustaining Superior Performance*. New York, NY: Free Press.

Porter, M.E. (2001). Strategy and the internet. *Harvard Business Review*, 79(3): 62–78.

Ritala, P., Baiyere, A., Hughes, M., & Kraus, S. (2021). Digital strategy implementation: the role of individual entrepreneurial orientation and relational capital. *Technological Forecasting and Social Change*, 171: 120961.

Roy, R., & Cohen, S.K. (2017). Stock of downstream complementary assets as a catalyst for product innovation during technological change in the US machine tool industry. *Strategic Management Journal*, 38(6): 1253–67.

Rumelt, R., Schendel, D., & Teece, D. (1994). *Fundamental Issues in Strategy: A Research Agenda*. Boston, MA: Harvard Business School Press.

Shapiro, C., & Varian, H.R. (1999). *Information Rules: A Strategic Guide to the Network Economy*. Boston, MA: Harvard Business School Press.

Sokol, D., & Zhu, F. (2021). *Harming Competition and Consumers Under the Guise of Protecting Privacy: An Analysis of Apple's iOS 14 Policy Updates*. Working Paper. https://papers.ssrn.com/sol3/papers.cfm?abstract_id=3852744.

Teece, D.J. (1986). Profiting from technological innovation: implications for integration, collaboration, licensing and public policy. *Research Policy*, 15(6): 285–305.

Volberda, H.W., Khanagha, S., Baden-Fuller, C., Mihalache, O.R., & Birkinshaw, J. (2021). Strategizing in a digital world: overcoming cognitive barriers, reconfiguring routines and introducing new organizational forms. *Long Range Planning*, 54: 102110.

Wind, J. (1997). Preemptive Strategies. In Day, G.S., Reibstein, D.J., & Gunther, R.E. (Eds.). *Wharton on Dynamic Competitive Strategy*: 256–276. New York, NY: Wiley.

Zhu, F., & Liu, Q. (2018). Competing with complementors: an empirical look at Amazon.com. *Strategic Management Journal*, 39(10): 2618–42.

# PART I

# DIGITAL STRATEGY AS DIGITAL BUSINESS MODEL CHOICE

# 1. Digital diversification

*Paolo Aversa and Francesca Hueller*

## INTRODUCTION

Diversification strategies have long been considered viable options to grow various kinds of businesses (Palich, Cardinal, and Miller, 2000). Adopting a diversification strategy traditionally corresponds to widening the organization's scope across multiple products and markets (Markides and Williamson, 1994, 1996; Porter, 1985; Rumelt, 1974). Whereas some firms can operate in a single market and be sustainable over time, many firms decide to diversify in terms of their product range, vertical integration, geographical presence, and customer engagement (see, for example, Collis and Montgomery, 1997; Grant, 2016; Puranam and Vanneste, 2016). The topic of diversification has traditionally corresponded to the emergence of corporations and multinational firms, pointing to diversification strategies as effective ways for firm growth, risk reduction, efficiency optimization, and performance enhancement—thus making it a core topic in strategic management for both theory and practice in the last 50 years (see Ahuja and Novelli, 2017, for a review). Although we still consider diversification a ubiquitous and viable strategy for firm growth and performance, scholars and practitioners alike wonder if and how, in today's digital domains, the implementation and the scope of diversification change (Menz et al., 2021).

The recent, pervasive diffusion of digital technologies (Appio et al., 2021; Cennamo et al., 2020; Volberda et al., 2021) has indeed opened new questions regarding the traditional role of diversification, while unveiling new opportunities for firms along new and old dimensions. Emerging digital technologies (e.g., artificial intelligence (AI), internet of things (IoT), blockchain, connected items) have helped companies that deployed a coherent digital strategy to succeed—often against major incumbents—and scale up by leveraging, among other factors, compelling and complex mechanisms of diversification, which move beyond the traditional types of offline diversification (Aversa et al., 2020)—see the cases of Google, Tesla or Amazon, among others.[1]

In addition, the breakthrough of digital solutions, frequently underpinned by the use of (big) data (George, Haas and Pentland, 2014; Hartmann and Henkel, 2020) and general-purpose digital technologies characterized by their applicability to a wide range of product-market settings (Bresnahan and Trajtenberg, 1995; Gambardella and McGahan, 2010), have blurred product, firm, and industry boundaries and affected firms' and industry's cost structure (Menz et al., 2021; Verhoef et al., 2021)—in turn bringing important implications for diversification. For instance, digitalization's impact on the firm's costs through automation and sharing digital assets increases firms' internal efficiency, reduces internal transaction costs, and enables superior scale and scope via diversification (Luo, 2021; Menz et al., 2021). This expansion, however, also increases managerial complexity and triggers relatedness mechanisms that—despite being not entirely new per se—operate quite differently in digital domains.

Some studies have started to grapple with such timely phenomena and suggested that, if successfully managed, digital diversification (DD) holds opportunities for performance enhancements (e.g., Menz et al., 2021; Sohl, Vroom, and McCann, 2020). However, from a theoretical standpoint, we still have a fragmented understanding about whether, how, and why our theoretical understanding and principles about traditional diversification need to be updated when investigating digital domains. We thus ask: What is different, if anything, in DD compared to traditional diversification (TD)?

To address this question, in the first place, we provide a definition of "digital diversification," and next, we disentangle and compare some of the basic mechanisms of diversification in traditional and digital domains. Second, we focus on the issue of related vs unrelated diversification in the two contexts and present mechanisms to explain how digitalization modifies the inverted U-shape curve representing the diversification–performance relationship in traditional domains, thus varying the relative importance of unrelated diversification in digital contexts. Third, we elaborate on some of these aspects and link them to two diversification dimensions, specifically (a) DD Locus: Supply Side vs Demand Side, and (b) DD Type: Product vs Business Model. Our work has overall a broadening objective, aiming to provide an initial, structured understanding to identify a coherent set of questions for further research. This is why in the final part of this chapter we will point to open issues for research and practice in DD and suggest an agenda of future opportunities for scholarly and industry research.

## TOWARDS A CONCEPTUALIZATION OF DIGITAL DIVERSIFICATION

Traditionally—and often by looking at non-digital settings—diversification has been conceptualized as the means by which firms can share resources, economize on transaction costs, or reduce economic risk, and it is usually classified into three types—see Ahuja and Novelli (2017), Ansoff (1957), Grant (2016), and Puranam and Vanneste (2016). The first type, "horizontal diversification," is traditionally defined as firms engaging in different industries offering additional products or services, perhaps by using related technologies (Su and Tsang, 2015; Wiersema and Bowen, 2008). Walt Disney Company provides a good example of horizontal diversification as it expanded its business from an animation industry to an amusement park, film production, and television industry, including Marvel Comics, television network ABC, and cable sports channel ESPN in its product portfolio. The second, traditionally known as "vertical diversification" (Block et al., 2016), implies the possibility for a firm to move upstream or downstream in the value chain, such as becoming or integrating other players in the chain. For example, Ikea not only controls much of the raw material production (i.e., upstream), ensuring a complete and sustainable vertical integration, but it also controls the manufacturing process and the final distribution to the consumer through its retail units (i.e., downstream). The third type is "geographical diversification" (Dagnino et al., 2019; Hitt, Hoskisson, and Kim, 1997), which entails expanding the firm into different geographical markets, usually in separate units in new regions or countries. Coca-Cola geographically diversifies its presence in more than 200 countries and territories, with the majority of its revenues coming from overseas sales, despite being an American brand. More recently, literature has claimed that firm diversification encompasses not only such traditional dimensions but also ways of combining different mechanisms of value creation and capture, thus implying distinct modes of customer engagement through "business model diversification" (see Ahuja and Novelli, 2016; Aversa, Haefliger, and Reza, 2017; Sohl, Vroom, and McCann, 2020).

For example, Formula 1 teams, in addition to racing with advanced cars and monetizing from race results, sell the same components used for the car—such as engines and gearboxes—to competitors, thus gaining access to valuable data about how those components perform—an intangible resource that can provide valuable insights to develop their own technology further, win more car races, and sell future parts at higher prices (for more details, see Aversa, Furnari, and Haefliger, 2015).

Early works on corporate strategy (e.g., Rumelt, 1974, 1982) highlighted the importance of considering the degree of relatedness (i.e., complementarity) among businesses as a proxy for successful and profitable diversification. Related diversification has traditionally been conceptualized as expanding a business into similar products and services or participating in a new industry that shares similarities with the industries in which the firm is already operating— which empirically is often investigated by looking at the similarity of the "standard industrial classification of economic activities" (in short, "SIC codes"). The underlying logic is that such similarities lead to "relatedness," which offers interdependencies and complementarities across multi-industry businesses sharing common resources, technologies, scope, and knowledge (e.g., Harrison et al., 2001; Markides and Williamson, 1994, 1996; Rumelt, 1982). For instance, as films and television are both two sectors of the broader media entertainment industry that share similar resources and infrastructures (recording studios, broadcasting technology, scripting competencies, distribution and advertising networks, etc.), Disney's acquisition of the television network ABC is a good example of related diversification. Conversely, unrelated diversification traditionally corresponds to expanding a business into very distant products and services or joining industries, markets, or sectors presenting different input–output configurations or limited synergies along with resources or capabilities (see, for example, Ahuja, Lampert, and Novelli, 2013; Bryce and Winter, 2009; Montgomery, 1982; Teece, 1977). Coca-Cola acquiring Columbia Pictures is a case of unrelated diversification, as the motion picture industry lacks—at least on the supply side—any evident similarity with the soft drinks industry in terms of production and distribution.

Diversification scholars seem to agree that the relationship between diversification relatedness and firm performance usually follows an inverted U-shape curve (Palich, Cardinal, and Miller, 2000), and thus, even considering some exceptions, a moderate level of relatedness across specific markets and customer segments is beneficial to diversified organizations. As relatedness increases, firms' opportunities to expand their scope—implying possible complementarities in production and consumption—will be more concentrated across specific markets and customer segments. It is important to notice, however, that the recent advancement of digital technologies is surprisingly providing new opportunities for firms to successfully extend their business even into *unrelated* activities (products, services, or business models) in a way that traditional approaches to corporate strategy cannot fully capture. Cases such as Amazon, Alphabet, Apple, Meta, Tesla, or Uber have challenged the traditional idea of relatedness in diversification and showed how activities that appear somewhat unrelated (e.g., running marketplaces, entering the healthcare sector, and sending rockets to space) might enjoy strong synergies when their value is created and captured through digital technologies. Hence, the development and support of digital tools (e.g., platforms, IoT, AI, machine learning), combined with the omnipresence of big data, create space for consumer and producer synergies from diversification and foster novel pathways for competitive advantage in digital contexts.

We define "digital diversification" (DD) as a digitally enabled type of product, service,[2] and business model diversification, which exploits opportunities from a firm's engagement with different digitally driven activities and offerings. While specific research on DD is still in its initial stage, management and strategy scholars' attention has been increasingly devoted to other very close and related phenomena in the digital world. In particular, platforms (e.g., Cennamo and Santalo, 2013; Cusumano, Gawer, and Yoffie, 2019; Rietveld and Eggers, 2018), also known as "multi-sided" business models as they connect multiple groups of stakeholders, have received bourgeoning attention. Platforms often connect to (and transact with) customer groups that are radically different and often part of distinct industries—think of Amazon connecting publishing houses with technology companies to deploy digital versions of books that are compatible with multiple devices, including its own Amazon Kindle. Scholars have also explored the competitive dynamics within a broader and heterogeneous competitive space of heterogeneous actors, which has been termed an "ecosystem" (see, for example, Adner and Kapoor, 2010; Gawer, 2009; Gawer and Cusumano, 2014; Jacobides, Cennamo, and Gawer, 2018), and the increasing role of data and analytics to support digital products, digital business models diversification, and competitive advantage across many industries (Adner, Puranam, and Zhu, 2019; Aversa et al., 2020; Menz et al., 2021). These trends all touch upon (directly or indirectly) multi-business initiatives and thus further raise timely questions on whether digital dimensions of diversification differ from the traditional types, while urging scholars to inquire if and why existing theory may be (in)sufficient to grasp this phenomenon.

Arguably, DD allows firms to take advantage of broadly redeployable assets such as data and digital general-purpose technologies that can be shared across different users, applications, and platforms while creating additional value that could not be realized in non-digital businesses. The distinct nature of these assets—whose costs and benefits greatly differ from tangible infrastructure and classic resources we learned to appreciate since the first Industrial Revolution—seems to suggest that DD may not entirely conflate with what we term here TD. But why exactly? A closer look at the main differences between TD and DD follows to respond to this question.

## Comparing Traditional Diversification vs Digital Diversification

As digitalization is altering the way firms diversify their businesses and compete, understanding how competition changes when we move from TD to DD is paramount. To foster a comprehensive and consistent understanding of the DD phenomenon, we follow Cennamo (2021: 267) into identifying a set of discrete, theoretically relevant dimensions along which we compare and contrast traditional vs digital diversification (see Table 1.1). We concentrate on different competition levels, drivers, foci, actions, and dynamics.

Ditto, diversification is traditionally conceptualized at the product level and corresponds to widening the organization's scope across multiple products and markets within a defined sector or industry (Markides and Williamson, 1994, 1996; Porter, 1985; Rumelt, 1974). DD, instead, is often implemented at the level of platforms or ecosystems, whose "boundaries span across multiple (traditionally defined) product markets and sectors" (Cennamo, 2021: 266). This implies that the competition logic can no longer be defined by the type of output produced or by the input that enables the production of goods and services (Jarillo, 1988); rather, it corresponds to extending the firm's engagement with a set of different yet interdependent actors, which span over a variety of product markets, sectors, and segments, or customer engagement

*Table 1.1*    *Comparing traditional diversification and digital diversification*

| | Traditional diversification | Digital diversification |
|---|---|---|
| Competition level | • Diversification is defined at the level of products within a given market or industry. | • Diversification is determined at the level of platform systems or ecosystems. |
| Competition driver | • Firm competitive position and sustainability. | • Customer value creation. |
| | | • Alignment of stakeholders participating in value creation. |
| Competitive analysis' focus | • Focus on the supply side. | • Focus on both the supply and demand side. |
| | • Analysis of the interfirm rivalry driving firm performance. | • Analysis of the multiple heterogeneous stakeholders participating in value creation and capture. |
| Competitive actions | • Provide products or services designed for a predefined use. | • Provide integrated solution(s). |
| | • New product(s) offering. | • New mechanism(s) of value creation, delivery, and capture independent of the product offering. |
| | • Product(s) pricing strategy. | |
| Competitive dynamics | • Competition across products and firms. | • Competition across platforms and ecosystems. |
| | • Multimarket competition. | • Platform single vs multihoming. |
| | | • Platform owner vs complementors. |
| | | • Complementors vs complementors. |
| Competitive advantage (sources) | • Producer synergies across multi-product businesses. | • Consumer and producer synergies. |
| | • Use of physical assets (difficult to redeploy across similar businesses). | • Use of digital assets (reproducible, transferable, and modular). |
| | • Increasing returns from related diversification. | • Increasing scope of resource (and capabilities) redeployment within and outside industries. |
| | | • Increasing returns from related and unrelated diversification and cost savings. |
| | | • Growing revenues through enhanced customer experience. |

mechanisms that may be new to the nature of a firm. Yet, whereas competition in TD is driven by the firm's willingness to search and sustain a competitive position within a given market or industry over time, the driving force of DD is value creation through greater consumption benefits and personalized experiences for platform users (Cennamo, 2021; Panico and Cennamo, 2015) and the search for multilateral alignment with all the (market and non-market; supply- and demand-side) actors who play a critical role in determining value creation and capture for the focal firm (Adner and Kapoor, 2016).

As the main competition driver moves from firms' competitive position and sustainability to value creation and stakeholders' alignment, the competitive focus also shifts. While TD overwhelmingly concentrates on supply-side advantages (see Markides and Williamson, 1996; Penrose, 1959), DD considers the critical role of external stakeholders, such as customers and complementors (see, for example, Cennamo, Ozalp, and Kretschmer, 2018; Kapoor and Agarwal, 2017; Tavalaei and Cennamo, 2020), and the related demand-side advantages (see Priem, Wenzel, and Koch, 2018; Ye, Priem, and Alshwer, 2012). In doing this, DD emphasizes opportunities to potentially realize digital synergies on both the supply side and demand side, as well as the role of platforms in bringing together heterogeneous stakeholders (e.g., Cennamo and Santalo, 2013; Rietveld, Schilling, and Bellavitis, 2019) and the diversification of customer-engagement mechanisms of value creation and value capture (i.e., business models) (e.g., Aversa et al., 2020; Sohl, Vroom, and McCann, 2020).

Accordingly, rather than being focused on the interfirm rivalry (i.e., rival firms, potential entrants, and substitutes) defining a firm's competitive position as in TD, DD necessitates a thorough analysis of the multiple stakeholders (e.g., competitors, customers, suppliers, complementors) participating in the business model (Aversa et al., 2020; Cozzolino, Corbo, and Aversa, 2021), and affiliating with multiple industries, platforms, or ecosystems at the same time (Tiwana, 2015; Zhu and Iansiti, 2012). This multilateral interdependence of relationships among firms in a vertical (i.e., upstream and downstream) and across verticals represents one critical difference between DD and TD. Compared to product-level diversification in traditional markets where the diversifying firms may focus just on one area (e.g., the product niche downstream or the production upstream in the value chain) (e.g., Adner and Kapoor, 2016; Porter, 1985), in digital contexts firms must consider all the relationships among stakeholders within and across different value chains (who may not have direct links to the focal firm) and, often, rewire those relationships to diversify successfully, at times introducing new business models (Aversa, Hervas-Drane, and Evenou, 2019; Visnjic, Jovanovic, and Raisch, 2021). In a nutshell, DD involves, to a greater extent, the need to design a related ecosystem strategy or to shape the ecosystem to its intended goals.

Another distinctive aspect of DD is the facilitated development of new digital activities and offerings that can proliferate at lower costs (e.g., app-based engagement, automated activity tracking) than expanding traditional offline experiences or brick-and-mortar activities (e.g., retailing, outsourcing). Digital companies can produce and deliver digitally-enabled goods—either online, offline solutions, or products—which are made more appealing by integrating technology into "smart" products or connected devices. These sometimes very different solutions (e.g., fitness watches monitoring calorie consumption and connected fridges automatically re-stocking groceries that support a specific diet) can share and exploit the same underlying web infrastructure, digital tools, and digital assets (biophysics information, credit card details, data on individual eating preferences, Wi-Fi and Bluetooth protocols)—"digital" complementarities that underpin what we consider digital product diversification. Besides, the use of digital products as the infrastructure to access, channel, and share relevant information across users (e.g., Google Search, Google Maps), and the possibility to leverage the data traffic generated by the users and providers to facilitate transactions and deliver customized products or solutions, sometimes delivered by external players in the ecosystem (e.g., Amazon Marketplace to deliver groceries and dietary food supplements), allow firms to establish multiple mechanisms of value creation, delivery, and capture (e.g., freemium models [see Chapter 6 for more details], subscriptions, product sharing) that are independent of the product offering; i.e., digital business models diversification. Likewise, the possibility of connecting to other core and peripheral products (which may drive new sources of value and money) to offer an enhanced and integrated solution to customers (e.g., Alexa or Google Home, Peloton bikes) enables decoupling between the product's direct benefits to its user and the ancillary benefits it can generate for customers, thus creating new monetization strategies that can be multiparty (e.g., the subscriptions embedded in Apple Health).

Notably, the sharing and redeployment of data in digital product and business model diversification represent a substantive difference compared to physical businesses leveraging traditional fixed assets. The reproducible, transferable, highly modular nature of digital assets affects the cost structure as we know it in TD and gives digital firms the chance to expand the usual scope of their diversification relatedness into domains that, seen under traditional assumptions, might look like hardly profitable (Rumelt, 1982). As a result, the source of competitive advantage shifts from increasing returns from mostly related diversification in traditional product markets to increasing returns from both related and seemingly unrelated diversification in digital contexts. The latter offers digital firms cost-saving through automation and resource redeployment, and consequently it represents a search for firms' growth opportunities and enhanced customer experience (Verhoef et al., 2021). It is thus important to discuss how the underlying relationship between relatedness and performance varies in moving from TD to DD and what are the drivers supporting this new phenomenon.

**Diversification Relatedness and Performance: What Changes in Digital Diversification?**

We thus consider how digital opens up new possibilities for firms to diversify into both *related* and *unrelated* businesses. From low-cost airlines offering car rentals, insurances, and hotel prices to online companies such as TripAdvisor and Airbnb floating the idea of booking flights as a backward integration, and Uber running Uber Eats to compete with Deliveroo, digitalization led many firms to add new unrelated products and services to their value chain. In particular, we focus on how digital assets allow firms to expand the scope of their resource redeployment within and beyond the firm's boundaries and explain mechanisms that may modify the classic inverted U-shape curve of diversification and performance (Palich, Cardinal, and Miller, 2000).

In traditional markets, when firms move from related diversification to unrelated diversification, the significant costs (e.g., control, coordination, diseconomies) from penetration into new product categories or markets (i.e., unrelated diversification) tend to overcome the benefits from diversification—diminishing the returns and decreasing the performance (Palich, Cardinal, and Miller, 2000). Put differently, the marginal costs of diversification increase dramatically when firms expand into activities with different input–output configurations (compared to expanding in categories where the firm already operates—i.e., related diversification), generating—after a certain point—penalties for increasingly unrelated diversification.

Nevertheless, what happens when firms move from related to unrelated diversification in digital markets may be quite different. If we consider, for example, that the costs of producing one additional unit of a physical product are—all other things being equal—substantially higher than those of creating a new digital product unit (e.g., duplicating and delivering audio or video streaming content, software programs—see Aversa, Hervas-Drane, and Evenou, 2019), we should expect the lower marginal costs to weaken the curvilinear mechanism and, therefore, flatten the U-shaped curve. But what mechanisms explain how DD challenges the scope of TD? What shifts the inverted U-shape curve, thus altering the logic of related vs unrelated diversification and its relation to firm performance?

We posit that seemingly unrelated diversification is more beneficial within the digital dimension than previously thought in TD. Competing in the "digital age" requires significant investments in the management of big data and digital technologies to compete effectively (Menz et al., 2021). These, despite often being associated with substantial initial costs, offer more efficient sharing and redeploying opportunities than physical assets (as the marginal costs are lower and, in the case of digital platforms, sometimes negligible), while returns could be exponential. Take, for example, Airbnb or Uber, which faced significantly high initial costs to construct the web infrastructure required to transmit their digital goods or solutions, but over time, connected thousands of potential hosts and travelers, drivers, and riders to their service at "near-zero" marginal costs. Accordingly, we argue that sharing digital assets (primarily in the form of big data) and leveraging digital tools (e.g., platforms, IoT, AI, machine learning) across businesses that do not (necessarily) transact with each other can increase the scope of resource redeployment (Sakhartov and Folta, 2015) within and outside the industry. This, in turn, generates better performance from diversification and changes the traditional inverted U-shape curve (see the dotted line in Figure 1.1) of relatedness and performance into an S-shaped curve (see the solid line in Figure 1.1). As explained, this happens through two main mechanisms: (1) cost reduction for resource redeployment (i.e., modularity of digital assets is superior to physical assets, thus requiring low costs to connect loosely coupled assets), and (2) increasing returns from seemingly unrelated diversification (i.e., a better understanding of consumer behavior is a strategic asset across multiple consumption experiences and industries, and machine learning allows it to perform on a vast scale).

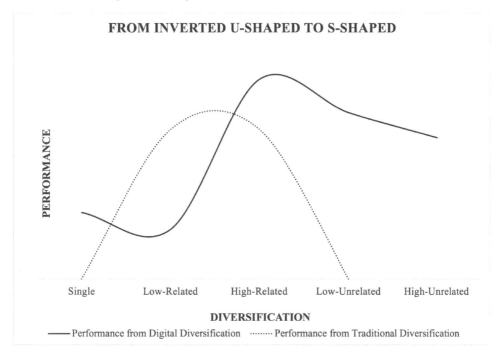

*Figure 1.1*      *Comparing traditional diversification U-shaped curve vs digital diversification S-shaped curve*

In redefining the inverted U-shaped curve, one needs to consider how modern digitalization allows firms to collect, analyze, and redeploy big data more effectively and at a fraction of the cost of physical assets. Today's digitalization tends to increase firms' internal efficiency through greater automation (Davenport and Ronanki, 2018) and better coordination between processes, in turn reducing the internal transaction and operating costs that arise from sharing assets across businesses and from the necessary decisional activities. This positively affects firms' performance by enabling organizations to quickly increase activities across both scale and scope[3] (Luo, 2021; Menz et al., 2021), and it favors growing revenues, as demonstrated by the advancement of "new giant" firms that dominate entire sectors (Menz et al., 2021). For an iconic example, consider how Amazon has redesigned the company around its AI and machine learning applications—like its warehouses being automated with smart robots and its Amazon Web Services (AWS) business—effectively reducing the internal transaction and coordination costs of its gigantic logistics to mobilize goods for the online Marketplace.

The high initial fixed costs and progressively low marginal costs, coupled with the low internal transaction and coordination costs, change the cost structure and shape the outcomes of diversification in digital markets, with a substantial effect on the possibility of expanding the scope of firms' diversification—therefore, its relatedness. Specifically, digital assets allow for more unrelated diversification as they facilitate entering markets previously considered to be "worryingly unrelated"—hence, flattening the inverted U-shaped curve after its tipping point (Haans, Pieters, and He, 2016). By comparing the two curves in Figure 1.1, one can appreciate that, in our theorization, while the inverted U-shaped pattern indicates that moderate levels of relatedness lead to optimal performance when it comes to DD, the best returns are achieved at high levels of related diversification and at limited (or low) levels of unrelated diversification.[4]

Figure 1.2 details how the cost structure (as theorized in Palich, Cardinal, and Miller, 2000) generated from digital assets redeployment and the benefits from enhanced consumption experience in digital markets underpin the S-shaped curve of DD. We follow the theorizing and testing of U-shaped models featured in Haans, Pieters, and He (2016) to redefine the curvilinear model. We suggest that the relationship between DD and firm performance results in an S-shaped model (e.g., Hashai, 2015) because of the interplay between (a) high initial fixed costs combined with (b) low marginal, (internal) transaction, and (c) coordination costs, and thanks to the (d) increasing diversification benefits when moving towards unrelated domains.

In particular, coordination costs are negligible at low or absent (i.e., single) levels of related diversification; however, as the fixed initial costs are higher than the benefits derived from synergies with limited product scope, this leads to suboptimal performance outcomes. For example, Airbnb's transition from a website where the founders originally rented out a few airbeds in their living room to a major platform infrastructure connecting hosts and travelers globally only two years later determined huge initial costs. Moving towards related diversification, the synergies from expanding a business into similar products increase significantly and overcome the rise in coordination costs, raising returns from diversification. Also, the low or even zero variable costs that characterize high levels of related diversification in digital contests allow firms to reach optimal performance outcomes. Back to our example, having set up its online infrastructure, Airbnb started to redeploy the same resources and capabilities to expand its offer from cheap rooms at more convenient prices (than hotels) to the world's most extraordinary homes. This comes at minimal marginal cost to Airbnb for serving a new offering.

For low levels of unrelated diversification, the benefits from diversification need to be balanced with growing coordination costs that lead to a slight decrease in performance outcomes as the unrelatedness increases. Nonetheless, returns from unrelated diversion are significantly higher than those expected from engaging in unrelated activities in TD (see Figure 1.1 for a comparison). This implies that DD allows for extended scope from unrelated diversification. As such, it followed that many digitally enabled firms started to pursue diversification away from their core products. Airbnb, for instance, expanded into offering online and real-world experiences to guests, transforming itself into a travel company. In doing so, it leverages the same underlying technology, web infrastructure, and data flow to access its users.

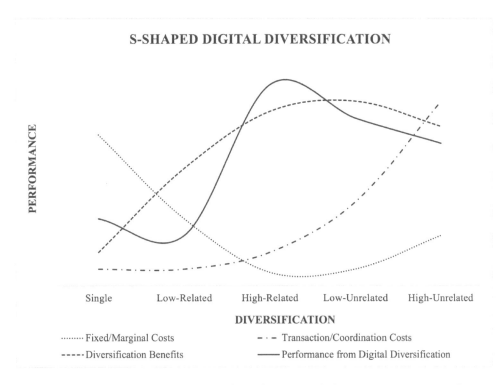

*Figure 1.2*   *Digital diversification S-shaped curve: underlying costs structure and benefits*

Yet, extensive unrelated diversification in digital contexts gives rise to considerable internal transaction and coordination costs, which, together with increasing marginal costs due to the very different nature of new products and markets in which firms penetrate, outweigh synergy effects, leading to more complexity, substitution effects, and causal ambiguity, and consequently decrease the performance from diversification. Take, for instance, the possibility for Airbnb to introduce flight and rental car bookings as a part of its services; this will bring costs deriving from managing numerous and different unrelated businesses that may limit the performance from diversification. For example, a customer booking both a flight and a flat through Airbnb might expect the company to take care of the flat re-booking in case the flight gets cancelled or moved—thus requiring a different, bigger, and possibly more costly customer service.

## THE MAIN DIMENSIONS OF DIGITAL DIVERSIFICATION

Based on some of these distinctive aspects, we characterize DD across two different broad dimensions: (1) DD Locus: Supply Side vs Demand Side and (2) DD Type: Product vs Business Model, and highlight opportunities and challenges with the support of a few examples.

*Table 1.2     Supply- and demand-side drivers of digital diversification*

|  | Drivers | Influence on value | Example |
|---|---|---|---|
| Supply-side | Resource complementarities. | Synergic use of a specific resource across multiple businesses. | Amazon Prime Video leverages Amazon Web Services Cloud for its streaming service and back-end infrastructure. |
|  | Capability complementarities. | Redeployment of a specific capability across multiple businesses. | Amazon uses its technological capabilities to develop proprietary high-tech products such as Amazon Fire TV and Fire Phone. |
| Demand-side | One-stop-shop effects. | Customers' reduction in search and transaction costs due to the engagement with multiple consumption experiences within the same firm. | Amazon customers can access a broad selection of products and services, stream video, buy electronics, and obtain cloud storage within the same website. |
|  | Network effects. | Increasing returns and transacted volume from affiliation for one customer group when another customer group from another business model increasingly engages. | Book publishers offering their e-book online for Amazon Kindle will benefit from the increasing presence of retailers in the Amazon Marketplace and vice versa. |

**Digital Diversification Locus: Supply Side vs Demand Side**

In digital contexts, whether a firm can create a competitive advantage from diversification depends to an ever-greater extent on its ability to exploit synergies within and outside the firm boundaries, thus concentrating the diversification locus on the producer (supply side) and the consumer (demand side). Diversifying a firm's portfolio by exploiting unique complementarities across specific resources and capabilities (i.e., supply side) and by providing superior advantages to the customer through one-stop shops and (indirect) network effects (i.e., demand side) represents a different, discrete, and viable diversification strategy. Table 1.2 summarizes the supply- and demand-side drivers of DD.

To explain the supply-side implications from diversification in digital domains, we draw on the resource-based view (RBV) of the firm (Barney, 1991; Wernerfelt, 1984)—i.e., one of the most widely established theoretical perspectives to explain internal sources of competitive advantage. The RBV framework suggests that firms should look inside their boundaries, at the inner resource and capability bundles (Chirico et al., 2011; Helfat and Peteraf, 2003), to find the sources of competitive advantage. Accordingly, the production or "supply-side" diversification focuses on the internal capabilities of firms to leverage and redeploy portfolio resources to contribute to the firm's core competencies across related products and markets and exploit strong synergies originated from common share assets, resources, and capabilities across businesses (Ahuja, Lampert, and Novelli, 2013; Teece, 1977, 1982).

Digitalization opens up new possibilities for firms to diversify into related as well as unrelated businesses, expanding into multiple activities with similar or different input–output configurations by sharing fundamental assets and leveraging digital tools across businesses that do not (necessarily) transact with each other. In particular, the proliferation of "general-purpose products or technologies" (Conti, Gambardella, and Novelli, 2019; Shermon and Moeen, 2019)—i.e., those broadly applicable across different uses and markets such as computing power, rapid prototyping, AI, or connectivity—and the emerging of a new intangible asset such as real-time (big) data (Adner, Puranam, and Zhu, 2019; George, Haas, and Pentland, 2014), has challenged many traditional strategic approaches to competitive positioning through the utilization of unique resources and capabilities (Teece, 2010).

Consider, for instance, how Amazon expanded into a plethora of unrelated businesses such as a marketplace, cloud services, electronics, video streaming, and more to become the Internet's main one-stop shop (Aversa et al., 2020). This is made possible, in part, by leveraging the same underlying technology and web infrastructure that the firm has already established, which, together with real-world user data, allows Amazon to benefit from supply-side complementarities. Integrating (and sharing across businesses) various digital assets is arguably more convenient than physical assets, as when shared data protocols and interfaces are in place, firms can enjoy quasi-modular coupling of different digital applications. Accordingly, the returns from synergies are often exponential, while the integrating costs are minimized compared to synergies from physical resource complementarities. For this reason, Amazon Prime Video leverages Amazon Web Services Cloud for its streaming service and back-end infrastructure—as does its direct competitor, Netflix (Aversa et al., 2020: 18). Likewise, Uber, traditionally offering only ride-sharing with vehicles, diversified into businesses such as bike-sharing (Jump) as well as food delivery (see Uber Eats) by leveraging digital multi-point localization technologies.

However, not all firms need to change their product offering to attract more demand and benefit from producer synergies; rather, they can make their offering available and valuable across different digital contexts to benefit from the synergic use of specific resources at the platform ecosystem level across multiple uses, while benefiting from different customer groups engaging across different platforms (Rietveld, Schilling, and Bellavitis, 2019). Such is the case of the Apple TV app, which went from being an Apple exclusive to a multi-platform title, available on the Android TV platform and other devices and platforms such as Amazon's Fire OS and LG's webOS—thus extending the app's compatibility to feature in the most prominent operating systems for smart TVs and streaming devices—what is also termed "multihoming" (Kretschmer et al., 2020). This permits taking full advantage of complementarity in production (Jacobides, Cennamo, and Gawer, 2018) by increasing the platform's value, while extending the app's value by the breadth of its multi-platform installation.

In recent times, strategy scholars have shifted their attention to customer interaction as key to firm value creation, value capture, and competitive advantage—defined as the "demand side" (Adner and Zemsky, 2006; Priem, 2007; Rietveld and Eggers, 2018; Ye, Priem, and Alshwer, 2012). The demand-side perspective builds on the premise that firms should exploit "consumer bundling preferences as the basis for firm strategies" (Ye, Priem, and Alshwer, 2012: 207) to leverage significant complementarities derived from effective mechanisms of customer engagement. Recognizing the centrality of customer engagement is core to any demand-side strategy, and in a digital context, it allows firms to overcome some of the traditional limitations related to offline/brick-and-mortar businesses (Amit and Zott 2001; Sawhney, Verona, and Prandelli, 2005)—e.g., limits to scalability, data accessibility, and consumption tracking (Aversa et al., 2020)—while it highlights some of the challenges related to diversification beyond product-markets.

To explain the demand-side implications of diversification in digital domains, we draw on the literature that takes the customer (group) as the focal point—i.e., the business model literature (for comprehensive recent reviews, see Klang, Wallnöfer and Hacklin, 2014; Massa,

Tucci, and Afuah, 2017)—to distinguish two fundamental and complementary mechanisms behind firm diversification moves: customer engagement via one-stop-shop effects (Kaufman, 1996) and (indirect) network effects (Economides, 1996; Milgrom and Roberts, 1990). The benefits of one-stop-shop effects have been well established in the marketing literature to indicate the possibility for the consumer to engage with a multitude of consumption experiences within the same point of sale (Kaufman, 1996; Messinger and Narasimhan, 1997). This potentially reduces consumers' search and transaction costs in the physical world. Network effects are equally well documented in economics (Economides, 1996; Economides and Katsamakas, 2006; Milgrom and Roberts, 1990) and have more recently gained prominence among business models regarding multi-sided markets (Rochet and Tirole, 2006; Sun and Tse, 2009) to explain the roles that multiple customer groups play for the pricing strategies and possibly the growth of the volume transacted in such contexts.

Digital technologies—when effectively designed and implemented—may support superior customer engagement and increasing demand-side complementarities, which facilitate the development of new digital experiences (e.g., new websites, new online functions, new apps) due to a more in-depth understanding of the customer group's preferences—often at lower costs than expanding traditional brick-and-mortar activities (e.g., new shops, new events, new real-life experiences). Above all, digital solutions allow firms to closely track consumers' experiences and collect large amounts of information to offer personalized and customized solutions while locking consumers across different consumption experiences—given the consumer's switching costs and the difficult portability of personal data, which provide superior customization within a specific system.

To understand the potential of the demand-side synergies, we consider how Amazon expanded its business models' portfolio, leveraging significant one-stop-shop and network effects (for more details, see Aversa et al., 2020). Amazon customers, notoriously, can engage with different consumption experiences, such as access to a broad selection of products, movie rentals, and online storage within the same website. At the same time, the growing offering of e-books for Amazon Kindle indirectly increases the presence of retailers in the Amazon Marketplace. These mechanisms, which are not mutually exclusive, create opportunities for Amazon to increase the adoption between and within customer groups, fostering firm growth, revenues, and ultimately competitive advantage (Aversa et al., 2020: 20). In doing so, Amazon attracts new customers to its platform, expanding its customer base over time, and yielding greater access to digital data. The latter can track consumers' experiences conveniently to enhance further data-driven customer profiling and customization, or be leveraged to offer new complements or complementary goods to take advantage of cross-selling and reduce customer acquisition costs. This, in turn, embeds the customer experience within the platform and creates significant lock-in opportunities. Hence, holding digital technologies and effectively managing big data allows firms to achieve potential additional revenues from higher corporate sales volume, protect themselves from losing customers to competitors, and sustain competitive advantage through a digitally driven strategy (Gregory et al., 2021).

**Digital Diversification Type: Product vs Business Model**

While vertical and geographical diversification might also benefit from the adoption of digital technologies, we feel that digitalization has reached its acme—and triggered substantive changes—when applied across two specific types: product and business model diversification.

*Table 1.3*      *Digital product vs digital business model diversification: classification and examples*

| | | Digital business model diversification — NO | Digital business model diversification — YES |
|---|---|---|---|
| **Digital product diversification** | **YES** | Multiple products / Single business model / e.g., Revolut. Product: multiple products (e.g., debit cards, virtual cards, commission-free stock trading, crypto, commodities, and other services). Business model: single business model (dyadic digital-only banking model). Other examples: Monzo, BBC online. | Multiple products / Multiple business models / e.g., Amazon. Product: multiple products (e.g., household goods, servers, digital content on-demand). Business model: multiple business models (Amazon Marketplace is a two-sided platform, Amazon Mechanical Turk is a crowdsourced dyadic service, Amazon Prime is an expedited shipping subscription model that complements Amazon Marketplace but is also bundled with an online-streaming content service, etc.). Other examples: Google, Apple. |
| | **NO** | Single product / Single business model / e.g., Lyft. Product: single service type (rides) with a wide coverage of multiple service classes (e.g., rides in regular vehicles, premium cars, SUVs). Business model: single business model (matchmaking business connecting drivers to riders). Other examples: Booking.com, Vrbo. | Single product / Multiple business models / e.g., Netflix. Product: single product type (video pay-per-view entertainment). Business model: dual business model (DVD-by-mail and video-on-demand streaming for a subscription fee). Other examples: Spotify, Tinder |

Accordingly, and as a matter of parsimony, we focus here on these two dimensions only. These types of diversification are not mutually exclusive; rather, they can interact in ways that are far from trivial. Notably, digital and traditional firms could be focused on a single product and a single business model (e.g., Lyft), diversified in terms of their product offering but engaging in a single business model (e.g., Revolut), or diversified in terms of their business models mobilizing the same product (e.g., Netflix); while others could be diversified along both digital product and business model dimensions (e.g., Amazon), which makes the assessment along a single diversification dimension more challenging—see Table 1.3 for a classification with related examples.

Adopting a diversification strategy conventionally indicates widening the organization's scope across multiple products or product lines and markets (Grant, 2016; Puranam and Vanneste, 2016) by sharing resources, technology, and knowledge. Accordingly, the core of traditional corporate strategies relies on the number of products and services included in a company's portfolio (see, for example, Granstrand, Patel, and Pavitt, 1997; Srivastava and Gnyawali, 2011). The rise of digital technologies has facilitated the development and offer of new digital activities and offerings, usually at lower cost than expanding traditional offline experiences—hence making horizontal or "product" differentiation even more attractive to digital companies. The latter can exploit the same web infrastructure and digital tools to produce and deliver other digitally enabled goods, which can include both online solutions (e.g., apps, bitcoins, online experiences) and offline products enhanced by digital technologies (e.g., IoT, connected items, 3D printers). Besides, the possibility to share and redeploy data remains—in digital product and business model diversification—a substantive difference compared to physical businesses, and it encompasses opportunities for efficient and effective scaling up.

To fully understand the potential offered by digital product diversification, we consider how an Internet giant like Google proliferated its digital offering and activities at limited cost by leveraging the same infrastructures and underlying technologies for its end-user products, such as Google Search, Maps, Gmail, and its Cloud Platform (GCP), to reach diverse Internet users through a single all-access limited account. Google initially started developing its leading service—i.e., the online search engine—in 1996. Afterward, it expanded its business into different Internet-related products and services such as Gmail, Google Drive, Google Search, and other online services such as Google Translate and Google Maps as a strategic cornerstone to becoming a one-stop venue for all Internet-related needs. Hence, Google's digital product diversification encompasses the creation and innovation of complementary Internet-related customer-facing properties (Google Maps, Gmail, etc.) to adapt to the technological break-through, extend its scope, and strengthen its competitive advantage while gaining a global reach limited only by Internet access and regulatory boundaries. In addition, Google corners diverse technology-dependent consumers by further diversifying its businesses into other industries and sectors that are dependent, to some extent, on its services and products—thus taking advantage of an ecosystem of businesses spanning various complementary product markets, wherein Alphabet, the parent company, acts as the orchestrator.

Recent years, however, have seen growing evidence that—beyond traditional types of diversification—firms can also deploy a portfolio of (at least two) business models—what has been recently labeled as business model diversification (Ahuja and Novelli, 2016; Aversa, Haefliger, and Reza, 2017; Snihur and Tarzijan, 2018; Sohl, Vroom, and McCann, 2020). Business models are traditionally defined as simplified representations of value creation and value capture (Aversa, Furnari, and Haefliger, 2015; Massa, Tucci, and Afuah, 2017; Teece, 2010; Zott, Amit, and Massa, 2011) and can be better appreciated when different customer engagements are mobilizing the same product in the digital space—as it is in the case of a pay-per-view or subscription model for movie rental.

The iconic case of Amazon Prime provides a good example to explain the chance offered by targeting the same market through different digitally driven ways of engaging with the customers (Ahuja and Novelli, 2016). Amazon Prime Video originally started operating in 2006 as an on-demand rental platform. Since then, Amazon has grown the subsidiary into a complete entertainment and sports SVOD platform (i.e., subscription video on demand), offering access to digital video content through a Prime membership. Unlike Netflix or Hulu, where all digital movies and TV shows come included with a subscription, Amazon Prime Video runs parallel video-on-demand (TVOD) offering temporary rentals for video content. This means that Amazon Prime Video subscribers can rent, buy, download, or stream movies or television shows (as an online Blockbuster) outside of their subscription on a pay-per-view basis. Hence, the TVOD represents a solution that may complement or substitute the original offering by using the same supply system (the Amazon Prime Video website) but engaging with the customer's needs differently. Orchestrating these two business models, Amazon Prime Video increases its market share through different value delivery and monetization mechanisms while collecting more information about how customers use and value its products and services. For this reason, Prime Video represents a challenge to the future of those streaming services operating only on subscription-based business models. Yet, more importantly, this case highlights that business model diversification can be enacted independently of other types of diversification, and it deserves distinct consideration.

In disentangling these two key dimensions, we also acknowledge that DD and digital resources allow the blending of online and offline services to serve the convenience and offer (virtually) limitless possibilities for diversification into new products and new business models[5] (Aversa et al., 2020). Hence, DD can also encompass digital and non-digital interplay, such as traditional, offline products enhanced by digital technologies and interdependencies between online vs offline experiences. For example, consider how adding a software component to a physical product can make the latter more appealing to an ever-increasing pool of digitally conscious consumers. Alexa or Google Home, due to the possibilities offered by the integration of technology in products and AI, enable making homes and products "smart" and simplifying consumers' lives through one of the most impactful innovations of this era, the IoT. Besides, think about how Amazon is attempting to further enhance its brick-and-mortar retail (e.g., Wholefoods), featuring one of the most advanced shopping technologies—which allows consumers to grab and go what they need without lines or checkout—while collecting offline and online data to improve the customer experience among all other unrelated businesses in its portfolio.

However, the interplay between digital and non-digital businesses may generate both complementarities and cannibalization. The case of Netflix—with its DVD-by-mail and streaming platform—has been extensively discussed and investigated in the literature of business models to illustrate how firms can leverage digital technologies to offer consumers different ways to engage with a focal proposition (watching rented movies) within the online and offline space (see, among others, Ahuja and Novelli, 2016; Teece, 2010). While selling DVDs and Blu-rays via offline retail and supplying films online as a streaming service may enhance positive complementarities for the firms providing the video content, cannibalization may occur at the product level if customers start to stream movies via Netflix's streaming platform rather than purchasing them as DVD rental service.

## DISCUSSION

In the last 50 years, diversification has surged as one of the key scholarly conversations in strategic management, and it has led to a major proliferation of empirical and theoretical studies (see Ahuja and Novelli, 2017). However, the increasing diffusion of digital technologies (Appio et al., 2021; Cennamo et al., 2020; Volberda et al., 2021) has challenged the traditional role of diversification and our understanding of these dynamics within firm boundaries and organizations—disclosing new drivers and dimensions that support firm growth through DD. Due to the technological breakthroughs, diversification can cross product and industry boundaries by integrating functionalities previously provided by different technologies, interconnecting digital and non-digital activities, and bringing together various stakeholders from previously separate industries to participate in the process of value creation and capture (Dattée, Alexy, and Autio, 2018; Tiwana, Konsynski, and Bush, 2010). As digital artifacts get increasingly permeable and open—and the product, industry, and organizational boundaries get more diffused—questions about how digital technologies enable, constrain, and shape the nature of diversification are gaining increasing importance.

Despite scholars having advanced valuable research to understand these timely phenomena, their contributions are somewhat fragmented and have not been so far combined to achieve a comprehensive and coherent understanding to clearly explain how and why our idea of diversification should be re-examined in digital domains. Hence, building on the extensive literature on corporate diversification and several iconic examples, we explained how digitalization urges us to move beyond our traditional understanding of corporate strategy and competitive dynamics at the firm level to explore diversification into digital contexts. We started by providing a conceptualization of "digital diversification" as a digitally enabled type of product, service, and business model diversification, which exploits opportunities from a firm's engagement with different digitally driven activities and offerings. Although the concept has already been practically investigated in empirical papers, to date a clear and theoretically informed definition of DD and an overview of its characterizing dimensions are missing. We then devoted particular attention to the foundations underpinning diversification in traditional and digital contexts, presented the most significant differences with traditional types of diversification (e.g., related vs unrelated diversification), and, finally, we focused on how DD differs between the supply and demand side, or for product vs business models; this allowed us to explain and contextualize the unique nature of DD.

We ultimately posit that DD moves from but does not fully conflate with TD; instead, it overcomes some of the traditional limitations related to offline or brick-and-mortar businesses by extending diversification opportunities beyond the firm's boundary and organization into areas of limited industry relatedness. Accordingly, firms operating and competing in digital contexts can improve their performance by expanding their scope in terms of the diversity or the breadth of their engagement with different related and unrelated digital solutions across businesses that do not necessarily transact with each other in one or multiple settings. The almost unlimited opportunities offered by diversification in digital contexts, in turn, put new demands on measuring DD and assessing a firm's digital portfolio's breadth in one or multiple settings.

**A Future Agenda for Digital Diversification**

Our discussions on the implications for theory and practice hint at future opportunities for research on DD and identify a research agenda for future studies within platforms and ecosystems, which combines both supply- and demand-side observations, implications originated by diversifying into new digital products or digitally enabled business models, as well as implications originated by diversifying into related and unrelated activities and offerings. Table 1.4 summarizes our main questions across areas that are relevant to DD, which we have more or less directly addressed in this chapter.

We presented mechanisms and provided reasons supporting firms' expansion of relatedness and increasing returns from seemingly unrelated diversification due to digitalization; we believe it might be interesting for future research to focus on the relationship between traditional and digital diversification and investigate how the value of relatedness varies across different diversification strategies, or for different degrees of digitalization. In exploring this trajectory, future studies could reveal how and under what conditions the traditional inverted U-shape curve representing diversification relatedness and performance shapes into an S-curve, or how the curve changes when firms pursue both digital and physical diversification at the same time (i.e., exploring implications for a cumulative effect). Furthermore, while in

*Table 1.4*     *A future agenda for digital diversification*

| Diversification dimensions | New research directions | Example |
| --- | --- | --- |
| Drivers: digital diversification vs traditional diversification | Investigate the relationship between traditional and digital diversification and how the value of relatedness varies across different diversification strategies. | • How does the relationship between diversification relatedness and firm performance vary for increasing degrees of digitalization?<br>• What are the implications of redeploying digital assets in traditional diversification?<br>• At which point does unrelated digital diversification lead to negative returns? |
| Supply side vs demand side in digital diversification | Disentangle supply- and demand-side complementarities and explore their mutual effect on diversification and, consequently, on performance. | • How do firms deploy and renew corporate capabilities, knowledge, and resources to manage digital diversification?<br>• What customer-focused mechanisms explain firms' diversification success and failure in digital contexts?<br>• How do the trade-offs and interplay firms face when combining supply- and demand-side strategies affect the performance? |
| Product vs business model in digital diversification | Investigate effective product and business model diversification strategies and their combined effect for novel pathways of value creation and creation. | • What are effective diversification strategies in the digital age?<br>• How do digital product and digital business model diversification relate to each other?<br>• What are the interdependencies between digital product and digital business model diversification, and how do they enhance firms' performance?<br>• How does the interplay between digital and non-digital diversification strategies impact firms' performance? |
| Platforms and ecosystems in digital diversification | Explore the significant role of platform owners and complementors diversification strategies and their implication on performance intraplatform and ecosystem competition. | • What are the platform owner diversification strategies associated with superior performance in platform-based ecosystems?<br>• Why are certain firms more successful at orchestrating or benefiting from their ecosystem?<br>• Under which conditions is adopting a diversification strategy associated with superior performance for complementors in platform-based ecosystems?<br>• Why are some complementors more likely to be accepted by other firms in an ecosystem? |

our study we advance that digitalization might lead to increasing returns from related and seemingly unrelated diversification, it is not clear at which point unrelated digital diversification leads to suboptimal or negative returns. In this regard, we recommend that future research should explore to what extent firms can diversify in unrelated domains using digital without significant performance penalties.

Since DD is mostly driven by the retention and redeployment of valuable data, we believe future research should focus on the importance of firms' capability to manage big data and new analytical tools to exploit novel ways of strategizing that differ from traditional corporate strategies. Thus, further studies exploring DD and *supply-side* implications should focus, for instance, on how firms deploy and renew corporate capabilities, knowledge, and resources to manage digital transformation while acknowledging digitalization's impact on the firm's boundary. The latter may have implications on the firm's internal organization and engagement with the actors in the ecosystem enabling the diversification and calling for possible reconsideration of existing theories in this strand. In addition, future research should investigate the *demand-side* implications to emphasize the importance of including environmental and external elements, such as customer engagement in an ecosystem structure, to explain firms' diversification success and failure in digital contexts. We suggest that DD calls for increased attention to the mutual effect of demand- and supply-side complementarities on diversification, two sides of the same coin that have often been studied in isolation. The combination of these two dimensions can unveil new and unique opportunities for realizing both producer and consumer synergies—whose value is critical for sustainable competitive advantage—and bring key implications for firm performance. For instance, on the supply side, a firm should be able to obtain, process, and store big data to track consumers and their preferences while identifying which experiences trigger more customer engagement mechanisms on the demand side. This means that producer and consumer synergies are leveraged simultaneously by firms—as a strategic cornerstone for further diversification—to offer consumers only products or services relevant to them. In this respect, we recommend considering the possible transition from a one-stop shop (effect) to a no-stop shop (effect), where consumers do not have to perform any action to receive products or services after their first engagement with the firm—thus reducing the intensity and granularity of interactions. This could be explored in the case of automatic, recursive purchases or subscription models across multiple lines of digital business.

Future studies on DD should contribute by clarifying what differs from TD, with particular attention to product and business model diversification, and reconsidering what is the optimal scale and scope for effective diversification strategies in digital settings. For example, we acknowledge that digital actors—such as Amazon, Google, or Disney—often engage with both product and business model diversification, making it difficult to disentangle the two aspects fully. Although distinguishing these two dimensions may not be straightforward, we suggest that, preferably, digital product and digital business model diversification can be combined, calling for novel pathways of value creation and capture. Besides, we also suggest that future studies should explore the interplay between DD and TD strategies and their implication on firms' performance. Here, scholars could observe how firms can expand their mobile application's value and standalone functionality not only by bundling with other apps but also by connecting them with smart products or connected devices (e.g., wearables such as Apple Watch, Fitbit, Garmin) to increase the value proposition beyond the digital or physical products per se. One should also acknowledge the possibility for those firms to capture value from the enhanced offering through different monetization mechanisms, such as single auto-renewable subscription services accessible through multiple apps or in-app purchases available in multiple platform versions of their app. In that case, scholars should explore the opportunities for firms derived from engaging with both product and business model diversification at the same time—an important aspect that deserves further investigation.

New research could also study the mechanisms and the underlying assumptions that TD cannot either explain or fully capture as proper and unique of digital contexts. Among those, the value and implications of business based on an "intangible" infrastructure, the pervasive redeployment of data assets, and the virtualization of consumption experiences should be taken into particular consideration. This will strengthen our understanding of DD as an omni-comprehensive view to explain diversification strategies that span and overcome the limitation of diversification in brick-and-mortar businesses. Therefore, we stress how understanding DD requires investigating firm-level dynamics as intertwined with higher-level changes, such as the emergence of platforms or ecosystems. This chapter underscores the significant role that multi-sided "platform" business models connecting multiple groups of stakeholders outside the boundary and the competitive dynamics within "ecosystems" play in the firm's decision to expand its presence into other domains. Hence, we also suggest that understanding the underlying mechanisms of the aforementioned one-stop shop and network effects across both product and business model diversification dimensions could explain why certain firms are more successful at orchestrating or benefiting from their ecosystem. At the same time, in disentangling diversification strategies in platforms and ecosystems, we also acknowledged how complementors' diversification could encompass more than one of these dimensions; i.e., they could be diversified in their product offering but not in platforms, or they could mobilize the same product engaging in different ways with different customers who engage across various platforms. This also represents a stepping stone to understanding why some complementors are more likely to be accepted (or not) by other firms and why some firms are more likely to hold a leadership role within an ecosystem.

## CONCLUSION

It is reasonable to challenge whether, after more than half a century of research on corporate strategy and diversification, we really need to update our understanding when approaching digital contexts. While we still consider many of the classic underpinnings highly informative and valuable, we claim that if TD principles were sufficient to fully comprehend and explain the entrance of new digital firms and their successful strategies in connecting seemingly unrelated businesses through digital technologies, we would not see so many traditional, resource-rich corporations—extremely experienced in the long-rooted "art" of brick-and-mortar diversification—failing to advance (or simply imitate) diversification strategies that much younger but digitally shrewd companies are pursuing. The disruption experienced by several traditionally diversified incumbents has pushed us to believe that we need—at least in part—to reconsider the underlying drivers of diversification in digital contexts. Still, we acknowledge our chapter is far from completing this ambitious task, and it offers (by design) more questions than answers. Nonetheless, we hope that by providing an initial definition and conceptualization of digital diversification, we may be able to lay some of the foundations for future scholars that aim to contribute to this growing debate, which holds promises to provide better, theoretically grounded explanations of this compelling phenomenon.

## NOTES

1.  Note that there are also examples that run counter to this trend. There are cases of big tech companies that have struggled to diversify despite having all the capabilities, as the latter were resource-intensive, suggesting that not all the big techs can swiftly diversify at scale. In addition, there are cases of companies successfully diversifying in traditional markets that have struggled to diversify in digital contexts—raising new demands on what is different in digital diversification vs traditional diversification.
2.  Note that hereafter—for a matter of brevity—whenever we say "products," we also imply "services."
3.  We acknowledge that it has been theorized and found that digitalization should reduce firm scale and scope as market-based transacting becomes more efficient (Menz et., 2021). However, we provide reasons supporting firms' expansion of scope due to digitalization and DD. Therefore, there

are arguments to support both an expansion and a contraction of firm boundaries (Afuah, 2003; Autio, Mudambi, and Yoo, 2021; Menz et al., 2021).

4.   Figure 1.1 clearly shows how performance reaches a lower optimization (or turning) point for moderate levels of relatedness in traditional markets and how performance declines when firms move from moderate levels of related diversification to unrelated diversification. Instead, we theorize that the optimization (or tipping) point from DD is reached at higher levels of related diversification, and it is higher in absolute terms, which implies greater returns from both related and unrelated diversification compared to TD. This suggests that the relationship between relatedness of diversification and performance becomes "steeper" (in DD) as the penalty for unrelated diversification in digital is significantly lower relative to physical diversification because of the importance of asset redeployment, cost-saving, and enhanced customer experience.

5.   As an aside, adding a service might be considered a new business model, such as servitization; however, there could be cases of companies adding new businesses where services are an important part, without changing business models per se. In other words, not every product and service diversification necessarily has to incorporate a new business model. For example, selling a digitally enabled product (e.g., cell phone or cleaning robot) and adding an AI chatbot for after-sale service is a digitally enabled case of servitization, but it is not a new business model.

# REFERENCES

Adner, R., and Kapoor, R. 2010. "Value Creation in Innovation Ecosystems: How the Structure of Technological Interdependence Affects Firm Performance in New Technology Generations." *Strategic Management Journal* 31 (3): 306–33. https://doi.org/10.1002/smj.821.

Adner, R., and Kapoor, R. 2016. "Innovation Ecosystems and the Pace of Substitution: Re-Examining Technology S-Curves." *Strategic Management Journal* 37 (4): 625–48.

Adner, R., Puranam, P., and Zhu, F. 2019. "What Is Different About Digital Strategy? From Quantitative to Qualitative Change." *Strategy Science* 4 (4): 253–61.

Adner R., and Zemsky, P. 2006. "A Demand-Based Perspective on Sustainable Competitive Advantage." *Strategic Management Journal* 27 (3): 215–39.

Afuah, A. 2003. "Redefining Firm Boundaries in the Face of the Internet: Are Firms Really Shrinking?" *Academy of Management Review* 28: 34–53.

Ahuja, G., Lampert, C.M., and Novelli, E. 2013. "The Second Face of Appropriability: Generative Appropriability and Its Determinants." *Academy of Management Review* 38 (2): 248–69.

Ahuja G., and Novelli, E. 2016. "Incumbent Responses to an Entrant with a New Business Model: Resource Co-Deployment and Resource Re-Deployment Strategies." In *Resource Redeployment and Corporate Strategy* (*Advances in Strategic Management*, Vol. 35), edited by T.B. Folta, C.E. Helfat and S. Karim: 125–53. Bingley: Emerald Group. https://doi.org/10.1108/S0742-332220160000035006.

Ahuja G., and Novelli, E. 2017. "Redirecting Research Efforts on the Diversification–Performance Linkage: The Search for Synergy." *Academy of Management Annals* 11 (1): 342–90.

Amit, R., and Zott, C. 2001. "Value Creation in E-Business." *Strategic Management Journal* 22 (6–7): 493–520.

Ansoff, H.I. 1957. "Strategies for Diversification." *Harvard Business Review* 35 (5): 113–24.

Appio, F.P., Frattini, F., Petruzzelli, A.M., and Neirotti, P. 2021. "Digital Transformation and Innovation Management: A Synthesis of Existing Research and an Agenda for Future Studies." *Journal of Product Innovation Management*, 38(1): 4–20.

Autio, E., Mudambi, R., and Yoo, Y. 2021. "Digitalization and Globalization in a Turbulent World: Centrifugal and Centripetal Forces." *Global Strategy Journal* 11: 3–16.

Aversa, P., Furnari, S., and Haefliger, S. 2015. "Business Model Configurations and Performance: A Qualitative Comparative Analysis in Formula One Racing, 2005–2013." *Industrial and Corporate Change* 24 (3): 655–76.

Aversa, P., Haefliger, S., Hueller, F., and Reza, D.G. 2020. "Customer Complementarity in the Digital Space: Exploring Amazon's Business Model Diversification." *Long Range Planning*: 101985.

Aversa, P., Haefliger, S., and Reza, D.G. 2017. "Building a Winning Business Model Portfolio." *MIT Sloan Management Review* 58 (4): 49–54.

Aversa, P., Hervas-Drane, A., and Evenou, M. 2019. "Business Model Responses to Digital Piracy." *California Management Review* 61 (2): 30–58. https://doi.org/10.1177/0008125618818841.

Barney, J. 1991. "Firm Resources and Sustained Competitive Advantage." *Journal of Management* 17 (1). https://doi.org/10.1177/014920639101700 1.

Block, J.H., Henkel, J., Schweisfurth, T.G., and Stiegler, A. 2016. "Commercializing User Innovations by Vertical Diversification: The User–Manufacturer Innovator." *Research Policy* 45 (1): 244–59.

Bresnahan, T.F., and Trajtenberg, M. 1995. "General Purpose Technologies 'Engines of Growth'?" *Journal of Econometrics* 65 (1): 83–108.

Bryce, D.J., and Winter, S.G. 2009. "A General Interindustry Relatedness Index." *Management Science* 55 (9): 1570–85.

Cennamo, C. 2021. "Competing in Digital Markets: A Platform-Based Perspective." *Academy of Management Perspectives* 35 (2): 265–91.

Cennamo, C., Dagnino, G.B., Di Minin, A., and Lanzolla, G. 2020. "Managing Digital Transformation: Scope of Transformation and Modalities of Value Co-Generation and Delivery." *California Management Review* 62 (4): 5–16.

Cennamo, C., Ozalp, H., and Kretschmer, T. 2018. "Platform Architecture and Quality Trade-Offs of Multihoming Complements." *Information Systems Research* 29 (2): 461–78. https://doi.org/10.1287/isre.2018.0779.

Cennamo, C., and Santalo, J. 2013. "Platform Competition: Strategic Trade-Offs in Platform Markets: Platform Competition." *Strategic Management Journal* 34 (11): 1331–50. https://doi.org/10.1002/smj.2066.

Chirico, F., Sirmon, D.G., Sciascia, S., and Mazzola, P. 2011. "Resource Orchestration in Family Firms: Investigating How Entrepreneurial Orientation, Generational Involvement, and Participative Strategy Affect Performance." *Strategic Entrepreneurship Journal* 5 (4): 307–26.

Collis, D.J., and Montgomery, C.A. 1997. *Corporate Strategy: Resources and the Scope of the Firm.* Chicago, IL: Irwin.

Conti, R., Gambardella, A., and Novelli, E. 2019. "Specializing in Generality: Firm Strategies When Intermediate Markets Work." *Organization Science* 30 (1): 126–50.

Cozzolino, A., Corbo, L., and Aversa, P. 2021. "Digital Platform-Based Ecosystems: The Evolution of Collaboration and Competition between Incumbent Producers and Entrant Platforms." *Journal of Business Research* 126: 385–400.

Cusumano, M.A., Gawer, A., and Yoffie, D.B. 2019. *The Business of Platforms: Strategy in the Age of Digital Competition, Innovation, and Power.* New York, NY: Harper Business.

Dagnino, G.B., Giachetti, C., La Rocca, M., and Picone, P.M. 2019. "Behind the Curtain of International Diversification: An Agency Theory Perspective." *Global Strategy Journal* 9 (4): 555–94.

Dattée, B., Alexy, O., and Autio, E. 2018. "Maneuvering in Poor Visibility: How Firms Play the Ecosystem Game When Uncertainty Is High." *Academy of Management Journal* 61 (2): 466–98. https://doi.org/10.5465/amj.2015.0869.

Davenport, T.H., and Ronanki, R. 2018. "Artificial Intelligence for the Real World." *Harvard Business Review*, January–February. https://hbr.org/2018/01/artificial-intelligence-for-the-real-world.

Economides, N. 1996. "The Economics of Networks." *International Journal of Industrial Organization* 14 (6): 673–99.

Economides, N., and Katsamakas, E. 2006. "Two-Sided Competition of Proprietary vs. Open Source Technology Platforms and the Implications for the Software Industry." *Management Science* 52 (7): 1057–71.

Gambardella, A., and McGahan, A.M. 2010. "Business-Model Innovation: General Purpose Technologies and Their Implications for Industry Structure." *Long Range Planning* 43 (2–3): 262–71.

Gawer, A. 2009. "Platform Dynamics and Strategies: From Products to Services." *Platforms, Markets and Innovation* 45: 57.

Gawer, A., and Cusumano, M.A. 2014. "Industry Platforms and Ecosystem Innovation: Platforms and Innovation." *Journal of Product Innovation Management* 31 (3): 417–33. https://doi.org/10.1111/jpim.12105.

George, G., Haas, M.R., and Pentland, A. 2014. *Big Data and Management*. Briarcliff Manor, NY: Academy of Management.

Granstrand, O., Patel, P., and Pavitt, K. 1997. "Multi-Technology Corporations: Why They Have 'Distributed' Rather than 'Distinctive Core' Competencies." *California Management Review* 39 (4): 8–25.

Grant, R.M. 2016. *Contemporary Strategy Analysis: Text and Cases Edition*. Chichester: John Wiley & Sons.

Gregory, R.W., Henfridsson, O., Kaganer, E., and Kyriakou, H. 2021. "Data Network Effects: Key Conditions, Shared Data, and the Data Value Duality." *Academy of Management Review* 47 (1). https://doi.org/10.5465/amr.2021.0111.

Haans, R.F.J., Pieters, C., and He, Z. 2016. "Thinking about You: Theorizing and Testing U- and Inverted U-Shaped Relationships in Strategy Research." *Strategic Management Journal* 37: 1177–95.

Harrison, J.S., Hitt, M.A., Hoskisson, R.E., and Ireland, R.D. 2001. "Resource Complementarity in Business Combinations: Extending the Logic to Organizational Alliances." *Journal of Management* 27 (6): 679–90.

Hartmann, P., and Henkel, J. 2020. "The Rise of Corporate Science in AI: Data as a Strategic Resource." *Academy of Management Discoveries* 6 (3): 359–81.

Hashai, N. 2015. "Within-industry Diversification and Firm Performance: An S-shaped Hypothesis." *Strategic Management Journal* 36 (9): 1378–1400.

Helfat, C.E., and Peteraf, M.A. 2003. "The Dynamic Resource-Based View: Capability Lifecycles." *Strategic Management Journal* 24 (10): 997–1010.

Hitt, M.A., Hoskisson, R.E., and Kim, H. 1997. "International Diversification: Effects on Innovation and Firm Performance in Product-Diversified Firms." *Academy of Management Journal* 40 (4): 767–98.

Jacobides, M.G., Cennamo, C., and Gawer, A. 2018. "Towards a Theory of Ecosystems." *Strategic Management Journal* 39 (8): 2255–76. https://doi.org/10.1002/smj.2904.

Jarillo, J. 1988. "On Strategic Networks." *Strategic Management Journal* 9 (1): 31–41.

Kapoor, R., and Agarwal, S. 2017. "Sustaining Superior Performance in Business Ecosystems: Evidence from Application Software Developers in the IOS and Android Smartphone Ecosystems." *Organization Science* 28 (3): 531–51. https://doi.org/10.1287/orsc.2017.1122.

Kaufman, C.F. 1996. "A New Look at One-Stop Shopping: A TIMES Model Approach to Matching Store Hours and Shopper Schedules." *Journal of Consumer Marketing* 13: 4–52.

Klang, D., Wallnöfer, M., and Hacklin, F. 2014. "The Business Model Paradox: A Systematic Review and Exploration of Antecedents." *International Journal of Management Reviews* 16 (4): 454–78.

Kretschmer, T., Leiponen, A., Schilling, M., and Vasudeva, G. 2020. "Platform Ecosystems as Meta-organizations: Implications for Platform Strategies." *Strategic Management Journal* 43 (3): 405–24.

Luo, Y. 2021. "New OLI Advantages in Digital Globalization." *International Business Review* 30: 1–8.

Markides, C.C., and Williamson, P.J. 1994. "Related Diversification, Core Competences and Corporate Performance." *Strategic Management Journal* 15 (S2): 149–65.

Markides, C.C., and Williamson, P.J. 1996. "Corporate Diversification and Organizational Structure: A Resource-Based View." *Academy of Management Journal* 39 (2): 340–67.

Massa, L., Tucci, C.L., and Afuah, A. 2017. "A Critical Assessment of Business Model Research." *Academy of Management Annals* 11 (1): 73–104.

Menz, M., Kunisch, S., Birkinshaw, J., Collis, D.J., Foss, N.J., Hoskisson, R.E., and Prescott, J.E. 2021. "Corporate Strategy and the Theory of the Firm in the Digital Age." *Journal of Management Studies* 58(7): 1695–1720.

Messinger, P.R., and Narasimhan, C. 1997. "A Model of Retail Formats Based on Consumers' Economizing on Shopping Time." *Marketing Science* 16 (1): 1–23.

Milgrom, P., and Roberts, J. 1990. "Rationalizability, Learning, and Equilibrium in Games with Strategic Complementarities." *Econometrica: Journal of the Econometric Society* 58 (6): 1255–77.

Montgomery, C.A. 1982. "The Measurement of Firm Diversification: Some New Empirical Evidence." *Academy of Management Journal* 25 (2): 299–307.

Palich, L.E., Cardinal, L.B., and Miller, C.C. 2000. "Curvilinearity in the Diversification–Performance Linkage: An Examination of over Three Decades of Research." *Strategic Management Journal* 21 (2): 155–74.

Panico, C., and Cennamo, C. 2015. "What Drives a Platform's Strategy? Usage, Membership, and Competition Effects." In *Academy of Management Proceedings*, 2015: 15942. Briarcliff Manor, NY: Academy of Management.

Penrose, E.T. 1959. *The Theory of the Growth of the Firm*. New York, NY: John Wiley & Sons Inc.

Porter, M.E. 1985. "Technology and Competitive Advantage." *Journal of Business Strategy* 5 (3): 60–78.

Priem, R.L. 2007. "A Consumer Perspective on Value Creation." *Academy of Management Review* 32 (1): 219–35. https://doi.org/10.5465/amr.2007.23464055.

Priem, R.L., Wenzel, M., and Koch, J. 2018. "Demand-Side Strategy and Business Models: Putting Value Creation for Consumers Center Stage." *Long Range Planning* 51 (1): 22–31.

Puranam, P., and Vanneste, B. 2016. *Corporate Strategy: Tools for Analysis and Decision-Making*. Cambridge: Cambridge University Press.

Rietveld, J., and Eggers, J.P. 2018. "Demand Heterogeneity in Platform Markets: Implications for Complementors." *Organization Science* 29 (2): 304–22. https://doi.org/10.1287/orsc.2017.1183.

Rietveld, J., Schilling, M.A., and Bellavitis, C. 2019. "Platform Strategy: Managing Ecosystem Value through Selective Promotion of Complements." *Organization Science* 30 (6): 1232–51.

Rochet, J., and Tirole, J. 2006. "Two-Sided Markets: A Progress Report." *RAND Journal of Economics* 37 (3): 645–67.

Rumelt, R.P. 1974. *Strategy, Structure, and Economic Performance*. Cambridge, MA: Harvard University Press.

Rumelt, R.P. 1982. "Diversification Strategy and Profitability." *Strategic Management Journal* 3 (4): 359–69.

Sakhartov, A.V., and Folta, T.B. 2015. "Getting beyond Relatedness as a Driver of Corporate Value." *Strategic Management Journal* 36 (13): 1939–59.

Sawhney, M., Verona, G., and Prandelli, E. 2005. "Collaborating to Create: The Internet as a Platform for Customer Engagement in Product Innovation." *Journal of Interactive Marketing* 19 (4): 4–17.

Shermon, A., and Moeen, M. 2019. *Zooming In or Zooming Out: Entrants' Product Usage Breadth in the Nascent Drone Industry*. Working paper, University of North Carolina, Chapel Hill.

Snihur, Y., and Tarzijan, J. 2018. "Managing Complexity in a Multi-Business-Model Organization." *Long Range Planning* 51 (1): 50–63.

Sohl, T., Vroom, G., and McCann, B.T. 2020. "Business Model Diversification and Firm Performance: A Demand-Side Perspective." *Strategic Entrepreneurship Journal* 14 (2): 198–223.

Srivastava, M.K., and Gnyawali, D.R. 2011. "When Do Relational Resources Matter? Leveraging Portfolio Technological Resources for Breakthrough Innovation." *Academy of Management Journal* 54 (4): 797–810.

Su, W., and Tsang, E.W.K. 2015. "Product Diversification and Financial Performance: The Moderating Role of Secondary Stakeholders." *Academy of Management Journal* 58 (4): 1128–48.

Sun, M., and Tse, E. 2009. "The Resource-Based View of Competitive Advantage in Two-Sided Markets." *Journal of Management Studies* 46 (1): 45–64.

Tavalaei, M.M., and Cennamo, C. 2020. "In Search of Complementarities within and across Platform Ecosystems: Complementors' Relative Standing and Performance in Mobile Apps Ecosystems." *Long Range Planning*, April: 101994. https://doi.org/10.1016/j.lrp.2020.101994.

Teece, D.J. 1977. "Technology Transfer by Multinational Firms: The Resource Cost of Transferring Technological Know-How." *Economic Journal* 87 (346): 242–61.

Teece, D.J. 1982. "Towards an Economic Theory of the Multiproduct Firm." *Journal of Economic Behavior & Organization* 3 (1): 39–63.

Teece, D.J. 2010. "Business Models, Business Strategy and Innovation." *Long Range Planning* 43 (2–3): 172–94.

Tiwana, A. 2015. "Evolutionary Competition in Platform Ecosystems." *Information Systems Research* 26 (2): 266–81.

Tiwana, A., Konsynski, B., and Bush, A.A. 2010. "Platform Evolution: Coevolution of Platform Architecture, Governance, and Environmental Dynamics." *Information Systems Research* 21 (4): 675–87. https://doi.org/10.1287/isre.1100.0323.

Verhoef, P.C., Broekhuizen, T., Bart, Y., Bhattacharyaa, A., Qi Dong, J.Q., Fabien, N., and Haenlein, M. 2021. "Digital Transformation: A Multidisciplinary Reflection and Research Agenda." *Journal of Business Research* 122: 889–901.

Visnjic, I., Jovanovic, M., and Raisch, S. 2021. "Managing the Transition to a Dual Business Model: Tradeoff, Paradox, and Routinized Practices." *Organization Science* 33 (5): 1964–89.

Volberda, H.W., Khanagha, S., Baden-Fuller, C., Mihalache, O.R., and Birkinshaw, J. 2021. "Strategizing in a Digital World: Overcoming Cognitive Barriers, Reconfiguring Routines and Introducing New Organizational Forms." *Long Range Planning* 54 (5): 102110.

Wernerfelt, B. 1984. "A Resource-based View of the Firm." *Strategic Management Journal* 5 (2): 171–80.

Wiersema, M.F., and Bowen, H.P. 2008. "Corporate Diversification: The Impact of Foreign Competition, Industry Globalization, and Product Diversification." *Strategic Management Journal* 29 (2): 115–32.

Ye, G., Priem, R.L., and Alshwer, A.A. 2012. "Achieving Demand-Side Synergy from Strategic Diversification: How Combining Mundane Assets Can Leverage Consumer Utilities." *Organization Science* 23 (1): 207–24.

Zhu, F., and Iansiti, M. 2012. "Entry into Platform-Based Markets." *Strategic Management Journal* 33 (1): 88–106. https://doi.org/10.1002/smj.941.

Zott, C., Amit, R., and Massa, L. 2011. "The Business Model: Recent Developments and Future Research." *Journal of Management* 37 (4): 1019–42.

# 2. The next frontier of digital business model innovation

*Ludovica Moi, Yanina Rashkova and Francesca Cabiddu*

## INTRODUCTION

Today, increasing global competition and challenges posed by the phenomenon of digital transformation have triggered in-depth changes in firms' products, roles, structures, and interactions and in specific business model innovation (BMI) (Cennamo et al., 2020; Chesbrough, 2010; Foss & Saebi, 2017; Hess et al., 2016; Verhoef et al., 2021).

People constantly use digital tools to share and receive real-time experiences and information (Islam et al., 2020; Zheng et al., 2020). In this regard, companies increasingly profit from adopting digital technologies to reconfigure their relationship with customers, revenue models, and operations and accomplish new value-creation opportunities (Parida et al., 2019; Rydén & El Sawy, 2019; Visnjic et al., 2018). Research on BMI raises the need for firms to look for ways to innovate and adapt to the new patterns and makeup of the marketplace with greater flexibility and quickness (Brand et al., 2021; Chen et al., 2015; Cucculelli & Bettinelli, 2015; Tavoletti et al., 2021). Scholars particularly outline the importance of upgrading skills and competencies to address fast-changing environmental dynamics better and enhance competitiveness (Bresciani et al., 2021). Other scholars assume that the ability to innovate BMs in response to major changes in the external environment may be a key dynamic capability (Zott et al., 2011). Among the core dynamic capabilities required in the digital transformation era, recent studies highlight the prominence of agility (Bresciani et al., 2021; Warner & Wäger, 2019). Agility is the firm's capacity to manage uncertainty, seize market opportunities, and reconfigure its resources in a timely fashion for greater customer value (Sambamurthy et al., 2003; Teece, 2010; Teece et al., 2016).

In particular, the role of agility as a key driver for BMI has been recognized in the literature under the concept of strategic agility, which encompasses three meta-capabilities (strategic sensitivity, leadership unity, and resource fluidity) necessary to accelerate BM renewal (Doz & Kosonen, 2010). However, our understanding about how strategic agility helps organizations to innovate and adapt their digital BMs to the changing conditions of the market is still limited (Battistella et al., 2017; Rachinger et al., 2019; Schneider & Spieth, 2013; Spieth et al., 2014; Verhoef et al., 2021). Prior literature has explored different types of capabilities in the context of digital transformation—e.g., team-specific cognitions, big data analytics, or networking capabilities (Ciampi et al., 2021; Hadjielias et al., 2021; Vrontis et al., 2020)—and the mechanisms through which such capabilities elicit innovation outcomes. Nevertheless, we still have little empirical and theoretical knowledge concerning the impact of strategic agility on digital BMI (Warner & Wäger, 2019).

In this chapter, we attempt to answer the following research question: "How does strategic agility enable organizations to innovate their digital business models?" We conduct an exploratory single-case study (Eisenhardt, 1989; Miles & Huberman, 1984; Yin, 1994), focusing the attention on the case of Clickio, a leading firm in programmatic marketing that offers innovative technological solutions for digital publishers.

By extending the literature on agility and BMI, our findings offer a structured analysis of the different ways in which strategic agility assists firms in accomplishing digital BMI to develop a more significant digital value proposition in shifting business contexts. This chapter has crucial implications for practice. It may help managers seeking to redefine their digital BM by learning more about how strategic agility can be embedded into their strategic and operational efforts to adapt to the uncertainty of today's complex and fast-changing landscape more effectively.

## THEORETICAL BACKGROUND

### Business Models and Digital Business Model Innovation

A BM is generally defined as a set of structured and interdependent elements through which organizations create and deliver value to customers (Zott et al., 2011). It encompasses the relationships between a firm and its overall stakeholders (e.g., customers, suppliers), as well as its internal units and departments (e.g., units, staff, teams), articulated in procedures and action routines (Battistella et al., 2017). Hence, a BM epitomizes the overall business architecture and related mechanisms set around a firm's value proposition generated to acquire target customers and entice them to pay, eventually converting these payments to profit (Foss & Saebi, 2018; Magretta, 2002; Teece, 2010).

Early management studies conceived BMs as a bundle of stable practices and ways of performing to ensure efficiency (Siggelkow, 2002). Their archetypes described well-known business logic that explains value creation, delivery, and capture mechanisms across industry contexts (Baden-Fuller & Morgan, 2010). Over time, scholars have started to recognize that the elements composing a firm's BM are not hard to change; instead, they evolve and continuously interact with each other to enhance a firm's sustained competitive advantage (Cavalcante, 2014; Doz & Kosonen, 2010; Magretta, 2002).

The shifting from conventional BMs to more dynamic BMs has been sharpened by the growing adoption of digital technologies in business contexts, and the recent trend of digitization of products and services, which strongly influenced changes in customer expectations and firms' capacity to generate revenues and earn profits (El Sawy & Pereria, 2013). Today, it is highly important for firms' survival and success to continuously reconfigure BMs (Johnson et al., 2008) to take advantage of new value-creating opportunities and modify BMs effectively and in a timely manner when an opportunity or threat arises. Moreover, the persistent re-examination of BMs helps to maintain innovativeness and reduces the risk of inertia towards change which often occurs when a company has been successful with the same strategy over time (Achtenhagen et al., 2013).

A growing research stream is related to BMI (Schneider & Spieth, 2013; Teece, 2010; Zott et al., 2011), delineating those "novel, non-trivial changes to the key elements of a firm's business model and/or the architecture linking these elements" (Foss & Saebi, 2018, p. 201). The innovations in such elements affect a firm's value creation, delivery, and capture and are important sources of competitive advantage as they are difficult to be imitated by others (Rachinger et al., 2019).

Digitalization is considered an important driver of BMI. Indeed, it is with digitalization that firms seek to "reinvent" their BM; e.g., redesigning or experimenting with new products and services, rethinking their value proposition, reconfiguring value delivery models, or reorganizing processes (Westerman et al., 2014). Employing technology within a firm's BM considerably amplifies its ability to discover new growth opportunities to satisfy latent customer needs (Teece, 2010). Furthermore, by leveraging digital technologies, firms have progressively revolutionized their relationship with customers, suppliers, and overall business networks (Pagani & Pardo, 2017; Schallmo et al., 2017). Technologies increase virtual touchpoints with customers and facilitate market entry (Verhoef et al., 2021).

Scholars define digital BMs as "the underlying business logic deliberately acknowledges the characteristics of digitization and takes advantage of them, both in interaction with customers and business partners, and in its internal operation" (Bärenfänger & Otto, 2015, p. 18). A digital BM's value proposition may articulate in the following dimensions: content (the selection of activities to be performed), structure (the way such activities are performed), and governance (who performs these activities) (Amit & Zott, 2012). In this conception, BMI occurs when at least one of these elements is set in a novel way (Zott, 2016). According to scholars, digital BMI can be driven by several factors, including, for instance, the novelty of the activity system, the lock-in mechanisms that create switching costs, the set of complementarities that connect different BM elements, and the efficiency which saves the costs of those interactions (Zott & Amit, 2017). With this study, we deepen the mechanisms through which strategic agility impacts digital BMI.

**Agility**

Agility originates as a software development methodology aimed at developing software adjusted to customers' needs (Lee & Xia, 2010; Lindstrom & Jeffries, 2004). Teams work closely with users, make tests in short iterative cycles, and continuously update projects based on users' feedback to deliver high-quality and timely innovations (Bianchi et al., 2020; Chan & Thong, 2009; Cooper, 2014).

Today, agility is viewed as a crucial capability to thrive and succeed in unpredictable business contexts (Prange, 2021). Agility epitomizes the dynamic capability to manage uncertainty (Teece et al., 2016), to "detect and seize market opportunities with speed and surprise" (Sambamurthy et al., 2003, p. 238). In particular, agility concerns the ability to modify and reconfigure existing assets and capabilities continuously, change the way of doing business, and enhance customer value creation (Lee et al., 2015; Lu & Ramamurthy, 2011; Rigby et al., 2016; Tallon & Pinsonneault, 2011; Teece, 2010), which is vital for firms' survival. Indeed, to navigate dynamic and unpredictable markets, firms need to be flexible to intensified competition and technological turbulence (Chakravarty et al., 2013; Lee et al., 2015). Firms displaying agility are able to constantly look for new ways to adapt to fluctuations in the market demand rapidly (Moi & Cabiddu, 2021a, 2021b). From a practical perspective, agility occurs in multiple ways, including faster product-service delivery, quicker decision-making processes, and the delivery of higher product or service quality (Mahadevan et al., 2019).

Despite the significant scholarly insights into the importance of agility and its implications for business strategy and performance, research on the relationship between strategic agility and BMI is still evolving. Scholars conceptualize strategic agility as a useful tool to innovate BM, consisting of "thoughtful and purposive interplay" between three dimensions: strategic sensitivity (the ability to perceive strategic developments), leadership unity (the ability to engage top managers to commit towards changes), and resource fluidity (the internal ability to quickly reconfigure and redeploy resources) (Doz & Kosonen, 2010, p. 371). Firms with strategic sensibility develop a sense of the future development of the market, for example, by participating in experiments and exploring different configurations of future products. Moreover, by building on careful evaluation of the current business model and its core competencies, firms are implementing additional business solutions that redefine the concept of the BM entity. Leadership unity is the cornerstone of BMI because without the collective commitment of all top managers to the new model, it is difficult to bring about the desired change. Only through respectful dialogue, empowerment, compassion, and clear communication of the importance of the "everyone on board" attitude can a BM be reconfigured effectively. And ultimately, firms need to ensure that they have the resources to implement the new BM. Since firms are often involved in complex processes and operations that are difficult to change, the ability to quickly and without damage reallocate the necessary resources will provide structural flexibility that is required for BMI. Despite the recognition from the literature of the importance of strategic agility to innovate BMs (Doz & Kosonen, 2010), research about the impact of strategic agility on digital BMI is still in its infancy (Verhoef et al., 2021). To address this gap, in the following sections we will empirically explore the mechanisms through which strategic agility contributes to innovating the content, structure, and governance of a firm's digital BM (Amit & Zott, 2012).

## METHODOLOGY

Since little is known about the relationship between strategic agility and digital BMI, the present study adopts an exploratory single-case-study research design (Eisenhardt, 1989; Miles & Huberman, 1984; Yin, 1994). Such a methodology allows us to investigate the topic in a real-world setting and get in-depth empirical insights useful to build a robust theoretical inference (Dyer & Wilkins, 1991; Eisenhardt, 1989) generalized via analytical reasoning (Yin, 2013).

### Case Selection

We opted for a purposive sampling approach, according to which the case study is strategically chosen based on its information richness and helpfulness concerning the phenomenon investigated (Patton, 2005). Since our research focused on digital BMs, we looked for a case study operating in the digital industry as a suitable research setting for addressing the theoretical purposes and research questions of this study. The further selection criterion was represented by the firm's implementation of strategic agility, encountered by one of the three authors who collaborate with the firm and have a privileged view of the internal processes. For example, the fast decision of the owner to implement the GDPR [General Data Protection Regulation] Consent Tool solution to react to the new European Union GDPR initiative that directly impacted the digital BMs of many enterprises (Ziegler et al., 2019) may be related to leadership unity. Following these criteria, we identified Clickio as a remarkable case for our study that would allow us to conduct empirical qualitative research on strategic agility in the digital BMI domain.

*Table 2.1*        *Summary of the primary data sources*

| Primary data sources | Description |
| --- | --- |
| In-depth interviews | 3 Semi-structured interviews were conducted with the Commercial Director (65 minutes), the Director of Commercial Operations (36 minutes), and the Publisher Development Director (46 minutes). |
| Field notes from observations | During the research period, the field researcher produced qualitative data recorded in an observation diary. |

Clickio is a leading international firm in programmatic marketing, with representatives in Russia, Italy, and the United Kingdom. It was founded in 2015 by a team of five people. Currently, it has more than 70 employees serving over 500 clients globally. Clickio is a platform that provides digital publishers with innovative solutions that help their sites grow efficiently and sustainably, and represents the first Google Certified Publishing Partner in Italy and Russia. In 2018, Clickio significantly innovated its BM by developing a consent management platform, offering it free of charge to all digital publishers.

**Data Collection**

To ensure comprehensive coverage of the phenomenon investigated, we triangulated data from multiple sources (Eisenhardt, 1989; Miles & Huberman, 1984). We collected primary data through participant and non-participant observations during meetings and team-building events. As one of the co-authors had a role of a participant as an observer and was involved in the firm's activities during the whole period of the research, we embraced a deep understanding of our research setting (Dyer & Wilkins, 1991; Hammersley & Atkinson, 2019). Primary data also included in-depth interviews with key informants who were highly knowledgeable in the field (Eisenhardt & Graebner, 2007). Interviews followed a semi-structured interview protocol (Strauss & Corbin, 1998). Examples of guiding interview questions were as follows: How do you organize the firm to create and deliver your value proposition to your customers? Which process do you follow when developing a new product?

Interviews were properly recorded, transcribed, and coded through NVivo 10 software. The interviews were conducted in June 2021, with each interview lasting between 35 and 65 minutes (Table 2.1).

Secondary data were collected through the company's website, blog, social media accounts, and press releases. Such data were gathered via Ncapture, the browser application of NVivo.

**Data Analysis**

When analyzing the data, we were guided by abductive reasoning, since some aspects of our research problem are already grounded in the existing literature, while others are hidden (Bandara et al., 2015). Thus, we approached the data inductively when looking for evidence of how strategic agility impacts digital BMI, while aggregate dimensions, namely structure, governance, and content (Amit & Zott, 2012), were established deductively from the BMI literature.

We based our analysis on moves of the categorization process (Grodal et al., 2020). At first, we approached data by identifying relevant concepts via open coding (Gibbs, 2007). Second, we iteratively analyzed data by dropping, merging, splitting, and relating categories.

During this coding stage, we triangulated secondary data with previously identified categories. First-order concepts were then grouped around a set of second-order categories to view data at a higher level of abstraction until reaching a saturation point (Strauss & Corbin, 1998). Finally, we grouped second-order concepts into overarching dimensions that captured the most important elements in a BMI process: structure, governance, and content (Amit & Zott, 2012). See examples of this process in Table 2.2.

Two co-authors performed the whole coding process independently and simultaneously. During each coding step, we ran a coding comparison query. We discussed any inconsistencies until achieving a Kappa coefficient higher than 0.80 (Miles & Huberman, 1984).

To ensure robust results, we applied the following criteria used in qualitative research: credibility, transferability, dependability, and confirmability (Bell et al., 2018; Lincoln & Guba, 2013). In particular, for the credibility criteria (which parallels internal validity or confidence in the trustworthiness of research findings), we performed respondent validation; i.e., we shared our findings with the participants and obtained the corroboration of the study results. The transferability criteria (i.e., the applicability of the results in other contexts) was assured by a detailed description of the context to guarantee the full apprehension and understanding of the research setting and drive an analytical generalization (Yin, 2013). Concerning dependability (i.e., consistency of research findings), two co-authors performed data analyses and data coding simultaneously and independently by triangulating the data from multiple sources. Finally, for confirmability (i.e., unbiased interpretation of the findings), in explaining our research findings, we incorporated direct quotes from our interviews. We supported our explanations with examples using the original data.

## FINDINGS

Clickio's digital BM, from our point of view, consists of three intertwining elements—i.e., content, structure, and governance (Amit & Zott, 2012)—that, taken together, contribute to defining how it creates and delivers value. By elaborating upon these dimensions, strategic agility is found to encourage the company's digital BMI in several ways. The details of our research findings are discussed in the following paragraphs. Study findings are organized in a theoretical framework in which the key mechanisms of strategic agility impacting digital BMI across such dimensions are represented (see Figure 2.1).

### Digital BMI of Content

The main purpose of Clickio is to help digital publishers to navigate through a vibrant digital ecosystem and overcome several challenges in providing a holistic business solution that ranges from an effective monetization strategy and data compliance to site performance and data analytics. This scope is enhanced by the firm's ability to understand environmental changes and sense future opportunities and threats (strategic sensitivity). Through a proactive attitude in addressing such problems faced by publishers, Clickio engages in analyzing overall customer needs comprehensively and develops products that cover them fully: "Products and services that help sites grow. From ads to site speed to GDPR consent—we got you covered" (Clickio website). Different from other competitors in the sector that fulfill only specific, individual customer needs, Clickio is able to sense and seize promptly what the

*Table 2.2*      *Data analysis process (code examples)*

| 1st coding stage | 2nd coding stage | Aggregate dimension |
|---|---|---|
| • Providing constant human support in approaching customers<br>"From a commercial point of view, it is very important that we provide a personal account manager, a point of reference with a person. Many companies offer the same services, same products, platforms but no personal contact. While with us every publisher is followed personally, so all the solutions we offer are designed for this publisher. It is a personal approach that, in my opinion, distinguishes us. Offering a personal account manager in our times is not done by all, and we want to keep the same personalization, the same human approach when expanding on new markets […] we are all on web, we are all online, but at the same time we are all people, we want to keep this model." (Director of Commercial Operations)<br>"Whether it's related to an issue on the site, advice on strategy or a simple question on industry trends, your personal account manager will be on hand to help." (Clickio's website) | Human-like approach | Structure |
| • Implementing co-creative processes during product development to enhance overall customer experience<br>"Therefore, I ask many questions to know the reality of the person in front of me, because, based on my knowledge of the company's tools or the expertise gained over the years, I could have solutions for their needs or simply receive input from them and, therefore, become a *trait d'union* with the company and bring back what the market needs internally." (Publisher Development Director)<br>"There is always a beta-testing phase where we offer a product for free to a part of our trusted publishers […] at the end of the beta-testing period, we collect the feedback from them […] so that we see if there are any improvements to be made, changes to be applied to the product itself." (Director of Commercial Operations) | Customer engagement in product development | Governance |

| 1st coding stage | 2nd coding stage | Aggregate dimension |
|---|---|---|
| • Making operations, interactions, and product usage easier and accessible to all customers<br>"To understand how much he [the publisher] earns, he needs to consult two or three different places [platforms], take the calculator, and do the sum to understand how much he earns with advertising. As a solution, we have thought to collect all this data in one place and offer this product which is called [Unified Reporting] to the publisher. It is much easier for him to have all the data collected from various sources in a single report." (Director of Commercial Operations)<br>"We have restructured and added a lot of information […] but also modified it and [tried] to translate it, let's say, for the publisher." (Commercial Director) | All-embracing simplification | Content |
| • Ensuring idea-sharing and effective communication across the teams<br>"Within the team, we communicate daily, hourly I would say […] in the sense that we always confront the ideas during the informal and weekly meetings." (Publisher Development Director)<br>"We use various tools […] we are all on the web, despite the [working] from home or office […] all our data and all our tools are online. We use Slack, where we create various communication channels with various groups and thematic issues, so we are able to communicate between and within teams very quickly." (Director of Commercial Operations) | Cross-team engagement | Governance |

market wants, to offer a product that, comprehensively and in an integrative manner, fixes customers' problems. Clickio positions itself as a solution provider that closes the gap between the technology and commercial dimensions of every digital creator business. Thus, it focuses on offering solutions—not merely products—to real problems by developing products and services adjusted to shifts in customer needs and preferences. As the Director of Commercial Operations claims, "All our products are very user friendly, quite easy to use, and the problems they solve are multiple." Empowered by proactive actions, Clickio underwent a radical shift from a traditional business model to a holistic business solutions provider that addresses customers' objectives over 360 degrees, and creates unique products of superior value, consolidating its position as a market leader: "a solution to solve all these problems, because, for each aspect that I mentioned, there are separated provider[s], whereas [Clickio product name] is a unique solution" (Publisher Development Director).

The ability of Clickio to quickly reallocate the necessary business assets (resource fluidity) is concretized in the type of business solution offered. Clickio has developed an all-embracing platform that "disrupts" the traditional conception of the value-in-use (i.e., customer's outcome that is achieved through that product) (Macdonald et al., 2011), thus implementing customizable value-in-use. Indeed, Clickio empowers clients to use its products independently without having constant contact with a company. The Director of Commercial Operations explains that "there is a basic version of every product, but it can be easily customized if it is requested. We are flexible enough in this sense to provide customization. For example, our product Prism is all custom, so we are very flexible in this regard," adding that, "thanks to our technology, we have created a system that allows many publishers to be independent when using our service, without the necessity to constant and direct support from people." With custom platform usage, Clickio exploits the early development of the market and the

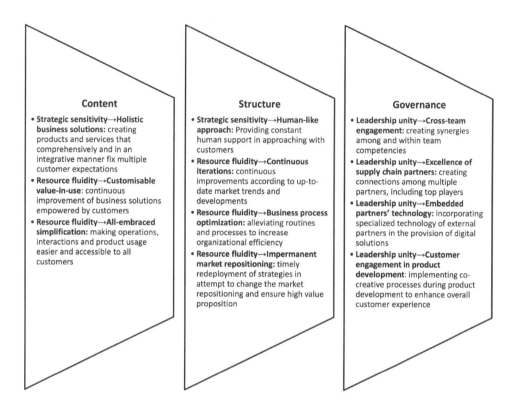

| Content | Structure | Governance |
|---|---|---|
| • **Strategic sensitivity→Holistic business solutions**: creating products and services that comprehensively and in an integrative manner fix multiple customer expectations<br>• **Resource fluidity→Customisable value-in-use**: continuous improvement of business solutions empowered by customers<br>• **Resource fluidity→All-embraced simplification**: making operations, interactions and product usage easier and accessible to all customers | • **Strategic sensitivity→Human-like approach**: Providing constant human support in approaching with customers<br>• **Resource fluidity→Continuous iterations**: continuous improvements according to up-to-date market trends and developments<br>• **Resource fluidity→Business process optimization**: alleviating routines and processes to increase organizational efficiency<br>• **Resource fluidity→Impermanent market repositioning**: timely redeployment of strategies in attempt to change the market repositioning and ensure high value proposition | • **Leadership unity→Cross-team engagement**: creating synergies among and within team competencies<br>• **Leadership unity→Excellence of supply chain partners**: creating connections among multiple partners, including top players<br>• **Leadership unity→Embedded partners' technology**: incorporating specialized technology of external partners in the provision of digital solutions<br>• **Leadership unity→Customer engagement in product development**: implementing co-creative processes during product development to enhance overall customer experience |

*Figure 2.1*    *A framework for strategic agility and digital business model innovation: content, structure, and governance*

latent needs of customers as the client acts as the designer of the end product and results, thus delivering high-quality services.

Moreover, quick reallocation of resources (resource fluidity) impacts the way Clickio supports the provision of services and products. Assisting publishers operating in a highly dynamic and complex marketplace, Clickio is driven by the idea that it is important to simplify operations, compressing time and resources needed to perform activities and stimulate innovation. The researcher who participated in the firm's daily routine noticed how this aspect of all-embracing simplification occurs in multiple ways. For instance, when Clickio communicates with its clients, all the materials (e.g., instructions, newsletters) are created to be understandable to the broad audience, regardless of the degree of tech literacy or knowledge. Also, Clickio offers a solution that combines data in one place to provide a unique, simplified report, thus solving issues in the management of multiple data sources. Even the platform's interface is developed to avoid unnecessary operations or steps. Furthermore, the most technologically sophisticated product of Clickio—the Consent Management Platform—is developed to "allow publishers to set up a consent workflow in minutes and be easy-to-use and very flexible," as reported on the corporate site. Thanks to these steps, the firm delivers new solutions quickly, significantly reducing the time and resources necessary to adapt to changes in customer needs and preferences.

## Digital BMI of Structure

Clickio successfully innovates its digital BM as it constantly looks for novel ways through which its core business activities are performed or connected, which is of extreme importance to compete in its dynamic and complex marketplace: "Our market is different from this morning. Tomorrow is different from today, sometimes completely [...] Clickio operates in a very dynamic market" (Publisher Development Director). Our findings reveal a range of innovative paths describing how Clickio creates and then distributes value to achieve its outstanding competitive advantage.

To gain a broader perspective about the future market development and successfully innovate its BM (strategic sensitivity), Clickio pays particular attention to the way it relates with clients. The fact that every task is performed within a virtual environment may risk amplifying the distance with customers, as people get frustrated by the huge number of options at their disposal and the continuous interactions with automated voices or systems. This aspect reduces empathy and augments the sense of detachment from the company with the risk of undermining the company's value creation and customer expectations towards hyper-customized products or services. To tackle this problem, Clickio engages in empathizing with customer feelings, adding the "personal" factor—i.e., emotional or psychological closeness—in the provision of its products or services, as the following quote exemplifies: "Clickio has always had a direct relationship with the customer, therefore not showing itself as just a technological company or in any case just a screen to relate to or a robot. We have always tried to put the human factor forward" (Commercial Director). By deploying such a human-like approach to be closer to customers, the firm enhances its ability to adjust its strategies and operations in response to market demand and gain strong reliability and trustworthiness. As the Publisher Development Director explains, it is true that there are several players in the marketplace which offer products or services of high quality. However, they often neglect to understand how important it is to create a human-like relationship with customers, especially when operating in a virtual environment. Clickio tries to fix this problem by providing personal account managers tailored to address customers' objectives with a human approach.

In the product development process, Clickio does not follow rigid and planned processes. Rather, it is committed to performing continuous iterations to align with the shifting market trends and development (resource fluidity). For instance, if during product development the company notices that the product is obsolete since customers do not require that product anymore, Clickio gives up that idea immediately to concentrate on something that better addresses what the demand looks for. The introduction of the GDPR represents an exemplar case of this BM's innovation process. The development of GDPR-compliant solutions did not belong to the competencies and technologies of Clickio. They were introduced later in response to a change in the needs of its customers. As a result, Clickio enriched its core competencies but also enlarged its market positioning considerably: "When we launched Clickio GDPR Consent Tool—now used by big publishers—at that moment, there was a big need, but no products available. A lot of people trusted us and received great support. Then, there was a chain reaction, which still continues today" (Commercial Director).

Another crucial aspect exemplifying how resource fluidity impacts Clickio's activity system is business process optimization. Clickio is open to constant and prompt optimization of its operations thanks to timely sharing of information and tightly connected teams and departments. Unlike traditional organizational structures based on rigid performance schemes,

Clickio's employees adopt more informal routines and processes to address issues, as the following quote explains: "Optimization is not only the service we offer but the way we run our business. If any step of the task or project can be simplified or optimized, we don't discuss a lot but implement changes easily" (Director of Commercial Operations).

Clickio's innovation in its BM's activity structure is also evident in the efforts made to cope with the recent Coronavirus pandemic, thanks to having different business model infrastructures in parallel (resource fluidity). Many companies were forced to reduce their advertising budget as market demand slowed down dramatically. In such a context, Clickio reacted promptly by searching for novel solutions to maintain customer value. As declared by the Publisher Development Director:

> In the time of pandemia, to ensure the same level of value proposition, we thought that we have to give additional solutions, and therefore more partnerships have been made with the vertical players of the market that do not belong to our classic offer. Thus, we posited ourselves as intermediaries that bring publishers additional solutions.

In this conception, Clickio was able to accomplish permanent market repositioning, which enabled the timely redeployment of strategies in an attempt to accommodate changing needs of clients. Clickio's BM was able to permanently run two separate modes of operating that ensured higher resilience during the pandemic.

**Digital BMI of Governance**

Empirical evidence uncovers multiple ways through which leadership unity, reached through a dynamic and collaborative working environment, impacts the main actors performing BMI. The company strongly relies on within-team competencies that, when merged together with fixing customer problems, enable it to discover more effective solutions to changes in customer requirements or unexpected situations. Different departments meet constantly (e.g., on a weekly basis) to brainstorm new ideas or to discuss how to improve products. The cross-team engagement enables the development of a clear and shared vision of the marketplace and supports greater customer satisfaction. As underlined by the Publisher Development Director, "If a publisher tells you 'I have this need,' but in my portfolio of products I have nothing to offer him, I always bring the information internally to ensure that my company can evaluate if it is convenient to develop such a product or service."

This collaborative attitude of Clickio can be found even in partnerships with excellent supply chain partners. To create greater customer value, the firm brings together premium ad partners and advertising networks, thus providing publishers with access to innovative solutions and products and enriching the experience of all market players. Notably, the value proposition of Clickio relies on the partnership with the main actor of the digital ecosystem, Google Inc. The collaboration with this prestigious partner enables the company to have early access to relevant information, such as new initiatives or regulations issued by Google, and, thus, be more competitive in the marketplace. Moreover, being a Google Certified Publishing Partner enhances Clickio's visibility as a reliable and trustworthy partner for publishers.

Not only does Clickio collaborate with other players, but, in some cases, the firm embeds the technology of other tech partners into its products. A peculiar example of how Clickio co-creates the value with external partners is described by the Commercial Director: "From the very beginning, we have relied on the technology of external partners that we have integrated into our platform. For example, the payment system takes place in total independence. So that our clients know that on a certain day of the month, without having to make any requests, they will receive the payment. While other competitors with a traditional system should exchange emails, send off the invoices … for us, the management of payments is fundamental, because innovative businesses cannot fail to have an automated payment system." By incorporating partners' technology in its business solutions, Clickio is able to create a win–win situation, as it delivers more valuable products while simultaneously saving costs, as the Director of Commercial Operations specifies: "If a website is located in the US and the server is located in Brazil or Russia, the response is slower, while if we have a server infrastructure in the US we can respond faster."

Even Clickio's customers are involved in the product development process. The firm gets inputs and feedback from its clients, co-creates products with them to ensure the building of products and services is tailored to solve their needs and requirements, and it also gets inspiration from customers to further innovate its BM: "There is always a beta-testing phase where we offer a product for free to a part of our trusted publishers […] at the end of the beta-testing period, we collect the feedback from them […] so that we see if there are any improvements to be made, changes to be applied to the product itself" (Director of Commercial Operations). By involving customer feedback, the firm has the opportunity to better engage in improving the overall customer experience, thinking about how to better serve its target market at large.

## DISCUSSION

BMI represents an increasing body of literature (e.g., Bhatti et al., 2021; Foss & Saebi, 2017, 2018; Iheanachor et al., 2021). However, more empirical studies about how strategic agility impacts digital BMI are still necessary (e.g., Warner & Wäger, 2019). In this chapter, we adopted an exploratory single-case-study research design to investigate how strategic agility enables organizations to innovate their digital BMs looking at the case of Clickio. Our study contributes to extending prior research in significant ways.

With our study, we contribute to deepening the different ways through which strategic agility, largely considered an important driver of BMI (Battistella et al., 2012; Bhatti et al., 2021; Brand et al., 2021; Doz & Kosonen, 2010), fosters firms to innovate the core dimensions of a digital BM. Prior literature emphasizes factors like novelty, lock-in mechanisms, complementarities, and efficiency as crucial for implementing BMI (Amit & Zott, 2012). We extend prior research by showing how the different meta-capabilities (i.e., strategic sensitivity, leadership unity, and resource fluidity) of strategic agility (Doz & Kosonen, 2010) impacts digital BMI with respect to the core dimensions of BM's content, structure, and governance (Amit & Zott, 2012).

In particular, prior literature highlights that strategic sensitivity means being able to perceive strategic developments (Doz & Kosonen, 2010). Our findings show that strategic sensitivity, enacted in a digital context, affects the type of activity performed (content) as it enables the creation of business solutions—i.e., products and services—that comprehensively satisfy multiple customer expectations. By distancing themselves from their traditional business model, firms can take a holistic view of future product development, which can significantly influence the development of innovative digital BM.

Moreover, in our study, strategic sensitivity directly affects the way activities are performed (structure) by rethinking the approach taken when communicating with clients. By implementing a human-like approach, firms are able to create more close relationships with clients, which allows them to excel in the competition and gain a competitive advantage. This is in accordance with previous literature that assumes that BMs represent management's conjecture about what customers want, how that value should be delivered, and how value should be captured (Teece, 2010).

Furthermore, resource fluidity, which implies adjusting resources and operations in a flexible manner in response to changes in BMs (Doz & Kosonen, 2010), impacts digital BMs' structure in important ways, namely continuous iterations, business processes optimization, and impermanent market repositioning. All these aspects enable companies to implement an activity system that comprehensively enhances the firm's ability to execute digital innovation in BMs in accordance with the latest market trends.

Moreover, resource fluidity impacts the type of activities performed through customizable value-in-use and all-embracing simplification that bring products of greater value thanks to the continuous improvements empowered by customers. In doing so, strategic agility is found to enhance the company's ability to bring outstanding customer satisfaction and foster business scalability. This result extends the comprehension of the various organizational capabilities that aid firms in the transformation of their BMs (Foss & Saebi, 2017).

Finally, as regards leadership unity, which represents the commitment towards BMI (Doz & Kosonen, 2010), this work proposes that cross-team engagement, together with excellent partnerships embedded in the firm's digital solutions, and deep customer engagement during the product development, complete a governance system that allows firms to develop adequate competencies and skills facilitating synergies over changing market dynamics, thus addressing innovation of a firm's BM successfully.

## Managerial Implications

From a managerial perspective, our research findings illustrate the importance of developing digital BMs based on strategic agility. Managers and practitioners need to innovate their digital BMs continuously to provide timely and more effective responses to market demand. On the one hand, they should encourage technology adoption throughout the organization. On the other hand, they need to embed agility into their strategic and operational efforts to adapt to the uncertainty of today's complex and fast-changing landscape more effectively. With this study, we provide guidance for assessing which kind of actions are appropriate to build an agile digital BMI, with a focus on content, structure, and governance dimensions.

## Limitation and Future Research

This study is subject to some limitations that could be addressed by future research. Indeed, further attention is needed to increase the understanding of strategic agility and digital BMI.

This study focuses on a single firm and industry; thus, our findings have few generalizations to other contexts. Therefore, researchers could extend our analysis to other sectors and explore whether further paths can be identified.

Furthermore, we based our analysis on the impact of strategic agility on digital BMI by considering the key dimensions of content, structure, and governance (Amit & Zott, 2012).

Although this framework is largely adopted by recent studies exploring BMI in a wide range of contexts (e.g., Pereira et al., 2022; Zhao et al., 2020), future studies could extend the impact of strategic agility on BMI by adopting other frameworks, and identifying new categories that could add more value to our results.

Moreover, it would be interesting to understand under which conditions it would be easier to innovate an existing BM for agile firms. Hence, future studies could investigate the role of environmental turbulence in the relationship between strategic agility and digital BMI adoption.

Finally, it would be interesting to understand what potential barriers or challenges to agility implementation in digital BMI can be recognized (e.g., high costs for digital transitions).

## REFERENCES

Achtenhagen, L., Melin, L., & Naldi, L. (2013). Dynamics of business models: Strategising, critical capabilities and activities for sustained value creation. *Long Range Planning, 46*(6), 427–42.

Amit, R., & Zott, C. (2012). Creating value through business model innovation. *MIT Sloan Management Review, 53*(3), 36–44.

Baden-Fuller, C., & Morgan, M.S. (2010). Business models as models. *Long Range Planning, 43*(2–3), 156–71.

Bandara, W., Furtmueller, E., Gorbacheva, E., Miskon, S., & Beekhuyzen, J. (2015). Achieving rigor in literature reviews: Insights from qualitative data analysis and tool-support. *Communications of the Association for Information Systems, 37*(1), 8.

Bärenfänger, R., & Otto, B. (2015). Proposing a capability perspective on digital business models. *Proceedings – 17th IEEE Conference on Business Informatics*, Vol. 2015, CBI, 17–25.

Battistella, C., Biotto, G., & De Toni, A.F. (2012). From design driven innovation to meaning strategy. *Management Decision, 50*(4), 718–43.

Battistella, C., De Toni, A.F., De Zan, G., & Pessot, E. (2017). Cultivating business model agility through focused capabilities: A multiple case study. *Journal of Business Research, 73*, 65–82.

Bell, E., Bryman, A., & Harley, B. (2018). *Business Research Methods*. New York, NY: Oxford University Press.

Bhatti, S.H., Santoro, G., Khan, J., & Rizzato, F. (2021). Antecedents and consequences of business model innovation in the IT industry. *Journal of Business Research, 123*, 389–400.

Bianchi, M., Marzi, G., & Guerini, M. (2020). Agile, stage-gate and their combination: Exploring how they relate to performance in software development. *Journal of Business Research, 110*, 538–53.

Brand, M., Tiberius, V., Bican, P.M., & Brem, A. (2021). Agility as an innovation driver: Towards an agile front end of innovation framework. *Review of Managerial Science, 15*(1), 157–87.

Bresciani, S., Huarng, K.H., Malhotra, A., & Ferraris, A. (2021). Digital transformation as a springboard for product, process and business model innovation. *Journal of Business Research, 128*, 204–10.

Cavalcante, S.A. (2014). Designing business model change. *International Journal of Innovation Management, 18*(2), 1450018.

Cennamo, C., Dagnino, G.B., Di Minin, A., & Lanzolla, G. (2020). Managing digital transformation: Scope of transformation and modalities of value co-generation and delivery. *California Management Review, 62*(4), 5–16.

Chakravarty, A., Grewal, R. and Sambamurthy, V. (2013). Information technology competencies, organizational agility, and firm performance: Enabling and facilitating roles. *Information Systems Research, 24*(4), 976–97.

Chan, F.K., & Thong, J.Y. (2009). Acceptance of agile methodologies: A critical review and conceptual framework. *Decision Support Systems, 46*(4), 803–14.

Chen, Y., Wang, Y., Nevo, S., Benitez, J., & Kou, G. (2015). Improving strategic flexibility with information technologies: insights for firm performance in an emerging economy. *Journal of Information Technology, 32*, 10–25.

Chesbrough, H. (2010). Business model innovation: Opportunities and barriers. *Long Range Planning*, *43*(2–3), 354–63.

Ciampi, F., Demi, S., Magrini, A., Marzi, G., & Papa, A. (2021). Exploring the impact of big data analytics capabilities on business model innovation: The mediating role of entrepreneurial orientation. *Journal of Business Research*, *123*, 1–13.

Cooper, R.G. (2014). What's next? After stage-gate. *Research-Technology Management*, *57*(1), 20–31.

Cucculelli, M., & Bettinelli, C. (2015). Business models, intangibles and firm performance: Evidence on corporate entrepreneurship from Italian manufacturing SMEs. *Small Business Economics*, *45*, 329–50.

Doz, Y.L., & Kosonen, M. (2010). Embedding strategic agility: A leadership agenda for accelerating business model renewal. *Long Range Planning*, *43*(2–3), 370–82.

Dyer, W.G., Jr, & Wilkins, A.L. (1991). Better stories, not better constructs, to generate better theory: A rejoinder to Eisenhardt. *Academy of Management Review*, *16*(3), 613–19.

Eisenhardt, K.M. (1989). Building theories from case study research. *Academy of Management Review*, *14*(4), 532–50.

Eisenhardt, K.M., & Graebner, M.E. (2007). Theory building from cases: Opportunities and challenges. *Academy of Management Journal*, *50*(1), 25–32.

El Sawy, O.A., & Pereira, F. (2013). *Business Modelling in the Dynamic Digital Space: An Ecosystem Approach*. Heidelberg: Springer.

Foss, N.J., & Saebi, T. (2017). Fifteen years of research on business model innovation: How far have we come, and where should we go? *Journal of Management*, *43*(1), 200–227.

Foss, N.J., & Saebi, T. (2018). Business models and business model innovation: Between wicked and paradigmatic problems. *Long Range Planning*, *51*(1), 9–21.

Gibbs, G.R. (2007). Thematic coding and categorizing. *Analyzing Qualitative Data*, *703*, 38–56.

Grodal, S., Anteby, M., & Holm, A.L. (2020). Achieving rigor in qualitative analysis: The role of active categorization in theory building. *Academy of Management Review*, *46*(3), 591–612.

Hadjielias, E., Dada, O.L., Cruz, A.D., Zekas, S., Christofi, M., & Sakka, G. (2021). How do digital innovation teams function? Understanding the team cognition-process nexus within the context of digital transformation. *Journal of Business Research*, *122*, 373–86.

Hammersley, M., & Atkinson, P. (2019). *Ethnography: Principles in Practice*. London: Routledge.

Hess, T., Matt, C., Benlian, A., & Wiesböck, F. (2016). Options for formulating a digital transformation strategy. *MIS Quarterly Executive*, *15*(2), 123–39.

Iheanachor, N., David-West, Y., & Umukoro, I.O. (2021). Business model innovation at the bottom of the pyramid: A case of mobile money agents. *Journal of Business Research*, *127*, 96–107.

Islam, A.N., Laato, S., Talukder, S., & Sutinen, E. (2020). Misinformation sharing and social media fatigue during Covid-19: An affordance and cognitive load perspective. *Technological Forecasting and Social Change*, *159*, 120201.

Johnson, M.W., Christensen, C.M., & Kagermann, H. (2008). Reinventing your business model. *Harvard Business Review*, *86*(12), 57–68.

Lee, G., & Xia, W. (2010). Toward agile: An integrated analysis of quantitative and qualitative field data on software development agility. *MIS Quarterly*, *34*(1), 87–114.

Lee, O.K.D., Sambamurthy, V., Kim, K.H., & Wei, K.K. (2015). How does IT ambidexterity impact organizational agility? *Information Systems Research*, *26*(2), 398–417.

Lincoln, Y.S., & Guba, E.G. (2013). *The Constructivist Credo*. Walnut Creek, CA: Left Coast Press.

Lindstrom, L., & Jeffries, R. (2004). Extreme programming and agile software development methodologies. *Information Systems Management*, *21*(3), 41–52.

Lu, Y., & Ramamurthy, K.R. (2011). Understanding the link between information technology capability and organizational agility: An empirical examination. *MIS Quarterly*, *35*(4), 931–54.

Macdonald, E., Wilson, H., Martinez, V., & Toossi, A. (2011). Assessing value-in-use: A conceptual framework and exploratory study. *Industrial Marketing Management*, *40*(5), 671–82.

Magretta, J. (2002). Why business models matter. *Harvard Business Review*, *80*, 86–92.

Mahadevan, D., Paquette, C., Rashid, N., & Ustinov, E. (2019). Building agile capabilities: The fuel to power your agile "body." McKinsey & Company: https://www.mckinsey.com/business-functions/organization/our-insights/building-agile-capabilities-the-fuel-to-power-your-agile-body#.

Miles, M.B., & Huberman, A.M. (1984). Drawing valid meaning from qualitative data: Toward a shared craft. *Educational Researcher*, *13*(5), 20–30.

Moi, L., & Cabiddu, F. (2021a). Leading digital transformation through an agile marketing capability: The case of Spotahome. *Journal of Management and Governance, 25*(4), 1145–77.

Moi, L., & Cabiddu, F. (2021b). An agile marketing capability maturity framework. *Tourism Management, 86*, 104347.

Pagani, M., & Pardo, C. (2017). The impact of digital technology on relationships in a business network. *Industrial Marketing Management, 67* (September 2016), 185–92.

Parida, V., Sjödin, D., & Reim, W. (2019). Reviewing literature on digitalization, business model innovation, and sustainable industry: past achievements and future promises. *Sustainability, 11*(391), 2–18.

Patton, M.Q. (2005). *Qualitative Research and Evaluation Methods*. Thousand Oaks, CA: SAGE.

Pereira, G.I., Niesten, E., & Pinkse, J. (2022). Sustainable energy systems in the making: A study on business model adaptation in incumbent utilities. *Technological Forecasting and Social Change, 174*, 121207.

Prange, C. (2021). Agility as the discovery of slowness. *California Management Review, 63*(4), 27–51.

Rachinger, M., Rauter, R., Müller, C., Vorraber, W., & Schirgi, E. (2019). Digitalization and its influence on business model innovation. *Journal of Manufacturing Technology Management, 30*(8), 1143–60.

Rigby, D.K., Sutherland, J., & Takeuchi, H. (2016). Embracing agile. *Harvard Business Review, 94*(5), 40–50.

Rydén, P., & El Sawy, O.A. (2019). How managers perceive real-time management: Thinking fast & flow. *California Management Review, 61*(2), 155–77.

Sambamurthy, V., Bharadwaj, A., & Grover, V. (2003). Shaping agility through digital options: Reconceptualizing the role of information technology in contemporary firms. *MIS Quarterly*, 237–63.

Schallmo, D., Williams, C., & Boardman, L. (2017). Digital transformation of business models: Best practice, enablers, and roadmap. *International Journal of Innovation Management, 21*(8), 1740014.

Schneider, S., & Spieth, P. (2013). Business model innovation: Towards an integrated future research agenda. *International Journal of Innovation Management, 17*(1), 1340001.

Siggelkow, N. (2002). Evolution toward fit. *Administrative Science Quarterly, 47*(1), 125–59.

Spieth, P., Schneckenberg, D., & Ricart, J.E. (2014). Business model innovation: State of the art and future challenges for the field. *R&D Management, 44*(3), 237–47.

Strauss, A., & Corbin, J. (1998). *Basics of Qualitative Research Techniques: Techniques and Procedures for Developing Grounded Theory*, 2nd ed. Thousand Oaks, CA: SAGE.

Tallon, P.P., & Pinsonneault, A. (2011). Competing perspectives on the link between strategic information technology alignment and organizational agility: Insights from a mediation model. *MIS Quarterly, 35*(2), 463–86.

Tavoletti, E., Kazemargi, N., Cerruti, C., Grieco, C., & Appolloni, A. (2021). Business model innovation and digital transformation in global management consulting firms. *European Journal of Innovation Management, 25*(6), 612–36.

Teece, D.J. (2010). Business models, business strategy and innovation. *Long Range Planning, 43*, 172–94.

Teece, D., Peteraf, M., & Leih, S. (2016). Dynamic capabilities and organizational agility: Risk, uncertainty, and strategy in the innovation economy. *California Management Review, 58*(4), 13–35.

Verhoef, P.C., Broekhuizen, T., Bart, Y., Bhattacharya, A., Qi Dong, J., Fabian, N., & Haenlein, M. (2021). Digital transformation: A multidisciplinary reflection and research agenda. *Journal of Business Research, 122*, 889–901.

Visnjic, I., Neely, A., & Jovanovic, M. (2018). The path to outcome delivery: Interplay of service market strategy and open business models. *Technovation, 72*, 46–59.

Vrontis, D., Basile, G., Andreano, M.S., Mazzitelli, A., & Papasolomou, I. (2020). The profile of innovation driven Italian SMEs and the relationship between the firms' networking abilities and dynamic capabilities. *Journal of Business Research, 114*, 313–24.

Warner, K.S., & Wäger, M. (2019). Building dynamic capabilities for digital transformation: An ongoing process of strategic renewal. *Long Range Planning, 52*(3), 326–49.

Westerman, G., Bonnet, D., & McAfee, A. (2014). *Leading Digital: Turning Technology into Business Transformation*. Boston, MA: HBR Press.

Yin, R.K. (1994). *Case Study Research: Design and Methods*, Applied Social Research Methods Series, Vol. 5. Thousand Oaks, CA: SAGE.

Yin, R.K. (2013). Validity and generalization in future case study evaluations. *Evaluation, 19*(3), 321–32.

Zhao, Y., Von Delft, S., Morgan-Thomas, A., & Buck, T. (2020). The evolution of platform business models: Exploring competitive battles in the world of platforms. *Long Range Planning, 53*(4), 101892.

Zheng, Y., Goh, E., & Wen, J. (2020). The effects of misleading media reports about COVID-19 on Chinese tourists' mental health: A perspective article. *Anatolia, 31*(2), 337–40.

Ziegler, S., Evequoz, E., & Huamani, A.M.P. (2019). The Impact of the European General Data Protection Regulation (GDPR) on Future Data Business Models: Toward a New Paradigm and Business Opportunities. In A. Aagaard (Ed.), *Digital Business Models: Driving Transformation and Innovation* (pp. 201–26). Cham: Springer.

Zott, C. (2016). How to innovate in business models: Changing the way the company does business. *IESE Alumni Magazine, 140*(January–March), 24–7.

Zott, C., & Amit, R. (2017). Business model innovation: How to create value in a digital world. *NIM Marketing Intelligence Review, 9*(1), 18–23.

Zott, C., Amit, R., & Massa, L. (2011). The business model: Recent developments and future research. *Journal of Management, 37*(4), 1019–42.

# 3. Crafting digital business models: an ongoing process of innovation and imitation

*Stephan von Delft and Yang Zhao*

## INTRODUCTION

The emergence of digital technologies, such as cloud computing and data analytics (Nambisan, 2017), has brought opportunities for the creation of new organizational forms (Adner et al., 2019; Cennamo et al., 2020; Iansiti and Lakhani, 2017; Teece, 2018). In music, Spotify creates value by allowing users to conveniently stream music, but also by making recommendations for new songs based on usage data; in healthcare, LunaDNA provides a member-owned digital ecosystem where patients can share their health data with selected organizations and be paid for it while helping advance scientific research; in gaming, Rovio, known for its popular iPhone game *Angry Birds*, has launched Rovio Stars, where it acts as a publisher for small third-party game developers and supports them with marketing and app store submissions.

Spotify, LunaDNA, and Rovio are examples of firms that have successfully crafted digital business models. "Digital business model" refers to the architecture of the value creation, delivery, and capture mechanisms of a firm, embodied in or enabled by digital technologies (Fichman et al., 2014; Soluk et al., 2021; Teece, 2010). As such, a firm's digital business model is a reflection of its realized digital strategy (Casadesus-Masanell and Ricart, 2011). A digital strategy is about creating customer value and competitive advantage in a constantly evolving digital world. That definition implies that the firm has made a choice about where to play and how to win in a digital ecosystem involving a distinctive set of activities that span the focal firm's boundaries. The resulting system of interdependent activities (Lanzolla and Markides, 2021) the firm implemented to leverage the capabilities of digital technologies is a reflection of its digital strategy, but it is not the strategy, it is the digital business model (Casadesus-Masanell and Ricart, 2010). Hence, one important purpose of a digital strategy is to answer the question of *what* digital business model to choose (Vendrell-Herrero et al., 2018; Weill and Woerner, 2018; Wirtz, 2019).

To illustrate this, consider a mobile game developer founded in 2017. At its foundation, the new digital venture decided to operate exclusively in Apple's App Store ecosystem and compete there through a particular digital business model. Choosing an ecosystem is a strategic choice that has consequences for the design of the firm's digital business model. For example, back in 2017, Apple only permitted transactions through its platform, thus barring app developers from directing customers to other ways to pay for a digital item or service. The choice of Apple's ecosystem implied that the game developer could not generate revenues from Apple users directly. It also likely captured less value from each transaction because Apple charged a commission on sales, which had consequences for the game developer's margin model (i.e., the contribution needed from each transaction to achieve the desired profits) and hence the value capture mechanism in its business model.

Fast forward to September 2021. Following a ruling by a federal judge in the US to ease restrictions on app developers, Apple was ordered to allow app developers to include links in their apps to other payment methods, eventually allowing complementors to its ecosystem to keep more of their profits. Our game developer now has an opportunity to develop its digital business model by steering customers to an outside website to complete transactions, thereby avoiding Apple's commission on sales. Again, the game developer's digital strategy will determine whether it adjusts its original business model or not. But its digital strategy also serves a second purpose: If the game developer decides to change its business model, the digital strategy will determine how it will develop its business model to seize the opportunity. The purpose of digital strategy is hence not only to decide what digital business model to choose, but also *how* to design the digital business model. The design of the digital business model is consequently a key means to implement digital strategy (Correani et al., 2020; Linde et al., 2020; Weill and Woerner, 2013).

In this chapter, we focus on this second important purpose of digital strategy and thus explore the question of how digital business models come into being and how they develop over time. This topic is important for new ventures that create their first digital business model (Ghezzi and Cavallo, 2020; Zott and Amit, 2007) as well as for established firms that undergo digital transformation (Ross et al., 2017; Warner and Wäger, 2019). The topic is also important at later stages of a digital firm's development. Whereas business models in traditional industries are fixed in place for years, if not decades, digital business models are subject to rapid displacement and, in extreme cases, outright disruption. This is because best practices and successful business model stories diffuse rapidly in the digital economy, eventually shortening business model life cycles. Digital firms hence need to have strategies in place to constantly develop their business models.

We start our discussion by providing an overview of the two principal ways to design digital business models identified in prior research: business model innovation and imitation. Both innovation and imitation are viable ways to form business models in the digital economy, and they are not mutually exclusive. Rather, they may be conceived of as two ends of a continuum along which real-world strategies to design digital business models lie. In this chapter, we integrate emerging and established research to develop this notion and explore strategies along the spectrum. These include pioneer, architect, blender, adapter, and copycat. We also discuss some of the basic principles and underlying mechanisms behind these strategies. The chapter concludes with a discussion of future research opportunities.

## TYPES OF STRATEGIES TO DESIGN DIGITAL BUSINESS MODELS

How digital business models form is a fundamental question of digital strategy and key to successful digital entrepreneurship. Prior research suggests several approaches to the design of a firm's business model. One approach, embedded in Schumpeterian innovation, conceives business model design as a process of innovation (e.g., Chesbrough, 2010; Foss and Saebi, 2017; Rachinger et al., 2019; Von Delft et al., 2019; Zott and Amit, 2007). This view suggests that the focal firm is the business model innovator and creates new ways of conducting economic exchanges to be unique and distinguish itself from rivals (Markides and Sosa, 2013). Business model innovation can occur by introducing new activities, and/or linking activities in novel ways, and/or creating new ways of governing activities (Amit and Zott, 2012). For example, the social media API[1] aggregation firm Gnip, which was acquired by Twitter in 2014, became a forerunner in building the real-time web by introducing a business model innovation based on collecting, packaging, and selling relevant data from social media websites in a novel way. Looking at Gnip's business model innovation, Sorescu (2017, p. 694) concludes that it "successfully leveraged [...] big data: their technology was able to sort through high variety, big volume data in real time, and extract only the portion that was of value to consumers."

While the focus on business model innovation as an agent of change reflects both the potential benefits that accrue to first movers and the dramatic impact of new business models on the competitive landscape, it tends to eclipse the role of imitation as an alternative way to form competitive business models. Prior research has, perhaps inadvertently, often considered business model imitation as a simple strategy, one only pursued by inferior copycats. Only more recently have scholars begun exploring imitation as a complementary approach to form viable business models (e.g., Amit and Zott, 2015; Frankenberger and Stam, 2020). By "business model imitation" we mean the borrowing of certain ingredients from another business model. For example, parts of Uber's ride-sharing model were successfully imitated by Didi, Go-Jek, and Grab in Asia. Following a business model imitation strategy can be an effective means of gaining competitive advantage, or as Davis and Aggarwal (2020) observe: "In the digital economy, innovators often lose out to more agile imitators who can leverage new know-how very quickly and creatively."

This chapter sets out to explore business model innovation and imitation strategies in the digital economy. But rather than exploring each approach separately (or even as a sharp binary choice), we suggest that the formation of digital business models consists of both innovation and imitation elements. To develop this notion, we begin by specifying what perfect business model innovation and perfect business model imitation would mean and under what conditions they would exist.

### Innovation and Imitation: Two Ends of a Continuum

For a digital business model to form through perfect innovation – that is, for the business model design to be completely novel to the world – two conditions would need to be satisfied. First, the digital business model must not reassemble any present or past business model of the organization. For established firms this would require a digital business model innovation to fundamentally deviate from the status quo of the existing (non-digital) business model, so that there is no ingredient of the old model to be recycled or re-used in the new model. The process of perfect innovation would hence require shifting, with the highest degree of radicalism, from an existing to a new business model (Massa and Tucci, 2014). For start-ups, this condition would mean that the design of the digital business model cannot be inspired by business models of ventures previously founded by the entrepreneur. Second, the process of perfect innovation would require forming a digital business model without influence from the external environment: Neither can the model, in full or part, be directly copied from another organization nor can the designer indirectly draw inspiration from existing business model designs suggested by external stakeholders (e.g., mentors, investors). Thus, perfect innovation would require a completely novel business model, one never seen before.

In practice, it is difficult to imagine that these conditions are fulfilled. Prior research on business model innovation in established firms suggests that total deviation from the established model may not be desirable. Instead, incumbents may want to create synergies between the old and the new model (Casadesus-Masanell and Tarziján, 2012; Kim and Min, 2015; Markides and Charitou, 2004). Moreover, Amit and Zott (2015) remind us that borrowing business models from other organizations is commonplace in the design of new business models. However, although we are unlikely to find a digital business model that forms through perfect innovation, some strategies to design digital business models do come rather close. For example, ArtistShare is widely recognized as the first crowdfunding platform that connects artists with fans. The platform enables artists to fund and promote their work by allowing the public to provide direct financial support, observe the creation of new artistic work, and gain access to additional material from an artist. Eventually ArtistShare became the blueprint for many crowdfunding platforms, such as KickStarter, IndieGoGo, and PledgeMusic.

For a digital business model to form through perfect imitation, the business model would have to be created by copying an existing business model in toto. Digital business models formed through perfect imitation, thus, completely reassemble the target of imitation. Again, we would expect the perfect imitation strategy to be as rare as the perfect innovation one. Organization theory and the wider strategy literature, for instance, suggest that imitation may be partial or error-prone, especially when coupled with factors such as complexity or causal ambiguity (Levinthal, 1997; Lippman and Rumelt, 1982; Posen et al., 2013; Rivkin, 2000). For example, whereas a new pricing mechanism in a business model can quickly be imitated by rivals, a complex system of interdependent and interlinked activities may not be imitated easily (Ethiraj et al., 2008; Zhao et al., 2020). In practice, we would therefore expect to see adaptations, of various degrees, to imitated business models. However, our own research and a small but growing body of literature suggests that some strategies to design digital business models do come rather close to perfect imitation, as when a fast follower aims to catch up with a business model innovator. For example, when the Samwer brothers founded Zalando in 2008 they borrowed heavily from Zappos.com's business model, eventually enabling the start-up to become a leading online fashion platform in Europe.

Thus, we would expect to find tendencies in the directions of perfect innovation and perfect imitation strategies to design digital business models rather than perfect forms of either. In effect, perfect innovation and perfect imitation strategies can be conceived of as the ends of a continuum along which real-world strategies to design digital business models lie. Such strategies would combine various aspects discussed above: The designer would introduce business model designs that are more or less novel, reassemble past or present business models of the organization to a certain degree, more or less draw inspiration from existing business models in or outside its home market, and proactively or reactively take on input from the environment in the design process.

Below we introduce different types of strategies to craft digital business models that fall along the spectrum (see Figure 3.1), beginning with those most reflective of the characteristics of a perfect innovation strategy and ending with those closest to the perfect imitation pole. Our aim is to explore the continuum, not to present an exhaustive typology, and to deliver insights on the strategic principles, prerequisites, and common pitfalls associated with each type.

## Pioneer Strategy

In the first type, called pioneer strategy, the organization leads in the introduction of new digital business models that create entirely new markets or create and exploit new opportunities

*Figure 3.1    Types of strategies to design digital business models along the continuum of perfect innovation and imitation*

in and across existing markets (Amit and Zott, 2012). Amazon, for example, started by selling books online but evolved its business model in terms of both markets (consumer goods, cloud computing, etc.) and geographies by introducing new activities to its business model (e.g., fulfillment by Amazon services for small businesses), novel linkages between activities (e.g., reinforcing existing and creating new structures through Prime), and new activity governance (e.g., allowing third parties to sell on its marketplace). Pioneers are frequently considered trendsetters, and – over time – their digital business model may become the "default solution" or "prototypical exemplar" (Aversa et al., 2019) in their domain of activity (e.g., Netflix's streaming model). For example, Clubhouse led the emergence of a new segment in the social media market by pioneering a social audio app that allows users to communicate in audio chat rooms, eventually becoming the trendsetter that many competing platforms followed (e.g., Facebook Live Audio Rooms, Reddit Talk, Spotify Live). In the digital economy, organizations following this strategy often introduce new platform business models (Zhao et al., 2020), where the pioneering firm takes a central position in an innovation ecosystem (Adner and Kapoor, 2010; Masucci et al., 2020). This does not imply that followers cannot build competing ecosystems, but once a pioneer has successfully established its ecosystem and locked-in value co-creation partners, switching costs are often high and it becomes challenging for followers to dethrone a pioneer in the same sector with a similar business model. Rather than following the pioneer, competitors could themselves become pioneers and disrupt the market leader (e.g., Apple vs Blackberry).

The principle behind the pioneer strategy is opportunity creation: The innovator drives the creation of new (ecosystem) value propositions in concert with partners and positions itself in such a way that it captures an often significant share of profits (e.g., Apple). As the driving force behind the invention of the new business model, the pioneer therefore requires strong dynamic capabilities not only to sense but also to shape and continuously develop the ecosystem (Ciampi et al., 2021; Helfat and Winter, 2011; Teece, 2007, 2018). This is because of the constantly changing nature of digital technologies and the ecosystem around which they are built (Nambisan et al., 2017; Yoo et al., 2012). For example, in a recent empirical study, Soluk et al. (2021) find that three specific dynamic capabilities are important in the context of digital business model innovation: knowledge exploitation capabilities, risk management capabilities, and marketing capabilities. Knowledge exploitation capabilities support pioneers in recognizing, internalizing, and exploiting internal and external knowledge. This allows pioneers to stay "tuned" with their ecosystem to continuously innovate their business model (Cennamo, 2021; Faraj et al., 2011; George et al., 2020). Pioneers also require risk management capabilities to manage threats (e.g., cyber risks) and uncertainties inherent in new digital business models (Nambisan et al., 2019). Finally, since pioneers deal with new customers or solve existing customers' problems in novel ways, they need marketing capabilities to gain insights on how ecosystems and customers function (Morgan et al., 2009; Nambisan et al., 2017).

Other strategic prerequisites for this strategy are a strong innovation orientation and the ability to engage in customer and complementor development. Consider the case of Rhapsody (today: Napster), a pioneering music streaming platform founded in 2001, which provides unlimited access to digital music for a flat monthly subscription fee. Rhapsody has created an ecosystem where it engages with songwriters, singers, bands, fans, producers, and tech start-ups to continuously innovate and drive the growth of the platform. In 2015, Rhapsody partnered with BandPage to use the music start-up's behavioral data algorithms to identify musicians' "super" fans and enable musicians to engage with their fans in real time. This collaboration helped musicians to reach, engage with, and monetize their fans, which created additional value for users on both sides of Rhapsody's platform. As this example illustrates, a pioneer strategy requires the pioneer to not only develop product or service content, but also collaborate with multiple stakeholders in the ecosystem to enrich the customer experience (Aversa et al., 2019; Luz Martín-Peña et al., 2018; Schiavone et al., 2021; Weill and Woerner, 2013). Furthermore, the pioneer requires a superior business model innovation process, which supports the organization in systematically exploring and experimenting with a variety of business model candidates to identify the most suitable model. Gupta and Bose (2019), for instance, observe that "pioneering digital ventures often experiment with multiple business models before converging on to a specific model." The importance of experimentation has frequently been highlighted in the extant business model literature (e.g., Andries et al., 2013; Bocken and Snihur, 2020; Konietzko et al., 2020; Sosna et al., 2010; Von Delft et al., 2019), but matters especially when digital firms pioneer new business models because of the complexity associated with novelty or even the immaturity of the underpinning digital technologies and market uncertainties. Here, incumbent firms that undergo digital transformation may have an advantage because they have "the resources to explore a variety of ideas and can more easily experiment with different processes and operations, which makes it more likely to discover a dominant model than a start-up is" (McGrath and McManus, 2020, p. 6).

To illustrate the pioneer strategy, consider the case of Xarvio, a digital farming solution that provides farmers with data on crop and soil health. In this digital business model, launched in 2016 by the chemical company BASF, Xarvio connects data, devices, and agrochemical solutions in a platform ecosystem. Recently, BASF extended its platform by introducing the Scouting App, which allows farmers to identify field stress from pictures of plants taken on their smartphone. It also added Field Manager, a new digital tool that provides farmers with cropping information and satellite data to predict plant health. A pioneer in the digital transformation of the global chemicals and agricultural industries, BASF continuously evolves its digital business model towards a ubiquitous farming solution. Moving beyond its core chemical business to assist farmers with disease and pest recognition and to offer tailored treatments based on current in-field conditions, BASF partnered with several companies for digital system development. For example, in 2020 BASF joined forces with engineering firm Bosch to provide target-based placement of seeds and application of fertilizer. In this partnership, Bosch contributes an Intelligent Planting Solution (IPS) system for automatic seeding control. The IPS is connected to the Xarvio Field Manager, which calculates exactly what and how much seed and fertilizer will provide the optimal yield. Ultimately, BASF orchestrates various complementors, eventually emerging as the leader of this new ecosystem.

The logic of a pioneer strategy rests on the assumption that the pioneer is first to introduce a business model innovation and can thus benefit from first-mover advantages. However, this comes with a considerable risk to the pioneer: neglecting innovation challenges in the environment. Innovation challenges exist for at least two reasons. First, pioneers introduce business model innovations that simultaneously affect "customers, suppliers, strategic partners and others who participate in a new activity system or are affected by it" (Snihur et al., 2021, p. 23). The pioneer requires external partners on both the supply and the demand side to adopt a new way of doing business – one which they are usually not yet familiar with, and which may not seem appropriate compared to traditional ways of conducting economic exchanges. Consider a financial technology company that aims to pioneer a new peer-to-peer money transfer business model. The company may struggle to gain support from customers and other ecosystem participants to successfully pioneer this new way of transferring money. Hence, a digital firm following a pioneer strategy may fail to acquire legitimacy for its new business model (Snihur et al., 2021). Before selling over the Internet became a legitimate business model, companies such as Amazon in retailing or Dow Corning in chemicals found it difficult to gain the acceptance of business model partners (Kashani and Francis, 2011; Santos and Eisenhardt, 2009). When key partners such as customers or investors are unfamiliar with core element(s) of a business model (e.g., online shopping), the pioneer might have a difficult time establishing its innovation. Second, a pioneer might be unable to develop the innovation ecosystem. As Adner and Kapoor (2010, p. 312) suggest: "When the focal innovation requires accompanying innovations in components, the focal firm's development challenges increase, as it now must overcome additional hurdles in specifying, sourcing, and integrating new components." From a business model perspective, challenges include failure to effectively coordinate and manage the set of multilateral relationships with complementors and customers as well as flaws in the design of the business model that concern the point of interaction with other ecosystem members' business models.

Moreover, although there are arguments for the benefits of leading in the introduction of new digital business models, prior research has shown that being first does not necessarily guarantee sustainable competitive advantage (Casadesus-Masanell and Zhu, 2013; Lieberman and Montgomery, 1998; Shankar et al., 1998). For example, although Rhapsody pioneered the music streaming business model, it later lost in competition with platforms like Spotify. Indeed, a common pitfall is for digital pioneers to become satisfied with the status quo and stop developing their business model. Our own research, for instance, shows that market leaders sometimes ignore competition because they are blinded by the "halo" of innovation (Zhao et al., 2020). Since business models do not operate in isolation, there is hence a risk of disregarding developments in the market, eventually losing in competition with fast-moving rivals. This issue is particularly acute in the digital economy, where the scope of competition and speed of change are considerably higher than in traditional industries (Urbach et al., 2017).

## Architect Strategy

In the second type of strategy, we relax the condition of clean sheet innovation that results in a new digital business model. Here, the firm draws on inspirations gained from external sources to introduce a business model innovation in its industry or home market. Because firms following this approach may use templates or archetypes of popular business models (e.g., razor-blade model) (Bocken et al., 2014; Bohnsack et al., 2014) to construct the business model, they can be called architect strategies.

In this case, the innovator relies on proven forms to build the business model. Consider the case of FlashMop, an Australia-based venture connecting busy households with local cleaners. The firm enables households to book a cleaner when they need one without having to wait, to rate and review cleaners, and to pay cashless and securely through an app. Called the "Uber of Home Cleaning" by Australian newspapers, FlashMop did use a proven business model from a company active in Australia to develop its business model. The use of proven forms is coupled with a strong orientation towards customers: The business model is formed in close dialogue with the target customer (Norton and Pine, 2013). Firms following this strategy must hence have a very good understanding of the customer's requirements (Chakravarty et al., 2014), often gained through direct interactions and observations. Whereas the pioneer needs to gain legitimacy and achieve alignment of activity flows between ecosystem members, the architect can rely on references to existing business logics and/or existing relationships to "buy in" customers and other transaction partners. For example, a company one of us worked with introduced a new product-as-a-service model, where it uses real-time data from its installed base of machines to predict when maintenance should be performed. While its customers were familiar with the concept of predictive maintenance and open to signing up to this new model (e.g., because they frequently used service contracts), building the new business model required the company to work closely together with its customers and build the model in several iterative steps. While the design concept of an architect is usually clear upfront, the full design (i.e., the final business model) is often not clear from the beginning. Although an architect might identify core elements of the activity system through which it creates, delivers, and captures value (e.g., by studying an existing solution in another market segment), it requires feedback from customers to put the different elements together in the "right" way. In other words, the architect uses insights gained from direct engagement with the customer to create interdependencies in the activity system step by step. In our example, the service company first used the data it collected to improve the quality of its machines as part of a digital transformation project rather than to immediately sell predictive maintenance services in a new business model. The new model unfolded only after several project workshops with its customers, starting with the creation of new activities to communicate the real-time status of machinery and ending with the identification of a new subscription-based payment method.

Because the business model design needs to unfold, the architect faces a degree of risk in the design undertaking. The architect can manage this risk by systematically probing and collecting feedback from customers and/or applying experiences from previous venturing activities (Keiningham et al., 2020). Whereas the pioneer exercises vision to shape the design space, the architect uses imagination and pragmatism to cope with, as opposed to challenge, the environment. The strategic principle behind the architect strategy is therefore opportunity discovery rather than creation. The architect strategy has a clear proactive but also some reactive elements (e.g., the service company mentioned earlier responded to an increasing "servitization" demand in the market, but proactively led the creation of the new business model).

An example for a company that has used an architect strategy to design its digital business model is the logistics and IT company Flaschenpost. Founded in 2014 by Dieter Büchel in Münster, Germany, as an on-demand beverage delivery company, it made headlines when it was acquired in 2020 for an estimated €1 billion by the Oetker Group. Büchel founded Flaschenpost because he was annoyed that he had to carry crates with water bottles purchased at grocery stores back to his home. Existing delivery services had, in his view, intransparent pricing models and slow delivery times.[2] Flaschenpost's value proposition is hence to make beverage home delivery easy and convenient: Customers order through a smartphone app or through Flaschenpost's website and receive their order within 2 hours. This delivery promise was at risk only two months after the foundation of the company, when Flaschenpost almost failed because it was too successful. The demand for its services skyrocketed and the firm had difficulties scaling its business model. While the value creation logic of on-demand business models, used by firms like Deliveroo or Grubhub, is well known and those models did inform the design of Flaschenpost's business model, building the model proved more challenging than originally anticipated. Büchel consequently decided to pause the development of the business model to systematically analyze customer behavior and requirements, eventually re-launching in 2016 (*Business Insider*, 2022). This exercise enabled the firm to better integrate digital and physical assets, enhance operations (e.g., implementation of semi-automatic warehousing, development of an algorithm to plan delivery routes), hire data analysts, and improve the customer experience (e.g., the app's layout). Eventually Flaschenpost took a classic on-demand delivery model and tailored it to market requirements, resulting in a successful business model innovation: As of 2021, the company receives seven million orders per year, delivers 150,000 crates per day, serves 150 German cities from 31 locations, and employs 13,500 people.

The logic of this strategy rests on the assumption that the architect can design a digital business model that is superior to existing (typically non-digital) solutions in a way that meets customer expectations and delivers value to both the innovator and its customers. However, there is a risk of underestimating the complexity of creating business model innovations. As the Flaschenpost example illustrates, even when drawing on popular templates and having evidence that the new value proposition is attractive, the design challenges are still considerable. Developing a scalable and reliable architecture of digital activities is not an easy task (Bharadwaj et al., 2013). It requires the architect to collaborate with customers to continuously adjust and fine-tune the new model (Achtenhagen et al., 2013; McGrath, 2010; Winter and Szulanski, 2001). Here, speed is not necessarily everything to the creation of a successful business model innovation. Instead, business model innovators may want to strategically "pause at learning plateaus to consolidate knowledge [...] and use steppingstones to make progress" (Ott and Eisenhardt, 2020, p. 2275). Thus, like constructing a new building, the architect may want to reflect on interim designs and check the coherence of the "structure" (e.g., fit between digital and physical assets). Failure to do so could result in an early commitment to a flawed business model innovation (Andries et al., 2013; Zhao et al., 2020). Moreover, even with a compelling business model innovation, it might be difficult for the architect to beat legacy systems, both internally and externally. Wessel and colleagues, for instance, observe that established companies often struggle to take advantage of new digital business models because they are constrained by their existing value chains: "A network of partners with fixed ways of doing business presents an external challenge" (Wessel et al., 2016, p. 6). They conclude that discovering opportunities to create new digital business models is not enough, but companies also need "to make difficult decisions that leave members of their legacy ecosystems behind" (Wessel et al., 2016, p. 8). For the architect this means carefully choosing who to involve and who not to involve in the design process.

## Blender Strategy

Now we relax the condition of innovation further. A digital business model can also be formed by blending different business model elements from sources inside and outside a digital firm's home market in a novel way. We use the term "blend" in an analogy with the production of spirits, where blending denotes the skilled mixing of different vintages and types of liquor. We hence refer to this strategy as "blending."

Digital business models developed through blending are often seen as inferior, compared to those developed through strategies closer to the perfect innovation pole. This notion, however, is simply incorrect. Blending a digital business model involves the complex mixing and orchestration of ingredients, and it can be a viable way to achieve leading positions in the digital economy (Frankenberger and Stam, 2020; Zhao et al., 2020). For example, Chinese Internet giant WeChat has, over the years, skillfully combined and integrated ingredients with many utility purposes, such as messaging, social media, mobile payment, and games, into a "super app business model," eventually enabling the firm to attract more than 1 billion monthly active users around the world (*Forbes*, 2019). Firms following a blender strategy require capabilities to complement various ingredients of their business model in such a way that it enhances the overall user experience. The focus is thus on consistency of the various business model parts: The blender's task is to bring out the best qualities of each of the business model's constituent elements by carefully balancing innovation and imitation. For example, the digital firm Meituan carefully integrated and balanced online group buying (OGB), on-demand delivery, accommodation, travel, leisure, and movie services by creating a "one-stop daily life services" platform. With the value proposition of "helping people eat better, live better," Meituan leverages its capability to address consumer needs across the whole local life services chain, thereby enhancing the overall customer experience. Blending digital business models is in part an art that needs to be learned over time – it is not a digital capability firms can acquire and plug into the organization. It requires the firm to be open-minded about learning from digital ventures in the wider digital economy, actively track and search for new business models, build the ability to understand the business models, and develop the mechanism to make innovative links between old and new business model ingredients.

To have a broad range of options available, the blender needs to search widely for new ingredients that can create value. This boundary-spanning search for new ingredients is both local (e.g., direct rivals) and, importantly, distant (e.g., in markets outside the firm's historic operating space), and it must be embedded in the firm's DNA. For example, in one of our recent research projects we observed that a digital venture in the UK frequently draws inspirations for its business model design from firms in China, Ireland, Japan, Spain, the US, and other locations – a boundary-spanning search that the firm embedded deeply in its corporate culture. Firms may also want to support the search through automation: Some of the master blenders we studied have developed sophisticated monitoring tools that automatically alert the top management to new features that create unusual traffic on rivals' platforms, eventually allowing the blender to quickly imitate and combine ingredients (Zhao et al., 2020).

To further illustrate the blender strategy, consider the case of the Singapore-based firm Grab. Founded in 2012, Grab started by providing mobile taxi-booking services, but soon incorporated Uber-like ride-sharing by attracting independent car and motorcycle drivers to its platform. From 2016 to 2018, Grab added food delivery, courier services, and e-scooter rentals to its transportation model. Grab also explored business models outside the transportation sector, which led it to discover digital payment services. Grab then further developed its business model to include digital payment, insurance, and financing services. In addition to Grab's expansion across industries, it also managed to break geographical boundaries. Here, Grab's superior capability to learn from companies in different countries played out. For example, Grab explored fintech services of the Indonesian online payment start-up Kudo and acquired it in 2017. Following its acquisition, Grab blended its existing payment system with Kudo's online financial service platform. Moreover, the learning culture of Grab emphasizes discovery and synthesis of intelligence across markets. This enables Grab to create a business model that solves common customer problems across Southeast Asian countries (e.g., the lack of public transportation during peak hours, limited use of credit cards), and also to embed its business model locally. Blending business model ingredients, Grab became the region's first "decacorn" (valuation greater than US$10 billion) in May 2021 (*Jakarta Post*, 2019).

Despite its potential, blending is, however, not without risks. On the one hand, a blender may unintentionally combine ingredients that are incompatible because of conflicts in the underlying value creation logic of activities (e.g., low-cost vs full-service). Moreover, even without direct conflicts between activities, a blender may still fail to create fit between the ingredients. This happens when the blender combines ingredients in such a way that they do not enhance their respective "flavors" (e.g., misfit between digital and non-digital elements). Lanzolla et al. (2021), for instance, recently noted that while attempting to blend physical and digital elements, local and distant search might not necessarily lead to a successful blend, a phenomenon they refer to as "search for the sake of search" (e.g., the early Google Labs searched broadly to achieve knowledge recombination yet closed in 2011 for a lack of results). In addition, in this volume, Lanzolla and colleagues show that the continuous blending of physical and digital reality depends on (1) the relation between the physical reality and the digital artefact and (2) the prevailing key logics in the development of the digital artefact. This further illustrates that blending a digital business model is not a simple task.

Another common pitfall in this strategy is to search too narrowly for business models to imitate. The boundary-spanning nature is key to successful blending: Digital firms that focus too much on their immediate home market and industry fail to exploit the full potential of blending and may hence lose in competition with blenders that have mastered the process of continuously creating a consistent business model by combining innovation and imitation across boundaries.

**Adapter Strategy**

In no strategy so far has imitation been at the core in the development of the digital business model. The next type is rather more clearly imitation-based. Here, the firm creates its business model mainly through imitation but develops some of the imitated elements further, thus displaying a certain degree of innovation and proactiveness. We can hence call this an "adapter strategy." Unlike an architect, an adapter would never commit to a major business model innovation. An adapter would also not balance innovation and imitation across boundaries. Instead, with its imitation efforts the adapter focuses on direct rivals, thus displaying a narrower view of the imitation space compared to the blender.

In this type, the firm learns about markets and effective ways to create, deliver, and capture value by borrowing from peers (McDonald and Eisenhardt, 2020). This dynamic process accelerates learning and enables the adapter to identify business model ingredients it believes are valuable and can be developed further, often to better serve niche markets. For instance, while many of its rivals operate online travel agent business models, the travel management company Key Travel adapted the business model of rivals by targeting a niche market: humanitarian, faith, and academic sectors. The company copied major parts from rivals to create its business model but added new activities (e.g., instead of promoting services to individual consumers, the account managers of Key Travel first get to know each client organization's travel requirements and then tailor travel services to the organization). By exclusively targeting the not-for-profit sector, Key Travel has acquired over 5,000 clients globally (Key Travel, 2023). A successful adapter strategy requires strong competencies in systematically studying and unpacking rivals' business models, which support the adapter in (1) quickly imitating rivals and (2) cherry picking those components of a rival's business model that add value to the adapter's business model. The adapter has a strong awareness of its core competencies, and it uses imitation to add business model ingredients that cater to those competencies.

For example, when the Chinese company Nuomi Wang created its OGB business model, it began by studying rivals' business models. It then picked several business model elements for imitation, such as activities to craft deals with local merchants and promote deals to consumers, but also linkages between elements in the business model (e.g., merchant relationship management and customer acquisition) and governance mechanisms (e.g., partnerships with merchants). Next, the company leveraged its core competencies as a social media company to develop some of the imitated elements further. For example, while Nuomi Wang broadly committed to the original OGB business model, it used its rich experience and competencies in social media to enhance deal promotion and consumer acquisition by encouraging consumers to post and share OGB deals on social media (the more consumers share, the greater the discount they could get). Consumers enjoyed interacting and because of this adaptation the user base grew significantly. Such evolutionary adjustments in the adapter strategy are the result of learning and action in real time (McDonald and Eisenhardt, 2020). The adapter needs strong capabilities to search for valuable solutions among competitors and to execute adaptations. The latter requires the adapter to have a vision of how improving the imitated ingredients can lead to optimal distinctiveness (Zhao et al., 2017) – being sufficiently similar to peers to be recognizable but different enough to be competitive. Whereas the architect uses value creation patterns (e.g., freemium, long-tail) to inform the formation of a new digital business model, it does not – in contrast to the adapter – rely on imitation from direct competitors to design its business model. Guided by a few basic design principles the architect is free to create an innovative system of activities. The adapter, on the other hand, imitates a rival's existing activity system and then selectively develops some features further.

Moreover, from a heuristics perspective (Bingham et al., 2007; Bingham and Eisenhardt, 2011), repeating imitative adaptation enables the adapter to learn the adaptation process from experience and also to develop simple rules to select business models for imitation and capturing adaptation opportunities quickly. Our research suggests that the more imitative the adaptation a digital firm carries out, the faster it masters the adaptation process. Implementing multiple adaptations over time allows adapters to learn from experience (e.g., learning why adaptations work) but also to take "a step back" and think about past and potential future adaptations holistically (e.g., reviewing how a particular adaptation worked and leveraging insights to inform future adaptation decisions).

To further illustrate the adapter strategy, consider the case of the online property portal Zoopla. Launched in 2007 in the UK, Zoopla began by imitating core ingredients from the business model of market leader Rightmove. Zoopla then adapted this two-sided property listing business model, which links estate agents with buyers and tenants, by adapting the valuation process of properties. In the original business model, the valuation of properties is done offline – i.e., not on the platform – but Zoopla developed a proprietary algorithm to provide estimated valuations on its platform. Using data from various sources, such as Royal Mail, Ordnance Survey, and Registers of Scotland, Zoopla analyzes millions of data points relating to property sales and home characteristics in local areas, thereby providing estimated valuations for 27 million UK homes.[3] This adaptation increased the user base (e.g., estimated valuations attracted potential homeowners, which would be linked to agents for the actual valuation) and helped Zoopla to strengthen network effects on its platform. Following an adapter strategy, Zoopla became one of the largest property portals in the UK.

As this example shows, imitating most of a rival's business model and then further developing some may be a basis to create competitive advantage. However, an adaptation strategy is not without risks. First, adapting the imitated ingredients can be time-consuming and distract the firm from other developments inside and outside the company. Moreover, the adapter may mistake a peripheral business model element for a core component, developing the wrong parts of the model, eventually losing in competition with more focused rivals. For example, Nuomi Wang found it challenging to decide whether OGB or social media was the core of its business model: the company spent time and money on developing the (peripheral) social media-based parts in its business model, but eventually neglected the development of (core) merchant relationships and service expansion beyond OGB deals. While Nuomi Wang focused on adapting what it believed to be the core parts of its business model, rivals overtook the distracted adapter. Despite acquisition by Baidu, Nuomi Wang never fully recovered and was eventually closed in December 2022 (*E-commerce Newspaper*, 2022).

## Copycat Strategy

All the strategies discussed so far have included a high to minor degree of innovation, but digital business models can form with almost no innovation as well; that is when digital firms develop their business models predominantly through imitation. The clearest case of this occurs when an entrant to a market clones or copies most of a rival's business model innovation. This type can be called "copycat strategy."

Imitation theory distinguishes between information- or rivalry-based imitation (Lieberman and Asaba, 2006; Semadeni and Anderson, 2010). An imitator following an information-based strategy to form business models copies from the competitor introducing a business model innovation on the assumption that the innovating firm has superior market knowledge: The imitator interprets the innovator's behavior as a signal for the attractiveness of a particular business model design (Casadesus-Masanell and Zhu, 2013; Gambardella and McGahan, 2010). In this type, the business model imitator follows direct competitors that are perceived to be "trendsetters." For example, after Sidecar pioneered a new peer-to-peer ride-sharing business model, it was successfully imitated by firms like Lyft and Uber. In contrast, rivalry-based business model imitation centers on keeping the status quo through imitation. In this type, the copycat aims to maintain competitive parity with close competitors. For example, the social network Instagram recently launched Instagram Stories, thereby integrating a popular feature from rival Snapchat into its own business model, and it rolled out a direct competitor to TikTok called Instagram Reels. Copycat strategies have in common that they are a reaction to a direct rival's innovation activity that creates value to users. The strategic principle behind this strategy is, thus, responsiveness.

For a copycat strategy to succeed, the strategy must fulfill several characteristics. First, the imitator must have a strong competitor orientation; i.e., the focus in the development of the business model is on beating competition rather than maximizing profits (Bendle and Vandenbosch, 2014). Therefore, copycat strategies can often be observed in early development stages of platform ecosystems, where a winner has not yet emerged and competing platforms need to grow the user base to generate network effects (Cennamo and Santaló, 2013; Zhao et al., 2020). Second, the imitator must be able to rapidly imitate the innovator. This requires intelligence about rivals' business models and the ability to quickly implement imitations, reflected in the need for superior monitoring and execution skills. For example, as mentioned above, Zalando rapidly imitated US online retailer Zappos.com, eventually enabling the firm to swiftly expand across Europe and establish a market-leading position, generating €7.98 billion in revenues and an operating income of €367 million in 2020 (Zalando, 2020). Third, the imitator requires an efficient business model imitation process. Copycats typically have a standardized imitation process to unlock learning curves and use high-resolution reporting to compare progress against a set of key performance indicators. For example, one of the copycats we studied (see Zhao et al., 2020) used the market leader as a benchmark and set monthly targets accordingly to guide imitative actions. Moreover, copycats learn imitation from process experience, which enables the copycat to identify a problem during business model imitation early and solve it through experience. This experience is a critical asset to succeed with copycat strategies. As Oliver Samwer, co-founder of Rocket Internet, once explained: "just as others have unique gift for the purest form of innovation, we might have a very good gift of execution" (Ekekwe, 2012). Finally, copycats usually attack by aggressively growing the copied business model.

An example for a digital firm that has used a copycat strategy to design its business model is Wimdu. Developed in the Internet start-up factory of Rocket Internet, the company launched 2011 in Germany as a clone of Airbnb. One hundred days after its launch – and supported by Rocket Internet's centralized team of seasoned coders, marketeers, and lawyers – Wimdu had already attracted 10,000 properties and was available in 15 languages (Sanchez, 2019). Wimdu also benefited from a $90 million investment from Rocket Internet. In June 2011, Airbnb issued a sharp statement: "a new type of scam has been brought to our attention: Airbnb clones posing as competition. We've discovered that [they] have a history of copying a website, aggressively poaching from their community, then attempting to sell the company back to the original" (TechCrunch, 2011). By 2012, Wimdu claimed 50,000 listings in over 100 countries, with over $100 million in expected revenues. However, in 2013, it began experiencing difficulties. In some regions, growth slowed down because of fierce competition with local rivals (e.g., Xiaozhu and Tujia in China) and regulatory bodies began scrutinizing its business practices. One year later its founders left, and the company remained behind growth targets. A merger with rival 9flats in 2016 did not aid the recovery and by 2018 Wimdu was forced to close.

As this example shows, copycat strategies come with a couple of challenges. First and foremost is the risk of completely disregarding innovation: exclusively focusing on imitation to grow the business model may result in a lack of vision. Thus, although copycat strategies can be a viable way to achieve growth, focusing on imitation for too long and failing to add, from time to time, (minor) innovations may bring copycat business models to an end. In other words, growing through imitation for the purpose of growth does not constitute a successful strategy to develop digital business models. Moreover, copycat strategies rest on the assumption that the copycat is able to rapidly scale the business model. Being unable to meet growth targets thus represents a serious threat. On the one hand, copycats need to grow faster than direct rivals, including the pioneer and other copycats. Indeed, the copycat strategy depends heavily on being the fastest. For example, the founder of an OGB firm in one of our studies (see Zhao et al., 2020) explained that they copied the market leader quickly because they were afraid of being left behind. He further explained that the decisions to copy and how to copy are typically made in days or even hours. On the other hand, copycats need to carefully manage growth expectations of (potential) investors. For example, in 2013/14 Wimdu was, despite a growth rate of 31 percent, not able to meet Rocket Internet's classification for a winning digital business (Ohr, 2015). Similarly, Facebook's TikTok clone Lasso was unable to dethrone TikTok and subsequently shut down in 2020.

This completes our discussion of strategies to design digital business models. In Table 3.1, we present a summary of major features of the identified strategies.

## EMERGING CONCLUSIONS AND FUTURE RESEARCH

In this chapter, we have discussed strategies to design digital business models to open up thinking and broaden views in academia and practice that remain framed in the image of business model innovation as the silver bullet to create viable ways of doing business in the digital economy, or as a sharp dichotomy between business models forming through either innovation or imitation. In contrast, in this chapter, we have shown the variety and complexity of business model formation processes. Different strategies, with various degrees of innovation and imitation, exist to create viable business models in the digital economy. In doing so, we offer a fresh perspective on digital strategy implementation. A focus on how digital business models form is particularly important for managers and entrepreneurs because they cannot stop at identifying a particular digital business model design but must inevitably deliver digital strategy by creating and constantly developing digital business models through innovation and imitation.

Although we used a wide range of established and emerging literature to develop our arguments and drew on various empirical observations to illustrate principles, strategic prerequisites, and common pitfalls of each strategy, more research along the spectrum of perfect innovation and imitation is clearly needed. This research can establish the boundary conditions of the strategies proposed here and further illuminate the theoretical mechanisms behind the various strategies. In the following we develop an agenda for future research on strategies to design digital business models. Table 3.2 provides an overview of the agenda and examples for potential research questions.

One new line of future inquiry this chapter opens concerns the strategies themselves: We believe more research on the *content* of strategies to design digital business models is needed. The strategies presented in this chapter are a starting point, but they are not a firm or exhaustive typology. Future research may, hence, set out to identify additional types of strategies, especially on the imitation end of the continuum since most research efforts have so far focused on innovation-based strategies (Foss and Saebi, 2017; Zott et al., 2011). However, as we have described, imitation-based strategies to design digital business models can deliver good outcomes. A better understanding of what imitation-based strategies exist can provide

*Table 3.1*    Strategies to design digital business models

| | Pioneer | Architect | Blender | Adapter | Copycat |
|---|---|---|---|---|---|
| Description | Digital business models formed by introducing new ways of doing business across markets and locations | Digital business models formed by drawing inspirations from existing designs to build innovations | Digital business models formed by combining ingredients across boundaries in novel ways | Digital business models formed by imitating ingredients and adapting some from rivals | Digital business models formed by replicating innovations from direct rivals |
| Examples | Amazon<br>Xarvio (BASF) | Flaschenpost<br>FlashMop | Grab<br>WeChat | Nuomi Wang<br>Zoopla | Wimdu<br>Zalando |
| Principle | Opportunity creation (ecosystem developing innovations; trendsetter) | Opportunity discovery (business model addresses unmet market needs) | Balance (consistency between various parts of the model) | Cherry picking (selecting elements to copy and develop some) | Responsiveness (reacting to rivals; fast follower) |
| Strategic prerequisites | • Innovation orientation<br>• Capabilities to develop customers and complementors<br>• Capabilities to build and shape ecosystems<br>• Superior business model innovation process | • Customer orientation<br>• Structured design process (from concept phase to full build)<br>• Capabilities to collaborate with key partners during the design process<br>• Strong project management skills | • Capabilities to identify business model ingredients across markets<br>• Imitation culture<br>• Mastering the blending process<br>• Capabilities to bring out the best qualities of each of the business model's parts | • Focus on core competencies<br>• Skills to unpack and understand rivals' business models<br>• Capabilities to adapt imitations<br>• Vision to further develop imitations to differentiate from rivals | • Competitor orientation<br>• Superior monitoring and execution skills<br>• Efficient business model imitation process<br>• Skills for aggressive growth of the business model |
| Common pitfalls | • Disregarding rivals' business models/dismissing imitation<br>• Stopping the development of the business model (e.g., complacency)<br>• Neglecting innovation challenges that reside in the firm's environment | • Underestimating the complexity of creating business model innovations (e.g., overcoming legacy systems)<br>• Focused commitment to a flawed business model innovation | • Combining conflicting ingredients (e.g., low-cost and full-service activities)<br>• Lack of fit between ingredients (e.g., imitated and innovated elements do not reinforce each other)<br>• Narrow search horizon | • Spending too much time on adapting the imitation(s) (surpassed by copycats or left-behind pioneers)<br>• Developing the wrong parts of the business model<br>• Developing the right parts of the business model but in a wrong way | • Dismissing innovation in the development of the business model<br>• Reacting too slowly<br>• Not meeting expectations (typically growth targets) |

*Table 3.2*       *An agenda for future research on strategies to design digital business models*

| Theme | Research direction | Examples |
|---|---|---|
| Digital business model design strategies: content | What design strategies exist along the spectrum? | • What capabilities underpin each strategy?<br>• How do cognitive microfoundations influence the choice of business model design strategies?<br>• Are business model design strategies mutually exclusive?<br>• What strategies do firms undergoing digital transformation use? |
| Digital business model design strategies: process | How do business model design strategies form? | • What is the role of top and middle managers in creating business model design strategies?<br>• What is the duration/length of different business model design strategies?<br>• How do firms move between different business model design strategies?<br>• How do firms learn business model design strategies? |
| Digital business model design strategies: context | When do business model design strategies emerge? | • When do firms move from one business model design strategy to another?<br>• How does the position of a firm in an ecosystem (e.g., leader vs complementor) affect the choice of business model design strategy?<br>• How does the life cycle of an ecosystem influence the choice of design strategy?<br>• How do firm characteristics (e.g., age, culture, size) influence the choice of business model design strategies? |
| Digital business model design strategies: outcomes | What are the results of business model design strategies? | • What digital business models emerge from each strategy, and why?<br>• What are performance implications of business model design strategies?<br>• What strategies enable a firm to rapidly scale its digital business model?<br>• What business model design strategies improve competitiveness? |

managers and entrepreneurs with more choices and assist them in the design of competitive digital business models. Moreover, future studies on the content of design strategies can contribute by exploring the mechanisms behind various strategies along the spectrum. For example, scholars could study the capabilities that underpin each strategy in more detail and explore the role of cognitive microfoundations in selecting strategies along the spectrum. Moving between the different strategies we have described can be another stream of research: Apple started as a pioneer but later mimicked Netflix's streaming business model when it added Apple TV+; Amazon pioneered e-commerce but later blended various new ingredients with its established model such as online grocery shopping and music streaming; Meituan started by copying Groupon, but adapted the business model by linking it with social media and location-based services; blended hotel booking, food delivery, and ride-sharing; and finally pioneered a data-based cloud platform for the digitalization of local merchants. Yet, we know very little about how firms move dynamically from one strategy to another. Besides, future studies on the interplay of different strategies could also explore whether combinations between strategies exist. An understanding of how different types of business model design strategies combine into each other and tend to sequence themselves over time could reveal a good deal about the design of digital business models.

A second line of future inquiry could focus on the *process* of how design strategies form. Building on research on strategy process (e.g., Fredrickson, 1983; Hutzschenreuter and

Kleindienst, 2006; Pettigrew, 1992; Van de Ven, 1992), this stream of future research could explore if findings from previous strategy process research apply in the digital economy and in particular to digital business model design strategies. Given that innovation ecosystems rarely emerge fully formed, do business model design strategies have to be emergent as well? Future studies can also explore the role of middle and top managers in the formation of the design strategies that we identified: Do pioneer strategies originate in the central vision of an entrepreneur or perhaps in plans of a firm's top management? Moreover, we have provided, first, plausible suggestions that learning plays a key role in several of the strategies to create digital business models (e.g., blending, copycat). How do digital firms learn business model design strategies? We have shown that firms can learn from experience, but could strategies also originate *in situ* when entrepreneurs or managers emerge in the moment? Given the fast-changing environment in which digital firms operate, perhaps entrepreneurs and managers need to decide while acting instead of deciding before acting? Could then design strategies be a pattern in a stream of improvisation? Answering these and related questions could help develop a better understanding not only about digital business models, but digital strategy more generally.

Another promising line of inquiry concerns the question of how the *context* of digital firms influences the types of strategies used to design the business model. A greater contextualization of research on digital business models can enrich future scholarship in the field because context (e.g., historic, temporal, spatial, cultural) provides opportunities for the creation of business models and sets boundaries to the design undertaking. For example, context can be both an asset and a liability, but context can also be influenced by business model innovation and imitation. Future research may, for instance, explore how the ecosystem influences the choice of strategy and the resulting business model design. As we have described, pioneers often shape the formation of new platform ecosystems and can take a dominant position therein. While we know a great deal about how ecosystem leaders compete through their business models, we know surprisingly little about how complementors create competitive business models vis-à-vis powerful ecosystem leaders. Do ecosystem leaders constrain how complementors form business models and influence, or even impose, the complementor's business model design? Or could a complementor perhaps capture more value by pioneering a new business model? To survive and proposer complementors need to interact with various players that constitute the ecosystem, but the underlying mechanisms through which the ecosystem shapes how complementors create, deliver, and capture value through their business models remains little understood and largely undertheorized. Overall, we need a better understanding of the boundary conditions of strategies to design digital business models: When do these strategies emerge? How do firm characteristics like age, culture, or size as well as characteristics of the environment (e.g., ecosystem life cycle, industry structure) influence design strategies?

Finally, we recommend future research to explore *outcomes* of strategies to design digital business models. For example, future research could investigate how the strategies identified here relate to certain business model designs. Using Amit and Zott's (2001) design themes, for example, are lock-in themes the result of architect strategies, do complementarities form through pioneering, or are efficiency-centered business models the result of copycat strategies? Future research on outcomes, especially quantitative studies, could also explore the effect of different strategies on firm performance (e.g., growth, market share) as well as other outcomes such as innovativeness.

Our conclusion is that strategies to design digital business models constantly meld innovation with imitation. Some strategies along the spectrum outlined in this chapter are more innovation-based, others are more imitation-based, and firms that utilize strategies along the spectrum have a rich repertoire to form digital business models.

## NOTES

1.    An application programming interface (API) is a connection between applications (e.g., computer programs).
2.    https://www.businessinsider.de/wirtschaft/startups/mit-bier-und-cola-zum-selfmade-millionaer-die -erfolgsgeschichte-von-flaschenpost-gruender-dieter-buechl-c/ (in German).
3.    https://www.theguardian.com/money/2011/jan/17/zoopla-consumer-app-of-week.

## REFERENCES

Achtenhagen, L., Melin, L., & Naldi, L. (2013). Dynamics of business models: Strategizing, critical capabilities and activities for sustained value creation. *Long Range Planning, 46*(6), 427–42.
Adner, R., & Kapoor, R. (2010). Value creation in innovation ecosystems: How the structure of technological interdependence affects firm performance in new technology generations. *Strategic Management Journal, 31*(3), 306–33.
Adner, R., Puranam, P., & Zhu, F. (2019). What is different about digital strategy? From quantitative to qualitative change. *Strategy Science, 4*(4), 253–61.
Amit, R., & Zott, C. (2001). Value creation in e-business. *Strategic Management Journal, 22*(6–7), 493–520.
Amit, R., & Zott, C. (2012). Creating value through business model innovation. *MIT Sloan Management Review, 53*(3), 41.
Amit, R., & Zott, C. (2015). Crafting business architecture: The antecedents of business model design. *Strategic Entrepreneurship Journal, 9*(4), 331–50.
Andries, P., Debackere, K., & Van Looy, B. (2013). Simultaneous experimentation as a learning strategy: Business model development under uncertainty. *Strategic Entrepreneurship Journal, 7*(4), 288–310.
Aversa, P., Hervas-Drane, A., & Evenou, M. (2019). Business model responses to digital piracy. *California Management Review, 61*(2), 30–58.
Bendle, N., & Vandenbosch, M. (2014). Competitor orientation and the evolution of business markets. *Marketing Science, 33*(6), 781–95.
Bharadwaj, A., El Sawy, O.A., Pavlou, P.A., & Venkatraman, N. (2013). Digital business strategy: Toward a next generation of insights. *MIS Quarterly, 37*(2), 471–82.
Bingham, C.B., Eisenhardt, K.M., & Furr, N.R. (2007). What makes a process a capability? Heuristics, strategy, and effective capture of opportunities. *Strategic Entrepreneurship Journal, 1*(1–2), 27–47.
Bingham, C.B., & Eisenhardt, K.M. (2011). Rational heuristics: The "simple rules" that strategists learn from process experience. *Strategic Management Journal, 32*(13), 1437–64.
Bocken, N.M., Short, S.W., Rana, P., & Evans, S. (2014). A literature and practice review to develop sustainable business model archetypes. *Journal of Cleaner Production, 65*, 42–56.
Bocken, N., & Snihur, Y. (2020). Lean startup and the business model: Experimenting for novelty and impact. *Long Range Planning, 53*(4), 101953.
Bohnsack, R., Pinkse, J., & Kolk, A. (2014). Business models for sustainable technologies: Exploring business model evolution in the case of electric vehicles. *Research Policy, 43*(2), 284–300.
*Business Insider* (2022). Mit Bier und Cola zum Selfmade-Millionär: Die Erfolgsgeschichte von Flaschenpost-Gründer Dieter Büchl. https://www.businessinsider.de/wirtschaft/startups/mit-bier-und -cola-zum-selfmade-millionaer-die-erfolgsgeschichte-von-flaschenpost-gruender-dieter-buechl-c/.
Casadesus-Masanell, R., & Ricart, J.E. (2010). From strategy and business models and onto tactics. *Long Range Planning, 43*(2–3), 195–215.

Casadesus-Masanell, R., & Ricart, J.E. (2011). How to design a winning business model. *Harvard Business Review, 89*(1/2), 100–107.

Casadesus-Masanell, R., & Tarziján, J. (2012). When one business model isn't enough. *Harvard Business Review, 90*(1/2), 132–7.

Casadesus-Masanell, R., & Zhu, F. (2013). Business model innovation and competitive imitation: The case of sponsor-based business models. *Strategic Management Journal, 34*(4), 464–82.

Cennamo, C. (2021). Competing in digital markets: A platform-based perspective. *Academy of Management Perspectives, 35*(2), 265–91.

Cennamo, C., & Santaló, J. (2013). Platform competition: Strategic trade-offs in platform markets. *Strategic Management Journal, 34*(11), 1331–50.

Cennamo, C., Dagnino, G.B., Di Minin, A., & Lanzolla, G. (2020). Managing digital transformation: Scope of transformation and modalities of value co-generation and delivery. *California Management Review, 62*(4), 5–16.

Chakravarty, A., Kumar, A., & Grewal, R. (2014). Customer orientation structure for Internet-based business-to-business platform firms. *Journal of Marketing, 78*(5), 1–23.

Chesbrough, H. (2010). Business model innovation: Opportunities and barriers. *Long Range Planning, 43*(2–3), 354–63.

Ciampi, F., Demi, S., Magrini, A., Marzi, G., & Papa, A. (2021). Exploring the impact of big data analytics capabilities on business model innovation: The mediating role of entrepreneurial orientation. *Journal of Business Research, 123*, 1–13.

Correani, A., De Massis, A., Frattini, F., Petruzzelli, A.M., & Natalicchio, A. (2020). Implementing a digital strategy: Learning from the experience of three digital transformation projects. *California Management Review, 62*(4), 37–56.

Davis, J., & Aggarwal, V.A. (2020). How Spotify and TikTok beat their copycats. https://hbr.org/2020/07/how-spotify-and-tiktok-beat-their-copycats.

*E-commerce Newspaper* (2022) Goodbye, Baidu Nuomi. https://www.dsb.cn/198131.html.

Ekekwe, N. (2012). When you can't innovate, copy. https://hbr.org/2012/05/when-you-cant-innovate-copy.

Ethiraj, S.K., Levinthal, D., & Roy, R.R. (2008). The dual role of modularity: Innovation and imitation. *Management Science, 54*(5), 939–55.

Faraj, S., Jarvenpaa, S.L., & Majchrzak, A. (2011). Knowledge collaboration in online communities. *Organization Science, 22*(5), 1224–39.

Fichman, R.G., Dos Santos, B.L., & Zheng, Z. (2014). Digital innovation as a fundamental and powerful concept in the information systems curriculum. *MIS Quarterly, 38*(2), 329–43.

*Forbes* (2019). WeChat becomes an e-commerce challenger in China with mini programs. https://www.forbes.com/sites/michellegrant/2019/10/28/wechat-becomes-an-e-commerce-challenger-in-china-with-mini-programs/.

Foss, N.J., & Saebi, T. (2017). Fifteen years of research on business model innovation: How far have we come, and where should we go? *Journal of Management, 43*(1), 200–227.

Frankenberger, K., & Stam, W. (2020). Entrepreneurial copycats: A resource orchestration perspective on the link between extra-industry business model imitation and new venture growth. *Long Range Planning, 53*(4), 101872.

Fredrickson, J.W. (1983). Strategic process research: Questions and recommendations. *Academy of Management Review, 8*(4), 565–75.

Gambardella, A., & McGahan, A.M. (2010). Business-model innovation: General purpose technologies and their implications for industry structure. *Long Range Planning, 43*(2–3), 262–71.

George, G., Merrill, R.K., & Schillebeeckx, S.J. (2020). Digital sustainability and entrepreneurship: How digital innovations are helping tackle climate change and sustainable development. *Entrepreneurship Theory and Practice,* 1042258719899425.

Ghezzi, A., & Cavallo, A. (2020). Agile business model innovation in digital entrepreneurship: Lean startup approaches. *Journal of Business Research, 110*, 519–37.

Gupta, G., & Bose, I. (2019). Strategic learning for digital market pioneering: Examining the transformation of Wishberry's crowdfunding model. *Technological Forecasting and Social Change, 146*, 865–76.

Helfat, C.E., & Winter, S.G. (2011). Untangling dynamic and operational capabilities: Strategy for the (n)ever-changing world. *Strategic Management Journal, 32*(11), 1243–50.

Hutzschenreuter, T., & Kleindienst, I. (2006). Strategy-process research: What have we learned and what is still to be explored. *Journal of Management, 32*(5), 673–720.

Iansiti, M., & Lakhani, K.R. (2017). Managing our hub economy. *Harvard Business Review, 95*(5), 84–92.

*Jakarta Post* (2019). How Grab Indonesia achieved decacorn status. https://www.thejakartapost.com/ adv/2019/03/01/how-grab-indonesia-achieved-decacorn-status-1551428831.html.

Kashani, K., & Francis, I. (2011). *Xiameter: The Past and Future of a "Disruptive Innovation".* International Institute for Management Development. Case IMD433-PDF-ENG. https://www.imd .org/research-knowledge/case-studies/xiameter-the-past-and-future-of-a-disruptive-innovation/.

Keiningham, T., Aksoy, L., Bruce, H.L., Cadet, F., Clennell, N., Hodgkinson, I.R., & Kearney, T. (2020). Customer experience driven business model innovation. *Journal of Business Research, 116,* 431–40.

Key Travel (2023). Why us. https://www.keytravel.com/why-us/.

Kim, S.K., & Min, S. (2015). Business model innovation performance: When does adding a new business model benefit an incumbent? *Strategic Entrepreneurship Journal, 9*(1), 34–57.

Konietzko, J., Baldassarre, B., Brown, P., Bocken, N., & Hultink, E.J. (2020). Circular business model experimentation: Demystifying assumptions. *Journal of Cleaner Production, 277,* 122596.

Lanzolla, G., & Markides, C. (2021). A business model view of strategy. *Journal of Management Studies, 58*(2), 540–53.

Lanzolla, G., Pesce, D., & Tucci, C.L. (2021). The digital transformation of search and recombination in the innovation function: Tensions and an integrative framework. *Journal of Product Innovation Management, 38*(1), 90–113.

Levinthal, D.A. (1997). Adaptation on rugged landscapes. *Management Science, 43*(7), 934–50.

Lieberman, M.B., & Asaba, S. (2006). Why do firms imitate each other? *Academy of Management Review, 31*(2), 366–85.

Lieberman, M.B., & Montgomery, D.B. (1998). First-mover (dis)advantages: Retrospective and link with the resource-based view. *Strategic Management Journal, 19*(12), 1111–25.

Linde, L., Sjödin, D., Parida, V., & Gebauer, H. (2020). Evaluation of digital business model opportunities: a framework for avoiding digitalization traps. *Research-Technology Management, 64*(1), 43–53.

Lippman, S.A., & Rumelt, R.P. (1982). Uncertain imitability: An analysis of interfirm differences in efficiency under competition. *Bell Journal of Economics, 13,* 418–38.

Luz Martín-Peña, M., Díaz-Garrido, E., & Sánchez-López, J.M. (2018). The digitalization and servitization of manufacturing: A review on digital business models. *Strategic Change, 27*(2), 91–9.

Markides, C., & Charitou, C.D. (2004). Competing with dual business models: A contingency approach. *Academy of Management Perspectives, 18*(3), 22–36.

Markides, C., & Sosa, L. (2013). Pioneering and first mover advantages: The importance of business models. *Long Range Planning, 46*(4–5), 325–34.

Massa, L., & Tucci, C. (2014). Business model innovation. *The Oxford Handbook of Innovation Management.* Oxford University Press, 420–41.

Masucci, M., Brusoni, S., & Cennamo, C. (2020). Removing bottlenecks in business ecosystems: The strategic role of outbound open innovation. *Research Policy, 49*(1), 103823.

McDonald, R.M., & Eisenhardt, K.M. (2020). Parallel play: Startups, nascent markets, and effective business-model design. *Administrative Science Quarterly, 65*(2), 483–523.

McGrath, R.G. (2010). Business models: A discovery driven approach. *Long Range Planning, 43*(2–3), 247–61.

McGrath, R., & McManus, R. (2020). Discovery-driven digital transformation. *Harvard Business Review, 98*(3), 124–33.

Morgan, N.A., Vorhies, D.W., & Mason, C.H. (2009). Market orientation, marketing capabilities, and firm performance. *Strategic Management Journal, 30*(8), 909–20.

Nambisan, S. (2017). Digital entrepreneurship: Toward a digital technology perspective of entrepreneurship. *Entrepreneurship Theory and Practice, 41*(6), 1029–55.

Nambisan, S., Lyytinen, K., Majchrzak, A., & Song, M. (2017). Digital innovation management: Reinventing innovation management research in a digital world. *MIS Quarterly, 41*(1), 233–8.

Nambisan, S., Wright, M., & Feldman, M. (2019). The digital transformation of innovation and entrepreneurship: Progress, challenges and key themes. *Research Policy*, *48*(8), 103773.

Norton, D.W., & Pine, B.J. (2013). Using the customer journey to road test and refine the business model. *Strategy & Leadership*, *41*(2), 12–17.

Ohr, T. (2015). 5 unexpected things Rocket Internet's annual report for 2014 reveals. https://www.eu-startups.com/2015/05/5-unexpected-things-rocket-internets-annual-report-for-2014-reveals/.

Ott, T.E., & Eisenhardt, K.M. (2020). Decision weaving: Forming novel, complex strategy in entrepreneurial settings. *Strategic Management Journal*, *41*(12), 2275–2314.

Pettigrew, A.M. (1992). The character and significance of strategy process research. *Strategic Management Journal*, *13*(S2), 5–16.

Posen, H.E., Lee, J., & Yi, S. (2013). The power of imperfect imitation. *Strategic Management Journal*, *34*(2), 149–64.

Rachinger, M., Rauter, R., Müller, C., Vorraber, W., & Schirgi, E. (2019). Digitalization and its influence on business model innovation. *Journal of Manufacturing Technology Management*, *30*(8), 1143–60.

Rivkin, J.W. (2000). Imitation of complex strategies. *Management Science*, *46*(6), 824–44.

Ross, J.W., Beath, C.M., & Sebastian, I.M. (2017). How to develop a great digital strategy. *MIT Sloan Management Review*, *58*(2), 6–9.

Sanchez, M. (2019). Imitation simply wasn't enough: A Wimdu post-mortem. https://www.eu-startups.com/2019/07/imitation-simply-wasnt-enough-a-wimdu-post-mortem/.

Santos, F.M., & Eisenhardt, K.M. (2009). Constructing markets and shaping boundaries: Entrepreneurial power in nascent fields. *Academy of Management Journal*, *52*(4), 643–71.

Schiavone, F., Mancini, D., Leone, D., & Lavorato, D. (2021). Digital business models and ridesharing for value co-creation in healthcare: A multi-stakeholder ecosystem analysis. *Technological Forecasting and Social Change*, *166*, 120647.

Semadeni, M., & Anderson, B.S. (2010). The follower's dilemma: Innovation and imitation in the professional services industry. *Academy of Management Journal*, *53*(5), 1175–93.

Shankar, V., Carpenter, G.S., & Krishnamurthi, L. (1998). Late mover advantage: How innovative late entrants outsell pioneers. *Journal of Marketing Research*, *35*(1), 54–70.

Snihur, Y., Zott, C., & Amit, R. (2021). Managing the value appropriation dilemma in business model innovation. *Strategy Science*, *6*(1), 22–38.

Soluk, J., Miroshnychenko, I., Kammerlander, N., & De Massis, A. (2021). Family influence and digital business model innovation: the enabling role of dynamic capabilities. *Entrepreneurship Theory and Practice*, *45*(4), 867–905.

Sorescu, A. (2017). Data-driven business model innovation. *Journal of Product Innovation Management*, *34*(5), 691–6.

Sosna, M., Trevinyo-Rodríguez, R.N., & Velamuri, S.R. (2010). Business model innovation through trial-and-error learning: The Naturhouse case. *Long Range Planning*, *43*(2–3), 383–407.

TechCrunch (2011). Airbnb freaks out over Samwer clones. https://techcrunch.com/2011/06/09/airbnb/.

Teece, D.J. (2007). Explicating dynamic capabilities: The nature and microfoundations of (sustainable) enterprise performance. *Strategic Management Journal*, *28*(13), 1319–50.

Teece, D.J. (2010). Business models, business strategy and innovation. *Long Range Planning*, *43*(2–3), 172–94.

Teece, D.J. (2018). Business models and dynamic capabilities. *Long Range Planning*, *51*(1), 40–49.

Urbach, N., Drews, P., & Ross, J. (2017). Digital business transformation and the changing role of the IT function. *MIS Quarterly Executive*, *16*(2), 1–4.

Van de Ven, A.H. (1992). Suggestions for studying strategy process: A research note. *Strategic Management Journal*, *13*(S1), 169–88.

Vendrell-Herrero, F., Parry, G., Bustinza, O.F., & Gomes, E. (2018). Digital business models: Taxonomy and future research avenues. *Strategic Change*, *27*(2), 87–90.

Von Delft, S., Kortmann, S., Gelhard, C., & Pisani, N. (2019). Leveraging global sources of knowledge for business model innovation. *Long Range Planning*, *52*(5), 101848.

Warner, K.S.R., & Wäger, M. (2019). Building dynamic capabilities for digital transformation: An ongoing process of strategy renewal. *Long Range Planning*, *52*(3), 326–49.

Weill, P., & Woerner, S.L. (2013). Optimizing your digital business model. *MIT Sloan Management Review*, *54*(3), 71–8.

Weill, P., & Woerner, S.L. (2018). *What's Your Digital Business Model? Six Questions to Help You Build the Next-Generation Enterprise*. Harvard Business Press.

Wessel, M., Levie, A., & Siegel, R. (2016). The problem with legacy ecosystems. *Harvard Business Review*, *94*(11), 68–74.

Winter, S.G., & Szulanski, G. (2001). Replication as strategy. *Organization Science*, *12*(6), 730–43.

Wirtz, B.W. (2019). *Digital Business Models: Concepts, Models, and the Alphabet Case Study*. Springer.

Yoo, Y., Boland, R.J., Jr, Lyytinen, K., & Majchrzak, A. (2012). Organizing for innovation in the digitized world. *Organization Science*, *23*(5), 1398–1408.

Zalando (2020). Annual report. https://corporate.zalando.com/en/investor-relations/key-figures-2020.

Zhao, E.Y., Fisher, G., Lounsbury, M., and Miller, D. (2017). Optimal distinctiveness: Broadening the interface between institutional theory and strategic management. *Strategic Management Journal*, *38*(1), 93–113.

Zhao, Y., Von Delft, S., Morgan-Thomas, A., & Buck, T. (2020). The evolution of platform business models: Exploring competitive battles in the world of platforms. *Long Range Planning*, *53*(4), 101892.

Zott, C., & Amit, R. (2007). Business model design and the performance of entrepreneurial firms. *Organization Science*, *18*(2), 181–99.

Zott, C., Amit, R., & Massa, L. (2011). The business model: Recent developments and future research. *Journal of Management*, *37*(4), 1019–42.

# 4.  The digitalization of physical reality: theoretical lenses to incorporate digitalization into management research

*Gianvito Lanzolla, Danilo Pesce and Christopher Tucci*

## 1.  DIGITALIZATION IN BUSINESS AND MANAGEMENT RESEARCH

In the early 2000s, digitalization was a fairly obscure construct. As shown in Figure 4.1, in just a few years digitalization has become a popular topic that fascinates both academics and practitioners in business and indeed all types of organizations. This growing popularity is not surprising. Digitalization is associated with several transformational outcomes for firms and their environments (World Economic Forum, 2020). A substantial body of research in several streams of the management literature has investigated the impact of digitalization on areas including management practice (Jarzabkowski and Kaplan, 2015; Sarker et al., 2019; Majchrzak and Griffith, 2020; Mousavi Baygi et al., 2021), organization and organizing (Yoo et al., 2012; Bailey et al., 2019; Kretschmer and Khashabi, 2020), firm boundaries (Nambisan et al., 2017; Lyytinen et al., 2020), business models (Teece, 2010; Massa et al., 2017; Lanzolla and Markides, 2021), partnerships (Adner, 2017; Dattée et al., 2018; Jacobides et al., 2018; Wang, 2021), innovation (Afuah and Tucci, 2012; Villarroel et al., 2013; Nambisan et al., 2020; Lanzolla et al., 2021), strategy (Bharadwaj et al., 2013; Berente, 2020; Hanelt et al., 2021), and the macro environment (World Economic Forum, 2020). In these studies, the digital technologies leading to digitalization have been conceptualized as general-purpose technologies (e.g., Gambardella and McGahan, 2010), based on their capabilities such as monitoring, control, connectivity, optimization, autonomy (Porter and Heppelmann, 2014, 2015), or for the degree of their technical properties—e.g., interoperability, speed (Bresnahan and Trajtenberg, 1995); or treated as mere contextual background. Granted, the vast majority of these studies focus on the use of digital technologies and on the implications of digitalization (e.g., Tilson et al., 2010) rather than on the technology per se.

We argue that the unsystematic conceptualization of the relationships between digital technology and digitalization has hampered the scope for comparing and contrasting extant research and developing integrative theoretical frameworks. In this chapter, we aim to address this gap and provide a conceptualization of the different ways in which the digitalization of physical reality can take place. First, based on a systematic analysis[1] of the business literature, we propose a taxonomy that reveals that the digitalization of physical reality leverages several digital technologies and outcomes ranging from full digitization—i.e., substitution of physical reality—to partial digitalization; i.e., complementarity between the legacy unit of physical reality and the digital artefact. We then show that partial digitalization of physical reality can rest on very different logics; i.e., simulation, emulation, and/or "feeling of presence." For all

83

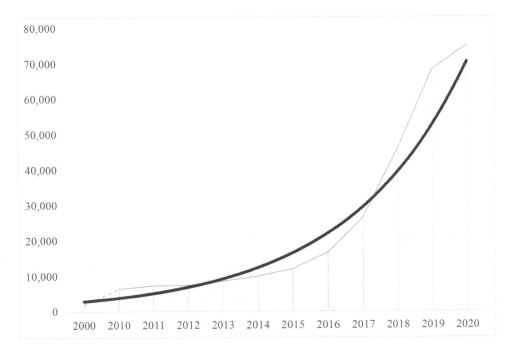

*Figure 4.1      Google Scholar results for "digitalization" or "digitalisation" over time*

these potential outcomes of digitalization, we highlight affordances as well as technical constraints to deliver on such affordances.

Second, the digitalization of the physical world does not happen one physical component
at a time, nor one component independently from another. We maintain that the interactions
among digitalized units of physical reality could be analyzed through the conceptual lens of
complexity theory. Borrowing from complexity theory, we identify three types of interactions,
which we label digital convergence, "phygital" convergence, and no convergence.

Overall, by providing a taxonomy of the outcomes of digitalization of single units of
physical reality and of their interaction, this chapter suggests that business and management
researchers open the black box of digitalization and be systematic and explicit in describing
the boundary conditions under which their research has been developed. We also propose
a research agenda for deepening the study of digitalization in order to inform business and
management research.

## 2.      THE DIGITALIZATION OF PHYSICAL REALITY

The process of digitalization of physical reality is realized through different technical processes
and technologies, hereafter called digitalization "technologies." The most common digitalization technologies include digitization, smartification, digital twins, augmented reality (AR),
virtual reality, and the metaverse. In what follows, we briefly describe these digitalization
technologies and their affordances, and we then provide an integrative taxonomic framework.

## 2.1     Digitization beyond Gravity: The De-Materialization of Physical Reality

Digitization is the process of changing from analog to digital form (Yoo, 2010). Converting text, videos, and music into digital form are all examples of digitization. Fully digitized artefacts acquire new properties vis-à-vis their physical earlier versions. Here we summarize some of the most salient properties that fully digitized artefacts acquire (please see the Appendix for supporting evidence).

### Editability
Full digitization allows the elements by which a digital artefact is made to be rearranged, while leaving its logical structure unchanged by deleting existing elements or adding new ones, modifying some of the functions of individual elements, and updating the content, items, or data fields. This is the case for digital repositories, whose utility is closely associated with constant updating. In this vein, editability intentionally makes digital artefacts incomplete throughout their lifetime and perpetually "under construction" in some sense, rendering their boundaries unknowable.

### Replicability
Full digitization allows the reproduction and distribution of each form of a digital artefact for (typically) an unlimited time and at virtually no cost. The classic example here might be the replicability of a song, perhaps via Spotify, at zero marginal cost. From the industrial perspective, another example is that of enterprise resource planning systems, which allow business processes to be replicated by replacing independent applications—unique for each function—with interrelated and standardized programs in functional modules.

### Modularity
Full digitization allows the elements by which digital artefacts are made to be decomposed—expanding the notion of modularity adopted from the physical world—and enabling the re-shuffling and the reorganization of these elements not only into new configurations, but also into unrelated use contexts. For example, software can be developed by different teams that work in parallel once the architecture has been defined.

### Granularity
Distinct from modularity, "granularity" refers to the "ingredients" from which blocks are made and describes the minute size and resilience of the elementary units or items by which a digital object is constituted. The granular constitution of digital artefacts is conveyed by the difference between their physical counterparts, which are non-granular blocks or elements bundled together in such a way that they are not readily decomposable or traceable as elementary units. In this vein, although modularity concerns relationships between blocks, granularity entails tracing composite units back to the most minute elements and operations of which they are made.

### Re-programmability
Full digitization allows a digital artefact to be released from its immediate use context by modifying its structure and repurposing it through a later binding of form and function. The re-programmability attribute builds on the Von Neumann computing architecture in terms

of enabling the separation of the semiotic functional logic of the digital artefact from the physical embodiment that executes it, thus allowing a digital artefact to perform a wide array of functions (such as calculation, communications, word processing, encryption, browsing, and so on). In contrast to manufacturing capability, the primary cost of digital development is limited to the hours of development thanks to the re-programmability characteristics of digital artefacts.

### Homogeneity

Full digitization allows any analog signal to be mapped to a set of binary numbers (discrete representation of data in bits of 0 and 1), thereby allowing any digital artefact to be stored, transmitted, processed, and displayed using the same digital devices and networks; e.g., location streaming services can be mixed with other services and content. Thus, the homogenization of data and the emergence of new media essentially separate the content from the medium. The homogenization of digital data at the service layer allows the emergence of new products and services through mashups across different product architectural boundaries. Therefore, devices, networks, services, and contents created for specific purposes are now being re-mixed to repurpose their usage.

### Traceability

Full digitization allows events and entities to be chronologically interrelated over time and space, thus leaving an unprecedented volume of digital traces as by-products which, in turn, can lead to new innovations that had not been anticipated by the original innovators or consumers; e.g., integrating and analyzing data from jogging exercises and using them to create personalized training plans. Such derivative innovations add new layers of affordances to the digital products and services. Indeed, the bulk of innovations in social and mobile media results from the generative use of their digital traces, now reflected in the popular idea of "big data."

### Interoperability

Full digitization enables data to be shared among different digital artefact formats by enabling their manipulation and expanding their accessibility over devices and platforms; e.g., the Nest self-learning thermostat that was designed with an application-programming interface that allows it to exchange information with other products, such as a smart lock. Whenever a homeowner enters his or her house, the smart lock communicates this information to the Nest thermostat, which then adjusts the temperature according to the homeowner's preferences.

### Speed

Full digitization enables the instant transmission of real-time data across a wide range of networks that generate, transform, and connect products and sensors by increasing speed and responsiveness and reducing latency. 5G is currently (2022) in the process of rollout with 6G under development, and they will enable a great improvement in bandwidth and latency that is predicted to lead to the emergence of new "Internet of Things" business models that will involve massive quantities of data and/or mission-critical processing. Self-driving cars and healthcare services will be among the beneficiaries, but wireless protocols will also pose a competitive challenge to fixed wireline services, which have historically been a cash cow for telecommunications companies.

**Synchronization**
Full digitization also enables synchronization; that is, synchronous communications between different data sources stored in different electronic memories at different "clock speeds." For instance, the "clock speed" of software development is generally much faster than that of traditional manufacturing; a software development team might create as many as ten iterations of an application in the time it takes to generate a single new version of the hardware on which it runs. Therefore, companies will need to synchronize these very different clock speeds of hardware and software development and will have to rethink many aspects of organizational structure, policies, and design principles.

**Accessibility/transferability**
Full digitization enables homogeneous and heterogeneous digital artefacts to be found and accessed through standardized protocols (such as an IP address and metadata), thereby enabling them to be enrolled in the global information infrastructure, the Internet. In this vein, connectivity also allows transferability by conveying changes in one part of the system to other parts of the system, or by distributing them to other system processes or objects.

**Ubiquity**
Finally, with its relatively inexpensive and ubiquitous connectivity, full digitization allows the types of information and knowledge that were not readily available in the past to be stored, mobilized, and interpreted anywhere; e.g., from a robot to a mechanical press, the performance of an industrial machine can be remotely monitored and adjusted by the end-users during operation. This offers users the unprecedented ability to customize the function, performance, and interface of products, and to operate them in hard-to-reach environments.

In isolation, and when combined with each other, these properties of digital artefacts make digital artefacts less subject to the constraints of the physical world; i.e., less subject to the constraints of "gravity."[2]

## 2.2    Smartification and Digital Twins: The Emulation at Scale of Physical Reality

According to Porter and Heppelmann (2014), smartification requires three core elements: (1) physical components comprising the product's mechanical and electrical parts; (2) sensors, microprocessors, data storage, controls, software, and, typically, an embedded operating system and enhanced user interface that amplify the capabilities and value of the physical components; and (3) connectivity components that amplify the capabilities and value of the smart components and enable some of them to exist outside the physical product itself.

Digital twins take smartification to the next level. They are adaptive models that emulate the behavior of a physical system in a virtual system exploiting real-time data to update itself along its lifecycle (Tao et al., 2018; Semeraro et al., 2021). In the commercial world, different variations of the term have emerged to highlight some specific aspects of this emulation (see below), and these include "digital model," "product avatar," and "digital shadow." These different digital twins differ mostly in the level of data integration between the physical and digital counterpart (Kritzinger et al., 2018).

Smartification and digital twins are two examples of digitalization technologies that build on emulation of physical reality to create digital copies of it. Emulation seeks to duplicate an object exactly as it exists in physical reality. For instance, Alemdar and Ersoy (2010) and

Porter and Heppelmann (2014, 2015) define emulation as the (complete) imitation of a physical object through sensors, computing, and networking technologies that allow the physical object to provide information about its environment, context, and behavior, thus enabling it to operate not only in the real world but also in a digital environment.

The performance of digital emulation depends not only on the accuracy of the emulation logics but also on the level of data synchronization. Tao et al. (2018) identified three key technical properties that might have an impact on data synchronization:

1. Real-time reflection: Two spaces exist in digital twins, physical space and virtual space. The virtual space is the real reflection of the physical space, and it can keep ultra-high synchronization and fidelity with the physical space.
2. Interaction and convergence in physical space, between historical data and real-time data, and between physical space and virtual space.
3. Self-evolution: Digital twins can update data in real time, so that virtual models can undergo continuous improvement through comparing virtual space with physical space in parallel.

The most recent advances in emulation have been based on the use of artificial intelligence. Smartification, digital twins and, more broadly, digital emulation overcome some of the constraints of the physical world by complementing the physical object with digital copies that acquire the properties of digitized artefacts. As such, emulation has the potential to decrease optimization costs in numerous ways, many of which were not previously possible (Porter and Heppelmann, 2014). For example, through emulation, algorithms and analysis can be applied to in-use or historical data to improve production, utilization, and efficiency. In wind turbines, for example, a sensor can adjust each blade at each revolution to capture maximum wind energy. And each turbine can be adjusted not only to improve its performance, but also to minimize its impact on the efficiency of neighboring ones.

## 2.3    Virtual Reality: Creating Virtual Worlds

Virtual reality occurs when digital representations stand for, and in some cases completely substitute, the physical objects, processes, or people they represent. For instance, Lyytinen (2021) defines "virtual embedding" as the agreed virtual representations of real-world phenomena such as an organization's assets, actors, entities in physical environments, and immaterial "objects" (e.g., money, equity). Virtualization enables spatial separation and independence between people and objects (or other people) through three core elements (Bailey et al., 2012): operating with or on representations, operating through representations, and operating within representations. According to Baskerville et al. (2020), virtualization results from pre-formatted, automated, and contingent "live actions" performed by software. Virtual reality is often associated with simulation. Simulation is the use of a mathematical or computer-based representation of a physical system for the purpose of studying constrained effects or how physical systems work. Crucially, it seeks to simulate some aspects of the physical systems but does not necessarily represent all the aspects or follow all the rules of the real environment. According to Bailey et al. (2012), simulation is important because it is through simulation that virtuality comes closest to replacing reality.

Referring to virtual reality, Baskerville et al. (2020) introduce the concept of "ontological reversal," in which the digital version is created first, and the physical version second (if needed)—e.g., 3D printing. With ontological reversal, non-physical digital objects are not only as real as physical objects; they are more "real." It used to be that the sale of a ticket (plane, train, concert, event) produced a physical ticket and a digital record of the transaction was stored in the company's information system as proof of the transaction. Today, physical tickets are no longer produced. Real tickets exist in the cloud. When a user needs physical proof of the real (non-physical) ticket, they can reproduce a physical copy of the non-physical item. The ontology of physical and digital has been reversed. With the ontological inversion, there is a temporal inversion in the way products are produced. The digital version is produced first, the physical version is produced when and where it makes sense (cf. Baskerville et al., 2020; Nambisan et al., 2020).

## 2.4   Augmented Reality and the Metaverse: Toward Digitalizing the Biological and Sensory Spheres

Porter and Heppelmann (2017) define AR as the process of transforming volumes of data and analytics into images or animations that are superimposed on the real world. The real-time use of information in the form of text, graphics, audio, and other virtual enhancements integrated with real-world objects is the element that differentiates AR from virtual reality. AR integrates and adds value to the user's interaction with the real world and does not simulate an interaction with the physical world as in virtual reality. The author Neal Stephenson succinctly summarizes such differences: "the purpose of VR is to take [people] to a completely made-up place, and the purpose of AR is to change your experience of the place that you're in" (Robinson, 2017). By overlaying digital information directly on real objects or environments, AR allows people to process the physical and digital simultaneously, eliminating the need to mentally bridge the two. That improves people's ability to rapidly and accurately absorb information, make decisions, and execute required tasks quickly and efficiently. AR also improves how users visualize and therefore access new monitoring data, how they receive and follow instructions and guidance on product operations, and even how they interact with and control the products themselves. According to Rasool et al. (2021), two key properties of AR are vividness and interactivity. Factors of vividness are sensory breadth and sensory depth. Sensory breadth is the number of sensory dimensions, and sensory depth is the resolution of each channel. How these sensory inputs come together—i.e., how they are mediated—creates the sense of vividness. Interactivity has to do with how the user can map and make their actions into the mediated environment persistent.

The metaverse takes augmented and virtual reality to the next level. "Metaverse" is a term created by Neal Stephenson in the 1992 novel *Snow Crash*. In the book, the protagonist Hiro enters a virtual reality called the metaverse as an escape from his physical reality living in a run-down container. Perhaps one of the first iterations of the metaverse was *Second Life* (2003). However, the concept of the metaverse began to take hold in 2020, when several platforms (including Facebook, which changed its name to Meta in 2021) imagined their own versions of the metaverse. The metaverse represents an evolution of social connection, an "embodied Internet," where the user is no longer a spectator but becomes an integral part of the experience of connection, communication, and transaction (Balis, 2022). According to Meta, the 3D spaces of the metaverse will allow users to socialize, learn, collaborate, work, play, shop, create, find communities, and grow their business through avatars that actually inhabit the virtual space, having a real "feeling of presence" (Meta Connect Conference,

2021). Balis (2022) points out that the immersive environment of the metaverse is an opportunity for consumer companies as well as industrial ones. For example, Nvidia is investing in forms of metaverse related to manufacturing and logistics to reduce waste and accelerate better business solutions. Microsoft is positioning its cloud services to engage forms of the metaverse where avatars and immersive spaces can infiltrate collaboration environments such as Teams. Nike and Louis Vuitton are investing in the most assertive part of the metaverse by investing in both building virtual retail environments for selling their physical products and creating virtual products and collectibles (e.g., virtual sneakers in NFTs, or non-fungible tokens) for the metaverse.

Some technologies underpinning the metaverse, such as ubiquitous and mobile supercomputing, neurotechnological brain enhancements, and genetic editing, seek to extend beyond physical reality by integrating the biological sphere and undoing the gravity that currently distinguishes the physical from the digital world. The digitalization of the "feeling of presence" promises to bring the digitalization of the physical world to the next stage in terms of affordances.

## 2.5   A Taxonomy of Outcomes of the Digitalization of the Physical World

Beyond the proliferation of technologies and commercial jargon, the review above allows us to highlight that the digitalization of the physical world, overall, has multiple potential outcomes. On one hand, in limited cases, digitalization can lead to full substitution of physical reality. On the other hand, digitalization can lead to outcomes where there is a degree of complementarity between the digital artefact and physical reality. Such degree of complementarity is mediated by the logics underpinning the digital artefacts: emulation, simulation, or "feeling presence"— and by the level of digital/physical (data) synchronization. In Figure 4.2, we show a taxonomy of potential outcomes of the digitalization of the physical world.

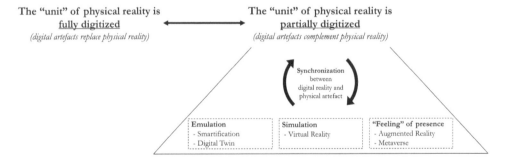

*Figure 4.2*    *Possible outcomes of digitalization of "units" of physical reality*

## 3.   INTERACTIONS AMONG UNITS OF DIGITALIZED PHYSICAL REALITY

As shown in Figure 4.2, the digitalization of physical objects may span full digitization to partial digitization; in other words, a physical "unit" (or "component" or "object") can be fully replaced by a digital one at one extreme, or the physical unit could be partially replaced by a digital artefact that complements the physical one. We call this substituting for physical reality or complementing physical reality and it can take the form, as mentioned above, of emulation, where one attempts to mimic the behavior and properties of a physical system; simulation, where one creates a digital reality independent of physical reality; or feeling of presence, where simulation is connected to some elements of physical reality.

However, the digitalization of the physical world does not happen one physical component at a time, nor is any one component typically fully independent of other ones. Thus, what happens when the different elements represented in our taxonomy interact with one another? What are the outcomes of these interactions? While our taxonomy in Figure 4.2 provides guidelines as to what should be considered when exploring the outcomes of digitalization in isolation, we claim that we also need a framework to explore their complex interactions. Complexity theory provides a suitable way to help think through interactions or interdependencies.

There are many ways of thinking about complexity, but most if not all of them refer directly or indirectly to whatever phenomenon is under consideration as a system (cf. Forrester, 1961), where the units or components have greater or lesser degrees of interdependencies between them. In other words, when something changes in one component of a system, to what degree does that change the other parts of the system? This varies considerably with the kind of system under consideration, from mechanical systems to biological systems to social systems (Massa et al., 2018). Of course, there is variance within these different kinds of systems (one single cell is much less complex than a human being, but both are more complex than, say, a table). In general, the more we move from a simpler system to a more complex one, the less the mere representation of the elements (components) of the system is sufficient to provide a complete picture to understand the whole system.

NK modelling (cf. Kauffman, 1993) has often been employed to describe different levels of complexity. Originally developed to understand the "fitness" of biological systems, $N$ refers to the number of attributes or components, and $K$ the interdependencies between components. If we start with mechanical systems, these can be broken down, from least complex to most complex (see Massa et al., 2018, for more detail), into static mechanical systems with no retroactivity, mechanical systems with predetermined dynamics, and mechanical systems with control mechanisms. It is at this last level of complexity where interdependencies are more pronounced and feedback loops develop (for example, different devices on an airplane that regulate the behavior of the aircraft). At a higher level of complexity, we move to biological systems with self-maintaining dynamics such as autopoiesis and many more interacting feedback loops. And finally, when we arrive at social systems, the number of feedback loops and interdependencies between the components, themselves biological systems, becomes even more pronounced and difficult to predict (Anderson, 1999; Massa et al., 2018).

Thus, a focus on the number and type of interdependencies is the key tenet of complexity theory and some related management streams (e.g., Anderson, 1999; Massa et al., 2018; Adner, Puranam, and Zhu, 2019; Siggelkow and Terwiesch, 2019). We claim that the concepts developed in complexity theory offer suitable lenses to study the interdependencies between the different outcomes of digitalization. For instance, complexity theory highlights the need to consider the role of different types of feedback loops and to what degree the system is constrained by physical components. In Table 4.1, building on these concepts we show how different interactions may lead to different types of convergence (Yoffie, 1996) between physical and digital reality.

*Table 4.1    Outcomes of the interaction among units of digitalized physical reality*

| | Fully digital artefact | Partially digital artefact | Physical artefact |
|---|---|---|---|
| Fully digital artefact | I | II | III |
| | Type of feedback loops among units: | Type of feedback loops among units: | Type of feedback loops among units: |
| | Continuous, synchronous, and autonomous | Continuous, yet not fully synchronous | Unidirectional flow/no loops |
| | No gravity | Gravity anchors | Gravity prevails |
| | Type of convergence: | Type of convergence: | Type of convergence: |
| | Digital convergence | Phygital convergence | No convergence |
| | Potential outcomes: | Potential outcomes: | Potential outcomes: |
| | ● Autonomous realities | ● Dual clock speed between digital and physical | ● Clock speed between digital and physical diverging at scale |
| | ● Emergence of new digital logics | | |
| | ● Self-reinforcing loops | ● Asynchronous | ● Decoupling |

Table 4.1 shows how a fully digital artefact interacts with a system in which some or all of the other units or components are fully, partially, or un-digitized. In the first column (I), when the component is fully digital and the rest of the system is too, we would characterize the situation as being subject to a continuous, synchronous, and autonomous feedback loop, since there would not be human intervention or the necessity of waiting for a mechanical system to complete a task. We would say that the physical world does not exert "gravity" toward the digital world in this situation. Examples of this situation could be a "smart contract" that is executed automatically in the future when certain conditions are met, or autonomous drone inspection leading to automatic insurance payouts. In terms of outcomes, we might call this column "autonomous realities" (imagine virtual reality not mediated through humans) in which new fully digital logics emerge and the feedback loops are self-reinforcing or self-correcting. Of course, one challenge in this column is the self-reinforced amplification of unintended consequences.

Column II shows the situation in which the focal artefact has been fully digitalized, but the rest of the system is only partially digitalized. Depending on the degree of human or mechanical intervention and the degree to which the digital components act as a complement to the physical ones, we would say that the physical elements of this system exert gravity on the digital ones. The feedback loops could still be continuous, but would not be fully synchronous, since automation would be more difficult, especially if people or batch-processing machines bottleneck decision-making and reactions. Examples of this particular situation might be digital twins, where outputs of sensors on a real piece of equipment are fed into a simulation to track the current state and predict future states. In the case of future predicted problems, an intervention (e.g., replacing a physical component) is then done in real life. In this case, we are concerned with the "dual clock" speeds of the digital vs the physical; for example, if problems were identified using a digital twin but the intervention was not done for some time. Thus, we speak of the asynchronous nature of the different processes.

Finally, Column III demonstrates the case of a fully digitalized component in a system where the rest of the components are entirely physical. Here we would say that "gravity" would constrain the digital element to a greater degree and feedback loops would be non-existent or very slow. An example would be a digital music player—e.g., the Apple iPod—that offers a one-way flow of information for storage of digitalized data. Fans can listen to their preferred music, but they cannot interact with it. This applies equally to Web 1.0 applications. In this case, we would argue that there would be no convergence between the digital and physical world, or at least it would be extremely slow, thus our characterizing the clock speed as "divergent at scale" with a "decoupling" of the digital element from the physical one(s).

## 4. INCORPORATING DIGITALIZATION INTO MANAGEMENT RESEARCH

In this chapter, we have argued that management research exploring the implications of digitalization should incorporate a more nuanced and systematic definition of digitalization. Digitalization is a multi-dimensional construct. For instance, the digitalization of physical reality may be based on logics ranging from emulation to simulation and may lead to very different outcomes; e.g., the digitalization of physical reality might result in full substitution of physical reality and/or in the complementarity between units of physical reality and related digital artefacts. Furthermore, interactions among digitalized units of physical reality generate feedback loops that lead to new—or even new and autonomous—forms of physical/digital convergence. Building on a systematic literature review, we have developed a taxonomy to classify the different forms of digitalization of units of physical reality (Figure 4.2), highlighted the affordances of such digitalized units, and developed a further taxonomy to classify outcomes when these units interact with one another (Table 4.1).

Extant (strategic) management research has mostly focused on the strategic and organizational implications of "using" digitalization (e.g., Adner et al., 2019; Berente, 2020; Nambisan et al., 2020; Hanelt et al., 2021). We have argued here that a more nuanced characterization of digitalization will help to reveal what goes on below the surface and that, as such, should lead to more precise boundary conditions as well as to more clearly surfacing the mechanisms through which digitalization enacts its "affordances" and contributes to the co-creation of new organizational realities. For instance, our taxonomy might inform research seeking to reveal the seemingly unlimited generativity of digitalization (Zittrain, 2008; Yoo et al., 2010; Yoo, 2012; Dattée et al., 2018; Lyytinen et al., 2018; Cennamo and Santaló, 2019; Pentland et al., 2022; Perreira et al., 2022) and provide indications on evolutionary trajectories; provide more nuance to the understanding of how social and technical elements jointly evolve in socio-technical systems (Tilson et al., 2010); inform strategy research on the capabilities, organizations, and management needed to leverage digitalization (e.g., Cennamo and Santaló, 2019; Lanzolla et al., 2021); and help the logics that could lead to business model innovation (cf. Massa and Tucci, 2014; Bohnsack et al., 2021) be more specific. To put it in more general terms, our taxonomies might help to more systematically understand how new forms of business realities are emerging and provide a framework to compare and contrast the rich digitalization research that is emerging. Crucially—and by implication—our taxonomies might also prove useful to provide input in designing digitalization technologies and digitalization governance systems that keep "humans in control" (United Nations, 2020) over digitalized reality, which we strongly believe is a core, and unnegotiable, ethical imperative.

## NOTES

1.  We reviewed the literature published in organization, management, and information systems journals using "digitalization" as a keyword. For comprehensiveness purposes, we also developed a list of synonyms and related processes and concepts including digitization, connectivity, datafication,

digital materiality, artificial intelligence, and digital artefacts. An initial Scopus search of 30 leading business and management journals covering several domains, such as general management, management science, information management, human resource management, innovation, marketing, organization studies, and strategy, with the identified keywords, returned 680 journal articles. We then read all the abstracts to identify the non-spurious articles; i.e., articles where our keywords were used with reference to the mechanisms studied in the paper and not just quoted as examples. This reduced the number of articles to 200.

2. Obviously, this is a metaphor and we are not referring to gravity in the sense of physics (exertion of force based on the mass of an object).

# REFERENCES

Adner, R. 2017. Ecosystem as structure: An actionable construct for strategy. *Journal of Management*, 43: 39–58.

Adner, R., Puranam, P., & Zhu, F. 2019. What is different about digital strategy? From quantitative to qualitative change. *Strategy Science*, 4(4): 253–61.

Afuah, A., & Tucci, C.L. 2012. Crowdsourcing as a solution to distant search. *Academy of Management Review*, 37(3): 355–75.

Alemdar, H., & Ersoy, C. 2010. Wireless sensor networks for healthcare: A survey. *Computer Networks*, 54(15): 2688–710.

Andersen, P.H. 2006. Regional clusters in a global world: Production relocation, innovation, and industrial decline. *California Management Review*, 49(1): 101–22.

Anderson, P. 1999. Complexity theory and organization science. *Organization Science*, 10(3): 216–232.

Angwin, D., & Vaara, E. 2005. Introduction to the special issue: "Connectivity" in merging organizations: Beyond traditional cultural perspectives. *Organization Studies*, 26(10): 1445–53.

Bahrami, H., & Evans, S. 2011. Super-flexibility for real-time adaptation: Perspectives from Silicon Valley. *California Management Review*, 53(3): 21–39.

Bailey, D.E., Leonardi, P.M., & Barley, S.R. 2012. The lure of the virtual. *Organization Science*, 23(5): 1485–504.

Bailey, D.E., Leonardi, P.M., & Chong, J. 2010. Minding the gaps: Understanding technology interdependence and coordination in knowledge work. *Organization Science*, 21(3): 713–30.

Bailey, D.E., Faraj, S., Hinds, P., Von Krogh, G., & Leonardi, P.M. 2019. Special issue: Emerging technologies and organizing. *Organization Science*, 30(3): 642–46.

Baldwin, C.Y. 2007. Where do transactions come from? Modularity, transactions, and the boundaries of firms. *Industrial and Corporate Change*, 17(1): 155–95.

Baldwin, C.Y., & Clark, K.B. 2000. *Design Rules, Vol. 1: The Power of Modularity*. Cambridge, MA: MIT Press.

Baldwin, C.Y., & Woodard, C.J.J. 2009. The architecture of platforms: A unified view. In *Platforms, Markets and Innovation*, ed. A. Gawer, 19–44. Cheltenham, UK and Northampton, MA, USA: Edward Elgar Publishing.

Balis, J. 2022. How brands can enter the metaverse. *Harvard Business Review*. https://hbr.org/2022/01/how-brands-can-enter-the-metaverse.

Bardhi, F., & Eckhardt, G.M. 2017. Liquid consumption. *Journal of Consumer Research*, 44(3): 582–97.

Barrett, M., Davidson, E., & Vargo, S.L. 2015. Service innovation in the digital age: Key contributions and future directions. *MIS Quarterly*, 39(1): 135–54.

Baskerville, R.L., Myers, M.D., & Yoo, Y. 2020. Digital first: The ontological reversal and new challenges for information systems research. *MIS Quarterly*, 44(2): 509–23.

Benkler, Y. 2006. *The Wealth of Networks: How Social Production Transforms Markets and Freedom*. New Haven, CT: Yale University Press.

Berente, N., 2020. Agile development as the root metaphor for strategy in digital innovation. In *Handbook of Digital Innovation*, eds. S. Nambisan, K. Lyytinen, & Y. Yoo, 83–96. Cheltenham, UK and Northampton, MA, USA: Edward Elgar Publishing.

Berente, N., Srinivasan, N., Yoo, Y., Boland, R.J., & Lyytinen, K. 2007. Binate diversity and the rolling edge of design networks. In 28th International Conference on Information Systems. Atlanta.

Bharadwaj, A., El Sawy, O.A., Pavlou, P.A., & Venkatraman, N.V. 2013. Digital business strategy: Toward a next generation of insights. *MIS Quarterly*, 37(2): 471–82.

Bohnsack, R., Kurtz, H., & Hanelt, A. 2021. Re-examining path dependence in the digital age: The evolution of connected car business models. *Research Policy*, 50(9): 104328.

Boland, R.J., Lyytinen, K., & Yoo, Y. 2007. Wakes of innovation in project networks: The case of digital 3-D representations in architecture, engineering, and construction. *Organization Science*, 18(4): 631–47.

Bose, R., & Luo, X. 2011. Integrative framework for assessing firms' potential to undertake Green IT initiatives via virtualization: A theoretical perspective. *Journal of Strategic Information Systems*, 20(1): 38–54.

Breschi, S., & Catalini, C. 2010. Tracing the links between science and technology: An exploratory analysis of scientists' and inventors' networks. *Research Policy*, 39(1): 14–26.

Bresnahan, T.F., & Trajtenberg, M. 1995. General purpose technologies "engines of growth"? *Journal of Econometrics*, 65(1): 83–108.

Cano-Kollmann, M., Cantwell, J., Hannigan, T.J., Mudambi, R., & Song, J. 2016. Knowledge connectivity: An agenda for innovation research in international business. *Journal of International Business Studies*, 47(3): 255–62.

Caridi-Zahavi, O., Carmeli, A., & Arazy, O. 2016. The influence of CEOs' visionary innovation leadership on the performance of high-technology ventures: The mediating roles of connectivity and knowledge integration. *Journal of Product Innovation Management*, 33(3): 356–76.

Cennamo, C., & Santaló, J. 2019. Generativity tension and value creation in platform ecosystems. *Organization Science*, 30(3): 617–41.

Chatterjee, D.D., Segars, A.H., & Watson, R.T. 2006. Realizing the promise of e-business: Developing and leveraging electronic partnering options. *California Management Review*, 48(4): 60–83.

Chester Goduscheit, R., & Faullant, R. 2018. Paths toward radical service innovation in manufacturing companies: A service-dominant logic perspective. *Journal of Product Innovation Management*, 35(5): 701–19.

Cross, R., Laseter, T., Parker, A., & Velasquez, G. 2006. Using social network analysis to improve communities of practice. *California Management Review*, 49(1): 32–60.

Dattée, B., Alexy, O., & Autio, E. 2018. Maneuvering in poor visibility: How firms play the ecosystem game when uncertainty is high. *Academy of Management Journal*, 61(2): 466–98.

Dhar, V., & Sundararajan, A. 2007. Information technologies in business: A blueprint for education and research. *Information Systems Research*, 18(2): 125–41.

Elberse, A. 2008. Should you invest in the long tail? *Harvard Business Review*, 86(7–8).

Fang, E. 2008. Customer participation and the trade-off between new product innovativeness and speed to market. *Journal of Marketing*, 72(4): 90–104.

Faulkner, P., & Runde, J. 2009. On the identity of technological objects and users innovation in functions. *Academy of Management Review*, 34(3): 442–62.

Faulkner, P., & Runde, J. 2011. The social, the material, and the ontology of non-material technological objects. In 27th European Group for Organizational Studies Colloquium. Gothenburg.

Fichman, R.G., Dos Santos, B.L., & Zheng, Z. 2014. Digital innovation as a fundamental and powerful concept in the information systems curriculum. *MIS Quarterly*, 38(2): 329–43.

Fleming, L., & Sorenson, O. 2004. Science as a map in technological search. *Strategic Management Journal*, 25(8–9): 909–28.

Forman, C., & Van Zeebroeck, N. 2019. Digital technology adoption and knowledge flows within firms: Can the Internet overcome geographic and technological distance? *Research Policy*, 48(8): 103697.

Forrester, J.W. 1961. *Industrial Dynamics*. Cambridge, MA: MIT Press.

Gambardella, A., & McGahan, A.M. 2010. Business-model innovation: General purpose technologies and their implications for industry structure. *Long Range Planning*, 43: 262–71.

Garud, R., Jain, S., & Tuertscher, P. 2008. Incomplete by design and designing for incompleteness. *Organization Studies*, 29(3): 351–71.

Gosain, S., Malhotra, A., & El Sawy, O.A. 2004. Coordinating for flexibility in e-business supply chains. *Journal of Management Information Systems*, 21(3): 7–45.

Grover, V., & Kohli, R. 2013. Revealing your hand: Caveats in implementing digital business strategy. *MIS Quarterly*, 37(2): 655–62.

Hanelt, A., Bohnsack, R., Marz, D., & Antunes Marante, C. 2021. A systematic review of the literature on digital transformation: Insights and implications for strategy and organizational change. *Journal of Management Studies*, 58(5): 1159–97.

Henfridsson, O., Mathiassen, L., & Svahn, F. 2014. Managing technological change in the digital age: The role of architectural frames. *Journal of Information Technology*, 29(1): 27–43.

Iansiti, M., & Lakhani, K.R. 2014. Digital ubiquity: How connections, sensors, and data are revolutionizing business. *Harvard Business Review*, 92(11): 90–99.

Jacobides, M.G., Cennamo, C., & Gawer, A. 2018. Towards a theory of ecosystems. *Strategic Management Journal*, 39: 2255–76.

Jarzabkowski, P., & Kaplan, S. 2015. Strategy tools-in-use: A framework for understanding "technologies of rationality" in practice. *Strategic Management Journal*, 36(4): 537–58.

Kallinikos, J. 2009. On the computational rendition of reality: Artefacts and human agency. *Organization*, 16(2): 183–202.

Kallinikos, J., Aaltonen, A., & Marton, A. 2010. A theory of digital objects. *First Monday*, 15(6): 1–22.

Kallinikos, J., Aaltonen, A., & Marton, A. 2013. The ambivalent ontology of digital artefacts. *MIS Quarterly*, 37(2): 357–70.

Kallinikos, J., & Mariátegui, J.C. 2011. Video as digital object: Production and distribution of video content in the internet media ecosystem. *Information Society*, 27(5): 281–94.

Kambil, A., & Van Heck, E. 1998. Reengineering the Dutch flower auctions: A framework for analyzing exchange organizations. *Information Systems Research*, 9(1): 1–19.

Kane, G.C., & Alavi, M. 2007. Information technology and organizational learning: An investigation of exploration and exploitation processes. *Organization Science*, 18(5): 796–812.

Kaschig, A., Maier, R., & Sandow, A. 2016. The effects of collecting and connecting activities on knowledge creation in organizations. *Journal of Strategic Information Systems*, 25(4): 243–58.

Kauffman, S.A., 1993. *The Origins of Order: Self-Organization and Selection in Evolution*. New York, NY: Oxford University Press.

Kim, S., & Anand, J. 2018. Knowledge complexity and the performance of inter-unit knowledge replication structures. *Strategic Management Journal*, 39(7): 1959–89.

Kolb, D.G. 2008. Exploring the metaphor of connectivity: Attributes, dimensions and duality. *Organization Studies*, 29(1): 127–44.

Kolb, D.G., Caza, A., & Collins, P.D. 2012. States of connectivity: New questions and new directions. *Organization Studies*, 33(2): 267–73.

Kretschmer, T., & Khashabi, P., 2020. Digital transformation and organization design: An integrated approach. *California Management Review*, 62(4): 86–104.

Kritzinger, W., Karner, M., Traar, G., Henjes, J., & Sihn, W. 2018. Digital twin in manufacturing: A categorical literature review and classification. *IFAC-PapersOnLine*, 51(11): 1016–22.

Krogh, G. von, Haefliger, S., Spaeth, S., & Wallin, M.W. 2012. Carrots and rainbows: Motivation and social practice in open source software development. *MIS Quarterly*, 36(2): 649–76.

Langlois, R.N. 2002. Modularity in technology and organization. *Journal of Economic Behavior & Organization*, 49(1): 19–37.

Lanzolla, G., & Markides, C. 2021. A business model view of strategy. *Journal of Management Studies*, 58(2): 540–53.

Lanzolla, G., Pesce, D., & Tucci, C.L. 2021. The digital transformation of search and recombination in the innovation function: Tensions and an integrative framework. *Journal of Product Innovation Management*, 38(1): 90–113.

Lazer, D., & Friedman, A. 2007. The network structure of exploration and exploitation. *Administrative Science Quarterly*, 52(4): 667–94.

Lee, J., & Berente, N. 2012. Digital innovation and the division of innovative labor: Digital controls in the automotive industry. *Organization Science*, 23(5): 1428–47.

Leonardi, P.M., & Bailey, D.E. 2008. Transformational technologies and the creation of new work practices: Making implicit knowledge explicit in task-based offshoring. *MIS Quarterly*, 32(2): 411–36.

Leone, M.I., & Reichstein, T. 2012. Licensing-in fosters rapid invention! The effect of the grant-back clause and technological unfamiliarity. *Strategic Management Journal*, 33(8): 965–85.

Lycett, M. 2013. "Datafication": Making sense of (big) data in a complex world. *European Journal of Information Systems*, 22(4): 381–6.

Lyytinen, K. 2021. Innovation logics in the digital era: A systemic review of the emerging digital innovation regime. *Innovation: Organization & Management*, 24(1): 13–34.

Lyytinen, K., & Yoo, Y. 2002. Research commentary: the next wave of nomadic computing. *Information Systems Research*, 13(4): 377–88.

Lyytinen, K., Nambisan, S., Yoo, Y., 2020. A transdisciplinary research agenda for digital innovation: Key themes and directions for future research. In *Handbook of Digital Innovation*, eds. S. Nambisan, K. Lyytinen, & Y. Yoo, 279–86. Cheltenham, UK and Northampton, MA, USA: Edward Elgar Publishing.

Lyytinen, K., Sørensen, C., & Tilson, D. 2018. Generativity in digital infrastructures: A research note. In *The Routledge Companion to Management Information Systems*, eds. D. Galliers & K. Stein, 253–75. New York, NY: Routledge.

Lyytinen, K., Yoo, Y., & Boland, R.J. 2016. Digital product innovation within four classes of innovation networks. *Information Systems Journal*, 26(1): 47–75.

Mabey, C., & Zhao, S. 2017. Managing five paradoxes of knowledge exchange in networked organizations: New priorities for HRM? *Human Resource Management Journal*, 27(1): 39–57.

Majchrzak, A., & Griffith, T.L. 2020. The new wave of digital innovation: The need for a theory of sociotechnical self-orchestration. In *Handbook of Digital Innovation*, eds. S. Nambisan, K. Lyytinen, & Y. Yoo, 17–40. Cheltenham, UK and Northampton, MA, USA: Edward Elgar Publishing.

Majchrzak, A., & Malhotra, A. 2013. Towards an information systems perspective and research agenda on crowdsourcing for innovation. *Journal of Strategic Information Systems*, 22(4): 257–68.

Majchrzak, A., Markus, M.L., Wareham, J., Lynne Markus, M., & Wareham, J. 2016. Designing for digital transformation: Lessons for information systems research from the study of ICT and societal challenges. *MIS Quarterly*, 40(2): 267–77.

Manovich, L. 2001. *The Language of New Media*. Cambridge, MA: MIT Press.

March, S., Hevner, A., & Ram, S. 2000. Research commentary: An agenda for information technology research in heterogeneous and distributed environments. *Information Systems Research*, 11(4): 327–41.

Mardon, R., & Belk, R. 2018. Materializing digital collecting: An extended view of digital materiality. *Marketing Theory*, 18(4): 543–70.

Massa, L., & Tucci, C.L. 2014. Business model innovation. In *The Oxford Handbook of Innovation Management*, eds. M. Dodgson, D. Gann, & N. Phillips, 420–41. New York, NY: Oxford University Press.

Massa, L., Tucci, C.L., & Afuah, A. 2017. A critical assessment of business model research. *Academy of Management Annals*, 11(1): 73–104.

Massa, L., Viscusi, G., & Tucci, C.L. 2018. Business models and complexity. *Journal of Business Models*, 6(1): 59–71.

Matusik, S.F., & Mickel A.E. 2011. Embracing or embattled by converged mobile devices? Users' experiences with a contemporary connectivity technology. *Human Relations*, 64(8): 1001–30.

Mazmanian, M. 2013. Avoiding the trap of constant connectivity: When congruent frames allow for heterogeneous practices. *Academy of Management Journal*, 56(5): 1225–50.

Mazmanian, M., Orlikowski, W.J., & Yates, J. 2013. The autonomy paradox: The implications of mobile email devices for knowledge professionals. *Organization Science*, 24(5): 1337–57.

Meta Connect Conference. 2021. The metaverse and how we'll build it together. https://www.facebookconnect.com/.

Mousavi Baygi, R., Introna, L.D., & Hultin, L., 2021. Everything flows: Studying continuous sociotechnical transformation in a fluid and dynamic digital world. *MIS Quarterly*, 45(1): 423–52.

Nambisan, S., & Sawhney, M. 2007. A buyer's guide to the innovation bazaar. *Harvard Business Review*, 85(6): 109.

Nambisan, S., Lyytinen, K., Majchrzak, A., & Song, M. 2017. Digital innovation management: Reinventing innovation management research in a digital world. *MIS Quarterly*, 41(1): 223–38.

Nambisan, S., Lyytinen, K., & Yoo, Y. 2020. Digital innovation: Towards a transdisciplinary perspective handbook of digital innovation. In *Handbook of Digital Innovation*, eds. S. Nambisan, K. Lyytinen, & Y. Yoo, 2–12. Cheltenham, UK and Northampton, MA, USA: Edward Elgar Publishing.

Ng, I.C.L., & Wakenshaw, S.Y.L. 2017. The Internet-of-Things: Review and research directions. *International Journal of Research in Marketing*, 34(1): 3–21.

Normann, R. 2001. *Reframing Business: When the Map Changes the Landscape*. Chichester: John Wiley & Sons.

Orlikowski, W.J., & Scott, S.V. 2008. Sociomateriality: Challenging the separation of technology, work and organization. *Academy of Management Annals*, 2(1): 433–74.

Orlikowski, W.J., & Scott, S.V. 2016. The algorithm and the crowd: Considering the materiality of service innovation. *MIS Quarterly*, 39(1): 201–16.

Overby, E. 2008. Process virtualization theory and the impact of information technology. *Organization Science*, 19(2): 277–91.

Pentland, B.T., Yoo, Y., Recker, J., & Kim, I. 2022. From lock-in to transformation: A path-centric theory of emerging technology and organising. *Organization Science*, 33(1): 194–211.

Peppard, J. 2018. Rethinking the concept of the IS organization. *Information Systems Journal*, 28(1): 76–103.

Perreira, J., Viscusi, G., & Tucci, C.L. 2022. *Crowd Forms of Organizing and Generativity Mechanisms*. Working paper, Imperial College Business School.

Pil, F.K., & Cohen, S.K. 2006. Modularity: Implications for imitation, innovation, and sustained advantage. *Academy of Management Review*, 31(4): 995–1011.

Porter, M.E., & Heppelmann, J.E. 2014. How smart, connected products are transforming competition. *Harvard Business Review*, 92(11): 64–89.

Porter, M.E., & Heppelmann, J.E. 2015. How smart, connected products are transforming companies. *Harvard Business Review*, 93(10): 53–71.

Porter, M.E., & Heppelmann, J.E. 2017. Why every organization needs an augmented reality strategy. *Harvard Business Review*, 95(6): 46–57.

Rai, A., & Sambamurthy, V. 2006. Editorial notes: The growth of interest in services management – Opportunities for information systems scholars. *Information Systems Research*, 17(4): 327–31.

Rasool, J., Molka-Danielsen, J., & Smith, C.H. 2021. Transitioning from transmedia to transreality storyboarding to improve the co-creation of the experience space. In *Proceedings of the 54th Hawaii International Conference on System Sciences* (p. 648).

Robinson, J. 2017. The sci-fi guru who predicted Google Earth explains Silicon Valley's latest obsession. https://www.vanityfair.com/news/2017/06/neal-stephenson-metaverse-snow-crash-silicon-valley -virtual-reality.

Sarker, S., Chatterjee, S., Xiao, X., Elbanna, A., 2019. The sociotechnical axis of cohesion for the IS discipline: Its historical legacy and its continued relevance. *MIS Quarterly*, 43(3): 695–719.

Schilling, M.A. 2000. Toward a general modular systems theory and its application to interfirm product modularity. *Academy of Management Review*, 25(2): 312–34.

Semeraro, C., Lezoche, M., Panetto, H., & Dassisti, M. 2021. Digital twin paradigm: A systematic literature review. *Computers in Industry*, 130: 103469.

Shapiro, C., & Varian, H.R. 1999. The art of standards wars. *California Management Review*, 41(2): 8–32.

Siggelkow, N., & Rivkin, J.W. 2005. Speed and search: Designing organizations for turbulence and complexity. *Organization Science*, 16(2): 101–22.

Siggelkow, N., & Terwiesch, C. 2019. *Connected Strategy: Building Continuous Customer Relationships for Competitive Advantage*. Boston, MA: Harvard Business Press.

Sørensen, C., & Landau, J.S. 2015. Academic agility in digital innovation research: The case of mobile ICT publications within information systems 2000–2014. *Journal of Strategic Information Systems*, 24(3): 158–70.

Svahn, F., & Henfridsson, O. 2012. The dual regimes of digital innovation management. In *45th Hawaii International Conference on System Sciences*, 3347–56. Maui.

Tao, F., Cheng, J., Qi, Q., Zhang, M., Zhang, H., & Fangyuan, S. 2018. Digital twin-driven product design, manufacturing and service with big data. *International Journal of Advanced Manufacturing Technology*, 94(9–12): 3563–76.

Teece, D.J. 2010. Business models, business strategy and innovation. *Long Range Planning*, 43: 172–94.

Teece, D.J. 2018. Profiting from innovation in the digital economy: Enabling technologies, standards, and licensing models in the wireless world. *Research Policy*, 47(8): 1367–87.

Tilson, D., Lyytinen, K., & Sorensen, C. 2010. Research commentary: Digital infrastructures – The missing IS research agenda. *Information Systems Research*, 21(4): 748–59.

Tiwana, A. 2008. Does technological modularity substitute for control? A study of alliance performance in software outsourcing. *Strategic Management Journal*, 29(7): 769–80.

Tiwana, A., Konsynski, B., & Bush, A.A. 2010. Research commentary: Platform evolution – Coevolution of platform architecture, governance, and environmental dynamics. *Information Systems Research*, 21(4): 675–87.

Trantopoulos, K., Von Krogh, G., Wallin, M.W., & Woerter, M. 2017. External knowledge and information technology: Implications for process innovation performance. *MIS Quarterly*, 41(1): 287–300.

United Nations. 2020. *UN75: Social Contract 2020: Toward Safety, Security, & Sustainability for AI World*. New York, NY: United Nations.

Villarroel, J.A., Taylor, J.E., & Tucci, C.L., 2013. Innovation and learning performance implications of free revealing and knowledge brokering in competing communities: Insights from the Netflix Prize challenge. *Computational and Mathematical Organization Theory*, 19(1): 42–77.

Wajcman, J., & Rose, E. 2011. Constant connectivity: Rethinking interruptions at work. *Organization Studies*, 32(7): 941–61.

Wang, P., 2021. Connecting the parts with the whole: Toward an information ecology theory of digital innovation ecosystems. *MIS Quarterly*, 45(1): 397–422.

World Economic Forum. 2020. *Digital Transformation: Powering the Great Reset*. Geneva: World Economic Forum.

Xue, L., Zhang, C., Ling, H., & Zhao, X. 2013. Risk mitigation in supply chain digitization: System modularity and information technology governance. *Journal of Management Information Systems*, 30(1): 325–52.

Yoffie, D.B., 1996. Competing in the age of digital convergence. *California Management Review*, 38(4): 31–53.

Yoo, Y. 2010. Computing in everyday life: A call for research on experiential computing. *MIS Quarterly*, 34(2): 213–31.

Yoo, Y. 2012. Digital materiality and the emergence of an evolutionary science of the artificial. In *Materiality and Organizing: Social Interaction in a Technological World*, eds. P.M. Leonardi, B.A. Nardi, & J. Kallinikos, 134–54. Oxford: Oxford University Press.

Yoo, Y., Boland, R.J., Lyytinen, K., & Majchrzak, A., 2012. Organizing for innovation in the digitized world. *Organization Science*, 23(5): 1398–408.

Yoo, Y., Henfridsson, O., & Lyytinen, K. 2010. The new organizing logic of digital innovation: An agenda for information systems research. *Information Systems Research*, 21(4): 724–35.

Zhang, L. 2016. Intellectual property strategy and the long tail: Evidence from the recorded music industry. *Management Science*, 64(1): 24–42.

Zhang, Z., Yoo, Y., Wattal, S., Zhang, B., & Kulathinal, R. 2014. Generative diffusion of innovations and knowledge networks in open source projects. In Thirty Fifth International Conference on Information Systems. Auckland, New Zealand.

Zittrain, J.L. 2006. The generative Internet. *Harvard Law Review*, 119(7): 1974–2040.

Zittrain, J.L. 2008. *The Future of the Internet and How to Stop It*. New Haven, CT: Yale University Press.

# APPENDIX

*Table 4A.1*     *Properties of digital artefacts*

| Properties | Exemplary references |
| --- | --- |
| Editability | (Shapiro & Varian, 1999; Zittrain, 2006; Kane & Alavi, 2007; Nambisan & Sawhney, 2007; Garud et al., 2008; Zittrain, 2008; Yoo, 2010; Yoo et al., 2010; Kallinikos et al., 2013; Kaschig et al., 2016) |
| Replicability | (Elberse, 2008; Kallinikos & Mariátegui, 2011; Kallinikos et al., 2013; Zhang, 2016; Ng & Wakenshaw, 2017; Mardon & Belk, 2018) |
| Modularity | (Baldwin & Clark, 2000; Schilling, 2000; Manovich, 2001; Langlois, 2002; Andersen, 2006; Pil & Cohen, 2006; Baldwin, 2007; Dhar & Sundararajan, 2007; Tiwana, 2008; Zittrain, 2008; Baldwin & Woodard, 2009; Tiwana et al., 2010; Yoo et al., 2010; Bahrami & Evans, 2011; Yoo, 2012; Kallinikos et al., 2013; Xue et al., 2013; Nambisan et al., 2017) |
| Granularity | (Manovich, 2001; Benkler, 2006; Kallinikos, 2009; Kallinikos et al., 2010; Tiwana et al., 2010; Yoo et al., 2010; Yoo, 2012; Majchrzak & Malhotra, 2013; Barrett et al., 2015; Chester Goduscheit & Faullant, 2018) Related constructs found in the literature: Decomposability: (Yoo, 2010; Yoo et al., 2010) |
| Re-programmability | (Kallinikos et al., 2010; Yoo, 2010; Yoo et al., 2010; Faulkner & Runde, 2009, 2011; Krogh et al., 2012; Lee & Berente, 2012; Yoo et al., 2012; Yoo, 2012; Kallinikos et al., 2013; Fichman et al., 2014; Henfridsson et al., 2014) Related constructs found in the literature: Computation: (Dhar & Sundararajan, 2007; Kallinikos & Mariátegui, 2011; Bailey et al., 2012) |
| Homogeneity | (Yoo et al., 2010; Yoo, 2012; Yoo et al., 2012) Related constructs found in the literature: Dematerialisation: (Normann, 2001; Lycett, 2013) |
| Traceability | (Yoo, 2010; Yoo et al., 2010; Kallinikos et al., 2013; Fichman et al., 2014; Lyytinen et al., 2016) Related constructs found in the literature: Memorizability: (Yoo, 2010; Yoo et al., 2010) |
| Interoperability | (March et al., 2000; Bailey et al., 2010; Kallinikos et al., 2010; Yoo, 2010; Yoo et al., 2010; Kallinikos & Mariátegui, 2011; Yoo et al., 2012; Bharadwaj et al., 2013; Grover & Kohli, 2013; Kallinikos et al., 2013; Porter & Heppelmann, 2014; Porter & Heppelmann, 2015; Majchrzak et al., 2016; Teece, 2018) |
| Pervasiveness | (Lyytinen & Yoo, 2002; Fleming & Sorenson, 2004; Berente et al., 2007; Kolb, 2008; Orlikowski & Scott, 2008; Wajcman & Rose, 2011; Afuah & Tucci, 2012; Kolb et al., 2012; Yoo, 2012; Yoo et al., 2012; Bharadwaj et al., 2013; Sørensen & Landau, 2015; Mabey & Zhao, 2017; Peppard, 2018) |
| Speed | (Kambil & Van Heck, 1998; Gosain et al., 2004; Siggelkow & Rivkin, 2005; Lazer & Friedman, 2007; Fang, 2008; Leonardi & Bailey, 2008; Leone & Reichstein, 2012; Svahn & Henfridsson, 2012; Yoo et al., 2012; Bharadwaj et al., 2013; Sørensen & Landau, 2015; Caridi-Zahavi et al., 2016; Lyytinen et al., 2016; Teece, 2018) Related constructs found in the literature: Responsiveness: (Matusik & Mickel, 2011; Wajcman & Rose, 2011; Mazmanian, 2013; Mazmanian et al., 2013) |
| Synchronization | (Angwin & Vaara, 2005; Chatterjee et al., 2006; Rai & Sambamurthy, 2006; Overby, 2008; Yoo et al., 2010; Yoo et al., 2010; Bose & Luo, 2011; Wajcman & Rose, 2011; Porter & Heppelmann, 2014; Porter & Heppelmann, 2015) |

| Properties | Exemplary references |
|---|---|
| Accessibility | (Zittrain, 2006; Boland et al., 2007; Overby, 2008; Zittrain, 2008; Yoo, 2010; Yoo et al., 2010; Kallinikos & Mariátegui, 2011; Matusik & Mickel, 2011; Kallinikos et al., 2013; Mazmanian, 2013; Mazmanian et al., 2013; Fichman et al., 2014; Barrett et al., 2015; Orlikowski & Scott, 2016; Bardhi & Eckhardt, 2017; Ng & Wakenshaw, 2017) |
| | Related constructs found in the literature: |
| | Addressability: (Yoo, 2010; Kallinikos et al., 2013; Fichman et al., 2014) |
| | Findability: (Kallinikos et al., 2010; Kallinikos & Mariátegui, 2011; Kallinikos et al., 2013) |
| Transferability | (Cross et al., 2006; Boland et al., 2007; Leonardi & Bailey, 2008; Zittrain, 2008; Bailey et al., 2010; Breschi & Catalini, 2010; Lee & Berente, 2012; Kallinikos et al., 2013; Majchrzak & Malhotra, 2013; Zhang et al., 2014; Cano-Kollmann et al., 2016; Mabey & Zhao, 2017; Trantopoulos et al., 2017; Kim & Anand, 2018; Forman & Van Zeebroeck, 2019) |
| Ubiquity | (Kolb, 2008; Yoo, 2010; Matusik & Mickel, 2011; Wajcman & Rose, 2011; Mazmanian et al., 2013; Iansiti & Lakhani, 2014; Sørensen & Landau, 2015; Mardon & Belk, 2018) |

# 5. Framing and reframing digital business models: the global messenger industry

*Sungu Ahn and Charles Baden-Fuller*

## INTRODUCTION

The digital world has been characterized by frequent technological advances that alter the way firms create and capture value (Yoo, Boland, Lyytinen, and Majchrzak, 2012, and the introduction to this volume). Specific innovations include the arrival of inexpensive personal computers (PCs), ubiquitous mobile devices, 4G followed by 5G connectivity, and inexpensive machine learning capabilities matched by inexpensive big data storage. These events (and others not mentioned) have altered the capabilities of digital firms and thus challenged firms to think about their business models (value creation and capture mechanisms) in a cycle of change that is far faster than that in more traditional industries.

How do incumbent and new firms respond to the challenges of continual technological change? In particular, how have firms chosen and adjusted their strategies and associated business models? In times of technological change, it is rarely obvious how managers (who might be entrepreneurs) should approach the challenge. The lack of obvious signals concerning correct choices stems from the fact that technology does not define the relevant business model; business models need to be constructed to mobilize technology (Baden-Fuller and Haefliger, 2013; Chesbrough and Rosenbloom, 2002). The framing of the business model is a cognitive process (Baden-Fuller and Morgan, 2010) because the business model choice is bound up with the strategy choice (Casadesus-Masanell and Ricart, 2010). The literature on strategy has long recognized that cognitive frames are a key component of the determinants of strategy choice (Aversa, Huyghe, and Bonadio, 2021; Doz and Kosonen, 2010; Gavetti and Rivkin, 2007; Kaplan, 2008; Martins, Rindova, and Greenbaum, 2015; Porac, Thomas, and Baden-Fuller, 1989; Spender, 1989; Tripsas and Gavetti, 2000).

When thinking about business models and the framing of business models, we pay attention to value creation and value capture combinations. In the context of digital enterprises, three choices are particularly salient. The first is the traditional pipeline model, where customers are charged directly for the service (often using a freemium model). The second is the advertising support model, where advertisers provide the revenues to support the services and advertising is often viewed as neutral or negative from the value creation standpoint. The third is the complementor model, where providers of value-added complementary services attached to the core product provide the revenues to support the service. These three models can (and often do) overlap and sometimes intertwine. They often play out differently in different contexts. However, conceptually, each has a different "logic"; that is, each is a "distinct business model" (in the terminology of Baden-Fuller and Morgan, 2010).

From where do these frames emerge? Two strands of thinking have emerged over the years: the nature of the firm and the nature of the environment. Regarding the first theme, the nature of the firm, Tripsas and Gavetti (2000), in their study of Polaroid, noted that different divisions of the organization tended to utilize similar business models, suggesting that a shared mindset was prevalent. Likewise, Chesbrough and Rosenbloom (2002) and Chesbrough (2010) noted that Xerox rarely deployed novel business models among its many innovative enterprises formed in its own incubator, also indicating a strong sense of shared framing. More recently, Aspara, Lamberg, Laukia, and Tikkanen (2013) highlighted the importance of internal interactions between different groups of managers in framing business model choices in the context of changing digital technology for mobile phones at Nokia. Luoma, Laamanen, and Lamberg (2022) have pushed further by introducing the importance of organizational routines as a basis for cognitive framing of strategies and business models, drawing heavily on the work of Feldman and Pentland (2003). These insights provide further theoretical framings for the role of internal managerial influences.

When dealing with the challenge of setting the business model (and associated strategies) for a wholly new enterprise, in wholly new industries, many hints but few definitive guides are available. First, the possible influence of the overall environment is stressed. Spender (1989) argued for an industry with established recipes. Following this theme, Porac, Thomas, and Baden-Fuller (1989) argued that the community to which firms belong can be the source of inspiration for the business model (labeled a strategic approach), a framing that was reinforced by local (rather than global) competitive forces. In this case, the community was Hawick, a small town in Scotland where most of the community of firms was located, particularly a local technical college devoted to assisting local firms to which most managers were affiliated. We also note that for new firms, the power of the local context in framing business model choices is moderated by the antecedents of the entrepreneur; that is, those coming from inside the industry are more likely to adopt existing frames (Narayan, Sidhu, Baden-Fuller, and Volberda, 2020).

Although competitive forces clearly play a part in choosing a business model, other factors are often at work, particularly for new entrepreneurial firms (Sund, Galvan, and Bogers, 2021). We know that choosing a business model is a cognitive act that involves a complex set of processes of modeling and framing that involves search and experimentation (Baden-Fuller and Mangematin, 2013; McGrath, 2010). In this respect, Ott, Eisenhardt, and Bingham (2017) suggested three processes, namely doing, thinking, or bricolage, and that activities are intertwined between thinking and acting when firms design what they do and then enact those designs, often with variations. However, these processes are deeply influenced by technological possibilities because strategies in general and business models in particular are constructions that mobilize technological possibilities (Baden-Fuller and Haefliger, 2013).

In other words, new firms can challenge the status quo when they construct their own framing. This occurs when entrepreneurs have a "Schumpeterian" approach to strategy, along the lines advocated by Teece (2018, 2020). These observations build on the earlier work of Baden-Fuller and Stopford (1992) and Spender (1989), who argued that firms can "break the mold" of "industry thinking" through deliberate action that leverages technological advances, opening up new strategy combinations.

Finally, the boundaries between established firms and new firms are not always clear. In a recent article by Murmann and Zhu (2021), an established player (Tencent) approached the challenge of setting a new business model for one of its divisions in a manner more akin to that of a new firm by creating an internal contest between different approaches and deliberately attempting to break the "established ways of thinking."

We explored these ideas through our study of 14 important actors in the global digital messenger industry, from its inception in the mid-1990s to the late 2010s. We found that during the first period of the PC technology era, the advertising-supported business model prevailed. It was only in Korea[1] that we found challenger business models: those of monetization via complementors, pioneered by SayClub and later adopted by Nateon-Cyworld. Our detailed probing of these complementor monetization strategies proved to be effective for the local Korean environment, but they were not exported to other countries by Korean firms (nor adopted by international rivals); thus, they did not impinge on other players in other locations.

When the PC technology shifted to mobile, the potential value of complementor strategies became more salient. New firms emerged to challenge existing players with novel business models in the United States, Korea, Japan, and China. WhatsApp was greatly successful in the United States, with its simple fee for service, an offer that seemed attractive owing to the focus of WhatsApp on delivering quality communication services and avoiding the negative aspects associated with advertising. In Korea, new players, particularly KakaoTalk, exploited the complementor business model successfully, and the results of our in-depth analysis suggest that quite different ways of thinking prevailed in this firm. KakaoTalk was followed (implicitly or explicitly) by Line in Japan and WeChat (Tencent) in China. The complementor business model strategy for mobile technology proved to be extremely successful in terms of profits and influence for Korean, Japanese, and Chinese firms, sidelining firms with the advertising business model.

In choosing their business models and associated strategies, the major US-based firms appeared to have been deeply influenced by the business models of their parent firm and slightly influenced by events in Korea, Japan, or China, despite the fact that their operations in these countries were significantly curtailed by local competition using different business models. More in-depth work must be undertaken to examine why the US messenger firms (particularly Yahoo! and Microsoft) were so set against exploring novel business models (of launching super apps) for the US market and why so many significant US players exited the messenger market by 2020, leaving a single actor, Facebook, and its wholly owned subsidiary WhatsApp, as the dominant player.

## METHODS AND APPROACH

To identify the important actors in the instant messenger industry and the key technologies and relevant communities that might influence the managerial cognition behind the critical decisions made by the various actors in the industry, we actively gathered primary and secondary data from various databases. Our approach was consistent with those used by previous researchers who similarly sought to understand managers' cognitive frames using interview transcripts, shareholder letters, and investor relation materials (Abrahamson and Hambrick, 1997; Barr, 1998; Barr, Stimpert, and Huff, 1992; Cho and Hambrick, 2006; Clapham and Schwenk, 1991; Eggers and Kaplan, 2009; Kaplan, 2008).

The instant messenger service has developed significantly since its first commercial inception in the late 1990s.[2] In its infancy, it allowed users to exchange only text messages, and over time, more capabilities were added to include the sharing of photographs, videos, and more recently a range of embedded digital services with the worldwide web enabled by a computer, a phone, or other mobile devices. This service has not only displaced the much older traditional mobile phone company texting service but also become the most popular digital service.

We divided our study of the industry into two periods: the PC and mobile technology periods. The first commercial launch of instant messenger services was linked to the emerging popularity of PCs and the associated access to the worldwide web. During this period, the penetration of instant messenger services was quite limited because of the lack of accessibility of PCs. The arrival of mobile phones and connectivity transformed the industry, as more people could access the service, which led to a sharp increase in its popularity. Mobile technology also requires new competencies in terms of app and service developments. Finally, mobile technology has opened up more positive novel business models. The original actors appeared to be challenged, and new actors arrived, displacing the original incumbents, many of whom were unable to adjust fully.

In our study, we also divided the industry by geography. Although digital messenger services can be transmitted across the globe, language, cultural, and other barriers partitioned the industry between the English-speaking North American and Asian markets, which have different characteristics and approaches.

While numerous messenger applications have been developed throughout industry history, we selected 14 messengers for this study on the basis of the following criteria: (1) popularities and representativeness and (2) polarities and unusual exhibitions of variances in traits (i.e., business model), which are prime subjects of the investigation (Miles and Huberman, 1994). Methodologically, our approach was to undertake a cross-case analysis to examine emergent patterns across cases (Eisenhardt and Graebner, 2007). We focused on whether and how frames of managerial cognition link to the development of business models (Kaplan, 2011; Walsh, 1995).

In our study, we first looked across all 14 firms to capture the extent to which established frames of reasoning explain events and where there are deviations. Our next step was to probe the exceptions, which in our case were the innovative entrants that broke the industry frames of thinking. Where we could explain the strategies and business model choices of a firm using well-established theories, we did not probe deeply into what was happening. Confirming a well-established understanding is not our purpose. However, where we found unexplained events – that is, where firms appear to be acting "with strong degrees of agency" that go against established theorizing – we probed much more carefully. In particular, we probed the examples of SayClub and KakaoTalk, two Korean firms that adopted novel business models for the industry, which were eventually copied by Line in Japan and WeChat (Tencent) in China. Combining this cross-sectional analysis with selective case studies of extremes follows the tradition of other researchers, such as Eisenhardt (1989).

## HISTORY OF THE INDUSTRY

### PC Age from 1999 to 2007

During the PC era, the first scale-based service in the United States was ICQ, offered by the Israeli Internet platform company Mirabilis in 1996. It was followed in the late 1990s by several US-based firms such as AOL (with AIM) in 1997, Yahoo! (with Yahoo Messenger!) in 1998, and shortly after by Microsoft (with MSN) in 1999. AOL and Yahoo! were both Internet companies whose strategies were centered on a portal offering various services. (ICQ was purchased by AOL in 1998 but appeared to have been left to run itself, at least initially, as an independent company.) AOL and Yahoo! relied on advertising as a means of monetizing their offerings. Both companies had established business models and ways of thinking, and it was natural that they should offer Internet-based messenger services as part of a wider platform of web directory services that included news, searches, and e-mails. An important feature of these portal companies was monetization via advertising, often in banner form, which allowed the firms to offer their free-to-use services. The attraction of the (advertising-supported) free service was obvious: traditional telephone and text communication, which were linked to landline calls and providers, imposed costs per usage and time, whereas instant messengers were free to use (albeit with advertising) and more flexible and provided a better service, provided that the users had Internet connections. The entry dates and take-up rates (a success metric) for our sample firms are given in Tables 5.1 and 5.2.

Microsoft, which offered its MSN Messenger in 1999, was founded as a software company in 1975, with the traditional software as the product business model. Prior to 1998, Microsoft had various Internet offerings that were all combined and relaunched in 1998 as an integrated portal, with new services that included MSN Messenger. The MSN portal did carry advertising banners, but the extent of the importance of these advertisements to Microsoft, which had substantial cash flows coming from its traditional operations, was unclear.

Between 1996 and 2005, AOL, MSN, and Yahoo! were the three most popular websites, according to worldwide statistics, which justifies the choice of these three firms to be part of our sample. We suggest that the business model choices of these three major early entrants were strongly influenced by their established corporate ways of doing things.

### Case Studies of Korean Challengers to Existing Framings

In the late 1990s, relatively unnoticed by Western companies and observers, important Korean messenger service companies emerged, including SayClub (and its follower Nateon-Cyworld), which adopted different business models compared with the US firms. The origins of SayClub, Neowitz's chat service, were carefully probed by Lee, Rho, Kim, and Jun (2007). The authors explained that the Internet company Neowitz was formed after the Korean financial crisis in the late 1990s, at which time the Korean government significantly altered the institutional environment for new digital firms and fostered a culture of challenging existing orders. Originally conceived as an Internet service provider, Neowitz ran a portal. Neowitz went on to form SayClub in 1999 as an Internet chat service after its other core business collapsed.

An important element of the story of SayClub's strategy and business model choices was that at the start in 1999, SayClub emulated the established US business models of Yahoo! and AOL, of monetization via advertising. Unfortunately for Neowitz, the Korean environment was not at that time favorable for digital advertising, so these attempts at running an advertising business model failed; instead, SayClub had to find a new route to monetizing the SayClub offering, which, according to Lee et al. (2007), was found through the selling of avatars.

The offering of avatars for a fee can be considered a route toward monetization of the free chat service through the use of complementary products, not necessarily for the chat service but for something that makes the chat service more attractive to users. The nature of the avatar feature is shown in Table 5.3, along with an explanation of how the avatar came about.

*Table 5.1*  Summary of the business models and performances of sample messenger applications

| | Messenger service name | Entry | Business model | Parent company | Performance and subsequent owners |
|---|---|---|---|---|---|
| Portal offer initially via PC | ICQ | 1996 | Advertising-based | Mirabilis (founders) AOL from 1998, $287 million Digital Sky from 2010, $187 million | Messenger revenues unknown, still operating in 2021 |
| | AIM | 1997 | Advertising-based | AOL from founding | Messenger revenues unknown, closed in 2017 |
| | Yahoo! | 1998 | Advertising-based | Yahoo! from founding | Messenger revenues unknown, closed in 2018 |
| | MSN | 1999 | Advertising-based | Microsoft from founding | Messenger revenues unknown, believed to be small, closed in 2014 |
| | SayClub | 2002 | Complementary-feature-based | Neowiz from founding | More than $10 million revenues at its peak |
| | Nateon-Cyworld | 2003 | Complementary-feature-based | SK Electronics founded Nateon in 1999 and bought Cyworld in 2003 | More than $100 million revenues in 2006 |
| Social network initially via PC | Myspace | 2009 | Advertising-based | MySpace from founding | Free service, supported by a platform that is advertising-based |
| | Facebook | 2008 | Advertising-based | Facebook from founding | Free service, supported by a platform that is advertising-based |
| Offer initially via mobile application | WhatsApp | 2009 | $1 annual subscription fees | WhatsApp (founders) Facebook from 2014, $19.3 billion | At one point, revenues exceeded $1 billion |
| | | 2016 | Free | | |
| | KakaoTalk | 2010 | Complementor-based | KakaoTalk from founding | 85% share of the Korean market |
| | | 2016 | Added-advertising-based | | More than $2 billion in revenue from 2018, listed a $10 billion valuation (2018) |
| | Line | 2011 | Complementor-based | Naver founder, bought by Softbank in 2021, undisclosed price | More than $1 billion in revenue since 2016, IPO (2016), $5.5 billion market |
| | WeChat | 2011 | Complementor-based | | More than $5.5 billion in revenue since 2017 |

*Table 5.2*   *Number of users for different messengers (in millions)*

| | PC application | | | | | | Web-based SNS* envlopment | | Mobile application | | | |
|---|---|---|---|---|---|---|---|---|---|---|---|---|
| | AIM | MSN | Yahoo! | ICQ | SayClub | Nateon-Cyworld | Myspace | Facebook | WhatsApp | Kakao Talk | Line | WeChat |
| 2000 | 16 | 4 | 5 | 8 | 5 | - | - | - | - | - | - | - |
| 2002 | 22 | 16 | 12 | 4 | 10 | - | - | - | - | - | - | - |
| 2006 | 53 | 27 | 22 | 15 | 6 | 18 | (1,000) | - | - | - | - | - |
| 2010 | 100 | 330 | 248 | 42 | - | 10 | (1,000) | (2,000) | 10 | 10 | - | - |
| 2013 | 75 | - | (55) | 11 | - | 7 | | (10,000) | 200 | 40 | 150 | 272 |
| 2016 | 50 | - | (50) | 11 | - | - | | (20,000) | 1000 | 49 | 220 | 890 |

*Notes:*   The figures for Myspace and Facebook are the total number of users of the platform; actual user data are not available. SayClub and Nateon-Cyworld users are South Koreans (Korean population, around 50 million). * Social network services.

*Source:*   Nielsen net ratings/annual reports.

> We don't know actually who suggested the avatar idea first ... During the group discussion within the division, we questioned whether users can express themselves with pictorial images in the digital space ... and the answer was to change the dress and fashion. That's how the avatar business was created. (Eun Ju Lee, founding team of SayClub, February 21, 2003, *Hankook Ilbo*)

The Korean online community liked this offer of a chat service supported by avatars, so much so that Neowitz became quite profitable. Indeed, Neowitz became an important Internet site for Koreans, rivaling bigger US firms. Neowitz deepened its commitment to providing complementary services for fees, rather than monetizing by advertising, by launching online gaming services that had features linked to the chat service in 2002. The gaming services linked to chat proved profitable.

Another important Korean digital firm, SK Communications, with its chat service Nateon, copied Neowitz by offering personal webpage services through Cyworld starting in 1999. Cyworld's personal webpages were easy to manage, as it was based on Flash players. Users could simply manage personal webpages with graphical interfaces (see Figure 5.1). Nateon-Cyworld copied SayClub in that it used the complementary services of avatars (and games) as the monetization route for messenger services. Nateon-Cyworld users had access to other users' personal webpages with one click. Nateon-Cyworld users could purchase various cyber items to decorate their Cyworld webpages. This means that unlike advertising-based messengers, Nateon messenger chose to create and capture values by providing complementary services. By 2006, Nateon-Cyworld achieved significant revenues of more than $100 million on a relatively modest-sized user base. In Figure 5.1, we also provide an explanation of Nateon-Cyworld's thinking about its messenger service Nateon.

> We identified any potential weakness of the avatar-based model and tried to think about a novel model that can improve the currently popular avatar model ... In contrast to the previous projects, we tried to create a new one focusing on design aspect. The new one was to complement and address the lacking aspect of the currently popular avatar-based model. (Director of Cyworld, Jiyong Park, December 9, 2002, *Jungle* magazine)

Like Twitter today, users can choose to follow each other and selectively reveal content according to their privacy settings. In this way, they manage relationships between their friends, and Nateon-Cyworld's service became one of the must-use services for young people in South Korea.

The pattern of innovations of the five major messenger service companies, namely ICQ, AOL (AIM), Yahoo!, and Microsoft (MSN), and their Korean counterparts, SayClub and Nateon-Cyworld, is explained and traced in Table 5.4 and Figure 5.2. Table 5.4 lists the major innovations and explains how they work and compares which complementary services generate revenues (advertising and emoticons) and which elements are merely value-adding features. Figure 5.2 traces the launch events of each major firm in the PC era. ICQ was the innovator for the US-based firms that initiated a radical framing for the US industry, and others in the United States followed ICQ. In the same figure, we trace the innovations of SayClub and Nateon-Cyworld, which were quite different on account of their focus on a wholly different monetization route, reinforcing the points made above that the Korean firms were "mavericks" in this period.

*Table 5.3*    *Complementary premium service offered by SayClub*

| Firm | "Breaking the mold" Business model | Quotes |
|---|---|---|
| SayClub | While most firms capture value with adverts, SayClub invented a complementary feature-based model to create and capture values based on digital avatars | "We don't know actually who suggested the avatar idea first … During the group discussion within the division, we questioned whether users can express themselves with pictorial images in the digital space … and the answer was to change the dress and fashion. That's how avatar business was created." <br>(Eun Ju Lee, founding team of SayClub, February 21, 2003, *Hankook Ilbo*) |
| Nateon-Cyworld | While the majority of firms capture value with adverts, Cyworld invented a complementary feature-based model based on personal webpages (scaled-down versions of instantly accessible personal webpages) | "We identified any potential weakness of the avatar-based model, and tried to think about [a] novel model that can improve the currently popular avatar model … In contrast to the previous projects, we tried to create a new one based focusing on design aspect. The new one was to complement and address the lacking aspect of the currently popular avatar based model … In contrast to the existing virtual community service, Cyworld is a privacy driven community based on real name and friends … If you think about 90's PC communities, you could see very brief profile introductions for each user … why don't we create this kind of space for users to express themselves with some digital items? That was the beginning of personal mini-room[s] or web-pages for each users … Before deploying the new model, we tried to think about ways to address possible rejections and anger by users … We decided to initiate the new model as an option for those who only want … and additionally, we provided a one-time free coupon where users can experience services." (Director of Cyworld, Jiyong Park, December 9, 2002, *Jungle* magazine) <br>"If you remember Cyworld service, it was meant to be university-club service. If you enter into any university-club service. If you enter into any university-club, people tend to spend time with like-minded human-beings, rather than with everyone. In this regard, I realized that [in the real world a] university club is just a channel where each person can interact with another … I thought that this can work in the digital space too … If you think about the complementary model, the logic is the same. Cyworld imposed fees on individual users rather than specific groups or communities. People tend to be frugal and stingy on group activities, while actively paying for their individual activities or hobbies." (Director of the Business Planning Division, Lee Ram, April 11, 2016, looking back at her career in Cyworld)* |

*Notes:*    SayClub users could purchase premium avatars to display on the messenger. *http://topclass.chosun.com/news/articleView.html?idxno=1482.

*Note:* Cyworld users could purchase various items to decorate their personal webpages linked to Nateon.
*Source:* Images reproduced with permission from Nateon.

*Figure 5.1    Complementary premium service offered by Nateon-Cyworld*

**Facebook and Myspace Entry**

In 2004/2005, about a decade after the founding of Internet portals and associated messenger services, two major US-based social networking companies, Facebook and Myspace, were launched with quite different business models from the traditional portals of AOL, Yahoo!, and MSN. The new business models were matchmakers among a community of users. In 2008,

*Table 5.4*   Design differences in complementary features

| Features | PC-based messenger | Mobile-based messenger |
| --- | --- | --- |
| Messaging | Allow instant messaging between PC users. Offers enterprise versions at premium costs. * | Allow instant messengers between mobile users. No advertising banner. |
| Banner advertisements | Users must watch for advertising banners (within the messaging service). | N/A |
| Emoticons | [Static emoticons] (within the messaging service) Emoticons complement the content of text messaging; they were used to complement text messengers' feelings and emotions. | *[Animated emoticons] – 3rd Emoticons with animated moving images can be substitutes for text messages; users can deliver content without text messages and complement text messengers. *Third-party developers develop diverse emoticons.* |
| Gaming | [Messengers as chatting applications for gaming] Messengers become chatting applications for already published games. No third parties developed gaming for messenger users. | *[Messengers as gaming intermediaries] – 3rd Messengers introduce new mobile games and allow users to play games together. The game experience is aimed at becoming a part of social interactions and communications. *Third-party developers develop games specifically tailored to messenger users.* |
| Voice/video chat | [Complementary features for communications] Messenger users can voice and video chat with each other. | Same as PC, but within the messaging service. |
| Personal webpages | [Personal profile of messenger users] (external portal service) Users can update their social posts (i.e., personal pictures and updates) to show to other messenger users. | Same as PC, but within the messaging service. |
| E-mail | [Complementary features for communication] Messenger users can also interact via e-mail. | N/A |
| User radio | [Messengers as broadcasting intermediaries] Messenger users can receive other users' personal radio/music broadcasting. | N/A |
| Search | [Independent] Central messengers have search banners, and users can search on assigned websites such as Google, Yahoo!, or MSN (linked to external portals). | [Independent/searching for messaging experiences] During messaging, users can search together in the chatting messenger and obtain information together. |
| Shopping | [Independent] (external portal service) Messenger users can do commercial shopping; a special shopping mall was set up for messenger users. | Messenger users can do commercial shopping for friends and send gifts (internal and external service). |
| Contents | [Independent] (external portal service) Messenger users post their own novels and animations and share them with other users for free. | *[Independent] – 3rd(external and separate service) Messenger users can purchase professional-level novels and animations. Third-party developers develop content for messenger users. |

| Features | PC-based messenger | Mobile-based messenger |
|---|---|---|
| Stock | [Independent] Messenger selectively shows stock prices and news. | [Independent] (external and separate services) Messenger platform users can share investment information and make recommendations for each other. |
| Chatbots/third-party messaging services (plug-in) | [Messenger as a direct channel between commerce and users] – 3rd Messenger allows various commercial companies to interact with users via messaging. Third-party developers develop diverse chatbots and send commercial information to users. | *[Messenger as a direct channel between commerce and users] – 3rd Same as the PC. |
| Music | N/A | *[Music for personal profiles and sharing] (internal feature) Users can upload premium music to their personal profile pages to express their statuses. |
| Open market | N/A | *[Independent] Allows users to exchange products and services. |
| Taxi brokerage | N/A | [Messaging complementary to taxi services] – 3rd(external and separate services) Users can send their ride information to family and friends for their safety. Third-party taxi owners offer taxi-riding services. |
| Payment | N/A | *[Independent] (internal and external services) Users can store credit card information and make payments in both online and offline stores. |
| Banking | N/A | *[Independent] (external and separate services) Users can join mobile banking services. Users can save and borrow through messenger banking. |

*Notes:* * indicates the primary source of revenue, *3rd* indicates the involvement of third-party complementors, *underline* indicates the same services with different value creation and capture design between the two generations.

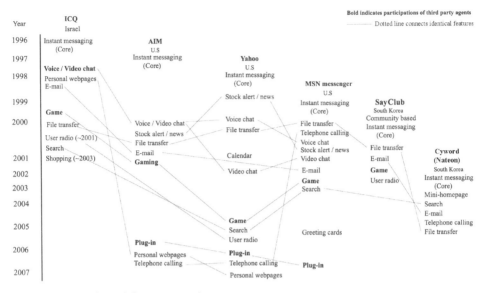

*Sources:*    Author web search from company sites.

*Figure 5.2    New service innovations deployed by ICQ, AIM, Yahoo!, and MSN between 1996 and 2007*

these firms quickly moved to incorporate messaging services into their platforms. For these new firms, the messenger feature was a natural extension of their matchmaking approach and had the effect of boosting user interactions (aimed at greater user lock-in into their platforms). These social media firms appeared to view the messenger service not as an "extra service" but rather as something integrated into the core offering of the platform. These moves proved to be successful, as Facebook's messenger function became so popular that the platform became a primary destination for online instant messaging during this PC era.

### Changes in Technology Regime and the Arrival of Smartphones

With the arrival of widely available smartphones in 2007, the communications industry (seen more broadly than just messenger services) went through significant dynamic changes. Rapid smartphone adoptions worldwide have widely enabled mobile computing and related software applications, including messenger services. The arrival of this technology significantly altered the attractiveness of the messenger service and its functionality. First, because the messenger service could be accessed "everywhere" from the smartphone, it became more attractive and competitive than the traditional mobile text and telephone. Second, because the mobile screen is more compressed, banner advertising became more intrusive to mobile phone users. Third, because of the capabilities of the mobile phone and its connectivity, numerous possibilities for connecting messaging app services to other apps on the phone platform emerged.

The initial effect of the arrival of the smartphone was that the incumbents, namely Facebook, Yahoo!, Microsoft, and others, were encouraged to develop smartphone messenger applications that emulated the PC offer. Initially, these firms did not significantly alter either the features of the PC messenger service or the business model approach. This lack of action signaled a closed mindset toward the new technology and its business model possibilities. By contrast, the novel technological platform stimulated wholly new approaches to mobile messenger services, including WhatsApp, WeChat, and KakaoTalk.

## WhatsApp

Founded in early 2009, WhatsApp (originally an independent company from Silicon Valley, California, and since 2014, a division of Facebook) adopted a different business model, avoiding advertising and focusing on value-added quality of delivery (e.g., encryption), with monetization through a fee.

The choice of strategy and business model for WhatsApp was a deliberate challenge to incumbents, with its novel construction of what was meant by "service." This novelty of think-ing is based on reframing the industry's deeply held assumptions about the messenger offering being a service that complements other services in a portal or social media platform that is offered for "free" within a wider advertising-supported environment, which might include explicit advertisements within the service itself.

The nature of this deliberate challenge to the existing industry order can be gauged by the speeches and statements of Jan Koum, the CEO of WhatsApp. He vocally condemned the industry's commitment to advertising and sought to find new ways to monetize his offering. The following quotation (albeit from 2012) neatly summarizes these views, which were also expressed elsewhere:

> Advertising isn't just the disruption of aesthetics, the insults to your intelligence, and the interruption of your train of thought … Your data isn't even in the picture. We are simply not interested in any of it … When people ask us why we charge for WhatsApp, we say, 'Have you considered the alternative?' (Jan Koum, CEO, WhatsApp Blog, 2012)

WhatsApp initially offered its service for a small positive price of $1 to assure users of an advertising-free environment, a strategy that initially yielded significant revenues. However, the "one-time fee" policy relied on new subscriptions, not continuing users. A little surpris-ingly, WhatsApp did not expand the suite of WhatsApp services beyond the simple messenger to include voice and video until after it was taken over by Facebook in 2014. After a short time, the fee dropped, and shortly after, WhatsApp was purchased by Facebook, which kept the same business model. This service was kept wholly separate from the core Facebook offering.

## Asian Super App KakaoTalk

In this last section on the history of the messenger industry, we discuss the emergence of a wholly new set of actors, the super apps KakaoTalk, Line, and WeChat, with a focus on KakaoTalk. KakaoTalk (the first mover, about which we have the most data) viewed the messenger service as a "portal in its own right"; that is, a portal within a portal, that offered a suite of services where monetization comes by supplying complementary services (rather than advertising; see Figure 5.3). KakaoTalk disrupted the Korean mobile industry by devel-oping the messenger service as a "super app" that challenged the two dominant firms, Apple (iOS) and Google (Android). A super app envelops the platform on which it sits. Super apps offer a suite of services within the mobile-phone-installed app that circumvents the other apps residing in the phone, sometimes disabling the features of the software platform itself. Table 5.5 summarizes the sequence of moves. The ability of super apps to undertake these moves is critically dependent on the fundamental software at the bottom of the stack, which is the software of the ARM chip.

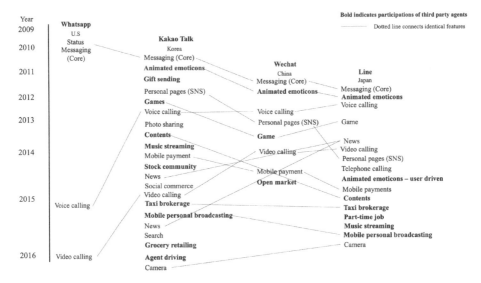

*Sources:*    Author web search from company sites.

*Figure 5.3*    *New service innovations deployed by WhatsApp, KakaoTalk, WeChat, and Line from 2009 to 2016*

To understand how KakaoTalk approached the challenge of developing its messenger service, we refer back to our interview with the founder, Lee Jae-Bum, and to public information about the founding of KakaoTalk on its website, supporting interviews with web developers who worked with the company for a long time, and the personal history of Lee Jae-Bum written by Steve J. Min (2021). We suggest that KakaoTalk, led by Lee Jae-Bum, pursued a sophisticated approach to identifying a business model that added value to customers at the same time as creating value for the company. This approach inevitably rejected the "advertising model" as the dominant way of capturing value.

The antecedents of KakaoTalk were a start-up company called IWILAB, which was founded around 2006 by Kim Bum-So, a venture capitalist who himself had started Hangame, a successful online games company. Kim Bum-So hired Lee Jae-Bum along with several others to develop new web-based services for both the United States and Korea. These services were based on various fees and supported by advertising. At the end of 2008, after the success of 3G mobile in the United States, Kim Bum-So directed his team to focus on mobile opportunities. 3G mobiles appeared in Korea by 2009, and Kim Bum-So quickly took the lead in developing a novel messenger app that was launched in March 2001.

*Table 5.5*   *Details of the KakaoTalk, Line, and WeChat complementor-based business models*

| Mobile messengers | KakaoTalk | Line | WeChat |
|---|---|---|---|
| Game | Take 20% of revenues from game revenues | Take 35% of total revenues | Take 30%–40% of total revenues |
| Content | Take 20% of revenues from content sales | Take 20% of revenues from content sales | - |
| Animated emoticons | Take 28%–35% of revenues from sales (the remaining portion goes to complementors) | Take 35% | Take 30%–60% of total revenues |
| Shopping | Take 3.5% of revenues | Take 10%–20% of total transaction | - |
| Gift sending | Take 15% | - | - |
| Payment | 3.5% of mobile payment transaction fees | 3.4%–3.5% of mobile payment transaction fees | 0.6% transaction fees with stores 0.01% user transaction charges |
| Part-time matching | - | $75–1,000 weekly posting charge | - |
| Music | $0.5 per music purchase | $75 monthly subscription fees | - |
| Hair shop | $50 initial registrations fee and $20 monthly subscription fees for hair salons | - | - |
| Commercial chatting | $0.015 per message | $24 for the first year $12 yearly charge afterward | $2,000 per business account |

Lee Jae-Bum explained his philosophy concerning how to build a business:

> In my view B2C businesses (need to be developed) in two stages. First, gathering traffic, which means creating a service that people want, and then with that traffic, pursuing monetization ... KakaoTalk was the result of 3 years of continuous attempts to develop and create a successful service (that generates traffic). During the initial period, we didn't think of the service as a platform but focused on gathering users with good services.

Lee Jae-Bum had worked for some years before the founding of KakaoTalk in Internet businesses supported by advertising, but even so, he had a sophisticated view concerning the monetization of Internet businesses:

> In 2010, March, KakaoTalk was released for the first time, and within a month we had gathered 1 million users [in a population of 50 million South Koreans]. Because of this rapid growth, we decided to pursue monetization. We initially decided to explore four business models: [monetization by] advertising, commerce, content and gaming. Gaming is a kind of content, but we knew gaming is a big business. We had two guiding principles for monetization ... Models that enable cooperating with partners; and models that are well aligned with the central messenger service, that do not [negatively impinge on the] messenger experience.

He continued:

> The "gift" function met the two criteria we set out. Developing the sending of gifts through the messenger function was not easy, and it required a partnership with KT [the Korean Telecommunications company]. [Fortunately] KT Giftshow was already available, so it was a relatively easy task [creating the gift function for the messenger] ... Following the gift function, we made several initiatives for commerce, advertising, and content and initiated attempts at several different business models. Although many of these features delivered value to the user, we were not able to reach a break-even point. So my final attempt, I created a new initiative around the game business ... The success of the Kakao game was more than my expectation, and this allowed us to find the answer to 'monetization.'

Discussions with Lee Jae-Bum and his colleagues made it clear that they all viewed advertising monetization strategies as value-destroying, especially in a mobile context where screen space is scarce and attention spans are fragile. The opening complementary service of emoticons was obvious for KakaoTalk, as it copied the earlier moves of SayClub and Nateon-Cyworld. However, the identification and mobilization of games, gifts, and other complementary services took much longer and required much more extensive planning, experimentation, and significant investments. Before KakaoTalk found profitable revenue sources, advertising banners were widely speculated to appear on mobile messengers (MTN, 2011). However, as the above-mentioned accounts indicate, KakaoTalk clearly rejects this idea.

In summary, we suggest that the pioneering moves regarding the complementor business model by SayClub (Neowitz) and Nateon-Cyworld (SK Communications) of the PC era were developed and deepened significantly by KakaoTalk in the mobile era. Line from Japan and WeChat (Tencent) from China followed the moves of KakaoTalk. We suggest that these moves were probably partly explicit copying and partly self-development. Murmann and Zhu (2021) claimed that WeChat was a pioneer. However, knowing that Tencent had many financial investments in Internet businesses in South Korea, and some intimate knowledge of KakaoTalk at this time, suggests to us that explicit copying of the pioneering moves of KakaoTalk was an element. These pieces of evidence along with the public quotes shown in

Table 5.6 suggest that the dominant Korean, Japanese, and Chinese players had complementor business models as their strategic logics.

## DISCUSSION

Our exposition of the history of the messenger industry identified two important periods, that related initially to PC technology and then to mobile technology, and the sequences of actions by the leading actors in these two periods. First, a significant number of entrants (especially AOL, Yahoo!, Microsoft, and Myspace) were established digital players diversifying from their existing activities into messenger services. These established digital players typically made choices about business models and strategies that were extensions of their strategies elsewhere in their businesses, choices that are wholly consistent with established theories relating to entrenched corporate logics set out at the start of the paper (Luoma et al., 2022; Tripsas and Gavetti, 2000).

We allocate more space in the history section to some important entrants, with particular emphasis on Neowitz (SayClub) and SK Electronics (Nateon-Cyworld) during the first period, and on WhatsApp and KakoTalk in the second period. These four firms are associated with innovative business models that challenge the existing incumbents, sometimes very success-fully. In the first period, that of PCs, two important entrants appeared from Korea, Neowitz (Sayworld) and SK Electronics (Nateon-Cyworld), which were largely local in influence. When one compares the framing of the business model choices of Neowitz with those of the traditional US incumbents, a clear picture of different framings is evident (see Tables 5.7 and 5.8). These Korean firms appeared to react to the fact that copying the incumbents was not possible due to local market conditions, and to be forced to adapt by processes that involved "reframing" through experimentation in a manner indicated by the existing literature (Hannah and Eisenhardt, 2018; Sosna, Trevinyo-Rodríguez, and Velamuri, 2010).

In the second period, two distinctive kinds of challenging entrants emerged. WhatsApp came from within the same community (Silicon Valley) that originated many of the leading digital incumbents. WhatsApp challenged along the lines indicated by Teece (2018), which sensed a new opportunity that was overlooked by the incumbents. However, after the initial success of this entrant (its revenue base quickly exceeded $1 billion), its approach was enveloped to parallel the more traditional actors, and its innovative trajectories were largely terminated. By contrast, the Asian challengers' actions led to some radical and fundamental alterations to the industry. Our probing into the history of KakaoTalk, demonstrably the leader among Asian firms in the mobile era, shows a different kind of approach. From the start, KakaoTalk sought to challenge the existing order. While KakaoTalk clearly engaged in experimentation, that experimentation appeared to be strongly "guided" by a cognitive perspective of challeng-ing the traditional order and establishing a wholly new approach and associated ecosystem. KakaoTalk's revenues quickly grew to $1 billion in a market that was one-fifth the size of the United States, generating as much as $15 in revenues from complementary products for the average customer, signaling remarkable success with a wholly different approach.

In our probing, we clearly recognize many competing suggestions as to how this framing came about. KakaoTalk is based in a community that is far from Silicon Valley physically and culturally but is associated with innovation in the digital domain. In addition, the changing technology landscape facilitated by the arrival of connectivity and more powerful computing

*Table 5.6*    Evidence of the cognitive processes of SayClub, Nateon-Cyworld, WhatsApp, KakaoTalk, Line, and WeChat

| Messenger | Quotes from top management |
|---|---|
| Sayclub | "[When creating the avatar-based model] we were also very not sure about the success of [a] cyber avatar based model. However, we were focusing on what our community users really want and how they can express themselves in the cyber community space. Internet technology fundamentally changed how people communicate and express." (Jinhwan Park, CEO of Neowitz, hosting the SayClub service) |
| Nateon-Cyworld | "[When creating the Cyworld business model] I did not think that people use [the] Internet to extract personal information for commercial purposes. Rather, I focused on the interactive aspects between [human beings] … I noted that when interacting with friends, people usually deliver small gifts to each other and view photo albums together." (Dong Hyung-Lee, creator of Cyworld) |
| WhatsApp | "Advertising isn't just the disruption of aesthetics, the insults to your intelligence and the interruption of your train of thought … Your data isn't even in the picture. We are simply not interested in any of it … When people ask us why we charge for WhatsApp, we say, 'Have you considered the alternative?'" (Jan Koum, CEO Blog, 2012) |
| Kakao | "In my view, B2C business mainly in two stages. First, gathering traffic (which means [create] a service that many people want), and second, with the traffic, pursue monetization … With Kakao, thinking that we have already achieved the first stage of gathering user traffics … I pursued monetization. We initially decided to pursue [a] business model (for profit) in four areas: adverts, commerce, contents, and gaming." (KakaoTalk former CEO Jae Bum-Lee) |
| Line | "Line capture[s] values currently from game[s], emoticons, and advertisements … We can better capture values … because we pursue platform strategies … We do not focus on simple value capture mechanisms such as … advertisements … We will continue to develop business models depending on local contexts." (Chief Marketing Officer Masuda Jun) |
| WeChat | "[The] major difference between WeChat and other chatting apps is that WeChat is not just chatting, WeChat is a social mobile platform, and WeChat already opened its API to third-party developers; that means any third-party apps can integrate with WeChat, and enjoy the big WeChat user base for their potential growth, as long as your app is welcomed by the users." (Louis Song, WeChat Manager, *Forbes*, 2013) <br> "[When talking about monetization] incubate and accelerate a variety of businesses within the ecosystem." (Managing Director Matthew Brennan, Inkstonenews, 2018) |

*Table 5.7*    *Excerpt of the business model analysis by Nateon-Cyworld executives at the time of new model creation (December 9, 2002)*

|  | Avatar-based model (previous industry-dominant model) | New model (mini-webpage and mini-room) |
|---|---|---|
| Advantages | • Identify user identities instantly<br>• Fun like playing with dolls<br>• Good integration with website | • Be able to understand users in depth<br>• Comprehensive and diverse content<br>• In line with transparencies of communities with private user data<br>• Can accumulate user histories |
| Disadvantages | • Masks are not in line with the transparencies of communities<br>• Not enough content aside from avatars<br>• Difficult to understand other users in depth<br>• Now a too-common model, with no room for differentiation | • Relatively large space on the web<br>• Relatively low intuition and instant configuration<br>• … |

*Source:* *Jungle Magazine* (translated), https://www.jungle.co.kr/magazine/6946.

also pushed firms to think outside the traditional industry's way of thinking. Our attempt to probe the antecedents of this thinking suggests a thorough pattern of intensive research, and interviews failed to come up with a single explanation. Multiple factors appear to be at work.

**Effectuation and Cognition**

Our Korean messenger firms provide good examples of effectuation strategies emphasized by Nambisan, Wright, and Feldman (2019) and Sarasvathy (2001). Mobile technology unlocked new possibilities, and firms became increasingly less bounded by space and time restrictions for value creation and capture, which have been primary concerns for brick-and-mortar businesses, reinforcing the point made by Baum, Locke, and Kirkpatrick (1998) and Kaplan (2011). Although the initial services lack both quality and quantity, they often found popular acceptance by users and successfully scaled up within 1–2 years. This approach and growth rate were difficult to imagine for non-digital businesses (Nambisan, Lyytinen, Majchrzak, and Song, 2017). Non-digital businesses often necessitate manufacturing facilities, R&D results, and marketing channels, which usually require prolonged periods before commercializing products and services. Careful planning and expert market research that signify customer adoptions have been prerequisites before commercialization (Brown and Eisenhardt, 1995). The conventional approach is thus to expect customer demand based on currently available and known information for the new product and assess the product–market fit accordingly (Kirzner, 1973; Shane, 2000). In this regard, the differences between digital and non-digital contexts become more vivid and clear.

Our contribution to the literature is our focus on the business model dimension of strategy and giving some granularity to effectuation strategies and their boundaries and drivers.

*Table 5.8*     *Evidence of the cognitive processes of ICQ, AOL (AIM), Yahoo!, and Microsoft (MSN)*

| Messenger | Quotes from top management |
|---|---|
| ICQ | "We have a central belief in the company that this [ICQ] is a social medium … build this as a medium, make this central and as a utility, make it [as] central in people's life as the telephone and the television, but with more value […] This year is really a year to [turn] that time online into page views, page views into impressions, and impressions into dollars." (Ted Leonsis, Former AOL President, BancBoston Robertson Stephens Tech 1999 Conference, CNET, 2002) |
| AIM | "My biggest job as a manager was to keep AIM alive internally, because every single executive vice president wanted to shut it down and kill it. They could not understand the concept of giving away for free something that was of real value to the paying subscriber base. […] Despite the effort … never sold a dollar of ad space." (Bosco, former manager of AIM messenger, Mashable, 2014) |
| Yahoo! | "As the number of our users has grown, so has our audience's appeal to major advertisers. To maximize this opportunity, we've developed new ways for marketing partners to integrate their messages into our communications products … Yahoo! Communications displayed five billion of these high-impact ads during the fourth quarter alone." (Yahoo! Annual Report, 2001) |
| MSN | "Communications continues to be the cornerstone of the Internet, and instant messaging is becoming a more prevalent way for people to communicate … We are excited to deliver our easy-to-use MSN Messenger Service to enable consumers to communicate with as many people as possible." (Brad Chase, Vice President of the Consumer and Commerce Group at Microsoft, Microsoft News, 1999)<br><br>"The premise in the early noughties was that the context in advertising was everything and that a social platform [where audience targeting was built on user data rather than on content context] could not be effective as a branding medium." (Chris Dobson, Former Vice President of Microsoft, Marketing Society, 2018) |

# CONCLUSIONS

The aim of our study was to probe the connections between business model thinking, technology, and cognition in the context of the messenger industry. We aimed to show that technology has a key role in this dimension and that the critical issue has been not digital compared with non-digital, but mobile compared with digital. Mobile technology has unlocked new business model possibilities, particularly those of monetization via complementors. In this industry, Korean firms, namely SayClub, Nateon-Cyworld, and, critically, KakaoTalk, unlocked the new business models through the development of complementor-based super apps. Surprisingly, the US messenger firms have not copied the innovations of Korean, Japanese, and Chinese firms, but this is yet to be fully explained. Our hint is that US firms have been blinded by corporate inertia and that new possibilities have been ignored, indicating policy questions and worries about the role of corporate inertia among some of the leading US digital firms.

# ACKNOWLEDGMENTS

We thank the editors and two anonymous reviewers for their insights and encouragement in writing this chapter and the executives of the firms who took the time to explain their business model choices. We also thank our colleagues at City University and our partners in our research projects for their assistance in this project. We acknowledge the funding support from Bayes Business School (formerly Cass), City, University of London, and RCUK grant "Building Better Business Models" EPSRC-EPK039695/1.

# NOTES

1. We are using "Korea" to refer to South Korea.
2. The technological development of instant messaging predates the commercial launch by many years: in the mid-1960s, the MIT Computation Center created the project called Compatible Time-sharing System, which allowed up to 30 users to send messages to each other.

# REFERENCES

Abrahamson, E., & Hambrick, D.C. (1997). Attentional homogeneity in industries: the effect of discretion. *Journal of Organizational Behavior*, 18(S1), 513–32.
Aspara, J., Lamberg, J.A., Laukia, A., & Tikkanen, H. (2013). Corporate business model transformation and inter-organizational cognition: the case of Nokia. *Long Range Planning*, 46(6), 459–74.
Aversa, P., Huyghe, A., & Bonadio, G. (2021). First impressions stick: market entry strategies and category priming in the digital domain. *Journal of Management Studies*, 58, 1721–60.
Baden-Fuller, C., & Haefliger, S. (2013). Business models and technological innovation. *Long Range Planning*, 46(6), 419–26.
Baden-Fuller, C., & Mangematin, V. (2013). Business models: a challenging agenda. *Strategic Organization*, 11(4), 418–27.
Baden-Fuller, C., & Morgan, M.S. (2010). Business models as models. *Long Range Planning*, 43(2–3), 156–71.

Baden-Fuller, C., & Stopford, J.M. (1992). *Rejuvenating the Mature Business: The Competitive Challenge*. Routledge.

Barr, P.S. (1998). Adapting to unfamiliar environmental events: a look at the evolution of interpretation and its role in strategic change. *Organization Science*, 9(6), 644–69.

Barr, P.S., Stimpert, J.L., & Huff, A.S. (1992). Cognitive change, strategic action, and organizational renewal. *Strategic Management Journal*, 13(S1), 15–36.

Baum, J.R., Locke, E.A., & Kirkpatrick, S.A. (1998). A longitudinal study of the relation of vision and vision communication to venture growth in entrepreneurial firms. *Journal of Applied Psychology*, 83(1), 43.

Brown, S.L., & Eisenhardt, K.M. (1995). Product development: past research, present findings, and future directions. *Academy of Management Review*, 20(2), 343–78.

Casadesus-Masanell, R., & Ricart, J.E. (2010). From strategy to business models and onto tactics. *Long Range Planning*, 43(2–3), 195–215.

Chesbrough, H. (2010). Business model innovation opportunities and barriers. *Long Range Planning*, 43, 354–63.

Chesbrough, H., & Rosenbloom, R.S. (2002). The role of the business model in capturing value from innovation: evidence from Xerox Corporation's technology spin-off companies. *Industrial and Corporate Change*, 11(3), 529–55.

Cho, T.S., & Hambrick, D.C. (2006). Attention as the mediator between top management team characteristics and strategic change: the case of airline deregulation. *Organization Science*, 17(4), 453–69.

Clapham, S.E., & Schwenk, C.R. (1991). Self-serving attributions, managerial cognition, and company performance. *Strategic Management Journal*, 12(3), 219–29.

CNET (2002). Ad banners seek home on ICQ. January 2.

Doz, Y.L., & Kosonen, M. (2010). Embedding strategic agility: a leadership agenda for accelerating business model renewal. *Long Range Planning*, 43(2–3), 370–82.

Eggers, J.P., & Kaplan, S. (2009). Cognition and renewal: comparing CEO and organizational effects on incumbent adaptation to technical change. *Organization Science*, 20(2), 461–77.

Eisenhardt, K.M. (1989). Making fast strategic decisions in high-velocity environments. *Academy of Management Journal*, 32(3), 543–76.

Eisenhardt, K.M., & Graebner, M.E. (2007). Theory building from cases: opportunities and challenges. *Academy of Management Journal*, 50(1), 25–32.

Feldman, M.S., & Pentland, B.T. (2003). Reconceptualizing organizational routines as a source of flexibility and change. *Administrative Science Quarterly*, 48(1), 94–118.

*Forbes* (2013). WeChat by Tencent: from chat app to social mobile platform. https://asia.nikkei.com/Business/Chinas-WeChat-has-big-retail-ambitions.

Gavetti, G., & Rivkin, J.W. (2007). On the origin of strategy: action and cognition over time. *Organization Science*, 18(3), 420–39.

Hannah, D.P., & Eisenhardt, K.M. (2018). How firms navigate cooperation and competition in nascent ecosystems. *Strategic Management Journal*, 39(12), 3163–92.

Inkstonenews (2018). The story of China's everything app. https://www.inkstonenews.com/tech/why-wechat-far-spent-force-despite-tencents-profits-dip/article/2159987.

Kaplan, S. (2008). Framing contests: strategy making under uncertainty. *Organization Science*, 19(5), 729–52.

Kaplan, S. (2011). Research in cognition and strategy: reflections on two decades of progress and a look to the future. *Journal of Management Studies*, 48(3), 665–95.

Kirzner, I.M. (1973). *Competition and Entrepreneurship*. University of Chicago Press.

Lee, K., Rho, S., Kim, S., & Jun, G.J. (2007). Creativity-innovation cycle for organizational exploration and exploitation: lessons from Neowiz – a Korean Internet company. *Long Range Planning*, 40(4–5), 505–23.

Luoma, J., Laamanen, T., & Lamberg, J.A. (2022). Toward a routine-based view of interfirm rivalry. *Strategic Organization*, 20, 433–46.

Marketing Society (2018). Interviews with Chris Dobson. https://www.marketingsociety.com/the-clubroom/interview-chris-dobson#7MymEjy0oFhqw5M2.97.

Martins, L.L., Rindova, V.P., & Greenbaum, B.E. (2015). Unlocking the hidden value of concepts: a cognitive approach to business model innovation. *Strategic Entrepreneurship Journal*, 9(1), 99–117.

Mashable (2014). The rise and fall of AIM, the breakthrough AOL never wanted. https://mashable.com/2014/04/15/aim-history/?europe=true#pmJbkDtDZPqn.

McGrath, R.G. (2010). Business models: a discovery driven approach. *Long Range Planning*, 43(2–3), 247–61.

Miles, M.B., & Huberman, A.M. (1994). *Qualitative Data Analysis: An Expanded Sourcebook.* SAGE.

Min, S.J. (2021). Personal history of Lee-Jae Baum, Noble Ambition Kings Bay Capital. https://nobleambition.wordpress.com/2011/07/12/korean-entrepreneurs-lee-jae-bum-of-kakaotalk/.

MTN (2011). Kakao's CEO LEE dreaming KakaoTalk as a global social hub. Available from: https://www.youtube.com/watch?v=blr6x2Ryxfk.

Murmann, J.P., and Zhu, Z. (2021). What enables a Chinese firm to create new-to-the-world innovations? A historical case study of intrafirm coopetition in the instant messaging service sector. *Strategy Science*, 6, 305–30.

Nambisan, S., Lyytinen, K., Majchrzak, A., & Song, M. (2017). Digital innovation management: reinventing innovation management research in a digital world. *MIS Quarterly*, 41(1).

Nambisan, S., Wright, M., & Feldman, M. (2019). The digital transformation of innovation and entrepreneurship: progress, challenges and key themes. *Research Policy*, 48(8), 103773.

Narayan, S., Sidhu, J., Baden-Fuller, C., and Volberda, H.W. (2020). Examining CEOs' business model schemas: a cognitive mapping of differences between insiders and outsiders. *New Horizons in Managerial and Organizational Cognition*, 4, 15–37.

Ott, T.E., Eisenhardt, K.M., & Bingham, C.B. (2017). Strategy formation in entrepreneurial settings: past insights and future directions. *Strategic Entrepreneurship Journal*, 11(3), 306–25.

Porac, J.F., Thomas, H., & Baden-Fuller, C. (1989). Competitive groups as cognitive communities: the case of Scottish knitwear manufacturers. *Journal of Management Studies*, 26(4), 397–416.

Sarasvathy, S.D. (2001). Causation and effectuation: toward a theoretical shift from economic inevitability to entrepreneurial contingency. *Academy of Management Review*, 26(2), 243–63.

Shane, S. (2000). Prior knowledge and the discovery of entrepreneurial opportunities. *Organization Science*, 11(4), 448–69.

Sosna, M., Trevinyo-Rodríguez, R.N., & Velamuri, S.R. (2010). Business model innovation through trial-and-error learning: the Naturhouse case. *Long Range Planning*, 43(2–3), 383–407.

Spender, J.C. (1989). *Industry Recipes.* Basil Blackwell.

Sund, K.J., Galvan, R.J., & Bogers, M. (2021). Exploring the connections between business models and cognition. *New Horizons in Managerial and Organizational Cognition*, 4, 1–13.

Teece, D.J. (2018). Business models and dynamic capabilities. *Long Range Planning*, 51(1), 40–49.

Teece, D.J. (2020). Hand in glove: open innovation and the dynamic capabilities framework. *Strategic Management Review*, 1(2), 233–53.

Tripsas, M., & Gavetti, G. (2000). Capabilities, cognition, and inertia: evidence from digital imaging. *Strategic Management Journal*, 21(10–11), 1147–61.

Walsh, J.P. (1995). Managerial and organizational cognition: notes from a trip down memory lane. *Organization Science*, 6(3), 280–321.

WhatsApp blog official webpage. https://blog.whatsapp.com.

Yoo, Y., Boland, R.J., Jr, Lyytinen, K., & Majchrzak, A. (2012). Organizing for innovation in the digitized world. *Organization Science*, 23(5), 1398–1408.

# 6.  Free(mium) strategies for digital goods
## Kevin J. Boudreau, Lars Bo Jeppesen and Milan Miric

## 1.    INTRODUCTION

The term "Freemium" is often used to describe a specific pricing and product strategy when multiple versions of a product are being offered: a superior version sold for a fee and a lower-quality (or feature-limited) version offered for free (or a very low price). This strategy can be observed through a variety of different approaches: feature-limited products where a full-featured version is sold at a high price (or through an update), while a version that has limited features is freely available; time-limited products where users have access to a full-featured product for a set period of time, and have to purchase a full version after the time trial expires; usage-limited products where users have access to a set number of free instances but are required to pay for a larger number of instances.

Offering tiered products (different quality tiers of the same product) is a long-established product design idea. One famous example is the case of printers, where the same printer technology was used to create a series of products at different price points. Since the quality differentiator was print speed, printer manufacturers would create a high-speed printer, then artificially slow down the printing speed in order to create lower-quality versions they could sell at lower prices (Deneckere & McAfee, 1996). However, with physical products, this approach could only be feasible in certain settings. With the growth of software and the internet from the 1980s and 1990s these tiered strategies became far more widespread (Hui & Chau, 2002). America Online (AOL) famously used to mail free demo (demonstration) disks to people or attach them to newspapers, providing users with a few hours of free online surfing, but also with the opportunity to pay if they wanted to spend more time online. Particularly during the period where software was distributed by disks and CDs, the strategy of providing a free demo (either feature- or time-limited) became the dominant model of marketing software. Consumers could try out a product before purchasing. This model remained largely unchanged until the early 2010s, when software consumption started shifting in two important ways. First, software purchases shifted to online sales, direct to consumers through storefronts such as the App Store. These storefronts made it possible to offer multiple versions of the same product, through creative features such as in-app purchases, which would allow consumers to access a free product and then purchase additional features or functionality. Second, software providers began to shift to more cloud-based services that are sold through a subscription or per-use basis. These service providers often offered a free version of their products which contained limited functionality, but then charged for more intense users.

Most digital products which we observe today have some freemium component. For example, newspapers provide only some articles for free, while others are behind a paywall. Sometimes, they provide a teaser of the article but require you to subscribe to read the rest of the article. Streaming services (Peacock, Hulu, Netflix, Paramount+) all have tiered approaches, either providing a free or discounted basic service (with either limited features or increased nuisance such as commercials) along with a premium service. Cloud storage providers such as Dropbox, Box and Google Drive are all based on a model of providing free storage to consumers, hoping that more demanding users will choose to upgrade to these tools. Mobile app stores such as Google Play or Apple's App Store are populated by products that offer some version of freemium strategies, either by having a pro and lite version of their products, or more commonly using in-app purchases to provide additional features. Many business-to-business services, such as the burgeoning sector of AI (artificial intelligence) services (machine translation, image detection, etc.), provide a free tier so that users can perform a set number of queries in a period of time, and have to pay for additional services.

Freemium in many ways represents more than just a pricing strategy. It affects how the products are designed (what features are included with which products). It creates a potential for wide-scale adoption of a product, even though very few users may become paying customers. This can impact the cost structure of a business, where a small number of paying customers have to offset the costs of a larger number of free customers (e.g., cloud storage companies have to keep the data of many free customers while being supported by a small number of paying customers). It emphasizes operations and efficiency from the perspective of software developers creating these products, over what may have traditionally been a creative-style, hit-driven industry in the past. These complex issues involving pricing decisions, product design decisions and organizational design decisions are often difficult to tackle in a single paper. Instead, most research papers focus on a particular aspect of freemium strategies, such as pricing. This makes it difficult to draw general conclusions about what are the situations when freemium is a viable strategy and what might be the other issues that firms want to consider when using these strategies, at least without reviewing this large and dispersed literature.

In this chapter, we provide an overview of the various streams of academic literature that have touched on the question of freemium. We then discuss the general conclusions that have emerged from the literature regarding when freemium strategies might be viable, and when they might not be. However, the academic literature on freemium is at times incongruent with the empirical reality we often see. As discussed above, there are numerous successful examples of freemium approaches, yet the academic literature highlights how this may be viable under very specific circumstances. To reconcile these differences, we further discuss what aspects of freemium strategies have only recently begun to be studied and why future research into these topics might help shed light on when and how freemium approaches are best used.

## 2.  DEFINING FREEMIUM STRATEGIES

Freemium strategies have been used to describe feature-limited products, time-limited products, usage-limited products, and multi-tiered products in general. A defining characteristic of these products, and a way of synthesizing these different definitions, is to see freemium as both a product design and pricing strategy, where firms offer a free version of their products (alongside some paid feature or version), which can enhance consumption of their products (either through more users and/or higher prices for premium features) but comes at a cost (either through cannibalized sales and/or costs of designing products for these strategies).

Freemium can be seen as an extension of multi-tiered product or product-line design strategies, as discussed in the example of printers above. However, what distinguishes freemium from these strategies is that a part of the product is available for free (zero price). In theory (as we discuss in the following section) firms can offer a version of their product at a lower price and do not have any particular reason for setting the price to zero. However, the empirical reality is that many (potentially even most) products that offer multiple versions set the price of the lower-quality version at zero. There might be a variety of reasons for this. Offering a zero price simplifies the process of price setting and allows firms to focus on optimizing the price of the higher-quality products. This might be particularly relevant for digital goods that can be purchased online in different geographical areas with different currencies, and therefore offering a free version might avoid a variety of transactional and accounting costs. Offering free versions makes it possible for consumers to try a product with minimal costs, which encourages a try-before-you-buy approach from customers that might be impeded by even a very low price. There may of course be consumer impressions associated with a free price, such that consumers might be cognitively more drawn to free products or might perceive free products as being naturally inferior (Shampanier, Mazar & Ariely, 2007). While this is beyond the scope of our particular focus, there is a rich literature in psychology and consumer behavior that has explored this issue (e.g., Raghubir, 2004).

Another reason why freemium strategies might be unique is that in theory, firms might equally be likely to benefit from subsidizing the consumption of the free product (set a negative price or paying consumers to try the product) as they are with setting a price for free. However, even though the empirical reality is that firms are setting their prices to zero, it does not imply that they are not designing their products such that consumers might benefit in other ways. Music streaming services offer their products for free but compete on other dimensions of product design such as the library of content that they provide, the fidelity of the content and other potential features to improve the consumer experience. Therefore, freemium provides a unique strategy based on offering a multi-tiered product constrained by having a free product offering, but considerably flexible with regard to the other features that might be implemented and offered.

## 3.   EXISTING RESEARCH ON FREEMIUM STRATEGIES

### 3.1   Theory Lens on Freemium Strategies

We begin our overview by considering the theoretical studies that have looked at freemium strategies. This is a good place to start for several reasons. First, these studies focus on the pricing decision given a single- or multi-tiered product offering. Second, these studies formalize the mechanism through which offering a free version influences the overall payoffs of a firm (e.g., larger user base, greater consumer understanding of product quality). This makes it possible to clearly articulate the tradeoff between the costs and benefits of freemium strategies. Finally, these theoretical studies link the consumer adoption decision (consumer utility function) and the firm product and pricing decisions (firm payoff function). The empirical papers we discuss later typically focus on only one of these aspects. Once we have discussed these stylized but highly informative theoretical representations of freemium strategies, we move on to discuss empirical papers in subsequent sections.

A precursor to the literature on freemium is the literature in economics–marketing–management that considered what can be referred to as product line design (Deneckere & McAfee, 1996; Moorthy & Png, 1992; Mussa & Rosen, 1978). This literature raised the concept that firms may benefit from creating value-subtracted versions of a high-quality product, which may be even more costly to produce than the original high-quality product (e.g., printers which are artificially slowed down). These papers focused primarily on physical products, where product-line design decisions basically refer to the price and quality of products they are going to be offering.

A number of follow-on studies focused on the use of such product-line design decisions but within the context of software (Bhargava and Choudhary, 2004; Krishnan & Gupta, 2001; Shapiro & Varian, 1998). This was an important context to consider because it had characteristics such as network effects, whereby the value of the product increased with the size of the user base, or quality uncertainty, where users were not able to understand the value of a software application until they had some time using it.

A further extension of these studies considered the specific (but commonly observable) case of a firm product line with a lower-quality (or value-subtracted) version of the products available for free (zero price). This zero price is important for two reasons. First, a zero price implies that the firm will generate no revenue from the lower-priced version of its products. Therefore, the benefits of the free version must be sufficiently large that they compensate for the lost revenues that result from this lower-quality version. Second, a zero price implies that competitors might also have to set a zero price for their products, as it is challenging to sell a product when your competitors are offering it for free. This market condition, where the prevailing price is zero, creates market conditions where firms have many users, but very few paying customers.

Cheng, Li and Liu (2015) model the optimal conditions where firms are best off providing a time-limited product, feature-limited product or hybrid of both. In their model, the core benefit arises from network effects which increase the value of the paid version of the product, with the overall number of users. Cheng and Liu (2012) consider a similar situation, but instead of network effects, study the information benefits of offering a free version: reduced uncertainty around product value. Appel, Libai, Muller and Shachar (2020) consider a variety of freemium models including either an ad-based free product or a paid version (in-app purchase on top of free products), and model the impact of sampling as a way of understanding the value of products.

Other studies have explored information diffusion from users to prospective users in the form of word-of-mouth diffusion about the value of a product (Niculescu & Wu, 2014; Dou, Niculescu and Wu, 2013). These studies highlight an important tradeoff at the heart of using freemium models. On the one hand, while a free product may enhance the user base of a company, it also cannibalizes the premium product lines as would-be customers will instead use the free version. The only way that this is feasible is if: (1) through network effects the value of the premium version increases with the size of a user base and therefore the firm can charge more for a premium product, as a consequence of having a free product with a large user base; (2) an information asymmetry exists which prevents consumers from understanding the true value of these products, and by being offered a free version, customers will understand the full value of the product and therefore be willing to pay more to acquire it. One important feature of these papers is that they consider a single firm in isolation (monopolist). Therefore, they do not consider how a pricing decision may interact with that of a competitor.

A small number of studies consider the use of a freemium strategy in a market with multiple firms (Zhang, Nan, Li & Tan, 2016; Etzion & Pang, 2014; Pang & Etzion, 2012). By adding a second firm to the model, consumers face a choice of whether they purchase a product from firm A or firm B (rather than in the monopolist case, where consumers face a choice of whether they purchase the product or not purchase anything). This means that consumer choices for which product to adopt are determined by the relative price and value of either product. Network effects provide an interesting complication to these models, where the value of a product increases with the size of the user base. Therefore, the price (response) functions in these models contain a tradeoff between the price charged and profitability (lower prices attract more users, but at a lower price). Contrary to the (more conventional) logic of the monopolist case which states that stronger network effects allow firms to simultaneously charge higher prices while attracting more consumers, the reality that these models highlight is that if firms charge higher prices, they will end up attracting fewer consumers to their products. This is part of the logic behind canonical models of competition under network effects (Katz & Shapiro, 1986), which show that it is optimal for firms to set low prices in the first period such that all consumers will adopt their products, so they may charge higher prices in subsequent periods. Otherwise, it would prove difficult to charge high prices and generate higher revenues under network effects. These studies consider tiered prices strategies, where firms can offer both a low-price/low-quality product and a high-price/high-quality product, but the utility of consumers would be derived from adopting either product (Zhang, Nan, Li and Tang, 2016; Etzion and Pang, 2014; Pang and Etzion, 2012). These papers do not explicitly consider free products, as that fixing prices to zero makes it difficult to solve a competition-on-a-line model. However, they convey the intuition behind freemium products. Namely, by offering a lower-priced version, firms can offset their competitors and increase their user base. At the same time, by offering a higher-priced version, they can extract higher revenues from those consumers that want to use premium features. These models play an important role in highlighting both the benefits of two-tiered or freemium strategies and also the importance of jointly considering freemium strategies, network effects and competitive interactions.

Shi, Zhang and Srinivasan (2019) focus explicitly on the case of freemium and highlight that even with strong network effects freemium is rarely optimal in a competitive setting. Instead, it may only be optimal in settings where a firm dominates the market, such that competitive pressures do not influence the product characteristics or the ability to set prices. Another important feature of this study is that it considers the optimal product quality regarding freemium. A second paper that studies this largely unexplored question is Li, Jain and Kannan (2019), which considers how product quality influences the degree to which freemium, in the form of free trial strategies, may be optimal. These results highlight how for higher-quality products, freemium strategies may be beneficial. However, for lower-quality products, offering free versions leads to cannibalization, which is difficult to offset with paid consumers.

**Summary of theoretical literature**
We began with the theoretical literature because it highlights the mechanisms and interactions between the decisions of firms and consumers. The key insight here is that freemium strategies are a useful way for companies to increase their user base but at a cost of cannibalizing their would-be paying customers. Therefore, in order for this to be a viable strategy (i.e., allow firms to generate higher revenues than not offering a free version), there needs to be some benefit from having a large user base. This can be through network effects increasing the utility of the products, word-of-mouth diffusion creating greater awareness or social features expanding the benefit of the network. Therefore, these aspects of product design have to be considered alongside the pricing strategy in order to successfully implement a freemium strategy. These studies reviewed in this section are summarized in Table 6.1.

*Table 6.1      Summary of freemium product strategies*

| Paper | Context | Type of study |
| --- | --- | --- |
| Shapiro & Varian (1998) | Theoretical foundation for selling information goods, including versioning as an effective way to design information products. | Theoretical |
| Cheng & Liu (2012) | Consider optimal conditions to offer a time-trial freemium strategy, to decrease product uncertainty. | Theoretical |
| Niculescu & Wu (2014) | Consider optimal conditions to offer a feature-limited version in comparison to seeding (offering the premium version for free to a sample of consumers). | Theoretical |
| Cheng, Li & Liu (2015) | Consider optimal conditions for feature-limited versus time-trial strategies. | Theoretical |
| Appel, Libai, Muller & Shachar (2020) | Consider differences between advertising-based versus freemium strategies. | Theoretical |
| Zhang, Nan, Li & Tan (2016); Etzion & Pang (2014); Pang & Etzion (2012) | Consider firms offering a product along with a complementary service. Consider the case of two competing firms offering both product and a service, versus just a product. Analogous to a firm offering a higher- and lower-quality product. | Theoretical |
| Shi, Zhang & Srinivasan (2019) | Consider freemium strategies explicitly with the additional caveat of an asymmetry between a market leader and follower. | Theoretical |
| Li, Jain & Kannan (2019) | Consider optimal designs of free sampling strategies, which are a variant of freemium strategies. | Theoretical |

## 3.2      Empirical Evidence for Freemium Strategies

Unlike the theoretical papers which consider both the consumer adoption decisions and the firm product design/pricing decisions, empirical studies generally focus on either the side of consumers (why consumers adopt a particular freemium product) or firms (what happens when firms offer a freemium product). Therefore, below we review these studies and summarize the main insights.

### Empirical studies of consumer adoption of freemium products

The theoretical literature on freemium strategies makes explicit assumptions about the ability of consumers to rationally observe and evaluate different alternatives. However, consumers often do not behave in such an idealized way, and the empirical studies of freemium strategies that have looked at consumers have primarily tried to understand the way in which consumers "perceive" these free offerings.

Rietveld (2018) studies how the use of freemium strategies is associated with consumer value, both using empirical evidence on video game sales and a randomized control trial that simulates the consumer purchase decision. The underlying theoretical arguments are that when firms freely reveal their products, it helps the consumers understand the value of these products. However, consumers incorrectly value these products and undervalue them when a free component is available, explained by prospect theory's "sunk cost" effect. There is a broader literature in marketing and psychology related to this phenomenon of how consumers perceive the value of free or promotional products (Shampanier, Mazar & Ariely, 2007; Raghubir, 2004). Niemand, Mai and Kraus (2019) consider competing consumer mentalities: one which argues that software and related products should intuitively be free, and another which argues that free products are inherently lower-quality and high-quality products should cost something. They provide evidence for both of these behaviors in consumers and highlight that individuals likely have different latent intuitions and therefore will perceive free products differently. Mäntymäki, Islam and Benbasat (2020) study the motivations of users to upgrade or retain their subscriptions, and find that upgrading and retention decisions are driven by different mechanisms. Upgrading to premium is often driven by the perception of value and price, as has been identified by other studies, while retention decisions are often driven by factors such as the availability of new content.

Fang, Zheng, Ye and Goes (2019) study the impact of social connections within freemium products and find evidence that greater social connections to other members of a community enhance the likelihood that individuals will pay for premium features. Relatedly, Gu, Bapna, Chan and Gupta (2021) find that introducing crowdsourced product features is associated with great product retention and user engagement, which further suggests that social (between-user) relationships may be a critical aspect of the consumer decision to upgrade to premium features.

The key insight from these studies is that in fact the consumer decision to adopt freemium products is based on a more complex set of behavioral factors that relate to how consumers perceive the value of products, given zero price. Therefore, the reality of understanding freemium choices potentially goes beyond any single mechanism. Additionally, different ways of implementing freemium strategies (e.g., time trial, feature-limited, social-interaction-limited) might emphasize different mechanisms relating to how consumers perceive the value of their products. For instance, for products that lend themselves naturally to community interactions, offering crowdsourced or social content may prove critical. Otherwise, for products that generate network effects based on interoperability but not social interaction per se, social features may not be as important.

### Empirical studies of firm use of freemium strategies

The other set of empirical papers that consider freemium strategies do not look at the decisions of consumers or how they might perceive freemium products. Instead, they try to study how the use of freemium products is associated with firm performance or product sales.

Rietveld (2018) paired a laboratory study of consumers' choices (discussed above) with observational data from the Steam marketplace for video games, which showed that titles that were sold through freemium strategies were associated with lower revenues despite being more widely used. This was consistent with the laboratory study, but also provided evidence consistent with the assertion of the theoretical literature that freemium strategies are often associated with greater use but lower revenues. Liu, Au and Choi (2014) find a similar pattern in studying mobile apps available on the Google Play (Android) store. Namely they find that offering a free trial of a high-quality version is associated with greater sales, suggesting that freemium products which allowed consumers to evaluate the high quality of the product led to greater sales and conversions from a free trial to a high-quality version. However, they did not find that high free download rankings were associated with greater sales, which indicates that simply having a large user base was not associated with higher revenues for freemium products. Lee, Zhang and Wedel (2021) study whether choosing to launch free, paid or both versions impacts the performance of mobile apps, based on a dataset of the 584 top-downloaded Android apps, and find that leading with the paid version is the most common launch strategy among this sample of successful titles. Runge, Wagner, Claussen and Klapper (2016) perform a large-scale field experiment on 300,000 users varying the types of freemium products provided and find that offering more features for free is associated with lower conversion but higher usage. Rietveld and Ploog (2021) study how the size of the network shapes whether freemium strategies will be successful, showing that freemium strategies may only be appropriate for markets with large networks (potential user base). These papers all point to the fact that freemium strategies are not associated with higher revenues overall, and suggest that freemium strategies may only be appropriate in certain situations.

Variants of freemium strategies have also been used to sell other forms of digital goods, other than software. Li, Jain and Kannan (2019) study the use of freemium strategies by booksellers who provide free trials for their products, and find that offering a free book with the opportunity to purchase a paperback version can lead to higher sales. However, they also find that this depends on the nature of the free products. If a high-quality free version is offered, then the sales of the paid version may be cannibalized, but this is greater for lower-quality titles. Lambrecht and Misra (2017) consider the timing of when firms may want to offer free products, and find that firms may benefit by offering free versions of their products, but in periods when demand is naturally high. The example they provide is sharing a sports newspaper for free during the season, when low-value (casual) fans are engaged, but charging during the off-season because this is the period when only high-value (hardcore) fans are engaged.

There has been related work also looking at the impact of free products on the domain of entertainment (music, movies and television). One aspect of these studies is that the free version was often not made deliberately available by the content creator. Instead, through piracy or other means, free versions of content have become available, and studies have attempted to understand the impact of these products on overall consumption and sales. Zhang (2018) studies the impact of relaxing DRM (digital rights management) measures around music that prevent sharing, and find that this is associated with 10 percent greater consumption, but particularly for the long tail (less popular albums). Similar patterns were supported by Peukert, Claussen and Kretschmer (2017), who find that the shutting down of a popular source of pirated movies decreased box-office revenues, which they attribute to the information diffusion effect that these free products provide. Similarly, Kretschmer and Peukert (2020) find that the shutting down of a service that provided free online music videos (similar to YouTube) reduced overall music record sales. However, these effects predominantly benefited more popular artists. Aguiar (2017) studies the introduction of a free use cap by the music streaming service Deezer and finds that this was associated with a decline in access to both lawful and unlawful alternative sources of music, suggesting that the free service helped to increase demand for these products. There are studies that have shown that the existence of these free products might in fact diminish the consumption of the premium products (Ma, Montgomery, Singh & Smith, 2014; Rob & Waldfogel, 2006, 2007).

A related instance can be the introduction of paywalls. Paywalls were introduced by many newspapers, which sought to move from an ad-based strategy where they provided free access to their newspaper articles to a subscription-based model where consumers would have to subscribe in order to read the articles. Several studies have exploited the introduction of a paywall by the *New York Times* (NYT) in order to evaluate whether restricting free content (the opposite of freemium) impacts consumption. Oh, Animesh and Pinsonneault (2016) study the rollout of the NYT paywall and find that this led to lower demand for online articles (less readership) and also weakened social conversations about these articles. However, much like the studies of piracy, they also document that this does not affect all products equally and that for niche (long-tail) products the impact of the paywall is greater. Pattabhiramaiah, Sriram and Manchanda (2019) look at the same rollout, and document the same decline in online readership, but additionally focus on positive spillover effects on the print subscription, which rises as a consequence of this paywall. Aral and Dhillon (2021) study the same setting but use a quasi-experiment that altered the paywall design. They similarly find that the introduction of a paywall reduced demand for online content but led to an increase in online subscriptions. Their calculations regarding the economic significance of these countervailing effects suggested that the newspaper was able to generate higher revenues once the paywall was introduced, despite lower traffic. These results provide further empirical evidence of how the availability of a free version reduces the overall demand for a particular product.

The main conclusion from reviewing these studies is that the impact of freemium strategies on performance is contingent on a variety of factors specific to that particular empirical context, such as the relative quality of the premium and free version (Li, Jain & Kannan, 2019; Liu, Au & Choi, 2014), the timing of when free versions might be offered (Lambrecht & Misra, 2017) or the nature of competition in the marketplace (Boudreau, Jeppesen & Miric, 2021). Additionally, the literature looking at piracy or paywall implementations indicates that free versus paid models might affect the consumption of mainstream versus long-tail products differently. Finally, these results may differ based on the types of products. Markets for software, books, newspapers, music and movies may respond differently to freemium strategies because of the inherent nature of the products. Therefore, it is helpful to have broad evidence on the impact of when freemium strategies are best used from a variety of settings.

### 3.3　Conclusions from Freemium Literature

The literature on freemium strategies straddles different academic disciplines, studies different implementations (types) of freemium strategies, and is often focused on a specific mechanism (e.g., network effects) or on providing evidence from a specific setting (e.g., mobile apps). This is understandable as it is challenging to integrate all of these complex issues within a single model, paper or dataset. Theory papers have often focused on explaining how a single mechanism (or channel) might jointly influence consumer adoption decisions and firm strategies. These studies highlight "when" freemium strategies might be most appropriate. Empirical papers fall into one of two categories. The first looks at how consumers evaluate freemium versus conventional offerings. The second looks at the impact of freemium strategies on either product demand or firm revenues. Understanding that each of these groups of studies has its own goal is in itself an important realization. Freemium (products, strategies, offers, etc.) is a broad label that applies to a variety of different approaches that may be effective under different conditions and affect consumption decisions differently. No single study applies to all implementations of freemium or has insights that may generalize to all potential contexts. This highlights the importance of having so many different studies that document and explore freemium in different settings, and the need for future work to further expand on these issues. In Table 6.2, we summarize the empirical papers studying freemium discussed above.

The main conclusion from the theoretical literature is that freemium is a strategy where firms are inherently cannibalizing their own revenue streams by offering a free product and should only do so in cases where this brings a clear benefit. The main conclusion from the empirical literature looking at the impact of using freemium strategies on product sales or firm revenues is that they are often associated with worse outcomes. This highlights that freemium strategies may be profitable, but only in a small set of cases. It certainly suggests that freemium should not be "the rule" but rather "the exception" when it comes to selling digital products.

*Table 6.2*     Summary of freemium product strategies

| Paper | Context | Type of study |
|---|---|---|
| Rietveld (2018) | Empirical evidence from freemium product offerings in the Steam marketplace, combined with a randomized control trial of consumer evaluations of freemium products. | Experimental and observational data |
| Niemand, Mai & Kraus (2019) | Study why freemium strategies are often ineffective by evaluating the perceptions of individuals to freemium product offerings. | Experimental |
| Mäntymäki, Islam & Benbasat (2020) | Evaluate how individuals value different aspects of software products and what impacts their decision to upgrade to premium features. | Observational data |
| Fang, Zheng, Ye & Goes (2019) | Study the impact of social interactions within a freemium mobile game, on the ability to convert users from free to premium features. | Observational data |
| Liu, Au & Choi (2014) | Analyze the association between using freemium strategies and product sales. | Observational data |
| Lee, Zhang & Wedel (2021) | Study the most common product strategies among the subset of top-downloaded titles. | Observational data |
| Runge, Wagner, Claussen & Klapper (2016) | Analyze the impact of freemium design by varying the way freemium strategies are designed in a large field experiment. | Experimental |
| Li, Jain & Kannan (2019) | Study free trials within publishing, finding conditions where offering a free version can be optimal. | Experimental |
| Lambrecht & Misra (2017) | Consider that firms may temporarily offer free content as a way of expanding demand for their products. | Observational data |
| Tidhar & Eisenhardt (2020) | Study the relationship between pricing strategy and organizational design, highlighting the conditions under which freemium strategies may be viable. | Observational data |
| Rietveld & Ploog (2021) | Study the effectiveness of freemium products in relation to market size, showing the limitation of freemium strategies in certain markets. | Observational data |
| Boudreau, Jeppesen & Miric (2021) | Study the impact of network effects and market position when using freemium strategies in comparison to paid-only strategies. | Observational data |

The empirical literature looking at consumer perceptions of freemium products highlights the additional complexity that arises from how consumers evaluate and perceive products that are available for free. This highlights the behavioral features which characterize "zero as a special price" (Shampanier, Mazar & Ariely, 2007) and why freemium strategies are more complex than tiered product strategies which bring with them their own challenges.

While this literature provides a number of important insights, it also raises a variety of questions: If, in fact, freemium strategies are only appropriate for certain situations, why are freemium products so common? How can we explain the examples of so many prominent companies that use freemium strategies (Spotify, Skype, Fortnite, Dropbox, etc.)? Additionally, does freemium require any organizational design choices or specific capabilities to go along with these pricing and product design decisions? We discuss these potential future strategies and questions below.

# 4.   POTENTIAL DIRECTIONS FOR FUTURE WORK INTO FREEMIUM STRATEGIES

While much is known and understood about freemium strategies, many avenues for research remain. Below, we highlight some areas where existing studies have begun to uncover important questions for freemium strategies. Yet, more work is needed to truly understand these issues.

## 4.1   How Market Position Impacts Whether Freemium Is a Viable Strategy

When academic papers (and specifically modeling papers) study the use of freemium strategies, particularly in relation to network effects, they do either for a monopolist firm, or for a symmetric duopoly (two firms with similar products). While this framework has led to a number of important insights, one aspect which it ignores is that realistically in a market some firms will be leaders (with the largest revenues or market share), and others followers (with a relatively lower share of sales and revenues). This is important for two reasons. First, firms with larger versus smaller installed bases may find it helpful to switch to freemium strategies at different points. Second, network effects amplify the advantage of the leader, while harming the followers.

There are very few studies that have considered the market position of firms in relation to freemium strategies. Shi, Zhang and Srinivasan (2019) show analytically how using freemium strategies may only be beneficial in cases where a market leader is dominant, and not beneficial for firms that are not market leaders (including followers). Boudreau, Jeppesen and Miric (2021) exploit a policy change that strengthened network effects, and observe how that impacted market leaders versus followers that used freemium. They find that network effects increased the advantage of leaders over followers, especially in settings where freemium strategies were used. Both studies point to the fact that freemium strategies will benefit leaders, while almost always harming followers (in comparison to the revenues they might have had in the absence of freemium strategies). Additionally, they point to the fact that freemium strategies might benefit leaders in their ability to gain an advantage over followers, but might not lead to higher revenues, consistent with what the broader empirical literature has shown.

The underlying reason behind this is that stronger network effects tie the success of firms to the size of their user base. This creates an incentive to lower prices in order to attract as many consumers as possible. However, unless one firm dominates all others (as is, in fact, the case in canonical models of competition under network effects – Katz & Shapiro, 1986), then the firm cannot raise prices and therefore might experience lower revenues even with a larger user base. Freemium strategies help to offset this, by allowing a firm to offer multiple versions. The free version can expand the user base, while the premium version can capitalize on the customers that are willing to pay for premium features. However, in that case, as well, the free version cannibalizes potential customers of the premium version, reducing would-be revenues, even despite a large market share.

This directly shapes the two issues described above in relation to freemium strategies. First, network effects amplify the advantage of the leader, and diminish those of the follower. Therefore, freemium strategies will allow market leaders to gain greater market share, and potentially greater revenues (in some cases). However, freemium strategies will diminish both the revenues and the market share of followers. Second, it raises the question of when do firms choose freemium strategies? For market leaders, an install-base advantage, as well as network effects, might be sufficient incentive to switch to freemium strategies. This might be especially attractive if a market leader believes that it can gain a sufficient market share that it can dominate in future periods. However, if competitors are attempting to challenge such a market leader, they also have an incentive to begin using freemium strategies. That is because for followers, offering a free version ensures that they can compete against the free version of the market leader. However, in general, the follower will be coerced into this strategy by a market leader, and may not find freemium strategies viable otherwise.

Therefore, it is important to realize that this use of freemium strategies can result from short-sightedness, whereby using a freemium strategy might be beneficial in the short term before competitors also switch to freemium. However, once an equilibrium occurs where all firms use freemium strategies, the payoffs for even leading firms may be lower than they were without freemium strategies. This pattern, which we jokingly call the "freemium death spiral," is an important pattern that may emerge where freemium strategies are used. Namely, firms may begin to switch to freemium strategies and strengthen network effects around their products to dominate all other competitors. However, if they do not manage to exclude other competitors from the market, and those firms shift to freemium strategies, then an equilibrium can emerge where all firms observe lower revenues than what would otherwise occur.

These patterns might explain what we observe in many markets where freemium strategies are used. For example, mobile app markets are populated by large numbers of freemium products, but all but a few large firms are able to be profitable and successful in this space. Dropbox, a leader in the cloud storage space and known for its freemium model, only became profitable in 2020 during the pandemic when demand for premium cloud products increased, and struggled to be profitable before, even when it commanded a considerable share of customers. Spotify struggled to be profitable with its freemium model, despite its virtual dominance of the streaming market.[1]

## 4.2    Designing an Organization around Freemium Product Strategies

A key aspect of strategy is the concept of "fit" between various firm activities (Siggelkow, 2011; Milgrom & Roberts, 1995). It is intuitive to characterize freemium strategies as a product/pricing decision. However, these decisions bring with them a variety of other choices that firms make to ensure that the surrounding organization fits with this pricing/product strategy. In their study of mobile app developers, Tidhar and Eisenhardt (2020) explore the importance of the fit between revenue models (including freemium) and other organizational decisions, highlighting how misalignment can be associated with worse performance. An illustration of this fact can be seen from the evolution of video game companies. The traditional model of video game development (from the industry launch until approximately 2010) was that game developers would create a new title, employing game designers, producers, artists, programmers and audio engineers to create a self-contained product (game). That product would then be put on sale either through physical means such as CDs or disks, or through a digital download. The product would not be updated or enhanced, with the exception of bug fixes or security updates. If the game developer wanted to offer new features, they would have to create an extension that would then be sold to owners of the original titles. Since approximately 2010, free-to-play games have emerged as a highly lucrative method of producing and marketing games. Examples include well-known titles such as *Fortnite*, *League of Legends*,

*World of Warcraft* and *Clash of Clans*. These products are not a fully contained release but instead are continuously updated with new features, characters, levels and extensions. This requires a team of developers that constantly creates new in-game content, sets prices and optimizes new product offers (e.g., clothing and outfits that players can buy in *League of Legends*). In addition, it requires a marketing team that continuously attracts new players, at a per-player cost, and an operational team to manage churn (loss of customers). Therefore, using these free-to-play strategies (a variant of freemium) implies a shift in terms of the organizational design, the structure of marginal and fixed costs, and the importance of marketing, continuously attracting users and managing churn. These costs may be considerable and are drastically different from those of the conventional model, where virtually all the development and marketing costs were incurred upfront. While the above examples are anecdotal, more exploration is needed to understand the full gamut of organizational decisions that have to be taken into account when freemium strategies are being used.

## 4.3    Supporting a Large Number of Non-Paying Customers

A key element of product design and pricing decisions is that certain customers have a higher value (or willingness to pay) than others. As a result, it may be more profitable to set higher prices in order to sell to a smaller number of customers. Conversely, freemium strategies are based on offering a version for zero price and so they imply having a larger number of customers, where most of the customers may be of low value (lower willingness to pay). While having a large number of "low value" customers may be helpful in increasing demand for the platform and allowing the firm to charge the "high value" customers, these low-value customers may bring with them some often unseen costs and unintended consequences.

First, freemium strategies imply a marginal cost that is not present with other types of sales strategies. For instance, freemium games require considerable effort on the part of game developers to provide server-based functionality and new features, updates and experiences. For example, freemium cloud storage providers (e.g., Google Drive, Dropbox) have to incur the storage costs of a large number of free-tier customers. Music streaming services such as Spotify have to incur costs each time a free customer plays a song (both royalties and infrastructure costs).

Second, freemium strategies imply that the majority of customers would not be "high value." Instead, a firm offering a freemium strategy would have to acquire a large number of "low value" customers to be able to capture a few "high value" customers. This implies that customer acquisition (marketing) costs for products with freemium strategies may be deceptively large (on average high cost to acquire on average low-value customers). While this is implied by some of the competition-on-a-line (Zhang et al., 2016; Pang & Etzion, 2012) models that consider multi-tiered strategies, it is often not translated into the verbal theory and more casual understanding of freemium strategies. As a result, freemium often has unseen costs that may need to be considered.

## 4.4    The Myth vs Reality of Freemium Strategies

Freemium strategies are often discussed with respect to a few highly successful examples. Products such as Google Drive, Spotify, *Fortnite*, etc., are often discussed as successes of freemium strategies. However, as the academic literature suggests, freemium strategies are only profitable in certain cases. In addition, a closer look at some of these cases suggests that they may not always be profitable. Spotify, Dropbox and other titles may enjoy huge user bases but have struggled to generate a profit. Video game titles such as *Fortnite* and *League of Legends* are examples of highly successful free-to-play (a variant of freemium) products. However, there are countless mobile apps using freemium strategies that struggle to make a profit. Therefore, this raises the question of whether freemium is, in turn, a viable strategy for all firms, and if not, then in which cases might freemium actually be viable? What has made some companies successful using freemium, where most firms seemingly fail? This is particularly relevant for entrepreneurial strategy, as we might wonder whether start-ups attempting to emulate the success of a few exemplarily freemium products and use freemium strategies are setting themselves up to fail.

## 5.    CONCLUSION AND SUMMARY

Freemium is an important strategy for selling digital products that is only likely to become more common in the future. This strategy is often discussed as a cunning way to both have a large number of users and charge high prices for premium products, especially in digital industries where network effects, compatibility, social interactions (word-of-mouth) and other characteristics create a tension between having a large number of users and profitability. In this chapter, we have attempted to provide a detailed review of the literature on freemium strategies and to highlight the conclusions from this literature, as well as the potential avenues for future work.

What is clear from our review is that the literature on freemium strategies is dispersed. Different studies consider different mechanisms, contexts and implementations of freemium strategies, making it challenging to form a unified theory of how freemium strategies work. However, this is not a problem. Each work that looks at a unique implementation of freemium strategies provides important theoretical and empirical evidence for how these strategies may be effective in these settings. It is helpful to understand what similarities and differences exist across software, music, movies, books and newspapers with regard to freemium services. One potential avenue for future research may be to distinguish the mechanisms that are present in different settings.

Additionally, there remain aspects of freemium studies that are understudied. We have highlighted some that have emerged from looking at the literature. However, there are potentially many other factors that can inform our understanding of what makes freemium strategies viable, and when they should be used.

In summary, freemium strategies are an important and common way of commercializing digital products. While much is understood about these strategies, a lot remains that has yet to be studied and there is an opportunity for future research to explore and disentangle these issues.

## NOTE

1.   https://www.bloomberg.com/news/articles/2020-05-07/dropbox-posts-first-net-income-on-rising -cloud-software-demand#xj4y7vzkg.

# REFERENCES

Aguiar, L. (2017). Let the music play? Free streaming and its effects on digital music consumption. *Information Economics and Policy*, *41*(December), 1–14.

Appel, G., Libai, B., Muller, E., & Shachar, R. (2020). On the monetization of mobile apps. *International Journal of Research in Marketing*, *37*(1), 93–107.

Aral, S., & Dhillon, P.S. (2021). Digital paywall design: Implications for content demand and subscriptions. *Management Science*, *67*(4), 2381–2402.

Bhargava, H.K., & Choudhary, V. (2004). Economics of an information intermediary with aggregation benefits. *Information Systems Research*, *15*(1), 22–36.

Boudreau, K., Jeppesen, L.B., & Miric, M. (2021). Competing on freemium: Digital competition with network effects. *Strategic Management Journal*, *43*(7), 1374–1401.

Cheng, H.K., Li, S., & Liu, Y. (2015). Optimal software free trial strategy: Limited version, time-locked, or hybrid? *Production and Operations Management*, *24*(3), 504–17.

Cheng, H.K., & Liu, Y. (2012). Optimal software free trial strategy: The impact of network externalities and consumer uncertainty. *Information Systems Research*, *23*(2), 488–504.

Deneckere, R.J., & McAfee, R.P. (1996). Damaged goods. *Journal of Economics & Management Strategy*, *5*(2), 149–74.

Dou, Y., Niculescu, M.F., & Wu, D.J. (2013). Engineering optimal network effects via social media features and seeding in markets for digital goods and services. *Information Systems Research*, *24*(1), 164–85.

Etzion, H., & Pang, M.S. (2014). Complementary online services in competitive markets: Maintaining profitability in the presence of network effects. *MIS Quarterly*, *38*(1), 231–48.

Fang, B., Zheng, Z., Ye, Q., & Goes, P.B. (2019). Social influence and monetization of freemium social games. *Journal of Management Information Systems*, *36*(3), 730–54.

Gu, Z., Bapna, R., Chan, J., & Gupta, A. (2021). Measuring the impact of crowdsourcing features on mobile app user engagement and retention: A randomized field experiment. *Management Science*, *63*(2), 1297–1329.

Hui, K.L., & Chau, P.Y. (2002). Classifying digital products. *Communications of the ACM*, *45*(6), 73–9.

Katz, M.L., & Shapiro, C. (1986). Technology adoption in the presence of network externalities. *Journal of Political Economy*, *94*(4), 822–41.

Kretschmer, T., & Peukert, C. (2020). Video killed the radio star? Online music videos and recorded music sales. *Information Systems Research*, *31*(3), 776–800.

Krishnan, V., & Gupta, S. (2001). Appropriateness and impact of platform-based product development. *Management Science*, *47*(1), 52–68.

Lambrecht, A., & Misra, K. (2017). Fee or free: When should firms charge for online content? *Management Science*, *63*(4), 1150–65.

Lee, S., Zhang, J., & Wedel, M. (2021). Managing the versioning decision over an app's lifetime. *Journal of Marketing*, *85*(6), 44–62.

Li, H., Jain, S., & Kannan, P.K. (2019). Optimal design of free samples for digital products and services. *Journal of Marketing Research*, *56*(3), 419–38.

Liu, C.Z., Au, Y.A., & Choi, H.S. (2014). Effects of freemium strategy in the mobile app market: An empirical study of google play. *Journal of Management Information Systems*, *31*(3), 326–54.

Ma, L., Montgomery, A.L., Singh, P.V., & Smith, M.D. (2014). An empirical analysis of the impact of pre-release movie piracy on box office revenue. *Information Systems Research*, *25*(3), 590–603.

Mäntymäki, M., Islam, A.N., & Benbasat, I. (2020). What drives subscribing to premium in freemium services? A consumer value-based view of differences between upgrading to and staying with premium. *Information Systems Journal*, *30*(2), 295–333.

Milgrom, P., & Roberts, J. (1995). Complementarities and fit strategy, structure, and organizational change in manufacturing. *Journal of Accounting and Economics*, *19*(2-3), 179–208.

Moorthy, K.S., & Png, I.P. (1992). Market segmentation, cannibalization, and the timing of product introductions. *Management Science*, *38*(3), 345–59.

Mussa, M., & Rosen, S. (1978). Monopoly and product quality. *Journal of Economic Theory*, *18*(2), 301–17.

Niculescu, M.F., & Wu, D.J. (2014). Economics of free under perpetual licensing: Implications for the software industry. *Information Systems Research, 25*(1), 173–99.

Niemand, T., Mai, R., & Kraus, S. (2019). The zero-price effect in freemium business models: The moderating effects of free mentality and price–quality inference. *Psychology & Marketing, 36*(8), 773–90.

Oh, H., Animesh, A., & Pinsonneault, A. (2016). Free versus for-a-fee: The impact of a paywall. *MIS Quarterly, 40*(1), 31–56.

Pang, M.S., & Etzion, H. (2012). Research note: Analyzing pricing strategies for online services with network effects. *Information Systems Research, 23*(4), 1364–77.

Pattabhiramaiah, A., Sriram, S., & Manchanda, P. (2019). Paywalls: Monetizing online content. *Journal of Marketing, 83*(2), 19–36.

Peukert, C., Claussen, J., & Kretschmer, T. (2017). Piracy and box office movie revenues: Evidence from Megaupload. *International Journal of Industrial Organization, 52*, 188–215.

Raghubir, P. (2004). Free gift with purchase: promoting or discounting the brand? *Journal of Consumer Psychology, 14*(1–2), 181–6.

Rietveld, J. (2018). Creating and capturing value from freemium business models: A demand-side perspective. *Strategic Entrepreneurship Journal, 12*(2), 171–93.

Rietveld, J., & Ploog, J.N. (2021). On top of the game? The double-edged sword of incorporating social features into freemium products. *Strategic Management Journal, 43*(6), 1182–1207.

Rob, R., & Waldfogel, J. (2006). Piracy on the high C's: Music downloading, sales displacement, and social welfare in a sample of college students. *Journal of Law and Economics, 49*(1), 29–62.

Rob, R., & Waldfogel, J. (2007). Piracy on the silver screen. *Journal of Industrial Economics, 55*(3), 379–95.

Runge, J., Wagner, S., Claussen, J., & Klapper, D. (2016). Freemium pricing: Evidence from a large-scale field experiment. *Humboldt University Berlin, School of Business and Economics, Institute of Marketing Working Paper.*

Shampanier, K., Mazar, N., & Ariely, D. (2007). Zero as a special price: The true value of free products. *Marketing Science, 26*(6), 742–57.

Shapiro, C., & Varian, H.R. (1998). Versioning: the smart way to sell information. *Harvard Business Review, 107*(6), 107.

Shi, Z., Zhang, K., & Srinivasan, K. (2019) Freemium as an optimal strategy for market dominant firms. *Marketing Science, 38*(1), 150–69.

Siggelkow, N. (2011). Firms as systems of interdependent choices. *Journal of Management Studies, 48*(5), 1126–40.

Tidhar, R., & Eisenhardt, K.M. (2020). Get rich or die trying … finding revenue model fit using machine learning and multiple cases. *Strategic Management Journal, 41*(7), 1245–73.

Zhang, L. (2018). Intellectual property strategy and the long tail: Evidence from the recorded music industry. *Management Science, 64*(1), 24–42.

Zhang, Z., Nan, G., Li, M., & Tan, Y. (2016). Duopoly pricing strategy for information products with premium service: Free product or bundling? *Journal of Management Information Systems, 33*(1), 260–95.

# PART II

# DIGITAL STRATEGY AS OPEN SYSTEMS DESIGN

# 7. Platform scope and value creation in digital platforms

*Ramya K. Murthy and Anoop Madhok*

## INTRODUCTION

In recent years, digital technologies have rapidly proliferated, bringing fundamental changes to how firms create and capture value, collaborate, and compete. Digital artifacts built using such technologies are generative as they continuously evolve through reuse, extension, and modification by multiple actors simultaneously with minimal coordination (Cennamo & Santaló, 2019; Zittrain, 2005). Often, at the core of such value co-creation are digital platform-based ecosystems (hereafter referred to as platform ecosystems or ecosystems) that simultaneously serve both as a central digital infrastructure to support co-creation as well as an organizational form to govern the actors involved (Jacobides et al., 2018; McIntyre et al., 2020; McIntyre & Srinivasan, 2017). Consequently, managing value co-creation in digital platform ecosystems is a vital facet of firm strategy in the digital era (Adner et al., 2019).

Digital platform ecosystems comprise a group of autonomous actors, called complementors, organized around the central digital platform infrastructure to co-create value with the platform sponsor (Chen et al., 2021; Kretschmer et al., 2020; McIntyre & Srinivasan, 2017). The digital platform sponsor faces two types of uncertainties (Tajedin et al., 2019) in co-creating value: First, being attracted rather than selected to participate in the ecosystem, the complementors are often *ex ante* unknown to the platform sponsor; and second, the complements developed by the complementors are also *ex ante* unknown. These two uncertainties have implications for value co-creation in the ecosystem as they shape the platform infrastructure design and ecosystem governance, modalities to secure commitment and cooperation of complementors for value co-creation, as well as the value proposition and identity of the digital platform ecosystem itself.

In this chapter, we aim to understand how the platform sponsor's choices of "platform scope" help manage the uncertainties of *ex ante* unknown complementors and complements and shape value co-creation in the platform ecosystem. The scope of the platform is a crucial tool to manage the two types of uncertainties as it signals value co-creation opportunities (Chen et al., 2021; Murthy & Madhok, 2021), defines complementors' access to shared resources for co-creation (Boudreau, 2010, 2017), shapes the platform sponsor's latitude to govern the ecosystem (Boudreau, 2017; McIntyre et al., 2020), and defines the market identity of the platform ecosystem (Cennamo, 2021). The value co-creation process begins with the platform sponsor, as the initiator of the ecosystem, choosing the product and market space in which to compete as well as choosing which parts of the value creation process to perform while opening the rest to the complementors. In essence, such a choice represents the platform scope, this being a key element of digital strategy as it plays a vital role in attracting and fostering external actors' participation and governing value co-creation within the ecosystem.

Platform scope constitutes technology, governance, and competition elements. Across the three streams of platform literature – technology management, economics, and strategy – we find three distinct conceptualizations of the scope of the platform: platform technology scope, platform sponsor scope, and platform market scope. The platform technology scope defines the platform components available to complementors. The technology boundaries enable and at the same time limit the complementors' innovation (Boudreau, 2012; Boudreau & Jeppesen, 2015; Boudreau & Lakhani, 2015). In contrast, the platform sponsor scope constitutes the choice of activities to be performed by the platform sponsor vis-à-vis the complementors, the assets owned, and the actors' extent of control (Boudreau, 2017; Gawer, 2020). Finally, platform market scope is the choice of products and markets that the platform ecosystem serves through its offerings (Cennamo, 2021). Whereas platform technology scope and platform sponsor scope relate to the internal scope choice of the actors' boundaries within the ecosystem, the platform market scope refers to the external scope choice of products and markets in which the firm chooses to compete. The choice of scope has key implications for value creation in ecosystems and the digital strategy of the actors. For instance, a choice of the platform sponsor to retain a broad scope would potentially make the technological interfaces less open, thereby allowing better control over critical assets and, therefore, more levers for platform governance (for example, a broad-scope Apple ecosystem as compared to a narrow-scope Android ecosystem of smartphones). However, such a choice of broad scope would mean that consumer utility would depend more on benefits accrued from the platform sponsor offerings.

This chapter contributes to the digital strategy, platforms, and firm scope literature. Our overview summarizes the current state of research on the topic of platform scope – encompassing technology, sponsor and market scope – and highlights the importance of the scope choice for digital strategy and value creation in platform ecosystems. In identifying the unique challenges of value co-creation in digital platforms, where platform scope is an integral aspect of the digital strategy of firms, we show how and why the platform sponsor's choice of boundaries vis-à-vis co-creating complementors and rivals is a critical strategic choice. Our analysis depicts platform scope as both similar to and yet distinct from extant notions of firm scope. We conclude by highlighting some salient areas to be addressed in future research on platform scope for a better understanding of digital strategy.

## DIGITAL STRATEGY AND VALUE CREATION IN DIGITAL PLATFORM ECOSYSTEMS

### Digitalization and Platform Ecosystems

Digital technologies encompass digitalized resources, assets, and information that together enable building modular digital artifacts which can be recombined into different end-products (Baldwin & Clark, 2000; Lusch & Nambisan, 2015). Digital artifacts are generative (Zittrain, 2005) in that they can be reused, modified, and extended by multiple actors simultaneously with minimal coordination and "continue to evolve in terms of their uses and functionalities depending on how they connect and integrate to other products and services" (Cennamo, 2021, p. 268; Yoo et al., 2010). Digitalization underscores a shift towards the digital representation of information, increased connectivity between multiple actors, and the ability to aggregate disjointed data (Adner et al., 2019). Whereas the generative nature of digital technologies drives innovation in end-products and value propositions, digitalized information and data aggregation enhance ease of increasingly costless connectivity as well as efficient and effective interaction between actors. For example, although generative smartphone operating systems support the development of millions of apps, insights from data aggregation are key to drive adoption as they enable the platform sponsor to connect the right apps with the consumers based on their preferences and usage behavior.

Digitalization has brought transformative processes that have resulted in fundamental shifts in how value is created. In essence, digitalization has enabled a shift in the locus of value creation from the core of the focal firm to co-creation with autonomous external actors. Since digital artifacts are perpetually in the making, the mere possibilities of combinations of the modular technologies make it impossible for a single firm to conceptualize and perform all the variations in-house. Thus, the focal firm seeks to leverage the distributed assets of external actors to perform variations of the underlying modular digital technologies. Often, a central infrastructure in the form of a digital platform, comprising core modules from the focal firm, is vital to foster building variations of the modules or value-enhancing complements. Platform sponsors leverage an ecosystem of autonomous external actors, called complementors, to co-create value without direct hierarchical control (Jacobides et al., 2018). The platform sponsors coordinate and organize the core offerings and complements into coherent value propositions through the digital platforms. Moreover, digital platforms serve as the "data hub channeling and integrating information from or to users and from or to multiple connected products and services" (Cennamo, 2021, p. 268). Hence, digital platforms are increasingly a core part of the digital strategy of the firm.

## Value Creation in Digital Platform Ecosystems

Whereas digital platform ecosystems offer the advantage of value co-creation, they also present two uncertainties for value creation – *ex ante* unknown complementors and *ex ante* unknown complements (Tajedin et al., 2019). Firstly, a digital platform infrastructure supports the independent production of value-enhancing complements through the extension of core modules without impacting the core itself (Cennamo & Santaló, 2019). This results in the development of an ecosystem of complementors and their products around the core platform (Gawer, 2014; McIntyre & Srinivasan, 2017). The complementors are free to produce their own products by leveraging the core platform and its open interfaces (Gawer, 2014; Tiwana et al., 2010). With this arrangement, multiple value propositions are possible (Dattée et al., 2018) when the consumer selects from competing complements and combines them with the platform offerings. However, and crucially, this arrangement implies that the platform sponsor does not know *ex ante which complements* would be produced around the platform. Secondly, the platform sponsor is unaware of the potential complementors for the platform. Modularity and open interfaces to the platform infrastructure mean that the platform modules are available to complementors to the extent that it is made available by the sponsor. Since no explicit agreement is required to begin producing complements, the platform sponsor has little knowledge of *which complementors* might potentially produce the complements. Thus, the platform sponsors face dual uncertainties in value co-creation in the ecosystems owing to *ex ante* unknown complementors producing *ex ante* unknown complements.[1]

The uncertainties of *ex ante* unknown complementors and their complements have multiple implications for value co-creation in the ecosystem. In a nutshell, the two uncertainties bring novel challenges at different stages of the value co-creation process – attracting complementors, co-creating value with them, and governing the ecosystem. First, the platform sponsor's design of the platform infrastructure and governance of the ecosystem should attract the participation of *ex ante* unknown complementors. Thus, the platform design and governance are crucial to value creation by the complementors and value appropriation for all the actors involved. Second, the platform sponsor must secure the commitment and cooperation of *ex ante* unknown complementors for value co-creation without invoking formal customized contracts or hierarchical control. Thereafter, the platform sponsor can govern the value co-creation process with only indirect and informal authority (Chen et al., 2021). Third, the platform sponsor has to manage *ex ante* unknown complements available on the platform for a coherent value proposition as well as nurture the "vigour" as well as identity of the ecosystem on an ongoing basis throughout the ecosystem lifecycle (Adner, 2017; Cennamo, 2021).

The uncertainties of *ex ante* unknown complementors and complements for value co-creation manifest similarly across both innovation and transaction types of platform ecosystems, in that the uncertainty from *ex ante* unknown complementors and the importance of attracting the "right" complementors is crucial for both types of platform ecosystems. The uncertainty from *ex ante* unknown complements is more evident in the innovation ecosystems, yet still important for transaction ecosystems. For instance, the innovation platform sponsor should consider the extent of interface openness to selectively support certain types of complements. Similarly, the transaction platform sponsor should consider platform design choices that support only certain types of transactions. Thus, with appropriate modifications, the arguments we advance apply to both the innovation and transaction platform ecosystems.

As we detail in the following section, platform scope is a crucial tool available to platform sponsors to manage the two uncertainties and enable value co-creation.

## DIGITAL PLATFORM SCOPE

The scope of the firm and its impact on firm performance has long been considered a key issue in strategic management research (Ahuja & Novelli, 2017; Conner, 1991; Rumelt et al., 1991). The choice of firm scope shapes a firm's strategies, the likelihood of survival, performance outcomes, and its competitive environment (Zenger et al., 2011). In digital platform ecosystems, the notion of platform scope has multiple dimensions and key implications for value creation and capture as well as for competition. The three streams of platform literature – technology management, economics, and strategic management perspectives (McIntyre & Srinivasan, 2017) – depict three distinct conceptualizations of platform scope that we term "platform technology scope," "platform sponsor scope," and "platform market scope." As detailed below, although the issue of platform scope has been addressed in each of the streams of the platform literature, their treatment of the topics has largely remained rooted in their respective foci.

### Platform Technology Scope

The technology management stream of the platform literature has focused on the technological and architectural aspects of the platform and their implications for the ecosystem. Broadly, in this stream of literature, "platform technology scope" refers to the platform technology components made available to complementors through the platform sponsor's design choices. Platform technology scope choices shape the complementors' participation decisions (Boudreau, 2012; Boudreau & Jeppesen, 2015; Boudreau & Lakhani, 2015) as well as the ability of the platform sponsor to govern the platform ecosystem for value creation and capture (Gawer, 2014; Tiwana, 2008; Tiwana et al., 2010). The platform technology scope encompasses platform technology design choices such as modularity, interface openness, and software development kits (SDKs).

Platform technology design choices have direct implications for value co-creation in platform ecosystems. The modularity of the platform infrastructure refers to a decoupled architecture of the core platform components to enable independent development of complements that do not interfere with the core or other complements and yet function as a whole (Baldwin & Clark, 2000; Tiwana, 2008). Overall, by sharing the platform resources through SDKs and application programming interfaces (APIs) (Chen et al., 2021), the platform sponsor chooses a more fluid technology boundary with the complementors, and therefore a narrow platform technology scope that promotes innovation in complements. The interfaces to the platform core components may be opened to allow the complementors to access and build complements over the core components. A narrow platform technology scope manifested through a modular platform architecture and more open interfaces improve complementors' innovation (Boudreau, 2010, 2017). In contrast, a narrow platform technology scope defined by a less modular platform architecture and more closed interfaces help the platform sponsor better control and capture value (Chen et al., 2021). However, the closing of the interfaces mean that several complements to the platform would no longer be available.

In a similar vein, platform sponsors offer SDKs to help complementors access the platform technology to design, develop, debug, and publish complements (Chen et al., 2021; Eaton et al., 2015). SDKs are an incentive to attract complementors to the platform ecosystem, though they often result in platform-specific investments that lock in the complementors to the focal ecosystem and reduce the compatibility of the complements with rival platform ecosystems.

In sum, the platform technology scope shapes the opportunities available to complementors for value co-creation by architecturally restricting access to platform technology components, interfaces, and SDKs. In doing so, the platform technology scope helps the platform sponsor address the uncertainties of value co-creation from *ex ante* unknown complementors and complements. The platform sponsor can selectively open parts of the core platform modules, interfaces, and SDKs such that they support the development of certain types of complements. Such a strategy may also be informed by the data generated and algorithms within the ecosystem. However, though critical, the technology scope does not suffice in and of itself and is supported by other pillars, such as platform sponsor scope.

## Platform Sponsor Scope

The success of a platform ecosystem is attributed to the potential of the platform sponsors and complementors to co-create value (Kapoor, 2018), with each actor performing different parts of the value co-creation process. Accordingly, the actor that performs a focal process retains control over the corresponding part of value creation. Such an arrangement begins with the platform sponsor, as the initiator of the ecosystem, choosing to perform parts of the value creation process itself while opening the rest to the complementors. In essence, platform sponsors choose their scope in the value creation process vis-à-vis the complementors, a choice that we term "platform sponsor scope." The choice of platform sponsor scope complements that of platform technology scope. As McIntyre et al. (2020) rightly point out, "while technology choices on platform design and interfaces have an influence on complementors' incentives to innovate, and can affect to some extent complementors' capability, they constitute only one of the levers of action that platform owners can manipulate. The scope of the platform [sponsor] is another lever of action" (p. 19). As we detail below, the strategy stream of platform literature has multiple treatments of platform sponsor scope that address key aspects of the digital strategy of the firm.

Researchers have described the platform sponsor scope as one of the key choices made at the outset as well as continually (Gawer, 2011; Gawer & Cusumano, 2008; Kapoor & Lee, 2013). As Cusumano and Gawer (2002) emphasize, the choice of platform sponsor scope is "not a one-time event because firms innovate continuously on their products and add new functionalities that may well have been performed previously by external firms." Early studies considered platform sponsor scope as the choice of complements to make internally as opposed to those left to complementors (Gawer, 2011; Gawer & Cusumano, 2008). In this treatment, a broad platform sponsor scope would depict a platform with several in-house complements, whereas a narrow scope would depict the availability of a wide range of third-party complements. Researchers have demonstrated that platform sponsors make in-house complements to kickstart network effects[2] and fill the gaps that are not addressed by third-party complementors (Cennamo, 2018; Hagiu & Spulber, 2013). For example, video game console manufacturers produce a few games in-house to attract consumers to the platform, which in turn attracts game developers to produce third-party games for the platform. However, such in-house complements can only enhance the quality and variety of complements within the ecosystem before the market takes off (Cennamo, 2018).

Another mode of scope choice that enables the platform sponsor to redefine its boundaries is directly entering the complementors' product spaces (Wen & Zhu, 2019; Zhu & Liu, 2018). For example, Amazon as the platform sponsor expands its scope vis-à-vis the complementors when it competes within their product categories using its own products. Researchers have demonstrated that the platform sponsor enters complementors' successful product spaces, particularly those having less platform-specific investments (Zhu & Liu, 2018). Such scope expansion by the platform sponsor discourages complementors' participation or influences them to shift their innovation to a different product space within the ecosystem. The complementors' decision to shift their innovation efforts within the ecosystem to a different product space is seen in dominant platform ecosystems (Wen & Zhu, 2019). Thus, platform sponsor scope choice influences complementors' participation behavior and their performance outcomes.

Platform sponsor scope is also addressed as a part of broader definitions such as the "vision that defines the ecosystem value proposition" (Dattée et al., 2018, p. 467; Iansiti & Levien, 2004) and an alignment structure comprising actors, their activities, positions, and information flows that materialize the value proposition (Adner, 2017). Whereas the blueprint or vision of the ecosystem defines the value proposition, the associated alignment structure aims to identify the ecosystem design and governance. In this treatment, the platform sponsor's compelling vision of the ecosystem is vital to attract the participation of ecosystem actors. However, in situations of high uncertainty where such value propositions may not be effectively envisioned *ex ante*, the platform sponsor scope choice evolves due to the collective discovery of the value propositions (Dattée et al., 2018).

In a more explicit treatment of boundaries, the platform sponsor scope is argued to comprise the assets owned, labor employed, and activities performed by the platform sponsor (Gawer, 2020). In this argument, platform sponsor scope is a key component of the digital strategy of firms and interacts with broader considerations such as the type of ecosystem and lifecycle stage. At a more granular level, platform sponsor scope comprises of: (i) the activities that the sponsor chooses to perform in-house while opening the others to complementors, and (ii) the sponsor's decision rights over complements (Murthy & Madhok, 2021). This treatment of platform sponsor scope encompasses prior conceptualizations as activities that underpin the delivery of the value proposition and form a key part of the alignment structure.

In sum, the platform sponsor scope is a boundary choice that shapes the participation decisions of complementors by signaling opportunities for value creation and capture in the platform ecosystem. The scope choice shapes the latitude that the sponsor has to govern the ecosystem, wherein the platform sponsor has complete control over the activities it performs internally and, moreover, can define rules on governance and decision rights that impact complementor participation. Thus, value creation in platform ecosystems involves not just direct but also indirect maneuvering by the platform sponsor, the lack of which may lead to the failure of ecosystems (Dattée et al., 2018; Tiwana, 2013; Tiwana & Konsynski, 2010).

## Platform Market Scope

Another conceptualization of platform scope concerns economic forces and the external scope of markets and products in which the platform ecosystem competes. We term this conceptualization of scope choice "platform market scope." The platform market scope choice has implications for managing the uncertainties in value co-creation as it shapes the identity and value proposition of the platform ecosystem as a whole and consequently attracts and fosters a desirable set of complementors and consumers to the ecosystem. Platform market scope, rooted in the economics stream of platform literature, is mostly addressed in relation to the product and market positioning of the platform ecosystem in relation to its competition (McIntyre et al., 2020). The dominant treatment here relates to the expansion of the market scope of the platform ecosystem and is often initiated by the platform sponsor. The platform market scope choice is a vital component of digital strategy as "firms that can capture and aggregate data from various sectors can unearth and exploit new kinds of synergies" to expand their scope of markets and products (Gawer, 2020, p. 6).

A platform sponsor may undertake platform market scope expansion to overcome entry barriers emerging from a rival's network effects and enter their market. Such an entry may be accomplished by platform envelopment where the focal platform sponsor bundles the features of the rival platform into its own offerings and targets the overlapping user base (Eisenmann et al., 2011). This expansion mode harnesses common components and user relationships by leveraging demand- and supply-side economies. Platform envelopment is beneficial to the envelopers as they gain market share by foreclosing the rival's access to users and thereafter leveraging network effects to drive growth. By leveraging product bundling, the platform sponsor expands the markets addressed by the offerings of the platform ecosystem. A prominent example of this type of scope expansion is Microsoft bundling its Windows Media Player with the Windows operating system for personal computers. This scope expansion enveloped the offerings of the RealNetworks media platform (Eisenmann et al., 2011).

Yet another way of platform market scope expansion involves the focal platform sponsor acquiring potential rival platform ecosystems to "curtail the target's innovation projects and pre-empt future competition" (Gawer, 2020, p. 6). Although this mode of market scope expansion is similar to non-digital firms, digital firms benefit from such acquisitions in terms of network effects and data aggregation from the target platform ecosystem. Facebook's acquisition of Instagram and WhatsApp are examples of such platform market scope expansion by Facebook.

Additionally, platform market scope comprises the decision to position as a niche or generalist platform ecosystem depending on whether they target specific groups of users or not (Seamans & Zhu, 2014). Platform market scope choice also shapes the distinctiveness of the platform ecosystem relative to its competition in terms of the type of complements and content available within the ecosystem (Cennamo, 2021; Cennamo & Santaló, 2013). Overall, the platform market scope is a key component in creating a unique platform market identity of the ecosystem from the perspective of the users.

**Integrated View of Digital Platform Scope**

Platform technology, sponsor, and market scope are distinct conceptualizations about firm boundaries in the platform literature. In accordance with their origins and respective interests, the three streams of platform literature have examined issues related to platform scope in a partial manner. The focus of the technology stream of research has largely remained on issues related to platform technology scope rather than platform sponsor scope. The economics stream of research on platform scope has focused on platform market scope, its expansion, and implications on competitive interaction but not on organizational and governance issues. Finally, the strategy stream of research has focused on the governance implications of the boundary between platform sponsors and complementors.

Yet, although they seem distinct choices and encompass different considerations, the three interact to influence the broader digital strategy and value co-creation. As Boudreau (2017) highlights, technology and platform sponsor boundaries vary distinctly but interact with each other to influence organizational and governance issues. Through an exhaustive literature review, Chen et al. (2021) argue that several elements of platform sponsor scope determine the design elements of platform technology scope. The platform sponsor establishes access control to determine to what extent complementors can join the platform ecosystem (an element of platform sponsor scope choice) by technologically restricting the use of boundary resources and platform interfaces (an element of platform technology scope). Another example from Chen et al. (2021) of the interaction between the scope choices relates to the platform sponsor requiring the use of its own SDKs to develop complements (an element of platform technology scope) and thereby reducing the compatibility of the complements with other rival platforms (an element of platform market scope).

Furthermore, in the digital context, the platform technology scope includes the boundaries in terms of ownership and access to transaction and user data as well as algorithms for analytics and governance. Digital platform ecosystems generate data about the actors involved in the form of reputation scores, ratings, reviews, interactions, and transactions among the actors (see Chapters 13 and 15, this volume). However, the accumulated data often rests within the boundaries of the platform sponsor (Clough & Wu, 2020). Such accumulated data coupled with artificial intelligence algorithms can create data network effects that drive participation and, therefore, value co-creation within the ecosystem (Adner et al., 2019). In this context, the platform technology scope choice encompasses the design choice of the extent to which the platform sponsor shares data and analytics with the complementors. However, as Chen et al. (2021) posit, such technology scope choices should be made in tandem with the sponsor scope choices that in turn shape governance within the ecosystem.

Despite providing a mapping of the platform technology and governance mechanisms, Chen et al. (2021) highlight that the implications of these choices on value co-creation are not fully understood. For example, there is debate on who captures the value created by harnessing these digital resources. On the one hand, as the owner of the data, the platform sponsor has a significant advantage in capturing such value (Clough & Wu, 2020). On the other hand, data sharing agreements and open platform interfaces are argued to offset such advantages (Gregory et al., 2021). Hence, the implications of technology scope choices in terms of data and algorithms and implications for platform sponsor scope are not fully understood, prompting calls for future research in this area.

In a recent effort to connect the seemingly separate but interdependent platform scope choices, Gawer (2020) considered the interaction between platform sponsor scope, platform sides, and interfaces and argued that these scope decisions are interdependent and need to be coherent for a successful digital strategy. From our perspective in this chapter, the "platform sides" may be viewed as one of the elements of platform market scope as it relates to pricing and network effects. Similarly, interfaces form one of the elements of platform technology scope. Although an important first step, this study does not consider the different underlying elements of platform technology and market scope, the governance implications of the scope choices, and the interaction between them. To emphasize the essential point, an integrated understanding of the implications of technology, sponsor, and market scope choices on value co-creation is necessary to better understand the phenomena. Thus, in the following sections, we discuss the implications of the scope choices on the broader digital strategy of firms and then highlight key areas for future research.

## IMPLICATIONS FOR DIGITAL STRATEGY

So far, we have provided an overview of the important role of digital platforms and platform scope in the digital strategy of firms. We now discuss the implications of digital platform scope for our extant understanding of the firm scope and value creation.

### Digital Strategy and Firm Scope

The scope of the firm has long been a central issue of strategic management as scholars have demonstrated its influence on key performance outcomes (Zenger et al., 2011). The conceptualization of digital platform scope differs from the firm scope literature involving hierarchical firms and hybrid arrangements like alliances. Platform technology and sponsor scope involve the choice of boundaries vis-à-vis the complementors who form an integral part of value co-creation in the ecosystem. These choices are similar and yet distinct to the traditional notion of firm scope. For instance, the conceptualization of platform sponsor scope as the choice of in-house complements vis-à-vis third-party complements is close to the make vs ally argument that has underpinned much of the scope of the firm literature in traditional firms (Parmigiani

& Mitchell, 2009; Parmigiani & Rivera-Santos, 2011; Shi et al., 2012). Yet, platform technology and sponsor scope choices differ from those of a traditional firm where the relationship between the actors involved is often arm's-length or transactional. This is because the platform ecosystems encompass an arrangement of interdependence. At the same time, the boundaries are distinct from those in hybrid organizational forms like alliances because the platform sponsor, as the focal economic actor, neither selects its partners nor establishes complex contracts involving firm scope.

Platform market scope is an external scope choice that is similar yet distinct to the scope choice of traditional firms in terms of products and markets to compete in. With fungible digital assets enabling easy entry into new markets and network effects helping to leverage economies of scale and scope, the boundaries between different products, markets and industries are less rigid (see Chapter 1, this volume; Adner et al., 2019; Gregory et al., 2021). For example, Amazon, which began as an e-commerce platform, soon leveraged its digital infrastructure of data centers to enter the cloud computing market. As Adner et al. (2019, p. 258) highlight, the "extreme fungibility [of digital assets] suggests that traditional notions of relatedness" in a focal firm's choice of products and markets to compete needs to be revisited.

Overall, whereas platform technology and market scope are explicit choices that shape innovation and market identity, respectively, platform sponsor scope is a boundary choice that shapes the ecosystem of actors around the platform. Thus, digital platform scope is a key element of digital strategy and a distinct kind of firm scope that is important for value creation in platform ecosystems.

**Value Creation under Uncertainty**

A fundamental challenge for firms crafting their digital strategy is the unique value creation challenge where the focal actor – platform sponsor in the case of a digital platform ecosystem – co-creates value with complementors but does not know *ex ante* who are the complementors or what their products may be. Digital platform ecosystems are argued to alleviate such uncertainties by the platform sponsor leveraging the market process to harness distributed knowledge of external actors, which is augmented with the sponsor's knowledge and capability to create value (Tajedin et al., 2019).

Digital platform scope serves as a basis to further examine heterogeneity in firm-designed markets, something we do not yet fully understand (Tajedin et al., 2019), and their performance implications. Platform scope captures how platform sponsors navigate the uncertainties of *ex ante* unknown complementors and complements to create value. The platform scope encompasses the platform sponsor's choice of value creation processes to perform internally while opening the other processes to complementors. It also involves the design choices of opening platform technology and data to complementors as well as the choice of products and markets to compete. Moreover, the choice of platform market scope also aids in making explicit the market identity of the platform ecosystems. Together, these choices informing platform scope serve as a tool to attract the *right* set of complementors to participate in the ecosystem by signaling the opportunities available for value creation and capture.

Importantly, the scope choice also shapes the sponsor's latitude to govern the ecosystem. The platform technology scope choice shapes how the complementors can leverage platform core modules and interfaces while indirectly restricting complement variability. Thus, the platform scope choices serve to foster a more *predictable* set of complements. Although the complementors can innovate within the boundaries defined by the platform scope choices, the variability in the type of complements is contingent on the scope choices as such choices place constraints on the level of access to platform technology, other actors, and the market. In other words, the heterogeneity in scope choices manifest in the variability of complements. In sum, the platform sponsor can overcome the uncertainties in value co-creation through their choice of scope to foster the right complementors and a predictable set of complements.

## DIRECTIONS FOR FUTURE RESEARCH

Platform scope is a key component of digital and platform strategy. Although some of the underlying considerations discussed above have been extensively studied in the platform literature, the topic of platform scope itself has received scant attention. The few studies that have focused on the boundaries of the platform ecosystem have tended to limit their focus to the aspects of interest pertinent to the respective stream of literature. We provide several directions for future research that can contribute to this important topic of digital strategy.

### Digital Strategy, Ecosystem Structure, and Dynamics

Digital platform ecosystems are at the core of the digital strategy of firms. Yet, it is not fully clear how the digital strategy takes shape alongside the structure and dynamics of the platform ecosystem. Scholars have extensively studied the role of ecosystem structure and governance in platform ecosystems. However, it is unclear how the different elements of structure and governance combine to shape value co-creation (Dushnitsky et al., 2020). This is particularly important because platform sponsors simultaneously choose the ecosystem structure and governance elements. Moreover, the digital strategy exemplified through the platform sponsor scope choice shapes the sponsor's latitude in ecosystem governance and the technology design of the platform ecosystem. Hence, it is vital to understand the interplay between platform ecosystems' structural elements and platform scope. Any such effort should also consider heterogeneity in platform ecosystems to better understand the antecedents of the scope choices and ecosystem structure.

Furthermore, it is also important to explore if and how platform scope choices impact the platform ecosystem dynamics. Much of the platform dynamics literature is based on the exhaustive examination of network effects. There is immense potential in understanding how the interactions between technology, sponsor, and market scope may impact the network effect dynamics. This line of research will be instrumental to building knowledge of scope choices alongside heterogeneity in user preferences. Recent studies (Jacobides et al., 2018; Tavalaei & Cennamo, 2020) have begun to shed light on the different types of complementarities and their implications for ecosystems. It would be vital to explore how scope choices interact with complementarities to shape the platform ecosystem structure and dynamics.

The notion of platform scope has implications for understanding digital strategy in terms of how focal actors can directly and indirectly influence value co-creation with external actors. Future studies can examine how the scope choice interacts with or influences broader digital strategies involving governance design choices in contexts other than digital platforms. This line of inquiry would also be fruitful to examine how the scope choices of a dominant player may shape entrepreneurial opportunities within the ecosystem. Another aspect of scope involves the broader boundary choice of the focal actor vis-à-vis other firms within the same market. Whereas much of the literature in this stream has focused on competitive positioning, there is scope to examine how this boundary choice interacts with the internal scope choice discussed above. Such an inquiry is particularly important for digital strategy because autonomous co-creators such as complementors often engage in multihoming or co-creation in multiple platform ecosystems simultaneously.

**Temporal Dimension of Digital Strategy**

Digital strategy, like other aspects of firm strategy, evolves over time and in response to changes in competition, complementor behaviors, and environmental factors. Digital platform scope is a choice made at the outset and continually (Cusumano & Gawer, 2002; Gawer, 2011) and therefore a key element to study along the temporal dimension. Gawer (2020) highlights the importance of the lifecycle stage in the scope choice. A key point of departure in the platform lifecycle is the market tipping point beyond which winner-take-all dynamics result in the dominance of one or a few platforms and the inevitable failure of the rest. A platform sponsor prioritizes value co-creation before the market tips with the hope of attracting participation and winning the race for network effects. Hence, during this period, the sponsor chooses its scope in a way that enhances transactions and innovation within the ecosystem. In contrast, after the market tips, the platform sponsors prioritize value capture, having achieved the benefits of network effects. During this period, the platform sponsor chooses its scope to facilitate profitability and market dominance (Gawer, 2020).

Although a good start, there is immense potential in exploring how each of the scope choices around technology, sponsor, and market boundaries evolve over time. Moreover, it is essential to understand if one or more of these elements of scope choices gain prominence at different stages of the lifecycle and the antecedents driving such selective importance of the scope elements. Such an examination should also consider how the scope choices co-evolve with the ecosystem structure and dynamics as well as the broader firm-level strategies of the platform sponsor. Furthermore, with the temporal dimension underexplored in the platform literature (Kretschmer et al., 2020), it is essential to empirically identify key lifecycle stages of the platform ecosystem from the perspective of digital strategy. Specifically, future research that can characterize specific lifecycle stages when data aggregation and digital assets bring transformative changes to the markets and industries would be of significant interest to policymakers and practitioners.

**Complementors' Strategies and Digital Platform Scope**

Although scholars have demonstrated that platform scope influences complementors' participation behavior, however with very few exceptions (Wen & Zhu, 2019; Zhu & Liu, 2018), we do not fully understand how complementors' strategies take shape in response to alternative scope choices. This is particularly relevant in contexts where complementors participate on multiple platforms with the same complements. In essence, this line of inquiry seeks to understand optimal scope choices and the relative importance of platform technology, sponsor, and market scope choices from the perspective of the complementors. Furthermore, as with much of the platform literature, there is huge potential to study the temporal dimension in this context. Specifically, understanding how complementors may respond to scope choices before and after the market tipping point is vital to understanding the power dynamics within the ecosystem. Such results will have implications for policymakers inclined to ensure a fair and competitive environment. Future studies can also examine the role of platform scope choice in shaping the ecosystem dynamics. A promising line of research involves exploring complementor strategies such as entry timing, pricing, and quality of complements under different types of network effects (symmetric vs asymmetric and data network effects) and complementarities (generic vs specific).

**Digital Strategy and Corporate Strategy**

With the growing importance of digital strategy, it is fundamental to understand how the broader firm-level strategies of the platform sponsor may interact with their digital strategy. One such important and potentially fruitful area of research relates to the interaction between the platform sponsor's corporate strategies and their digital strategy. Despite adopting the organizational logic of harnessing co-creation by autonomous complementors within their ecosystems, platform sponsors engage in alliances and joint ventures much like a traditional firm and often simultaneously. Whereas platform scope, particularly the platform technology and sponsor scope, is a choice made vis-à-vis the complementors, there exists the possibility of selectively modifying platform scope through inter-organizational arrangements. Although platform sponsors leverage the complementors' intellectual property, resources, and knowledge through their complements, several examples show that platform sponsors also depend on alliance partners. For example, GE, as the platform sponsor, announced partnerships with several firms and launched a four-tiered partnership program in its effort to encourage the development of complementary products for its internet of things (IoT) platform, GE Predix, even as it offered open APIs to its platform that the autonomous complementors can use to develop their products. Future studies can examine how the platform sponsor's corporate strategies interact with their scope choices and how these choices may shape complementors' strategies and overall ecosystem performance.

In conclusion, with the proliferation of digital technologies and the central role of platform ecosystems, it is important to explore different perspectives to enrich our understanding of the underlying elements and their manifestations. Notwithstanding the importance of technology and economics-based perspectives, novel considerations on digital platform ecosystems have raised new questions and provided opportunities to address ongoing debates not addressed by earlier work. This chapter, encompassing the notion of platform scope in informing digital strategy, is one such perspective that can trigger novel insights and has important managerial implications.

## NOTES

1. Of course the sponsor may know of some complementors or may even selectively invite specific actors to participate. Broadly speaking, however, the essential point remains that it largely does not know *ex ante* which actors will choose to participate and in what manner.
2. Network effects is a condition where the value an actor derives from participating in a platform increases when a greater number of actors participate on the same side (termed "direct network effects") or on other sides (termed "indirect network effects") of the platform (Katz & Shapiro, 1994; Rochet & Tirole, 2003). Consequently, a large number of actors on one side can attract more

actors to participate on the same or other sides of the platform. This dynamic results in a positive loopback such that more participation attracts even more actors.

# REFERENCES

Adner, R. (2017). Ecosystem as structure: An actionable construct for strategy. *Journal of Management*, *43*(1), 39–58. https://doi.org/10.1177/0149206316678451.

Adner, R., Puranam, P., & Zhu, F. (2019). What is different about digital strategy? From quantitative to qualitative change. *Strategy Science*, *4*(4), 253–61. https://doi.org/10.1287/stsc.2019.0099.

Ahuja, G., & Novelli, E. (2017). Redirecting research efforts on the diversification–performance linkage: The search for synergy. *Academy of Management Annals*, *11*(1), 342–90. https://doi.org/10.5465/annals.2014.0079.

Baldwin, C.Y., & Clark, K.B. (2000). *Design Rules: The Power of Modularity*. MIT Press.

Boudreau, K.J. (2010). Open platform strategies and innovation: Granting access vs. devolving control. *Management Science*, *56*(10), 1849–72. https://doi.org/10.1287/mnsc.1100.1215.

Boudreau, K.J. (2012). Let a thousand flowers bloom? An early look at large numbers of software app developers and patterns of innovation. *Organization Science*, *23*(5, SI), 1409–27. https://doi.org/10.1287/orsc.1110.0678.

Boudreau, K.J. (2017). *Platform Boundary Choices & Governance: Opening-Up While Still Coordinating and Orchestrating* (Entrepreneurship, Innovation, and Platforms, Vol. 37). Emerald Group. https://doi.org/10.1108/S0742-332220170000037009.

Boudreau, K.J., & Jeppesen, L.B. (2015). Unpaid crowd complementors: The platform network effect mirage. *Strategic Management Journal*, *36*(12), 1761–77. https://doi.org/10.1002/smj.2324.

Boudreau, K.J., & Lakhani, K.R. (2015). "Open" disclosure of innovations, incentives and follow-on reuse: Theory on processes of cumulative innovation and a field experiment in computational biology. *Research Policy*, *44*(1), 4–19. https://doi.org/10.1016/j.respol.2014.08.001.

Cennamo, C. (2018). Building the value of next-generation platforms: The paradox of diminishing returns. *Journal of Management*, *44*(8), 3038–69. https://doi.org/10.1177/0149206316658350.

Cennamo, C. (2021). Competing in digital markets: A platform-based perspective. *Academy of Management Perspectives*, *35*(2), 265–91. https://doi.org/10.5465/amp.2016.0048.

Cennamo, C., & Santaló, J. (2013). Platform competition: Strategic trade-offs in platform markets: Platform Competition. *Strategic Management Journal*, *34*(11), 1331–50. https://doi.org/10.1002/smj.2066.

Cennamo, C., & Santaló, J. (2019). Generativity tension and value creation in platform ecosystems. *Organization Science*, *30*(3), 617–41. https://doi.org/10.1287/orsc.2018.1270.

Chen, L., Tong, T.W., Tang, S., & Han, N. (2021). Governance and design of digital platforms: A review and future research directions on a meta-organization. *Journal of Management*, 01492063211045023. https://doi.org/10.1177/01492063211045023.

Clough, D.R., & Wu, A. (2020). Artificial intelligence, data-driven learning, and the decentralized structure of platform ecosystems. *Academy of Management Review*, *47*(1). https://doi.org/10.5465/amr.2020.0222.

Conner, K.R. (1991). A historical comparison of resource-based theory and five schools of thought within industrial organization economics: Do we have a new theory of the firm? *Journal of Management*, *17*(1), 121.

Cusumano, M.A., & Gawer, A. (2002). The elements of platform leadership. *MIT Sloan Management Review*, *43*(3), 51–8.

Dattée, B., Alexy, O., & Autio, E. (2018). Maneuvering in poor visibility: How firms play the ecosystem game when uncertainty is high. *Academy of Management Journal*, *61*(2), 466–98. https://doi.org/10.5465/amj.2015.0869.

Dushnitsky, G., Piva, E., & Rossi-Lamastra, C. (2020). Investigating the mix of strategic choices and performance of transaction platforms: Evidence from the crowdfunding setting. *Strategic Management Journal*, smj.3163. https://doi.org/10.1002/smj.3163.

Eaton, B., Elaluf-Calderwood, S., & Sorensen, C. (2015). Distributed tuning of boundary resources: The case of Apple's iOS service system. *MIS Quarterly*, *39*(1), 217–43.

Eisenmann, T., Parker, G.G., & Van Alstyne, M.W. (2011). Platform envelopment. *Strategic Management Journal*, *32*(12), 1270–85. https://doi.org/10.1002/smj.935.

Gawer, A. (2011). *Platforms, Markets and Innovation*. Edward Elgar Publishing.

Gawer, A. (2014). Bridging differing perspectives on technological platforms: Toward an integrative framework. *Research Policy*, *43*(7), 1239–49. https://doi.org/10.1016/j.respol.2014.03.006.

Gawer, A. (2020). Digital platforms' boundaries: The interplay of firm scope, platform sides, and digital interfaces. *Long Range Planning*, 102045. https://doi.org/10.1016/j.lrp.2020.102045.

Gawer, A., & Cusumano, M.A. (2008). How companies become platform leaders. *MIT Sloan Management Review*. http://sloanreview.mit.edu/article/how-companies-become-platform-leaders/.

Gregory, R.W., Henfridsson, O., Kaganer, E., & Kyriakou, H. (2021). Data network effects: Key conditions, shared data, and the data value duality. *Academy of Management Review*, *47*(1). https://doi.org/10.5465/amr.2021.0111.

Hagiu, A., & Spulber, D. (2013). First-party content and coordination in two-sided markets. *Management Science*, *59*(4), 933–49. https://doi.org/10.1287/mnsc.1120.1577.

Iansiti, M., & Levien, R. (2004). Strategy as ecology. *Harvard Business Review*, *82*(3), 68–78.

Jacobides, M.G., Cennamo, C., & Gawer, A. (2018). Towards a theory of ecosystems. *Strategic Management Journal*, *39*(8), 2255–76. https://doi.org/10.1002/smj.2904.

Kapoor, R. (2018). Ecosystems: Broadening the locus of value creation. *Journal of Organization Design*, *7*(1), 12. https://doi.org/10.1186/s41469-018-0035-4.

Kapoor, R., & Lee, J.M. (2013). Coordinating and competing in ecosystems: How organizational forms shape new technology investments. *Strategic Management Journal*, *34*(3), 274–96. https://doi.org/10.1002/smj.2010.

Katz, M.L., & Shapiro, C. (1994). Systems competition and network effects. *Journal of Economic Perspectives*, *8*(2), 93–115.

Kretschmer, T., Leiponen, A., Schilling, M., & Vasudeva, G. (2020). Platform ecosystems as meta-organizations: Implications for platform strategies. *Strategic Management Journal*, *43*(3), 405–24. https://doi.org/10.1002/smj.3250.

Lusch, R.F., & Nambisan, S. (2015). Service innovation: A service-dominant logic perspective. *MIS Quarterly*, *39*(1), 155–75.

McIntyre, D.P., & Srinivasan, A. (2017). Networks, platforms, and strategy: Emerging views and next steps. *Strategic Management Journal*, *38*(1), 141–60. https://doi.org/10.1002/smj.2596.

McIntyre, D.P., Srinivasan, A., Afuah, A., Gawer, A., & Kretschmer, T. (2020). Multi-sided platforms as new organizational forms. *Academy of Management Perspectives*, *35*(4). https://doi.org/10.5465/amp.2018.0018.

Murthy, R.K., & Madhok, A. (2021). Overcoming the early-stage conundrum of digital platform ecosystem emergence: A problem-solving perspective. *Journal of Management Studies*, *58*(7), 1899–932. https://doi.org/10.1111/joms.12748.

Parmigiani, A., & Mitchell, W. (2009). Complementarity, capabilities, and the boundaries of the firm: The impact of within-firm and interfirm expertise on concurrent sourcing of complementary components. *Strategic Management Journal*, *30*(10), 1065–91. https://doi.org/10.1002/smj.769.

Parmigiani, A., & Rivera-Santos, M. (2011). Clearing a path through the forest: A meta-review of interorganizational relationships. *Journal of Management*, *37*(4), 1108–36. https://doi.org/10.1177/0149206311407507.

Rochet, J.-C., & Tirole, J. (2003). Platform competition in two-sided markets. *Journal of the European Economic Association*, *1*(4), 990–1029.

Rumelt, R.P., Schendel, D., & Teece, D.J. (1991). Strategic management and economics. *Strategic Management Journal*, *12*, 5–29.

Seamans, R., & Zhu, F. (2014). Responses to entry in multi-sided markets: The impact of Craigslist on local newspapers. *Management Science*, *60*(2), 476–93. https://doi.org/10.1287/mnsc.2013.1785.

Shi, W. (Stone), Sun, J., & Prescott, J.E. (2012). A temporal perspective of merger and acquisition and strategic alliance initiatives: Review and future direction. *Journal of Management*, *38*(1), 164–209. https://doi.org/10.1177/0149206311424942.

Tajedin, H., Madhok, A., & Keyhani, M. (2019). A theory of digital firm-designed markets: Defying knowledge constraints with crowds and marketplaces. *Strategy Science*, *4*(4), 323–42. https://doi.org/ 10.1287/stsc.2019.0092.

Tavalaei, M.M., & Cennamo, C. (2020). In search of complementarities within and across platform ecosystems: Complementors' relative standing and performance in mobile apps ecosystems. *Long Range Planning*, 101994. https://doi.org/10.1016/j.lrp.2020.101994.

Tiwana, A. (2008). Does technological modularity substitute for control? A study of alliance performance in software outsourcing. *Strategic Management Journal*, *29*(7), 769–80. https://doi.org/10 .1002/smj.673.

Tiwana, A. (2013). *Platform Ecosystems: Aligning Architecture, Governance, and Strategy*. Morgan Kaufmann.

Tiwana, A., & Konsynski, B. (2010). Complementarities between organizational IT architecture and governance structure. *Information Systems Research*, *21*(2), 288–304. https://doi.org/10.1287/isre .1080.0206.

Tiwana, A., Konsynski, B., & Bush, A.A. (2010). Research commentary: Platform evolution – Coevolution of platform architecture, governance, and environmental dynamics. *Information Systems Research*, *21*(4), 675–87. https://doi.org/10.1287/isre.1100.0323.

Wen, W., & Zhu, F. (2019). Threat of platform-owner entry and complementor responses: Evidence from the mobile app market. *Strategic Management Journal*, *40*(9), 1336–67. https://doi.org/10.1002/smj .3031.

Yoo, Y., Henfridsson, O., & Lyytinen, K. (2010). Research commentary: The new organizing logic of digital innovation – An agenda for information systems research. *Information Systems Research*, *21*(4), 724–35. https://doi.org/10.1287/isre.1100.0322.

Zenger, T.R., Felin, T., & Bigelow, L. (2011). Theories of the firm–market boundary. *Academy of Management Annals*, *5*(1), 89–133. https://doi.org/10.1080/19416520.2011.590301.

Zhu, F., & Liu, Q. (2018). Competing with complementors: An empirical look at Amazon.com. *Strategic Management Journal*, *39*(10), 2618–42. https://doi.org/10.1002/smj.2932.

Zittrain, J.L. (2005). The generative internet. *Harvard Law Review*, *7*, 1975–2040.

# 8. A user guide to centralized, adaptive and decentralized ecosystems

*Andrew Shipilov, Nathan Furr and Francesco Burelli*

As the forces of digitalization and globalization are bringing down barriers between products, industries and geographies, ecosystems are becoming an important organization form in the 21st century. Some ecosystems represent billions in market value and others are poised to create billions. Companies rely on ecosystem development strategies as a part of their digital transformation. However, we have few conceptual tools to understand ecosystems, let alone design and manage them.

Ecosystems have attracted significant interest from researchers and practitioners alike. Jacobides et al. (2018) define ecosystems as groups of independent firms that are linked through non-generic complementarities. Kapoor (2018) defines ecosystems as a set of actors that contribute to the focal offer's user value proposition. In the corporate world, executives are using the metaphor of ecosystems as a rallying call for developing and executing digital strategies. For example, transformation from a bank to a group of platforms and ecosystems has been the critical pillar of DBS' strategy. Likewise, "ecosystem thinking" underlies the strategy of Haier, the white appliance maker.

But the broad use of the term "ecosystem" in both academic research and practitioner discourse risks confusion, as everything that involves the firm and its external environment can mistakenly be labeled "an ecosystem." It is important to understand how ecosystems are different from other mechanisms through which the firm manages its dependencies with the external environment, in order to apply the appropriate strategy and tactics. One would also want to understand to what extent ecosystems are synonymous with other strategic options, such as platforms or alliances. These questions go beyond academic debates. As scholars, we are in the business of developing analytical frameworks that should help practitioners make sense of the new business phenomena and develop better strategies. Hence, if ecosystems were the same as alliances or platforms, then traditional frameworks for thinking about achieving competitive advantage through collaboration or building multi-sided markets should suffice. However, if ecosystems were unique forms of organizing, perhaps we would need different analytical frameworks to analyze and act upon them.

In this chapter, we clarify the differences between ecosystems, platforms and alliances. We borrow from graph theory to develop a typology of different ecosystems: centralized, adaptive and decentralized. We also propose Ecosystem Canvas[1] as a conceptual tool that helps both researchers and practitioners to understand different business models of ecosystems. We hope that these clarifications, and the introduction of Ecosystem Canvas, can help academics to better structure their argumentation and business executives to identify future opportunities for value creation and value capture in ecosystems.

## WHAT ECOSYSTEMS ARE AND WHAT THEY ARE NOT

Ecosystems consist of several building blocks. First, there should be multiple actors, most commonly firms. Second, their businesses should be standalone, offering value propositions that exist, and be commercially viable, on the market on their own. Third, they also need to be linked to one another through non-generic complementarities. These complementarities are investments for mutual adaptation and coordination (Jacobides, Cennamo and Gawer, 2018). For example, when GoJek (a delivery service) becomes a part of DBS' (financial) ecosystem, the two independent companies collaborate with one another using Application Program Interfaces (API). These APIs allow DBS' customers to order delivery services from GoJek. APIs are technical enablers to the collaboration between the two organizations, with the non-generic complementarity consisting of the underlying co-investment of the two companies in the development of their APIs and their closed business relationships within their value chains. Finally, ecosystems tend to be organized around some customer value proposition. Again, in GoJek's case, the value proposition is in the seamless delivery of services, ranging from food to backrubs. DBS' value proposition is in seamless financial services for which customers do not need to go to the physical bank branch. The motto that characterizes this value proposition is "making banking invisible." DBS has also been working with other companies in the ecosystem of financial services, like Kasisto (developer of conversational artificial intelligence, or AI, technology for banking services) or FWD Insurance (a provider of online insurance solutions).[2]

Of course, APIs are not the only technologies that make ecosystems possible. On the front end, different elements of digital ecosystems can be connected through shared digital IDs (think Apple ID), through loyalty programs (e.g., Vitality's bonus points for healthy living) or through a common CRM (customer relationship management) software. On the back end, digital ecosystems are run from the cloud either when the orchestrator owns the cloud infrastructure (e.g., Google) or when the infrastructure is rented (e.g., Salesforce rents Amazon Web Services, or AWS, from Amazon). For non-digital ecosystems, collaboration is often made possible through inter-operability, connection standards and other coordinating mechanisms.

In general, digitalization in the form of algorithms, sensors, distributed computing, cloud, APIs and other related technologies allow broad search and recombination space for innovations made to enclose a customer journey into a single ecosystem so that the customer does not have the need to switch to a different one. Once inside, the customer can enjoy the benefits of inter-device coordination, autonomous systems, virtual reality (VR) and seamless access to content as well as easy payment for all of these services (Lanzolla, Pesce and Tucci, 2021).

The DBS example is interesting not only because it illustrates the broad spectrum of services that an ecosystem can address, but also because it helps illustrate potential confusions. For example, does DBS have a platform or an ecosystem? Is the collaboration with GoJek described as part of an alliance strategy or a part of an ecosystem strategy?

Platforms, alliances and ecosystems are similar because they are means through which firms deal with dependencies in their external environment. They are different depending on the way through which these dependencies are managed. A platform is a business model that connects different parties via a central intermediary, like a software or hardware platform, and in doing so it eliminates some frictions from the market (Cennamo and Santalo, 2013). For example, GoJek is a platform that connects providers of services (restaurants, drivers, massage therapists) to the consumers by channeling touchpoints through an app interface and making it possible for providers to access a wider pool of reachable and addressable potential customers and vice versa. In contrast to that, the part of the traditional bank in which a customer puts money into the account and earns interest while a bank lends this money to a different customer who wants to buy a car is not a platform because the borrower and the depositor do not interact; rather the bank is shuffling resources from one activity to another. By contrast, DBS Car Marketplace is a platform, because it directly connects the buyer and the seller and allows them to complete a transaction, including benefiting from financial services products as needed.

Ecosystems can be, and frequently are, organized around a platform, but not always. GoJek's began as a platform connecting motorbike riders to passengers. It then expanded into offering food delivery and personal services that all would arrive on a motorbike. This was an example of transitioning a platform into an ecosystem. Once the company offered financial services in collaboration with BCA Finance, GoJek solidified its ecosystem business model. By contrast, the ecosystem supporting electronic automobiles is not coordinated or controlled by a platform. This leads to a distinction between platform and non-platform mediated ecosystems.

Alliances differ from ecosystems because the former are based on formal agreements to collaborate while the latter are based on non-generic complementarities that may not have a formal agreement (Shipilov and Gawer, 2020). When Renault and Nissan formed an ill-fated joint venture in the late 1990s, this was a pure alliance. Pfizer and BioNTech's collaboration to create, manufacture, market and distribute a vaccine for COVID-19 is an alliance, which by itself cannot be considered an ecosystem. If we observe all of the alliances and joint ventures that Pfizer has made with its partners, we will be able to talk about Pfizer's alliance network, not Pfizer's ecosystem. In general, every alliance is likely to be based on top of some non-generic complementarities accompanied by a formal agreement (Gulati, Nohria and Zaheer, 2000). However, while ecosystem dependencies are also built upon non-generic complementarities, there may not be formal alliance relationships to coordinate activities. For example, with a few exceptions, most of the electric vehicle charging networks upon which electric car performance depends are not created through formal alliance networks, but through independent parties.

These distinctions matter because they allow us to be precise when we are talking about different strategies that companies use to manage dependencies with their external environments. These distinctions can also help us better understand each mode of external dependency management. We can borrow ideas from more developed research perspectives that characterize alliance networks, for example, and use them to develop a better understanding of modes of dependence management where the research is comparatively less developed. For example, Shipilov and Gawer (2020) suggest applying ideas and concepts from graph theory, which historically has been used to understand alliance networks, to understand the structure of an ecosystem. But graph theory can also help us recognize how differences in the structures of ecosystems imply different strategies for the firms involved.

# CENTRALIZED, ADAPTIVE AND DECENTRALIZED ECOSYSTEMS

Graph theory is a science of networks. It assumes that there are actors connected by relationships. The key theoretical prediction of graph theory is that the structure of relationships is more than the sum of individual relationships. When three actors are connected through social ties, graph theory predicts that these three connections will create behavioral mechanisms that go above and beyond the sum of three individual relationships. While such a connected "triad" will involve three bilateral relationships, connections will also lead to the emergence of trust and improved communication among all triad members (Borgatti et al., 2009). Using graph theory, we can create a "taxonomy" of ecosystems, which in turns yields different ecosystem strategies appropriate for creating and capturing value. More specifically, it can sharpen our understanding of the business models behind different types of ecosystems.

Centrality is one of the fundamental concepts in graph theory. An actor is central to the extent that many other central actors have built relationships to that actor (Bonacich, 2007). Ecosystems are not about individual actors; they are mostly concerned with properties of the entire system. Hence, we need to consider not just centrality from the toolkit of graph theory, but also the notion of centralization. A network is highly centralized when a single actor has many more ties than the other actors, on average. A "star" is a prototypical example of a centralized network where all actors are connected to a single actor. By contrast, in a decentralized network there is not a single dominant actor. Instead, many actors are connected to one another, but without any central connection. One can also imagine intermediate scenarios where a small group of actors which are connected to one another have a higher average number of ties as compared to the majority of actors (Wasserman and Faust, 1994).

If we think of ecosystems as groups of firms and links between them as non-generic complementarities, then the comparison between centralized and decentralized networks can translate into a comparison between centralized and decentralized ecosystems. The degree of centralization will affect technological and strategic properties of ecosystems. In this case, the structure of interdependencies will mediate the effects of the ecosystem's technological organization on ecosystem outcomes. Many of the most common ecosystem examples discussed broadly (and that often command high stock market valuations) are centralized ecosystems. For example, Apple has a centralized ecosystem where all developers depend on App Store to promote their apps to the customers. Content providers depend on Apple for distribution of their content through either Apple Music or Apple TV. Amazon is another example: customers depend on Amazon to connect them to sellers of physical or digital products; content owners depend on Amazon to link them to customers; companies also depend on Amazon to obtain cloud solutions at Amazon Web Services.

At the other extreme, there are decentralized ecosystems, such as the ecosystem of web technologies for e-commerce. Every website uses dozens or more web technologies. Some are used for hosting, others are for payment, yet others are used to display attractive fonts on the web. These technologies are developed by different companies, ranging from the familiar Google or Facebook to less familiar GoDaddy (provider of listing solutions) to even less familiar Cloudflare (optimizer of the speed of website loading). The dependencies among technologies are not focused on a single provider, and no single firm dominates the ecosystem, unlike Apple or Amazon dominating theirs (Burford, Shipilov and Furr, 2021).

In the middle of these extremes, there are what Furr and Shipilov (2018) labeled "adaptive ecosystems." Unlike centralized ecosystems, these ecosystems have a group of firms at the core, and not a single firm. Unlike decentralized ecosystems, the core firms are linked with one another in the adaptive ecosystem, and they work together in order to create a value proposition for the customer. For example, Philips, Salesforce and Radboud University Hospital created an adaptive ecosystem when they agreed to work together to build Philips Healthsuite: an ecosystem created to provide remote monitoring of health for chronically ill patients. While usually people with heart or lung problems or other chronic ailments would have had to be monitored in the hospitals, wearable technologies connected to the cloud allow long-distance patient monitoring and alerts to their caregivers should some health parameters deviate from the normal range. In this ecosystem, Philips brings the expertise of manufacturing wearable devices, Salesforce provides data analytics capabilities while Radboud University Hospital provides an initial pool of patients to test the technologies as well as assisting in research and development. Other members of the ecosystem that depend on the three core players involve third-party hospitals that use these technologies, third-party wearable device developers and insurance companies that provide Heathsuite as a part of the package for their customers. Other examples of adaptive ecosystems include those based on co-innovation agreements, such as those pursued by Cisco and partners such as Airbus and DHL (Furr, O'Keeffe and Dyer, 2016).

Although Shipilov and Gawer (2020) talked about centralized and adaptive ecosystems, their omission of decentralized ecosystems is an inherent limitation. This is because both centralized and adaptive ecosystems assume that all ecosystems are orchestrated by someone: be that by a single firm, as is the case in the centralized ecosystem, or by a group of firms, as is the case in the adaptive ecosystem. Decentralized ecosystems are interesting because they are not orchestrated by anyone. Any firm can join a decentralized ecosystem. Such ecosystems typically operate better if they are facilitated by common standards, which can be encoded at the level of industry rules or technology rules, such as an API or compatible programming language. Some firms might be relatively more dominant than the others in the decentralized ecosystem: there may be more e-commerce web technologies developed by Amazon, Google and Facebook than those developed by GoDaddy; however, no firms explicitly collaborate with one another on a regular basis to develop or market individual technologies. Customers of e-commerce ecosystems can pick and choose individual components for their own websites. They can either pay their developers or get these technologies for free (as would be the case with open-source technologies). These are the types of ecosystems most often discussed as "innovation ecosystems" (Granstrand and Holgersson, 2020) in that they have no centralized actors but are critical to deliver an innovation, such as the solar photovoltaic (PV) ecosystem (Kapoor and Furr, 2015). For example, for an end user to generate electricity from a solar PV system requires a significant ecosystem of component and complement providers, such as manufacturing equipment and materials to create solar panels, inverters to convert direct current to alternating current, and balancing of systems to connect that system to the grid. No central firm coordinates these many components and complements, although industry standards and regulation help facilitate coordination (Furr and Kapoor, 2018).

Because of the active coordination, adaptive and centralized ecosystems are more likely to be built around platform-based business models as compared to the decentralized ecosystems. That is, Apple, Amazon, Healthsuite and others use a platform at the core of their value proposition. Platform business models are valuable to the extent they can harness network effects:

*Table 8.1*      *Comparison of centralized, adaptive and decentralized ecosystems*

|  | Centralized | Adaptive | Decentralized |
|---|---|---|---|
| Degree of centralization | High: single orchestrator | Medium: small group of orchestrators | Low: no one dominates |
| Mechanisms of coordination | Standards actively set by the orchestrator – APIs, ecosystem access policies | Standards actively set by the orchestrators – APIs, ecosystem access policies | Common standards: industry or technology rules, API, programming languages |
| Platform-based models | Yes (e.g., Apple Store) | Yes (e.g., Philips Healthsuite) | No |

the more users use the system, the greater is the value that can be created for every additional user. Orchestrators in centralized and adaptive ecosystems are uniquely positioned to capture value from the network effects. Apple and Amazon obtain fees from every transaction made on their platform; Apple also sells hardware that makes its platform service possible. Healthsuite can capture value from their platform by selling user contracts to hospitals and insurance companies. By contrast, decentralized ecosystems are less likely to have a central mechanism, such as a platform, for capturing value from network effects. Some firms in the e-commerce technologies ecosystem make money by selling their web components, others (like Google or Facebook) provide them as free complements for developers to drive traffic to their revenue-generating services, such as search for Google or social media for Facebook.

Table 8.1 summarizes comparisons among these three different types of ecosystems.

## ECOSYSTEM CANVAS

Given that ecosystems come in different shapes and sizes, one needs help to make sense of their complexities. This is why we have developed a tool, Ecosystem Canvas (Shipilov and Burelli, 2021). This tool has two purposes. First, it helps describe an ecosystem on a single slide. This helps executives to make sense of underlying complexities and understand their company's place in an ecosystem. Is the ecosystem centralized, adaptive or decentralized? Second, it can help you build an ecosystem. The canvas depicts all of the components that should be in place for an ecosystem to exist and to create value for different stakeholders. If one of the components is missing, then an ecosystem will not live up to its full potential. Ecosystem Canvas is similar to the Business Model Canvas developed by Alex Osterwalder in that it is designed to be a graphic tool to discuss a business model. But Ecosystem Canvas is different because it is specifically targeted at describing or developing an ecosystem business model where other firms in the canvas are not necessarily buyers or suppliers for one another, but rather are the players with complementary business models. While Ecosystem Canvas was originally introduced in a short blog post, we would like to elaborate on it here, highlight its applications to different business cases and use it as a tool not only for comparing different ecosystems, but also as a tool for the development of ecosystem strategies.

Our research shows that the task of constructing an ecosystem can be simplified to two critical questions: (1) what do we want to do? And (2) who is needed to make it happen? To answer the first question, we need to understand what is the customer journey that the ecosystem wants to address. This customer journey is a sequence of activities, transactions and experiences that the ecosystem will deliver to its customers.

Figure 8.1 contains an example of what an Ecosystem Canvas would look like for an ecosystem called Philips Healthsuite.

This is an adaptive ecosystem that is built by Philips with its partners Salesforce.com and Radboud University Medical Center. The customer journey comprises monitoring of the patients' vital signs outside of the hospital using wearable technology. The customer persona is a representation of a client who would benefit from the transactions, activities or experiences within the customer journey living with a chronic condition. The Healthsuite ecosystem caters to patients with chronic health conditions: cancer, diabetes, chronic obstructive pulmonary disorder (COPD). An ecosystem's value to the customer comprises the value that the customer obtains from being catered to inside an ecosystem as opposed to the outside of the ecosystem. In the case of Healthsuite, the value resides in unobtrusive monitoring of their health by wearable devices. The information from these devices is analyzed by the algorithms developed by Philips, Salesforce and Radboud UMC and the results are communicated to the patients and their caregivers as well as to the hospital where they are being monitored. Off-the-shelf wearables, such as an iPhone, are not designed to capture the complexity of chronic conditions, whereas the Healthsuite's wearables are designed with the specific chronic conditions in mind.

Next, we want to understand who are the competitors (i.e., other ecosystems, other platforms or other standalone offerings). There are two kinds of competitors to think about: direct and indirect. Direct competitors are similar value propositions provided by other ecosystems or platforms. Siemens has been working to build similar solutions and direct competitors to Philips' Healthsuite in the healthcare space. Indirect competitors could be Apple and Google, which could build their own health apps, but such apps are quite generic and are not in general vetted by the healthcare providers. Finally, there are substitutes; for example, to keep the patient in the hospital, which becomes increasingly impractical due to the high costs of healthcare and psychological hardships to the patients.

Finally, we want to understand how our ecosystem will be monetized. This can be done in many ways, such as directly through collecting payments from transactions happening inside the ecosystem. Apple directly monetizes its ecosystem by levying a 30 percent charge on purchases in App Store. The ecosystem can also be monetized indirectly, such as through selling its data (or access) to the third parties. Google is paying Apple 15 billion dollars a year (as of 2021) to be a default search engine in the iPhone or in an iPad;[3] this is an example of an indirect monetization of an ecosystem. In case of Philips Healthsuite, monetization happens through renting the ecosystem's services. When the participation in this ecosystem is a part of an insurance plan that has been underwritten either by the state or by a commercial insurance provider, every additional customer becomes a source of incremental revenue. More customers mean more revenue and, even more importantly, more data, which means more accurate predictions about the state of the health of future customers. But it bears noting that, regardless of the monetization model or ecosystem type, ecosystems need to generate sufficient long-term value capture to hold ecosystems' participants together. Although an ecosystem orchestrator may temporarily reallocate value to another player to jump start the ecosystem, there needs to be a long-term monetization model to act as a "glue" to keep the ecosystem together (Furr and Shipilov, 2018).

Next, one needs to turn to the questions of which participants are needed in the ecosystem. Usually, participants in ecosystems take one of five distinct roles: orchestrator, core partner(s), technology enabler, complementors and resellers. The orchestrator is a firm that owns and understands the key value proposition for the customer. The core partner(s) provide the core

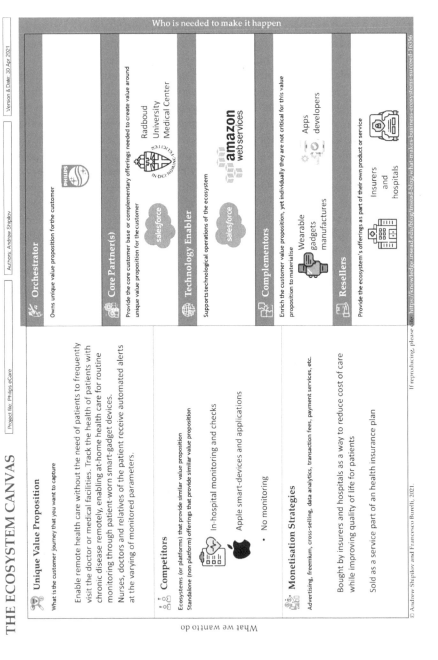

*Figure 8.1    Philips HealthSuite*

customer base or complementary offerings needed to create value around the unique value proposition for the customer. Technology enablers provide underlying ecosystem elements but do not provide the core value proposition itself nor do they typically have a central stake in the ecosystem value proposition itself. Complementors and resellers provide additional products or services that add value, but they are different from core partners because their removal does not reduce value proposition as drastically as removal of a core partner.

The distinction between centralized, adaptive and decentralized ecosystems is based on who is playing the orchestrator and core partner(s) roles. In the centralized ecosystem, the orchestrator is a single firm which does not have a core partner. Apple's or Amazon's ecosystem is an example of a centralized ecosystem because for the most part all of the ecosystem's activities are organized by the single firm—Apple or Amazon respectively. Philips' Healthsuite is an adaptive ecosystem because it has a core orchestrator (Philips) and the two core partners Salesforce.com and Radboud University Medical Center. Salesforce.com is a core partner because it provides data analytics capabilities; Radboud UMC is a core partner because it provides a core customer base. Finally, in a decentralized ecosystem there are no orchestrators but instead core partners and technology enablers. For example, in the decentralized solar PV ecosystem there is no orchestrator but instead core partners like module manufacturers as well as technology enablers like the makers of the equipment that PV module manufacturers depend upon (Furr and Kapoor, 2018). Alternatively, in the decentralized e-commerce ecosystem we described above, there are no orchestrators but rather technology enablers like Google, Facebook, Alibaba, etc.

Regardless of ecosystem type, no ecosystem can exist without complementors. They provide products or services that enrich the customer's value proposition, but they are not key for the value proposition to materialize. In the Philips Healthsuite example, the complementors are the companies that make wearable medical devices or potentially those that develop the code for the software that works with these devices. In the case of Apple's centralized ecosystem, the complementors are the developers of apps for the iOS devices. In the case of the decentralized solar PV ecosystem, complementors include providers of services to owners of solar PV installations as well as the cables and racks to connect and install PV systems.

Resellers represent the final role that is needed to make an ecosystem happen. Most frequently, these are the firms that provide an ecosystem's offering as a part of their own product and service. When an insurance company proposes the use of Philips Healthsuite to its clients (e.g., insured individuals and/or their employees), then they are the resellers of this ecosystem's offerings. Likewise, when the other hospitals want to sign up to using this ecosystem, they also become resellers. Radboud is not a reseller because it helps develop and test the new technology that underpins the functioning of the Healthsuite.

## ADAPTIVE vs CENTRALIZED ECOSYSTEM COMPARISON

Let us take a look at another comparison between centralized and adaptive ecosystems, this time in the domain of VR headsets.[4] Meta (also commonly known as Facebook, which is used interchangeably here) is one of the dominant players in this industry and is developing a centralized ecosystem. Its canvas is depicted in Figure 8.2, while the canvas of a competing, adaptive VR ecosystem orchestrated by Pico is depicted in Figure 8.3.

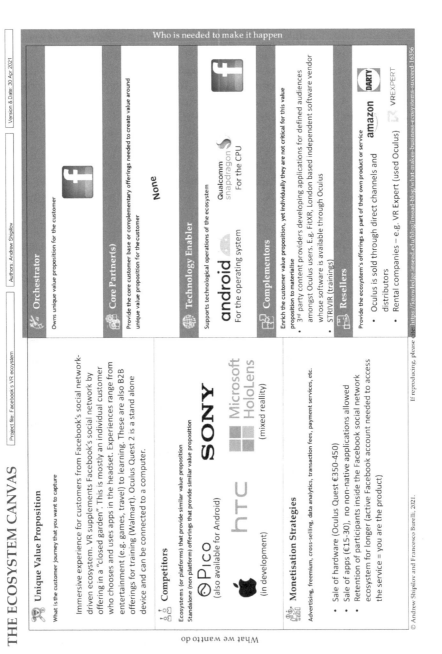

*Figure 8.2*　　*Facebook's centralized VR ecosystem*

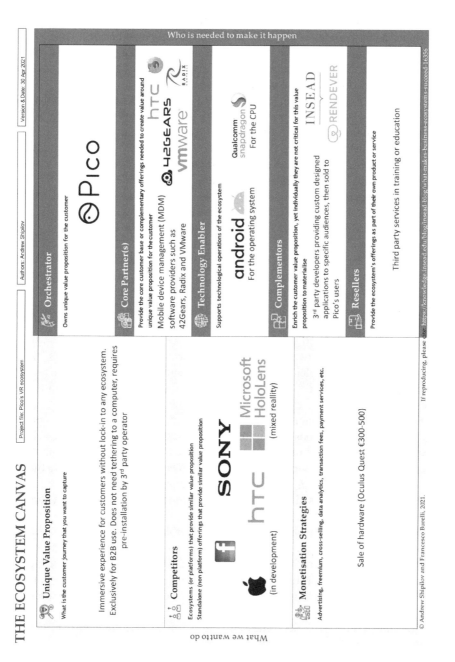

*Figure 8.3    Pico's adaptive VR ecosystem*

The unique value proposition of Meta's VR ecosystem is the immersive experience for customers who exist within Meta's Facebook social network-driven advertising ecosystem. VR supplements Facebook's social network offering in a "closed garden." This is mostly an individual customer who chooses and uses apps in the headset. Experiences range from entertainment (games and travel) to learning. There are also business-to-business (B2B) offerings for training. For example, Walmart used Oculus technology to train its associates to work with inventory in its stores and related warehouses. The Meta device requires logging in to the eponymous social network; otherwise one cannot use the headset.

There are quite a few competitors in this space. First, it is Pico and its ecosystem that we will describe below. Next, Apple and Microsoft are making forays into VR: Microsoft is working on the Hololens technology that represents a mixed-reality solution, while Apple has a super secretive project that has not yet seen the light of day. Sony is probably the most direct competitor; it has integrated its PlayStation console with the VR headset.

Meta follows multiple monetization strategies. First, it sells Oculus hardware for 350–450 dollars. Second, it also makes money on the sale of apps, such as games or educational or virtual travel software. These are sold for 15–30 dollars. Finally, it also monetizes its users' social networks through advertising. After all, if one cannot use Oculus without a Meta/Facebook account, then one has to become a "product" for Meta. This is a great business model because individuals pay for the privilege of being the product for Meta and Facebook!

The centralized nature of this ecosystem is apparent by examining the right-hand column of the Ecosystem Canvas. The orchestrator is Meta and it does not have another core partner. Technology enablers include Android for the operating system and the Qualcomm chipset as a central processing unit (CPU). The complementors are content providers that design apps for a particular audience and sell them to Oculus users. One example is FitXR, which is an independent London-based software vendor. It provides fitness apps for users. STRIVIR is an example of another complementor that develops software for training; in fact, it was the provider that helped Walmart develop the software for its store and warehouse training simulations.[5]

Pico is also developing VR, but its ecosystem is different. Pico's unique value proposition is to provide a B2B product (as opposed to primarily a business-to-consumer product). The proposition involves providing an immersive experience for customers without locking them into any ecosystem. A customer can purchase a device on its own, but it would require a third-party operator to pre-install software for the specific need. Among competitors we see a list similar to that for Meta. Monetization is different: Pico monetizes its ecosystem primarily through the sales of hardware that costs between 300 and 500 dollars.

The adaptive nature of this ecosystem is apparent on the right-hand column. Pico is the orchestrator that owns a unique value proposition for the customer. The core partners are HTC and Firefox. HTC provides Pico a solution (Viveport) to transfer content from the central servers onto the VR headset. Firefox is a free browser developed by the Mozilla Foundation. A user can port their Firefox settings from the desktop to the VR headset and synchronize web browsing across the two devices.

For the technology enablers, Pico relies on Android as an operating system, Qualcomm for the CPU and Tobii Spotlight Technology for rendering VR experiences. Tobii tracks a person's gaze in real time, which helps develop unique user experiences.[6] Complementors involve content developers that design applications for a particular audience and then sell them to Pico's users. INSEAD is one of many complementors as it developed a number of

VR educational simulations that can be used in the classroom without forcing participants to have their own Facebook accounts. And the resellers involve third-party services that provide training and education offerings.

The choice of the ecosystem depends on the capability of the potential orchestrator as well as on the dynamism of the external environment. If the orchestrator has all the resources needed to build an ecosystem and is relatively certain that the same resources will be required when the environment changes, then a centralized ecosystem is probably the right one. If the environment changes very rapidly and the orchestrator is not sure that it has all the right resources, then adaptive is the best (Furr and Shipilov, 2018).

If a potential orchestrator only has a set of components that others can use, but these components do not comprise a fully-fledged solution, then participation in a decentralized ecosystem as a technology enabler would probably suffice. For example, Google does not orchestrate the entire e-commerce ecosystem; it provides a set of highly useful components, such as Google Analytics, and then lets other technology providers develop their own components that work with Google Analytics. This tool is monetized through a freemium model: whereas small businesses can use this service without paying a monthly charge, the usage of more advanced functionality (that is frequently of interest to larger firms) requires a monthly payment.

## DECENTRALIZED ECOSYSTEMS

Decentralized ecosystems, by virtue of not being coordinated by any core participating partner, are potentially the most ambiguous of the three types of ecosystems. The characteristics of the value proposition enabled by the ecosystem become vaguer at the risk of having the definition be improperly used to define communities of companies operating within an industry or a value chain. Ecosystems of this type are also occurring less frequently than the other two. Following the line of the two previous examples within a technology and software theme, let us use the open-source software value propositions as the example of a decentralized ecosystem: Linux, the open software operating system whose canvas is depicted in Figure 8.4.

While the original video drivers for Linux were not suitable for VR applications, this is changing rapidly with developments of drivers, applications and devices currently available. However, they are not at the same stage of maturity and geographical supply as those functioning on other operating systems, hence the number of applications; e.g., games are not yet comparable to those available for other operating systems. This being said, Linux is a perfect example of a decentralized ecosystem with no orchestrator.

Linux's kernel was developed as a project by Linus Torvalds, a Finnish-American software engineer, in 1991, initially for educational purposes as an alternative to another operating system, MINIX, that was deemed too limited in its functionalities. Both MINIX and Linux originate from developers looking to create non-proprietary alternatives to an earlier operating system that was designed to be free to distribute.[7]

Linus Torvalds initiated Linux's open-source network, which was the kickstart of one of the best examples of a decentralized ecosystem. Torvalds created the Linux Kernel, which then, by virtue of the additional tools, drivers, programs and services developed by a community of developers, evolved into an operating system being used for a wide range of applications, including running the vast majority of search engines globally. The communities of developers,

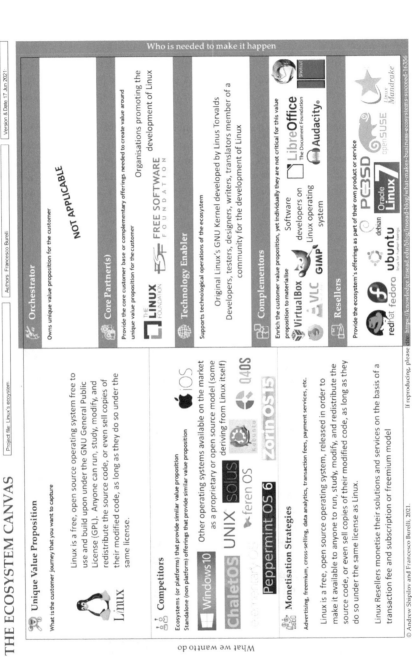

*Figure 8.4    Linux decentralized ecosystem*

many working on a voluntary basis, enable core functional parts of Linux—e.g., the drivers, utilities and programs—which are the technology enablers to the decentralized ecosystem.

Linux's unique value proposition consists in the provision and maintenance of an open-source operating system available to anyone to use and build upon on an open-source basis. Programmers can work on the source code to improve it, add features to it or fix parts as long they as they share the source code without charging a license fee for it. The ultimate purpose is to make a free software resource available to all.

Linux's competitors include a wide range of operating systems. These include proprietary, commercial solutions such as Microsoft's Windows and Unix, as well as other open-source operating systems that were developed based on Linux's kernel to the point of taking on a life of their own, such as Debian, Kubuntu and Debian-derived Q4OS.

There are no monetization strategies for the core of Linux itself as the community keeps developing it for the purpose of openness and upholding the principles of open-source software. While these ideological and moral bases apply to the core of the Linux's operating system, some developers and a number of Linux resellers offer their solutions and services with a transaction fee (e.g., packaged software offered for purchase), subscriptions (e.g., for services and support), or a freemium model, in which the operating system is offered for free but it is optimized to run specific applications. The latter is, for example, the case with Oracle Linux, a free-to-use operating system that is optimized to run Oracle Database, Oracle applications and Oracle Engineered Systems.

As mentioned above, the technical enablers are all the developers, testers, designers, writers and translators who are members of the various Linux communities and who contribute with their time and effort to the ongoing upgrade and improvement of the operating systems. Within these communities there are some major ones who are upholding the principles of open-source software and promoting the development of Linux: among those there are the Linux Foundation and the Free Software Foundation. Given the relevance and the influencing weight of these organizations, these play the role of core partners within the ecosystem. While these core partners have a stronger voice within the ecosystem, it is to be noted that they do not have decisioning or sanctioning authority as they lie with the wider community of participants.

Complementors are developers providing free and paid-for applications ranging from software automation (e.g., Libre Office, media players Audacity and VLC, web browsers such as Firefox) and other applications needed to complement the operating system and enable its full operativity. In this category there are developers such as Keith Packard and Dave Arlie, who are working on enabling VR devices on Linux.[8] Some hardware providers are also part of this category as they offer their kits with the needed drivers to operate on Linux, such as Half-Life's installment Alyx and Valve's own VR system, the Valve Index.[9]

Resellers package the Linux operating system with a suite of applications and accessory software and provide it as an off-the-shelf or service solution. Companies in this group include Linux Redhat, Oracle Linux 7, Debian, Linux Mandrake and others. Among all parties and type of companies mentioned so far, resellers are those who are mostly monetizing their solutions out of all the participants in Linux's ecosystem.

There is no orchestrator in this ecosystem. While the Linux kernel is trademarked by Linus Torvalds, in line with the open-source software guidelines there is no central owner or authority who is controlling access to, or participation in, the Linux community. It is self-managing and still guarantees conformity to the building principles and functionality for newly introduced developments. This lack of an orchestrator is what makes the ecosystem decentralized.

Other decentralized ecosystems include groups of complementary but uncoordinated organizations that develop on the basis of geographical proximity, around a scientific or technological center; e.g., a university with a strongly defined topical specialization. Industrial districts are also examples of such a type of self-organizing ecosystems developing around geographically localized spin-offs and short value chains of highly specialized manufacturing.

All three types of ecosystem configuration are highly evolutionary and change over time, often morphing into each other or becoming a business as a complement of other ecosystems. Airbnb is an example of a platform business model built on a centralized network that is used as a foundation for the establishment of other complementary centralized ecosystem business models. These, combined, are evolving all together into a wider customer journey, ecosystem proposition. There might have been an orchestrator at the core of a decentralized ecosystem at its very onset, much like Linus Torvalds started Linux. However, once the orchestrator has established the value proposition and overcome initial technological challenges, the ecosystem can continue developing on its own in a decentralized fashion. Likewise, a decentralized ecosystem may result from the evolution of the adaptive ecosystem to the point of full openness and full availability to all to participate, contribute and use the value proposition provided by the ecosystem to everyone. The difference to the adaptive ecosystem is in the nature of the commercial and participation agreements between the parties; whereas, in a decentralized ecosystem, participation is not controlled by any company within the ecosystem.

## SO WHAT? ECOSYSTEM CANVAS FOR STRATEGIZING

One can use the canvas just for describing and contrasting different ecosystems. However, its uses do not stop there. One can follow the same set of questions laid out in the canvas to construct the ecosystem from scratch. As many companies use ecosystem thinking as a pillar of their strategy and digital transformation, they need to know where to start. The canvas offers several useful questions to describe future ecosystems. Specifically, one would always need to know the value proposition of the new ecosystem, the customer journey that it is supposed to capture and the customer persona, as well as developing a cogent description for the value to customers. Any ecosystem creator would also need to know the results of comparing it to competition, which would involve benchmarking to competitive characteristics of platforms and non-platform businesses. The questions of direct and indirect monetization also need to be addressed. And of course, one needs to be very clear about which company will play which role in the ecosystem: who is/are the orchestrator, core partners, technology enabler, complementors and resellers.

The canvas can also be a useful tool to develop strategies for different ecosystems, as part of an emerging effort to define ecosystem management strategies (Cennamo, 2021). For example, if a value proposition of an existing ecosystem or the profile of its customer is not clear, then the canvas will nudge the strategist to clarify that. If an ecosystem has limited competition from other ecosystems, platforms or standalone business offerings, then this is good news that can translate into higher prices that could be charged in order to monetize it. However, if the competition is high, then monetization can be based either on low direct transaction fees or primarily through the indirect channels. The canvas can also pose a question to the strategist of whether the ecosystem should be centralized or one could invite core partners. If the orchestrator is currently providing its own technological infrastructure, does it make sense to outsource this to another player? Alternatively, if an ecosystem is based on someone else's technological solution, such as AWS or Azure, does it make sense to continue, or can the orchestrator provide this infrastructure better on its own? A periodic audit of complementors as well as a discussion as to whether an ecosystem will sell itself or it requires resellers would also be important parts of strategy discussion for any orchestrator or a core partner of an ecosystem.

## CONCLUSIONS

In this chapter, based on the principles of graph theory, we identified three types of ecosystems: centralized, adaptive and decentralized. We also offered a tool, Ecosystem Canvas, that can provide a visual representation of an ecosystem's components: its value proposition, competitive landscape and monetization strategies, as well as the critical roles that are needed for making ecosystems happen. Theoretically, this chapter contributes to the discussion about taxonomies of ecosystems (e.g., Shipilov and Gawer, 2020) and to the research on how ecosystems actually matter for firm performance (Burford, Shipilov and Furr, 2021).

One major limitation of our theory is that it has not been empirically validated. That is, we are not aware of empirical work that would compare performance differentials between centralized, adaptive and decentralized ecosystems. The second limitation is that we make no predictions about different ecosystem management strategies. A leader who manages a centralized ecosystem is likely to require different skills than someone who manages an adaptive ecosystem. Furthermore, a leader whose company is a complementor to a centralized, adaptive and decentralized ecosystem is also likely to require different skills. This also applies to the other levels of organizations, notably to their boards. Corporate governance consists of monitoring, strategy and legitimacy functions (e.g., Filatochev and Lanzolla, this volume) and directors in charge of companies that compete in centralized, adaptive and decentralized ecosystems are likely to require different skills in exercising these functions. Fortunately, these two limitations open up extensive opportunities for the future empirical research, both in terms of linking ecosystem structures to firm performance and elucidating different skillsets across different functional areas in companies that are required by different ecosystem configurations.

Despite these caveats, we hope that this work helps in developing the theory of ecosystems as well as in engaging with practitioners who use the ecosystem lens to think through their company's digital transformation.

## NOTES

1. Template available for download from: https://knowledge.insead.edu/sites/www.insead.edu/files/images/ecosystem_canvas_-_guidelines_template_v2.pdf.
2. https://www.marketresearch.com/GlobalData-v3648/DBS-Bank-Fintech-Ecosystem-11962276/.
3. https://www.forbes.com/sites/johanmoreno/2021/08/27/google-estimated-to-be-paying-15-billion-to-remain-default-search-engine-on-safari/?sh=65354aca669b.
4. This section is based on the material in the INSEAD case study "Which Ecosystem for INSEAD VR Initiative?", written by Andrew Shipilov, Brian Henry and Alon Epstein.
5. https://www.strivr.com/resources/customers/walmart/.
6. https://vr.tobii.com/foveated-rendering/.
7. https://www.digitalocean.com/community/tutorials/brief-history-of-linux.

8.    https://lwn.net/Articles/748208/.
9.    https://boilingsteam.com/the-state-of-virtual-reality-on-linux/.

# REFERENCES

Bonacich, P. (2007). Some unique properties of eigenvector centrality. *Social Networks*, *29*(4), 555–64.
Borgatti, S.P., Mehra, A., Brass, D.J., & Labianca, G. (2009). Network analysis in the social sciences. *Science*, *323*(5916), 892–5.
Burford, N., Shipilov, A.V., & Furr, N.R. (2021). How ecosystem structure affects firm performance in response to a negative shock to interdependencies. *Strategic Management Journal*, *43*(1), 30–57.
Cennamo, C. (2021). Competing in digital markets: A platform-based perspective. *Academy of Management Perspectives*, *35*(2), 265–91.
Cennamo, C., & Santalo, J. (2013). Platform competition: Strategic trade-offs in platform markets. *Strategic Management Journal*, *34*(11), 1331–50.
Furr, N., & Kapoor, R. (2018). Capabilities, technologies, and firm exit during industry shakeout: Evidence from the global solar photovoltaic industry. *Strategic Management Journal*, *39*(1), 33–61.
Furr, N., O'Keeffe, K., & Dyer, J.H. (2016). Managing multiparty innovation. *Harvard Business Review*, *94*(11), 76–83.
Furr, N., & Shipilov, A. (2018). Building the right ecosystem for innovation. *MIT Sloan Management Review*, *59*(4), 59–64.
Granstrand, O., & Holgersson, M. (2020). Innovation ecosystems: A conceptual review and a new definition. *Technovation*, *90*, 102098.
Gulati, R., Nohria, N., & Zaheer, A. (2000). Strategic networks. *Strategic Management Journal*, *21*(3), 203–15.
Jacobides, M.G., Cennamo, C., & Gawer, A. (2018). Towards a theory of ecosystems. *Strategic Management Journal*, *39*(8), 2255–76.
Kapoor, R. (2018). Ecosystems: Broadening the locus of value creation. *Journal of Organization Design*, *7*(1), 1–16.
Kapoor, R., & Furr, N.R. (2015). Complementarities and competition: Unpacking the drivers of entrants' technology choices in the solar photovoltaic industry. *Strategic Management Journal*, *36*(3), 416–36.
Lanzolla, G., Pesce, D., & Tucci, C.L. (2021). The digital transformation of search and recombination in the innovation function: Tensions and an integrative framework. *Journal of Product Innovation Management*, *38*(1), 90–113.
Shipilov, A., & Burelli, F. (2021). What makes business ecosystems succeed? INSEAD Knowledge. https://knowledge.insead.edu/strategy/what-makes-business-ecosystems-succeed.
Shipilov, A., & Gawer, A. (2020). Integrating research on interorganizational networks and ecosystems. *Academy of Management Annals*, *14*(1), 92–121.
Wasserman, S., & Faust, K. (1994). *Social Network Analysis: Methods and Applications*. Cambridge University Press.

# 9. Inquiry into digital peer-to-peer platforms

*Oksana Gerwe and Rosario Silva*

## INTRODUCTION

With the rise of companies like eBay, Etsy, Airbnb, BlaBlaCar, TaskRabbit, Udemy, etc., the digital peer-to-peer (P2P) platform business model has become an increasingly prevalent form of exchange across sectors and industries. The concept of digital P2P platforms has been put under the spotlight by the general press, incumbents and the society at large (Colby & Bell, 2016). P2P e-commerce, accommodation, transportation, on-demand household services, on-demand professional services, education and collaborative finance are some of the fastest growing sectors of the global economy (PWC, 2016). Multibillion-dollar evaluations of companies that afford economic benefits to millions of private individuals, who in the past had few if any opportunities to bring to market their assets or skills, reflect the economic and the strategic impact of P2P digital platforms. High participation and usage of such platforms by suppliers and consumers show their influence on the way we work, live and consume (Colby & Bell, 2016; Täuscher, 2019).

Given the magnitude and the impact of the digital P2P platforms, academic research on this new phenomenon has been rapidly evolving and now urgently needs to be solidified and clarified (Benjaafar, Kong, Li & Courcoubetis, 2018; Casadesus-Masanell & Hervas-Drane, 2010; Cullen & Farronato, 2021; Einav, Farronato & Levin, 2016). This is hardly surprising given the heterogeneity of firms and sectors that have adopted P2P business models (Täuscher & Laudien, 2018). Since the advancement of the digital P2P platforms is expected to continue at an accelerated pace and the theoretical development of this topic in the management literature is particularly scarce, in order for research in this field to go forward, it is important to have a clear view of the concept of digital P2P platforms and the different types that comprise their heterogeneous universe.

Considering the scale and the far-reaching implications of the P2P platforms on the one hand, and the lack of clarity on the subject in the management research on the other hand, there is a need to integrate existing knowledge in this area. The goal of the current chapter is to answer three research questions: (1) what is a digital P2P platform, (2) how can digital P2P platforms be classified and (3) what are the main strategic decisions related to digital P2P platforms. Importantly, systematic classification of diverse P2P platforms is needed not only to interpret but also to better predict various outcomes for platforms' owners and their participants. Furthermore, given the heterogeneity of P2P platforms and their unique features compared to other types of digital platforms, we need to develop a more nuanced understanding of the strategic decisions related to attracting, matching and retaining peer-providers and consumers.

## DEFINITION OF DIGITAL P2P PLATFORMS

The traditional way of conducting business between a business supplier and an individual con-sumer (B2C) has been disrupted by two different though related phenomena: the spectacular rise of digital platforms and adoption by many of them of P2P ways of exchange as a powerful alternative to B2C transactions.

The literature has defined a platform business as "a business based on enabling value-creating interactions between external producers and consumers" (Parker, Van Alstyne & Choudary, 2016, p. 5). Platforms provide the infrastructure and set the governance conditions that facil-itate the transactions between different sides (Parker et al, 2016). Chen and colleagues define digital platforms as a type of platform that serves as a "digital interface and utilizes digital technologies to facilitate interactions between different parties" (Chen, Tong, Tang & Han, 2022, p. 149). Digital platform businesses rely on digital technologies and connectivity to create "value by facilitating connections across multiple sides, subject to cross-side network effects" (Gawer, 2021, p. 2). The platform typically does not own the assets that underlie the transaction, such as real estate on accommodation platforms or cars on ride-hailing platforms, but plays the role of a matchmaker by facilitating the interactions between both sides (Einav et al., 2016). Instead, the platform owns the digital interface (a website, an app and the associated IT resources and capabilities) where the connection between the supplier and the consumer occurs (Gawer, 2021).

A digital P2P platform connects two types of actors: peer-providers and peer-consumers. We use the term "peer-provider" to refer to the actor that provides access to a particular asset via the digital platform, such as an individually owned property on Airbnb's platform or dog-walking help on TaskRabbit (Benoit, Baker, Bolton, Gruber & Kandampully, 2017). These are predominantly micro players, individuals, who often operate on an occasional basis; not established businesses or firms (Gerwe & Silva, 2020). Peer-consumers, in turn, form another side of the P2P platform as they seek to access particular goods or services. These are also individuals, usually ordinary citizens, not business consumers or wholesale buyers. The term "peer" in this context differentiates this type of exchange from B2C or business-to-business (B2B) transactions and refers to individual suppliers or consumers, whose operations are usually small in scale and do not represent an established business, company or corporation (Gerwe, Silva & de Castro, 2020).[1] Comparison between Amazon and Etsy, for example, illustrates the differences between B2C and P2P digital platforms. Both platforms facilitate sales of goods, but in the case of Amazon providers are usually established businesses, while on Etsy the goods are provided by enterprising individuals selling their arts and crafts on a small scale.

Digital P2P platforms have reduced entry costs, facilitating the possibility for millions of dispersed individual suppliers to bring their goods and services to market, changing the competitive landscape for business that traditionally provided services and delivered goods in different sectors. For example, by June 2021, Airbnb had 4 million hosts that offered their homes for short-term rent in the accommodation sector,[2] where historically the bulk of supply came from hotels and bed-and-breakfast operators. At the same time, Lyft had 2 million drivers, disrupting the traditional taxi operators;[3] TaskRabbit allowed 140,000 individuals (the so-called "taskers")[4] to offer their time and skills in assisting customers with errands and chores in the household services sector as an alternative to traditional cleaning companies or businesses that provide personal assistant services.

P2P platforms create value by reducing the time and the effort that large numbers of fragmented customers and peer-providers need to find each other and interact (Benjaafar et al., 2018; Einav et al., 2016). Additionally, by unlocking supply that is latent in the market but would be untapped without the platform, digital P2P platforms create new markets (i.e., ride-sharing, carpooling, crowdfunding, video-sharing, etc.). Underused physical assets, spare time or hidden talents of people that in the past would not be productive can now be targeted as sources of supply to create value for peer-providers, consumers and the platform.

Summing up the points above, a digital P2P platform can be defined as a digital interface that uses digital technologies to facilitate transactions between peer-providers and peer-consumers.

## CLASSIFICATION OF DIGITAL P2P PLATFORMS

Digital P2P platform businesses span multiple industries and economic sectors. Unlike other types of platforms, digital platforms rely on the digital interface (a website or a mobile app) to facilitate the transaction. Importantly, the assets that can be accessed through the digital platform can be digital (such as videos, photos, reports, etc.) or non-digital (such as accommodation facilities, means of transportation, human skills and talents, crafts, consumer products, etc.). Once the diversity among digital P2P platforms is recognized, the necessity to find a way to classify them becomes apparent. We posit that they can be categorized in a systematic way based on three salient dimensions of the transactions that they facilitate: (1) type of asset that underlies the transaction (i.e., physical, human, digital asset or money), (2) mode of transaction (i.e., only online, or online plus offline) and (3) monetary compensation to peer-provider (i.e., present or absent). Each dimension captures the main differentiating features between digital P2P platforms and represents a strategic choice that the platform makes before its launch and has direct implications for the platform's capacity to scale up, the heterogeneity of quality in the transactions and the risk of disintermediation. Table 9.1 includes some examples of different types of platforms.

### Type of Asset that Underlies the Transaction

Digital P2P platforms facilitate a wide array of transactions in which the asset type that underlies the transaction can be a physical asset, a human asset, a digital asset or money. Based on the type of assets, we can identify different types of digital P2P platforms:

- P2P physical asset platforms are those in which peer-providers bring their physical assets for transaction with others, such as real estate (e.g., Airbnb, Booking.com, Couchsurfing), cars (e.g., Turo) and new or second-hand products to sell (e.g., Etsy, eBay or Poshmark) (Gerwe & Silva, 2020; Vallas & Schor, 2020).
- P2P service platforms are platforms in which peer-providers offer a service to users. These platforms rely on human assets, such as time and skills (e.g., TaskRabbit), professional abilities and knowledge (e.g., Superprof, Skillshare, Busu) or a combination of physical and human assets (e.g., BlablaCar, Lyft).
- P2P digital content platforms make it possible for a large base of producers to provide access to created content (i.e., videos, ideas, photos, music) to other individuals (Casadesus-Masanell & Hervas-Drane, 2010), such as Pinterest, TikTok and YouTube.

*Table 9.1*     *Types of P2P platforms*

| Asset involved in the transaction | Space in which the transaction takes place | The transaction involves money | Example of firms | Examples of categories |
|---|---|---|---|---|
| Physical asset | Online | Money-based | Hurr | Peer-to-peer clothing rental |
| | | | Poshmark | Peer-to-peer resale (used clothes) |
| | | Money-based | Ebay | Peer-to-peer e.commerce |
| | | | Etsy | |
| | | | Taobao.com | |
| | Offline & online | Money-based | Airbnb Booking | Peer-to-peer real estate rental |
| | | | HomeAway | |
| | | | Turo | Peer-to-peer car rental |
| | | | Getaround | |
| | | | Peerrenters.com | |
| | | | Sparetoolz | Peer-to-peer tool rental |
| | | | Wallapop | Peer-to-peer online flea market |
| | | Non-money-based | Couchsurfing | Peer-to-peer home exchange |
| Service | Online | Money-based | Verbling | Peer-to-peer learning |
| | | | iTalki | |
| | | | Duolingo | |
| | | | Skillshare | |
| | Offline & online | Money-based | Care.com | On-demand household services |
| | | | Taskrabbit | |
| | | | Lyft | Ride-sharing |
| | | | Blablacar | Carpooling |
| | | | Nimber | Peer-to-peer delivery service |
| | | | Airbnb | Peer-to-peer home-sharing |
| | | Non-money-based | Couchsurfing | Peer-to-peer home exchange |
| Digital content | Online | Money-based | Udemy | Peer-to-peer learning |
| | | | iStockphoto | Peer-to-peer digital good sales |
| | | Non-money-based | Pinterest | Peer-to-peer image, video and |
| | | | YouTube | live streams sharing |
| | | | Twitch | |
| Money | Online | Capital plus interest rate | Prosper | Peer-to-peer lending platforms |
| | | | LendingClub* | |
| | | Equity | WeFunder | Equity crowdfunding |
| | | | EquityNet | |
| | | Other type of reward | Kickstarter | Reward-based crowdfunding |
| | | | GoFundMe | platforms |
| | | | Indiegogo | |
| | | | Patreon | |
| | | | Paypal | Peer-to-peer payments |
| | | | Venmo | |

*Note:* * In 2020, Lending Club acquired Radius Bank and announced that by the end of that year, it would no longer operate as a peer-to-peer lending platform.

- P2P money transactions platforms are those in which peer-providers bring their monetary contributions to fund or to lend to people that need money for a project, a charitable cause, a new business, etc. Some examples of crowdfunding platforms can be GoFundMe and Kickstarter, while Prosper is an example of a crowdlending platform. This type also includes the P2P payments platforms, such as Venmo.

The type of asset that is offered on the platform has direct implications for the potential pool of peer-providers that a particular platform can access to establish its operations and, therefore, for the potential growth of the platform. For example, only people willing to share their homes may act as peer-providers on Couchsurfing; only individuals willing to rent daily their spare cars may participate in Turo, and people willing to share their specialized knowledge or skills may offer services on Busu, the language learning platform. However, other platforms can enjoy an almost unconstrained supply, such as YouTube, in which almost anyone can upload a video, or even Kickstarter or Prosper, in which individuals need little spare money to participate. For instance, at Kickstarter the minimum amount for US-based projects that backers need to pledge to a project is $1 (Kickstarter, 2021). At Prosper, individuals need a minimum investment of just $25 to become an investor (Prosper, 2021). Thus, the type of asset that underlies transactions on a particular platform inherently creates barriers for entry to this platform and sets its scaling-up limits. As such, it seems easier to scale digital content and money transaction platforms than physical asset and service platforms, as the pool of peer-providers with digital assets or small amounts of cash is almost infinite while not every individual has a service to provide or physical asset to rent out or sell.

The type of asset also influences the motivations of users and peer-providers to join and stay with a platform, which is a relevant aspect of the digital platform strategy and its ability to scale up (McIntyre, Srinivasan & Chintakananda, 2021). During the early stages of its operations, a platform needs to attract a large base of providers; thus, it is important for the platform to understand factors that drive providers to join the platform. Extant literature shows that the motivations of peer-providers to participate in a P2P platform depend on the platform's type (Gerwe & Silva, 2020). For instance, Uber's drivers value the income and the flexibility of working for Uber (Hall & Krueger, 2018), while the reasons for individuals to engage in Airbnb hosting are money and the possibility to meet new people and establish social connections (Ikkala & Lampinen, 2015). Regarding the motivations to produce content for P2P digital content platforms, like YouTube, recent research shows that extrinsic motivations often associated with work, like earning money or gaining more prestige, are less important than intrinsic motivations, like socialization or enjoyment, which are more often related to leisure activities (Törhönen, Sjöblom, Hassan & Hamari, 2020). Finally, the crowdfunding literature shows that individuals' motivations to fund projects are, for instance, the desire to help others, support causes or be part of a community (Gerber & Hui, 2016). Thus, in order to attract participants and ensure that they stay on the platform, it is important for the digital P2P platform to understand and manage motivations of its peer-providers and consumers.

One important characteristic of P2P markets is the high degree of heterogeneity of both providers and their assets (Einav et al., 2016). Unlike traditional B2C business models, where quality is more standardized and often tied to a particular company brand, digital P2P platforms welcome a wide range of providers whose offerings may vary greatly in terms of quality. High heterogeneity on both sides is a distinctive feature of the digital P2P platforms that needs to be carefully taken into account and closely tracked by the platform managers when they design the platform strategy. In fact, low control over service quality is noted in extant research as one of the reasons for P2P platform failure (Täuscher & Kietzmann, 2017). It is not surprising that many digital P2P platforms over time push for an increased professionalization of peer-providers to increase the quality in the transactions. For example, Uber now has specific requirements for the age and condition of vehicles that can be used by drivers to provide services via this platform (Uber, 2021).

The risk of disintermediation is one of the highest threats for platforms' survival (Zhu & Iansiti, 2019). Disintermediation occurs when users and suppliers connect directly, bypassing the platform. This problem explains the failure of household services platforms, like Homejoy: Once house cleaners find enough clients and clients find good house cleaners, they do not need the platform anymore and start transacting directly (Zhu & Iansiti, 2019). We claim that the risk of disintermediation is higher on the digital P2P service platforms that may facilitate a strong bond between the same pair of a user and a supplier. For instance, in household services platforms, in which the regular, continuous interaction between the house cleaner and the user promotes a strong relationship between them; or in learning/education services platforms, in which it is likely that the tutor and the user develop a durable relationship.

## Mode of Transaction: Only Online or Online Plus Offline Transactions

A digital P2P platform facilitates transactions between peer-providers and consumers. On some platforms transactions are completely online, like buying something via Etsy or eBay, doing an online task via Upwork, sharing images via Pinterest or borrowing money from Prosper. However, on other digital P2P platforms, the transaction starts online with the exchange of information between individuals and the decision to close the deal between them, but the final service occurs offline, in the real world. For instance, in the P2P carpooling platform BlaBlaCar, the user searches online for information about the rides and the profiles of drivers. The user also has the possibility to connect online with the driver before and after booking a ride. The user books and pays for the ride online. However, the final service occurs offline, when the driver and the user travel together sharing a ride.

We posit that purely online P2P platforms can scale faster than those platforms on which transactions occur offline. While purely online platforms can be very accessible for all users, platforms that facilitate offline transactions require consumers and peer-providers to be located in a specific geographic location. Recent research shows that the number of providers on platforms that combine offline with online may depend on the specific macro-economic conditions of the city (Gerwe et al. 2020). This sets another constraint to the scaling-up potential of the platform.

Within the category of P2P platforms that combine online with offline, there is another characteristic of offline transactions that can limit a platform's growth as it is related to the scope of the network effects. The network effects have a local reach when the nature of the services exchanged is local and time-sensitive (Cullen & Farronato, 2021; Zhu & Iansiti, 2019). For instance, the network effects in carpooling and ride-sharing platforms will be local, as users and drivers interact on demand. Both sides need to personally meet immediately, in a specific location, at a set moment in time. Local network effects imply that only the number of users and providers that are located close to each other create value for the other side. The existence of local network effects limits the possibility for one platform to achieve a winner-take-all effect. By contrast, when users and providers do not need to personally meet immediately, as in the case of eBay, the network effects will be global, which means that users get value from the growth of the platform with new users from around the world.

The distinction between purely online and online with offline transactions on P2P platforms also has implications for the quality of the transaction. When the transaction takes place offline, the platform has less control over its quality. When providers and users interact face to face, such as in a carpooling, ride-sharing or home-sharing platform, the quality of the

*Table 9.2*      *Different types of rewards for peer-providers on digital P2P platforms*

| Type of reward | Example |
|---|---|
| Money | Airbnb, eBay, Taobao, Udemy |
| Social | Couchsurfing |
| Equity | WeFunder |
| Tangible rewards, such as a copy of a video/experiences | Kickstarter |
| Intangible rewards: attention, reputation, influence | Wikipedia |

final service is more uncertain as it depends on the interpersonal engagement between both sides (Kyprianou, 2018). Thus, to guarantee that the transactions are of a desired quality, the platform needs to actively manage quality expectations and delivery by means of articulating certain quality standards in the community of platform users, establishing measures to encourage good quality and discourage or penalize bad quality. Peer-provider and consumer ratings and online communities of peer-providers (i.e., designated Uber or Airbnb forums) are some of the widely used mechanisms for quality management across different digital P2P platforms.

Finally, the presence or absence of the offline component in the transactions on a digital P2P platform has different implications for the risk of disintermediation on a particular platform. For instance, in platforms in which individuals can access or exchange digital content, like YouTube or Pinterest, individuals can upload their videos, ideas, etc., and users can watch them without any direct connection between them. Crowdfunding and crowdlending platforms are also designed in a way in which both sides do not need to connect directly to complete the transaction. In this case, the value is created entirely within the platform, which allows the platform owner to have more control over it, and more possibilities to monetize the transaction as it is more difficult to have the disintermediation problem (i.e., that both sides bypass the platform and connect directly). However, on the majority of the P2P platforms where the peer-providers make accessible their physical assets, transfer them or deliver a service to the user, both sides need to engage in a direct connection in order to complete the transaction. For instance, Airbnb hosts need to interact directly with the guest to communicate the address and give them instructions about their stay. Other platforms, like TaskRabbit, Lyft, BlaBlaCar, Couchsurfing, Verbling, etc., facilitate a direct connection between peer-providers and users. This means that the platform has less control over the transaction and, as a result, it faces greater risks of disintermediation. Therefore, the platform needs to create trust in both its own characteristics and between individuals to encourage them to connect with others and to remain on the platform.

## Monetary Compensation

Another dimension that characterizes digital P2P platforms is whether the transaction involves a monetary payment from the consumer to the peer-provider (Fitzmaurice & Schor, 2015; Sundararajan, 2016). Some platforms facilitate transactions that do not involve any monetary exchange between peer-providers and consumers, such as Couchsurfing, where guests stay with hosts for free; YouTube, where users watch videos for free; or Kickstarter, where users receive money from the backers but they do not need to return the money nor pay them an interest rate. However, other platforms are money-based, such as Airbnb, where guests pay for the accommodation provided by hosts. Table 9.2 offers some examples of the different types of rewards that peer-providers can get for their participation in a P2P platform.

The presence (or absence) of monetary compensation from consumers to providers has a direct effect on the platform's growth and the possibility of creating network effects. On the one hand, free access to goods or services can encourage customers to join the platform, which can be helpful, at least at the launch of the platform, to create positive network effects (i.e., a large number of customers will be valuable for the peer-providers). On the other hand, when the transaction does not involve any monetary compensation for the peer-providers, their motivation to join and participate in the platform can be lower, unless the platform offers other ways to compensate peer-providers for their effort (i.e., YouTubers can receive a monetary compensation based on the payments made by advertisers). It is not surprising that the presence of financial compensation of peer-providers on Airbnb has been identified as one of the important explanatory variables when comparing the scale of this platform with, for instance, Couchsurfing, where there are no monetary incentives for peer-providers' participation.

The presence (or absence) of monetary compensation also has implications for the quality of assets and/or services that would be offered on the platform. We believe that financial payoffs are likely to ensure a higher quality of services and assets that are accessible on a digital P2P platform, compared to a similar competitor that does not have financial compensation built into the system. Furthermore, monetary compensation for transactions on the P2P platform affects the way a platform can capture value from these transactions. If we compare Couchsurfing with Airbnb, for example, Airbnb's decision to allow compensation for every transaction allows the platform to earn a fee from each booking, while a freemium model of Couchsurfing makes the monetization for the platform more challenging.

## STRATEGIC DECISIONS OF DIGITAL P2P PLATFORMS

Digital P2P platforms share some commonalities with other types of digital platforms, such as B2B or B2C platforms, and, therefore, may face similar strategic decisions common to digital platforms in general (Gawer, 2021). In order to successfully operate, grow and achieve network effects, digital platforms need to formulate and execute strategies regarding attracting, matching and retaining users on the two sides to the platform. However, the P2P nature of transaction gives rise to a number of unique features and strategic decisions characteristic of this setting. The fact that suppliers and consumers on the two sides of the P2P platform represent the multitude of fragmented individuals, not established businesses or firms, has unique implications for strategic choices made by the P2P platforms across different companies and over time. Below we explore strategic choices characteristic of digital P2P platforms around three main areas: (1) facilitation of frictionless entry of consumers and of peer-providers with heterogeneous quality, (2) the match between them and (3) the retention of both types of users within the platform.

### Attracting Both Sides to the P2P Platform

Some of the largest public companies in the world are digital P2P platforms such as eBay, Airbnb, Pinterest or Etsy (*Fortune*, 2021). These platforms create value by reducing market entry and transaction costs, which are those costs that "impede mutually advantageous interactions and exchanges" (Evans & Schmalensee, 2016, p. 209). For example, before the entry of Couchsurfing, Airbnb and Love Home Swap, it was difficult for a property owner to share their home with a stranger, and for an individual to share a place with the owner, because there were large costs for finding each other, ensuring safety, making the payment, etc. (Farronato & Fradkin, 2018). These platforms offered digital solutions that made it easy for peer-providers to join the new marketplace and to transact there.

### Ease of joining the platform

Since the participants on both sides of digital P2P platforms are typically micro players, not professional businesses or firms, the ease of entry and joining a P2P platform is critical. Individual peer-providers may not have the sophisticated knowledge or skills that professional market players would. Thus, an easy-to-join and easy-to-use platform helps users to affiliate with the platform. Indeed, a professional retailer is much more likely to have the right motivation, skills and knowledge to join Amazon, for example, than a host from a small town in Spain who wants to share an empty bedroom via Airbnb. Thus, the choice of the user-facing digital design on P2P platforms needs to ensure maximum ease of use, efficiency and attractiveness to appeal to a wide range of non-professional participants.

### Piggybacking strategy

Similar to other digital platforms, P2P platforms face the chicken-and-egg problem since it is difficult to simultaneously attract both sides, peer-providers and consumers, as the value of the platform for each of them depends on the existence of the other side. To build the initial base of users, digital P2P platforms may rely on a piggybacking or "growth hacking" strategy – importing users from other networks, to establish their first population of providers and/or consumers. Airbnb, for example, applied this strategy to increase its growth early on with the option "Publish on Craigslist" (Dou & Wu, 2021). On the Airbnb website hosts got an option to publish their Airbnb listings on Craigslist, and potential guests responding to the listing could still contact the host through Airbnb. This way a new platform can quickly address the problem of attracting one side of users, which will then start attracting the other side, creating network effects and generating value. This is particularly relevant when attracting non-professional peer-providers.

### Side-switching strategy

Furthermore, unlike B2C platforms where the roles of suppliers and consumers are generally fixed, to encourage growth of one side of the platform, P2P platforms can follow a strategy of side switching (Parker et al., 2016). P2P platforms can encourage consumers to join the provider side of the platform, and providers, the consumer side. For instance, a user of YouTube can also produce content; a Couchsurfing user can be a host in their home town and a guest at a travel destination. If every user on the demand side also becomes a user on the supply side, the platform will need less effort to achieve the scale necessary to create network effects.

The design of the platform can ensure that side switching is easy, reversible and costless (Gazé & Vaubourg, 2011). For instance, a user of PayPal can both receive and send money; similarly, on eBay a user can buy or sell items without the need to create a new account (Gazé & Vaubourg, 2011). The P2P resale marketplace Poshmark provides a good example of a platform that has grown more easily thanks to its side-switching strategy. Its IPO prospectus highlights how side switching facilitates its growth:

Buyers often convert to becoming sellers after experiencing the ease and value of selling on our marketplace. At any time, a user may be a buyer, a seller or both. This high velocity flywheel of community engagement drives strong monetization potential and an attractive business model with efficient user acquisition dynamics. Of all buyers who activated between 2012 and 2018, 34% of these buyers also activated as sellers by year end 2019, and of all sellers who activated between 2012 and 2018, 39% of these sellers activated as buyers by year end 2019. (Poshmark IPO Prospectus 2021, p. 2)

## Managing the quality of peer-providers

It is important to ensure that the platform grows by attracting users with whom the other users want to interact (Evans & Schmalensee, 2016). This implies the need to balance the mere frictionless entry with the entry of valuable users (i.e., users with whom other users want to interact). To ensure the entry of valuable users, digital P2P platforms may limit access by establishing some control mechanisms; that is, some rules or guidelines for judging whether a peer-provider should be allowed onto the platform (Thies, Wessel & Benlian, 2018). Platforms may also actively encourage peer-providers to increase their quality. Some platforms make investments to support peer-providers and help them become more professional in their platform-related operations. For instance, in 2015, Airbnb launched a dynamic pricing tool to suggest an optimal price for each listing (Oskam, Van de Rest & Telkamp, 2018). Similarly, platforms may encourage the development of communities of peer-providers where useful information and ideas will be shared by platform users.

## Ecosystem with third-party providers

Successful digital P2P platforms can strategically manage the ecosystem around its main service so that the engagement of additional participants can facilitate the entry of peer-providers. Platforms may actively encourage the emergence of other complements (e.g., third-party developers) that help peer-providers enter and operate successfully on the platform. For instance, in 2018, Airbnb launched the "Preferred Software Partner" program to identify those software providers who could offer the best tools for hosts (Airbnb, 2021). In this case, the platform owner needs to make a strategic decision on which services it will provide within the platform and which services will be managed via an ecosystem of other complements that help peer-providers to improve their main service.

To develop an attractive ecosystem, the platform must provide the resources that help third-party developers to create complementary assets (Ghazawneh & Henfridson, 2012). The information systems literature refers to such resources as platform boundary resources, such as application programming interfaces, or APIs (Ghazawneh & Henfridson, 2012). For P2P platforms with a very high number of peer-providers, digital boundary resources play a key role, as they ensure that peer-providers can independently manage their participation in the platform without unduly burdening the platform owner with queries or concerns.

An API makes it possible for developers to access and integrate the functionality of the platform with other applications and to create new applications. When digital platforms open their APIs to external developers, they facilitate development of new services compatible with the platform, expanding its functionalities (Gawer, 2021). In the design of the API, the platform needs to balance continuous control over the platform with the benefits of developing new complementary services that increase the value for their users. For instance, in 2017 Airbnb launched its official Airbnb API, which provides users with a tool called OAuth, an open protocol that enables hosts to update the content and the rates of their listings via a single app.

Although Airbnb has opened up its digital interface, it does not lose control over the platform, as it strictly controls the partners who have access to the API documentation (Reynolds, 2020).

Taken together, the ease of joining the platform, piggybacking, side switching, managing quality and building the ecosystem around the main service form the portfolio of strategic choices that digital P2P platform managers can use to effectively attract peers to join the platform.

## Matching Peer-Providers and Consumers

The high heterogeneity and fragmentation of peer-providers and consumers on digital P2P platforms implies higher search costs (Li & Netessine, 2020). As the platform grows and more users and peer-providers join the platform and the heterogeneity of offerings increases, the efficiency of matching may go down (Li & Netessine, 2020). However, the value of the P2P platform to its users is directly linked to its ability to facilitate a good match out of the multiple discrete options present on the two sides of the platform. Thus, it is necessary to manage the possible congestion and resulting inefficiencies by improving platform design and by taking into account that users on both sides are not professional business actors but ordinary enterprising individuals (Arnosti, Johari & Kanoria, 2021; Horton, 2019; Shi, 2021).

### Platform design

The design of the platform can help users share information, reducing the uncertainty about the quality, reliability and relevance of heterogenous users and offerings. More specifically, design of the matching mechanisms can reduce the hassle of the search process. P2P platforms can use different designs of the matching features: one side searches (e.g., Airbnb's guests search apartments), both sides search (e.g., Care.com allows individuals who need care and those who need a job to search for each other) and centralized matching (e.g., Uber and TaskRabbit recommend a limited number of providers to each user) (Shi, 2021). The platform may play an active role in creating and finetuning the categorization of the offerings, such as different categories of properties on accommodation platforms or rides and vehicles on ride-sharing platforms.

Xu & Chau (2018) analyzed how a design feature of a P2P lending platform that facilitates direct communication (e.g., a feature called "comment" that allows lenders to post questions and request information, and borrowers to respond) affected the odds of the funding success. Their results show that direct communication increases trust and the probability of matching: the more responses a borrower makes to the comments, the more likely the listing will attract sufficient funding.

Extant research offers evidence of matching inefficiencies. Some researchers claim that consumers may spend time and effort checking profiles of peer-providers but the latter would end up unavailable and reject consumer requests, which ultimately leads to consumers' disappointment (Arnosti, et al., 2021; Fradkin, 2017; Horton, 2019). For instance, Fradkin (2017) shows that Airbnb hosts reject guests very often both because of their lack of availability and their preferences. Up to 42 percent of inquiries regarding bookings get rejected on Airbnb. These rejections lead guests to abandon the platform. In addition, research offers evidence of discriminatory practices on digital P2P platforms such as Airbnb, Uber and Lyft (Cui, Li & Zhang, 2020; Edelman, Luca & Svirsky, 2016).

To reduce matching inefficiencies, scholars propose interventions in the platform's design. For instance, Arnosti et al. (2021) show that restricting the number of choices can lead to a better outcome, because it reduces the effort to find a suitable match.

**Mechanisms of digital trust and reputation**
Digital P2P platforms have grown thanks to the introduction of innovative mechanisms of digital trust and reputation, such as rating systems, insurance, digital payment mechanisms, verification of the identity of both sides, certification of the quality of the provider, etc., that reduce risks for both sides of P2P transactions (Cusumano, Gawer & Yoffie, 2019; Einav et al., 2016). Unlike B2C or B2B settings, where the consumer would usually be a more vulnerable side in the transaction and is therefore protected by the traditional customer protection mechanisms, on P2P platforms both peer-providers and consumers bear substantial risks in the transaction. For example, the Airbnb guest takes substantial risks by agreeing to stay with a stranger; but the Airbnb host also takes significant personal risks and risks to her assets by offering accommodation to a stranger (Gerwe & Silva, 2020).

Introduction of digital trust mechanisms by the platform reduces asymmetry of information that in the past limited P2P transactions to members of the family or neighborhood and increases the likelihood of a successful match between peer-providers and consumers (Gerwe & Silva, 2020; Täuscher, 2019). Empirical research on eBay confirms that reputation systems increase trust (Pavlou & Dimoka, 2006; Resnick & Zeckhauser, 2002), though some studies show the drawbacks of these systems as consumers are more reluctant to post negative feedback (Masterov, Meyer & Tadelis, 2015), which may lead to reputation inflation. For instance, Zervas, Proserpio and Byers (2021) found that the average Airbnb property rating is 4.7 stars, with 94 percent of all properties having a star-rating of either 4.5 stars or 5 stars in 2015. Overall, more research is needed about ways to improve the reputation systems (Dai, Jin, Lee & Luca, 2018).

**Active governance and control**
In addition to introducing digital mechanisms to create and maintain trust in digital P2P transactions, the platform itself can actively shape and manage behavior of its customers and peer-providers through active governance and control choices. Platforms can create and popularize a code of conduct and guidelines to set expectations for user behavior on the platform (Täuscher, 2017). Also, platform owners can encourage establishment of communities of users where platform-related standards and practices can be shared and discussed in a P2P fashion. The platform can set incentives for desired behavior and sanctions for bad behavior, including outright bans of poorly behaving platform users. For example, Uber may permanently ban drivers who are breaking the expectations of courteous or safe driving, and passengers with consistently low ratings due to bad behavior during rides.

Overall, different elements of platform design, the use of mechanisms of digital trust and reputation as well as the instruments of active governance and control increase the likelihood of a good match between peer-providers and consumers on digital P2P platforms.

**Retaining Customers and Peer-Providers within the P2P Platform**

Similar to other digital platforms, P2P platforms need to retain users within the platform to be able to capture value created on the platform. If users can easily switch to another platform (i.e., multi-homing) or bypass the platform by connecting directly between them (i.e., disintermediation), platforms will lose the opportunity to capture value. Thus, managers of digital P2P platforms need strategies to discourage multi-homing and disintermediation.

**Multi-homing**

Given the explosion of digital P2P platforms, their ability to maintain differentiation is critical for their growth and survival, especially when they face more intense competition (Srinivasan & Venkatraman, 2018). Multi-homing – that is, the decision of a peer-provider or a consumer to affiliate with multiple platforms – may reduce differentiation across platforms, leading to intense competition for retaining members on both sides (Rochet & Tirole, 2003).

Multi-homing is a common phenomenon on some P2P platforms, such as ride-sharing (Yu, Mo, Xie, Hu & Chen, 2021). Again, the heterogeneity of both consumers and peer-providers, which is characteristic of P2P settings, may involve a range of factors that can influence the level of multi-homing. In order to design a strategy that counteracts the tendency to multi-home, platforms need to understand the drivers of multi-homing behavior in their specific context. For instance, recent research using drivers' data from ride-sharing platforms located in Hangzhou (China) found that the driver's socio-demographic characteristics, income level, bonus income and work-time-related factors (e.g., the time gap of order dispatching and wait time) are critical factors that affect drivers' decision to switch to another platform (Yu et al., 2021). The authors suggest that improving the matching process would be one possible way to reduce the time gap between orders, which will decrease the likelihood of switching to another platform.

One strategy to decrease multi-homing is to differentiate the platform's functionalities and technological features (Cennamo, Ozalp & Kretschmer, 2018; McIntyre, Srinivasan, Afuah, Gawer & Kretschmer, 2021). We posit that adding new interactions and services is one way to enhance the value created by the P2P platform, attract new users and retain them. An important strategic decision in this case is about the scope of the platform, as the value for users might increase due to expansion of scope of their providers (Cennamo, 2021). Some platforms may specialize in one core transaction, as in the case of Couchsurfing, which focuses on home-sharing, in contrast to Airbnb, in which peer-providers offer a wide range of accommodation options (i.e., an entire place, private rooms, hotel rooms and shared rooms). Other platforms may follow an envelopment strategy, combining their own functionality with the functionality of other platforms (Eisenmman, Parker & Van Alstyne, 2011). For instance, eBay was able to develop and achieve impressive scale thanks to PayPal, a digital payment platform that ensured trust at the point of payment for goods or services. Another way to enhance the value of the platform for both sides, mitigating the risk of multi-homing, is through boosting data-driven network effects (Gregory, Henfridsson, Kaganer & Kyriakou, 2021). A better matching process is an effective way to keep the interest of both the consumer and peer-provider in continued participation in the platform. As consumers and peer-providers do more transactions, the platform learns about their preferences, which will allow it to offer more accurate recommendations in the future. The positive value creation loop will encourage customers and peer-providers to stay exclusively on this platform.

**Risk of disintermediation**

Besides multi-homing, P2P platforms need to manage the risk of disintermediation. Recent research shows that in the context of an online freelance marketplace, as a platform improves trust between both sides it increases the risk of disintermediation (Gu & Zhu, 2021). Given that platforms need to create trust to grow, the evidence suggests that platforms need to develop some strategies to avoid the disintermediation. Gu and Zhu (2021) propose some examples of strategies that platforms can follow to decrease the disintermediation risk, such as the verification and control of host data adopted by Airbnb or the decision of Thumbtack, a P2P platform that connects consumers with local home repair specialists, to charge fees to peer-providers when customers respond to their quotes; that is, before both sides agree to do the transaction. Future research can explore the effectiveness of different strategies to avoid disintermediation.

## CONCLUSION

The emergence and expansion of digital P2P platforms has substantially transformed the competitive landscape where traditional B2C and B2B ways of transacting used to dominate. Since the advancement of the P2P businesses is expected to continue at an accelerated pace, and the academic research on this topic is still scarce due to its relative novelty, it is critical to develop a clear view of what we understand under digital P2P platforms and systematize their heterogeneous universe in order to better predict various outcomes that concern P2P platforms and its participants.

In this chapter we first define digital P2P platforms as those that use digital technologies to facilitate interactions between peer-providers and peer-consumers. The term "peer" differentiates this type of exchange from B2C or B2B transactions and describes individual suppliers or consumers, whose operations are usually small in scale and do not represent an established business or corporation. Moreover, we offer a systematic classification of digital P2P platforms based on three salient dimensions: asset that underlies the transaction (physical, human, digital asset or money), mode of transaction (only online, or online plus offline), and monetary compensation (present or absent). A platform's decisions regarding these dimensions have significant strategic implications for its ability to scale up, the level of quality that it would be able to offer in its transactions and the risk of disintermediation.

Having analyzed distinctive features of the P2P context, we highlight a set of relevant strategic decisions that digital P2P platforms can use in order to ensure their success with respect to attracting, matching and retaining users on both sides of the platform. Given the scant empirical research, future research could explore the effectiveness of strategies to reduce both multi-homing and disintermediation in the context of digital P2P platforms. Future research may consider additional strategies that platforms can use in order to increase their value creation and value capture ability, such as the scope of the platform in terms of diversification and profitability potential. Taken together, the definition of digital P2P platforms, their classification and the analysis of some strategic decisions will allow researchers to conceptualize with greater clarity nuanced processes and outcomes that take place in the digital P2P ecosystems and improve the explanatory and predictive power of the inquiries that are much needed in this highly relevant area of research.

## NOTES

1.  We acknowledge that the distinction between a P2P and B2C platform can sometimes be fuzzy, as on P2P platforms there can be professional players present along with peer-providers. For example, on Airbnb, professional property managers and even hotels can offer their assets next to individuals who share their spare bedroom with travellers. However, it is important to note that for businesses, digital platforms usually serve as an additional channel for their operations, while for peer-providers this is the only way to enter the market and get visibility and clients. That is why P2P business models only became widely spread with the proliferation of digital platforms. Without the latter, peer-providers would have not had a chance to enter the market.
2.  https://news.airbnb.com/about-us/.
3.  https://www.ridester.com/lyft-stats/.
4.  https://www.taskrabbit.co.uk/careers.

## REFERENCES

Airbnb (2021). Our preferred software partners. https://www.airbnb.es/d/software-partners?

Arnosti, N., Johari, R., & Kanoria, Y. (2021). Managing congestion in matching markets. *Manufacturing & Service Operations Management*, *23*(3), 620–36.

Benjaafar, S., Kong, G., Li, X., & Courcoubetis, C. (2018). Peer-to-peer product sharing: Implications for ownership, usage, and social welfare in the sharing economy. *Management Science*, *65*(2), 477–93.

Benoit, S., Baker, T.L., Bolton, R.N., Gruber, T., & Kandampully, J. (2017). A triadic framework for collaborative consumption (CC): Motives, activities and resources & capabilities of actors. *Journal of Business Research*, *79*, 219–27.

Casadesus-Masanell, R., & Hervas-Drane, A. (2010). Peer-to-peer file sharing and the market for digital information goods. *Journal of Economics & Management Strategy*, *19*(2), 333–73.

Cennamo, C. (2021). Competing in digital markets: A platform-based perspective. *Academy of Management Perspectives*, *35*(2), 265–91.

Cennamo, C., Ozalp, H., & Kretschmer, T. (2018). Platform architecture and quality trade-offs of multi-homing complements. *Information Systems Research*, *29*(2), 461–78.

Chen, L., Tong, T.W., Tang, S., & Han, N. (2022). Governance and design of digital platforms: A review and future research directions on a meta-organization. *Journal of Management*, *48*(1), 147–84.

Colby, C., & Bell, K. (2016). The on-demand economy is growing, and not just for the young and wealthy. *Harvard Business Review*. https://hbr.org/2016/04/the-on-demand-economy-is-growing-and -not-just-for-the-young-and-wealthy.

Cui, R., Li, J., & Zhang, D. (2020). Reducing discrimination with reviews in the Sharing Economy: Evidence from field experiments on Airbnb. *Management Science*, *66*(3), 1071–94.

Cullen, Z., & Farronato, C. (2021). Outsourcing tasks online: Matching supply and demand on peer-to-peer internet platforms. *Management Science*, *67*(7), 3985–4003.

Cusumano, M.A., Gawer, A., & Yoffie, D.B. (2019). *The Business of Platforms: Strategy in the Age of Digital Competition, Innovation, and Power.* New York, NY: Harper Business.

Dai, W., Jin, G.Z., Lee, J., & Luca, M. (2018). Aggregation of consumer ratings: An application to Yelp. com. *Quantitative Marketing and Economics*, *16*(3), 289–339.

Dou, Y., & Wu, D.J. (2021). Platform competition under network effects: Piggybacking and optimal subsidization. *Information Systems Research*, *32*(3), 820–35.

Edelman, B., Luca, M., & Svirsky, D. (2016). Racial discrimination in the sharing economy: Evidence from a field experiment. Working Papers, Harvard Business School Division of Research.

Einav, L., Farronato, C., & Levin, D.J. (2016). Peer-to-peer markets. *Annual Review of Economics*, *8*(1), 615–35.

Eisenmann, T., Parker, G., & Van Alstyne, M. (2011). Platform envelopment. *Strategic Management Journal*, *32*, 1270–85.

Evans, D.S., & Schmalensee, R. (2016). Why winner-takes-all thinking doesn't apply to the platform economy. *Harvard Business Review*, 4. https://hbr.org/2016/05/why-winner-takes-all-thinking-doesnt -apply-to-silicon-valley.

Farronato, C., & Fradkin, A. (2018). The welfare effects of peer entry in the accommodation market: The case of Airbnb. NBER Working Paper No. 24361.

Fitzmaurice, C., & Schor, J. (2015). Collaborating and connecting: The emergence of the sharing economy. In: Reisch, L., and Thogersen, J., Eds., *Handbook of Research on Sustainable Consumption*. Cheltenham, UK and Northampton, MA, USA: Edward Elgar Publishing, 410–25.

*Fortune* (2021). Fortune 500. https://fortune.com/fortune500/.

Fradkin, A. (2017). Search, matching, and the role of digital marketplace design in enabling trade: Evidence from Airbnb. https://ssrn.com/abstract=2939084 orhttp://dx.doi.org/10.2139/ssrn.2939084.

Gawer, A. (2021). Digital platforms' boundaries: The interplay of firm scope, platform sides, and digital interfaces. *Long Range Planning*, *54*(5), 1–16.

Gazé, P., & Vaubourg, A.-G. (2011). Electronic platforms and two-sided markets: A side-switching analysis. *Journal of High Technology Management Research*, *22*(2), 158–65.

Gerber, L., & Hui, J. (2016). Crowdfunding: How and why people participate. In: Méric, J., Maque, I., and Brabet, J., Eds, *International Persepectives on Crowdfunding*, Bingley: Emerald Group, 37–64.

Gerwe, O., & Silva, R. (2020). Clarifying the sharing economy: Conceptualization, typology, anteced-ents, and effects. *Academy of Management Perspectives*, *34*(1), 65–96.

Gerwe, O., Silva, R., & Castro, J. de (2020). Entry of providers onto a sharing economy platform: Macro-level factors and social interaction. *Entrepreneurship Theory and Practice*, *46*(4). https://doi .org/10.1177/1042258720903404.

Ghazawneh, A., & Henfridsson, O. (2012). Balancing platform control and external contribution in third-party development: The boundary resources model. *Information Systems Journal*, *23*(2), 173–192.

Gregory, R., Henfridsson, O., Kaganer, E., & Kyriakou, H. (2021). The role of artificial intelligence and data network effect for creating user value. *Academy of Management Review*, *46*(3), 534–51.

Gu, G., & Zhu, F. (2021). Trust and disintermediation: Evidence from an online freelance marketplace. *Management Science*, *67*(2), 794–807.

Hall, J.V., & Krueger, A.B. (2018). An analysis of the labor market for Uber's driver-partners in the United States. *ILR Review*, *71*(3), 705–32.

Horton, J.J. (2019). Buyer uncertainty about seller capacity: Causes, consequences, and a partial solution. *Management Science*, *65*(8), 3518–40.

Ikkala, T., & Lampinen, A. (2015). Monetizing network hospitality: Hospitality and sociability in the context of Airbnb. *Proceedings of the 18th ACM Conference on Computer Supported Cooperative Work & Social Computing* (pp. 1033–44). Vancouver: ACM.

Kickstarter (2021). What is the minimum and maximum amount I can pledge to a project? https://help .kickstarter.com/hc/en-us/articles/360037565033-What-is-the-maximum-amount-I-can-pledge-to-a -project-.

Kyprianou, C. (2018). Creating value from the outside in or the inside out: How nascent intermediaries build peer-to-peer marketplaces. *Academy of Management Discoveries*, *4*(3), 336–70.

Li, J., & Netessine, S. (2020). Higher market thickness reduces matching rate in online platforms: Evidence from a quasiexperiment. *Management Science*, *66*(1), 271–89.

Masterov, D., Meyer, U., & Tadelis, S. (2015). Canary in the e-commerce coal mine: Detecting and predicting poor experiences using buyer-to-seller messages. *Proc. 16th ACM Conf. Econom. Comput.* (Association for Computing Machinery (ACM), New York).

McIntyre, D., Srinivasan, A., Afuah, A., Gawer, A., & Kretschmer, T. (2021). Multi-sided platforms as new organizational forms. *Academy of Management Perspectives*, *35*(4), 566–83.

McIntyre, D.P., Srinivasan, A., & Chintakananda, A. (2021). The persistence of platforms: The role of network, platform, and complementor attributes. *Long Range Planning*, *54*(5), 1–12.

Oskam, J., Van der Rest, J.-P., & Telkamp, B. (2018). What's mine is yours – but at what price? Dynamic pricing behavior as an indicator of Airbnb host professionalization. *Journal of Revenue & Pricing Management*, *17*, 311–28.

Parker, G.G., Van Alstyne, M.W., & Choudary, S.P. (2016). *Platform Revolution: How Networked Markets Are Transforming the Economy and How to Make Them Work for You.* New York, NY: W.W. Norton & Company.

Pavlou, P.A., & Dimoka, A. (2006) The nature and role of feedback text comments in online marketplaces: Implications for trust building, price premiums, and seller differentiation. *Information Systems Research, 17*(4), 392–414.

Poshmark IPO Prospectus (2021). https://www.sec.gov/Archives/edgar/data/1825480/000119312520320132/d66583ds1.htm.

Prosper (2021). Home page. https://www.prosper.com/invest#sec-3.

PWC (2016). Future of the sharing economy in Europe. http://www.pwc.co.uk/issues/megatrends/collisions/sharingeconomy/future-of-the-sharing-economy-in-europe-2016.html.

Resnick, P., & Zeckhauser, R. (2002) Trust among strangers in internet transactions: Empirical analysis of eBay's reputation system. *Advances in Applied Microeconomics, 11*, 127–57.

Reynolds, I.J.H. (2020). Airbnb API. https://www.zibtek.com/blog/airbnb-api/.

Rochet, J.-C., & Tirole, J. (2003). Platform competition in two-sided markets. *Journal of the European Economic Association, 1*(4), 990–1029.

Shi, P. (2021). Optimal matchmaking in two-sided marketplaces. USC Marshall School of Business Research Paper. https://ssrn.com/abstract=3536086.

Srinivasan, A., & Venkatraman, N. (2018). Entrepreneurship in digital platforms: A network-centric view. *Strategic Entrepreneurship Journal, 12*(1), 54–71.

Sundararajan, A. (2016). *The Sharing Economy: The End of Employment and the Rise of Crowd-Based Capitalism.* Cambridge, MA: MIT Press.

Täuscher, K. (2017). Leveraging collective intelligence: How to design and manage crowd-based business models. *Business Horizons, 60*(2), 237–45.

Täuscher, K. (2019). Uncertainty kills the long tail: Demand concentration in peer-to-peer marketplaces. *Electronic Markets, 29*(4), 649–60.

Täuscher, K., & Kietzmann, J. (2017). Learning from failures in the sharing economy. *MIS Quarterly Executive, 16*(4), 253–63.

Täuscher, K., & Laudien, S.M. (2018). Understanding platform business models: A mixed methods study of marketplaces. *European Management Journal, 36*(3), 319–29.

Thies, F., Wessel, M., & Benlian, A. (2018). Network effects on crowdfunding platforms: Exploring the implications of relaxing input control. *Information Systems Journal, 28*(6), 1239–62.

Törhönen, M., Sjöblom, M., Hassan, L., & Hamari, J. (2020). Fame and fortune, or just fun? A study on why people create content on video platforms. *Internet Research, 30*(1), 165–90.

Uber (2021). Eligible vehicles in New York City. https://www.uber.com/us/en/drive/new-york/get-started/eligible-vehicles/.

Vallas, S., & Schor, J.B. (2020). What do platforms do? Understanding the gig economy. *Annual Review of Sociology, 46*(4), 273–94.

Xu, J.J., & Chau, M. (2018). Cheap talk? The impact of lender-borrower communication on peer-to-peer lending outcomes. *Journal of Management Information Systems, 35*(1), 53–85.

Yu, J., Mo, D., Xie, N., Hu, S., & Chen, X. (2021). Exploring multi-homing behavior of ride-sourcing drivers via real-world multiple platforms data. *Transportation Research: Part F, 80*, 61–78.

Zervas, G., Proserpio, D., & Byers, J.W. (2021). A first look at online reputation on Airbnb, where every stay is above average. *Marketing Letters, 32*(1), 1–16.

Zhu, F., & Iansiti, M. (2019). Why some platforms thrive and others don't. *Harvard Business Review, 97*(1), 118–25.

# 10. Value creation in digital platform business models: value conceptualizations, value dimensions and value logics

*Richard Reinsberg, Birgit A.A. Solem and Per Egil Pedersen*

## INTRODUCTION

Anecdotical evidence suggests that Jeff Bezos and his colleagues drew the basic mechanisms of Amazon's business model on a napkin (Keidel, 2005; Stone, 2013). This sketch is based on the flywheel concept, described in Collins' (2001) book *Good to Great*, and illustrates how a great customer experience leads to more customer visits; more customers increase the volume of sales, which again attracts even more third-party sellers to the site, paying commissions on their sales. This growth allows Amazon to better utilize resources of fixed-costs operations (fulfillment centers, computer servers) and enables it to lower the prices (Keidel, 2005; Stone, 2013). In fact, the drawing includes two virtuous cycles that cover two specific but different value logics. The first logic suggests that scale creates value through lower costs and higher volumes – as for all large firms. The second logic suggests that product variety, enabled by complementors, creates value through a better customer experience. This latter logic relies on Amazon being a digital platform company benefiting from network effects, as it is the complementors that provide the variety. Thus, the model is an example of how generic and platform-specific value logics are meticulously integrated to support the overall value creation of digital platform businesses.

While extant platform literature has identified numerous individual sources of value creation, the relationships between them and, as illustrated by the "Bezos napkin," how sources of value creation are turned into value delivery and value capture are less explored. In fact, several scholars have raised the need to get a clearer understanding of the overall value creation mechanisms supporting the digital platform companies and the implications for users and society in a broader sense (Cusumano, 2020, p. 11; McIntyre et al., 2020a, p. 8). This chapter builds on previous reviews of the digital platform literature (e.g., McIntyre & Srinivasan, 2017; Rietveld & Schilling, 2020; Sriram et al., 2015; Thomas et al., 2014) and a systematic literature review covering the platform literature across strategy, management, innovation and marketing journals ranked by the Chartered Association of Business Schools (CABS). After examining 1,361 articles in the period up to June 2021, 166 articles were analyzed in detail to identify any value conceptualizations and the underlying value logics of digital platforms and their ecosystem of users. We thereby extend previous work on value dimensions in platform companies (e.g., Cennamo, 2018, 2021), and describe different "conceptualizations of value"; i.e., platform-related factors suggested to provide value. We relate our classification of platforms to the multi-sided transaction market, and as such, our focus is transaction platforms. Then, by using the business model construct that covers the way organizations operate to create, deliver, and capture value (Teece, 2010), we structure the value conceptualizations as sources of value creation, means of value delivery and mechanisms of value capture – what we term the "value dimensions" of a digital platform business model. This includes value from interactions and transactions between the platform and its network of exchange partners in favor of a value network perspective (Massa & Tucci, 2021).

On this basis, we then discuss how and why these value dimensions are linked together in systematic relationships – what we term "value logics." These logics describe beliefs about how platform companies create value, including how the interplay of resources and capabilities affects value creation and delivery, and how value is captured both through efficiency measures and differentiating advantages, as the Bezos napkin clearly illustrates. We exemplify with four fundamental value logics and identify if and how these are specific to platform business models compared to traditional pipeline business models. Finally, we discuss how the value logics may unfold with platforms and are theorized using extant theory in strategic management, such as the firm positioning, resource-based and capability perspectives, and how research on platform-specific value logics may inform these perspectives.

## KEY VALUE CONCEPTUALIZATIONS

In this section, we organize and present the key value conceptualizations revealed from the systematic literature review according to the three value dimensions of a business model (Teece, 2010). We differentiate between value conceptualizations referring to (1) potential sources of value creation; (2) means of value delivery, focusing on use value; and (3) mechanisms of value capture, including exchange value for the (platform) firm (Bowman & Ambrosini, 2000; Eggert et al., 2018; Lepak et al., 2007). Thus, this list represents the most frequently mentioned conceptualizations in the platform literature that explicitly focus on value, grouped into overall (second-order) value conceptualizations. It is therefore not a complete nor exhaustive list of factors or elements that may provide opportunities for value creation, delivery or capture, as the purpose is to shed light on key conceptualizations and any relationships between them. In the next section, we then structure these factors into value logics to provide an overall understanding of how value is created in a platform business model.

### Sources of Value Creation

Among the main sources of potential value creation in the platform literature are network effects, complementors, economies of scale and scope, and capabilities. Platforms, and actors in their corresponding ecosystems, rely on specific mechanisms to enhance the value potential of these sources.

Digital platforms are characterized by the presence of strong network externalities, or "network effects" (Evans, 2003; Hagiu, 2007; Katz & Shapiro, 1985) that function as a fundamental, underlying mechanism of how platform value is created (Tura et al., 2018). Direct network effects (Gawer, 2014; Gawer & Cusumano, 2014) arise when the possibility or benefit of network participation for a user depends on the other network users on the same side of the market (Steiner et al., 2016; Wallbach et al., 2019). On the other hand, indirect network effects arise when the different sides of a market benefit from the size or the characteristics of the other side of the market (Boudreau & Jeppesen, 2015; Hagiu, 2014; Rochet & Tirole, 2003). Network effects create value through reach (where the size of the networks on both sides enables reach and matching) and through value-creating interactions (between complementors and/or customers) at either one or both sides of the market.

Complementors (also named "third-party producers" or "third-party sellers") become an important source of value to platforms due to the content they are offering (Boudreau & Jeppesen, 2015; Cusumano, 2012; Ozalp et al., 2018; Wen & Zhu, 2019). By utilizing the size of the "complementor network" and their innovative capabilities (i.e., complementor innovation), platforms facilitate the generation of a potentially very large number of innovations. Due to growing demand or heterogeneity on the customer side for complementors' products – strengthening the indirect network effect – complementors become a source of value creation on behalf of the platform (Gawer & Cusumano, 2014; McIntyre et al., 2020b; Panico & Cennamo, 2020).

Size and economies of scale as conceptualizations become sources of value creation due to the platforms' ability to reach a large potential customer base (Chu & Manchanda, 2016; Cusumano & Gawer, 2002; Edelman, 2014). That is, a platform that accumulates a large user base can deliver value through improved matching of supply and demand. Value from size and scale is also created through growth and scale-up capabilities (Abdelkafi et al., 2019; Gawer & Henderson, 2007).

Economies of scope are a generic source of value creation (Broekhuizen et al., 2019; Eisenmann et al., 2011; Parmentier & Gandia, 2017), but in a supply-side platform context, scope benefits are created by utilizing platforms' "excess capacity" (Eckhardt et al., 2019; Perren & Kozinets, 2018) or through efficiencies in "resource utilization" (Ritala et al., 2014), exemplified by how Airbnb creates new markets based on previously untapped resources (Täuscher & Laudien, 2018). On the demand side, scope benefits are created by utilizing information about customers (as a digital asset), applying it to differentiate and serve heterogeneity in demand. For example, Amazon both utilizes customer data to drive cross-selling and successfully expands its offerings with additional services (e.g., Prime) (Hänninen et al., 2019).

Capabilities are also considered as sources of value creation (Eloranta & Turunen, 2016; Parker et al., 2016; Zhang & Tang, 2019), either through *generic* dynamic capabilities related to identifying opportunities for innovation (Helfat & Raubitschek, 2018; Teece, 2018), or by more *platform-specific* capabilities (Cenamor et al., 2019; Perks et al., 2017; Ramaswamy & Ozcan, 2018a). Examples of the latter include customer orientation that refers to the platforms' culture and capability to analyze, serve and satisfy the needs of both the buyer- and seller-side customers (Chakravarty et al., 2014; Clauss et al., 2019; Kollmann et al., 2020; Ramaswamy, 2020), and capabilities for analyzing big data (i.e., data of transactions, user behavior, complementor behavior) for the purpose of bringing value to both the platform and all its users (Hänninen et al., 2018; Nuccio & Guerzoni, 2019; Trabucchi & Buganza, 2020). Also, relationship management and governance are capability-based sources of value creation as they relate to how the platform orchestrates and controls activities in an ecosystem of complementors and partners (Bazarhanova et al., 2019; Eloranta & Turunen, 2016; Laczko et al., 2019). At last, pricing appears as a final capability-based source of value creation in the platform context (Eisenmann et al., 2006; Hagiu, 2009; Roger & Vasconcelos, 2014), primarily used as a coordination mechanism between the sides of the platform for growth (Parker & Van Alstyne, 2005; Rochet & Tirole, 2003).

## Means of Value Delivery

Among the value conceptualizations in the platform literature that can be considered means of value delivery include the value of reach and matching supply and demand, the price advantage, the variety and quality of products delivered, the platform quality, the perceived trust and the convenience of using the platform.

In delivering the use value of reach and matching supply and demand (Eckhardt et al., 2019; Hein et al., 2019), platforms rely on a core functionality that facilitates interactions and transactions on the platform and across its user sides (Tavalaei & Cennamo, 2020; Yang et al., 2020). This includes both transaction fulfillment, segmentation opportunities, market access, security issues and improved services (Cennamo, 2018; Yang et al., 2020), as well as providing easy-to-use search functions, reducing customers' "search costs" (Caldieraro et al., 2018; Hein et al., 2020).

While highlighting pricing as a value-creating source in the previous sub-section, a different conceptualization of price in the platform literature is that it also functions as a means of value delivery to customers demonstrated through lower prices (Edelman, 2014; Rangaswamy et al., 2020; Reinartz et al., 2019; Zervas et al., 2017). An increasing volume of complementors in a platform market increases the competition, which lowers the prices of competing products, thus benefiting the customers.

Product variety and product quality are also suggested as crucial elements in delivering value to customers. Product variety is a characteristic of the variety of the content produced and offered (i.e., in a broader sense) by complementors and/or customers. A greater variety of products (or services) provided by the complementors (Cenamor et al., 2013; Zhu & Iansiti, 2012) enables a match to a broader set of the customers' heterogeneous preferences, which may serve to further increase network effects (Cennamo, 2018; McIntyre & Srinivasan, 2017). As for product variety, product quality relates to the quality of the content produced and delivered to customers but relies on complementors' ability to innovate and improve the quality.

Another type of quality is platform quality, which relates to the customers' perception of the quality of the complementors and/or the platform itself (McIntyre & Srinivasan, 2017), and stems from customers' interaction with the platform. Thus, the strength of the network is not solely determined by the number of users, but also by the quality of the interactions (Hagiu, 2014).

Further, trust is also a means of value delivery as it serves as a mediating factor in all kinds of interactions and exchanges (i.e., complementor–customer, platform–complementor, customer–customer) (e.g., Clauss et al., 2019; Täuscher & Laudien, 2018). Because interactions on a platform often occur between strangers (Rangaswamy et al., 2020), it becomes crucial for a platform as an intermediator to incentivize trustworthy behavior. Accordingly, the higher the requirement for trust, the higher the degree of platform intermediation is needed (Perren & Kozinets, 2018).

Lastly, convenience functions as a means of value delivery (to all platform participants), substantiated by the platform. Platforms deliver or increase search convenience by providing convenient access, and the ability to match differentiated goods and services with the unique needs of their users (Eckhardt et al., 2019; Yrjölä et al., 2017). Platforms deliver or increase purchase convenience by providing efficient and convenient facilitation of transactions (Hein et al., 2020; Willing et al., 2017), and platforms deliver or increase use convenience by offering benefits such as rapid response and delivery, and automation of marketing and consumer processes (Crittenden et al., 2017; Reinartz et al., 2019).

**Mechanisms of Value Capture**

Among the mechanisms suggested by the platform literature to capture (exchange) value from sources of value creation and means of value delivery are efficiencies, such as reduced transaction and production costs, market power, and differentiation enabling price premiums and customer loyalty. Some of the mechanisms directly reflect captured exchange value, such as cost reductions, whereas others rely on specific and often implicit mechanisms of how the conceptualization is used to capture exchange value. For example, when loyalty is used to earn excess profits, and market power is used to negotiate lower purchasing costs.

Reduced transaction costs is mainly a generic value capture mechanism of efficiency (Abdelkafi et al., 2019; Hagiu, 2014; Helfat & Raubitschek, 2018), theorized from transaction cost economics (Williamson, 1985). The general assumption is that platforms, like any firm, seek to reduce the transaction and production costs of many routine activities (Rangaswamy et al., 2020). However, due to reduced costs of matching supply and demand (Abdelkafi et al., 2019; Hagiu, 2014), and increasing returns from scale (due to network effects), platforms may encounter lower transaction costs than traditional pipeline businesses (Lehdonvirta et al., 2019; Liu et al., 2020). Thus, this element is strongly related to the concepts of size and scale, including scale benefits of fixed-costs operations (Eisenmann et al., 2006, 2011; Porter, 2001).

Value capture is also related to growth, through increased market size, developing new markets or increased market power. This is especially evident if the market is characterized by a winner-take-all outcome (McIntyre et al., 2020b) where the market tends to converge on a single, dominant platform due to network effects (Basaure et al., 2020; Hossain & Morgan, 2013). As a result of increased market power, and even monopoly power (Spinello, 2005), platforms capture value beyond scale efficiencies through pricing, market entry in complementors' spaces and increased switching costs (Zhu, 2019; Zhu & Liu, 2018), or by leveraging existing user bases to enter new markets through "platform envelopment" (Eisenmann et al., 2011, p. 13).

Value capture from differentiation includes price premium, price differentiation and price discrimination to optimize revenues and profits (Nuccio & Guerzoni, 2019; Rangaswamy et al., 2020). For example, Airbnb controls the price, and thus maximizes its profits while simultaneously limiting competitors' market power (Zervas et al., 2017). Platforms also capture value through diversification and new revenue streams. Examples include Uber's supply-side extension Uber Eats, and Amazon's diversification into highly profitable cloud services (Nuccio & Guerzoni, 2019). Finally, customer loyalty and repurchase intention are both identified as value capture mechanisms for a platform (Clauss et al., 2019; Eckhardt et al., 2019).

## FROM VALUE CONCEPTUALIZATIONS TO VALUE LOGICS

In contrast to the traditional theories of strategy, such as the resource-based view (Barney, 1991; Peteraf, 1993) or the positioning view (Porter, 1980, 1985, 1996), where research has centered on value capture for the firm, and value creation is seen as a supply-side responsibility (Massa et al., 2017), the business model concept defines value creation as both a supply- and demand-side phenomenon (Aversa et al., 2021), where value is created not only by producers, but also by customers and other members of the value-creating ecosystem. In this perspective, competitive advantage can be resource- and activity-based, in the supply and/or demand side (Massa et al., 2017), and it acknowledges the complexity of the relationship between potential sources of value creation and value capture (Laczko et al., 2019). Thus, while the previous section indicated single elements of value creation, delivery and capture, more extensive and complex relationships also exist between these three dimensions, where a source of value may be exploited through different combinations of value delivery and value capture mechanisms.

For example, as the Bezos napkin demonstrates,[1] when complementors provide product variety on the platform that meets the needs of heterogeneous customers it enables price differentiation or discrimination as a mechanism of value capture. In other words, the managerial implications of theory suggest that advantages are obtained through the reliance on a particular logic of value creation and capture rather than an individual element of value (e.g., resources), and that a platform's business model may rely on different combinations of such value logics. The term "value logic" borrows from previous work on logics in strategic management, such as institutional and dominant logics (Ocasio & Radoynovska, 2016; Prahalad & Bettis, 1986), and we define it as the collective or shared beliefs about relationships between the dimensions of value in an ecosystem of participants on a platform. In the business model literature (Massa et al., 2017), logics (e.g., core logic, company logic, business logic) are often considered integral parts of a business model and some authors have even equaled logics to business models (e.g., economic logic; Magretta, 2002, p. 4). However, in the most widespread configurational perspectives on the business model concept (e.g., activities, resources and capabilities) (Zott & Amit, 2010, p. 217), value logics reflect the fundamental beliefs about the relationship between dimensions of value that underlie the business model as a configuration (ibid., p. 219). Thus, also for digital platforms, value logics serve the purpose of supporting the platform business model as a configuration of activities, resources and capabilities, and guide the design of platform architecture, governance structure and performance management systems. Even though we claim that value logics are generalizations of empirical relationships believed to be true by platform ecosystem participants – sometimes with performative implications (Garud et al., 2018), they are not validated theory. But as we will demonstrate later in this chapter, the validity of individual casual relationships inferred by value logics may be supported by established explanatory theories in strategic management. Table 10.1 illustrates four fundamental value logics with selected examples (sub logics) according to how the literature has suggested complete or partial relationships between value dimensions. These examples are not mutually exclusive, and they are provided for an illustrative purpose, meaning several similar empirical relationships may exist within each value logic. In addition, we specify whether each value logic is specific to a platform context, or represents relationships known from generic value logics that apply to businesses without platform or intermediary characteristics.

The scale-driven value logic builds on the assumption that the value of the platform increases with the size of the network, either by the number of users on the same or the other side, and is related to network effects but not necessarily dependent on this for the creation of value. Two examples of this logic are presented in Table 10.1. The first of these is based on value creation through size and growth and corresponds to the first value logic of Bezos' napkin introduced in the opening of this chapter. Here, size and scale are the sources of value that is delivered to the customers through lower prices, and enable value capture through cost efficiencies. This is due to economies of scale of fixed-costs operations, reduced costs

*Table 10.1*     *Examples of logics of value creation*

| Logic | Sources of value creation | Means of value delivery | Mechanisms of value capture | Platform-specific logic? |
|---|---|---|---|---|
| Scale-driven value logic | Economies of scale | Low price | Efficiencies<br>Market power | No |
| | Size of customer network | Reach<br>• Matching supply and demand<br>• Reduced customer search costs | Efficiencies<br>• Increasing returns to scale<br>• Reduced transaction costs<br>Market power | No/Yes |
| Interaction-driven value logic | One-sided customer interactions | Quality of interactions<br>Reduced customer transaction costs | Differentiation<br>• Interaction-driven revenues | No |
| | Reviews and ratings | Trust<br>Reduced search costs<br>Convenience | Differentiation<br>• Price premium<br>• Customer loyalty<br>• Innovation and product entry | Yes/No |
| Complementor-driven value logic | Complementor network size | Product variety<br>Reduced search costs<br>Convenience | Efficiencies<br>• Reinforcing network effects/ platform growth<br>Differentiation<br>• Pricing<br>• Customer loyalty | Yes |
| | Complementor innovation | Product quality | Efficiencies<br>• Reduced inventory risk<br>Differentiation<br>• Pricing<br>• Customer loyalty | Yes |
| Scope-driven value logic | Excess capacity | Variety and quality through supply-side extensions | Differentiation<br>• Diversification<br>• New revenue streams | No |
| | Big data analysis | Fulfillment of (broader) customer needs<br>Service offerings<br>Personalization and customization | Differentiation<br>• Pricing<br>• New revenue streams<br>• Customer loyalty | No/Yes |

because of volume discounts, or reduced costs from utilizing existing assets or resources across families of products (Gawer & Cusumano, 2014; Ordanini & Pol, 2001; Reinartz et al., 2019). In addition to delivering a lower price, this also enables value capture for the platform through efficiencies (by dividing the savings between price and profits) and market power. This logic is not specific to a platform but would apply to any business and follow the general economies of scale rationale. In the second example, size is related to reach because a platform that accumulates a large user base delivers value through improved matching of supply and demand (reach) and by reducing the search costs for the customer (Edelman, 2014; Eisenmann et al., 2011; Yang et al., 2020). This value is then captured through increased efficiencies and reduced transaction costs (Edelman, 2014; Eisenmann et al., 2011; McIntyre et al., 2020b). Similar to our first example, this logic is not specific to platforms; however, in a business model that relies on the combination of this logic with a complementor-driven logic described below, value effects increase due to indirect network effects, turning demand-side scale into supply-side benefits (Eisenmann et al., 2011; McIntyre et al., 2020b).

The interaction-driven value logic is based on the fundamental idea that same- and cross-side interactions, respectively and by themselves, serve as sources of value. This logic is differentiated from scale-driven logics in that it is not reaching other users, but the quality of the interactions between them, enabled by the platform, that represent the basic means of value. Two examples of this logic are reflected in the relationships between value dimensions presented in Table 10.1. The first of these can be illustrated by one-sided networks where the users interact by exchanging similar content. However, instead of focusing on the value of reaching many similar users as in a purely scale-driven logic, the one-sided interaction-driven value logic focuses on the quality of interactions, the social value from participating in networks (i.e., recognition, belonging) and the reduction in customers' transactions costs. This logic is often implicit in network research on online forums, clearly articulated in research on information platforms (e.g., social media), but less prominent in research on transaction platforms. Thus, this type of logic is generic to network services facilitating interaction where value is captured through, for example, subscription-based revenues (Enders et al., 2008), but when cross-sided interactions are facilitated, the logic appears as platform-specific. Another example of the interaction-driven logic is how platforms make customer interactions into a source of value through reviews and ratings of complementors' services or products. These affordances enable value delivery through trust, improved user experience (convenience) and reduced search costs, consequently utilized extensively by platform companies such as Airbnb, eBay, Taobao, TripAdvisor and Uber for differentiation purposes (Curchod et al., 2020; Lehdonvirta et al., 2019; Ramaswamy & Ozcan, 2018b; Zhang et al., 2012). These interactions also enable signaling of user needs, expectations and content requests to complementors that may drive revenue from future transactions through innovations (Eckhardt et al., 2019; Hukal et al., 2020). Also, as the platform obtains information about customer needs and complementor resources, this can be aggregated and used in product entry decisions (Zhu & Iansiti, 2012), and in the exercise of power amplifying the value capture mechanisms of other value logics.

The two examples of the complementor-driven value logic in Table 10.1 encompass the sheer number of complementors and complementors' innovativeness. The first example reflects the second value logic of Bezos' napkin where a wide variety of products (and services) creates value through a better customer experience. This logic is strongly linked to indirect network effects, specific to a platform-based business model, and is different from scale logics in that the source of value originates from complementors that operate with a high degree of autonomy on digital platforms. The complementors provide the selection (variety) that enables the matching of heterogenous customer needs (Cennamo, 2018), reduces customer search costs and improves the convenience of use (Eckhardt et al., 2019; McIntyre & Srinivasan, 2017). This improved customer experience then serves to further increase network effects, efficiently fueling additional platform growth. Furthermore, because higher variety potentially means less competition, this could also drive higher rent extraction (Hagiu, 2009). In the second example, we highlight the value delivery of product quality. Since platform firms usually do not have sufficient capabilities, resources or complete systems in-house, they depend on the availability and innovativeness of the complementary products and services. Value creation then expands beyond the conventional economics of supply and demand of goods and services, to include value creation co-created with a network of actors (Ramaswamy & Ozcan, 2018a). The more high-quality products presented at the platform, the greater the benefits to users from using the platform and its complementary products (Cennamo, 2018), securing or raising the overall reliability, profitability and competitive advantage of the platform through price premiums or increased customer loyalty (Lee et al., 2018; Nuccio & Guerzoni, 2019; Tellis et al., 2009). Additionally, having complementors provide the quality and innovativeness of the products shifts the inventory risk from the platform to the complementors (Hänninen et al., 2019), and also enables the platform to reach new markets by leveraging complementors' architectures and networks (McIntyre & Srinivasan, 2017).

The scope-driven value logic is characterized by relying on the uniqueness of the assets, labor or activities controlled by the platform firm as the source of value. It includes platform architecture, openness and governance, and applies many of the underlying principles of the resource-based view and the theory of dynamic capabilities. In the first example, we have highlighted how value is created by utilization of excess capacity which goes beyond the traditional focus of capacity planning (Laczko et al., 2019; Porter, 2001), delivered through diversification and supply-side extensions (e.g., Uber Eats, Amazon Web Services). For the platform company, this differentiation represents new revenue streams as well as potential risk reduction through diversification of the product portfolio. In the second example, we have highlighted the scoped capability of insight and big data analysis as a source of value creation. Different from big data as a resource, where size drives the volume of data in a scale-based logic, this logic focuses on how big data are utilized through analytical capabilities; for example, in value delivery through personalization and product recommendations (Hänninen, 2020; Hänninen et al., 2019). It also supports the development of customers' heterogeneous preferences (e.g., "long tail assortments"), a form of market development stimulating ever-increasing heterogeneity and, consequently, growth. As a result, the platform captures more value of the market with segmentation and price optimizations (Nuccio & Guerzoni, 2019), increases efficiencies through improvement of internal processes (Hein et al., 2019), and facilitates the identification of new business opportunities and new revenue streams (Hukal et al., 2020; Willing et al., 2017). While both examples are typically reflected in digital business models, they are not platform-specific logics. However, the logic becomes platform-specific when data is collected and combined across the ecosystem. Then, third-party data is effectively converted into first-party data for the platform that strengthens the value delivery of matching supply and demand compared to traditional pipeline businesses (Rangaswamy et al., 2020).

## DISCUSSION

While we have documented four fundamental value logics found in the platform literature, the variation and complexity of the examples in Table 10.1 reflect logics as comprehensive beliefs that are difficult to validate and defend with precise theory. Strategy theory provides several lenses for observing and measuring the validity of different value logics but there is not a simple mapping between value logics and theoretical lenses in strategic management. Value logics may include beliefs about several causalities on which a particular strategy theory may have focused, and found empirical support for one, or a few. An example is how the resource-based view (RBV) supports the validity of the relationship between big data, dynamic capabilities and performance (Wamba et al., 2017). Consequently, using different theories from the strategy field may be necessary when researchers try to explain why different platform business models – relying on different value logics – succeed (Cennamo, 2021).

We follow the distinction of four lenses in strategy research (Priem, 2007), add dynamic capabilities to the set, and discuss how generic and platform-specific elements of value logics can be theorized using transaction costs, RBV, dynamic capabilities, positioning and demand-side strategy perspectives.

"Transaction cost theory," or "transaction cost economics" (TCE) (Williamson, 1985), is used in articles theorizing scale-, interaction- and complementor-driven logics. Among the generic strategic management issues discussed using this theory are governance structures and complementarity. However, the platform literature offers new insight in TCE by suggesting that digital platforms offer new governance structures not covered along the traditional market–hybrid–hierarchy dimension (Reimers et al., 2019). For example, digital platforms resemble a public market structure under private exchange with value logics allowing market power as a value capture mechanism to take new forms – and potentially threaten traditional market regulation (Calvano & Polo, 2021). Platforms also enable new forms of complementarity to form in ecosystems of actors not previously discussed in strategy literature using TCE; i.e., identifying relationships within ecosystems that do not fit into the classical firm–supplier relationship (Jacobides et al., 2018). Thus, TCE supports the platform-specificity of the complementor-driven logics exemplified in Table 10.1.

RBV (Barney, 1991; Peteraf, 1993) is naturally used to theorize scope-driven logics, but also, somewhat surprisingly, interaction- and complementor-driven logics. Using RBV to support the validity of the complementor-driven logic illustrates how the platform literature broadens the debate on the locus of value creation (Kapoor, 2018) to include external complementor and even cross-network resources (Sun & Tse, 2009). How big data represent valuable resources in scope-driven logics is demonstrated in numerous studies (e.g., Hänninen et al., 2019), but it is somewhat surprising that few of them explicitly inform the debate on the characteristics of resources (e.g., valuable, rare, inimitable, organized) in the RBV (e.g., Braganza et al., 2017). The reason, however, is the complementarity between big data as a material resource, and big data analytics and culture as organizational resources in value creation (Dubey et al., 2019) – an understanding that contributes to general research on material/organizational complementarity in RBV (Wiengarten et al., 2013).

This leads to literature theorizing scope-driven value logics using both general theory of organizational capabilities (OC) (Madhok, 1996) as well as more specific theory of dynamic capabilities (DC) (Teece, 2007). Here, the platform literature on value creation contributes to the identification of unique capabilities of relevance to digital strategic management. Examples include ecosystems orchestration capabilities, also used to theorize complementor-driven logics (Helfat & Raubitschek, 2018) as well as recently developed digital-specific concepts at the intersection between information, marketing and strategic management research, such as big data analytics capabilities (Mikalef et al., 2018) and big data marketing affordances (De Luca et al., 2021). However, dynamic capabilities "underpin not only value creation but also value capture by platform leaders" (Helfat & Raubitschek, 2018, p. 1391; Teece, 2018) because integrative capabilities improve ecosystem orchestration and reduce transaction costs.

While all logics in Table 10.1 share some theoretical underpinnings from the firm positioning perspectives focusing on barriers to competition, generic strategies and value aggregation (Porter, 1980, 1985), extensive theorizing based on this perspective is found in scale-, interaction- and complementor-driven logics. Early work on platforms pointed to network effects as an alternative barrier to entry than those discussed for traditional industries (Katz & Shapiro, 1994), but of the four sources of value creation in e-business suggested using firm positioning perspectives (Amit & Zott, 2001), "lock-in" is given less attention in current platform value logics. Instead, the platform literature on value creation seems to *combine* different elements of the firm positioning perspective; for example, as when Cennamo (2021) elegantly integrates differentiation and scale considerations in a two-dimensional framework showing that platform value is created through both platform identity and growth under the logics of distinctiveness and scale. This demonstrates how value logics form a basis for theorizing platform-specific extensions of Porter's (1980) generic strategies.

Finally, reflecting the increasing attention to use value in the platform literature on value creation, demand-side perspectives are gaining attention. This perspective has developed at the intersection of marketing and strategy, and consequently marketing scholars dominate this part of the platform literature. With long traditions for "means-end analysis" and modeling mediated and complex causal chains, there is often closer correspondence between value logics and the models used to theorize them here than in other perspectives. Examples include the value creation framework of Reinartz et al. (2019) and value model of Steiner et al. (2016), both published in a leading marketing journal, but with obvious relevance to digital strategy. Models theorizing customer-driven logics often include direct measurement of use value as it is perceived by platform users, particularly customers (e.g., Clauss et al., 2019) relying on well-developed measurement principles and scales. Also, research on value co-creation in this perspective covers diverse conceptualizations of value, offers deep insight into the various actors involved in its creation and is now also applied in platform contexts (e.g., Perren & Kozinets, 2018; Ramaswamy & Ozcan, 2018b). In responding to the calls to understand the "benefits of platform businesses to users and society" (Cusumano, 2020, p. 11), these perspectives on platform use value may also prove useful to strategic management.

Going back to Bezos' napkin, the drawing illustrates how value for customers, complementors and the platform firm interacts through combinations of value logics of both generic and more platform-specific character. In fact, in the case of Amazon, not only two but most of the introduced logics underlie the business model, and as we have discussed, some of these value logics appear connected, which reinforces the effect of each logic (e.g., when complementor-, interaction- and scale-driven logics reinforce each other). Therefore, depending on the context and the business environment, we may find that different combinations of value logics underly different business models across companies and business areas. For example, the business model of the fashion retail platform Zalando relies on scale-, complementor- and scope-driven value logics, but not particularly on the interaction-based logic. This is different from, for example, the business model of Airbnb, which contrastingly relies heavily on the interaction-based logic, in combination with scale, complementor and scope logics. Still, they both achieve high business performance. Further, Amazon also connects value logics across business models, like when the underlying value logics of Amazon's Marketplace are connected to the underlying value logics of Amazon's Web Services (Ritala et al., 2014). Thus, this illustrates the complexity of how a platform-based business model differs from traditional business models in how value logics support the business model configuration of activities, resources and capabilities.

## CONCLUSION

To better understand the uniqueness and benefits of digital platform business models, this chapter provides a comprehensive overview of value conceptualizations in alignment with the business model dimensions of value creation, delivery and capture in the digital platform context. We have introduced the concept of value logics as shared beliefs about relationships between the dimensions of value and documented four fundamental value logics that underlie platform-specific or generic business models, namely the scale-, interaction-, complementor- and scope-driven value logics. Instead of giving an extensive or complete overview of all variants of these logics, we have presented examples of how and why some of these variants are specific to digital platform business models. As such, these value logics are generalizations of complex empirical relationships believed to be valid by the ecosystem of participants on a platform, and as we have demonstrated, also by authors of the literature on platform value creation. However, more research is needed to empirically map out the actual managerial beliefs, and compare these with our value logics, to provide a better picture of how managers think about value creation in digital platform business models. Even though the value logics are not validated theory, we demonstrate support for many of the causalities underpinning the value logics in explanatory strategy theory and discuss how the platform literature on value creation contributes to development or extension of these theoretical perspectives. Although the value logics we have documented are mainly based on literature studying the transaction platform context, we believe they are relevant to other types of platforms (information and innovation platforms) (Cennamo, 2021), as well as to other digital businesses, and can serve as useful tools in analyzing and understanding digital business strategy.

## NOTE

1. While we define value logics as beliefs about complex relationships that require validation, both in the example of Bezos' napkin and in the platform literature, our presentation uses a form where we assume their validity can be or has been confirmed.

## REFERENCES

Abdelkafi, N., Raasch, C., Roth, A., & Srinivasan, R. (2019). Multi-sided platforms. *Electronic Markets*, *29*(4), 553–9.

Amit, R., & Zott, C. (2001). Value creation in e-business. *Strategic Management Journal*, *22*(6–7), 493–520.

Aversa, P., Haefliger, S., Hueller, F., & Reza, D.G. (2021). Customer complementarity in the digital space: Exploring Amazon's business model diversification. *Long Range Planning*, *54*(5), 101985.

Barney, J. (1991). Firm resources and sustained competitive advantage. *Journal of Management*, *17*(1), 99–120.

Basaure, A., Vesselkov, A., & Töyli, J. (2020). Internet of things (IoT) platform competition: Consumer switching versus provider multihoming. *Technovation*, *90–91*, 102101.

Bazarhanova, A., Yli-Huumo, J., & Smolander, K. (2019). From platform dominance to weakened ownership: how external regulation changed Finnish e-identification. *Electronic Markets*, *30*, 525–38.

Boudreau, K.J., & Jeppesen, L.B. (2015). Unpaid crowd complementors: The platform network effect mirage. *Strategic Management Journal*, *36*(12), 1761–77.

Bowman, C., & Ambrosini, V. (2000). Value creation versus value capture: Towards a coherent definition of value in strategy. *British Journal of Management*, *11*(1), 1–15.

Braganza, A., Brooks, L., Nepelski, D., Ali, M., & Moro, R. (2017). Resource management in big data initiatives: Processes and dynamic capabilities. *Journal of Business Research*, *70*, 328–37.

Broekhuizen, T.L.J., Emrich, O., Gijsenberg, M.J., Broekhuis, M., Donkers, B., & Sloot, L.M. (2019). Digital platform openness: Drivers, dimensions and outcomes. *Journal of Business Research*, *122*, 902–14.

Caldieraro, F., Zhang, J.Z., Cunha, M., & Shulman, J.D. (2018). Strategic information transmission in peer-to-peer lending markets. *Journal of Marketing*, *82*(2), 42–63.

Calvano, E., & Polo, M. (2021). Market power, competition and innovation in digital markets: A survey. *Information Economics and Policy*, *54*, 100853.

Cenamor, J., Parida, V., & Wincent, J. (2019). How entrepreneurial SMEs compete through digital platforms: The roles of digital platform capability, network capability and ambidexterity. *Journal of Business Research*, *100*, 196–206.

Cenamor, J., Usero, B., & Fernández, Z. (2013). The role of complementary products on platform adoption: Evidence from the video console market. *Technovation*, *33*(12), 405–16.

Cennamo, C. (2018). Building the value of next-generation platforms: The paradox of diminishing returns. *Journal of Management*, *44*(8), 3038–69.

Cennamo, C. (2021). Competing in digital markets: A platform-based perspective. *Academy of Management Perspectives*, *35*(2), 265–91.

Chakravarty, A., Kumar, A., & Grewal, R. (2014). Customer orientation structure for Internet-based business-to-business platform firms. *Journal of Marketing*, *78*(5), 1–23.

Chu, J., & Manchanda, P. (2016). Quantifying cross and direct network effects in online consumer-to-consumer platforms. *Marketing Science*, *35*(6), 870–93.

Clauss, T., Harengel, P., & Hock, M. (2019). The perception of value of platform-based business models in the sharing economy: determining the drivers of user loyalty. *Review of Managerial Science*, *13*(3), 605–34.

Collins, J. (2001). *Good to Great: Why Some Companies Make the Leap and Others Don't*. HarperCollins.

Crittenden, A.B., Crittenden, V.L., & Crittenden, W.F. (2017). Industry transformation via channel disruption. *Journal of Marketing Channels*, *24*(1–2), 13–26.

Curchod, C., Patriotta, G., Cohen, L., & Neysen, N. (2020). Working for an algorithm: Power asymmetries and agency in online work settings. *Administrative Science Quarterly*, *65*(3), 644–76.

Cusumano, M.A. (2012). Platforms versus products: Observations from the literature and history. In S.J. Kahl, B.S. Silverman & M.A. Cusumano (Eds.), *Advances in Strategic Management* (Vol. 29, pp. 35–67). Emerald Group.

Cusumano, M.A. (2020). Guidepost: The evolution of research on industry platforms. *Academy of Management Discoveries*, *8*(1).

Cusumano, M.A., & Gawer, A. (2002). The elements of platform leadership. *MIT Sloan Management Review*, *43*(3), 51–8.

De Luca, L.M., Herhausen, D., Troilo, G., & Rossi, A. (2021). How and when do big data investments pay off? The role of marketing affordances and service innovation. *Journal of the Academy of Marketing Science*, *49*(4), 790–810.

Dubey, R., Gunasekaran, A., Childe, S.J., Blome, C., & Papadopoulos, T. (2019). Big data and predictive analytics and manufacturing performance: Integrating institutional theory, resource-based view and big data culture. *British Journal of Management*, *30*(2), 341–61.

Eckhardt, G.M., Houston, M.B., Jiang, B., Lamberton, C., Rindfleisch, A., & Zervas, G. (2019). Marketing in the sharing economy. *Journal of Marketing*, *83*(5), 5–27.

Edelman, B. (2014). Mastering the intermediaries: Strategies for dealing with the likes of Google, Amazon, and Kayak. *Harvard Business Review*, *92*(6), 86–92.

Eggert, A., Ulaga, W., Frow, P., & Payne, A. (2018). Conceptualizing and communicating value in business markets: From value in exchange to value in use. *Industrial Marketing Management*, *69*, 80–90.

Eisenmann, T., Parker, G., & Van Alstyne, M.W. (2006). Strategies for two-sided markets. *Harvard Business Review*, *84*(10), 92–101, 149.

Eisenmann, T., Parker, G., & Van Alstyne, M. (2011). Platform envelopment. *Strategic Management Journal*, *32*(12), 1270–85.

Eloranta, V., & Turunen, T. (2016). Platforms in service-driven manufacturing: Leveraging complexity by connecting, sharing, and integrating. *Industrial Marketing Management*, *55*, 178–86.

Enders, A., Hungenberg, H., Denker, H.-P., & Mauch, S. (2008). The long tail of social networking: Revenue models of social networking sites. *European Management Journal*, *26*(3), 199–211.

Evans, D.S. (2003). Some empirical aspects of multi-sided platform industries. *Review of Network Economics*, *2*(3), 191–209.

Garud, R., Gehman, J., & Tharchen, T. (2018). Performativity as ongoing journeys: Implications for strategy, entrepreneurship, and innovation. *Long Range Planning*, *51*(3), 500–509.

Gawer, A. (2014). Bridging differing perspectives on technological platforms: Toward an integrative framework. *Research Policy*, *43*(7), 1239–49.

Gawer, A., & Cusumano, M.A. (2014). Industry platforms and ecosystem innovation. *Journal of Product Innovation Management*, *31*(3), 417–33.

Gawer, A., & Henderson, R. (2007). Platform owner entry and innovation in complementary markets: Evidence from Intel. *Journal of Economics and Management Strategy*, *16*(1), 1–34.

Hagiu, A. (2007). Merchant or two-sided platform? *Review of Network Economics*, *6*(2).

Hagiu, A. (2009). Two-sided platforms: Product variety and pricing structures. *Journal of Economics and Management Strategy*, *18*(4), 1011–43.

Hagiu, A. (2014). Strategic decisions for multisided platforms. *MIT Sloan Management Review*, *55*(2), 71–80.

Hänninen, M. (2020). Review of studies on digital transaction platforms in marketing journals. *International Review of Retail, Distribution and Consumer Research*, *30*(2), 164–92.

Hänninen, M., Mitronen, L., & Kwan, S.K. (2019). Multi-sided marketplaces and the transformation of retail: A service systems perspective. *Journal of Retailing and Consumer Services*, *49*, 380–88.

Hänninen, M., Smedlund, A., & Mitronen, L. (2018). Digitalization in retailing: Multi-sided platforms as drivers of industry transformation. *Baltic Journal of Management*, *13*(2), 152–68.

Hein, A., Schreieck, M., Riasanow, T., Setzke, D.S., Wiesche, M., Böhm, M., & Krcmar, H. (2020). Digital platform ecosystems. *Electronic Markets*, *30*(1), 87–98.

Hein, A., Schreieck, M., Wiesche, M., Böhm, M., & Krcmar, H. (2019). The emergence of native multi-sided platforms and their influence on incumbents. *Electronic Markets*, *29*(4), 631–47.

Helfat, C.E., & Raubitschek, R.S. (2018). Dynamic and integrative capabilities for profiting from innovation in digital platform-based ecosystems. *Research Policy*, *47*(8), 1391–99.

Hossain, T., & Morgan, J. (2013). When do markets tip? A cognitive hierarchy approach. *Marketing Science*, *32*(3), 431–53.

Hukal, P., Henfridsson, O., Shaikh, M., & Parker, G. (2020). Platform signaling for generating platform content. *MIS Quarterly*, *44*(3), 1177–1205.

Jacobides, M.G., Cennamo, C., & Gawer, A. (2018). Towards a theory of ecosystems. *Strategic Management Journal*, *39*(8), 2255–76.

Kapoor, R. (2018). Ecosystems: Broadening the locus of value creation. *Journal of Organization Design*, *7*(1), 12.

Katz, M.L., & Shapiro, C. (1985). Network externalities, competition, and compatibility. *American Economic Review*, *75*(3), 424–40.

Katz, M.L., & Shapiro, C. (1994). Systems competition and network effects. *Journal of Economic Perspectives*, *8*(2), 93–115.

Keidel, R.W. (2005). Strategize on a napkin. *Strategy & Leadership*, *33*(4), 58–9.

Kollmann, T., Hensellek, S., de Cruppe, K., & Sirges, A. (2020). Toward a renaissance of cooperatives fostered by Blockchain on electronic marketplaces: A theory-driven case study approach. *Electronic Markets*, *30*(2), 273–84.

Laczko, P., Hullova, D., Needham, A., Rossiter, A.M., & Battisti, M. (2019). The role of a central actor in increasing platform stickiness and stakeholder profitability: Bridging the gap between value creation and value capture in the sharing economy. *Industrial Marketing Management*, *76*, 214–30.

Lee, J.Y., Fang, E., Kim, J.J., Li, X., & Palmatier, R.W. (2018). The effect of online shopping platform strategies on search, display, and membership revenues. *Journal of Retailing*, *94*(3), 247–64.

Lehdonvirta, V., Kässi, O., Hjorth, I., Barnard, H., & Graham, M. (2019). The global platform economy: A new offshoring institution enabling emerging-economy microproviders. *Journal of Management*, *45*(2), 567–99.

Lepak, D.P., Smith, K.G., & Taylor, M.S. (2007). Value creation and value capture: A multilevel perspective. *Academy of Management Review*, *32*(1), 180–94.

Liu, Y., Chen, D.Q., & Gao, W. (2020). How does customer orientation (in)congruence affect B2B electronic commerce platform firms' performance? *Industrial Marketing Management*, *87*, 18–30.

Madhok, A. (1996). Crossroads: The organization of economic activity – Transaction costs, firm capabilities, and the nature of governance. *Organization Science*, *7*(5), 577–90.

Magretta, J. (2002). Why business models matter. *Harvard Business Review*, *80*(5), 86–92.

Massa, L., & Tucci, C.L. (2021). Innovation and Business Models. *Oxford Research Encyclopedia of Business and Management*. https://oxfordre.com/business/view/10.1093/acrefore/9780190224851.001.0001/acrefore-9780190224851-e-296.

Massa, L., Tucci, C.L., & Afuah, A. (2017). A critical assessment of business model research. *Academy of Management Annals*, *11*(1), 73–104.

McIntyre, D.P., & Srinivasan, A. (2017). Networks, platforms, and strategy: Emerging views and next steps. *Strategic Management Journal*, *38*(1), 141–60.

McIntyre, D.P., Srinivasan, A., Afuah, A., Gawer, A., & Kretschmer, T. (2020a). Multi-sided platforms as new organizational forms. *Academy of Management Perspectives*, *35*(4).

McIntyre, D.P., Srinivasan, A., & Chintakananda, A. (2020b). The persistence of platforms: The role of network, platform, and complementor attributes. *Long Range Planning*, 101987.

Mikalef, P., Pappas, I.O., Krogstie, J., & Giannakos, M. (2018). Big data analytics capabilities: A systematic literature review and research agenda. *Information Systems and e-Business Management*, *16*(3), 547–78.

Nuccio, M., & Guerzoni, M. (2019). Big data: Hell or heaven? Digital platforms and market power in the data-driven economy. *Competition and Change*, *23*(3), 312–28.

Ocasio, W., & Radoynovska, N. (2016). Strategy and commitments to institutional logics: Organizational heterogeneity in business models and governance. *Strategic Organization*, *14*(4), 287–309.

Ordanini, A., & Pol, A. (2001). Infomediation and competitive advantage in B2B digital marketplaces. *European Management Journal*, *19*(3), 276–85.

Ozalp, H., Cennamo, C., & Gawer, A. (2018). Disruption in platform-based ecosystems. *Journal of Management Studies*, *55*(7), 1203–41.

Panico, C., & Cennamo, C. (2020). User preferences and strategic interactions in platform ecosystems. *Strategic Management Journal*, *43*(3), 507–29.

Parker, G.G., & Van Alstyne, M.W. (2005). Two-sided network effects: A theory of information product design. *Management Science*, *51*(10), 1494–1504.

Parker, G.G., Van Alstyne, M.W., & Choudary, S.P. (2016). *Platform Revolution: How Networked Markets Are Transforming the Economy and How to Make Them Work for You*. W.W. Norton & Company.

Parmentier, G., & Gandia, R. (2017). Redesigning the business model: From one-sided to multi-sided. *Journal of Business Strategy*, *38*(2), 52–61.

Perks, H., Kowalkowski, C., Witell, L., & Gustafsson, A. (2017). Network orchestration for value platform development. *Industrial Marketing Management*, *67*, 106–21.

Perren, R., & Kozinets, R.V. (2018). Lateral exchange markets: How social platforms operate in a networked economy. *Journal of Marketing*, *82*(1), 20–36.

Peteraf, M.A. (1993). The cornerstones of competitive advantage: A resource-based view. *Strategic Management Journal*, *14*(3), 179–91.

Porter, M.E. (1980). *Competitive Strategy: Techniques for Analyzing Industries and Competitors*. Free Press.

Porter, M.E. (1985). *Competitive Advantage: Creating and Sustaining Superior Performance*. Free Press.

Porter, M.E. (1996). What is strategy? *Harvard Business Review*, *74*(6), 61–78.

Porter, M.E. (2001). Strategy and the Internet. *Harvard Business Review*, *79*(3), 62–78, 164.

Prahalad, C.K., & Bettis, R.A. (1986). The dominant logic: A new linkage between diversity and performance. *Strategic Management Journal*, *7*(6), 485–501.

Priem, R.L. (2007). A consumer perspective on value creation. *Academy of Management Review*, *32*(1), 219–35.

Ramaswamy, V. (2020). Leading the experience ecosystem revolution: Innovating offerings as interactive platforms. *Strategy and Leadership*, *48*(3), 3–9.

Ramaswamy, V., & Ozcan, K. (2018a). Offerings as digitalized interactive platforms: A conceptual framework and implications. *Journal of Marketing, 82*(4), 19–31.

Ramaswamy, V., & Ozcan, K. (2018b). What is co-creation? An interactional creation framework and its implications for value creation. *Journal of Business Research, 84*, 196–205.

Rangaswamy, A., Moch, N., Felten, C., Van Bruggen, G., Wieringa, J.E., & Wirtz, J. (2020). The role of marketing in digital business platforms. *Journal of Interactive Marketing, 51*, 72–90.

Reimers, K., Guo, X., & Li, M. (2019). Beyond markets, hierarchies, and hybrids: An institutional perspective on IT-enabled two-sided markets. *Electronic Markets, 29*(2), 287–305.

Reinartz, W., Wiegand, N., & Imschloss, M. (2019). The impact of digital transformation on the retailing value chain. *International Journal of Research in Marketing, 36*(3), 350–66.

Rietveld, J., & Schilling, M.A. (2020). Platform competition: A systematic and interdisciplinary review of the literature. *Journal of Management, 47*(6), 159–77.

Ritala, P., Golnam, A., & Wegmann, A. (2014). Coopetition-based business models: The case of Amazon.com. *Industrial Marketing Management, 43*(2), 236–49.

Rochet, J.-C., & Tirole, J. (2003). Platform competition in two-sided markets. *Journal of the European Economic Association, 1*(4), 990–1029.

Roger, G., & Vasconcelos, L. (2014). Platform pricing structure and moral hazard. *Journal of Economics and Management Strategy, 23*(3), 527–47.

Spinello, R.A. (2005). Competing fairly in the new economy: Lessons from the browser wars. *Journal of Business Ethics, 57*(4), 343–61.

Sriram, S., Manchanda, P., Bravo, M.E., Chu, J., Ma, L., Song, M., Shriver, S., & Subramanian, U. (2015). Platforms: A multiplicity of research opportunities. *Marketing Letters, 26*(2), 141–52.

Steiner, M., Wiegand, N., Eggert, A., & Backhaus, K. (2016). Platform adoption in system markets: The roles of preference heterogeneity and consumer expectations. *International Journal of Research in Marketing, 33*(2), 276–96.

Stone, B. (2013). *The Everything Store: Jeff Bezos and the Age of Amazon*. Random House.

Sun, M., & Tse, E. (2009). The resource-based view of competitive advantage in two-sided markets. *Journal of Management Studies, 46*(1), 45–64.

Täuscher, K., & Laudien, S.M. (2018). Understanding platform business models: A mixed methods study of marketplaces. *European Management Journal, 36*(3), 319–29.

Tavalaei, M.M., & Cennamo, C. (2020). In search of complementarities within and across platform ecosystems: Complementors' relative standing and performance in mobile apps ecosystems. *Long Range Planning*, 101994.

Teece, D.J. (2007). Explicating dynamic capabilities: The nature and microfoundations of (sustainable) enterprise performance. *Strategic Management Journal, 28*(13), 1319–50.

Teece, D.J. (2010). Business models, business strategy and innovation. *Long Range Planning, 43*(2–3), 172–94.

Teece, D.J. (2018). Profiting from innovation in the digital economy: Enabling technologies, standards, and licensing models in the wireless world. *Research Policy, 47*(8), 1367–87.

Tellis, G.J., Yin, E., & Niraj, R. (2009). Does quality win? Network effects versus quality in high-tech markets. *Journal of Marketing Research, 46*(2), 135–49.

Thomas, L.D.W., Autio, E., & Gann, D.M. (2014). Architectural leverage: Putting platforms in context. *Academy of Management Perspectives, 28*(2), 198–219.

Trabucchi, D., & Buganza, T. (2020). Fostering digital platform innovation: From two to multi-sided platforms. *Creativity and Innovation Management, 29*(2), 345–58.

Tura, N., Kutvonen, A., & Ritala, P. (2018). Platform design framework: Conceptualisation and application. *Technology Analysis and Strategic Management, 30*(8), 881–94.

Wallbach, S., Coleman, K., Elbert, R., & Benlian, A. (2019). Multi-sided platform diffusion in competitive B2B networks: Inhibiting factors and their impact on network effects. *Electronic Markets, 29*(4), 693–710.

Wamba, S.F., Gunasekaran, A., Akter, S., Ren, S.J.-f., Dubey, R., & Childe, S.J. (2017). Big data analytics and firm performance: Effects of dynamic capabilities. *Journal of Business Research, 70*, 356–65.

Wen, W., & Zhu, F. (2019). Threat of platform-owner entry and complementor responses: Evidence from the mobile app market. *Strategic Management Journal, 40*(9), 1336–67.

Wiengarten, F., Humphreys, P., Cao, G., & McHugh, M. (2013). Exploring the important role of organizational factors in IT business value: Taking a contingency perspective on the resource-based view. *International Journal of Management Reviews, 15*(1), 30–46.

Williamson, O.E. (1985). *Economic Institutions of Capitalism*. Free Press.

Willing, C., Brandt, T., & Neumann, D. (2017). Electronic mobility market platforms: A review of the current state and applications of business analytics. *Electronic Markets, 27*(3), 267–82.

Yang, Z., Diao, Z., & Kang, J. (2020). Customer management in Internet-based platform firms: Review and future research directions. *Marketing Intelligence and Planning, 38*(7), 957–73.

Yrjölä, M., Rintamäki, T., Saarijärvi, H., & Joensuu, J. (2017). Consumer-to-consumer e-commerce: Outcomes and implications. *International Review of Retail, Distribution and Consumer Research, 27*(3), 300–315.

Zervas, G., Proserpio, D., & Byers, J.W. (2017). The rise of the sharing economy: Estimating the impact of Airbnb on the hotel industry. *Journal of Marketing Research, 54*(5), 687–705.

Zhang, S., & Tang, T. (2019). Managing same-side and cross-side innovations in two-sided platforms. *Marketing Intelligence and Planning, 37*(7), 770–90.

Zhang, X., Luo, J., & Li, Q. (2012). Do different reputation systems provide consistent signals of seller quality: A canonical correlation investigation of Chinese C2C marketplaces. *Electronic Markets, 22*(3), 155–68.

Zhu, F. (2019). Friends or foes? Examining platform owners' entry into complementors' spaces. *Journal of Economics and Management Strategy, 28*(1), 23–8.

Zhu, F., & Iansiti, M. (2012). Entry into platform-based markets. *Strategic Management Journal, 33*(1), 88–106.

Zhu, F., & Liu, Q. (2018). Competing with complementors: An empirical look at Amazon.com. *Strategic Management Journal, 39*(10), 2618–42.

Zott, C., & Amit, R. (2010). Business model design: An activity system perspective. *Long Range Planning, 43*(2), 216–26.

# 11. Digital competition and user engagement: how do the user engagement strategies of social media platforms contribute to value creation?

*Ioanna Constantiou*

## INTRODUCTION

In recent years, several social media platforms (SMPs) – for example, Facebook, Twitter, Snapchat, and TikTok – have increased their market dominance. These platforms have been hailed for the rapid growth of their market shares for many reasons, but especially due to the size of their networks (Parker et al., 2016). Network size is only one of the key ingredients of SMPs' success. Keeping participants active on the platform is equally important in the light of low switching costs, which challenge the traditional strategy of locking in users (Farrell & Klemperer, 2007). Besides, the easy accessibility to SMPs' networks facilitates users' multi-homing. Competition among SMPs intensifies when multi-homing is common among users (Zhu & Iansiti, 2019). As digital competition intensifies, SMPs have to consider new strategies for maintaining their user base and increasing the platform's value for all participants.

Cultivating user engagement with a platform has become a key element in formulating SMPs' strategy (Hollebeek et al., 2019). When participants use a platform frequently, they generate value not only by using the platform's core features, but also by leaving digital traces of their activities on the platform. These digital traces can be the source of developing new functionalities, applications, or features generating value to the platform, third parties, or the app developers, and creating value for the end users. User engagement has been postulated as the emotional, cognitive, and behavioral investment of a user in a brand or technology (Hollebeek, 2011; Hollebeek et al., 2014), and is considered vital for the digital platform's survival (Parker et al., 2016). SMPs that fail to engage users may be abandoned, while increasing user engagement helps in attaining superior platform performance outcomes, including users' loyalty, positive word of mouth (Ray et al., 2014), and continuous use of the platform (Hollebeek et al., 2019). Thus, SMP strategies must go beyond attracting new users and ensure that current users remain active and engaged with the platform in the long term.

User engagement manifests in the greater use of, and contributions to, an SMP. That is, users interact and share content readily and voluntarily with others, as well as cognitively and emotionally bonding with SMPs (Hollebeek & Chen, 2014), contributing to value creation (Brodie et al., 2013; Hollebeek et al., 2019). Besides, the more users engage with an SMP, the more valuable it becomes to other users, as well as increasing the opportunities for service innovation (Dou et al., 2013; Iansiti & Lakhani, 2020) such as the design of innovative, data-based services by the platform, or other forms of value creation, including personalized recommendations (Iansiti & Lakhani, 2020). Other platform participants, such as advertisers and application developers, also capture part of the value generated from the increased number of users and their active participation through indirect network effects (Parker et al., 2016). This chapter focuses on user engagement and value creation; the value generated and captured by other participants is outside the scope of the chapter. The chapter aims to unpack how the user engagement strategies of SMPs contribute to value creation, and identify their impact on digital competition.

A successful user engagement strategy should consider the users' interactions with technological features from a multidimensional perspective (Hollebeek, 2011; Hollebeek et al., 2014), and their impact on the SMP's perceived value. The SMP's decisions about which technological features to introduce have a direct influence on the user engagement strategies (Liu et al., 2017). The chosen technological features afford a range of interactions for users and these affordances shape unique communication practices in each SMP. These practices build a specific image for the SMP that becomes a determining factor for user engagement, and contribute to its perceived value. Thus, the SMP's digital competition strategies that determine its position in the digital landscape may involve differentiation based on the unique communication practices established from user engagement.

This chapter starts by offering a conceptualization of user engagement in terms of the depth and breadth of user interactions with the platform's services. User engagement does not involve high switching costs because of foregone investments of money, time, or data, but a continuous stimulation of user participation. The main arguments are then presented, building on a comparison of two seemingly contradicting user engagement strategies of SMPs: content persistence and content perishability. This is followed by a brief account of value creation strategies and positioning of user engagement in this context. Finally, the chapter presents the conditions under which user engagement strategies contribute to value creation for SMPs and the implications for digital competition, and concludes by depicting the corresponding research directions.

## DEFINING USER ENGAGEMENT

The original conceptualization of user engagement comes from the human–computer interaction research field. It refers to users' experience with technology that goes beyond usability (O'Brien & Toms, 2008) and describes individuals becoming captivated by technology. Several studies have investigated user engagement from a user-centric perspective (O'Brien & Cairns, 2016) and mainly examined how users' perceptions about technological features and their goals influence their engagement (Chen & Cheung, 2019). However, user engagement in human–computer interaction has been treated largely as an abstract concept (Ray et al., 2014). In the digital platforms literature, user engagement is a concept that encompasses a set of measurements of user actions on a platform (Voorveld et al., 2018). This view has become popular due to the abundance of data on user behavior available on platforms, and emerging mechanisms to generate value for such data (Alaimo & Kallinikos, 2017). This stream of literature highlights the behavioral dimension of user engagement. Behavioral engagement in SMPs has been investigated at a platform level through the frequency of visits or time spent on an SMP (Gummerus et al., 2012; Hollebeek et al., 2014), or at a content level, through users' creation and consumption of content, as well as their direct responses to original content (e.g., responding, liking, commenting, sharing) (Gummerus et al., 2012; Li & Xie, 2020).

The concept of customer engagement has been developed into a theoretically and empirically validated construct in the marketing field. Customer brand engagement is rooted in marketing and social psychology, and is described as "the level of an individual customer's motivational, brand-related and context-dependent state of mind characterized by specific levels of cognitive, emotional and behavioural activity in direct brand interactions" (Hollebeek 2011, p. 790). The three dimensions of engagement provide a holistic view of individual's interactions with the brand. This conceptualization offers the adequate theoretical lens to analyze user interactions with the SMP's features and reveal how they contribute to value creation. User engagement is defined as a user's brand-related state of mind, characterized by specific cognitive, emotional, and behavioral manifestations in interactions with platform features. Platform features refer to different services and applications developed and offered by the focal SMP.

The cognitive dimension refers to users' positive or negative thoughts and reflections on specific interactions with the SMP's features (Hollebeek & Chen, 2014). For example, positive thoughts and considerations are involved regarding how to compose a status update for Facebook and which features to include in it. In contrast, reading someone's post and considering how to express disagreement may involve negative cognitive reactions.

The emotional dimension refers to users' positively or negatively valenced affect in such interactions (Hollebeek & Chen, 2014). This includes either positive feelings, such as enjoyment or pride (Hollebeek et al., 2014), or negative feelings, such as uncertainty, doubt, and frustration with technology (O'Brien & Toms, 2008).

Lastly, the behavioral dimension involves the energy, effort, and time spent (Hollebeek & Chen, 2014) on the interactions with an SMP's features.

Overall, the three different perspectives of user engagement clearly stipulate that the focus is the individual user of the social media network that adopted the platform to build a social network and communicate with other individual users. This clear focus of user engagement theories has implications for the platform strategy and the value creation. The proposed view of user engagement, depicting a multidimensional concept, underlines the need to combine the brand focus with a focus on the technological features and their affordances in order to unpack the complex process that takes place every time a user interacts with the platform's features. Considering the cognitive and emotional reactions of the user, it is possible to identify new sources of value creation, such as user attention, which can become a valuable resource for innovation. Such identification allows SMPs to develop user engagement strategies to shape new communication practices. These strategies could contribute to the platform's image and increase its perceived value by creating representative communication practices which are directly related and identified in the focal SMP. For example, Instagram is used, strategically, to share content with followers to communicate a message about a product or place, and the content is thoroughly developed to look almost professional (Voorveld et al., 2018). Snapchat is used for sharing an intimate picture with a very close group of friends to reveal a momentarily emotional state. The content is not curated in any way and the user's motivation is often spontaneous (Morlok et al., 2018).

## SMPs' FEATURES AND USER ENGAGEMENT

The user engagement strategies of SMPs vary, but the main objective in the digital environment is to generate data on user behavior and reveal users' needs in specific situations and times. The technology features of an SMP enable and constrain user actions by affording a number of use scenarios (Leidner et al., 2018). The most prominent feature is content persistence, which allows users to engage with the content in numerous ways. Recently, the opposite feature of content perishability has emerged as an alternative means of user engagement. In the following, the two key features for user engagement with SMPs are used as examples to show how SMPs' user engagement strategies contribute to competition.

Promoting user engagement on SMPs has long been thought of as requiring persistent content (Boyd, 2010). The assumption has been that when users interact socially online, they want their shared content to remain online permanently, unless they delete it manually. So, SMPs foster engagement by enabling users to upload content, express "likes," and comment on and share content that remains available on the platform (Alaimo & Kallinikos, 2017). Combined with the ability to react to content shared by others, users may also engage with gamification features, when, for example, more information or quantifications of the impact a particular post had on the user social network are available (e.g., viewed-by figures). These numbers may motivate users to share more content and become strategic by considering, for example, how to introduce content using specific text, or even paying an amount of money to have the post visible to more people. These reactions could be cognitively or emotionally driven. All the actions/reactions generate more data for the SMP, which becomes more efficient at predicting users' needs, and thus personalizes the offerings. The platform capitalizes on the data network effects (Gregory et al., 2021).

User engagement with specific platform features could create either positive or negative reactions. If the platform elicits more negative reactions than positive ones, it may challenge user satisfaction and loyalty and thus reduce the intentions to continue using the platform. User engagement strategy should balance between introducing new features while maintaining positive interactions for users. Despite the allure of data network effects (Gregory et al., 2021) which could lead to the design of a user engagement strategy to generate continuous streams of user data for value creation, there is a pitfall of negative user interactions. In particular, the introduction of new platform features may generate low-quality data or build on redundant or non-representative user actions in the platforms. For example, SMPs may consider the introduction of a thumbs-down button to indicate the dislike of content, such as a video on YouTube (Khan, 2017), but this notably valuable data could hamper the user motivation to freely express oneself through personal posts or pictures on SMPs.

A recent paradigm shift in SMP design has challenged these presumed benefits of content persistence (Cavalcanti et al., 2017). This involves the integration of perishable content features that make shared content disappear after a short period of time by default (Chen & Cheung, 2019). First introduced by Snapchat in 2011, perishable content features have since been implemented by other popular SMPs such as Facebook, Instagram, WhatsApp, and LinkedIn; market reports expect them to continue to gain popularity (Norcross, 2018). The growing popularity of perishable content features offers opportunities to SMPs to design new features, but the effects on user engagement are yet unknown. Initial empirical research provides controversial findings, indicating positive user reactions (e.g., fun or willingness to share personal information) and negative user reactions (e.g., annoyance, loss, and regret) (Piwek

& Joinson, 2016). Perishable content features affect the emotional, cognitive, and behavioral dimensions of user engagement (Cavalcanti et al., 2017). This is manifested through new user behaviors in social media. Perishable content features may change user engagement in terms of directing attention to specific activities on the platform – e.g., users being focused while reading a message that will gradually disappear – or user behaviors by affording new possibilities; e.g., spontaneous content sharing. Perishable content highlights the importance of user attention that interacts with the brand in experiential ways, such as using sponsored filters to decorate a picture.

Perishable content features appear to complement rather than substitute persistent content features (Morlok et al., 2018). While mundane or private content is shared through perishable content features, users tend to switch to persistent SMPs or features to share information they regard as memorable and not too private. SMPs' strategy of introducing new platform features has recently shown a trend of combining persistent and perishable content features so users can choose which content to share via which feature. This strategy is being pursued by formerly persistent SMPs such as Facebook and Instagram, and might prove more successful in the long run than Snapchat, which relies heavily on perishable content features. Empirical findings suggest that the most interesting areas of application for perishable content features are contexts in which providers aim to encourage users to effortlessly share content on a regular basis and promote fast, intensive, yet short-lived communication; an example could be the online dating context (Voorveld et al., 2018). In contrast, contexts in which users share important and valuable content or engage in deep communication (e.g., between a company and a customer in a service context) are less suitable for perishable content features (Voorveld et al., 2018).

Recent examples of SMPs' user engagement strategies introducing perishable content features highlight the challenge when the platform offers mainly persistent content. Different combinations of persistent and perishable content of the major SMPs indicate experimentation and attempts to imitate the successful features of competitors such as Snapchat. In 2019, YouTube introduced an option for content creators with more than 10,000 subscribers to share YouTube Stories, which can be liked and commented on before they disappear after seven days. Since 2017, WhatsApp users have been able to share photos and videos in the status feature for 24 hours, while in 2020 the "disappearing messages" feature was introduced. The messages are automatically deleted in a chat after seven days if the feature is activated for particular chat settings. In Instagram, since 2016 users have been able to share stories (i.e., photos or videos) that last 24 hours, and live videos in Instagram Stories, which disappear after ending. Since 2016, Facebook has offered a live video feature; the video is automatically deleted after the stream ends. Since 2017, users have been able to share Facebook Stories (i.e., photos or videos), which disappear after 24 hours. Since 2020, there has been a Vanish Mode on Facebook Messenger. Messages and pictures disappear after being seen, when Vanish Mode is switched on in the chat settings of the particular chat. This feature is only available in a few countries for the time being.

## CONCEPTUALIZING VALUE IN SMPs

SMPs are communication platforms originally developed to connect people by building social networks and allowing users to establish and maintain communications with others. Hence, SMPs have not been designed as two- or multi-sided platforms. However, SMPs' strategy to exploit the abundance of data generated by users' interactions with the platform features has transformed them into multi-sided platforms which facilitate advertisers or other third parties by pooling large numbers of participants and matching their needs. For example, SMPs use data about each user's behavior in the platform – e.g., digital traces – which are aggregated, encoded and computed into valuable input for advertisers that would then target the appropriate audience of users in the SMP (Alaimo and Kallinikos 2017). Understanding how value is shared among the SMP and its participants is important; however, this chapter focuses on user engagement and how value is created in the SMPs.

The concept of value creation refers to the total value being created for the user from their participation in the platform. Adapting the conceptualizations of Brandenburger and Stuart (1996), value creation refers to value received or perceived by the user of the SMP, and it is distinguishable from value capture, which refers to the portions of value received by the SMP or other parties. The relation between value creation and value capture is not as direct in SMPs as for businesses in a value chain where value is first created and then captured by the involved parties. In the case of multi-sided platforms, one should account for the multiple user groups interacting in the platform; the individual users, the complementors, and the advertisers. For example, Facebook generates value by providing an interface that facilitates communications and interactions through information-sharing among participants, which creates value through network and data network effects, while it captures value by generating revenues through advertising. Since user engagement literature focuses on the individual as a user of the platform and the reactions or experiences from services and features used, the reference group in the case of value creation are the individual users. In particular, user engagement strategies are investigated from the SMP's perspective to create value and maintain user involvement with the platform. Besides, it is important to limit the focus to value creation and not value capture since user engagement contributes to the first.

User engagement strategies highlight the intrinsic value of the platform through the introduction of new features which aim to increase frequency of interactions (Voorveld et al., 2018). When the features involve positive emotional and cognitive engagement, they broaden user interactions on the platform. The more users interact with the platform features, the higher the probabilities that they reveal additional potential uses the features afford, and entrench their communications practices in the focal SMP. This can also lead to new communications practices that represent the platform and shape its image for the users. For example, when Snapchat was launched it promoted the perishability content feature through Snaps (i.e., pictures of very short videos) and created new communication practices whereby users could share the mundane content of everyday life with a very close circle of friends and low inhibitions, since the content is deleted within seconds.

## VALUE CREATION AND USER ENGAGEMENT STRATEGIES

A major challenge for SMPs is that people download the application and use it for a short while, and then become inactive, without abandoning the application. A number of SMPs motivate user creativity through interactions with technological features. From promoting special tools to creating and enhancing the content shared to including gamification features, the platforms attempt to increase user interactions with the platforms by adding to their perceived

*Table 11.1*     *The different perspectives of user engagement and their implications for value creation*

| Engagement type | Definition | Literature | Examples of engagement strategies | Mechanisms of value creation |
|---|---|---|---|---|
| User engagement as a human–computer interaction | Users' experience with technology, and describes how they become captivated by technology | O'Brien & Toms, 2008; O'Brien & Cairns, 2016; Ray et al., 2014; Chen & Cheung, 2019 | Introduction of buttons to react to content shared (e.g., like, celebrate)<br><br>The personalized wall interface (e.g., personal information, representative pictures) | SMP's features motivate user to interact with and leave digital traces which become data about personal preferences to be used for new features and more personalization |
| User engagement as a user interaction with the platform | A set of measurements of user actions on a platform | Gummerus et al., 2012; Voorveld et al., 2018; Li & Xie, 2020 | Gamification features (e.g., percentage of CV completion on LinkedIn, number of views on a post)<br><br>Features for nudging (e.g., asking on a status update "How do you feel today?") | SMP's features that aim to intensify the frequency of user interactions with them and contribute to the development of innovative data-driven services |
| User engagement adapted from customer brand engagement | A user's brand-related state of mind, characterized by specific cognitive, emotional, and behavioral manifestations in interactions with platform features | Hollebeek, 2011; Brodie et al., 2013; Hollebeek & Chen, 2014; Hollebeek et al., 2014 | • *Cognitive*<br>Introduce features with different time duration of content availability (e.g., Snaps lasting few seconds, Stories lasting 24 hours)<br>• *Emotional*<br>Introduce features evoking emotional reactions to posts shared by other users (e.g., love button, or emoji)<br>• *Behavioral*<br>Introduce gamification features quantifying the impact of content shared in the user's network | • *Cognitive*<br>Content features that intend to capture the attention of the user to the SMP and increase time spent on it and contribute to the development of innovative services targeted to user preferences<br>• *Emotional*<br>Increase the user interaction with the content of others, increase the frequency of visits to the SMP and time spent, and contribute to the development of innovative services<br>• *Behavioral*<br>Features that aim to increase the frequency of updating and sharing content and contribute to the development of innovative data-driven services |

value. Table 11.1 offers an overview of the different perspectives of user engagement, the corresponding strategies, and the mechanisms of value creation.

Different forms of user engagement may attract different types of input from users while maintaining their loyalty to the platform. Focusing only on the behavioral dimension of user engagement may lead to excessive data from the use of a platform's features. However, the quality of such data may be low since they do not represent natural user behavior but are derived from artificially stimulated users by employing specific tools or mechanisms. For example, platform tools that aim to engage users in a flow state or repetitive behavior through gamification may create harm – e.g., addictive behaviors – because of hyper-engagement (Thorpe & Roper, 2019). Alternatively, user engagement that builds on multidimensional interactions with the platform's features, including emotional and cognitive ones, may create a stronger connection between users and the platform and increase the perceived values of the platform for the user. When the engagement is not about data, it might be about user attention (Davenport & Beck, 2000). Attracting and increasing user attention in the platform could be valuable for advertisers or other third parties. SMPs can generate revenue by monetizing user attention either from advertising (e.g., influencer model) or views of content in YouTube. User attention might be more valuable than data collection when a third party aims, for example, at cognitive stimulation of users or experiencing a brand, and is not raising high privacy concerns as data-sharing strategies do. Since user attention is another value-generating resource for SMPs and it is scarce, the SMPs compete on attracting and maintaining it through different user engagement mechanisms.

Users' perceptions for each platform are shaped by their experiences and engagement with its features. User subscriptions in two or more SMPs that have similar key features, and build their social networks with the same core – i.e., close ties and different sizes – are indications that such SMPs are used in parallel and for different purposes. In other words, SMPs offer different practices of communicating in different contexts. The ways users contribute to value creation in the platform will enrich the specific communication practices that create the platform's image.

## USER ENGAGEMENT AND DIGITAL COMPETITION

SMPs are competing in an environment characterized by network effects and "winner-takes-all" market dynamics (Eisenmann et al., 2006). The introduction of the other sides, such as advertisers and third parties, generates more value to SMPs. For example, SMPs may capture value from the user data by selling aggregated information to advertisers (Alaimo & Kallinikos, 2017) or third-party developers exploiting indirect network effects and offering services to the platform users (Parker et al., 2016). Van Alstyne et al. (2016) argued that in these environments platform owners have to make smart choices about access (whom to let onto the platform) and governance (or control what consumers, third-party providers, and competitors are allowed to do there). This view focuses on coordination strategies, as well as their effects on platform competition, complementors' incentives to join the platform or provide higher-quality complements, or user utility (e.g., Cennamo & Santaló, 2013; Cennamo, 2021).

SMPs coexist in an environment where multi-homing is dominant among users. Multi-homing originates from empirical studies focusing on digital products with quantifiable adoption and switching costs, such as gaming consoles and gaming platforms (Cennamo et al., 2018). The concept is adapted to account for the user establishing a very similar network of connections in competing SMPs. This user behavior challenges the opportunity of SMPs to generate value by offering similar services to the same users or exposing them to the same complementors, or advertisers.[1] However, SMPs could view user multi-homing as an opportunity for generating value and capitalize on the complementarities of a user choosing to post the same content on more than one platform. The role of multi-homing in relation to user engagement should be further investigated since the digital environment creates a dilemma to SMPs. Multi-homing could lead SMPs to invest in creating barriers and strategies to prevent users from creating similar social networks in competitors' platforms, or SMPs could accept multi-homing as a new condition in the digital environment and focus on exploiting it while looking for differentiation strategies. Users' multi-homing (Zhu & Iansiti, 2019) may limit the "winner-takes-all" dynamics and lead to the coexistence of multiple similar platforms (Cennamo & Santaló, 2013; Cennamo, 2021). Multi-homing limits lock-in, and attenuates the ability of the platform owner to capture the value they create (Cennamo et al., 2018).

These arguments build on the extrinsic value of the network (McIntyre & Chintakananda, 2014) and tend to undermine the intrinsic value. User engagement underscores the importance of intrinsic value, especially when considering the platform's features that motivated users engage with. SMPs compete in different dimensions and need to consider how to coexist. Recent studies have depicted the platform owner as an orchestrator (e.g., Cennamo, 2021) who shapes the market's direction to build a distinctive position in a specific area. This involves creating "meaning" for participants by attracting and steering the focal attention towards features that should be regarded as valuable. In this context the focus of the platform is on shaping interactions and aligning users' incentives towards contributing to the market's shared assets – platform reputation and identity and the intended platform's goals (Cennamo & Santaló, 2013; Jacobides et al., 2018; Cennamo, 2021). User engagement strategies are closely related to this view. The users' interactions with the platform features are meant to create positive experiences and motivate recurring use, and hence the continuous generation of data, or attracting attention. These sources available to the SMP can be combined with third parties' assets, exploiting indirect network effects.

User engagement strategies of SMPs reveal new aspects of digital competition where user behavior in the platform becomes a source of value either through data from digital traces or time spent when the user's attention is captured in the platform. These resources are available to the platform but are not owned by the platform. They are valuable and unique but have a dynamic nature and can be lost if the users stop engaging with the platform. User engagement strategies are the key mechanisms of maintaining and increasing these new types of resources. The value creation potential of these resources depends on a number of strategic considerations about the user engagement strategies.

First, SMPs should consider how to balance the users' switching costs with the stimulation of user engagement in the platform since both underlying strategies aim at users' retention. Entrenching users to the SMP's service by creating additional costs of switching may not be sustainable in the long run and may lead the users to completely switch to a similar alternative platform which they already use in the context of multi-homing.[2] Switching costs may differ for different user activities or roles. Switching costs are higher for content creators (e.g., Instagram Influencers, YouTubers) than content users. Additionally, the underlying communication practices represented by the SMP would raise different types and intensities of switching costs (e.g., LinkedIn versus Instagram). Switching costs depend on the flexibility of moving data and connections from one SMP to another. Building a closed platform is almost impossible in the current digital environment. When an SMP focuses on user engagement features and tools, users may experience positively the interactions with that SMP and increase the frequency of use and time being present on it. For example, sharing specialized content on LinkedIn which is commented on and liked by other users of the SMP may increase the user's positive experience with the platform and even shape his or her identity as an expert in a particular area.

Second, SMPs should explore the potential of integrating these new value-generating resources to innovate and in particular the new features' development in order to differentiate their service offerings. Users' interactions with the SMP's features may reveal new uses or new sources of value, such as attention. These differentiation strategies may be short-lived since in the digital environment it is easy to imitate strategies and replicate resources. However, what is unique in this case is the SMPs' ability to build a particular image by establishing and extending specific communication practices for their users. SMPs could differentiate their evolutionary trajectories and align the user engagement strategies to steer user interactions towards enhancing the communications practices that better represent their image. For example, LinkedIn is viewed as a destination for professionals, and Instagram is viewed as a destination for influencers. The SMPs could innovate by providing features for the specific audience they attract in order to improve their experience and retain them.

Third, despite the appeal of easily imitating and replicating specific technology features, SMPs should consider the distinct communication practices they offer to users through their platform. SMPs should decide whether the introduction of a new feature would strengthen or weaken their image by considering user engagement and its impact in long-term benefits or negative outcomes. For example, introducing personal emoticons in LinkedIn may create negative cognitive and behavioral engagement by unnecessarily increasing the number of possible reactions to content. Similarly, introducing a feature like Snaps in Facebook would work against the communication practice of sharing persistent content, which is the main practice characterized by Facebook.

SMPs offer most of their core services to users for free and aim at increasing use frequency and time spent with services or features as means of generating data or attention. User engagement strategies are designed to meet this objective and hence motivate the users to contribute in value creation by interacting with the SMP's features. Striking the right balance between stimulating the user interactions with the SMP's features and maintaining the perceived value of these interactions is not a simple task. For the behavioral dimension this refers to an increase in use frequency without hyper-engaging the user in a compulsive or addictive habit. The latter would not contribute to value creation since data generated would represent not actual behaviors but artificially stimulated ones. In relation to the emotional dimension, this refers to activating positive emotions and avoiding features that could raise stress levels in terms of content's time availability or negative reactions from the social network. The latter could activate a vicious cycle where the user would behave in a non-representative way, compromising the quality of data and challenging other users. In relation to the cognitive dimension, SMPs' features should not increase cognitive overload. SMPs' use involves hedonic motivations (Van Koningsbruggen et al., 2017) and increasing cognitive effort for the use of specific features may have adverse effects on user engagement.

Overall, user engagement strategies are depicted as tools of managing the individual interactions with the platform which constitute a key ingredient of the new resources for value creation; i.e., behavioral data and user attention. Focusing on different dimensions of user engagement and combining them with the platform features would contribute to advancing competition between SMPs based on differentiation. This is not changing the competition paradigm, but underlines different trajectories along the current paradigm, questioning the logic of hyper-competition and continuous innovation resulting from imitation strategies. User engagement strategies suggest a different approach to differentiation and user retention that builds on the technological features and the underlying affordances of the focal platform. When the SMP's features are aimed at generating behavioral data and attracting user attention they contribute to the new sources for value generation.

*Table 11.2*    *Suggestions for future theoretical and empirical work*

| Potential future theoretical developments | Potential future empirical investigations | Potential research questions |
| --- | --- | --- |
| The interplay of user engagement strategies and switching costs in SMPs | | |
| • Understanding the interplay of user engagement and switching costs strategies in SMPs' competition<br>• Understanding the tradeoffs of user engagement and switching costs in SMPs' strategies for value creation | • Identifying the impacts of user engagement strategies and lock-in strategies on user's retention<br>• Understanding how multi-homing influences the interplay of user engagement and switching costs | • How does multi-homing affect user engagement strategies?<br>• How do user engagement and switching costs interact in SMPs' competition?<br>• How do SMPs' user engagement strategies contribute to users' retention? |
| Value creation and value capture in SMPs and user engagement strategies | | |
| • Understanding how user engagement increases value for other participants in the SMPs<br>• Theorizing the relationships between user engagement strategies, value creation, and value capture | • Exemplifying how user engagement strategies generate value to other participants in the SMPs (e.g., complementors, advertisers)<br>• Identifying how the user engagement strategies contribute to value capture by SMPs | • How do user engagement strategies contribute to an SMP becoming a system of value creation?<br>• How do user engagement strategies contribute to value capture by SMPs? |
| User engagement strategies and SMPs' competition | | |
| • Understanding how user engagement strategies contribute to the SMPs' differentiation strategies<br>• Understanding the relation between user engagement strategies and SMPs' competition | • Exemplifying how user engagement strategies shape the SMPs' images<br>• Identify new communication practices enabled by user engagement strategies for SMPs | • What are the SMPs' features enabling user engagement and shaping the differentiation strategies?<br>• How do user engagement strategies shape communication practices regarding SMPs? |

## CONCLUSIONS AND FUTURE WORK

The theory put forward in this chapter requires further development and empirical work. The areas that need to be addressed most urgently are summarized in Table 11.2, which presents subjects for future theoretical developments, future empirical investigations, and specific research questions. More generally, the conceptualization of user engagement that entails changes in the SMPs' strategy calls for a review of extant theories that view SMPs as multi-sided platforms, and at the same time requires new theorizing around SMPs as systems of value creation. Future empirical investigations should focus on examining the usefulness of this approach in its ability to distinguish user engagement strategies from other types of curation strategies offered by SMPs, and in evaluating its applicability in wide-ranging empirical contexts.

Table 11.2 presents a research agenda on some key aspects to focus on and the knowledge gaps as well as the departure points shifting the field's conversation and pushing the boundaries of current knowledge. Digital competition among SMPs is intense, and this is evidenced by the lengths to which SMPs will go to sustain and increase their dominance in the long run. Short-lived hype does not indicate that an SMP is successful. Thus, SMPs should investigate and choose the right combinations of technological features that allow them to create value from users' participation. The current convergence on offering similar features may intensify the competition even more, although users' reactions indicate a different trend in the environment. Differentiating user engagement strategies could bring new revenue sources and change the intensity of competition. User engagement strategies allow SMPs to build a unique image based on the specific communications practices they represent. These practices are developed based on the users' interactions with technological features, and are enabled by the user engagement strategies of SMPs.

## NOTES

1.   Consider the example of a user browsing online for a particular retailer brand. This search result will follow the user in any SMP they go as a banner advertisement, until their next search.
2.   For example, a user stops using Skype and switches to WhatsApp or Messenger.

## REFERENCES

Alaimo, C., & Kallinikos, J. (2017). Computing the everyday: Social media as data platforms. *Information Society*, *33*(4), 175–91.
Boyd, D.M. (2010). Social Network Sites as Networked Publics: Affordances, Dynamics and Implications, in *A Networked Self: Identity, Community, and Culture on Social Network Sites*, Z. Papacharissi (ed.), Routledge, 39–58.
Brandenburger, A.M., & Stuart, H.W., Jr (1996). Value-based business strategy. *Journal of Economics & Management Strategy*, *5*(1), 5–24.
Brodie, R.J., Ilic, A., Juric, B., & Hollebeek, L. (2013). Consumer engagement in a virtual brand community: An exploratory analysis. *Journal of Business Research*, *66*(1), 105–14.
Cavalcanti, L.H.C., Pinto, A., Brubaker, J.R., & Dombrowski, L.S. (2017). Media, meaning, and context loss in ephemeral communication platforms: A qualitative investigation on Snapchat, in *Proceedings of the 2017 ACM Conference on Computer Supported Cooperative Work and Social Computing*, 1934–45.
Cennamo, C. (2021). Competing in digital markets: A platform-based perspective. *Academy of Management Perspectives*, *35*(2), 265–91.
Cennamo, C., Ozalp, H., & Kretschmer, T. (2018). Platform architecture and quality trade-offs of multi-homing complements. *Information Systems Research*, *29*(2), 461–78.
Cennamo, C. & Santaló, J. (2013). Platform competition: Strategic trade-offs in platform markets. *Strategic Management Journal*, *34*(11), 1331–50.
Chen, K.J., & Cheung, H.L. (2019). Unlocking the power of ephemeral content: The roles of motivations, gratification, need for closure, and engagement. *Computers in Human Behavior*, *97*, 67–74.
Davenport, T.H., & Beck, J.C. (2000). Getting the attention you need. *Harvard Business Review*, *78*(5), 118–26.
Dou, Y., Niculescu, M.F., & Wu, D.J. (2013). Engineering optimal network effects via social media features and seeding in markets for digital goods and services. *Information Systems Research*, *24*(1), 164–85.
Eisenmann, T., Parker, G., & Van Alstyne, M.W. (2006). Strategies for two-sided markets. *Harvard Business Review*, *84*(10), 92.
Farrell, J., & Klemperer, P. (2007). Coordination and lock-in: Competition with switching costs and network effects. *Handbook of Industrial Organization*, *3*, 1967–2072.
Gregory, R.W., Henfridsson, O., Kaganer, E., & Kyriakou, H. (2021). The role of artificial intelligence and data network effects for creating user value. *Academy of Management Review*, *46*(3), 534–51.
Gummerus, J., Liljander, V., Weman, E., & Pihlström, M. (2012). Customer engagement in a Facebook brand community. *Management Research Review*, *35*(9), 857–77.
Hollebeek, L.D. (2011). Demystifying customer brand engagement: Exploring the loyalty nexus. *Journal of Marketing Management*, *27*(7–8), 785–807.
Hollebeek, L.D., & Chen, T. (2014). Exploring positively-versus negatively-valenced brand engagement: A conceptual model. *Journal of Product & Brand Management*, *23*(1), 62–74.

Hollebeek, L.D., Glynn, M.S., & Brodie, R.J. (2014). Consumer brand engagement in social media: Conceptualization, scale development and validation. *Journal of Interactive Marketing, 28*(2), 149–65.

Hollebeek, L.D., Srivastava, R.K., & Chen, T. (2019). SD logic-informed customer engagement: Integrative framework, revised fundamental propositions, and application to CRM. *Journal of the Academy of Marketing Science, 47*(1), 161–85.

Iansiti, M., & Lakhani, K.R. (2020). *Competing in the Age of AI: Strategy and Leadership when Algorithms and Networks Run the World.* Harvard Business Press.

Jacobides, M.G., Cennamo, C., & Gawer, A. (2018). Towards a theory of ecosystems. *Strategic Management Journal, 39*(8), 2255–76.

Khan, M.L. (2017). Social media engagement: What motivates user participation and consumption on YouTube? *Computers in Human Behavior, 66,* 236–47.

Leidner, D.E., Gonzalez, E., & Koch, H. (2018). An affordance perspective of enterprise social media and organizational socialization. *Journal of Strategic Information Systems, 27*(2), 117–38.

Li, Y., & Xie, Y. (2020). Is a picture worth a thousand words? An empirical study of image content and social media engagement. *Journal of Marketing Research, 57*(1), 1–19.

Liu, D., Santhanam, R., & Webster, J. (2017). Toward meaningful engagement: A framework for design and research of Gamified information systems. *MIS Quarterly, 41*(4), 1011–34.

McIntyre, D.P., & Chintakananda, A. (2014). Competing in network markets: Can the winner take all? *Business Horizons, 57*(1), 117–25.

Morlok, T.N., Constantiou, I., & Hess, T. (2018). Gone for better or for worse? Exploring the dual nature of ephemerality on social media platforms. In *Proceedings of the 26th European Conference on Information Systems (ECIS)*, Association for Information Systems. AIS Electronic Library (AISeL).

Norcross, N. (2018). Social media and content marketing trends that will shape 2018. *Forbes* (January 11). https://www.forbes.com/sites/forbesagencycouncil/2018/01/11/social-media-and-content -marketing-trends-that-will-shape-2018/#4314d34e33d7.

O'Brien, H., & Cairns, P. (2016). *Why Engagement Matters.* Springer International.

O'Brien, H.L., & Toms, E.G. (2008). What is user engagement? A conceptual framework for defining user engagement with technology. *Journal of the American Society for Information Science and Technology, 59*(6), 938–55.

Parker, G.G., Van Alstyne, M.W., & Choudary, S.P. (2016). *Platform Revolution: How Networked Markets Are Transforming the Economy and How to Make Them Work for You.* W.W. Norton & Company.

Piwek, L., & Joinson, A. (2016). What do they Snapchat about? Patterns of use in time-limited instant messaging service. *Computers in Human Behavior, 54,* 358–67.

Ray, S., Kim, S.S., & Morris, J.G. (2014). The central role of engagement in online communities. *Information Systems Research, 25*(3), 528–46.

Thorpe, A.S., & Roper, S. (2019). The ethics of gamification in a marketing context. *Journal of Business Ethics, 155*(2), 597–609.

Van Alstyne, M.W., Parker, G.G., & Choudary, S.P. (2016). Pipelines, platforms, and the new rules of strategy. *Harvard Business Review, 94*(4), 54–62.

Van Koningsbruggen, G.M., Hartmann, T., Eden, A., & Veling, H. (2017). Spontaneous hedonic reactions to social media cues. *Cyberpsychology, Behavior, and Social Networking, 20*(5), 334–40.

Voorveld, H.A., Van Noort, G., Muntinga, D.G., & Bronner, F. (2018). Engagement with social media and social media advertising: The differentiating role of platform type. *Journal of Advertising, 47*(1), 38–54.

Zhu, F., & Iansiti, M. (2019). Why some platforms thrive and others don't. *Harvard Business Review,* January–February.

# 12. Platform governance as a social movement

*Thomas Huber, Thomas Kude, Jan Lepoutre and Julien Malaurent*

## INTRODUCTION

Platforms tend to show winner-take-all dynamics and lead to monopolistic structures, which has led to fierce debates about how to best rein in the power of platform owners (Hurni et al. 2021). In recent years, this has resulted in calls to regulate and break up digital platforms (Dolata 2020, Popiel and Sang 2021). Even though regulation and antitrust efforts are powerful tools in hands of governments and supranational institutions, ever since the rise of the "Bork doctrine" these have been one-sidedly geared toward consumer welfare (Bork 1993, Khan 2016). However, the monopoly power of platforms does not only work upstream, leading to potential harm for consumers; they also possess downstream monopoly power because platformization of industries often implies sharp power imbalances between very few platform owners and a potentially large number of third-party providers (Hurni et al. 2021). Due to these sharp power imbalances, platform owners can govern their ecosystems of third-party developers in a top-down fashion (Foerderer et al. 2018, Huber et al. 2017, Hurni et al. 2021). For example, by setting standards and defining the rules of the ecosystem, platform owners define the constraints within which third parties act (Foerderer et al. 2018, Ghazawneh and Henfridsson 2013). In recent years, such downstream monopoly power of platform owners has gained public attention in the context of online marketplaces such as Apple's App Store and Google's Play Store (Parker et al. 2020). For example, third-party developers who want their apps listed in these app stores have to comply with a wide range of criteria unilaterally defined by Apple and Google, respectively (Huber et al. 2017, Parker et al. 2020).

Given the systematic power and resource asymmetries of platform ecosystems, the large majority of third-party providers is necessarily weak in isolation. As a result, in some platform industries, third-party providers have turned to collective action. For example, the International Association for SAP Partners (IS4P) has the explicit goal to "exert more influence on SAP".[1] The formation of such collective action initiatives is relevant because collectives can create a counterweight to the monopolistic power of platform owners and, thus, address some of the issues associated with extreme power asymmetries. Despite this importance, we know relatively little about the process through which such collective initiatives are formed and exert impact.

This chapter is a first step to address this gap by studying the emerging social movement against Apple's App Store rules from summer 2016 till summer 2021. Insights discussed in this chapter are mostly based on secondary data and have been complemented by one interview with a top-level executive from the association France Digitale.[2] The secondary data includes official documents published by Apple (i.e., press releases, websites, the App Store Review Guidelines, and all changes and extensions to the App Store Review Guidelines since 2014), as well as articles from newspapers, websites, and blogs. We are reflexive about the caveats of our current dataset, which mainly relies on secondary data. In further research, we plan to broaden our empirical investigation to additional secondary and primary evidence. We used our data to construct a rich narrative of the incidents that spurred collective action efforts among third-party developers, to carefully trace when and how these efforts emerged, who was involved or contributed to these efforts, and the goals they pursued. Overall, our findings show how various individuals and organizations that were initially disconnected and isolated became part of an emerging social movement, whose constituents became increasingly interconnected and organized. We show how this movement forced Apple into changing some of its App Store rules and influenced regulatory initiatives in the European Union (EU) and the US.

With this chapter, we contribute to the ongoing debate on platform governance, platform regulation, and digital innovation. By beginning to unpack the collective action processes leading to the emergence of a social movement, we contribute to a new bottom-up understanding of platform governance that provides important insights for entrepreneurs, platform owners, and scholars interested in platform governance and policy implications. The chapter is organized as follows. The next section introduces the literature on platform governance from the perspective of platform owners as well as complementors before presenting our research framework of collective action as a participant-driven, bottom-up governance mechanism. Then, we reconstruct the emerging social movement against Apple's App Store rules covering the time period of 2016–2021. We conclude with a brief discussion of implications for the platform governance literature, regulators, and practitioners.

## PLATFORM GOVERNANCE

The governance concept is used to capture a wide variety of managerial mechanisms and practices used and enacted in a number of different contexts such as large multi-divisional firms ("corporate governance") (Aguilera et al. 2008, Shleifer and Vishny 1997), outsourcing relationships ("outsourcing governance") (Al-Azad et al. 2010, Huber et al. 2013, Lioliou et al. 2014), and particular departments ("IT governance") (Tiwana et al. 2013, Weill and Ross 2004). The particular mechanisms and practices that constitute governance differ considerably from one context to the other. For example, corporate governance is concerned with the structure of boards and the influence of different shareholders (Aguilera et al. 2008), while outsourcing governance is concerned with design characteristics of formal contracts and the level of trust between outsourcing partners (Benaroch et al. 2016).

The focus of this study is on platform governance defined as the mechanisms to ensure desirable behavior of the third-party developers or complementors participating in a platform ecosystem (Tiwana 2015). What makes platform governance unique is that the relationship between platform owner and a particular platform participant is usually characterized by substantial asymmetry (Kude et al. 2008). By building an ecosystem of platform participants, platform owners engage in a one-to-many relationship. That is, platform owners draw value not from the relationship with one particular platform participant, but from the mass of all participants. Therefore, platform owners are less dependent and face less threat of opportunistic behavior from individual complementors (Hurni et al. 2021, Kude et al. 2011). As a consequence, platform owners are in a position in which they can design and enforce governance mechanisms in a top-down fashion and with a focus on the overall ecosystem of complementors (rather than on individual complementors) (Foerderer et al. 2018, Möhlmann et al. 2020). The platform governance mechanisms implemented by platform owners are generally geared toward two interconnected goals (Foerderer et al. 2021). First, governance mechanisms aim at enabling platform participants to independently and autonomously contribute products and services that complement the platform. Second, while platform participants develop and create their services independently and autonomously, governance mechanisms in addition aim at controlling the behaviors and contributions of platform participants to ensure alignment.

In the context of digital platforms that build the foundation for others to innovate, enabling governance mechanisms allow for generativity, in terms of unforeseen innovation by complementors (Boudreau 2010). Platform owners can increase the generativity of their platform and the surrounding ecosystem through providing access to various types of resources (Kude and Huber 2021). On the one hand, platform owners grant access to the platform itself as the technological foundation. As mentioned above, platforms are designed in a modular way and the ease and effectiveness with which complementors can access the platform's functionality and data through application programming interfaces (APIs) are critical enablers of a platform's generativity. Thus, APIs provide one type of boundary resources, which are an important component of platform governance (Ghazawneh and Henfridsson 2013).

On the other hand, platform owners can increase the platform's generativity by granting access to knowledge that enables complementors to build add-ons. Such knowledge is transmitted through knowledge boundary resources, which range from personalized support via contact persons in call centers to scalable self-service systems (Foerderer et al. 2019). Generally, access to resources is often stratified, such that various partner levels exist. For example, enterprise software platforms often have multiple partner levels. As complementors move up this partner hierarchy, they obtain access to more valuable resources enabling new avenues for the cocreation of value (Wareham et al. 2014).

Second, the mechanisms used by platform owners to control platform participants can be broadly classified into two categories—those that aim at controlling behavior and contributions at the individual level as well as those that aim at ensuring the quality of the overall system. Mechanisms that aim at ensuring the behavior of individual platform participants can focus on input control, output control, or behavioral control (Wiener et al. 2020). Input control means that participants and contributions are scrutinized before they are granted access to the platform. Behavioral control means that the activities of users are observed and inspected. Output control means that the result of a service is verified *ex post* (Foerderer et al. 2021, Wiener et al. 2020). For example, Uber relies on background checks of drivers (input control), a rating system where riders rate their experience after the service is completed (output control), and algorithmic control based on collected ride data (behavioral control) (Möhlmann et al. 2020, Wiener et al. 2020). In a similar vein, platform owners operating app stores exert output control by only granting those apps the right to be listed on the App Store that comply with certain technical, content, commercial, and design criteria (Tiwana 2015).

In addition to controlling the behavior of individuals, control mechanisms also aim at ensuring the coherence of the overall system. This system-level control is particularly important for digital platforms that go beyond matchmaking to also build the foundation or digital real estate for others to innovate (Kude and Huber 2021, Parker et al. 2016). In this case, those that use the digital platform will usually rely on the platform itself and a set of complementary solutions. For instance, iPhone users use a bundle of services consisting of the operating system, iOS, along with a number of downloaded apps. In such a context, it is of critical importance that the overall system will function well, and the various apps will seamlessly integrate with the platform to provide a coherent user experience. Various platform governance mechanisms have been discussed to achieve this goal, including APIs that channel and restrain the way platform functionality can be used, or design guidelines that give recommendations and standards for how complementary solutions are expected to be built and designed (Tiwana 2015).

Although platform governance is mostly seen to be driven by the focal platform owner, an emerging stream of research provides first indications that third-party complementors are not necessarily passive bystanders; instead, platform participants have agency when it comes to platform governance. For example, Eaton et al. (2015) examined Apple and its app developers and revealed that in the early days of the App Store, third parties were able to influence the design of platform resources such as cross-compilers, thereby protecting their own interests. Resonating with this insight, Huber et al. (2017) found that complementors in the enterprise software industry may tie their businesses closely to a platform owner to obtain access to resources beyond what is stipulated by the partner program. In a similar vein, the work of Hurni et al. (2021) foregrounds the importance of self-determined and proactive complementors that often take a key role in reorienting platform partnerships when situations change.

## COLLECTIVE ACTION AS A PARTICIPANT-DRIVEN GOVERNANCE MECHANISM

We build on prior work that has recognized the agency of platform participants when it comes to platform governance as well as existing studies that have acknowledged the unilateral dependence of individual platform participants. We focus attention on collective action as one particular strategy by platform participants aimed at countervailing some of the platform owner's strict control over its ecosystem. Our research framework is shown in Figure 12.1.

We argue that collective actions of platform participants can emerge from actions of individual and collective actors as they become increasingly interconnected and coordinated (Lim 2012, Oh et al. 2015). To trace the emergence of collective action, we distinguish two dimensions. On the one hand, the actions of actors may differ in their geographical reach. Actions may be rather local initiatives, consisting of actors from a specific geographical region and focusing on issues specific to that region. Actions may also be global and independent of local idiosyncrasies. On the other hand, these actions may be carried out by different types of actors that operate at different levels. Actions may be carried out by individual persons or companies that may only be loosely connected. However, as individuals and companies begin to interact more closely and in a more coordinated fashion, actions may be carried out by more formal institutions such as coalitions and interest groups (Faik et al. 2016).

Thus, we distinguish six types of actions as shown in Figure 12.1: individual initiatives at the local level or at the global level, organizational initiatives at the local level or at the global level, or more formal institutionalized initiatives with a local focus or with a global focus. By mapping empirically observed actions into the six fields of Figure 12.1 and showing how the actions in different fields are connected, we will study how collective action emerges and evolves over time.

The goal of collective actions of third-party participants in platform ecosystems is to influence the views and behaviors of relevant actors. Similar to the actions of third parties, these relevant actors are situated and operate at different levels. At the institutional level, collective

actions may aim to change the views and behaviors of policymakers or any kind of supranational or national institution. At the individual and organizational level, a primary target of
collective action is the platform owner organization and its future behavior. Other actors at the
individual and organizational level may be other platform participants and consumers.

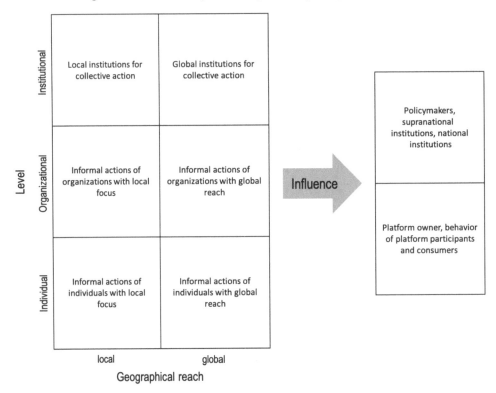

*Figure 12.1    Framework to study collective action of third-party complementors*

## The Emergence of a Movement Against Apple's Governance of the App Store

### App Store review: key issues from a developer perspective

A key mechanism through which Apple governs its ecosystem of third-party developers is
the "App Store review" process. Apple sees this process as a mechanism to "provide a safe
experience for users to get apps and a great opportunity for all developers to be successful."
In this process, every newly released app and every app update is reviewed by Apple's App
Store review team. To successfully pass through the App Store review process, every app
submitted to the App Store has to fulfill a number of criteria set forth in the App Store Review
Guidelines.[3] The guidelines specify a wide range of criteria related to an app's visual design,
user interface, technical architecture, and content (e.g., disallowed content such as pornogra-
phy). This chapter focuses on those guidelines that touch on fundamental questions related to
the business model of a third-party developer; i.e., guidelines that stipulate how an app can be

monetized. Table 12.1 summarizes the key stipulations related to the monetization of apps as set forth in the App Store Review Guidelines.

In recent years, the monetization guidelines have come under scrutiny by developers because they can cause a variety of issues for these developers (see Table 12.1 for details on the specific issues). Especially, four inter-related issues are frequently and widely raised. First, for basically all transactions of digital goods and services that take place within the app, app developers have to pay a commission, which in most cases amounts to 30 percent. Second, for "pure" software companies the only way to avoid the 30 percent commission is to opt in to the "reader app" category, which is exempted from the 30 percent rule. However, apps falling into the "reader" category have to be extremely limited in their feature set. Specifically, to qualify as a "reader app," the app is only allowed to surface content that was purchased previously and outside the app—whereas other rather basic features such as selling of digital content and account creation are not allowed within the app. Third, reader apps are not allowed to "link out"; i.e., they are not allowed to inform the user about the fact that account creation, adding of alternative payment methods, and purchasing of new digital content can only happen outside the app. Fourth, because the App Store stands between the user of an app and the third-party developer and acts as the one-and-only distribution platform for apps, Apple "owns" the customer relationship. This means that while developers get 70 percent of the value of all transactions of digital goods and services that are sold through the app or the App Store, the direct customer relationship is between Apple and the user—not between the third-party developer and the user.

Since the early days of the App Store there has been a dormant dissatisfaction among developers as to how Apple governs the App Store. While in the early 2010s the top issue among developers was the duration of the app approval process, the criticism shifted over time to the above-mentioned monetization rules. App developers complained about these rules and their seemingly arbitrary enforcement from the App Store's inception. However, spurred by high-profile conflicts between Apple and major streaming apps, criticism grew from 2016 onwards, as will be shown in the subsequent sections.

### Formulating discontent in the wake of the Spotify and Netflix incidents

A wave of outrage was unleashed when two high-profile streaming apps decided to become "dumb" reader apps. The first was Spotify, the world's largest music streaming service. To be allowed to stop using Apple's in-app purchase system (IAP) and thus circumventing the "Apple Tax," Spotify had to remove the "sign-up" feature from its app, along with any hint or link as to where users would be able to sign up. Spotify publicly expressed discontent: On June 26, 2016 it sent legal complaints about its treatment in the App Store not only to Apple but a number of lawmakers in the EU as well as the US that were known for their critical stance about big tech.

The media heavily covered these quarrels between Apple and Spotify, often framing them as an important battlefield in the wider streaming wars in which Apple and Spotify, along with companies like Netflix and Amazon, were major combatants. Yet, while many outlets noted that Apple's 30 percent commission was considerable, published opinion noted that taking commissions for customer acquisitions is a common business practice. In fact, Spotify's criticism was regularly framed as hypocritical due to its long history of paying out only tiny fees to the creators (musicians) on its own platform.

*Table 12.1*     *App Store monetization rules for software products and services and key issues for developers*

| Rule | Description of the rule | Implications of the rule for developers | Issues for developers |
|---|---|---|---|
| The 30 percent commission, aka the "Apple Tax" (see App Store Review Guidelines, Section 3.1) | If developers want to sell digital goods through the App Store, they have to use Apple's payment system, called "in-app purchase," and whenever this payment system is used, Apple takes a defined cut of 30 percent from the transaction.* | Developers have to pay a 30 percent commission for all paid digital goods and services purchased through the app, including the initial app purchase, app subscription fees, paid app updates, and a broad range of in-app sales such as paid premium features, paid premium content, in-game currencies, digital gift cards, vouchers, and tips to developers or digital content creators. Developers do not have to pay a commission for:<br>• digital goods and services offered for free.<br>• physical goods and services; i.e., "goods or services that will be consumed outside the app" (e.g., Uber rides, train tickets, and physical goods sold through the Amazon app). | The 30 percent fee is considered to be too high. The scope of the 30 percent commission is considered to be too broad. |
| The "reader app" exemption (see App Store Review Guidelines, Section 3.1) | Reader apps—i.e., apps that "allow a user to access previously purchased content or content subscriptions (specifically: magazines, newspapers, books, audio, music, video, access to professional databases, VoIP [Voice over Internet Protocol], cloud storage, and approved services such as educational classroom management apps)"—are exempted from the mandatory use of "in-app purchase." | If the app qualifies as a "reader app," they can use alternative payment methods and thus do not have to pay a commission. If developers opt to use an alternative payment method, they need to collect the users' payment information outside the app. | The "reader app" exemption is considered to be flimsy, creating considerable uncertainty as to whether an app is eligible (e.g., Dropbox is a "reader app" but messaging apps are not). The enforcement of the exemptions through Apple can appear arbitrary (e.g., Basecamp's project management software is a "reader app" but its email service is not). Apple's own apps and services can always use "in-app purchase" without having to pay a commission. |

| Rule | Description of the rule | Implications of the rule for developers | Issues for developers |
|------|------------------------|------------------------------------------|------------------------|
| No linking out (see App Store Review Guidelines, Section 3.1.1) | Apps selling digital goods and services are strictly forbidden to direct or even notify users that alternative payment options might be available outside the App Store; i.e., apps may not include buttons, external links, or other calls to action that direct customers to purchasing mechanisms other than "in-app purchase." | App developers have no means to make users aware of the possibility that the app's full functionality can only be unlocked outside the app. | Even if developers are exempted from the mandatory use of "in-app purchase" their ability to monetize digital products and services outside the App Store is severely limited. Apps that use alternative payments have to introduce friction into the user experience because in order to sign up to the app and enter alternative payment information, users have to leave the app. |
| Apple owns the customer relationship | When apps use "in-app purchase" the direct customer relationship is between Apple and the end user—not between the third-party developer and the end user; i.e., Apple performs billing, payment processing, and refunding. | App developers do not know who their customers are: They usually do not know who exactly bought the app and are not allowed to contact their customers other than through the app itself. App developers can only access sales and usage information pertaining to their app in aggregated form through an Apple service called App Store Connect (previously iTunes Connect). | Developers are stripped away from almost all traditional means of managing customer relationships. If developers decide to abandon the iOS platform, they also abandon their complete iOS customer base, creating strong lock-in. |

*Notes:* For certain categories of apps the commission is lower (usually 15 percent). Unless explicitly mentioned in our case story, the focus of this study is on apps to which the 30 percent commission applies/applied.

Starting in 2018, Netflix—at the time the highest grossing app of the App Store—began A/B testing a "reader app" in 30 markets outside the US. In December of that year, Netflix transformed into a reader app globally. The new start screen only showed the following message: "How do I watch Netflix? Members that subscribe to Netflix can watch here in the app." This move was widely discussed in the Apple blogosphere[4] and commented on by famous third-party developers such as Marco Arment, Jay Freeman, and Dave Verwer. In particular, bloggers and podcasters that are close to Apple's developer community, such as John Gruber's *Daring Fireball*, Jason Snell's *Six Colors*, Jim Dalrymple's *Loop Insight*, and Rene Ritchie's *Vector* and *Debug* podcasts, started to criticize Apple for how it treated third-party developers. At that time, the blogosphere and individual developers showed particular dismay over the "no linking out" rule, which was seen as much more problematic for the large number of small developers than for the small number of "heavyweights" such as Spotify and Netflix—simply because most users are well aware of Netflix's and Spotify's websites and can guess that this is where they can sign up. The blogosphere's arguments and criticism were partly taken up by the wider tech press (e.g., *The Verge*, *TechCrunch*, and *Wired*) and the business press (e.g., the *Wall Street Journal* and *Financial Times*) as well as the popular press (e.g., the *New York Times* and *Washington Post*) also heavily covered the "streaming wars." However, the press outlets were more narrowly covering the fact that Apple had recently become a competitor to both Spotify (via Apple Music) and Netflix (via Apple TV+), whereas the main concern of the blogosphere and famous iOS developers was the broader issue of Apple's relationship with developers.

**Apple's rules come under wider scrutiny in the wake of the Basecamp and Epic controversies**

The public debate about Apple's treatment of particular apps and its ecosystem of developers reached new heights when the small development company Basecamp was about to launch its new email service Hey. Basecamp is well regarded in Apple's developer community due to its eponymous project management software and its web application framework Ruby on Rails—both of which are widely used in the iOS development community. For a long time, Basecamp had marketed software under the exemption for "reader apps" so that it did not have to pay a 30 percent commission to Apple. At first, its new email service Hey was also accepted under this exemption, but when Basecamp submitted an update of this app to the App Store review process, Apple pulled this decision back—even though the update was apparently unrelated to any rules of the reader category. This put the spotlight on what was widely perceived as arbitrary decisions surrounding the reader category. For example, *The Verge* wrote:

> Now we're in full pretzel mode. Dropbox is a 'reader app' somehow and therefore exempt? 3.1.3(a) [of the App Store Review Guidelines] refers to 'reader' mode, but it also has an eminently interpretable clause that includes 'approved services.' I cracked a joke about the No True Scotsman logical fallacy, but more I think about it, the more it applies.

The public controversy about the App Store now began to shift its focus away from the "streaming wars" between Apple and a small number of heavyweight apps toward a more fundamental issue important for all developers; i.e., Apple's perceived arbitrariness in designing and applying its rules.

Only a few weeks later, another high-profile app-developer tapped into and further fueled this controversy: Epic—the company behind the wildly popular game *Fortnite*—sneaked a hidden and dormant functionality into the update. Once woken up, the hidden functionality was a clear violation of the App Store Review Guidelines: It equipped *Fortnite* with its own alternative in-app payment system. In consequence, Apple pulled the app from its store.

**App developers start coalescing against Apple**

Epic accompanied its public fallout over the App Store monetization rules with a public relations campaign that included anti-Apple "commercials" that were reminiscent of Apple's famous "1984" spot—but with reversed roles. Now it was Apple that was framed as the powerful oppressor and Epic took the role of the rebellious liberator. In addition, Epic led the foundation of the Coalition of App Fairness (CAF) in September 2020. Among the 13 founding members of the CAF were Basecamp and Spotify but also other major app developers such as the streaming service Deezer and Match group (the maker of Tinder). The CAF advocates against the "arbitrary, draconian policies that are applied in a capricious manner, unfair transaction fees (also known as an 'app tax'), and monopolistic control" by Apple. It also explicitly criticizes Apple for forcing "developers to sell through the App Store and use its in-app purchasing system."[5]

The CAF was successful in putting the spotlight on how Apple treated its third-party developers: Its founding, and its criticism of Apple and the demands that it formulated, received world-wide media attention. Yet, in its early days the CAF was first and foremost driven by rather large and mainly US-based companies. A high-ranking executive from France Digitale—the leading European start-up association representing over 2,000 digital entrepreneurs and investors—described the CAF as being "biased" and "very, very transatlantic." Yet, he saw the CAF and the "backlash against Apple" that it created as an opportunity to tip regulation in favor of small start-ups from Europe.

> It's very important to us because otherwise the regulator is going to regulate us the same way [it] is regulating the big tech and that we don't want. (Interview, France Digitale top executive)

Accordingly, France Digitale joined the CAF in February 2021, which was widely covered by both French (e.g., *Dimanche*, *Le Figaro*, *Le Monde*) and international press. France Digitale's top executive felt that France Digitale would provide something to the CAF that it was lacking by then; i.e., direct access to French and European regulators:

> I don't think it's obnoxious or arrogant to say that we have a direct line with the Commissioner Breton,[6] and with ministry 'Bercy'[7] in France ... [We are] the most influential tech industry group in Brussels.[8]

France Digitale joined the CAF with the goal of lobbying for the key goals of its start-up members, which it had elicited from the bottom up:

> We had several start-ups bringing up issues and we basically made a synthesis out of all these complaints ... We tend to be a pragmatic people in the start-up community. We were not particularly happy about the situation and we just want to find solutions. The very first thing is that we need Apple to open up its payment system. The second point is the 30% [commission]. The others ... [other platform owners] make a distinction between start-ups and larger third-party providers.

Shortly after France Digitale had become an official member of the CAF, it filed its own lawsuit against Apple and joined another lawsuit as a plaintiff. Both lawsuits accused Apple of self-preferencing because Apple's own apps do not have to follow the same rules as those from third-party developers. Irrespective of what the courts would decide, the CEO of France Digitale was optimistic that either outcome would be a win for his organization:

> we will either have a very clear condemnation of Apple's violation of existing competition law, or proof that the current law does not allow digital giants to be touched. (Nicolas Brien, CEO France Digitale, official press statement)

**Apple and regulators respond to the movement**
In this section, we outline how Apple and regulators responded to the general dismay of developers and their attempts to collectively organize against Apple. First, Apple performed multiple revisions of its rules: For app developers with an annual revenue below 1 million USD, Apple cut the commission to 15 percent. Moreover, it clarified the scope of the "reader app" category and introduced three additional app categories that were explicitly exempted from the mandatory use of the IAP system and thus the "Apple Tax." In addition, Apple introduced a right to appeal; i.e., app developers became able to ask Apple to review or reconsider its decisions about whether an app violates guidelines. Years of public dispute between Apple and its developers did not go unnoticed by regulators either: "We follow, for instance, the hearings on the Epic's case very closely" (Margrethe Vestager,[9] *New York Times*, June 10, 2021). Both

in the US and the EU, major legislative initiatives emerged that aim to address problematic business practices of platform owners toward their developers (see, for example, the Digital Markets Act[10] in the EU and various anti-monopoly bill proposals for the US[11]). In addition to the level of the 30 percent fee, and the preferential treatment of the platform owner's own apps, regulators now became increasingly concerned about what appears to be a minor detail in the App Store Review Guidelines; i.e., the "no linking out rule":

> And also, if for instance, you're then Spotify, you cannot tell your subscribers that you can get it without the commission fee if you sign up via the Spotify website … So even though you could avoid the commission fee signing up via the website, you're not being told that this is possible. (Margrethe Vestager, *New York Times*, June 10, 2021)

## DISCUSSION

Our study is among the first to illustrate an important but relatively recent facet of platform governance: collective actions initiated by third-party providers in a bottom-up fashion. Our empirical example is a case in point of such an initiative as it shows how collective actions form across multiple organizational levels in the complex and multifaceted environment of Apple and its App Store. Our case shows that the opposition to the rather rigid rules started at the level of individual developers and development companies, which was then picked up by the global blogosphere. The thoughts of this blogosphere were then echoed in the wider popular press, increasing attention even further. Interestingly, this beginning movement was then joined by larger app developers.

On the one hand, these larger developers piggybacked on this movement to push the debate toward their own interest. Indeed, it appears clear that in this movement, some large developers were self-interested (see Spotify) and hid themselves behind the social movement while pushing for their own interests, without necessarily caring about the prosperity of the ecosystem as a whole. On the other hand, the presence of such powerful actors helped the cause to move forward and gain further popularity and support. In this process, the local and global activities at the individual and organizational level were taken up by institutional actors—both local and global. An example of a local institution is France Digitale, which represents start-ups in France. An example of an institution at the global level is the CAF, which was founded by some of the larger complementors, but later also joined by France Digitale. These institutional initiatives raised awareness in the popular press, but also affected policy makers and convinced Apple to adjust some of the rules. Figure 12.2 summarizes our findings by symbolizing how the social movement against Apple's App Store rules emerged through the interconnected actions of actors operating on different levels and possessed different reach.

Our study has several implications and provides ample opportunities for future research. In particular, our work extends the growing literature on platform governance, which has so far mostly been focused on the perspective of platforms' owners (Baldwin et al. 2000, Boudreau 2010, Gulati et al. 2012, Parker and Van Alstyne 2005). Our study complements the existing literature by demonstrating that platform governance can be influenced by complementors; i.e., platform governance is not necessarily a top-down approach driven by platform owners— it can also emerge from the bottom up. Our case shows that such initiatives emerge over time and span local and global activities and activities at the individual, organizational, and

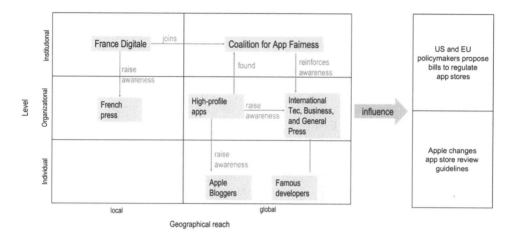

*Figure 12.2    Emergence of collective actions in the Apple case*

institutional level. This makes us suggest that future research could take a process perspective and develop a process theory on such emergent, multi-level dynamics.

Our study also has important implications for practice. For complementors, who want to engender change in the ecosystem, our findings show that simply opposing a platform owner and stating this publicly will likely not be enough. To make a difference, complementors need to actively involve other parties—small and large at both the local and global level—and then act as if they were one entity. This is a challenging task that requires careful orchestration among these independent actors and a sensitivity for opportunities to engage in and perform protests.

Our study also has important implications for platform owners, as it shows that managing complementors goes beyond enabling and controlling, but also includes sensing, supporting, and being responsive to complementor initiatives. Platform owners should be aware of this and actively include continuous monitoring of such dynamics in their day-to-day activities. If platform owners see this as an advantage to sense the wishes and issues of platform participants, then attending to initiatives and institutions formed by platform participants could actually be a competitive advantage and a valuable information challenge. It is also important for platform owners to realize that despite the power imbalance and asymmetric relationship, the maturity of the platform business model will make initiatives of platform participants more common and something that needs to be considered in the governance of platforms.

## NOTES

1. https://www.ia4sp.org/en/successgoals/.
2. https://francedigitale.org/.
3. Apple updates these guidelines on a regular basis. For our analysis we refer to those App Store review guidelines relevant at the time of our cases. For this specific section, we thus refer to the App Store review guidelines published in June 2016.
4. This blogosphere consists of countless blogs focused on a wide variety of issues such as rumors about new products and services (e.g., macrumors.com), product reviews (e.g., Macworld), and practical tips (e.g., igeeksblog.com).

5.    https://appfairness.org/wp-content/uploads/2020/12/about-coalition-01052021.pdf.
6.    Thierry Breton is the EU Commissioner for the Internal Market; i.e., the head of the regulation body responsible for establishing a level playing field across the EU single market on which small and medium-sized businesses and start-ups grow.
7.    The Ministry of Economy and Finance is informally referred to as "Bercy." It is the key government entity for the regulation of the economy, including the regulation of competition and small businesses.
8.    Brussels is the de facto capital of the EU.
9.    Margrethe Vestager is the Executive Vice President of the European Commission and the Commissioner for Competition, who leads the EU's strategy on small and medium-sized businesses and start-ups, as well as "Europe Fit for the Digital Age" strategy.
10.    https://ec.europa.eu/competition/sectors/ICT/digital_markets_act.html.
11.    https://cicilline.house.gov/press-release/house-lawmakers-release-anti-monopoly-agenda-stronger -online-economy-opportunity.

## REFERENCES

Aguilera, R.V., Filatotchev, I., Gospel, H., and Jackson, G. 2008. "An Organizational Approach to Comparative Corporate Governance: Costs, Contingencies, and Complementarities," *Organization Science* (19:3), pp. 475–92.
Al-Azad, S., Mohiuddin, M., and Rashid, M. 2010. "Knowledge Transfer in Offshore Outsourcing and International Joint Ventures (IJVs): A Critical Literature Review from Cross-Cultural Context," *Global Journal of Strategies and Governance* (1:1), pp. 41–67.
Baldwin, C.Y., Clark, K.B., and Clark, K.B. 2000. *Design Rules: The Power of Modularity*. MIT Press.
Benaroch, M., Lichtenstein, Y., and Fink, L. 2016. "Contract Design Choices and the Balance of Ex-Ante and Ex-Post Transaction Costs in Software Development Outsourcing," *MIS Quarterly* (40:1), pp. 57–82.
Bork, R. 1993. *The Antitrust Paradox: A Policy at War with Itself*. Free Press.
Boudreau, K. 2010. "Open Platform Strategies and Innovation: Granting Access Vs. Devolving Control," *Management Science* (56:10), pp. 1849–72.
Dolata, U. 2020. "Internet–Platforms–Regulation." Working Paper. https://www.sowi.uni-stuttgart.de/ dokumente/forschung/soi/soi_2020_2_Dolata.Internet.Platforms.Regulation.pdf.
Eaton, B., Elaluf-Calderwood, S., Sørensen, C., and Yoo, Y. 2015. "Distributed Tuning of Boundary Resources," *MIS Quarterly* (39:1), pp. 217–44.
Faik, I., Bhattacharya, P., and Phan, T. 2016. "From Collective Sensemaking to Collective Mindfulness: The Evolution of Online Social Movements," *Academy of Management Proceedings*, p. 18089.
Foerderer, J., Heinzl. A, and Kude, T. 2021. "Plattformökosysteme." Working Paper. University of Mannheim.
Foerderer, J., Kude, T., Mithas, S., and Heinzl, A. 2018. "Does Platform Owner's Entry Crowd Out Innovation? Evidence from Google Photos," *Information Systems Research* (29:2), pp. 444–60.
Foerderer, J., Kude, T., Schuetz, S.W., and Heinzl, A. 2019. "Knowledge Boundaries in Enterprise Software Platform Development: Antecedents and Consequences for Platform Governance," *Information Systems Journal* (29:1), pp. 119–44.
Ghazawneh, A., and Henfridsson, O. 2013. "Balancing Platform Control and External Contribution in Third-Party Development: The Boundary Resources Model," *Information Systems Journal* (23:2), pp. 173–92.
Gulati, R., Wohlgezogen, F., and Zhelyazkov, P. 2012. "The Two Facets of Collaboration: Cooperation and Coordination in Strategic Alliances," *Academy of Management Annals* (6:1), pp. 531–83.
Huber, T.L., Fischer, T.A., Dibbern, J., and Hirschheim, R. 2013. "A Process Model of Complementarity and Substitution of Contractual and Relational Governance in IS Outsourcing," *Journal of Management Information Systems* (30:3), pp. 81–114.

Huber, T.L., Kude, T., and Dibbern, J. 2017. "Governance Practices in Platform Ecosystems: Navigating Tensions between Cocreated Value and Governance Costs," *Information Systems Research* (28:3), pp. 563–84.

Hurni, T., Huber, T.L., and Dibbern, J. 2021. "Power Dynamics in Software Platform Ecosystems," *Information Systems Journal* (32: 2), pp. 310–43.

Khan, L.M. 2016. "Amazon's Antitrust Paradox," *Yale Law Journal* (126), p. 710.

Kude, T., Dibbern, J., and Heinzl, A. 2008. "Complementarity, Relation-Specific Investment, and Opportunism: Explaining Asymmetric Governance Modes in Hub-and-Spoke Networks within the Enterprise Application Software Industry," *Proceedings of JAIS Theory Development Workshop.* Information Systems Department in Weatherhead School of Management at Case, pp. 8–25.

Kude, T., Dibbern, J., and Heinzl, A. 2011. "Why Do Complementors Participate? An Analysis of Partnership Networks in the Enterprise Software Industry," *IEEE Transactions on Engineering Management* (59:2), pp. 250–65.

Kude, T., and Huber, T. 2021. "Responding to Platform Owner Moves: A 14-Year Qualitative Study of Four Enterprise Software Complementors." Working Paper. ESSEC Business School.

Lim, M. 2012. "Clicks, Cabs, and Coffee Houses: Social Media and Oppositional Movements in Egypt, 2004–2011," *Journal of Communication* (62:2), pp. 231–48.

Lioliou, E., Zimmermann, A., Willcocks, L., and Gao, L. 2014. "Formal and Relational Governance in IT Outsourcing: Substitution, Complementarity and the Role of the Psychological Contract," *Information Systems Journal* (24:6), pp. 503–35.

Möhlmann, M., Zalmanson, L., Henfridsson, O., and Gregory, R.W. 2020. "Algorithmic Management of Work on Online Labor Platforms: When Matching Meets Control," *MIS Quarterly* (45:4), pp. 1999–2022.

Oh, O., Eom, C., and Rao, H.R. 2015. "Research Note: Role of Social Media in Social Change: An Analysis of Collective Sense Making During the 2011 Egypt Revolution," *Information Systems Research* (26:1), pp. 210–23.

Parker, G., Petropoulos, G., and Van Alstyne, M. 2020. "Digital Platforms and Antitrust." Working Paper 06/2020. Bruegel.

Parker, G.G., and Van Alstyne, M.W. 2005. "Two-Sided Network Effects: A Theory of Information Product Design," *Management Science* (51:10), pp. 1494–1504.

Parker, G.G., Van Alstyne, M.W., and Choudary, S.P. 2016. *Platform Revolution: How Networked Markets Are Transforming the Economy and How to Make Them Work for You.* W.W. Norton & Company.

Popiel, P., and Sang, Y. 2021. "Platforms' Governance: Analyzing Digital Platforms' Policy Preferences," *Global Perspectives* (2:1).

Shleifer, A., and Vishny, R.W. 1997. "A Survey of Corporate Governance," *Journal of Finance* (52:2), pp. 737–83.

Tiwana, A. 2015. "Evolutionary Competition in Platform Ecosystems," *Information Systems Research* (26:2), pp. 266–81.

Tiwana, A., Konsynski, B., and Venkatraman, N. 2013. "Special Issue: Information Technology and Organizational Governance: The IT Governance Cube," *Journal of Management Information Systems* (30:3), pp. 7–12.

Wareham, J., Fox, P.B., and Cano Giner, J.L. 2014. "Technology Ecosystem Governance," *Organization Science* (25:4), pp. 1195–1215.

Weill, P., and Ross, J.W. 2004. *IT Governance: How Top Performers Manage IT Decision Rights for Superior Results.* Harvard Business Press.

Wiener, M., Cram, W.A., and Benlian, A. 2020. "Technology-Mediated Control Legitimacy in the Gig Economy: Conceptualization and Nomological Network," in Hirschheim, R., Heinzl, A., and Dibbern, J. (Eds), *Information Systems Outsourcing.* Springer, pp. 387–410.

# PART III

# DIGITAL STRATEGY AS DATA USE

# 13. Strategizing with data: data-based innovations and complementarities

*Cristina Alaimo and Aleksi Aaltonen*

## INTRODUCTION

Strategy making and implementation have always depended on data. The collection and analysis of data about internal and external matters have furnished the means by which organizations make sense of their past, map their current environment, and make projections to the future. Yet, the nature and volume of available data, together with their modalities of production, circulation, and use, have changed dramatically over the last two decades, calling for a reassessment of how data figure in strategy. Massive amounts of digital data are produced by social media, transaction processing systems, sensor and transportation networks, everyday gadgets, and backend infrastructures of various sorts under mixed and often unknown conditions that differ from those under which data were traditionally produced for strategizing (Alaimo and Kallinikos 2022). Much of the data are then further repurposed, aggregated, packaged, and exchanged between parties, rendering their status as 'facts' increasingly ambiguous (Alaimo et al. 2020a; Jones 2019; Martin 2015). Adding to these concerns, the time horizon of digital data has shortened dramatically, which sits rather uneasily with the promise of strategy as the source of long-term organizational success, not to mention that the heterogeneous and dispersed production and use of data gives rise to a volatile business environment that can be difficult to pin down by tools and metrics traditionally used for strategizing (Constantiou and Kallinikos 2015; Kallinikos and Constantiou 2015).

Importantly, the challenges that digital data pose to strategy making and implementation cannot be adequately addressed from the dominant perspective that sees data narrowly as resources to be harvested and fed into analytics or, more generally, business processes. It is common to believe that big digital data offer advantages to firms mostly because of their scale and scope, whereas dictums such as 'more data better decisions' (see, for example, Chen et al. 2012) and other similar ideas often rest on the false premise that data are no more than carriers of facts and that their procurement and use have a direct impact on value creation (Bradley et al. 2021; Gregory et al. 2021). Yet, digital data do not exist as natural resources awaiting to be exploited and their ownership is hardly a source of strategic advantage as such. Businesses that can turn digital data into a strategic advantage do so because they build extensive technological and organizational capabilities to engage in data production internally or, as increasingly happens, as a part of larger ecosystems that take charge of the entire data value chain, including operations such as data production, maintenance, circulation, analytics, and reuse (Alaimo et al. 2020a). Many of the challenges in strategizing with digital data arise from the fact that digital artifacts are constantly in the making (Kallinikos et al. 2013). Rather than being disembodied and fixed facts about a domain of reality such as customers or markets, as data science typically assumes, data are better seen as carriers of potential meaning and value that can be realized only if certain technological and organizational conditions are met (Aaltonen and Tempini 2014).

While data have undoubtedly been part of business and expressed some of these characteristics before, the rapidly evolving digitalization of economy cuts across industries, physical locations, and regulatory domains, putting data at the heart of business and strategy. Advertising, retail, and finance are just a few examples of industries in which strategic efforts are now implemented with data and through data, and are increasingly governed by platforms that spend considerable effort on harvesting and analyzing data (Aaltonen et al. 2021; Alaimo 2022; Alaimo and Kallinikos 2017, 2021; Monteiro and Parmiggiani 2019). Under these circumstances, digital data are no longer just a resource that organizations use for strategizing but the very medium through which work is done and value is produced. As most business processes and resources are transformed into data, or "datafied," they become visible, actionable, and manageable only through various sorts of data artifacts. In summary, when data take the center stage and become both the main objects of business and the medium through which things are done, the ways in which existing conceptions of strategy making and implementation have incorporated data may become inadequate for successful strategizing.

In this chapter, we discuss the challenges that digital data pose for strategizing. We argue that a successful appreciation of the digital transformation of strategy requires us to look at data as more than a resource feeding analytics or, more generally, business processes. To contextualize our discussion, we first briefly recount the co-evolution of strategy making and implementation together with the kind of data that has served these activities. Data have always been both an economic resource and an important medium of sensemaking and organizing (Alaimo et al. 2020a; Alaimo and Kallinikos 2021, 2022; Jones 2019; Monteiro and Parmiggiani 2019), yet the current literature largely focuses on the former (data-as-resource) at the cost of the latter (data-as-medium). We show how traditional tools, methods, and ways to incorporate data into strategizing are bound with data that are collected and processed under conditions that may not hold anymore. Differently from earlier forms of data that used to feed strategy making and implementation, much of digital data originate from fast, automated cycles of data production that often lie outside the control of traditional expertise and strategy tools that may therefore need to be adapted or altogether abandoned. Second, we unpack the properties of digital data as cognitive artifacts and outline the characteristics of their production, which are shaped by the attributes of digital technology and the fact that data are increasingly produced and collected outside established classifications and methodological procedures. This raises several questions regarding how to incorporate and make data serve strategizing. We illustrate the change of paradigm by drawing upon two case studies.

The cases shed light on how much formal strategy processes are affected by the changing nature of data. The first case shows how data-based innovation is premised on new datawork practices that organizations need to put in place to disambiguate and validate the facts that digital data represent. Without this datawork, strategy making remains an empty conceptual exercise that will hardly result in competitive advantage (Aaltonen et al. 2021). The second case shows the role of data complementarities in platform ecosystem emergence. Instead of hoarding and using its own data, the platform leader orchestrates data flows between ecosystem participants and thus establishes the conditions to produce innovative data-based services and a novel market to distribute them (Alaimo et al. 2020b). Three key takeaways emerge from our case illustrations. The first concerns the importance of datawork and data complementarities. By implementing appropriate datawork practices, firms can respond to the unbundled and heterogenous characteristics as well as the shortened lifespan of data. Data do not have intrinsic strategic value, but their potential strategic value needs to be actively created through datawork practices, fostering data complementarities, or by other means. The second point is linked to the fact that data and data-based innovation – that is, the possibility of innovating with new forms of data (as a resource) and through data (as a medium) – redefine traditional tools and processes of strategy making. For many digital-era companies such as those operating in platform ecosystems, strategic decisions evade traditional market definitions and value chain thinking (Jacobides et al. 2018; Porter 2001). Ideas such as the existence of stable markets, the assumption that resources are clearly defined entities that can be situated either outside or inside the boundaries of organizations, seem not to hold the explanatory power they once had. In the illustrative cases we present, data take a constitutive role in creating and managing new kinds of complementarities, resources, and markets that do not exist prior to their making and whose functioning cannot be explained by recourse to traditional frameworks. The third takeaway concerns regulation. Data and digital market regulation will have a massive impact on the possibilities of innovating and strategizing with data (Cennamo and Sokol 2021). Still-current approaches to regulation seem to rely on traditional categories and narrow conceptions of data as mere economic resources. Data exhibit characteristics that change constantly and condition value creation and value capture in ways which necessitate an informed and flexible approach that considers both the opportunities and the risks linked to data at different stages along their journey. Ultimately, we believe, strategy making in the digital age must address the issue of how data substantially rewrite existing views of organizations and their environments.

## DATA AND STRATEGY

The evolution of strategy and strategy making coincides, to a substantial degree, with the establishment and diffusion of various records, tools, concepts, and techniques for monitoring organizational operations, analyzing the external environment, and elaborating possible scenarios for action (Hopwood 1987; Yates 1989). If strategy is seen both as the actions taken by organizations and as the processes by which actions are decided, recorded, and assessed, then strategy cannot be studied apart from the data which support those decisions and actions, and their recording and evaluation (Gavetti and Levinthal 2000; Gavetti and Rivkin 2007; March 1999; Mintzberg 1987; Mintzberg et al. 2003; Porter 1996). Beyond what may be a specific approach to strategy and strategy making, the very idea that a set of decisions and actions of organizations may result in recognizable patterns at the organizational or industrial level is linked to the ways these patterns can be made visible and communicated (Pfeffer and Sutton 2006). Strategy is both a conceptual and practical exercise that has always rested on data of some sort (Mintzberg et al. 2020; Porter 1985). Even when strategy is considered as embodied in a firm's activities, rules, and routines, it is data, data production, storage, and communication that can make it visible and comparable across time and contexts (Gavetti and Rivkin 2007; Nelson and Winter 1982; Yates 1989). In this respect, data, and their dynamics and characteristics, have been essential in defining and supporting many foundational concepts upon which different approaches to strategy rest.

Classic approaches to strategy, the design school and positioning school (Mintzberg 1990) understand strategy as an exercise of matching internal organizational resources to external environment, so that the organization can identify opportunities and threats which, in turn, may be developed into elaborate plans to gain competitive advantage. To do so, organizations and strategy researchers have produced data and developed tools and models to read internal and external organizational environments, and to support the search for a strategic fit between them. As internally generated data became key instruments of administration (see Chandler 1977, p. 104), they created the conditions for the development of further administrative tasks (Beniger 1986; Yates 1989) and for the emergence of core ideas of strategy. For instance, the very notion of organizational strengths and weaknesses gained traction thanks to the concurrent development of administrative data and models for the assessment of internal resources. As the mapping and understanding of internal resources and external environment developed (Porter 1980, 1985) by embracing cognitive skills, know-how, and IT assets, so did the understanding of strategy to espouse more sophisticated ways to capture competitive advantage; for instance, in the form of dynamic capabilities. The idea of dynamic capabilities takes the notion of 'best fit' to frame the strategic relation between internal resources and external opportunities and develops several data-driven procedures to discover, hypothesize, and assess how to best achieve and, importantly, maintain competitive advantage in a changing environment (Teece 2007).

The fundamental role of data in constituting ideas of strategy is evident in popular approaches to strategizing, yet it takes an even more critical role in formal methods. In strategic planning (Ackoff 1983; Ansoff 1965), for instance, data are essential to the assessment of the external and internal conditions of the firm and in the production of forecasting about future conditions. A predict-and-prepare approach (Ackoff 1983, p. 59) can be effectively undertaken only if there are enough data of the right kind. On the other hand, such data need to be prepared and produced with the aim of predicting internal states and the business environment, using specific procedures that validate the power of those predictions based on the data. As a result, data production often become so tightly coupled with the aims of assessment, evaluation, and prediction that the exercise of data production and validation may become more important than strategy itself. The result of strategic planning is, to use Mintzberg's words, a numbers game that in the end has little to do with strategy as a source of competitive advantage (Mintzberg 2000; Mintzberg et al. 2020).

## THE STANDARD VIEW OF DATA

Despite the historical relevance of data in constituting the conditions for strategy and, on the other hand, the novelty of digital data and their implications for strategizing, much of the literature views digital data merely as factual inputs or at best as valuable resources that will enrich the existing strategy-making process and boost the usual strategy tools and frameworks to reveal opportunities for competitive advantage (Abbasi et al. 2016; Chen et al. 2012). Such a view is usually coupled with an understanding of data that goes rarely beyond framing data as 'raw' facts that are to be refined through analytical or, more generally, computational processes (see Gitelman 2014 for a rebuttal). We may call this straightforward if usually unspoken conception of data the 'standard view' by which data are taken to be a foundational entity serving as input to analytics (Aaltonen and Penttinen 2021; Jones 2019).

No matter the amount of work and decisions associated with the cleaning, structuring, or fitting of data for use, the data tokens are simply taken to represent external facts in the standard view. The ambiguous links of data with the events they are meant to represent are either dismissed or treated as a matter of representational truthfulness, basically by something that can be solved by adding more data or more accurate data (Hazen et al. 2014; Lee et al. 2002; Wang and Strong 1996). Jones (2019, p. 5) notes how such a perspective is reflected in textbook definitions that describe data as 'raw facts that describe a particular phenomenon' (Haag and Cummings 2013, p. 508), 'a series of facts that have been obtained by observation or research and recorded' (Bocij et al. 2008, p. 794), or 'raw facts that can be processed into accurate and relevant information' (Turban 2006, p. G-3). The standard view is useful for performing statistical and other analytical operations with data, but it is all but blind to the novelty of digital data in terms of the specificities of their cycles of production, circulation, and reuse, and how the digital makeup of data is changing the broader relationship of data with the organizational reality and the environmental conditions they supposedly stand for. Reflecting the underlying standard view, data science and analytics copes with data as predominantly factual entities that can be variously processed, cross-referenced, aggregated, and computed by mostly automated operations to deliver one or another insight. While tacitly assumed to be carriers of meanings and knowledge that is 'discovered' through analytics, in practice the nature of data as the output of production process oriented by business aims, existing knowledge, industry standards, and technological developments is rarely acknowledged.

Economics has extended and updated the concept of digital resources in an attempt to deal with novel dynamics triggered by the digital economy, theorizing data as intangible economic resources. In this view, digital data are seen as 'non-rival' assets (Shapiro and Varian 1999) that are non-depletable upon use and, therefore, infinitely reusable. The consequences of non-rivalry are then often theorized in terms of costs. Data-based goods can be costly to develop but once in place they can be often reproduced or repurposed with little or no additional cost (Brynjolfsson and McAfee 2014; Varian 2010). Concepts adopted from economics have been central to frame the dynamics of the digital age, including the promise of digital platforms and ecosystems (see, for example, Gregory et al. 2021; Parker et al. 2016; Shapiro and Varian 1999). Progressive datafication – that is, the transformation of business processes, actions, and resources into data – means that data constitute an increasingly critical asset for many businesses and are now reputed by many to be the primary (re)sources of competitive advantage (Baesens et al. 2016; Chen et al. 2012). Data and the dynamics of the digital economy are very different from those that marked the economics of the industrial age, yet the general approach remains bounded to the view of data as input resources that can be processed and combined to achieve economic or strategic goals. This resource-driven view of data is also dominant in the literature on digital innovation, digital strategy, and digital platforms and ecosystems, which largely leaves unpacked what kind of resources data are, how they are produced today and how their digital nature changes the relationship between data and strategy making.

## PROCESSUAL APPROACH TO DIGITAL DATA

Data are human-made artifacts, a cognitive and communicative medium used to select, encode, and record events in particular formats that allow exchanges between social agents and support practices that are variously linked to knowledge production, organizing, and, indeed, strategizing (Beniger 1986; Kallinikos 1999, 2007; March 1999; Mintzberg et al. 2020; Yates 1989; Zuboff 1988). Viewing data as a medium of cognition and communication, in addition to data being resources, helps us understand why digital data are transforming many of the processes and practices taking place in organizations, including strategizing. Taking a broader perspective on data has become critical today when massive amounts data are, first, produced by various internet-based systems, infrastructures, and connected devices under varied conditions that are not readily inspectable and, second, constantly repurposed, aggregated, and exchanged across organizational settings (Alaimo et al. 2020a; Clarke 2016; Ekbia et al. 2014; Floridi 2012; Jones 2019). As data travel across contexts, such as when social media data are used for credit scoring (Huang et al. 2017), their reuse impinges upon several issues linked to data quality, reliability, and value that cannot be tackled by organizations in a similar manner to before (Kallinikos and Constantiou 2015).

Working with data across boundaries and along their entire life cycle is riddled by ambiguities, institutional approaches, and organizational aims which do play a fundamental role in shaping how organizations can draw insights, inferences, or predictions from data (Aaltonen and Tempini 2014; Aaltonen et al. 2021; Alaimo and Kallinikos 2021, 2022; Monteiro and Parmiggiani 2019; Passi and Jackson 2018). For instance, even when data are produced autonomously from sensor devices or machines their production is always shaped by specific technological designs and business decisions. Someone must decide which kind of events are worthy to be recorded and how. Yet, various intentions and decisions inscribed into data tend to be obfuscated by the complex and dispersed technological infrastructure supporting data making. This also brings additional work in the subsequent phases of the data life cycle such as cleaning, structuring, and transforming data that often require a great deal of interpretive effort, decision making, and collaboration across teams and businesses. Furthermore, repurposing of data is an increasingly diffused practice in data-intensive environments. Data may be bought and sold in data marketplaces via novel intermediaries such as data management platforms, data market providers, or data brokers, which diffuse the practice of relying on the work of data intermediaries during subsequent phases of data production and use. Business may not have or want to build in-house capabilities to store, manage, or analyze their data, and some of the most crucial phases of data analysis such as aggregation and structuration must be constantly negotiated across industries and fields, and increasingly with regulators and public agencies.

It follows that strategic use of data cannot be a mere technological or statistical endeavor as analytics are never performed on 'raw' data but on different kinds of data artifacts that are assembled and managed through data cleaning, structuring, aggregation, and active maintenance. We have elsewhere advanced a processual view of data which illustrates the complexities of the data life cycle and accounts for its dynamic and embedded nature (see, for example, Aaltonen et al. 2021; Alaimo et al. 2020a). Importantly, data are not valuable or usable all the time in the same way, but their characteristics of editability, portability and re-contextualizability change along the process of data production, circulation, and reuse (see Figure 13.1). Briefly, editability confers to data the possibility of being recurrently reusable without which much of data-based innovation would not be possible. Portability means that the same data types are usable across settings, platforms, organizations, and ecosystems and, thus by implication, re-contextualizable in the sense of it being possible for them to be used outside the domain linked to their origin or conventional use. Taken together these attributes make digital data quite different from traditional data and condition their utility and relevance for strategizing.

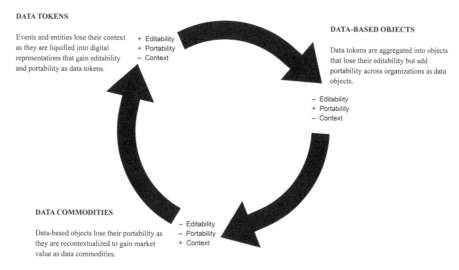

DATA TOKENS

Events and entities lose their context
as they are liquified into digital
representations that gain editability
and portability as data tokens.

+ Editability
+ Portability
− Context

DATA-BASED OBJECTS

Data tokens are aggregated into objects
that lose their editability but add
portability across organizations as data
objects.

− Editability
+ Portability
− Context

DATA COMMODITIES

Data-based objects lose their portability as
they are recontextualized to gain market
value as data commodities.

− Editability
− Portability
+ Context

*Source:*   Adapted from Aaltonen et al. (2021).

*Figure 13.1   A process theory of data commodification*

The current big data industrial complex also contributes to change the processes of data production, circulation, and use in ways that bear consequences for traditional strategy making and implementation (Martin 2015). First, the production, circulation, and reuse of data happening across contexts and organizational settings means that data are assembled from heterogenous sources (i.e., organizational context and industries, technologies, devices, standards, etc.). For instance, in manufacturing industries that are adopting Internet of Things (IoT) solutions, digital data from manufacturing machines, internal accounting and financial data, and real-time machine performance data are combined to elaborate predictions on the quality of production or on the lifespan of mechanical devices (Jovanovic et al. 2021). The criss-crossing of contexts and sources blurs clear-cut distinctions that have dominated strategy and strategy making so far (Constantiou and Kallinikos 2015). When data are combined constantly and from several sources that cut across organizational and even industry boundaries, clear distinctions between firms and environments become unstable and it becomes problematic to establish what a 'best fit' would exactly mean for achieving and maintaining competitive advantage (Teece 2007).

Second, the cycles of data production can be remarkably fast. The constant real-time production of data, characteristic of internet-era and digital devices, makes the time horizon of many types of digital data very short. This sits uneasily with the idea of data as the source of long-term organizational success through the planning and elaboration of 'sustainable advantage' over organizational rivals (Constantiou and Kallinikos 2015). For instance, the real-time flow of data characterizing digital advertising has completely reshaped existing concepts, indicators, and measures that have traditionally been used by marketers and publishers to decide on marketing efforts. Today, concepts such as 'audience' have been radically altered by the possibilities of real-time aggregation of behavioral and other data coming for mobile devices, search engines, and social media (Aaltonen and Tempini 2014; Napoli 2011). These data, and

*Table 13.1      Characteristics of digital data production, circulation, and (re)use*

| | |
|---|---|
| Heterogenous | Data are assembled from different organizational context and industries, using different technologies, devices, and standards. |
| Fast | Data are produced in real time and on a continuous basis. This means that the time horizon of many types of digital data is very short as they will be quickly outdated by novel cycles of data production. |
| Unbundled | Data production is not bounded any longer to specific procedures and institutionalized expertise. Data production is not tied up to its use; any kind of data is in principle usable for any kind of purpose. |

the new kind of data-based audience they construct, in turn, may not last beyond the moment in which individuals browse a specific type of content. As 'audience' becomes a real-time entity the consequences of the shift cascade on the whole advertising industry, and in particular, impact strategic media buying and planning (Alaimo 2022).

Third, the modalities of data production, circulation, and reuse are not bounded any longer to specific procedures and institutionalized expertise. Importantly, the objectives of data analytics do not drive data collection anymore, as the collection of data has become 'unbundled' from their subsequent use (Alaimo and Kallinikos 2022). As mentioned already in our 'Data and strategy' section, data used to be tied to specific expertise, institutionalized approaches, and organizational practices that have significantly contributed to constructing the meaning of the data (Desrosières 1998; Porter 1995). From the perspective of strategizing, this means that digital data are no longer the result of strict planning requirements to find the 'right kind' of data or the well-tested outputs of consistent procedures to map internal organizational operations or resources. Reading the actual conditions of internal resources or external environments via digital data requires moving away from existing expertise toward more hybrid approaches that acknowledge the fundamental role of technology in giving form to data. For instance, the proliferation of data will likely require updating expertise and outsourcing some data work to third-party software companies and, to some extent, cognitive technologies. As artificial intelligence (AI) systems and external partners gradually replace internally operated models and methods, along with organizations increasingly relying on external data, managers need to be cognizant of the changing meaning of strategy in a datafied environment. The more data procurement and analytics can be outsourced to external parties, the less they alone can be a source of competitive advantage.

## STRATEGIZING WITH DIGITAL DATA: TWO ILLUSTRATIVE EXAMPLES

We draw from two case studies to illustrate and elaborate the points we have made about strategizing with digital data. The first case focuses on the relentless datawork organizations need to engage in when dealing with the heterogenous and unbundled nature of data production (Aaltonen et al. 2021; Aaltonen and Tempini 2014). It is only through such datawork practices that data become the objects of a new kind of work which is constituted by cleaning, validating, repairing, and re-analyzing data artifacts to maintain the stability and reliability they otherwise tend to lack (Passi and Jackson 2018). The case narrates how datawork, which is tightly linked with the characteristics of data as digital resources, critically enables novel processes of strategy making and implementation. The second case illustrates the role of data complementarities in fostering innovation in digital platform ecosystems (Alaimo et al. 2020b). We show how an innovative digital platform ecosystem emerges and is formed around data complementarities that arise from combining different data from different sources and lead to the production of novel data-based goods (Alaimo et al. 2020b; see also Ritala and Karhu, this volume). The case shows how the process of harnessing data complementarities is anything but trivial and requires the development of shared practices and governance mechanisms, technological functionalities, and cognitive infrastructures able to support the production, use, and commercial exchange of data and related services.

## Data-Based Innovation

We studied an innovative telecommunications operator that created a novel advertising channel and products by repurposing telecommunications data. The company positioned itself at the intersection of telecommunications and advertising industries by turning mobile sub-scribers into an advertising audience through the reuse of data from the network infrastructure (Aaltonen et al. 2021; Aaltonen and Tempini 2014). Consumers joined the telecommunica-tion service by allowing the company to relay marketing messages to their mobile phones in exchange for a quota of free communications, whereas advertisers paid for having their advertisements delivered to consumers using the service. The core innovation was thus made possible by the company harnessing data that are traditionally used for billing and maintaining the network infrastructure to measure consumer attention, thereby effectively transforming mobile messaging into an advertising medium. In short, the entry into the traditionally heavily data-driven market for advertising audiences was based on repurposing an extant data resource.

The data from the network infrastructure turned out, however, to be rather different artifacts than traditional data on audience such as the data produced by offline audience measurement arrangements or even internet advertising. The extremely detailed data from the network infrastructure would in principle allow the company to identify and interact with each indi-vidual consumer using the service, but the data as such do not constitute a meaningful object of exchange in the market for advertising audiences. What the company did not foresee about the data as a strategic resource is that turning the data into something that would meaningfully communicate the quantity and quality of messaging recipients to advertisers would take a lot of going back and forth between industry partners and the way the data was produced and represented. The main difficulty was to convince the advertisers that digital data represented a 'real' audience. This was largely due to the semiotic attributes and instability of digital data as carriers of facts, produced outside institutionalized audience measurement arrangements and repurposed from infrastructure belonging to a different industry.

Traditionally, the data for audience measurement used to be produced by dedicated ratings agencies that operate long-established arrangements for observing people's media consump-tion, whereas the data from the network infrastructure come effectively unbundled and unvali-dated for any such aim. The data had to be strategically re-contextualized to serve the business model and setting, which entailed a substantial amount of datawork to construct a valid audience or, as we call it, a new type of data commodity for the market. For instance, estab-lishing simple metrics such as response rate or the reach of advertising turned out to be not just a matter of counting the data tokens but essentially a negotiation about what do such concepts mean in the new setting. Indeed, if the audience would have simply existed 'out there' waiting to be brought to the market using the available, extremely detailed data, it should not have required the amount of datawork that we see in the case. Rather than measuring the audience using the data, it would seem more appropriate to say that the company manufactured the audience from the data.

The case illustrates how the transition from carefully designed data collection arrangements tailored for a specific purpose under strictly regulated institutional conditions to a setting in which data are aggressively repurposed for new uses gives rise to strategic opportunities but also makes it insufficient to treat data narrowly as cognitive input to analytics. While the company used some advanced analytics in its operations, the majority of datawork concerned contextualizing and fixing the meaning of data itself. To this end, one might argue that persistent ambiguities in data result from a failure to properly apply processes and methods developed to record or manage data, but in the case we analyzed the difficulties also signaled a creative struggle to produce something new out of the data artifacts. The risk is that strategizing that operates exclusively from the standard view of data becomes blindsided by those who can create and harness new types of data and understand what capabilities organizations need to become and remain competitive.

## Data Complementarities

In the second case, we studied the evolution of a platform that leveraged data to drive innovation and foster the emergence of a digital ecosystem. TripAdvisor, which is one of the most well-known social media platforms in the travel and hospitality industry, moved from being by-and-large a thematic search engine and advertising company to an influential social media platform dedicated to tourism, and finally to a complex service ecosystem which provides content to users; data analytics to hotels and partners; advertising; price comparisons; hotel, restaurant, and tours booking services; personalization services; and so on (Alaimo et al. 2020b). The twenty-year evolution of TripAdvisor shows a continuous effort in innovating with data that led to several emerging strategic opportunities.

In each of the three stages of TripAdvisor's evolution the key resources the platform used to form new business relations were data leveraged through datawork and data-based technologies. What we found, however, is that each of the stages was strategically linked to different types of data. In the first stage, TripAdvisor accumulated domain-specific travel data which were already available from various online sources (e.g., hotel and destination data). In the second stage the company generated new kinds of data from heterogenous user interactions on TripAdvisor's platform (e.g., reviews, ratings, comments, preference data). To this day, the capabilities of social data production developed during the second stage of TripAdvisor's evolution remain pivotal to its market position and its identity (Cennamo 2021). However, the overall ecosystem emerged only when the platform was able to orchestrate the production, circulation, and exchange of several kinds of transaction data among different partners. These, combined with the already existing travel data and social data, led to the emergence of data complementarities which were used to develop real-time personalized data-based services for different ecosystem actors such as end-users, hotels, marketers, content producers, online travel agencies (OTAs), and internet booking engines (IBEs), among others.

The ecosystem actors participated largely interchangeably as data producers and data consumers, and as the platform developed new features and services, their role and position in the ecosystem kept shifting as a result. TripAdvisor's multilateral relationships with its ecosystem actors were primarily forged in data, attesting to the power of digital data as a key resource and medium through which interdependencies are formed and managed. The interdependencies were negotiated and orchestrated dynamically via data and data-based technologies such as application programming interfaces (APIs). Because of this, TripAdvisor has been able to establish value-reinforcing relationships among ecosystem actors that cannot be captured by the classic definitions of partners, clients, or competitors. Managed by data, such interdependent, dynamic, and complex relationships led to novel ecosystem configurations and the creation of novel markets (Adner 2017; Iansiti and Levien 2004; Jacobides et al. 2018).

Differently from other kinds of complementarities, data complementarities can be forged among any kind of resources or activities from any field or industry. Data are in principle, if not in practice, always relatable to other data and their relatability does not follow generic–specific distinctions or modular organization principles (Jacobides et al. 2018). Data tokens disregard the functional, physical, or cognitive makeup of existing resources, activities, or outputs and instead work under the logic that governs the production and use of data. Consequently, data-based complementarities do not follow the rules of other types of complementarities.

The case illustrates how the process of harnessing data complementarities is anything but trivial and requires the development of shared practices and governance mechanisms, technological functionalities, and cognitive infrastructures able to support the production, use, and commercial exchange of data and related services. Ecosystems are novel inter-organizational configurations that emerge to coordinate the production of innovative data-based goods. To coordinate the allocation of those novel data goods and services that the ecosystem produces, traditional market mechanisms are seldom efficient. The case of TripAdvisor shows that rather than 'entering new markets' or 'matching supply- and demand-side actors,' data platforms create their own novel markets which operate by using data and data governance as coordination and control mechanisms for the allocation of data-based resources and goods.

## THE CHANGING PARADIGM OF STRATEGY

Data always entail a particular view of the world that they may help materialize, such as when the data are used to describe the organizational external environment, or to prescribe and validate step-by-step strategic plans. In this respect, data have never been just the recording of organizational facts or of organizations' external conditions but have always been coupled with several conventions, organizational aims, and technological capabilities that shape how and what facts are recorded and give meaning and value to business practices related to data, including strategizing (Alaimo and Kallinikos 2022). Data on the external environment made sense because they rested on the assumption that the environment was a sufficiently stable entity that could be understood via a specific set of data and indicators, and that such indicators would continue to give a reasonable representation of the environment over time (see, for example, Desrosières 1998; Porter 1995).

With digital technologies the properties of data and their role as strategic resources is bound to change dramatically. Data become more heterogenous, more ephemeral, and less dependent on traditional expertise, models, and frameworks. Such conditions make data more ambiguous in their traditional role as factual inputs to analytics serving strategy making and planning. Automated, fast, and dispersed cycles of data production, circulation, and reuse happen outside the control of firms and by pulling together resources, activities, and outputs across firms and industry boundaries. The datafication of work, organizational processes, and the business environment make data artifacts an increasingly prominent part of the reality that they are set to describe. These characteristics of data and data production challenge the standard view of data and the idea that successful strategy can be unlocked by more or better data. Instead, the properties of digital data make them often unfit to sustain long-term, clear-cut models or plans that could be turned into measurable procedures to achieve competitive advantage (Constantiou and Kallinikos 2015). Three key points emerge from our illustrative cases that help further define the challenge that strategizing confronts in an increasingly datafied business environment.

The first strategic takeaway is the importance of datawork and data complementarities. By implementing appropriate datawork practices, firms can respond to the unbundled and heterogenous characteristics as well as to the shortened lifespan of data. Data do not have intrinsic strategic value, but their potential strategic value needs to be actively created through datawork practices or by harnessing data complementarities. The two cases are quite explicit in this regard. The first case shows how a telecommunication operator, a small company operating in a traditional domain, developed an innovative entry to media industry by repurposing data from the network infrastructure. Without various forms of datawork, the company would have not been able to transform network data tokens into data commodities that had value for marketers as audiences (Aaltonen et al. 2021). The case of TripAdvisor is a story of a successful platform that eventually grew into a complex ecosystem. Its success is, however, not given by mere access to data but, as the case shows, by how TripAdvisor has actively fashioned platform functionalities, internal capabilities, and multilateral relationships with other ecosystem actors to produce, exchange, and use data enabling ecosystems actors to create and capture value (Alaimo et al. 2020b). Instead of hoarding and using data from the ecosystem by itself, the platform owner orchestrated data flows between ecosystem participants and thus made it possible for new kinds of complementarities to emerge. In this sense, data complementarities question the idea of data network effects that simply emerge from a platform owner's AI capacity to turn data harvested from the platform into user value (Gregory et al. 2021).

These remarks challenge standard economic approaches to data that unduly simplify the embedded, distributed, and dynamic processes of data production and the multiple and complex ways these connect to strategic value creation and capture. The cases point out how strategizing is tightly linked with the organizational and inter-organizational capacity to work with data, which raises significant challenges for digital strategy making that must be addressed both theoretically and empirically. Organizations that develop relevant capabilities to work with data and to orchestrate inter-organizational data flows to support novel types of complementarities are more likely to build competitive advantage than those that rely narrowly on data as factual inputs to AI-driven strategy making and implementation. To this end, future research needs to reflect upon the boundary conditions of strategy in a datafied organizational environment. As data and digital technology become the cognitive and economic infrastructure of most industries the meaning of strategy shifts and may become different for different firms and industries.

The second point is linked to ideas such as the existence of stable markets, the assumption that resources are clearly defined entities that can be situated either outside or inside the boundaries of organizations, or that competitors and collaborators are distinguishable from one another and remain fixed over time, which are increasingly put into test by the novel dynamics of the digital economy (Aldrich and Pfeffer 1976). Instead, what we are seeing is a much more volatile and uncertain socioeconomic environment where these categories are blurred.

In this environment, data assume a central role in strategizing that is nevertheless different from the earlier times. The cases we presented both exemplify how the issue of market positioning or the entry in new markets have changed. Market positioning has been a traditionally well-developed aspect of strategy and, sometimes, even a regulated endeavor that is preceded by an extensive analysis and knowledge of all the actors involved, followed by a process based on detailed step-by-step procedures and models (Porter 1980, 1985; Mintzberg et al. 2020). In the cases we presented, data do not only support analysis, planning, or strategic decision making, but they also take a constitutive role in creating and managing new kinds of complementarities, resources, and markets. The market for mobile messaging-based advertising in the first case and the market for new personalized real-time data-based hospitality services in the second case do not exist prior to the making of the innovative data-based services and their mechanisms of production and commodification. To understand how novel markets emerge as a result of the data-based dynamics and operations, strategy making and implementation must incorporate an expanded view of digital data that goes beyond the standard conception of data as factual inputs to analytics or, more generally, business processes. Markets that efficiently allocate data-made services and goods exhibit mechanisms that differ both from traditional markets and from industrial or software-based platforms (Alaimo and Kallinikos 2022).

The final, third point concerns regulation. So far data production, circulation, and (re)use have been an unregulated and opaque territory and a fertile ground for questionable market practices and platform power struggles. On the other hand, current approaches to regulation do not seem to consider the innovative potential of digital data and the change of paradigm they require. Approaches to data regulation and digital market regulation are still being made with the aid of traditional categories and the standard view of data as mere economic resources. The processual view of data we have put forward necessitates a different and more flexible approach which considers the opportunities and risks linked to data at different stages along their journey. Data exhibit characteristics that change constantly and condition value creation and value capture. Furthermore, the fast, distributed, and heterogeneous nature of data production calls for rules and regulation which are flexible enough to guarantee innovation, complemented by standards to increase regulatory resilience and sustainability for all the users involved across domains (Cennamo et al. 2022; Cennamo and Sokol 2021; Larouche and de Streel 2021). Although strategy scholars have recently started engaging with the issue of platforms and ecosystems regulation (Cusumano et al. 2021), few have dealt with the novelty of digital data, datawork practices, and emerging dynamics that they introduce. In complex and volatile environments where heterogenous actors interact (e.g., individuals, firms, public institutions, and so on) and whose interactions are increasingly transformed into data and coordinated through the data and digital technologies, the links between social life, economic activities, and regulation will become tighter, more interdependent, and practiced on less obvious grounds.

## CONCLUSIONS

The production of digital data presents characteristics that profoundly differ from how data were traditionally produced and perceived in strategy making and implementation activities. Data-based innovation and complementarities as instances of strategic opportunities that emerge with digital data (as a resource) and through digital data (as a medium) are critical examples of how data can drive strategy beyond providing facts about the internal and external environment. Seizing new opportunities requires, however, a perspective that goes beyond the standard view of data and pays due attention to the characteristics of digital data as human-made artifacts of continuous making. As a result, some of the traditional concepts and processes of strategy making need to be reconsidered and used with stricter boundary conditions in mind. For instance, subsuming data under the broad category of non-rival goods overlooks many relevant and distinct attributes that make digital data artifacts an increasingly important medium of socioeconomic life. The shortcomings of such an approach become evident when it is called to give an account of key economic and market dynamics of the digital age. Most digital companies that operate in platform ecosystems, for instance, can hardly be understood through the lens of classic market definitions; when they enter new markets, they often do so by using data to create a novel space for value-creating relationships and exchanges, which are then orchestrated through even more data.

# REFERENCES

Aaltonen, A., Alaimo, C., & Kallinikos, J. (2021). The making of data commodities: Data analytics as an embedded process. *Journal of Management Information Systems, 38*(2), 401–29.

Aaltonen, A., and Penttinen, E. (2021). What Makes Data Possible? A Sociotechnical View on Structured Data Innovations. In *Proceedings of the 54th Hawaii International Conference on System Sciences (HICSS)*, pp. 5922–31.

Aaltonen, A., & Tempini, N. (2014). Everything counts in large amounts: A critical realist case study on data-based production. *Journal of Information Technology, 29*, 97–110.

Abbasi, A., Sarker, S., and Chiang, R.H.K. (2016). Big data research in information systems: Toward an inclusive research agenda. *Journal of the Association for Information Systems, 17*(2), i–xxxii.

Ackoff, R.L. (1983). Beyond prediction and preparation [I]. *Journal of Management Studies, 20*(1), 59–69.

Adner, R. (2017). Ecosystem as structure: An actionable construct for strategy. *Journal of Management, 43*(1), 39–58.

Alaimo, C. (2022). From people to objects: the digital transformation of fields. *Organization Studies, 43*(7), 1091–114. https://journals.sagepub.com/doi/10.1177/01708406211030654.

Alaimo, C., & Kallinikos, J. (2022). Organizations decentered: Data objects, technology and knowledge. *Organization Science*. Article in advance (forthcoming). https://pubsonline.informs.org/doi/pdf/10.1287/orsc.2021.1552.

Alaimo, C., & Kallinikos, J. (2021). Managing by data: Algorithmic categories and organizing. *Organization Studies, 42*(9), 1385–1407.

Alaimo, C., & Kallinikos, J. (2017). Computing the everyday: Social media as data platforms. *Information Society, 33*(4), 175–91.

Alaimo, C., Kallinikos, J., & Aaltonen, A. (2020a). Data and Value. In Nambisan, S., Lyytinen, K., & Yoo, Y. (eds.) *Handbook of Digital Innovation*, Cheltenham, UK and Northampton, MA, USA: Edward Elgar Publishing, pp. 162–78.

Alaimo, C., Kallinikos, J., & Valderrama, E. (2020b). Platforms as service ecosystems: Lessons from social media. *Journal of Information Technology, 35*(1), 25–48.

Aldrich, H.E., & Pfeffer, J. (1976). Environments of organizations. *Annual Review of Sociology, 2*(1), 79–105.

Ansoff, H.I. (1965). *Corporate Strategy: An Analytic Approach to Business Policy for Growth and Expansion*. New York, NY: McGraw-Hill.

Baesens, B., Bapna, R., Marsden, J.R., Vanthienen, J., & Zhao, J.L. (2016). Transformational issues of big data and analytics in networked business. *MIS Quarterly, 40*(4), 807–18.

Beniger, J. (1986). *The Control Revolution: Technological and Economic Origins of the Information Society*. Cambridge, MA: Harvard University Press.

Bocij, P., Greasley, A., & Hickie, S. (2008). *Business Information Systems: Technology, Development and Management for the e-Business*, fourth ed. Harlow: Pearson Education Limited.

Bradley, V.C., Kuriwaki, S., Isakov, M., Sejdinovic, D., Meng, X.-L., & Flaxman, S. (2021). Unrepresentative big surveys significantly overestimated US vaccine uptake. *Nature, 600*, 695–700.

Brynjolfsson, E., & McAfee, A. (2014). *The Second Machine Age: Work, Progress, and Prosperity in a Time of Brilliant Technologies*. New York, NY: W.W. Norton & Company.

Cennamo, C. (2021). Competing in digital markets: A platform-based perspective. *Academy of Management Perspectives, 35*(2), 265–91.

Cennamo, C., Kretschmer, T., Constantinides, P., Alaimo, C., & Santaló, J. (2022). Digital platforms regulation: An innovation-centric view of the EU's Digital Markets Act. *Journal of European Competition Law & Practice*. https://doi.org/10.1093/jeclap/lpac043.

Cennamo, C., & Sokol, D.D. (2021). Can the EU regulate platforms without stifling innovation? *Harvard Business Review*. https://hbr.org/2021/03/can-the-eu-regulate-platforms-without-stifling-innovation.

Chandler, A.D. (1977). *The Visible Hand: The Managerial Revolution in American Business*. Cambridge, MA: Harvard University Press.

Chen, H., Chiang, R.H.L., & and Storey, V.C. (2012). Business intelligence and analytics: From big data to big impact. *MIS Quarterly, 36*(4), 1165–88.

Clarke, R. (2016). Big data, big risks. *Information Systems Journal, 26*(1), 77–90.

Constantiou, I.D., & Kallinikos, J. (2015). New games, new rules: Big data and the changing context of strategy. *Journal of Information Technology, 30*(1), 44–57.

Cusumano, M., Gawer, A., & Yoffie, D. (2021). Can self-regulation save digital platforms? *Industrial and Corporate Change*. Forthcoming.

Desrosières, A. (1998). *The Politics of Large Numbers: A History of Statistical Reasoning*. Cambridge, MA: Harvard University Press.

Ekbia, H., Mattioli, M., Kouper, I., Arave, G., Ghazinejad, A., Bowman, T., Suri, V.R., Tsou, A., Weingart, S., and Sugimoto, C.R. (2014). Big data, bigger dilemmas: A critical review. *Journal of the American Society for Information Science and Technology, 66*(8), 1523–45.

Floridi, L. (2012). Big data and their epistemological challenge. *Philosophy and Technology, 48*(2), 103–21.

Gavetti, G., and Levinthal, D. (2000). Looking forward and looking backward: Cognitive and experiential search. *Administrative Science Quarterly, 45*(1), 113–37.

Gavetti, G., & Rivkin, J.W. (2007). On the origin of strategy: Action and cognition over time. *Organization Science, 18*(3), 420–39.

Gitelman, L. (2014). *Raw Data Is an Oxymoron*. Cambridge, MA: MIT Press.

Gregory, R.W., Henfridsson, O., Kaganer, E., & Kyriakou, H. (2021). The role of artificial intelligence and data network effects for creating user value. *Academy of Management Review, 46*(3), 534–51.

Haag, S., & Cummings, M. (2013). *Management Information Systems for the Information Age*, ninth ed. New York, NY: McGraw-Hill Irwin.

Hazen, B.T., Boone, C.A., Ezell, J.D., & Jones-Farmer, L.A. (2014). Data quality for data science, predictive analytics, and big data in supply chain management: An introduction to the problem and suggestions for research and applications. *International Journal of Production Economics, 154*, 72–80.

Hopwood, A.G. (1987). The archeology of accounting systems. *Accounting, Organizations and Society, 12*(3), 207–34.

Huang, J., Henfridsson, O., Liu, M.J., & Newell, S. (2017). Growing on steroids: Rapidly scaling the user base of digital ventures through digital innovation. *MIS Quarterly, 41*(1), 301–14.

Iansiti, M., and Levien, R. (2004). *The Keystone Advantage: What the New Dynamics of Business Ecosystems Mean for Strategy, Innovation, and Sustainability*. Boston, MA: Harvard Business School Press.

Jacobides, M.G., Cennamo, C., & Gawer, A. (2018). Towards a theory of ecosystems. *Strategic Management Journal, 39*, 2255–76.

Jones, M. (2019). What we talk about when we talk about (big) data. *Journal of Strategic Information Systems, 28*(1), 3–16.

Jovanovic, M., Sjödin, D., & Parida, V. (2021). Co-evolution of platform architecture, platform services, and platform governance: Expanding the platform value of industrial digital platforms. *Technovation*, 102218.

Kallinikos, J. (2007). *The Consequences of Information: Institutional Implications of Technological Change*. Cheltenham, UK and Northampton, MA, USA: Edward Elgar Publishing.

Kallinikos, J. (1999). Computer-based technology and the constitution of work: A study on the cognitive foundations of work. *Accounting, Management & Information Technology*, 9(4), 261–91.

Kallinikos, J., Aaltonen, A., & Marton, A. (2013). The ambivalent ontology of digital artifacts. *MIS Quarterly*, 37(2), 357–70.

Kallinikos, J., & Constantiou, I.D. (2015). Big data revisited: A rejoinder. *Journal of Information Technology*, 30(1), 70–74.

Larouche, P., & de Streel, A. (2021). The European Digital Markets Act: A revolution grounded on traditions. *Journal of European Competition Law & Practice*, 12(7), 542–60.

Lee, Y.W., Strong, D.M., Kahn, B.K., & Wang, R.Y. (2002). AIMQ: A methodology for information quality assessment. *Information & Management*, 40(2), 133–46.

March, J.G. (1999). *The Pursuit of Organizational Intelligence: Decisions and Learning*. Cambridge, MA: Blackwell.

Martin, K.E. (2015). Ethical issues in the big data industry. *MIS Quarterly Executive*, 14(2), 67–85.

Mintzberg, H. (2000). *The Rise and Fall of Strategic Planning*. London: Pearson Education.

Mintzberg, H. (1990). The design school: Reconsidering the basic premises of strategic management. *Strategic Management Journal*, 11(3), 171–95.

Mintzberg, H. (1987). *Crafting Strategy*. Boston, MA: Harvard Business School Press.

Mintzberg, H., Ahlstrand, B., & Lampel, J.B. (2020). *Strategy Safari*. London: Pearson.

Mintzberg, H., Ghoshal, S., Lampel, J., & Quinn, J.B. (2003). *The Strategy Process: Concepts, Contexts, Cases*. London: Pearson Education.

Monteiro, E., & Parmiggiani, E. (2019). Synthetic knowing: The politics of the Internet of Things. *MIS Quarterly*, 43(1), 167–84.

Napoli, P.M. (2011). *Audience Evolution: New Technologies and the Transformation of Media Audiences*. New York, NY: Columbia University Press.

Nelson, R.R., and Winter, S.G. (1982). *An Evolutionary Theory of Economic Change*. Cambridge, MA: Belknap.

Parker, G.G., Van Alstyne, M., & Choudary, S.P. (2016). *Platform Revolution*. New York, NY: W.W. Norton & Company.

Passi, S., & Jackson, S.J. (2018). Trust in data science: Collaboration, translation, and accountability in corporate data science projects. *Proceedings of the ACM on Human-Computer Interaction*, 2(CSCW), 1–28.

Pfeffer, J., and Sutton, R.I. (2006). *Hard Facts, Dangerous Halftruths, and Total Nonsense: Profiting from Evidence-Based Management*. Cambridge, MA: Harvard Business School Press.

Porter, M.E. (2001). The Value Chain and Competitive Advantage. In D. Barnes (Ed.), *Understanding Business: Processes*. London: Routledge, pp. 50–66.

Porter, M.E. (1996). What is Strategy? *Harvard Business Review*, 74(6), 61–78.

Porter, M.E. (1985). *Competitive Advantage: Creating and Sustaining Superior Performance*. New York, NY: Free Press.

Porter, M.E. (1980). *Competitive Strategy: Techniques for Analyzing Industries and Competitors*. New York, NY: Free Press.

Porter, T.M. (1995). Trust in Numbers: The Pursuit of Objectivity in Science and Public Life. Princeton, NJ: Princeton University Press.

Shapiro, C., & Varian, H.R. (1999). *Information Rules: A Strategic Guide to the Network Economy*. Boston, MA: Harvard Business School Press.

Teece, D.J. (2007). Explicating dynamic capabilities: The nature and microfoundations of (sustainable) enterprise performance. *Strategic Management Journal*, 28(13), 1319–50.

Turban, E. (2006). *Information Technology for Management: Transforming Organizations in the Digital Economy*, fifth ed. Hoboken, NJ: Wiley.

Varian, H.R. (2010). Computer mediated transactions. *American Economic Review*, 100(2), 1–10.

Wang, R.Y., & Strong, D.M. (1996). Beyond accuracy: What data quality means to data consumers. *Journal of Management Information Systems*, 12(4), 5–34.

Yates, J. (1989). *Control through Communication: The Rise of System in American Management*. Baltimore, MD: Johns Hopkins University Press.

Zuboff, S. (1988). *In the Age of the Smart Machine: The Future of Work and Power*. New York, NY: Basic Books.

# 14. Profiting from data products

*Llewellyn D.W. Thomas,[1] Aija Leiponen and Pantelis Koutroumpis*

## INTRODUCTION

Although a handful of digital platforms have generated massive profits from data via online search, social networks, and e-commerce, most companies that have historically had access to vast amounts of data, such as financial intermediaries, telecommunications operators, and utilities, have struggled to commercialize and capture value from their data. Still, there is strong evidence that "data products"—defined as collections of data that are tradeable (also called "data commodities"; see Aaltonen, Alaimo & Kallinikos, 2021)—can offer significant value (Brynjolfsson, Collis & Eggers, 2019; Nakamura, Samuels & Soloveichik, 2017), to the extent that accountants and statistical agencies have considered new methods to measure their true economic importance (Byrne & Corrado, 2020; Collins & Lanz, 2019).

In this chapter we develop a conceptual framework for analyzing why some firms succeed and others fail to create data products that generate significant profits. We outline strategic challenges in amassing market power with data products and adapting business models to control data markets. To do so, we first explore the economic attributes of data products and compare them against those of information products such as content and algorithm (software) products to highlight their strategic implications.

Second, we describe how the attributes of data products influence the processes of value creation and capture. We show that value creation not only depends on data quality but also on complementary data and identifiability that are not critical for information products such as content and algorithms. On the other hand, value capture from data products hinges on the ability to exclude others from using the data product and the complementary assets, particularly through access to complementary data, information, skills, and technologies (and platform design). While excludability is a central strategic challenge for all digital innovations, complementarities feature more prominently as sources of market power for data products than for information products.

Third, we characterize feasible business models for data products (Teece, 2010; Zott & Amit, 2010). As the economic attributes and drivers of market power of data products are different from those of traditional information products, data product strategies and business models will differ from those for digital content or software. We show that feasible business models seek to ensure that the control over complementary data, information, technology, and/ or skills does not adversely impact data value creation.

*Table 14.1      Data products vs information products*

| | Data products | Information products | |
|---|---|---|---|
| | (Raw) data | Content | Algorithm (software) |
| Type of observation | Codified observation | Codified expression; i.e., observations with structure, relationships, and meaning | Codified instruction for achieving an outcome |
| Role in value creation | Intermediate input into a process of transformation | Consumption or use in production | Method of transformation |
| Experience good | Yes | Yes | Yes |
| Credence good | Yes | No | No |
| Value capture | Nearly unexcludable | Partially excludable | Partially excludable |
| IP (intellectual property) available | Trade secrecy; weak copyright in some jurisdictions | Copyright | Copyright; patents in some jurisdictions |

## DATA PRODUCTS VERSUS INFORMATION PRODUCTS

Data and information are closely related concepts. Data can be analyzed to generate information, and components of information can be categorized into variables and structured into a dataset. On a fundamental level, both data and information are systematic representations of reality or imagination.[2] To provide a sharp distinction between data and information, we focus on the notion of an "observation," an elemental unit of representation (see Table 14.1 for a summary). An observation can be as simple as a single measurement of temperature using a device such as a thermometer. The temperature reading can be recorded as "data" into a storage system such as a notebook or a computer. We define a unit of data as a *codified observation fixed in a tangible medium*. An observation is not data unless it is codified and recorded.[3] When a person only looks at the thermometer and notices the reading, the tacit observation does not become data. A data product, in turn, is a collection of data units that are tradeable.

In this view, information, in contrast, consists of related and interpreted observations (data). For example, the temperature reading could become information by connecting it with other observations such as the date and time of the reading and interpreting it in the context of similar observations in previous years. Thus, a unit of data, say "30 degrees Fahrenheit," becomes information: "It was a cold day; 30 degrees Fahrenheit on the first day of June was unusual even for northern Maine." When data are connected to other data in a specific context, and codified into an expression, it becomes information (cf. Aaltonen & Tempini, 2014). Information is thus *codified expression fixed in a tangible medium*. It may contain data as part of the expression, and if such expression is also original, it may qualify for copyright protection. As such, an information product is a codified and fixed expression that is tradeable.

Some forms of codified expression can provide instructions designed to achieve a specific outcome. For example, a computer program may consist of codified expression in the form of an algorithm. We distinguish such algorithmic forms of information from content. While algorithms can also be content—for example, cooking recipes can consist of original expression and at the same time take the form of an algorithm ("bring the sauce to a boil and then pour it over the vegetables")—they are a unique subset of content that is often used to transform data into information. Algorithms are typically not consumed for their expression value but for their value of generating outcomes. Thus, we define information in the form of algorithms as *codified instructions fixed in a tangible medium*. Algorithms differ from content in that they usually do not contain observations and thus are devoid of meaningful data.

Summarizing, from an economic perspective data can be viewed as an input into the creation of information, often with the help of algorithms. Information can, in turn, be used in a context of production or service delivery to improve productivity, utility, or performance.[4] This implies, however, that data, as codified observations, are not useful alone, because their transformation into information requires understanding of the relations between the observations (Bellinger, Castro & Mills, 2004; Rowley, 2007). Economically, data are thus an *intermediate input* into a process of transformation. Information products, in contrast, are often consumed as such (Linde & Stock, 2011). Information products are generally final products in that they are not designed at the outset to be transformed or combined with other products to create final products.[5]

## DATA PRODUCT VALUE CREATION

As data have become integral to business operations, awareness is growing of their strategic importance. For instance, data analytics can lead to improved business performance through new business insights and faster and better decisions (DalleMule & Davenport, 2017; Davenport, Barth & Bean, 2012; McAfee & Brynjolfsson, 2012; Van Rijmenam, Erekhinskaya, Schweitzer & Williams, 2019). Data can also enable value-adding extensions to existing products or services, or the development of entirely new data-based products and business models (Foss & Saebi, 2017; Parmar, Mackenzie, Cohn & Gann, 2014; Sorescu, 2017; Wixom & Ross, 2017). This has led some to claim that data are becoming the new capital of the twenty-first century, and that personal data are a new asset class (Hammell et al., 2012; Schwab, Marcus, Oyola, Hoffman & Luzi, 2011). In this section we explore what kind of an asset data are.

### Data Value Chain

Data do not create value simply by existing. Data add value in an economic system through three sequential stages: data building, information creation, and production/operations (Crockett, 2002; Goodridge & Haskel, 2015). Data are usually collected or compiled to describe a phenomenon of interest that can be observed (see Figure 14.1). Some activity takes place in the real world (e.g., temperature variation, urban mobility, social interaction, web browsing) and the purpose of collection is to analyze and understand the activity or the subjects. To achieve this, the phenomenon is sampled and the collection of observations is instrumented through surveys, application programming interfaces (APIs), sensors, or other special sensing equipment. The collected observations are stored as raw data. In the data-building stage, value is created out of raw data by transforming them into data products available in a format that is structured and available for analysis. The information creation stage involves generating insights about the relationships among variables in data through analytical processes such as statistics, sentiment analysis, or machine learning applied to data. Finally, in the third stage, the full economic value of data are realized when the information products are applied in a commercial context, either as products and services delivered to customers, or to enhance or inform other products, processes, or services.

## Data Characteristics Enhancing Value Creation

There are several characteristics of data that enhance the value created, as illustrated in Figure 14.1. The value of data depends on their quality and identifiability, and the availability of complements such as complementary data, information products, analytical technologies, and skills. While the value of information also depends on its quality, identifiability and complementary goods play a much less central role.

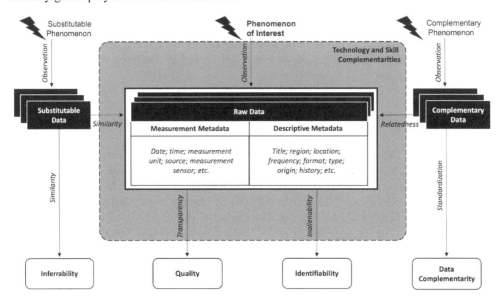

*Figure 14.1    Attributes of data products influencing value creation*

## Quality

Data products, like information products, tend to have incomplete transparency regarding their quality, as they are "experience goods" where the quality can only be ascertained upon consumption (see Figure 14.1). For example, it is difficult to determine whether a person will enjoy a movie until they have watched it. Data products may even be "credence goods," meaning their quality can only be verified after a longer period of use or indirectly through comparison against characteristics of similar data. Upon browsing through a data product, it may be impossible to assess whether the observations are correct or useful for a specific purpose. Such opacity of quality creates challenges in the commercialization of information goods, and these challenges are accentuated for data goods.

Many experience and credence good markets have introduced mechanisms to help users assess quality. For example, consumers may rely on contracts or partial disclosure through mechanisms such as warranties, samples, recommendation engines, and the reputation and branding of the goods to form expectations about their quality. Experience goods can thus be successfully commercialized if meta-information (metadata) is available and helps characterize the goods. The social, contractual, and economic mechanisms of previews, reviews, warranties, and reputations also address the credence good aspect of data products. Thus, "enough" information about the data product can be made available to provide sufficient transparency.

As a method of providing "enough" information, "metadata" are critical in the commercialization of data (see Figure 14.1). For example, it helps to know how and by whom the data in the product were collected to evaluate its quality. In the case of data products, quality is less about the match with the consumer's personal preferences and more about the match with the user's needs in terms of the structure, format, coverage, and accuracy of the data product. Coverage and accuracy can be partially revealed through a description of the data collection method. Therefore, for data products, metadata that annotate the characteristics of the constituent data enable an assessment of the methods applied to collect and compile the data product. Without information about how the raw data were collected ("measurement" metadata), such as the measurement units, measuring equipment, and the source, and information about the attributes of the raw data ("descriptive" metadata), such as the descriptive name, format, and history, potential users will not be able to interpret the inference arising from the observations.

An important descriptive metadata for value creation are "provenance" metadata. To assess the quality and thus value of a data product, it may be essential to know how the data supplier obtained the data product—to understand its history. Provenance informs a potential data consumer about the activities, transactions, and conditions under which the data product was created, organized, and acquired. Without a complete historical record that provides transparent provenance, the credibility of the metadata, or even legality of the data product itself, might suffer in the eyes of the potential consumer. In comparison, the requirement for provenance is less pressing for information products—the assessment of the quality and value of content such as a movie or a song is much less dependent on knowing the history of the information product itself.

Thus, in distinction to information products, metadata are much more strongly complementary with data products (as depicted in Figure 14.1), as the quality of the data product can be relatively transparent if high-quality metadata are available. Consequently, both the measurement and descriptive metadata are vital to understanding the value of data products. Without descriptive metadata which describe provenance, it will be difficult to use the data product in any meaningful way. Measurement metadata, in turn, allow the assessment of whether data collection has been biased or flawed in some way and can help evaluate whether the generated insights inform the purpose of the data analysis. The lack of either type of metadata creates an obscure representation of the phenomenon of interest (cf. Figure 14.1). Meanwhile, an information product such as content or an algorithm may still be consumed without any sample, warranty, or other form of metadata.

### Identifiability

The value of a data product also critically depends on the connection between the raw data and the phenomenon being observed, an attribute that is not salient for information products. As detailed in Figure 14.1, data products are collected to describe phenomena that can be observed. In the context of weather, the data may be collected by a temperature gauge, a specific sensor in a specific location. Thus, the weather observation is pointing to that specific location, even though the observation itself—the temperature reading—does not contain location data. In many cases the phenomenon being observed is a person or an organization, and the observations are connected to that person or organization. In other words, data are always "inalienably" connected to the object of measurement through relationships that are separate from the data themselves (see Figure 14.1).

"Inalienability" is an established legal concept used to describe legal entitlements that cannot be traded away (Calabresi & Melamed, 1972). Certain protections such as basic human rights to bodily integrity are inalienable in the sense that they cannot be contractually taken away in most modern countries—such contracts would not have legal validity. We adopt and extend the notion of inalienability in a technical sense to describe the idea that an observation is always connected to something outside of itself that is being observed. Data inalienability is closely related to the notion of privacy—while privacy is a property that relates to the data subject, inalienability is an attribute of the data product itself. Inalienability is also related to identifiability. When an observation is inalienable from the data subject, the data subject is highly identifiable. Data inalienability thus creates value because it makes the data subjects identifiable, contributing to the predictive power of analytics. Data aggregation and anonymization can weaken inalienability but the value of the set of observations still depends on the identities of the observed entities: the more transparent the identity of the observed entity is, the more valuable are the observations.

Thus, data inalienability itself is a source of value because it allows the connection of adjacent data points to the data subject and thereby enhancing the analytical power to generate very specific information and insights. It is much more valuable to have data about the health of individuals in a specific location than data about the average health of residents in that location. Nevertheless, although it would be difficult to predict the specific health outcomes for individuals from aggregated health data, if such aggregate data were combined with other individual-level data such as the residents' daily patterns of mobility, it would be relatively easy to infer these. This shows how the value of identifiability is related to the value of complementary data.

**Inferrability**
The value of a data product is influenced by whether the raw data can be inferred from other substitute sources, or what has also been called "information leakage" (Acemoglu, Makhdoumi, Malekian & Ozdaglar, 2019). For a data source to substitute for a focal data product, its representation of the empirical phenomenon must have sufficient similarity to the representation of the phenomenon of interest of the data product (see Figure 14.1). Take the example of the address of an individual. Although such data may be restricted due to privacy concerns, location data which show the location of the individual at nighttime can act as a substitute to knowing the residential address. As such, the market value of a data product is dependent on the availability of data which can substitute for the focal data product that describes the phenomenon of interest—the more difficult it is to infer the phenomenon of interest, the more value the data product itself will have.

High inferrability thus implies that there are close substitutes that provide similar insights and reduce the market value of the focal data product (cf. Acemoglu et al., 2019). For information products, the availability of close substitutes, such as other movies within the same genre, also reduces the market value of the focal good. However, the logic of substitution is different for information products and data products. In the case of information products, substitution is between somewhat similar consumption experiences. For data products, inferrability implies the opportunity to recreate the missing data by analyzing other data products. Inferring missing data thus usually requires an analytical step, whereas consuming a substitute information product does not typically require additional procedures.

## Complementary data

The economic value of a data product also depends on the availability of *related* data from complementary phenomena (see Figure 14.1). While an information product usually has standalone value (think of a movie or a software program), the value of a single data observation typically depends on access to additional related data such as a time series or a cross section (or both) of the same variable. More broadly, the economic value of a data product depends not only on the quality of the observation itself and its metadata, but also on the availability of complementary data from other phenomena that can be combined with the focal data product (see Figure 14.1). For example, to measure inflation, the US Bureau of Labor Statistics collects price data within more than 200 product categories for several hundred commodities in each category,[6] and providers of consumer behavior data and analysts such as Experian assess consumer profiles via a panel of over 500 personal and behavioral indicators coming from several different sources.[7] Similarly, although mapping data, such as that provided by Google Maps, are useful for finding directions, they gain much of their value from the ability to link with other data sources, such as traffic conditions or restaurant locations. These examples highlight that the value of a single observation is strongly complementary with other related observations. The value of each dataset is amplified by the possibility of combination with the others. Consequently, as data products can serve multiple purposes for analysis and insights, standardization allows further reuse.

## Technology and skill complementarities

Finally, the value of a data product requires the availability of complementary technologies and skills to be able to collect, curate, secure, and maintain the raw data, metadata, and data products themselves (see Figure 14.1). As well as the skills and technologies required to manage the data products, complementary technologies and skills are also required to create actionable insights out of the dataset. These include human judgment to design models that can analyze the data product and software programs and computer resources to run such models. Thus value creation from data products requires both data management and analytical resources, although data products can certainly be commercialized (e.g., through trading) without analytics (Koutroumpis, Leiponen & Thomas, 2020; Thomas & Leiponen, 2016).

## DATA PRODUCT VALUE CAPTURE

Given the factors that enhance value creation from data discussed in the previous section, we now outline the factors that influence "appropriability," or the degree to which firms will be able to capture the returns on their investments in creating data products. This requires the ability to differentiate and control; in other words, to generate market power. Value creation in data products builds on the attributes of the data product itself, but the complementary elements are also crucial in realizing the value (Pisano & Teece, 2007; Teece, 1998). When commercializing a data product, a firm can accumulate power by a number of mechanisms: by controlling the data product itself, by controlling the complementary data and information products that are required to capture value (such as the metadata that inform consumers about the sources, procedures, and provenance associated with the data product or the standards which allow it to be utilized), or by controlling the complementary technologies and skills (such as the analytical tools needed to generate the insight or the platform that enables the data to be processed, combined, and distributed). Next, we examine each of these sources of market power.

## Control of the Data Product

In economics, information products such as content and algorithms are characterized as "nonrival." Nonrivalry means that one person's consumption does not prevent simultaneous consumption by other consumers, nor does it diminish the amount available to other consumers (Varian, 1998). Digitized information products are nonrival because, unlike cars that can only be driven by one party at a time, digital information can simultaneously be used in many different locations by many different people. Like information products, data products are inherently nonrival—one person's use of digital data does not exclude another from using them, nor does it reduce the utility of use to others at other times. However, use by others may influence the commercial value of the data or information product. As such, firms wish to strategically control the access of others to their data products.

Information products are considered to have "partial excludability" (see Table 14.1). Excludability refers to the ability to exclude others from consumption, and the greater the potential to exclude, the greater the potential value capture, because the creator has more control who gets access to it. For nonrival products, excludability primarily depends on the legal regime and has generally been supported through trade secrets, various contractual control rights, and intellectual property rights (DeLong & Froomkin, 2000; Varian, 1998). Intellectual property rights such as patents and copyrights offer some protection for information products.[8] Patents protect an invention that is an industrial application of a novel technical insight; for example, in the form of instructions embedded in software algorithms. Copyrights protect the original expression of an idea, including instructions. Both content- and algorithm-based information products are primarily protected by copyright, although algorithms may also have patent protection (particularly in the US). However, copyright is a relatively weak intellectual property right, especially in the digital environment, and, consequently, digital content and software industries have been marred with thorny lawsuits for years (for good discussions, see Lessig, 1999, 2008).

Compared with information products, the usage of a data product is even more challenging to legally exclude. Observations from a database can be streamed or shared, or the order of the observations or variables may be substantially altered, or the observations may be combined with others, after which it may be impossible to detect where the data originated. Data and databases can be legally protected under copyright, but this protection is weak (see Table 14.1). For databases, copyright typically primarily protects the whole structure and organization of the database, not the individual observations it contains (e.g., it is not possible to copyright a number or a word; a specific sequence of numbers or words could be copyrighted, but not if the sequence is altered). The extent of the protection varies by jurisdiction, with the US having no specific copyright protection for databases, Australian copyright law protecting databases, and the Canadian approach somewhere in the middle (Zhu & Madnick, 2010). The European Union database right also seeks to protect the non-copyrightable aspects of databases; for example, when the data are provided in a different order or in a manipulated format.

Nevertheless, it is difficult to prove that a set of observations originates from a protected database as data can in many cases be independently collected and individual facts are not protected by intellectual property rights, although they can be kept trade secrets.

In the US, courts have deemed compilations of data copyrightable when the process of selecting or arranging the data requires subjective judgment (Mattioli, 2014). The Second Circuit of the US Federal Court has stated that data "[s]election implies the exercise of judgment in choosing which facts from a given body of data to include in a compilation."[9] According to the US Copyright Office, data arrangement "refers to the ordering or grouping of data into lists or categories that go beyond the mere mechanical grouping of data as such, for example, the alphabetical, chronological, or sequential listings of data."[10] However, legal scholars agree that such protection is unlikely to prevent unwanted copying. Imitators could rather easily expropriate individual data points without copying their specific arrangement or selection within the database. In several court cases, decisions held no infringement even though defendants copied substantial amounts. Some have argued that after the landmark "Feist" case in 1991,[11] it is difficult in the US to prevent a competitor from taking substantial amounts of material from copyrighted collections of data and using it in a competing product (Wald, 2002). Because of this lack of a legal form of protection (intellectual or other property rights), data products are mainly protected by secrecy, often reinforced by contractual agreements. As such, in contrast to information products, data products per se are barely excludable, and any control of data products themselves usually depends on contract enforcement.

## Control of Complementary Data and Information Assets

Although direct control of a data product is challenging, control of the complementary data and information products can create some market power. For example, metadata can be critical to convey the value of the data product to a potential consumer, and therefore the ability to control the metadata can confer significant market power. Whereas it is difficult to track the use and dissemination of individual data products and enforce use restrictions, as described above, there might be more powerful legal tools, including trade secrecy and copyrights, to address illegal copying of metadata documentation, especially if distributed separately from the data product. Thus, one could conceivably offer the data product openly but limit the dissemination of the metadata to verified commercial partners. Indeed, Mattioli (2014) has proposed that data protection rights could be centered on metadata rather than the data product itself.

Another method for firms to capture value from data products is through the control of the standards that define both the data product and the metadata and influence the complementarity with other data products. While it might not be possible (or desirable) to control the data product itself, the standards by which it is encoded may be protected by intellectual property rights or trade secrets. By controlling the standard through which the utility of either the data product or its metadata can be realized, the ability to capture some of the value of the data product can result. For example, many file formats are proprietary, and the owners of those file formats, such as the owner of AutoCAD software, can prevent any subsequent use of the data product for uses other than design, thereby ensuring they capture the value in any use of those standards.

Yet another method to capture value from a data product may be to control any strongly complementary data that enhance the value of the resource in question. Here, one might attempt to limit the distribution of a unique proprietary data product to a smaller number of clients while widely disseminating an open data product that is more easily available or even in the public domain.

**Control of Complementary Technology and Skills**

A further route to capture value from a data product is through control of the complementary technologies and skills that the data product relies upon. While many of the essential analytic tools, algorithms, and machine learning methods are available as open-source software or otherwise in the public domain—for example, due to scientific publication—these can also include proprietary resources and capabilities that can be protected as trade secrets. Thus, one method for value capture consists of opening the data product but retaining control of relevant models and algorithms through secrecy. This strategy is well known in the open-source software context where businesses such as Red Hat and Anaconda thrive on complementarities between open and proprietary capabilities and might enable value appropriation at a large scale.

Data exchange platforms can become powerful by leveraging access to a dynamic resource or an ecosystem of data partners (cf. Thomas, Autio & Gann, 2014). While old data or long-standing exchange relationships rarely depend on a platform that enables new connections, in a dynamic environment where data products and their associated sources change frequently, a trading platform can add value by enabling search, standards, and contractual templates for efficient matching and trading (Koutroumpis et al., 2020; Pallais, 2014). For example, Bloomberg has attempted to build such a data platform for data products from multiple vendors.[12] If successful in gaining critical mass, such a platform could become very profitable, but there are no known examples yet of successful dedicated data exchange platforms.

Consumer platforms, such as Facebook and Google, provide services that offer unique access to a dynamic data resource (cf. Cennamo, 2020). In doing so they are maintaining control over the means of data collection. While their main value propositions are not based on data trading (and hence differentiating them from dedicated data product exchange platforms discussed above), data access and analytics substantially enhance the value propositions, especially for advertisers. In this case, data products are indirectly commercialized through information services, and the data themselves do not need to be revealed.

## BUSINESS MODEL IMPLICATIONS

A successful business model for data products is built upon a differentiated position in the data ecosystem that the firm can sufficiently control and leverage (cf. Jacobides, Knudsen & Augier, 2006; Teece, 2010). To build this differentiated position, business models seek value creation opportunities by ensuring quality through metadata, reducing inferrability (as similar data products reduce market value), and maximizing identifiability. A successful business model also seeks to ensure that the data product is complementary with other relevant data, information, technologies, and skills.

When the data product can be controlled, then a successful business model is possible by directly licensing the data product, so long as the data product itself is sufficiently valuable to justify the inherent transaction costs. However, when the data product cannot be controlled,

*Table 14.2*    *Data product business models*

| Business model | Data supply | Data factory | Data service | Data platform |
|---|---|---|---|---|
| Description | Selling a data product | Using data analytics and skills to create and sell information products | Providing complementary tools and services that improve data held by third parties | Acting as a two-sided platform to become a bottleneck to access data held by third parties |
| Data value creation opportunity | When data product is particularly valuable due to quality or identifiability | When data product is freely available (non-excludable) or is not particularly valuable | When third-party data product can be enhanced through complementary data | When there is friction in the marketplace for valuable data products |
| Data value capture mechanism | Excludability; secrecy | Complementary data and information; complementary technology and skills | Complementary technology and skills; standardization | Excludability; complementary technology and skills |
| Transaction method | Data licensing | Subscription | Software licensing; subscription | Subscription |
| Firm types | Large/established | Any size with model and software skills | Usually large enough to guarantee "trust" | Usually large to maintain bottleneck control |
| Capabilities required | Strong contract enforcement expertise | Analytics and technology expertise | Technology and standardization expertise | Technology expertise |
| Risks and opportunities | Product differentiation and cyber security | Scalability of complementary data and subscription model | Leveraging industry standards and metadata control | Illicit copying and entry from other entities with comparative advantages |
| Examples | Experian consumer credit reporting; Vodafone mobility data; Maersk shipping data | Meltwater for market sentiment analysis; CB Insights for technology trends; Estated for real estate data | ID Analytics for credit and identity risk | QuantHouse for financial data; Prognos for clinical outcomes |

then a successful business model requires control of at least one of the complementary resources so that value can be captured (Teece, 1986). Thus, when the data product is not excludable, successful data business models prominently feature complementarities as sources of market power. Furthermore, feasible business models need to ensure that the control over data, information, skill, and technology complementarities does not adversely impact data value creation. For instance, business models that overly restrict the ability to analyze data (for example, by limiting skill or technology complementarities through control of a standard) will weaken value creation opportunities. The innovator thus needs to ensure that they keep alive the proverbial goose that lays the golden egg: that the ultimate value being captured is greater under the control strategies than without them, despite the negative impact on value creation. In this section we review how different business models resolve this tradeoff between value creation and value capture (see Table 14.2 for a summary).

## Data Supply Business Models

When a data product has significant value because of its unique quality or identifiability, the main commercialization route is via licensing agreements (see Table 14.2). Licensing results in data supply business models that are based on provision of a data product that others may reuse while the licensor maintains control over it (Thomas & Leiponen, 2016). This is quite common in industries such as communications, media, and entertainment; for example, a telecommunications firm such as Vodafone can sell the mobility data generated by its customers to a firm that provides traffic information (cf. Tosi, 2017). Alternatively, it may be possible to make available the organization's "exhaust data" produced by unrelated business transactions (Manyika et al., 2011); for example, transport companies such as Maersk can collect data on global product shipments and license data to supplement business and economic forecasts.[13]

As these business models do not rely on control of complementary data, information, technology, and/or skills, the value capture does not adversely impact data value creation. However, while data licensing can be lucrative, it is a challenging way to monetize data products (Wixom & Ross, 2017). The necessary condition for these data supply-based business models is the excludability of the data product, necessitating a capacity for strong contract enforcement. Data licensing involves high transaction costs due to negotiation and contracting, and hence is only warranted for high-value data (Mayer & Argyres, 2004). Valuable data are typically highly identifiable, and thus confidential and sensitive, further accentuating the need for protection. To protect the licensed data, firms normally rely on secrecy and contractual arrangements to commercialize their data products and associated metadata, as it makes no sense to license data products to parties whom the seller cannot monitor or who do not seek to maintain their reputation and branding. To establish such licensing business models requires extensive resources and skill in initiating, negotiating, and enforcing the agreements. Hence, data licensing arrangements will primarily be pursued by organizations that are large, well known, and highly reputable, and whose contracting practices and services are well developed and reasonably transparent.

An example of the data licensing business model is Experian, a consumer credit reporting agency that collects and aggregates data on over one billion people and businesses.[14] As consumer credit data are inalienable (the value of the data largely comes from the clear identity of the data subjects, and the subjects are often relatively easy to re-identify from aggregated data), the business and ethical risks of trading these private data are high. Consider the fallout from the 2017 data breach of Equifax, a similar business, involving the personal data, including full names, social security numbers, birth dates, addresses, and, in some cases, driver license numbers, of 145.5 million US Equifax consumers. The company lost 35 percent of its market capitalization, or USD$6 billion, over the week after the breach becoming public, and the stock price stayed on a lower level thereafter.[15] Thus, licensing confidential data products requires contracts with strict enforceability. As high transaction costs make this bilateral marketplace rather inefficient (Koutroumpis et al., 2020), the data products need to have low inferrability to be valuable, generating market power due to their uniqueness. Overall, data licensing agreements will be limited to large and highly reputable companies providing access to differentiated and high-value data products.

## Data Factory Business Models

The data factory business model is based on firms leveraging control of complementary data and information products and complementary skills and technologies to produce derivative information products (see Table 14.2). While these business models rely on control of complementary data, information, technology, and skills, they avoid decreasing the value of the data product by focusing on data that are widely available or are unable to be controlled. Value is captured by leveraging concentrated and excludable skills and technology that generate insights out of the open or non-excludable data.

For a data factory business model to be successful, the generated insights need to be in high demand. For instance, a desirable competitive position may be created through a tailored combination of data products and software tools, leveraging analytics for data to create derivative information products that are usually provided through subscription. Whereas each client solution is unique, this strategy depends on the scalability of the process by developing data analytics and information product delivery to customers. Here, business models are based around the control of the complementary expertise to develop the analytic services that create human-readable information products, such as visualizations and mashups. This approach requires the development of complementary information products, such as software and analytical models, which can be made excludable through the protection of intellectual property. A particularly large part of the development cost is the process of discovering the customer's data needs and appropriate analytical tools. Further, firms need to ensure an efficient and highly automated data on-boarding process, as this can be critical for long-term success. However, with a steady stream of subscription-based clients, this data factory business model can be lucrative.

There are many fast-growing data companies based on the combination of open data products and proprietary analytics. For example, Meltwater provides an analytic service for market sentiment based on publicly available social media data. Similarly, CB Insights predicts what the next technology trend will be relying on data from funding rounds for technology start-ups, App Annie estimates the impact of new versions on downloads and revenues through the application of proprietary software and analytics on data on the open app market, and Estated simply sells subscriptions to APIs that deliver aggregated US real estate property data so that real estate businesses can find the open property data they require. Estated digitizes, organizes, maps, and serves public property ownership records from US counties. Thus, although the data are publicly available, the process of efficiently retrieving and digitizing public records is excludable and highly complementary to the open data available in each locale.

### Data Service Business Models

The data service business model involves providing complementary tools and services, via subscription or, more rarely, through software licensing, to improve the data products held by third parties (see Table 14.2). While these business models rely on the control of complementary technology and skills, they avoid decreasing the value of the data product by focusing on improving the complementary technology, and not basing value capture on data products themselves. This means that firms can build a desirable competitive position when it is difficult to appropriate value directly from a data product. Thus, these business models rely on the control of critical complementary technologies to add value to the data product of a third party.

For instance, one potential data service business model is providing provenance validation and certification and auditing services, to ensure that the integrity and the quality of data products are maintained. Similarly, businesses can provide a "trust" infrastructure, such as identity management services between individuals and merchants who wish to use and/or collect data (Moiso & Minerva, 2012; Schwab et al., 2011). To address privacy concerns or General Data Protection Regulation (GDPR) compliance, such business models offer products and services that ensure the compliance with data governance practices by searching for data products that contain identifiable information for individuals and ensuring that the customer meets regulatory or privacy demands.[16]

An example of such complementary services is ID Analytics, which collects clients' event data, such as credit applications, and builds a data consortium by integrating these data to create a more comprehensive industry-level credit and identity risk data product than any single client could do alone. The event data of a single client is thus strongly complementary with those of other clients. Such data management business models can also focus on the provision of reliable and robust metadata, adding value to raw or semi-raw data by improving the efficiency, interpretability, and overall functionality of the data. In this case, value is created through aggregation of complementary data and by improving the quality of the data product and its metadata. Value is captured through control of complementary assets, in this case the procedures to gain and sustain the trust of the clientele as a neutral and reliable third-party service. These business models attempt to resolve a source of failure in the market for data products. When the relevant, complementary data products are dispersed, or when desirable insights require sophisticated tools, these types of complementary services can create value by efficiently enabling their integration.

Another approach to developing data service business models is to leverage control over data and analytical standards, such as a proprietary file format. Here proprietary software tools—such as data converters that transform data from one proprietary format to another or analyze data using a particular technique—can be sold to customers. Such standards and analytic techniques (such as artificial intelligence) advance at dizzying speeds and many of the standards and methods are offered as open source or are made available in the public domain through scientific conferences and publications. However, once the current flurry of scientific progress slows down, it is possible that a greater share of the analytic innovations will be protected and privatized through secrecy and patents. For instance, the number of patents issued in the US Patent and Trademark Office that refer to artificial intelligence (including machine learning) have grown substantially since 2002.[17] While the earliest patents date from the 1980s, most of them were granted since 2015, and annual machine learning patents issued grew ten-fold between 2009 and 2018.

Thus, in the future it is conceivable that data service business models will shift toward patent-protected software strategies. Nevertheless, firms have ongoing innovation opportunities in facilitating the adoption of advanced techniques in the enterprise environment. For example, the Anaconda distribution of the Python and R open-source programming languages, which enable large-scale data processing, predictive analytics, and scientific computing, is designed for enterprise-class deployments and has been commercialized accordingly.

**Data Platform Business Models**

The data platform business model involves profiting from a multisided platform. Firms can seek to acquire platform control to become the bottleneck that provides access to critical data products to suppliers and consumers, even when they do not hold or control those resources themselves (Cennamo, 2020; Thomas et al., 2014). Data platform business models leverage the control of the technology that links these two sides of the market, although some can also seek to profit from control of data products (excludability). This means that firms can build a desirable competitive position regardless of whether they can appropriate value directly from a data product.

While the excludability problems apply to data platforms as much as bilateral data transactions (Koutroumpis et al., 2020), data platforms can become essential sources of time-sensitive data products such as those from financial markets. When success in algorithmic trading depends on nanosecond advantages in data access, customers are willing to pay a lot to cut down latency by small fractions of a second. Providing the lowest latency to public sources of data products such as stock markets can then become a significant competitive advantage. Companies such as QuantHouse collocate their operations within major financial markets to offer algorithmic traders ultra-low-latency data product access and hosting services.

Alternatively, firms can focus on a sectoral theme and collect, aggregate, and repurpose data products. To that effect, firms build platforms that search, cross reference, and contextualize data to find correlations, identify efficiencies, or visualize complex relationships. The most common examples of data aggregators are price comparison services, such as the travel search engine Kayak. Other examples include healthcare start-ups such as Prognos that integrate clinical, payment, public health, and behavioral data to help other businesses manage the costs of licensing and analyzing clinical outcomes data. In principle, general data trading through "eBay-like" platforms is also possible, although these seem to be scarce because excludability is very challenging for this type of platform (Koutroumpis et al., 2020).

As with data service business models, this business model depends on some friction in the marketplace that the data platform can alleviate. However, with current technology it is very difficult on a public platform to exclude parties from retrieving and further sharing the data products. Therefore, the platform must generate some unique (differentiated) value from compiling disparate data resources with analytical methods that would be difficult for competitors to replicate. The platform might also apply some methods to restrict views of the raw data and thereby increase the cost of illicit copying of the data resources.

## CONCLUSION

In this chapter we have provided a conceptual foundation for strategies to commercialize data products. We characterized the economic nature of data products and distinguished them from information products. We highlighted quality, inferrability, and identifiability as key attributes of data products. We illustrated how data products differ from content- and algorithm-based information products. We showed that in contrast to content or algorithms, the value of data products often depends on additional, complementary, and potentially unique, digital assets. These include metadata, other data and information products, analytic tools, and distribution platforms. Such complementarities arise because data products are almost always intermediate goods. Firms need to ensure that data products are curated, manipulated, analyzed, and reported, to create valuable and unique information products. Therefore, commercialization strategies for data products may focus on controlling either the data product itself or some of the complementary digital assets.

However, controlling the data product itself is often tricky because of the limited legal tools to protect data assets. This results in significant transaction hazards, and thus the excludability of data products themselves relies primarily on secrecy and contracts. Consequently, firms may be inclined to focus on internal data innovation by creating data products that are internally sourced and used. While this approach might support data product commercialization through provision of other digital services such as search and social network platforms

(Cennamo & Santalo, 2013; Eisenmann, 2008; Hagiu & Yoffie, 2009), if data innovation only occurs within firm boundaries, then the broader economy may miss out on opportunities to innovate by connecting disparate but complementary data from different organizations. Thus, from a societal welfare perspective, sole reliance on within-firm data innovation is suboptimal, and large-scale markets or sharing arrangements for data products would "lift all boats," provided confidentiality and privacy concerns could be adequately addressed.

Hence, to maximize the social value of data products, there need to be ways to profitably combine complementary data products held by different parties. While highly valuable data products can be directly commercialized through bilateral contractual licensing arrangements, most data product business models focus on controlling one of the complementary digital assets. Complementarities among data products and other digital assets give rise to a few viable strategies to commercialize data resources beyond the immediate analytic needs of the data holding company itself. Such assets may include compilations of related data, tools, analytical services, or distribution channels, which may be able to garner enough market power to create sustainable business models even though excludability of data itself is limited.

In conclusion, markets for data products can be complex and opaque, because the valuation of data products usually depends on complementary digital assets. When the data product cannot be controlled, the power in markets for data products arises from business models that enable controlling such complementary assets, technologies, and activities.

## NOTES

1.  The authors are listed in reverse alphabetical order.
2.  For instance, the US National Academies of Science define data as facts, numbers, letters, and symbols that describe an object, idea, condition, situation, or other factors (National Research Council, 1999; Uhlir & Cohen, 2011).
3.  This aligns with Aaltonen & Penttinen's (2021) assertion that data do not *have* a structure but are made by a structure that confers data their capacity to represent contextual facts.
4.  This aligns with Ackoff's (1989: 3) suggestion that data consists of "symbols that represent the properties of objects and events," whereas "information consists of processed data."
5.  This is not to say that information goods are never combined with other information or data to create a subsequent final good. For instance, music can be added to the score of a movie. The point is that they are typically not designed at the outset to be intermediate goods.
6.  https://www.bls.gov/cpi/questions-and-answers.htm#Question_10.
7.  http://www.experian.co.uk/marketing-services/solutions/targeting/consumer-data.html.
8.  Trademarks also offer (very) limited protection by attaching a legally protected symbol to the information or data good.
9.  *Key Publications, Inc. v. Chinatown Today Publishing Enters., Inc.*, 945 F.2d 509, 513 (2d Cir. 1991).
10. Guidelines for Registration of Fact-Based Compilations 1 (Rev. Oct. 11, 1989).
11. *Feist Publications, Inc., v. Rural Telephone Service Co.*, 499 U.S. 340 (1991).
12. https://www.bloomberg.com/professional/product/platform-data-distribution/.
13. http://fortune.com/2014/09/18/global-trade-economic-indicator/.
14. https://en.wikipedia.org/wiki/Experian.
15. https://www.wired.com/story/equifax-breach-response/.
16. See https:// www .mediapost.com/ publications/ article/ 310355/ egnyte -offers -cross -european -compliance-platform.html; https://www.egnyte.com/.
17. https:// www .uspto .gov/ about -us/ news -updates/ new -benchmark -uspto -study -finds -artificial -intelligence-us-patents-rose-more.

# REFERENCES

Aaltonen, A., Alaimo, C., & Kallinikos, J. 2021. The making of data commodities: Data analytics as an embedded process. *Journal of Management Information Systems*, 38(2): 401–29.

Aaltonen, A., & Penttinen, E. 2021. *What Makes Data Possible? A Sociotechnical View on Structured Data Innovations*. Paper presented at the 54th Hawaii International Conference on System Sciences, Hawaii.

Aaltonen, A., & Tempini, N. 2014. Everything counts in large amounts: A critical realist case study on data-based production. *Journal of Information Technology*, 29(1): 97–110.

Acemoglu, D., Makhdoumi, A., Malekian, A., & Ozdaglar, A. 2019. Too much data: Prices and inefficiencies in data markets. *National Bureau of Economic Research Working Paper Series*, No. 26296.

Ackoff, R.L. 1989. From data to wisdom. *Journal of Applied Systems Analysis*, 16, 3–9.

Bellinger, G., Castro, D., & Mills, A. 2004. Data, information, knowledge, and wisdom. http://www.systems-thinking.org/dikw/dikw.htm.

Brynjolfsson, E., Collis, A., & Eggers, F. 2019. Using massive online choice experiments to measure changes in well-being. *Proceedings of the National Academy of Sciences*, 116(15): 7250–55.

Byrne, D., & Corrado, C. 2020. Accounting for innovations in consumer digital services: It still matters. In C. Corrado, J. Haskel, J. Miranda & D.E. Sichel (Eds.), *Measuring and Accounting for Innovation and the Twenty-First Century*, Vol. 78: 471–517. Cambridge, MA: National Bureau of Economic Research.

Calabresi, G., & Melamed, A.D. 1972. Property rules, liability rules, and inalienability: One view of the cathedral. *Harvard Law Review*, 85(6): 1089–1128.

Cennamo, C. 2020. Competing in digital markets: A platform-based perspective. *Academy of Management Perspectives*, 35(2): 265–91.

Cennamo, C., & Santalo, J. 2013. Platform competition: Strategic trade-offs in platform markets. *Strategic Management Journal*, 34(11): 1331–50.

Collins, V., & Lanz, J. 2019. Managing data as an asset. *CPA Journal*, 89(6): 22–7.

Crockett, L. 2002. Fundamental issues in honors teaching: Data, information, knowledge, and wisdom on the wired campus. In C.L. Fuiks & L. Clark (Eds.), *Teaching and Learning in Honours*: 21–32. Lincoln, NB: National Collegiate Honors Council.

DalleMule, L., & Davenport, T.H. 2017. What's your data strategy? *Harvard Business Review*, 95(3): 112–21.

Davenport, T.H., Barth, P., & Bean, R. 2012. How "big data" is different. *MIT Sloan Management Review*, 54(1): 43–6.

DeLong, J.B., & Froomkin, A.M. 2000. Speculative microeconomics for tomorrow's economy. In B. Kahin & H.R. Varian (Eds.), *Internet Publishing and Beyond: The Economics of Digital Information and Intellectual Property*: 6–29. Cambridge, MA: MIT Press.

Eisenmann, T.R. 2008. Managing proprietary and shared platforms. *California Management Review*, 50(4): 31–53.

Foss, N.J., & Saebi, T. 2017. Business models and business model innovation: Between wicked and paradigmatic problems. *Long Range Planning*, 51(1): 9–21.

Goodridge, P., & Haskel, J. 2015. How does big data affect GDP? Theory and evidence for the UK. *Imperial College Business School Discussion Paper*. London: Imperial College Business School.

Hagiu, A., & Yoffie, D.B. 2009. What's your Google strategy? *Harvard Business Review*, 87(4): 74–81.

Hammell, R., Bates, C., Lewis, H., Perricos, C., Brett, L., & Branch, D. 2012. Open data: Driving growth, ingenuity and innovation. *Deloitte Analytics Briefing Note*: 1–36. London: Deloitte.

Jacobides, M.G., Knudsen, T., & Augier, M. 2006. Benefiting from innovation: Value creation, value appropriation and the role of industry architectures. *Research Policy*, 35(8): 1200–221.

Koutroumpis, P., Leiponen, A., & Thomas, L.D.W. 2020. Markets for data. *Industrial & Corporate Change*, 29(3): 645–60.

Lessig, L. 1999. Code is law. *Industry Standard*, 18.

Lessig, L. 2008. *Remix: Making Art and Commerce Thrive in the Hybrid Economy*. London: Bloomsbury Academic.

Linde, F., & Stock, W.G. 2011. *Information Markets: A Strategic Guideline for the I-Commerce*. New York, NY: De Gruyter Saur.

Manyika, J., Chui, M., Brown, B., Bughin, J., Dobbs, R., Roxburgh, C., & Byers, A.H. 2011. Big data: The next frontier for innovation, competition, and productivity. In McKinsey Global Institute (Ed.), *McKinsey Global Institute Report*: 1–156. N.p.: McKinsey.

Mattioli, M. 2014. Disclosing big data. *Minnesota Law Review*, 99: 534–84.

Mayer, K.J., & Argyres, N.S. 2004. Learning to contract: Evidence from the personal computer industry. *Organization Science*, 15(4): 394–410.

McAfee, A., & Brynjolfsson, E. 2012. Big data: The management revolution. *Harvard Business Review*, 90(10): 60–66, 68, 128.

Moiso, C., & Minerva, R. 2012. *Towards a User-Centric Personal Data Ecosystem: The Role of the Bank of Individuals' Data*. Paper presented at the 2012 16th International Conference on Intelligence in Next Generation Networks, ICIN 2012, October 8–11, 2012, Berlin, Germany.

Nakamura, L., Samuels, J., & Soloveichik, R. 2017. Measuring the "free" digital economy within the GDP and productivity accounts. *ESCoE Discussion Paper*. London: Economic Statistics Centre of Excellence.

National Research Council. 1999. *A Question of Balance: Private Rights and the Public Interest in Scientific and Technical Databases*. Washington, DC: National Academy Press.

Pallais, A. 2014. Inefficient hiring in entry-level labor markets. *American Economic Review*, 104(11): 3565–99.

Parmar, R., Mackenzie, I., Cohn, D., & Gann, D.M. 2014. The new patterns of innovation. *Harvard Business Review*, 92(1/2): 86–95.

Pisano, G.P., & Teece, D.J. 2007. How to capture value from innovation: Shaping intellectual property and industry architecture. *California Management Review*, 50(1): 278–96.

Rowley, J. 2007. The wisdom hierarchy: Representations of the DIKW hierarchy. *Journal of Information Science*, 33(2): 163–80.

Schwab, K., Marcus, A., Oyola, J.R., Hoffman, W., & Luzi, M. 2011. *Personal Data: The Emergence of a New Asset Class*. Cologny: World Economic Forum.

Sorescu, A. 2017. Data-driven business model innovation. *Journal of Product Innovation Management*, 34(5): 691–96.

Teece, D.J. 1986. Profiting from technological innovation: Implications for integration, collaboration, licensing. *Research Policy*, 15(6): 285–305.

Teece, D.J. 1998. Capturing value from knowledge assets: The new economy, markets for know-how, and intangible assets. *California Management Review*, 40: 55–80.

Teece, D.J. 2010. Business models, business strategy and innovation. *Long Range Planning*, 43(2–3): 172–94.

Thomas, L.D.W., Autio, E., & Gann, D.M. 2014. Architectural leverage: Putting platforms in context. *Academy of Management Perspectives*, 28(2): 198–219.

Thomas, L.D.W., & Leiponen, A. 2016. Big data commercialization. *IEEE Engineering Management Review*, 44(2): 74–90.

Tosi, D. 2017. Cell phone big data to compute mobility scenarios for future smart cities. *International Journal of Data Science and Analytics*, 4(4): 265–84.

Uhlir, P.F., & Cohen, D. 2011. Internal document. Board on Research Data and Information, Policy and Global Affairs Division, National Academy of Sciences.

Van Rijmenam, M., Erekhinskaya, T., Schweitzer, J., & Williams, M.-A. 2019. Avoid being the turkey: How big data analytics changes the game of strategy in times of ambiguity and uncertainty. *Long Range Planning*, 52(5): 101841.

Varian, H.R. 1998. Markets for information goods. *IMES Discussion Paper Series*, Vol. 99-E-9. Tokyo, Japan: Institute for Monetary and Economic Studies, Bank of Japan.

Wald, J. 2002. Legislating the golden rule: Achieving comparable protection under the European Union database directive. *Fordham International Law Journal*, 25(4): 987–1038.

Wixom, B.H., & Ross, J.W. 2017. How to monetize your data. *MIT Sloan Management Review*, 58(3): 10–13.

Zhu, H.W., & Madnick, S.E. 2010. Legal challenges and strategies for comparison shopping and data reuse. *Journal of Electronic Commerce Research*, 11(3): 231–9.

Zott, C., & Amit, R. 2010. Business model design: An activity system perspective. *Long Range Planning*, 43(2–3): 216–26.

# 15. Capturing value from data complementarities: a multi-level framework

*Paavo Ritala and Kimmo Karhu*

## 1. INTRODUCTION

For contemporary organizations, data are now the single most important strategic resource. Data are collected in almost all settings, ranging from individual users' preferences in online marketplaces to continuous monitoring of industrial equipment performance through ubiquitous sensors. Importantly, given the huge volume of data collected from multiple sources, it becomes clear that "data seldom matter in [the] singular" (Alaimo & Kallinikos, 2021, 3) and that "data are seldom solely strategic resources that exist internal to the boundaries of any individual firm" (Gregory et al., 2021b). Increasingly, organizations combine different data sets into "data objects" of sufficient stability (Alaimo & Kallinikos, 2021), including credit scores, user profiles, employee profiles, viewability metrics, and digital twins (virtual versions of physical machinery). Furthermore, data resources are typically a by-product of a process or an intermediate good that is then combined and transformed into other "information goods" ranging from scientific reports to advertisements (Koutroumpis et al., 2020). This in turn points to the existence and relevance of "data complementarities," which we define here as the added value creation potential of combining different data sets into actionable and meaningful goods, objects, and artifacts. This chapter explores how firms can capture value from such data complementarities in different settings.

The potential of data complementarities is increased with combinatorial breadth; indeed, data resources are often combined across organizational boundaries to make them more meaningful (Clough & Wu, 2022; Gregory et al., 2021b). For instance, an online service user profile typically combines behavioral data from service use (e.g., clicks, purchases, likes) with click-through data for different advertisers and usage data from other web services. Similarly, a contemporary car's infotainment center includes sensor-based data on fuel consumption and other vehicle-specific metrics, as well as data from external services (e.g., traffic information, enriched location information such as location of the next charging station, music, and other entertainment services). Global supply chains are now also optimized by the use of demand and supply data, logistics information, and continuous real-time monitoring across multiple parties (Yan & Wang, 2012). Finally, digital platforms like TripAdvisor combine complementarities across multiple ecosystem actors, including hotel data, destination data, and user reviews (Alaimo et al., 2020).

There are several reasons for the strategic centrality of data for modern organizations and the consequent extent of data collection and combination. Unlike knowledge, which tends to be sticky and costly to reproduce (Grant, 1996), data fundamentally resemble a public good that can be reproduced and used by multiple actors simultaneously at little or no cost. Relatedly, data are by nature "nonrival" (Jones & Tonetti, 2020) in that they are undiminished when used by multiple actors. Ideally, then, data can increase opportunities to create and capture value for multiple organizations and individuals, driving complementary and competitive innovation across different industries and ecosystems (Yoo et al., 2010).

However, a number of significant barriers and tensions can restrict value capture from data complementarities. When viewed as a strategic resource, mobilizing data across organizational boundaries is often frowned upon because of competitive concerns (Cho & Jun, 2013; Ghoshal et al., 2020; Jones & Tonetti, 2020) and the limited availability of relevant intellectual property regimes (Koutroumpis et al., 2020). Additionally, customer-specific data collection and analytics are subject to regulatory and contractual conditions (Leonard, 2014) that further restrict the mobility of data resources, even in the case of internal data sharing across organizational units and functions. In an ideal world, all of these hindrances can be overcome because "at a technological level, data is infinitely usable" (Jones & Tonetti, 2020, p. 2819). However, while this may be true in theory, in practice data sharing and resulting complementarities still fall short of their potential.

While existing studies have discussed utilization of data complementarities in the context of digital platforms (Alaimo et al., 2020), there is yet no systematic account of how firms might capture value from complementarities across different data sets in different organizational contexts and at different levels of analysis. To bridge this gap, we describe a framework for capturing value from four distinct types of data complementarity across the classic continuum between hierarchy and markets (Williamson, 1985): intra-firm (hierarchy), bilateral contractual relationships, platform ecosystems, and data markets. In conclusion, we briefly illustrate the use of data complementarities in the health care sector and outline some implications for research and practice.

## 2.   DATA RESOURCES AND DATA COMPLEMENTARITY

Data resources are of value to organizations in three distinct ways. First, the variety in data, or in statistical terms "variance," is the fundamental source for inferring information from the data using statistical means (all machine learning and artificial intelligence-based, or AI-based, methodologies are fundamentally based on statistical methods, even the very advanced ones). A second related factor is the sheer increase in data volume for similar cases in a given context; increasing $N$ increases the statistical significance of the analysis and strengthens interpretation. Finally, data has potential for complementary value when different types of data sets are combined and recombined in different ways (Alaimo et al., 2020; Kallinikos et al., 2013; Yoo et al., 2010). We focus here on this third aspect as the foundation for data complementarities. Simply stated, data can be combined with other types of data to produce complementary value beyond that of the two data sets separately. This aligns with the definition of complementarities in the resource-based view of the firm (e.g., Adegbesan, 2009; Harrison et al., 2001), but data's distinctive features can produce complementarities of much greater scope and scale and for a larger number of actors than other resource types.

Unlike knowledge resources, which are often heterogeneous in terms of expression, all data are composed of zeros and ones, leading to data homogenization (Yoo et al., 2010) allowing for easy dissemination and combination of data. Relatedly, Alaimo et al. (2020) highlighted data's inherent editability, portability, and recontextualizability, noting that data can serve as a highly contextual carrier of meaning, so allowing different organizations working alone or together to create and capture value from data in multiple heterogeneous ways. While software and data share many affordances as digital resources, including easy transferability and editability, data differ from software in that they are not executable or reprogrammable alone. However, software and algorithms enable the value of data complementarities to be captured by transforming data as intermediate goods or by-products into information goods (Koutroumpis et al., 2020) or by aggregation into sufficiently stable and actionable data objects (Alaimo & Kallinikos, 2021).

How, then, do firms differ in their ability to capture value from data complementarities? One relevant issue is the development of machine learning and analytics capabilities as a significant source of productivity differences in firms' utilization of data (Clough & Wu, 2022; Gregory et al., 2021a). As data become a strategic resource, firms have moved from a value chain model to a logic of continuous improvement and learning based on data and analytics (Schildt, 2020). The classical way that value can be captured from data is to collect data about the business (e.g., products, users, and machines) and then use analytical capabilities (e.g., statistical analysis, visualization, and machine learning) to improve either the firm's operations or the product itself. Improved analytical capabilities can also help to improve data-driven decision making (see, for example, Brynjolfsson & McElheran, 2016), typically realized in the form of dashboards for monitoring production line status or as models for predictive maintenance (Porter & Heppelmann, 2014). Dashboards and predictive maintenance models are instances of data objects (Alaimo & Kallinikos, 2021)—sufficiently stable aggregates or bundles of complementary data sets. Other examples of products or services that benefit from data complementarities include smart connected products (Porter and Heppelmann, 2014) such as self-driving cars (e.g., Tesla) or tractors that not only prepare a field but simultaneously collect vast amounts of data that help to optimize farming operations. Finally, data have inherent value as a saleable asset; for example, consumer behavior data are immensely valuable for other firms targeting a similar customer base or for advertising firms seeking to enhance targeting. Indeed, there is evidence of growing market-based exchange for customer data (Koutroumpis et al., 2020).

While all forms of data complementarity are important, the potential to capture value becomes more scalable and generative (Thomas & Tee, 2021) when those complementarities cross organizational boundaries. As one obvious example, customer data become much more useful for targeted online advertising when combined across different sources and use patterns. In the same way, predictive maintenance solutions typically use sensor-based and other data from multiple industrial providers (Alaimo & Kallinikos, 2021); in the simplest case, the machinery is situated at the customer firm's site, and the data are analyzed by the provider. However, different component providers may supply distinct modules that also collect data, facilitating complementarities in which a synchronized "digital twin" can be used to predict maintenance needs, process disruptions, and performance improvements on the basis of ongoing data collection. In such scenarios, data may cross organizational boundaries multiple times, but the complementarities are created at the level of a data object operated by the focal firm. Finally, the full nonrival potential of data is unlocked and potential societal benefits are maximized when shared and accessed in a broader market, ideally in a "many-to-many" setting (Koutroumpis et al., 2020; for discussion, see Jones & Tonetti, 2020).

## 3.   CAPTURING VALUE FROM DATA COMPLEMENTARITIES: A MULTI-LEVEL FRAMEWORK

In developing a multi-level framework for capturing value from four types of data complementarity in distinct organizational contexts, we began from Williamson's (1985) classic conception of the different organizing forms for economic activity, including hierarchies, markets, and the "hybrid organizations" that lie between these two extremes. In both the classical model and the framework proposed here, hierarchies are intra-organizational contexts, in which data ownership is clear, and "internal" complementarities are created from data owned and collected by the firm. At the other extreme, in data markets (e.g., Koutroumpis et al., 2020), data are freely bought and sold; in the case of "open data" markets, there is free mobility of data as a public resource. In this type of market, firms can capture what we call "unbounded" data complementarities that are not for the most part planned, designed, or restricted beforehand.

While Koutroumpis et al. (2020) interpreted "data markets" as broadly including all kinds of transactional data sharing, we identify two distinct hybrid organizational forms between the extremes of hierarchy and market, following Shipilov and Gawer's (2020) distinction between (bilateral) contractual networks and ecosystems. In our framework, bilateral contractual relationships refer to inter-organizational contexts in which data sharing, integration, and ownership are contractual and bilaterally negotiated by independent organizational entities to capture "relational" data complementarities. This differs from our second "hybrid" context, the platform ecosystem, in which the orchestrator of a digital platform establishes a governance model, architectural control mechanisms and rules, and related boundary resources (see, for example, Karhu & Ritala, 2021; Thomas et al., 2014) that determine how data are collected and used on the platform. As a platform can distribute economic activity and related data collection and generate network externalities among its users, the platform owner can capture "supermodular" data complementarities (cf. Jacobides et al., 2018).

The initial overview of the framework is provided in Table 15.1, where we briefly describe data complementarities and implications for value capture at each organizational context. In interpreting Table 15.1 and the discussion that follows, it is important to note that rather than proposing a tightly exclusive taxonomy, our framework advances a typology in which the four "layers" of data complementarities and related challenges may sometimes overlap and share features. To that extent, the proposed typology is more like a continuum from hierarchy to market, in which the nature of data complementarity and the associated value capture challenges change in moving between the two extremes. The four types are illustrated by examples from the public and private sectors.

### Internal Data Complementarities in a Hierarchy

While analyses of data complementarities have to date focused mainly on inter-organizational settings (Alaimo et al., 2020), we believe that the same value creation mechanisms operate in intra-firm contexts. In practice, firms are essentially collectives characterized by bundles of internal complementarities—a defining feature of their idiosyncrasy (Alexy et al., 2018)—and this logic also extends to intangible resources (Grant, 1996). On that basis, it makes sense to begin our analysis by examining data complementarities in hierarchies—that is, within the boundaries of an organizational entity.

*Table 15.1*     *Four types of data complementarity in distinct organizational contexts*

|  | Internal | Relational | Supermodular | Unbounded |
|---|---|---|---|---|
| Organizational context | Hierarchy | Bilateral contractual relationship | Platform ecosystem | Data market |
| Role of focal firm | Sole owner and curator of data resources | Party to a bilateral agreement establishing conditions for combining data across organizational boundaries | Orchestrator of a platform ecosystem collecting data resources from participants via a digital platform | Participant in open market exchange of data resources |
| Source of data complementarity | Complementary organization-specific data resources combined from different data sets | Complementary data resources from different organizations combined on the basis of bilateral agreements | Complementary data resources collected from ecosystem actors via a centralized platform | Data complementarities defined case by case in markets where providers and users are matched |
| Realization of complementary value | Improved firm performance; improved value proposition for products or services | Improved firm performance; improved value proposition for products or services | Improved platform value proposition; increased "data network effects" | Value captured via market mechanism (for-profit) or from open data by individual actors (non-profit) |
| Key value capture challenges | Setting up firm-specific processes and developing capabilities to collect, integrate, analyze, and exploit data resources | Legal, technical (interoperability), and competitive concerns regarding data sharing and negotiating value capture | Power imbalance and privacy issues; developing boundary resources to coordinate ecosystem data complementarities at arm's length | Data curation, homogenization, and standardization of data-sharing interfaces and frameworks |
| Examples | Internal data including customer order history, product search, and shopping cart activity used to optimize shipping at Amazon.com (Erevelles et al., 2016) | Supply chain data used to improve logistical efficiency (Yan & Wang, 2012) Predictive maintenance service improvement for equipment based on sensor data owned by the producer (Porter & Heppelmann, 2014) | Complementarities across hotel data, destination data, and user reviews on the TripAdvisor platform (Alaimo et al., 2020) | Amazon AWS Data Exchange:[a] find, subscribe, and use third-party data in the cloud Open bioinformatic databases like EMBL-EBI (Cantelli et al., 2021); European Union (EU) Data Spaces[b] |

*Notes:*    [a] https://aws.amazon.com/data-exchange/. [b] https://digital-strategy.ec.europa.eu/en/policies/strategy-data.

We contend that "internal" data complementarities occur when different sets of organizational data are combined and recombined in ways that create value beyond that created by those data sets alone. For instance, marketing and customer service teams might provide the production and logistics teams with data about which types of offerings generate most attention. In leading data-oriented companies like Amazon.com, combinations of different customer data types (e.g., product search and order history) are integrated seamlessly and augmented by algorithms that optimize utilization of these different data sets (see, for example, Erevelles et al., 2016).

These firm-specific combinations of data can be seen to produce intra-organizational relational rents; as in the original conceptualization of relational rents (Dyer & Singh, 1998), intra-organizational relational rents are produced when idiosyncratic resources are combined, exchanged, and co-developed. To produce such rents by exploiting data resources, the organization must overcome data integration challenges, as well as any organizational barriers to data sharing, by developing enhanced capabilities and frameworks for utilizing and integrating data. One important element of organizational analytics capability is "combinatory capability" (see also Kogut & Zander, 1992): the capacity to integrate, harmonize, and process data sets to capture the available complementarities. In this regard, big data analytics (De Mauro et al., 2018; Gupta & George, 2016; Mikalef et al., 2019) and AI (Gregory et al., 2021a) are key organizational capabilities, which are required in sync with other organizational arrangements to enable the collection, integration, and aggregation of data resources. The key issue here is to clarify the role of such capabilities in extracting firm-specific internal rents from data (Clough & Wu, 2022) while potentially creating value for the user base and other stakeholders (Gregory et al., 2021b).

Intra-organizational data sharing and integration is not without its challenges. Like organizational knowledge, organizational data often end up in silos as a consequence of specialization and local optimization. For instance, the marketing department, the accounting department, and the R&D team may all have completely different sets of data, often in different formats or databases. This means that organizational actors are likely to encounter significant difficulties in accessing the different interfaces and information systems that deal with internal processes. Indeed, unlike inter-organizational contexts, the challenges of intra-organizational data sharing rarely relate to contractual issues or competitive concerns but rather to how data can be integrated across organizational stakeholders to create value. Data siloing is especially apparent in large incumbent organizations, all the more so in the public sector, where the multiple independent units and functions of vast and complex entities like city authorities are supported by disparate information systems (see, for example, Bundred, 2006). Another challenge for organizations of every kind is how to deal with personal data. In Europe, the General Data Protection Regulation (GDPR) limits how personal data can be processed by public and private sector actors, and specific user consent is needed before sharing or processing personal data.[1] For public sector organizations in particular, other challenges include laws that prohibit analysis of social and health care data together, and these must be kept entirely separate.

### Relational Data Complementarities in Bilateral Contractual Relationships

As in intra-organizational contexts, "relational" data complementarities in bilateral contractual relationships between firms have significant potential to create value and generate relational rents (Dyer & Singh, 1998) when combining data sets generates value beyond that produced by individual data sets alone. This potential is as huge as it is obvious, and data sharing is often a key requirement for relationship building and achieving the goals of an alliance or network (Biggemann, 2012). In business-to-business settings, for instance, sharing of logistics or quality data across supply chains is crucial for supply chain safety and operational efficiency.

In principle, given the unlimited reprogrammability (with the use of software) and the inherent homogenization of data (Yoo et al., 2010), relational data complementarities have huge potential. Additionally, the nonrival features of data mean that there "are potentially large gains to data being used broadly" (Jones & Tonetti, 2020, p. 2819). For instance, Ciccullo et al. (2021) demonstrated how data sharing in the agri-food supply chain reduced food loss and waste for all of the actors involved, and Shaw et al. (2017) have discussed the potential of data sharing for port resilience and disaster planning. These cases highlight the available inter-organizational relational rents (Dyer & Singh, 1998; Lavie, 2006) when firms establish infrastructures, mechanisms, and practices for data sharing. In essence, these relational rents depend on the ability to harness relational data complementarities across organizational boundaries.

In our view, the potential for relational data complementarities is seriously underutilized, which would explain the rarity of known cases of data sharing (especially "horizontally" among peers) beyond supply chain contexts, where data sharing is more common. One reason for this lack of utilization relates to competitive concerns, as data are difficult to protect using intellectual property mechanisms (Koutroumpis et al., 2020) and are therefore often seen as a firm-specific asset, leading to non-disclosure (Cho & Jun, 2013; Ghoshal et al., 2020), with potentially suboptimal results (Jones & Tonetti, 2020). Firms also encounter a range of technical and organizational barriers to data sharing, again leading to organizational data silos and suboptimization (Shaw et al., 2017). As a related issue, privacy concerns mean that personal data cannot always be moved across organizational boundaries, especially when a customer does not give their consent. However, that barrier is removed if consent is granted, as in third-party targeted ads based on customer consent, for instance. It is also worth noting that the GDPR imposes further restrictions on the public sector; as there is typically an inherent power imbalance between the data subject and the public sector actor, consent cannot be so freely utilized.

## Supermodular Data Complementarities in Platform Ecosystems

In platform markets (also known as two-sided or multi-sided markets), platform users join a digital infrastructure that connects them to other users (Cennamo, 2021). The dominant model is the centralized platform market, in which a central organization (often called the platform or ecosystem "orchestrator"; see Thomas & Ritala, 2021) coordinates an ecosystem of users and complements (as in Google Android), users and producers (as in Uber), or users who are peers (as in Facebook). The platform orchestrator—typically a for-profit firm—often owns customer access and related customer and usage data and is therefore best placed to both create and capture value from the platform market (Clough & Wu, 2022). Platform users benefit from the network effects generated by the platform; the more users there are on one side of the platform, the more valuable the platform will be to users on the same side (as in the case of Facebook) or on the other side (as in the case of buyers and suppliers on a marketplace platform). Gregory et al. (2021a, 2021b) have recently argued that these regular network effects are boosted by "data network effects" that accumulate when platform-specific AI-capabilities are used to improve the offering for all platform users.

Platforms are typically built as modular structures, where a platform orchestrator builds a platform core, and actors at the periphery join by means of boundary resources such as user interfaces or application programming interfaces (Karhu & Ritala, 2021). What, then, is the source of the platform ecosystem's data advantage? We argue that it lies in the ecosystem's complements—the "modules" (Jacobides et al., 2018) that provide a continuous stream of data to the platform orchestrator. For instance, Netflix integrates usage data from different content items (i.e., modules) on the platform for continuous learning and service improvement (Verganti et al., 2020). In such cases, even if the module providers (in Netflix's case, content providers) create those modules, the data flowing from their use are owned by the platform owner (Netflix). The modular platform structure and related complementarities can be characterized as "supermodularity" (Jacobides et al., 2018); on that basis, we refer to data complementarities in platform ecosystem contexts as "supermodular" data complementarities. Here, providers of complements (e.g., content, applications, products) control their own economic production, promoting significant innovation at the periphery, even if the data flow toward the core.

The centralized platform model produces data complementarities within the boundaries of a platform ecosystem and under the control of the platform orchestrator. The platform orchestrator collects and governs a "data lake," takes ownership of user data, and supplies platform participants with complementarities in the form of same- or cross-side network effects, creating additional value by constant improvement of platform offerings through data network effects (Gregory et al., 2021a). The key benefit of this model is its scalability; through efficient matching of supply and demand and curation of user interactions, a platform can potentially create a virtuous cycle of increasing network effects and user value on all sides of a multi-sided market (Cennamo, 2021). In a centralized model, then, data complementarities rely heavily on the platform orchestrator's ability to collect, combine, and productize data from different platform actors to increase user value for different stakeholders, ultimately capturing value for the platform owner while at the same time incentivizing complementors to remain on the platform (Clough & Wu, 2022). The online advertising market is a good example of how data are used to create and capture value in a platform ecosystem. Customer data are collected by the platform owner from different sources (e.g., users of Google search) and bundled together for sale to organizations that can enhance ad targeting. In such cases, the platform owner collects data using the "many-to-one" model before reselling those data to advertisers using the "one-to-many" model (Koutroumpis et al., 2020).

In addition to the challenges discussed above for internal and relational data complementarities, the platform model involves data collection on a massive scale and at arm's length, requiring strategic deployment of various legal and technical boundary resources (Karhu et al., 2018). To control for data usage and ownership, platforms must make careful choices regarding the openness of their governance model (Cennamo, 2021; Karhu & Ritala, 2021; Thomas et al., 2014). From a societal perspective, platforms' massive data use may also create power asymmetries (Cutolo and Kenney, 2021) or, in the worst case, surveillance capitalism (Zuboff, 2019). Giga platforms like Amazon, Google, and Facebook have essentially become "data monopolies" that policy makers struggle to deal with.

## Unbounded Data Complementarities in Data Markets

In data markets, participants exchange data resources on the open market for compensation (see, for example, Koutroumpis et al., 2020) or free of charge in the case of open data (Kitchin, 2014). In the former case, data are bought and sold by firms that can see value in a given set of data—for example, consulting and research firms selling customer preference data and user profiles for a particular industry. In the latter case, the data become a public good and fully realize their potential as a nonrival resource (Jones & Tonetti, 2020) providing potential use cases for any aspiring user of such data. For instance, open data is increasingly provided by public actors and aggregated in projects, such as OpenStreetMap,[2] and various open bioinformatic databases, such as EMBL-EBI.[3]

In the data markets described above, firms can capture "unbounded" data complementarities. By "unbounded" we mean wide-ranging complementarities that can be achieved through open market exchange, which are not typically planned, designed, or restricted beforehand by the data providers, and where use cases are not often or necessarily known *ex ante*. Instead, data complementarities are defined and realized case by case after data have been transacted (in the case of for-profit data markets) or acquired (in the case of open data markets).

However, aggregating third-party data incurs the cost of adaptation and ensuring quality for the new context. For that reason, data governance and quality become an issue in the (open) market model and require some means of data curation (see, for example, Cavanillas et al., 2016). To avoid or automate this process, unbounded data complementarities in data markets are facilitated by homogenization of data resources and standardization of data-sharing interfaces (see, for example, Kovacs et al., 2016). Another challenge is that sellers may not truthfully reveal the origin and overall quality of the data, and buyers may disregard the terms for use, so degrading the data's value (Koutroumpis et al., 2020).

For the above reasons, Koutroumpis et al. (2020, p. 654) noted that "no 'eBay for data' has emerged" other than the dark web's illegal data markets for credit card information and the like. However, this environment is changing rapidly; among notable recent developments, Amazon AWS has launched a data exchange that "makes it easy to find, subscribe to, and use third-party data in the cloud."[4] As of the end of 2021, this market was offering thousands of data products from hundreds of providers. As another example, the European startup Datarade[5] offers commercial data from 2,000-plus providers in 300-plus categories. In addition to these emerging commercial data markets, there are established open data markets based on cities, such as Helsinki Region Infoshare (Jaakola et al., 2015) and London Datastore, with close to 1,000 data sets in each. Finally, bioinformatics is a leader in the utilization of open data; for example, EMBL-EBI has a massive 390 petabytes of data and an estimated use value of £5.5 billion per annum (Cantelli et al., 2021), illustrating the massive value potential of unbounded data complementarities in open market settings.

At government level, as part of the European strategy for data, the EU is aiming to create a digital single market for data, including common European data spaces for health, agriculture, and finance. The ultimate goal is to make more data available for use in the economy while allowing the companies and individuals who generate the data to retain control. Various communities and collectives are also working to standardize broadly shared governance principles and technological infrastructures for data transactions and sharing in true many-to-many fashion. These include the MyData.Org[6] movement, the International Data Spaces Association,[7] and the Gaia-X project.[8] All of these projects and communities aspire to resolve the challenges of data privacy and ownership and to develop mechanisms that will enable data owners to capture value while facilitating wider data dissemination.

## 4. AN ILLUSTRATION: DATA COMPLEMENTARITIES IN THE HEALTH CARE SECTOR

An aging population will increase health care demand and organizing costs, posing a major future challenge for the public sector. One way of making services more effective and efficient is to improve how healthcare data are used. The following examples of the four types of data complementarity in this sector serve to illustrate the utility of our multi-level framework.

Increased data sharing is expected to be a key feature of future health care provision, both for private sector providers and for public–private collaboration (see, for example, Casey et al., 2016; Tortorella et al., 2021). Collaboration will require data sharing across intra- and inter-organizational silos and boundaries. This affords significant opportunities but is also likely to highlight significant barriers in ensuring data security, privacy, and interoperability. At present, regulatory barriers in the health care sector limit the potential for unlocking complementary value from the available data; for example, health care data can generally be analyzed only for the purpose for which they were originally collected. The examples presented here portray the potential of data sharing in the health care sector, especially in relation to data complementarities.

Health care is a particularly appropriate context in which to analyze data complementarities. We, human beings, the objects of health care services, are biochemical organisms, in which all distinct organisms are often dependent from each other, providing a natural source for complementarities (i.e., rather than treating individual health one aspect at a time, healthcare benefits from understanding the whole biochemical system). In bioinformatics, a biochemical pathway is an example of a data object—a digital twin of a human being—to which we can attach measurement data in much the same way as sensor data are attached to a machine's digital twin. Figure 15.1 shows one small part of such a pathway, illustrating the potential of data complementarities for health solutions related to sensory perception.

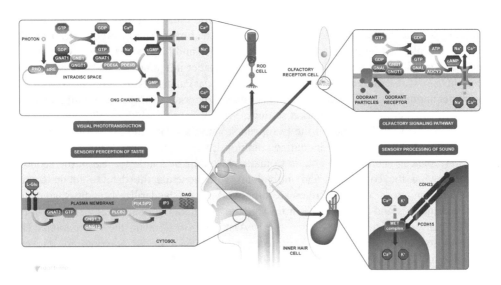

*Source:* "Sensory Perception" by Reactome is licensed under CC BY 4.0: https://reactome.org/content/detail/R-HSA-9709957.

*Figure 15.1   Biochemical pathway for sensory perception as an example of data complementarity*

Regarding internal data complementarities, public and private sector health care providers typically offer distinct health care services involving highly specialized healthcare professionals (e.g., gastroenterologists, endocrinologists). Individual health care records and the service history of earlier visits are often useful when deciding how to treat the patient's current condition. However, while specialized healthcare is important and often effective, many diseases benefit from a more holistic approach, and the various treatments offered by different units can benefit from data sharing within the organization to produce additional complementary value and support more patient-centric models of care. Another source of internal data complementarities in health care is the use of relevant data in distinct but complementary contexts. For example, as social problems and health issues are often interlinked, social care data (e.g., employment services) and other types of social data (e.g., social media) can complement health care data (Spagnoletti et al., 2015).

In the private sector, one example of relational data complementarity is how pharmaceutical companies collaborate during drug development. Different companies specialize in specific development phases or specific technologies, and they gain more value by collaborating with others in selected areas than by trying to do everything in-house. One recent and timely example is the development of COVID-19 vaccines, where highly specialized small firms like BioNtech collaborated with more established firms like Pfizer to produce vaccines in super-fast time through in-depth data sharing.

Public–private partnership has been offered as one solution to address the public sector sustainability gap in the health care sector. In such a setting, the overall treatment of a patient consists of various services offered by public and distinct private sector organizations. To unleash data complementarities in this context, there must be a means of sharing data across organizations. In Finland, for example, a centralized national health care data repository and platform called My Kanta[9] enables data sharing between public and private sector actors, including pharmacies, private health clinics, and occupational health care providers. This shared data resource allows patients to make flexible use of public and private health providers without any need for cross-consultation or repeated blood samples or doctor visits. This may ultimately lead to a platform market based on an open multi-sided platform model with supermodular data complementarities, where private and public sector providers could offer complementary services.

Another example of supermodular data complementarities in the health care sector is the various health tracking solutions and smart watches offered by companies, such as Apple and Suunto, or other wearable devices, such as the Oura Ring. These devices enable users to collect health data and track their outdoor activities; users benefit from sharing this data with their peers, and platform owners can collect massive amounts of data that can be used to improve their devices' accuracy—for example, how well the Oura ring measures sleep quality. Sometimes, completely new and unexpected features emerge from data collection, such as the ability to recognize the early signs of COVID-19 from body temperature data.[10] Furthermore, providers of smart watches can enable third-party complementors to develop applications based on, for example, heart rate and training regime data.

An example of unbounded data complementarities in the health care sector are various bioinformatic platforms, such as the EMBL-EBI and Reactome pathway knowledge base mentioned above (Croft et al., 2014). Reactome data, which consist of hundreds of thousands of proteins, complexes, and reactions between them forming more than 20,000 biochemical pathways, are annotated and curated in decentralized fashion, and the open license makes them freely available for anyone to use for any purpose. To illustrate the potential for data complementarities in this data market context, consider again the example (Figure 15.1) of pathways for human sensory perception, which demonstrates how data from one sensory system can complement data from another. For instance, if one lab conducts experiments on visual phototransduction (top left, Figure 15.1) and another focuses on sound processing (bottom right,

Figure 15.1), the two labs can unleash complementarities from their data by referring to the Reactome database to identify reactions connecting these pathways.

## 5.    CONCLUSION

In this chapter, we have described a multi-level framework for capturing value from data complementarities. For managers and firms involved in developing and implementing digital strategies, the relevance of data complementarities is clear. As firms collect ever more data from customers, processes, and the ubiquitous sensors now embedded in machines and products, developing the requisite capabilities to aggregate, compile, and make sense of those data should be a key priority. As well as showing how firms can reap data complementarities internally, we have demonstrated the importance of data acquisition across organizational boundaries. The key decision is no longer whether to collect data but how and from where, and how to put it to productive use. We believe our chapter offers a useful point of departure for conducting such decisions.

The chapter also serves as a point of departure for future research. Conceptualizing data complementarities as the added value creation potential of combining different data sets into actionable and meaningful goods, objects, and artifacts, we argue that data complementarity is a scale-free concept that spans a continuum ranging from the intra-firm hierarchy to the open data market. As data complementarities have previously been examined mainly in platform contexts (Alaimo et al., 2020), we sought to extend the concept to different levels of analysis, arguing that data complementarities differ qualitatively at different levels and present different opportunities and challenges. Accordingly, we elaborated a multi-level model for capturing value from four types of data complementarity: internal (hierarchy), relational (bilateral contractual relationship), supermodular (platform ecosystem), and unbounded (data market).

In the intra-firm context, data complementarities begin to accumulate when different organizational data sets (e.g., sales, manufacturing) are combined. Based on the logic of the resource-based view (Schmidt & Keil, 2013), this complementarity refers to the higher returns that accrue when one resource is combined with another. The idiosyncratic combinations created by these resource bundles in turn form the basis for firm differentiation (Alexy et al., 2018). These resources include organization-specific data sets and, in particular, the organization's capacity to interpret, analyze, and learn from those data (Gregory et al., 2021a).

In inter-organizational settings, combining data sets across different silos and boundaries can provide data complementarities unique to a particular supply chain or a network, as in the case of logistics optimization, for example. However, relational data complementarities in bilateral relationships or broader contractual networks remain rare because of the competitive, technical, and legal challenges associated with data exchange across organizational boundaries.

We also showed how platform ecosystems as a form of organizing (Kretschmer et al., 2020) resolve many of the challenges restricting the realization of data complementarities in contractual relationships and networks. In this context, data complementarities can be scaled up significantly if different data sources are effectively collected and curated, as in the case of TripAdvisor, for example (Alaimo et al., 2020). Platforms based on centralized governance models provide a clear framework for data ownership (often to the benefit of the platform owner) and facilitate value creation for platform users and complementors, resulting optimally in a virtuous growth cycle.

Finally, we demonstrated how for-profit and open data markets afford opportunities for unbounded data complementarities. While data markets involving true market-based exchange remain nascent (see Koutroumpis et al., 2020), we note a number of emergent frameworks and initiatives that show potential for more extensive and broader-based data sale and exchange. Importantly, in open data markets, data providers do not typically restrict how data are used, so creating the conditions for truly nonrival value creation (Jones & Tonetti, 2020).

We also explained how firms can capture value from data. At the most basic level, firms can profit from collecting and analyzing data (such as customer data) and deploying appropriate analytics (Gregory et al., 2021a) to enhance their ability to capture value (Clough & Wu, 2022). That improved ability is reflected in better targeting of customer advertising or profit maximization by selecting the optimal revenue model (Huotari & Ritala, 2021). Given the nonrival nature of data (Jones & Tonetti, 2020), value capture is likely to improve significantly when data are shared and combined across organizational boundaries. However, in these broader contexts, new challenges also emerge, which we have elaborated throughout this chapter (see Table 15.1). Inter-organizational bilateral relationships often involve contractual and competitive challenges, leading to underutilization of data complementarities and fewer opportunities for value capture. While centralized platform markets are one well-known solution, setting up a platform necessarily involves other governance challenges (Cennamo, 2021). Furthermore, while data markets ideally lead to wide-ranging or unbounded data complementarities, the challenge is to ensure value capture for both providers and acquirers of those data.

Future research should further investigate the interplay between data complementarities and value capture. Wide-ranging data complementarities have significant potential for value creation and capture, but this may be hindered by technical difficulties, competitive concerns (Jones & Tonetti, 2020), or customer data privacy issues. How data complementarities are created and organized and who captures that value are topics that remain underexplored. Additionally, while we have outlined four archetypal organizational contexts for data complementarities, future research should further explore the potential of different data markets (Koutroumpis et al., 2020) and of both centralized and decentralized platform models (e.g., Vergne, 2020).

## NOTES

1. https://gdprinfo.eu/.
2. https://www.openstreetmap.org/.
3. https://www.ebi.ac.uk/.
4. https://aws.amazon.com/data-exchange/resources/.
5. https://datarade.ai/.
6. https://mydata.org/.
7. https://internationaldataspaces.org/.
8. https://www.data-infrastructure.eu/GAIAX/Navigation/EN/Home/home.html.
9. https://www.kanta.fi/en/my-kanta-pages.
10. https://ouraring.com/blog/early-covid-symptoms/.

## REFERENCES

Adegbesan, J.A. (2009). On the origins of competitive advantage: Strategic factor markets and heterogeneous resource complementarity. *Academy of Management Review*, *34*(3), 463–75.

Alaimo, C., & Kallinikos, J. (2021). Organizations decentered: Data objects, technology and knowledge. *Organization Science*, *33*(1), 19–37. https://doi.org/10.1287/orsc.2021.1552.

Alaimo, C., Kallinikos, J., & Aaltonen, A. (2020). Data and value. In Nambisan, S., Lyttinen, K., & Yoo, Y. (Eds), *Handbook of Digital Innovation*. Cheltenham, UK and Northampton, MA, USA: Edward Elgar Publishing, 162–78.

Alexy, O., West, J., Klapper, H., & Reitzig, M. (2018). Surrendering control to gain advantage: Reconciling openness and the resource-based view of the firm. *Strategic Management Journal*, *39*(6), 1704–27.

Biggemann, S. (2012). The essential role of information sharing in relationship development. *Journal of Business and Industrial Marketing*, *27*(7), 521–6.

Brynjolfsson, E., & McElheran, K. (2016). The rapid adoption of data-driven decision-making. *American Economic Review*, *106*(5), 133–39.

Bundred, S. (2006). Solutions to silos: Joining up knowledge. *Public Money and Management*, *26*(2), 125–30.

Cantelli, G., Bateman, A., Brooksbank, C., Petrov, A.I., Malik-Sheriff, R.S., Ide-Smith, M., Hermjakob, H., Flicek, P., Apweiler, R., Birney, E., McEntyre, J. (2021). The European Bioinformatics Institute (EMBL-EBI) in 2021. *Nucleic Acids Research*, *50*(D1), D11–D19.

Casey, C., Li, J., & Berry, M. (2016). Interorganizational collaboration in public health data sharing. *Journal of Health Organization and Management*, *30*(6), 855–71.

Cavanillas, J.M., Curry, E., & Wahlster, W. (Eds) (2016). *New Horizons for a Data-Driven Economy*. Cham: Springer International.

Cennamo, C. (2021). Competing in digital markets: A platform-based perspective. *Academy of Management Perspectives*, *35*(2), 265–91.

Cho, M., & Jun, B.H. (2013). Information sharing with competition. *Economics Letters*, *119*(1), 81–4.

Ciccullo, F., Cagliano, R., Bartezzaghi, G., & Perego, A. (2021). Implementing the circular economy paradigm in the agri-food supply chain: The role of food waste prevention technologies. *Resources, Conservation and Recycling*, *164*, 105114.

Clough, D.R., & Wu, A. (2022). Artificial intelligence, data-driven learning, and the decentralized structure of platform ecosystems. *Academy of Management Review*, *47*(1) 184–9.

Croft, D., Mundo, A.F., Haw, R., Milacic, M., Weiser, J., Wu, G., … & D'Eustachio, P. (2014). The Reactome pathway knowledgebase. *Nucleic Acids Research*, *42*(D1), D472–D477.

Cutolo, D., & Kenney, M. (2021). Platform-dependent entrepreneurs: Power asymmetries, risks, and strategies in the platform economy. *Academy of Management Perspectives*, *35*, 584–605.

De Mauro, A., Greco, M., Grimaldi, M., & Ritala, P. (2018). Human resources for big data professions: A systematic classification of job roles and required skill sets. *Information Processing & Management*, *54*(5), 807–17.

Dyer, J.H., & Singh, H. (1998). The relational view: Cooperative strategy and sources of interorganizational competitive advantage. *Academy of Management Review*, *23*(4), 660–79.

Erevelles, S., Fukawa, N., & Swayne, L. (2016). Big data consumer analytics and the transformation of marketing. *Journal of Business Research*, *69*(2), 897–904.

Ghoshal, A., Kumar, S., & Mookerjee, V. (2020). Dilemma of data sharing alliance: When do competing personalizing and non-personalizing firms share data. *Production and Operations Management*, *29*(8), 1918–36.

Grant, R.M. (1996). Toward a knowledge-based theory of the firm. *Strategic Management Journal*, *17*(S2), 109–22.

Gregory, R.W., Henfridsson, O., Kaganer, E., & Kyriakou, H. (2021a). The role of artificial intelligence and data network effects for creating user value. *Academy of Management Review*, *46*(3), 534–51.

Gregory, R.W., Henfridsson, O., Kaganer, E., & Kyriakou, H. (2021b). Data network effects: Key conditions, shared data, and the data value duality. *Academy of Management Review*, https://doi.org/10.5465/amr.2021.0111.

Gupta, M., & George, J.F. (2016). Toward the development of a big data analytics capability. *Information & Management*, *53*(8), 1049–64.

Harrison, J.S., Hitt, M.A., Hoskisson, R.E., & Ireland, R.D. (2001). Resource complementarity in business combinations: Extending the logic to organizational alliances. *Journal of Management*, *27*(6), 679–90.

Huotari, P., & Ritala, P. (2021). When to switch between subscription-based and ad-sponsored business models: Strategic implications of decreasing content novelty. *Journal of Business Research*, *129*, 14–28.

Jaakola, A., Kekkonen, H., Lahti, T., & Manninen, A. (2015). Open data, open cities: Experiences from the Helsinki Metropolitan Area. Case Helsinki Region Infoshare www.hri.fi. *Statistical Journal of the IAOS*, *31*, 117–22.

Jacobides, M.G., Cennamo, C., & Gawer, A. (2018). Towards a theory of ecosystems. *Strategic Management Journal*, *39*, 2255–76.

Jones, C.I., & Tonetti, C. (2020). Nonrivalry and the economics of data. *American Economic Review*, *110*(9), 2819–58.

Kallinikos, J., Aaltonen, A., & Marton, A. (2013). The ambivalent ontology of digital artifacts. *MIS Quarterly*, *37*(2), 357–70.

Karhu, K., Gustafsson, R., Lyytinen, K. (2018). Exploiting and defending open digital platforms with boundary resources: Android's five platform forks. *Information Systems Research*, *29*, 479–97.

Karhu, K., & Ritala, P. (2021). Slicing the cake without baking it: Opportunistic platform entry strategies in digital markets. *Long Range Planning*, *54*(5), 101988.

Kitchin, R. (2014). *The Data Revolution: Big Data, Open Data, Data Infrastructures and Their Consequences*. Los Angeles, CA: SAGE.

Kogut, B., & Zander, U. (1992). Knowledge of the firm, combinative capabilities, and the replication of technology. *Organization Science*, *3*(3), 383–97.

Koutroumpis, P., Leiponen, A., & Thomas, L.D. (2020). Markets for data. *Industrial and Corporate Change*, *29*(3), 645–60.

Kovacs, E., Bauer, M., Kim, J., Yun, J., Le Gall, F., & Zhao, M. (2016). Standards-based worldwide semantic interoperability for IoT. *IEEE Communications Magazine*, *54*(12), 40–46.

Kretschmer, T., Leiponen, A., Schilling, M., & Vasudeva, G. (2020). Platform ecosystems as meta-organizations: Implications for platform strategies. *Strategic Management Journal*, *43*(3), 405–24. https://doi.org/10.1002/smj.3250.

Lavie, D. (2006). The competitive advantage of interconnected firms: An extension of the resource-based view. *Academy of Management Review*, *31*(3), 638–58.

Leonard, P. (2014). Customer data analytics: Privacy settings for "Big Data" business. *International Data Privacy Law*, *4*(1), 53–68.

Mikalef, P., Boura, M., Lekakos, G., & Krogstie, J. (2019). Big data analytics capabilities and innovation: The mediating role of dynamic capabilities and moderating effect of the environment. *British Journal of Management*, *30*(2), 272–98.

Porter, M.E., & Heppelmann, J.E. (2014). How smart, connected products are transforming competition. *Harvard Business Review*, *92*(11), 64–88.

Schildt, H. (2020). *The Data Imperative: How Digitalization Is Reshaping Management, Organizing, and Work*. Oxford: Oxford University Press.

Schmidt, J., & Keil, T. (2013). What makes a resource valuable? Identifying the drivers of firm-idiosyncratic resource value. *Academy of Management Review*, *38*(2), 206–28.

Shaw, D.R., Grainger, A., & Achuthan, K. (2017). Multi-level port resilience planning in the UK: How can information sharing be made easier? *Technological Forecasting and Social Change*, *121*, 126–38.

Shipilov, A., & Gawer, A. (2020). Integrating research on interorganizational networks and ecosystems. *Academy of Management Annals*, *14*(1), 92–121.

Spagnoletti, P., Resca, A., & Sæbø, Ø. 2015. Design for social media engagement: Insights from elderly care assistance. *Journal of Strategic Information Systems*, *24*(2), 128–45.

Thomas, L.D., Autio, E., & Gann, D.M. (2014). Architectural leverage: Putting platforms in context. *Academy of Management Perspectives*, *28*(2), 198–219.

Thomas, L.D., & Ritala, P. (2021). Ecosystem legitimacy emergence: A collective action view. *Journal of Management*. https://doi.org/10.1177/0149206320986617.

Thomas, L.D., & Tee, R. (2021). Generativity: A systematic review and conceptual framework. *International Journal of Management Reviews*. https://doi.org/10.1111/ijmr.12277.

Tortorella, G.L., Saurin, T.A., Fogliatto, F.S., Rosa, V.M., Tonetto, L.M., & Magrabi, F. (2021). Impacts of Healthcare 4.0 digital technologies on the resilience of hospitals. *Technological Forecasting and Social Change, 166*, 120666.

Verganti, R., Vendraminelli, L., & Iansiti, M. (2020). Innovation and design in the age of artificial intelligence. *Journal of Product Innovation Management, 37*(3), 212–27.

Vergne, J.P. (2020). Decentralized vs. distributed organization: Blockchain, machine learning and the future of the digital platform. *Organization Theory, 1*(4), 2631787720977052.

Williamson, O.E. (1985). *The Economic Institutions of Capitalism: Firms, Markets, Relational Contracting*. New York, NY: Free Press.

Yan, R., & Wang, K.Y. (2012). Franchisor–franchisee supply chain cooperation: Sharing of demand forecast information in high-tech industries. *Industrial Marketing Management, 41*(7), 1164–73.

Yoo, Y., Henfridsson, O., & Lyytinen, K. (2010). Research commentary: The new organizing logic of digital innovation – An agenda for information systems research. *Information Systems Research, 21*(4), 724–35.

Zuboff, S. (2019). *The Age of Surveillance Capitalism: The Fight for a Human Future at the New Frontier of Power*. London: Profile Books.

# 16. Data control coordination in cloud-based ecosystems: the EU GAIA-X ecosystem

*Niloofar Kazemargi, Paolo Spagnoletti, Panos Constantinides and Andrea Prencipe*

## 1.  INTRODUCTION

As a key enabler of digital transformation in many industrial sectors (Vial, 2019), organizations are increasingly adopting cloud services to access resources that would otherwise be prohibitively expensive to develop in-house (Marston et al., 2011; Mell & Grance, 2011). Cloud computing enables on-demand access to shared digital resources and capabilities (e.g., software applications, platforms and infrastructures). It eliminates costly in-house IT investments and lengthy installation (Mell & Grance, 2011) and enhances organizational agility through the rapid deployment, scalability and accessibility of cloud services (Marston et al., 2011).

A "cloud-based ecosystem" is a set of organizations involved in dynamic collaborations enabled by data access, storage and processing activities distributed across multiple software applications, platforms and infrastructures. Cloud-based ecosystems are structured as a set of complex relationships and data distributed among different actors. For example, in the financial sector, banks have recently adopted various collaboration models that can be combined with the existing IT infrastructures of banks to offer new financial services. There are multiple actors within these cloud-based ecosystems, including incumbent or challenger banks (e.g., HSBC vs Monzo), which stand as customers; cloud service providers (CSPs) (e.g., Amazon, Alphabet, Microsoft), which develop, control and govern cloud services; public authorities that regulate and supervise banking activities; and third parties that support the activities of other actors either through training or providing technology and knowledge (Basole & Park, 2018).

In such cloud-based ecosystems, however, there are legal, privacy and security concerns (Khan et al. 2019). Cloud resources are owned, provided, maintained and controlled by CSPs in collaboration with third parties, which are outside the client firm's organizational boundaries. This means that client firms have little control over the access, storage and processing of data in the cloud with negative implications for value co-creation opportunities. Schneier (2013, p. 2) identifies data control as a key issue in cloud-based systems: "[Some cloud providers] give our data to the government without notice, consent, or a warrant; almost all sell it for profit," because "companies … act in their own self-interest and not in their users' best interest." Considering cloud users, data owners, service providers and government and regulatory bodies perspectives all together, data control is even more difficult to achieve in cloud-based ecosystems in which paradoxical tensions characterize different and sometimes conflicting expectations of ecosystem actors (Constantinides et al., 2018; Tilson et al., 2010). We define "data control" as the control over the data access, storage and processing activities of different actors in relation to the digital strategies of each actor.

Despite a proliferation of research on platform ecosystems (e.g., Adner, 2017; Jacobides et al., 2018), few studies have specifically examined the role of data control in value co-creation. Data control has been traditionally intended as a means to protect data assets from privacy and security violations within organizational boundaries (Lowry et al., 2017). While organizations increasingly rely on distributed data to create value, they need to address the tension between sharing and protecting data (Anderson et al., 2017). Similarly, in cloud-based ecosystems, where the value creation logic has shifted from a closed vertically integrated model to multisided platforms, data protection must be balanced with data sharing needs. Though data sharing exposes sensitive data to external parties, it also offers opportunities for value capture by reducing distribution, transaction and search costs and enables innovation through cross-boundary collaboration (Nambisan et al., 2017; Pagani, 2013; Vial, 2019). Therefore, when successfully orchestrated, data control activities offer heterogeneous actors the possibility to exploit the innovation potential of their complementary digital resources and capabilities.

In this chapter, we focus on the formative stage of cloud-based ecosystems to examine how actors coordinate data control activities to co-create value. We develop a conceptual model of data control coordination in cloud-based ecosystems by drawing on an expository instantiation of the formation of the European Union (EU) GAIA-X ecosystem. Our model shows that cloud-based ecosystems entail control bottlenecks: uncoordinated data control constrains value creation. To resolve data control bottlenecks, thus, coordination among actors across a cloud-based ecosystem is needed and multilateral agreements on data control must be established *before* engaging in innovative activities that lead to value co-creation. Data control coordination is a precursor to generating complementarities between ecosystem actors. We illustrate how data control contributes to achieve alignment over the ecosystem for it to start operating, overcoming bottlenecks and unleashing value opportunities from complementarities. We conclude by discussing key implications for further research on digital strategy in cloud-based ecosystems.

## 2.    VALUE CO-CREATION IN CLOUD-BASED ECOSYSTEMS

In business ecosystems, value is co-created by actors that share their resources and capabilities to achieve a common goal (Jacobides et al., 2018). Ecosystem actors are autonomous organizations that rely on other actors who are specialized in the development and production of complementary resources and capabilities (Adner, 2017). Actors co-specialize their resources and capabilities to build complementarities in the ecosystem and co-create value across industries and organizational boundaries (Lusch & Nambisan, 2015). However, the formation of ecosystems frequently spawns bottlenecks that require coordination to enable value creation.

Bottlenecks are constraints on the emergence or growth of an ecosystem and can arise due to different (often conflicting) interests and expectations on the resources and capabilities to be exchanged and co-specialized. Research suggests that controlling the bottlenecks often leads to the successful strategic positioning of firms within an ecosystem (Baldwin, 2014; Hannah & Eisenhardt, 2018; Kapoor, 2018). Unless these bottlenecks are resolved, there are issues in both value creation and value capture. The bottlenecks constrain value co-creation within the ecosystem and also hamper value capture since value is captured primarily by actors in control of bottlenecks. Bottlenecks can be resolved by aligning the incentives for producing complementary services (Masucci et al., 2020). The coordination efforts made by ecosystem actors in aligning their interests and expectations lead to the establishment of mutual agreements that remove bottlenecks, resulting in the enhanced performance and orderly growth of the ecosystem (Adner, 2017).

We consider a "cloud-based ecosystem" as a special type of ecosystem in which a set of organizations gather, store and process data on a cloud infrastructure to co-create value. Cloud services are fundamental in supporting digital strategies through various sourcing models such as software-as-a-service (SaaS), platform-as-a-service (PaaS) and infrastructure-as-a-service (IaaS) (Marston et al., 2011; Mell & Grance, 2011). Such models enable on-demand access to shared digital resources that substantially extend the scale and speed of business strategies for cloud service users (Bharadwaj et al. 2013). Moreover, cloud services expand the scope of digital business strategies involving third parties in the exchange of digital resources and capabilities (Bharadwaj et al., 2013; Rai et al., 2012).

In cloud-based ecosystems, value co-creation is based on multisided and multilayered business models and requires complex and dynamic coordination both within and across ecosystem actors. First, focal firms need standardized processes, centralization and control to facilitate integration and attain global efficiency (Sklyar et al., 2019). Cloud services enable such integration by providing access to back-end resources and capabilities that are seldom available locally because of the considerable investments needed. Second, across firm boundaries, cloud services require the precise alignment of business models to redesign value creation, value delivery and value capture processes. For instance, coordination is needed to ensure that technology solutions successfully interact with product–service–software systems of other companies (Kohtamäki et al., 2019) through cloud services. Third, cloud technologies and infrastructures also facilitate business model experimentation and horizontal knowledge spill-overs. Ecosystem actors engage in bottom-up initiatives and sensemaking to understand specific ecosystem dynamics and repair bottlenecks. For instance, a cloud service provider can allow a rival platform's user to interact with its own platform as part of either a competitive or collaborative strategy (Eisenmann et al., 2009; Ondrus et al., 2015). Therefore, a closer look at how digital resources and capabilities are integrated in cloud-based ecosystems can offer insights on value co-creation (Lusch & Nambisan, 2015).

## 3. DATA CONTROL IN CLOUD-BASED ECOSYSTEMS

As data are increasingly becoming key resources for digital strategy implementation, retaining control over data among ecosystem actors becomes a major organizational concern. Data access, storage and processing (e.g., analytics, visualization, encryption, transmission) are the key activities of cloud-based ecosystems, all of which lead to value co-creation when successfully performed and orchestrated among ecosystem actors (Nambisan et al., 2017). Organizations can, in fact, benefit from the enhanced data storage and processing capabilities offered by specialized CSPs to rapidly innovate their services and scale up business. However, the distributed nature of data storage and processing activities in cloud-based ecosystems creates interdependencies among multiple actors and raises issues of availability, data integrity, quality, heterogeneity, privacy and governance. These issues require coordination among actors with different interests, preferences and expectations (De Bruijn & Janssen, 2017; Tilson et al., 2010; Vial, 2019).

By "data control" we mean the control over the data access, storage and processing activities of different actors in relation to their digital strategies. Data control plays a dual role in cloud-based ecosystems. On one side, data are objects of control since each actor must protect data assets from threats to their privacy, intellectual property and security (Ahmad et al., 2021; Spiekermann et al., 2015). In other words, each actor not only needs to address their digital strategy, but also enact and exert control over data to protect data assets (Anderson et al. 2017). On the other side, data are also a means to exert control over other actors, such as when data-driven decision-making supports cyber security operations (Baskerville et al., 2014; Lodi et al., 2014). In cloud-based ecosystems, a single organization does not have full data control, since data storage and processing are distributed to actors outside a firm's boundaries (Paquette et al., 2010; Subashini & Kavitha, 2011).

What renders the relationships among actors even more complex is the partial control over data in a cloud-based ecosystem; each actor manages and controls data based on the adopted cloud service models. For instance, a cloud service provider may, for efficiency reasons, outsource some data storage or data processing capabilities to third parties which contribute to value co-creation in the ecosystem (Basole & Park, 2018; Pagani, 2013; Sandberg et al., 2020). Furthermore, the way an actor processes and exchanges data might not be aligned with other actors and can cause conflicting situations. The actions and decisions of one actor can be in favor of its own interests, while they can be seen as policy violations by other actors (Vial, 2019). Any data breach can cause negative consequences not only for ecosystem actors – in terms of financial losses, interruptions in business continuity or damage to organizational reputation – but also for the beneficiaries of ecosystem services (Kallinikos et al., 2013; Newell & Marabelli, 2015; Vial, 2019). Therefore, the mismatched conditions on data control, underlying data storage and processing in cloud-based ecosystems, introduce bottlenecks that may hamper the ecosystem formation. When such bottlenecks are successfully resolved, data control complementarities can be leveraged by ecosystem actors to co-create value.

In the following sections, we illustrate the concepts of control bottlenecks, data control coordination and data control complementarities in the context of GAIA-X, a collaborative project aimed at creating a federated, cloud-based ecosystem in Europe.

## 4.    METHOD AND CASE DESCRIPTION

We chose GAIA-X as an illustrative case (Yin, 2009) to discuss data control in cloud-based ecosystems. GAIA-X is a collaborative initiative between European companies to create and develop a federated, cloud-based ecosystem in Europe. So far, GAIA-X involves more than 400 European and non-European organizations. As a European initiative, GAIA-X involves a diverse set of actors such as governments, CSPs, businesses and academia to develop shared requirements for data infrastructure. The mission of the project is to define and implement common standards for managing data in cloud-based ecosystems through a federated data infrastructure. Such data infrastructure needs to fulfill data control requirements and at the same time encourage innovation. This reflects the European view on the importance and the role of data in the digital economy.[1] By ensuring that data are accessed, stored and exchanged in compliance with shared requirements, GAIA-X promises to set up new opportunities for digital strategies and value creation. The GAIA-X project is organized around 10 different domains: agriculture, energy, finance, geoinformation, health, industry 4.0, mobility, public sector, smart cities and smart living. Within each domain, several use cases were developed to illustrate usage scenarios for such federated cloud-based infrastructures and services.

To explore the role of data control and how it can be coordinated to co-create value, we first collected secondary data such as press releases, reports and use cases (for sources of evidence, see the Appendix). To gain better insights, we conducted formal interviews and had informal conversations with officers at the GAIA-X association, including service providers and cloud users. In addition, we attended seminars and meetings related to the GAIA-X project. Notes were taken during all these interviews and events that were transcribed, coded and analyzed using the NVivo software package. We first identified order codes, then aggregated codes into second-order themes and finally aggregated theoretical categories (Gioia et al., 2013).

## 5.  AN ILLUSTRATIVE CASE: DATA CONTROL COORDINATION IN GAIA-X

In this section, we discuss how this ecosystem is forming through three phases: namely, identifying control bottlenecks, achieving mutual agreements and coordinating data control, and finally developing data control complementarities.

### 5.1  Identifying Control Bottlenecks

In creating value from data there are bottlenecks which constrain the emergence and growth of digital ecosystems (Adner, 2012; Baldwin, 2014). Ecosystem actors involved in GAIA-X have identified several bottlenecks (see Table 16.1) that we summarize here.

A major bottleneck faced by GAIA-X is the legal compliance of CSPs in accessing, storing and processing data. Here we find two main challenges to the compliance of data control activities with rules and regulations issued by regulators and public bodies. A first challenge is the cross-sector compliance on data control. It is challenging for a data owner (e.g., a public administration organization) to ensure that its CSPs are compliant with sector-specific norms on data control that apply to the cloud service user. In particular, in highly regulated markets such as finance, public administration and healthcare, cloud service users need to ensure that service providers are compliant with sector-specific regulations. For instance, access and exchange of data in the healthcare sector can create serious legal issues between CSPs and public healthcare institutions. The former, in fact, may trade data generated on their cloud infrastructure to pharmaceutical and insurance companies without explicit consent from the recipients of public healthcare services. A second challenge is related to cross-country legal compliance. It is challenging for data owners to ensure that data control activities performed by CSPs in other countries are compliant with regulations that apply to the cloud service users (e.g., GDPR,[2] NIS). For instance, under the NIS Directive,[3] both European cloud service users having critical infrastructure (e.g., energy, banking, health and transport) and their CSPs are obliged to report any "significant" cyber incident to relevant authorities within 72 hours of detection. Such legal concerns are exacerbated by the lack of a comprehensive legal framework on data control. Although over the last few years we have witnessed several regulations and policies evolving and coming into force, ambiguity for interpretation within regulations may lead to noncompliance. For instance, uncertainty with respect to the scope of data portability

*Table 16.1*     *Data control bottlenecks in cloud-based ecosystems*

| Bottlenecks | Description | Examples from GAIA-X |
| --- | --- | --- |
| Cross-sector and cross-country legal compliance on data control | Cloud service users cannot ensure that their CSPs are compliant with sector-specific norms on data control that apply to cloud service users. European cloud service users cannot ensure that their non-European CSPs are compliant with EU regulations on data control (e.g., General Data Protection Regulation, or GDPR, and Network & Information Systems Regulations, or NIS). | • Highly regulated markets: finance, public administration, and healthcare<br>• Critical infrastructure directive (NIS)<br>• Insufficient clarity about the applicable jurisdiction |
| Data sovereignty on access, storage and processing | Lack of transparency and sovereignty over stored and processed data. Lack of complete control over stored and processed data and also the decision on who is permitted to have access to it. | • Data processing to train machine learning algorithms in non-transparent ways<br>• Data centers located in a different country with respect to the cloud service user (decentralized processing locations)<br>• Attribution of cyberattacks |
| Data interoperability | Multiple stakeholders have difficulties in exchanging data and infrastructure services because of an absence of widely accessible interfaces. | • Multiple technology stacks<br>• Data portability issues when data owners want to give access to another cloud service provider (lock-in)<br>• Sector-specific data spaces and lack of ontology |

right under the Article 20 of GDPR is not well defined (Krämer, 2020), which renders legal compliance difficult.

Another bottleneck faced by GAIA-X is sovereignty on data access, storage and processing. "Data sovereignty" refers to "the complete control over stored and processed data and also the independent decision on who is permitted to have access to it."[4] In the European context, few dominant non-European providers (especially American) own and control the key cloud infrastructure and services. In other words, the European service users have a limited control over data in cloud infrastructures and platforms. This is amplified by the lack of transparency on how data generated by European citizens and organizations are stored and processed by service providers. Data processing may enhance the ability of firms to improve the quality of existing services. However, actors may engage in anti-competitive practices that reduce innovation and erode consumer welfare. For instance, some CSPs can obtain a competitive advantage by training machine learning algorithms with datasets enriched with large amounts of customer data and hence improve the quality of services in ways that actors with restricted access to data cannot (Parker et al., 2021). However, this can result in excessive data collection and cost-saving actions that reduce data protection and the quality of services. Another undesired outcome might be self-preferencing when transaction platforms use data generated on their platforms for predicting and manipulating user behaviors in favor of their interests (Crémer et al., 2019). Finally, there is a concern over the physical location of infrastructures (i.e., data centers), especially for sectors with sensitive data such as finance, that may become unavailable for problem resolution outside the control of crisis management institutions linked to the data owners.[5] This can be exacerbated as data are replicated in multiple locations for redundancy purposes and data centers are distributed across geographic boundaries. Such locations might include countries in which there are political conflicts; there is simply no transparency about the physical locations of data and data centers. This may also lead to the problem of attribution that challenges law enforcement agencies when dealing with international cybercrime.

A third bottleneck faced by GAIA-X is "data interoperability." This refers to "the ability of several systems or services to exchange information and to use the exchanged information mutually" (GAIA-X, 2021[6]). Data interoperability problems arise in the absence of widely accessible interfaces. Service providers often use proprietary formats and interfaces through which other organizations access data and applications to develop new services. This hinders the interactions among actors to integrate and use data. For example, interoperability across infrastructures, applications and data is challenged by multiple technology stacks offered and managed by various service providers. This negatively influences value co-creation from data, as each actor relies on others' capabilities and resources at different technology stacks (Basole & Park, 2018). In addition, proprietary interfaces increase the complexity of data exchange from one service provider to another and may lead to lock-in situations. Other examples of interoperability bottlenecks are due to the lack of common data ontologies within and across sectors.

In summary, although cloud-based ecosystems provide opportunities for value co-creation, these opportunities are challenged by control bottlenecks regarding heterogeneous expectations about how other actors access, store and process data.

When bottlenecks are not resolved, data control resources and capabilities are vertically integrated within separate supply chains. In these cases, value is created only through an aggregate of buyer–supplier relations without creating a specific structure of relationships and alignment among actors (Jacobides et al., 2018). This value system constrains value capturing for all the involved stakeholders. Cloud service users are not given the opportunity to choose and recombine their resources and capabilities with other actors. Each cloud service provider competes with other vertically integrated service providers to expand its user base. However, in the absence of collaboration within and across sectors, the market potential of each actor remains limited to its own user base, which often leads to failures in attaining the critical mass of users required to activate the network externalities of a digital platform strategy. For instance, the lack of technology standards, regulation, cooperation with financial institutions and privacy concerns among the consumers are some of the key factors that explain the failure of many attempts to establish successful mobile payment solutions (Ondrus et al., 2015), such as Monero, K-merce and Zoop.

Acknowledging the possibility of collapsing the efforts to isolated hierarchies, GAIA-X aims to establish a set of coordination mechanisms between consumers and providers of cloud services to resolve the data control bottlenecks. Multiple European stakeholders are engaged in the definition of architecture requirements for an array of federated services enabling data-driven innovation (GAIA-X, 2020b[7]). Although ecosystem actors involved in GAIA-X recognize the fundamental role played by CSPs such as Microsoft, Amazon and Google, a key assumption is that value can be generated in the cloud-based ecosystem only if coordination mechanisms that dynamically resolve the issues of data control are in place.

*Table 16.2*       *Data control coordination domains in cloud-based ecosystems*

| Bottleneck | Coordination domains | Examples of coordination mechanisms from GAIA-X |
|---|---|---|
| Cross-sector and cross-country legal compliance on data control | Rules and policies | Rights and Obligations of Participants Onboarding and Certification |
| Data sovereignty on access, storage and processing | Data security | Identity and trust Sovereign data exchange |
| Data interoperability | Service platform | Federated catalogue |

## 5.2    Achieving Mutual Agreements and Coordinating Data Control

We identify three domains of coordination through which ecosystem actors achieve mutual agreements to resolve data control bottlenecks: namely, rules and policies, data security and service platforms. In this section, we illustrate how GAIA-X members aim to resolve each control bottleneck by establishing a set of coordination domains (see Table 16.2).

To resolve the issues of cross-sector and cross-country legal compliance on data control, the GAIA-X members agreed on a set of rules and policies that established the rights and obligations of participants, onboarding and certification schemas. Although the European regulations were in place, the complexity and differences of the regulations across sectors demand further efforts to develop a shared framework that specifies the expected behavior of actors. Apart from the policies underlying EU values, certain requirements are included. Some examples of these rules and policies are data protection that refers to the processing of personal data in compliance with the EU GDPR and portability and reversibility preconditions for exchange of non-personal data. Another key element is security requirements that refer to compliance with information security policies such as cryptography and physical infrastructure security. Equally important are transparency of contracts, including specific terms and conditions in contracts addressing requirements for data exchange. These rules and policies enable each actor to achieve a deeper understanding of the expectations and requirements of other actors on data control. This reduces uncertainty for actors and in turn allows them to adjust their resources and capabilities more effectively in compliance with agreed rules and policies. Such rules and policies target the entire technology stack from the cloud infrastructure containing data to the cloud-based software and data. One coordination mechanism is onboarding and certifications to ensure an acceptable level of conformity to the shared framework. This means that a service provider seeking to offer services needs to illustrate its compliance with rules and policies either through "self-description" or certifications and attestation. Another coordination mechanism is defining rights and obligations for either service providers or service consumers; for instance, both "must fulfill GAIA-X Service agreements" (GAIA-X, 2020b, p. 19).

A second coordination domain introduced to resolve the data sovereignty bottleneck in GAIA-X is data security. The essential objective is retaining control over data storage, processing and access, which requires an environment of mutual trust where actors decide on the usage of cloud resources and services. The primary coordination mechanisms adopted are identity and trust management to ensure users' authentication and authorization. Before giving access to data resources and capabilities, negotiation of data agreements between providers and consumers plays an important role to coordinate actors and ensure the fulfillment of mutual expectations on terms and conditions. Another coordination mechanism is data usage policies. During data exchange, data logging provides continuous monitoring of data usage by using logging systems over transactions to keep records of data provided, data received, policies enforced and policy-violating messages. This enables monitoring of data usage and checks if actors follow the rules and obligations or violate them. By extension, this enhances the transparency of data usage.

A third coordination domain is the service platform, referred to as the "federated catalogue" in GAIA-X. By developing a federated catalogue of assets[8] and services, different providers list their offers which would be accessible by service consumers. This enables service consumers to search and find the best-matching offers and to monitor for relevant changes in those offers. Through the service platform, different services at the respective technology stacks can be combined to address specific requirements and avoid lock-in. Such service platforms trigger the use of open and standardized formats and interfaces (i.e., application programming interfaces, or APIs) to facilitate interactions between actors. Arguably, here one challenge lies with incentives for participation and the governance of competing interests, a key theme in the platform ecosystem literature (Huber et al., 2017; Tiwana et al., 2010; Wareham et al., 2014; Zhang et al., 2020).

In resolving the data control bottlenecks, ecosystem actors need to define and agree on a set of coordination mechanisms by means of achieving mutual agreements. This set of mutually agreed coordination mechanisms becomes the "alignment structure" between ecosystem actors, their positions and flows (Adner, 2017) in regard to data control. Only by arriving at this alignment structure does the ecosystem begin to form and only then can ecosystem actors begin to develop complementarities toward value co-creation. Based on the early stages of the formation of the GAIA-X ecosystem, we submit that this alignment structure is flexibly negotiated and agreed upon around the identified coordination domains, *not* the coordination mechanisms. The domains constitute the broader contexts of concern and are directly linked to the control bottlenecks. The coordination mechanisms are the executable activities that bring to bear the efficacy of domain principles at specific localities. While coordination domains are similar across industrial sectors, the coordination mechanisms need to be adapted to sector-specific requirements due to the level of data sensitivity or regulatory frameworks.

## 5.3 Developing Data Control Complementarities

Coordination mechanisms enable ecosystem actors to co-specialize their resources and capabilities (Jacobides et al., 2006). "Co-specialization" refers to the adjustment of capabilities and resources to agreed organizational, technical and legal requirements. The three coordination domains enable each actor to revisit its capabilities and resources in order to ensure the alignment of data exchange and processes within the ecosystem. For example, in the GAIA-X ecosystem, actors need a comprehensive understanding of the common rules and policies; they need to expand their knowledge about standards, rules and policies and develop the relevant skills to fulfill security expectations (i.e., expanding intangible resources). Another example of developing specialized capabilities is using a common specification language (e.g., ODRL[9]) to describe the usage restrictions of data and services in a transparent way understandable for all actors. Without such specific resources and capabilities provided by each actor, data control cannot be achieved. This means that data exchange and eventually the development of innovative services will materialize in a very limited way. Data control, hence, is an important complementarity for the emergence of digital service ecosystems which is achieved by specific capabilities and resources provided by different actors. The conformity with data control requirements and the allocation of specific resources and capabilities to data control contribute to the emergence of digital services based on shared, accessed data. Indeed, actors' fulfillment of data control requirements enables further data sharing through cloud services within the ecosystem.

In the GAIA-X ecosystem, the national hubs in each country are the main contact points for users operating in different sectors. Each national hub is mainly responsible for identifying service users' requirements and thus is in a strategic position to manage "in-situ rights" to access end-user data (Cabral et al., 2021; Parker et al., 2021). The national hubs play a particularly active role in collecting and evaluating use cases. These use cases illustrate potential scenarios where control over data storage, access and process are addressed through analysis of sector-specific requirements and including relevant rules and standards. One example of a use case in manufacturing was Collaborative Condition Monitoring (CCM). Unlike the traditional supply chain in which data are gathered and analyzed by original equipment manufacturers (OEM), the use case demonstrates how analytics on data collected from different companies using artificial intelligence (AI) can result in added value for all companies. For example, companies can increase the life cycle of machines and components by ensuring control over data access and process (GAIA-X, 2020a[10]). By underscoring the importance of data control, use cases encourage actors in developing and using different cloud-based solutions in compliance with control requirements before accessing and using data. Thus, coordination mechanisms enable the development of data control complementarities among and between ecosystem actors.

Although coordination mechanisms aim at aligning data-related activities of multiple actors, the use cases demonstrate the need for further coordination requirements as each industrial sector deals with specific control requirements. This becomes even more challenging when actors need to interact across sectors. It is challenging to achieve unilateral agreement across different sectors, or what GAIA-X calls "data spaces," following the European Data Strategy (IDSA, 2021). A data space is defined as "a federated data ecosystem within a certain application domain and based on shared policies and rules" (IDSA, 2021, p. 7). The challenge of specifying legal, operational and functional agreements as well as technical standards for such data spaces is that individuals and organizations usually act in multiple ecosystems concurrently, and therefore are not limited to sharing data within a single data silo or data space (IDC, 2020). Thus, defining the boundaries of a data space, whether in healthcare, banking, manufacturing or other sectors, is a challenging task. For example, the recent Digital Markets Act (DMA) has tried to overcome this challenge by defining "gatekeepers" not by means of their activities within a single data space, but rather by means of their financial turnover and absolute size thresholds. As expert reports on the DMA have noted, however, this definition needs to be accompanied by more specific policies on "forbidden behaviors to which only extreme considerations would justify an exception" and "practices which are in principle considered anti-competitive but for which a pro-competitive justification is possible, with the gatekeeper bearing the burden of proof for that efficiency defense" (Cabral et al., 2021: p. 3). Thus, although broad coordination mechanisms can be reached, further context-specific practices are needed to coordinate data control within each data space (e.g., data portability may entail different trade-offs in healthcare versus manufacturing). One reason is that the dominant service providers are often reluctant to adjust their services and infrastructures to the EU common framework unless they are convinced of the likelihood of future revenue streams.

Moreover, there may be tensions between participants from different countries, or industrial sectors. Finally, the lack of a suitable legal framework results in delays in the achievement of agreements.

As the GAIA-X ecosystem shows, there is not one data ecosystem, but rather multiple data ecosystems across data spaces, from healthcare to finance and from manufacturing to public administration. Data travel across these data spaces and are both a resource and a medium of signification, in that they generate new meanings of, and relationships between, other resources exchanged within the ecosystem (Alaimo et al. 2020b). Thus, what was previously agreed as an effective data control coordination mechanism between ecosystem actors within a specific data space becomes contested by other actors in other data spaces. As discussed above, coordination mechanisms may be contested in light of data control complementarities that lead to anti-competitive behaviors across data spaces. In summary, data control complementarities may challenge previously agreed coordination mechanisms in cloud-based ecosystems as they may entail distinct trade-offs for different data spaces.

In the next section we elaborate on these points by developing a process model of data control coordination in cloud-based ecosystems. We discuss our own contributions and implications for further research in digital strategy and platform ecosystems as well.

## 6.    CONTRIBUTIONS AND IMPLICATIONS

In this chapter, we have examined how heterogeneous actors coordinate data control activities in cloud-based ecosystems to co-create value. Drawing on the GAIA-X case, we develop a conceptual model of data control coordination in cloud-based ecosystems. Our model shows that coordination among actors across a cloud-based ecosystem starts by resolving data control bottlenecks in multilateral agreements *before* engaging in innovative activities that lead to value creation. Data control is a precursor which generates complementarities between ecosystem actors. Although we use GAIA-X as an illustrative case, the conceptual model can be transferred to other contexts where value creation relies extensively on data sharing enabled by cloud services. Our work offers theoretical advances on platform ecosystems and practical implications on digital strategy. Figure 16.1 illustrates our model.

First, our process model contributes to research on platform ecosystems by focusing on the early stage of the formation of nascent ecosystems. Nascent ecosystems are in an early stage of formation or reformation (Hannah & Eisenhardt, 2018), as in the example of the GAIA-X federated ecosystem, but also the recent reformation of the banking ecosystem through mobile payment platforms, challenger banks and API providers, as well as new regulations such as the Payment Services Directive 2 (PSD2). During this formative stage, coordination is not orchestrated by a lead or keystone firm (Gawer & Henderson, 2007; Iansiti & Levien, 2004). Rather, during this stage, ecosystem actors are still trying to ascertain what is at stake, which resources and capabilities would be beneficial for each actor and how they can begin to coordinate activities toward co-specialization. Most importantly, as we show in the GAIA-X case, during this formation stage, ecosystem actors begin to acknowledge their heterogeneous interests and expectations which pose significant control bottlenecks to the ecosystem. Previous research has shown that controlling the bottlenecks often leads to the strategic positioning of firms within an ecosystem (Baldwin, 2014; Hannah & Eisenhardt, 2018; Kapoor, 2018; Masucci et al., 2020). Unless the bottlenecks are resolved, value is captured by those in

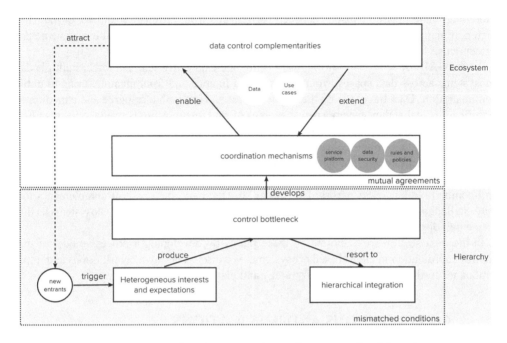

*Figure 16.1    A process model on data control coordination in cloud-based ecosystems*

control, leaving many ecosystem actors with no choice but to resort to hierarchical models of value creation. For instance, the failure to resolve control bottlenecks impacts the scalability of mobile payment services to platform ecosystems (Ondrus et al., 2015). Whereas the literature on nascent ecosystems focuses on performance bottlenecks (Hannah & Eisenhardt, 2018), our study focuses on data control bottlenecks, which, as we show, can make or break the ecosystem. As the GAIA-X case shows, data control cannot rest with a single actor nor a set of dominant actors because that situation can generate significant control bottlenecks. Ecosystem actors need to collectively agree on a set of data control coordination mechanisms that are distributed based on operational and technical standards, as well as legal rules and regulations. This sets a precedent for a distributed orchestration of the ecosystem.

Second, our model contributes to the recent debate on antitrust and competition in platform ecosystems (Krämer, 2020; Parker et al., 2021). Many of the commentaries on antitrust have focused on the anti-competitive practices of platform owners (or gatekeepers) on third parties, such as tying, bundling and self-preferencing. Our case extends this focus to data control coordination mechanisms which cut across data spaces or domains of use, but also specific applications or APIs. For example, much discussion within the DMA (Article 6) has been focused on the ways by which Google ties and bundles its proprietary set of applications and APIs for Google Mobile Services (i.e., Google Play Store, Google Search, Google Chrome, YouTube and Google Maps) on all Android devices. Although there can be benefits to coordinating an ecosystem by allowing a platform owner to tie and bundle services together (Parker et al., 2021), there are significant anti-competitive effects from the exclusive control of data generated from those services. Data is both a medium and a resource (Alaimo et al., 2020b). Data is part of an architectural configuration of a platform ecosystem (e.g., data generated from Google Maps), but it is also a medium for constructing completely new services (e.g., data from Google Maps fed into Airbnb). Thus, as the GAIA-X case illustrates, data control coordination above and beyond the architectural configuration of an ecosystem becomes even more relevant.

Our process model places emphasis on the role that data control coordination mechanisms have on value creation and capture. Specifically, as the GAIA-X case shows, such coordination mechanisms can lead to both unique and supermodular data control complementarities (cf. Jacobides et al., 2018). First, unique complementarities emerge from co-dependencies between the data resources and capabilities of diverse ecosystem actors. For example, providers of mobile financial services can co-specialize with mobile app developers and achieve unique complementarities through open APIs (Gomber et al., 2018; Kazan et al., 2018). Such unique complementarities would not be possible without first coordinating data control between these parties. Second, supermodular complementarities emerge as the value of one set of resources and capabilities increases when combined with others: "more of A makes B more valuable" (Jacobides et al., 2018, p. 2262). In such complementarities, the value of A influences the value of B, but A is not a necessary pre-condition for B. For instance, the GAIA-X case shows that coordinated data control often results in reduced costs and increased efficiency for actors in accessing, storing and processing data. The more actors are involved in such data control activities, the more the value of digital services increases for GAIA-X and sub-ecosystems within and across data spaces.

Certainly, as discussed earlier, there are trade-offs across the operational and technical standards, as well as legal rules and regulations upon which coordination rests (Miller & Toh, 2020). For example, it is not yet clear "whether data portability would lead to more or less competition and innovation in established digital markets per se" (Krämer, 2020, p. 19). It is also not clear how data sovereignty could be achieved, given the trade-offs between the benefits and costs of signing up for services by large CSPs that leverage data-enabled network effects versus signing up with small, local CSPs (Cabral et al., 2021). These trade-offs challenge the existing coordination mechanisms requiring more situated mutual agreements. This is where polycentric governance may prove useful (Constantinides, 2012; Constantinides & Barrett, 2015), as coordination domains can be broadly defined to allow for the tailoring of coordination mechanisms to local circumstances. In particular, the proposal to introduce "in-situ" data rights, where different users, from individuals to producers of services, gain rights to use data in their respective localities – i.e., without porting those outside a given platform – thus preserving innovation while reducing the sovereignty risk, is a step in the right direction (Martens et al. 2021).

Third, our chapter contributes to digital strategy research by focusing on the shift towards data-centric ecosystems that are based on cloud services, as opposed to specific organizational boundaries. This has implications for data strategy, as organizations need to rethink their data control activities to reap the benefits of data as means to structure their relationships in a digital ecosystem. Data control activities become then a strategic element for organizations that rely on data to realize their value propositions. These organizations have to align their data strategy with business's strategy to expand their value creation. Our model shows that data-driven innovation starts by identifying data control bottlenecks and then developing coordination mechanisms to resolve such bottlenecks. To capture value from the ecosystem, internal and external resources and capabilities need to be re-organized. Resolving data control bottlenecks allows actors to use cloud services for data access, storage and processing, which eventually leads to new opportunities for value creation. Outcomes of such value creation can be cost reduction through real-time data access and automation, efficiency and scaling up of IT resources and infrastructures, agility in coping with changes, and innovations such as augmented reality objects and AI-based services.

Finally, future research can apply our model to analyze how coordination on data control can influence the nature and locus of opportunity discovery and pursuit in entrepreneurial ecosystems (Autio et al., 2018; Steininger, 2019). In fact, cloud-based ecosystems can potentially attract new actors and lead to the creation and scaling up of new ventures in remote geographical locations with many potential implications for policy makers, entrepreneurs and investors. For instance, policy makers can recognize the wider role of cloud-based ecosystems as hotbeds of business model innovation and for the diffusion of radical, digitally enabled business models in the economy in rural areas and in developing countries. Moreover, complementarities on data control can inform new venture location decisions and give rise to specialized structures and cluster-specific knowledge that support business model experimentation and venture scale-up (Ali et al., 2017).

## 7.    CONCLUSION

In this chapter, we elaborated on the key elements of a process model of the formation of cloud-based ecosystems, while placing emphasis on data control coordination. Our model shows that coordination among actors across a cloud-based ecosystem starts by resolving data control bottlenecks in multilateral agreements, before engaging in innovative activities that lead to value creation. Our model contributes to research on platform ecosystems strategy and recent debates on antitrust issues and identifies important topics for further research.

By means of conclusion, we discuss a set of managerial implications for digital strategy formulation. Depending on their organizational objectives, managers need to decide how to address the data control bottleneck. This decision directly influences the value creation in terms of scope, scale, time-to-market and/or novelty of products and services. If managers perceive the data control bottleneck as a threat to data protection, they resort to hierarchical integration of data control activities. Although such a hierarchical system guarantees the full control over data access, storage and processing, value creation is constrained at the traditional dyadic level. However, managers may opt to engage in a digital ecosystem strategy and contribute to resolve the data control bottleneck. Resolving the data control bottleneck requires the efforts of ecosystem members to collectively define and mutually agree on a set of coordination mechanisms. An ecosystem approach to resolve data control bottlenecks allows actors to exchange resources and capabilities to co-create value. Resolving data control bottlenecks presents new possibilities to activate network externalities, scale services, explore new technologies and business opportunities, and offer innovative and complex value propositions building on other actors' value-added services (Fuller et al., 2019). Our findings also show that managers cannot focus solely on their firm's strategy. Instead, a shift from a focus on firms' strategy to a focus on an ecosystem's strategy may lead to long-term benefits.

Our model underlines that value creation from data is increasingly enabled by cloud services. Thus, managers need to ensure service providers or data users (accessing, storing or processing data) all act in conformity with regulations and the organizational strategy. Understanding the role of data control within an ecosystem will attract more organizations to specialize their data control activities and allow the ecosystem to expand the scope of value creation without compromising data asset protection.

## ACKNOWLEDGEMENTS

We would like to thank the GAIA-X community and especially Mr. Aniello Gentile, an EU board member of the GAIA-X project, and CY4GATE, a cybersecurity company partner of the GAIA-X project, for the kind support in helping us with this project.

## NOTES

1. https://ec.europa.eu/info/sites/info/files/communication-european-strategy-data-19feb2020_en.pdf.
2. See European Commission (2016). Regulation (2016/679/EU) on the protection of natural persons with regard to the processing of personal data and on the free movement of such data, and repealing Directive 95/46/EC (General Data Protection Regulation). *Official Journal of the European Union*, L119/1, 1–88.
3. https://www.enisa.europa.eu/topics/nis-directive.
4. According to GAIA-X (2020a), the definition of data sovereignty is adopted from "Digital Sovereignty and Artificial Intelligence – Preconditions, Responsibilities and Recommendations for Action," Focus Group "Digital Sovereignty in a Connected Economy," 2018; "Digital Sovereignty in the Context of Platform-Based Ecosystems," Focus Group "Digital Sovereignty in a Networked Economy," 2019; and also from "Role Model 2030 for Industry 4.0: Structuring Digital Ecosystems Globally," Plattform Industrie 4.0, 2019. See GAIA-X (2020a).
5. One recent example is a fire at a physical cloud datacenter located in France that disrupted public administration services in other countries. https://www.reuters.com/article/us-france-ovh-fire-idUSKBN2B20NU.
6. https://www.gaia-x.eu/sites/default/files/2021-05/Gaia-X_Architecture_Document_2103.pdf.
7. https://www.data-infrastructure.eu/GAIAX/Redaktion/EN/Publications/gaia-x-technical-architecture.pdf?__blob=publicationFile&v=5.
8. According to GAIA-X (2021), "An Asset can be a Data Asset, a Software Asset, a Node or an Interconnection Asset" (p. 11). "A Data Asset is an Asset that consist of data in any form and necessary information for data sharing. A Node is an Asset and represents a computational or physical entity that hosts, manipulates, or interacts with other computational or physical entities. A Software Asset is a form of Assets that consist of non-physical functions. An Interconnection is an Asset that presents the connection between two or multiple Nodes" (p. 12).
9. W3C. ODRL Information Model 2.2 [W3C Recommendation 15 February 2018]. https://www.w3.org/TR/odrl-model/.
10. https://www.data-infrastructure.eu/GAIAX/Redaktion/EN/Publications/gaia-x-driver-of-digital-innovation-in-europe.pdf?__blob=publicationFile&v=8.

## REFERENCES

Adner, R. (2012). *The Wide Lens: A New Strategy for Innovation*. New York, NY: Penguin.
Adner, R. (2017). Ecosystem as structure: An actionable construct for strategy. *Journal of Management*, 43(1), 39–58. https://doi.org/10.1177/0149206316678451.
Ahmad, A., Maynard, S.B., Desouza, K.C., Kotsias, J., Whitty, M.T., & Baskerville, R.L. (2021). Cybersecurity incident response in organizations: An exploratory case study and process model of situation awareness. *Computers & Security*, 101, 102–22.

Alaimo, C., Kallinikos, J., & Aaltonen, A. (2020a). Data and Value. In Nambisan, S., Lyytinen, K., & Yoo, Y. (Eds) *Handbook of Digital Innovation* (pp. 162–78). Cheltenham, UK and Northampton, MA, USA: Edward Elgar Publishing.

Alaimo, C., Kallinikos, J., & Valderrama, E. (2020b). Platforms as service ecosystems: Lessons from social media. *Journal of Information Technology*, 35(1), 25–48.

Ali, A., Warren, D., & Mathiassen, L. (2017). Cloud-based business services innovation: A risk management model. *International Journal of Information Management*, 37(6), 639–49. https://doi.org/10.1016/j.ijinfomgt.2017.05.008.

Anderson, C., Baskerville, R.L., & Kaul, M. (2017). Information security control theory: Achieving a sustainable reconciliation between sharing and protecting the privacy of information. *Journal of Management Information Systems*, 34(4), 1082–1112. https://doi.org/10.1080/07421222.2017.1394063.

Autio, E., Nambisan, S., Thomas, L.D.W., & Wright, M. (2018). Digital affordances, spatial affordances, and the genesis of entrepreneurial ecosystems. *Strategic Entrepreneurship Journal*, 12(1), 72–95.

Baldwin, C.Y. (2014). *Bottlenecks, Modules and Dynamic Architectural Capabilities*. Harvard Business School Finance Working Paper No. 15-028. https://doi.org/10.2139/ssrn.2512209.

Baskerville, R., Spagnoletti, P., & Kim, J. (2014). Incident-centered information security: Managing a strategic balance between prevention and response. *Information and Management*, 51(1), 138–51. https://doi.org/10.1016/j.im.2013.11.004.

Basole, R.C., & Park, H. (2018). Interfirm collaboration and firm value in software ecosystems: Evidence from cloud computing. *IEEE Transactions on Engineering Management*, 66(3), 368–80. https://doi.org/10.1109/TEM.2018.2855401.

Bharadwaj, A., El Sawy, O.A., Pavlou, P.A., & Venkatraman, N. (2013). Digital business strategy: Toward a next generation of insights. *MIS Quarterly*, 37(2), 471–82.

Cabral, L., Haucap, J., Parker, G., Petropoulows, G., Valletti, T., & Van Alstyne, M. (2021). *The EU Digital Markets Act: A Report from a Panel of Economic Experts*. Brussels: Publication Office of the European Union. https://doi.org/10.2760/139337.

Constantinides, P. (2012). *Perspectives and Implications for the Development of Information Infrastructures*. Hershey, PA: IGI Global.

Constantinides, P., & Barrett, M. (2015). Information infrastructure development and governance as collective action. *Information Systems Research*, 26(1), 40–56. https://doi.org/http://dx.doi.org/10.1287/isre.2014.0542.

Constantinides, P., Henfridsson, O., & Parker, G. (2018). Platforms and infrastructures in the digital age. *Information Systems Research*, 7047, 1–20. https://doi.org/10.1287/isre.2018.0794.

Crémer, J., de Montjoye, Y.-A., & Schweitzer, H. (2019). *Competition Policy for the Digital Era*. Report for the European Commission. Brussels: European Commission.

De Bruijn, H., & Janssen, M. (2017). Building cybersecurity awareness: The need for evidence-based framing strategies. *Government Information Quarterly*, 34(1), 1–7.

Eisenmann, T.R., Parker, G., & Van Alstyne, M. (2009). Opening Platforms: How, When and Why? In Gawer, A. (ed.) *Platforms, Markets and Innovation* (Vol. 6, pp. 131–62). Cheltenham, UK and Northampton, MA, USA: Edward Elgar Publishing.

European Commission (2016). Regulation (2016/679/EU) on the protection of natural persons with regard to the processing of personal data and on the free movement of such data, and repealing Directive 95/46/EC (General Data Protection Regulation). *Official Journal of the European Union*, L119/1, 1–88.

Fuller, J., Jacobides, M.G., & Reeves, M. (2019). The myths and realities of business ecosystems. *MIT Sloan Management Review*, 60(3), 1–9.

GAIA-X (2020a). *GAIA-X: Driver of Digital Innovation in Europe: Featuring the Next Generation of Data Infrastructure*. Brussels: GAIA-X. https://www.data-infrastructure.eu/GAIAX/Redaktion/EN/Publications/gaia-x-driver-of-digital-innovation-in-europe.pdf?__blob=publicationFile&v=8.

GAIA-X (2020b). *Technical Architecture*. Brussels: GAIA-X. https://www.data-infrastructure.eu/GAIAX/Redaktion/EN/Publications/gaia-x-technical-architecture.pdf?__blob=publicationFile&v=5.

GAIA-X (2021). *Architecture Document*. Brussels: GAIA-X. https://www.gaia-x.eu/sites/default/files/2021-05/Gaia-X_Architecture_Document_2103.pdf.

Gawer, A., & Henderson, R. (2007). Platform owner entry and innovation in complementary markets: Evidence from Intel. *Journal of Economics & Management Strategy*, 16(1), 1–34.

Gioia, D.A., Corley, K.G., & Hamilton, A.L. (2013). Seeking qualitative rigor in inductive research: Notes on the Gioia methodology. *Organizational Research Methods*, 16(1), 15–31.

Gomber, P., Kauffman, R.J., Parker, C., & Weber, B.W. (2018). On the fintech revolution: Interpreting the forces of innovation, disruption, and transformation in financial services. *Journal of Management Information Systems*, 35(1), 220–65. https://doi.org/10.1080/07421222.2018.1440766.

Hannah, D.P., & Eisenhardt, K.M. (2018). How firms navigate cooperation and competition in nascent ecosystems. *Strategic Management Journal*, 39(12), 3163–92. https://doi.org/10.1002/smj.2750.

Huber, T.L., Kude, T., & Dibbern, J. (2017). Governance practices in platform ecosystems: Navigating tensions between cocreated value and governance costs. *Information Systems Research*, 28(3), 563–84. https://doi.org/10.1287/isre.2017.0701.

Iansiti, M., & Levien, R. (2004). *The Keystone Advantage: What the New Dynamics of Business Ecosystems Mean for Strategy, Innovation, and Sustainability*. Boston, MA: Harvard Business Press.

IDC (International Data Corporation) (2020). *Final Study Report: The European Data Market Monitoring Tool Key Facts & Figures, First Policy Conclusions, Data Landscape and Quantified Stories*. N.p.: Lisbon Council and International Data Corporation. https://datalandscape.eu/sites/default/files/report/D2.9_EDM_Final_study_report_16.06.2020_IDC_pdf.pdf.

IDSA (International Data Spaces Association) (2021). *Design Principles for Data Spaces*. Position Paper, Version 1.0, April 2021, OpenDei. Dortmund: International Data Spaces Association. https://design-principles-for-data-spaces.org/.

Jacobides, M.G., Cennamo, C., & Gawer, A. (2018). Towards a theory of ecosystems. *Strategic Management Journal*, 39(8), 2255–76. https://doi.org/10.1002/smj.2904.

Jacobides, M.G., Knudsen, T., & Augier, M. (2006). Benefiting from innovation: Value creation, value appropriation and the role of industry architectures. *Research Policy*, 35(8), 1200–221.

Kallinikos, J., Aaltonen, A., & Marton, A. (2013). The ambivalent ontology of digital artifacts. *MIS Quarterly*, 37(2), 357–70.

Kapoor, R. (2018). Ecosystems: broadening the locus of value creation. *Journal of Organization Design*, 7(1). https://doi.org/10.1186/s41469-018-0035-4.

Kazan, E., Tan, C., Lim, E.T.K., Sørensen, C., & Damsgaard, J. (2018). Disentangling digital platform competition: The case of UK mobile payment platforms. *Journal of Management Information Systems*, 35(1), 180–219. https://doi.org/10.1080/07421222.2018.1440772.

Khan, F., Kim, J.H., Moore, R., & Mathiassen, L. (2019). Data Breach Risks and Resolutions: A Literature Synthesis. In *Twenty-Fifth Americas Conference on Information Systems*, Cancun (pp. 1–10).

Kohtamäki, M., Parida, V., Oghazi, P., Gebauer, H., & Baines, T. (2019). Digital servitization business models in ecosystems: A theory of the firm. *Journal of Business Research*, 104, 380–92.

Krämer, J. (2020). Personal data portability in the platform economy: Economic implications and policy recommendations. *Journal of Competition Law & Economics*, 17(2), 263–308. https://doi.org/10.1093/joclec/nhaa030.

Lodi, G., Aniello, L., Di Luna, G.A., & Baldoni, R. (2014). An event-based platform for collaborative threats detection and monitoring. *Information Systems*, 39, 175–95.

Lowry, P.B., Dinev, T., & Willison, R. (2017). Why security and privacy research lies at the centre of the information systems (IS) artefact: Proposing a bold research agenda. *European Journal of Information Systems*, 26(6), 546–63. https://doi.org/10.1057/s41303-017-0066-x.

Lusch, R.F., & Nambisan, S. (2015). Service innovation: A service-dominant logic perspective. *MIS Quarterly: Management Information Systems*, 39(1), 155–75. https://doi.org/10.25300/MISQ/2015/39.1.07.

Marston, S., Li, Z., Bandyopadhyay, S., Zhang, J., & Ghalsasi, A. (2011). Cloud computing: The business perspective. *Decision Support Systems*, 51(1), 176–89. https://doi.org/10.1016/j.dss.2010.12.006.

Martens, B., Parker, G., Petropoulos, G., & Van Alstyne, M.W. (2021). *Towards Efficient Information Sharing in Network Markets*. TILEC Discussion Paper No. DP2021-014. https://doi.org/10.2139/ssrn.3956256.

Masucci, M., Brusoni, S., & Cennamo, C. (2020). Removing bottlenecks in business ecosystems: The strategic role of outbound open innovation. *Research Policy*, 49(1), 103823. https://doi.org/10.1016/j.respol.2019.103823.

Mell, P., & Grance, T. (2011). *The NIST Definition of Cloud Computing: Recommendations of the National Institute of Standards and Technology*. Gaithersburg, MD: U.S. Department of Commerce.

Miller, C.D., & Toh, P.K. (2020). Complementary components and returns from coordination within ecosystems via standard setting. *Strategic Management Journal*, 43(3), 627–62. https://doi.org/10.1002/smj.3143.

Nambisan, S., Lyytinen, K., Majchrzak, A., & Song, M. (2017). Digital innovation management: Reinventing innovation management research in a digital world. *MIS Quarterly*, 41(1), 223–38. https://doi.org/10.25300/MISQ/2017/41.

Newell, S., & Marabelli, M. (2015). Strategic opportunities (and challenges) of algorithmic decision-making: A call for action on the long-term societal effects of "datification." *Journal of Strategic Information Systems*, 24(1), 3–14. https://doi.org/10.1016/j.jsis.2015.02.001.

Ondrus, J., Gannamaneni, A., & Lyytinen, K. (2015). The impact of openness on the market potential of multi-sided platforms: A case study of mobile payment platforms. *Journal of Information Technology*, 30(3), 260–75.

Pagani, M. (2013). Digital business strategy and value creation: Framing the dynamic cycle of control points. *MIS Quarterly*, 37(2), 617–32.

Paquette, S., Jaeger, P.T., & Wilson, S.C. (2010). Identifying the security risks associated with governmental use of cloud computing. *Government Information Quarterly*, 27(3), 245–53. https://doi.org/10.1016/j.giq.2010.01.002.

Parker, G., Petropoulos, G., & Van Alstyne, M.W. (2021). *Platform Mergers and Antitrust*. Boston University Questrom School of Business Research Paper No. 376351. https://doi.org/10.2139/ssrn.3763513.

Rai, A., Pavlou, P.A., Im, G., & Du, S. (2012). Interfirm IT capability profiles and communications for cocreating relational value: Evidence from the logistics industry. *MIS Quarterly*, 36(1), 233–62.

Sandberg, J., Holmström, J., & Lyytinen, K. (2020). Digitization and phase transitions in platform organizing logics: Evidence from the process automation industry. *MIS Quarterly: Management Information Systems*, 44(1), 129–53. https://doi.org/10.25300/MISQ/2020/14520.

Schneier, B. (2013). You have no control over security on the feudal internet. *Harvard Business Review Blog*, June 6. http://blogs.hbr.org/cs/2013/06/you_have_no_control_over_s.html.

Sklyar, A., Kowalkowski, C., Tronvoll, B., & Sörhammar, D. (2019). Organizing for digital servitization: A service ecosystem perspective. *Journal of Business Research*, 104, 450–60.

Spiekermann, S., Acquisti, A., Böhme, R., & Hui, K.-L. (2015). The challenges of personal data markets and privacy. *Electronic Markets*, 25(2), 161–67.

Steininger, D.M. (2019). Linking information systems and entrepreneurship: A review and agenda for IT-associated and digital entrepreneurship research. *Information Systems Journal*, 29(2), 363–407.

Subashini, S., & Kavitha, V. (2011). A survey on security issues in service delivery models of cloud computing. *Journal of Network and Computer Applications*, 34(1), 1–11. https://doi.org/10.1016/j.jnca.2010.07.006.

Tilson, D., Lyytinen, K., & Sørensen, C. (2010). Digital infrastructures: The missing IS research agenda – Research commentary. *Information Systems Research*, 21(4), 748–59.

Tiwana, A., Konsynski, B., & Bush, A.A. (2010). Platform evolution: Coevolution of platform architecture, governance, and environmental dynamics. *Information Systems Research*, 21(4), 675–87. https://doi.org/10.1287/isre.1100.0323.

Vial, G. (2019). Understanding digital transformation: A review and a research agenda. *Journal of Strategic Information Systems*, 28(2), 118–44. https://doi.org/10.1016/j.jsis.2019.01.003.

Wareham, J., Fox, P.B., & Cano Giner, J.L. (2014). Technology ecosystem governance. *Organization Science*, 25(4), 1195–1215.

Yin, R.K. (2009). *Case Study Research: Design and Methods*. Thousand Oaks, CA: SAGE.

Zhang, Y., Li, J., & Tong, T.W. (2020). Platform governance matters: How platform gatekeeping affects knowledge sharing among complementors. *Strategic Management Journal* 43(3), 599–626.

# APPENDIX: DATA SOURCES

*Table 16A.1    Sources of data used*

| Source of evidence | Description |
| --- | --- |
| Documentation | ● GAIA-X website |
| | ● Press release |
| | ● Blogs (digital sovereignty and innovation) |
| | ● Publications and articles |
| Seminars | ● Information webinars and events (x4) |
| Use cases | ● 65 use cases from different sectors (e.g., health, finance, energy, agriculture) |
| Articles | ● Newspapers and magazines (around 30 pages) |
| Interviews and informal conversations | ● Interviews with EU board member of the GAIA-X project (x2) |
| | ● Informal conversation with GAIA-X community (x3) |

# PART IV

# DIGITAL STRATEGY AND THE NEW MANAGERIAL IMPERATIVES

# 17. "Open source corporate governance" in the era of digital transformation

*Igor Filatotchev and Gianvito Lanzolla*

## INTRODUCTION

The pervasive diffusion, adoption and use of digital technologies – often referred to as digital transformation or the fourth industrial revolution – has triggered profound changes in the economy, society and institutions (World Economic Forum, 2016). Not surprisingly, a rich "digital transformation" academic literature has emerged to shed light on these changes. For instance, digital technology adoption has been linked to increased organizational experimentation and to the emergence of new sociotechnical practices (e.g., Almirall and Casadesus-Masanell, 2010; Bailey et al., 2012; Brunswicker et al., 2019; Yoo et al., 2010); and to the rewiring of firm business models into open ecosystems (Casadesus-Masanell and Zhu, 2013; Cennamo, 2018; Cennamo and Santaló, 2013, 2019; D'Aveni et al., 2010; Jacobides et al., 2018; Parker et al., 2016; Porter and Heppelmann, 2014; Zhu and Furr, 2016; Zhu and Iansiti, 2012). Overall, extant literature has also highlighted that the organizational outcomes of the digital transformation are far from being unidirectional, unambiguous and always positive (e.g., Lanzolla, Pesce, & Tucci, 2021). As a result, managerial strategies in the digital domain are associated with increasing uncertainties for companies, their shareholders and other stakeholders.

Traditionally, shareholders have relied on corporate governance to align with management and, ultimately, enhance firm value. Legacy corporate governance has long been based on the "closed system" framework that is predominantly centered on the idea of aligning the interests of managers (agents) and shareholders (principals) through a series of internal and external mechanisms and practices (Eisenhardt, 1998). More recently, there has been a transition from the perhaps over-stylized principal/agent model to an "open system" approach to corporate governance (Filatotchev et al., 2021). "Open system" governance seems potentially more helpful to align different stakeholders when companies need to strategize and execute strategy in rapidly changing technologies and regulatory environments. Yet, despite these recent developments, we know very little regarding effective corporate governance in the era of digital transformation (Filatotchev et al., 2020).

To shed more light on this topic, in this chapter, by integrating the digitalization and corporate governance literatures, we elaborate on the implications of digital technology's adoption and use for the corporate governance functions. We consider three distinct corporate governance functions (Chatterjee et al., 2003; Daily et al., 2003; Fama and Jensen, 1983; Filatotchev et al., 2003; Westphal, 1999). The monitoring and control function refers to the board's role in overseeing managerial (over-)discretion. The strategy function refers to the role of the board, investors, the auditors and other governance participants in providing management with expertise and access to resources and support in identifying the firm's strategic goals and a roadmap to deliver on them. The legitimacy function refers to the role of corporate governance in ensuring compliance with national codes and regulations, as well as broader societal expectations with regard to conducting business responsibly. Our analyses reveal that digital technology has an ambivalent impact on corporate governance functions (and legacy practices), and we identify the key challenges that should be addressed (summarized in Table 17.1).

By building on the emergent open system approach to corporate governance (Aguilera et al., 2008; Filatotchev et al., 2021), we claim that, to tackle the new realities of openness, interdependencies, dynamism, and fluidity brought forward by digital technology diffusion and use, companies should adopt a multi-stakeholder "open source" approach to corporate governance (hereafter referred to as open source governance). Our open source governance builds on two core principles: (a) the need to systematically increase complementarities among internal and external stakeholders in both governance and strategy, and (b) the need to purposely balance short-term compliance and long-term legitimacy among broader groups of the firm's stakeholders. We show the implications of these two principles for governance practices and highlight the differences vis-à-vis the legacy governance's practices. Overall, open source governance shifts emphasis from the over-narrow agency perspective towards developing a system of interactions between the company and its ecosystem. A key part of open source governance is associated with transition to a reliance on "strategic" rather than "financial" controls within the firm's governance mechanism. We claim that these changes are needed if boards are to remain relevant and effective.

Finally, we highlight a research agenda to develop the open source corporate governance approach further. For instance, one point in this research agenda includes "decision-rights partitioning" – i.e., how decision-making authority is split between the company's owners/shareholders and community members or, in other words, the degree of centralization/decentralization of the decision-making process. Other points that we highlight include how to increase transparency and accountability, as well as how to include checks and balances on powerful actors in the era of digitalization.

## HOW DOES DIGITAL TRANSFORMATION IMPACT CORPORATE GOVERNANCE FUNCTIONS?

To understand the impact of digital technology adoption and diffusion on corporate governance functions, the first problem involves conceptualizing digital technology. There are many digital technologies and a lot of evocative jargon – e.g., cloud computing, big data analytics, artificial intelligence (AI), Internet of Things, 5G connectivity, augmented reality. In the absence of frameworks that can capture holistically the novelty of digital technologies, a more pragmatic approach is to focus on the transformational capabilities that digital technologies introduce. Here, we focus on two prevailing transformational capabilities: pervasive connectivity (often enabled by the Internet of Things and broadband) and intelligent automation (often enabled by AI and cloud technologies). Taken individually, automation and connectivity do not introduce particularly new transformational capabilities for firms. For instance, the first industrial revolution was spurred by automation, and organizations and businesses have sought connections, used data and tried to automate since the early days of that revolution. But while these capabilities in isolation are not particularly new, their interaction and pervasiveness are transformational both of the environment in which companies operate (World Economic Forum, 2016) and of companies' activity systems (Teece, 2010). As such, pervasive

*Table 17.1    Digital transformation and corporate governance challenges*

| Functions of corporate governance | Challenges presented by digitalization |
|---|---|
| Monitoring function | • The illusion of objectivity in monitoring; |
| | • Opacity of the digital monitoring infrastructure itself (e.g., path dependency, filtering); |
| | • The blurring of the organizational boundaries and functions and, with it, of the focal points of the monitoring functions – e.g., what should be monitored? |
| | • The disconnect between the pace of changes in the business environment, strategic choices, strategy execution choices, related risks and the monitoring systems themselves. |
| Strategy function | • Challenges to build new resources and assets at the intersection of the digital and physical worlds, and disposal of legacy assets; |
| | • Increased tension between knowledge recombination/integration vs knowledge specialization; |
| | • Increasing need for experimentation; |
| | • The simultaneous participation in different "ecosystems" for value co-delivery. |
| Legitimacy function | • The firm's exposure to poly-centric regulatory environments; |
| | • Regulatory "vacuum areas" become a target of regulatory action; |
| | • New regulatory approaches in defining what constitutes a "market failure". |

connectivity and intelligent automation have multilevel implications for the corporate governance functions. Table 17.1 summarizes such multilevel challenges. Below we elaborate on these challenges further.

## Digital Technologies and the Challenges for the Monitoring Function

The business press is dotted with examples of failures to monitor and prevent serious managerial misconduct even in companies equipped with sophisticated automated monitoring systems. Consider, for instance, the UBS rogue trader or the UK Libor-fixing scandals. Far from eliminating risks arising from managerial discretion, digital technologies compound traditional risks of information systems – e.g., implementation risks – with new ones. These new risks take three forms. First, monitoring via digital technologies is often based on "algorithms" that, no matter how sophisticated they might be, are based on "learning", using available data, and on "learning sets", which are not always transparent to the final users (Kellogg et al., 2020; Zuboff, 2019). Our research shows that company boards often have a "deistic" faith in the "objectivity" of such monitoring capabilities, sometimes with mixed results. Second, the outputs of this automated monitoring are not always fully transparent (e.g., Lanzolla et al., 2021). Increasingly, even the developers themselves admit that the outcomes of their "learning sets" are unpredictable. As such, these digital monitoring systems introduce a new degree of volatility in the organizations. It follows that it might be challenging to build alignment between such (unpredictable) automated monitoring systems and the company's monitoring goals. Third, it is increasingly challenging to monitor risks in the inter-connected "organic" ecosystems (e.g., Jacobides et al., 2018; Kellogg et al., 2020). For instance, organizations as self-contained entities with well-defined and well-guarded boundaries are becoming less prevalent since companies find themselves more and more involved in ecosystems – i.e., the networks of suppliers, consumers and platforms that need to be engaged via digital technologies in order to (co)deliver and enhance a firm's value proposition. Companies such as KPMG,

Zurich and the Russell Group are developing computational algorithms powered by big data and analytics that might make monitoring systemic risks in such ecosystems more effective. However, our research shows that these algorithms are often based on legacy logics which are not robust enough to predict the outcomes of complex interactive (often nested) ecosystems. By 2030, it is estimated that over half of the world's population will be online (Euromonitor, 2015), and 29.42 billion devices will be connected in Internet of Things solutions (Statisa, 2023). Every attempt a stakeholder makes to address a problem triggers responses from other stakeholders in the ecosystem, which are not always predictable.

The challenges of relying on digital technologies for monitoring are augmented by the abrupt pace of change. Moore's law predicts that computing power should double in performance every 18/24 months, and it is still viewed as a reliable method of calculating future trends. In a nutshell, this means that everything that is transformed digitally is likely to double in performance every 1.5–2 years. This increased technological pressure tends to undermine any legacy advantages and business models and exposes companies to the need to change their strategies at a faster pace than in the past (this implies that operational, tactical and strategic risks – see Figure 17.1 – also change at different speeds). Yet, new strategic choices require not only new resources, capabilities and business models, but also new key performance indicators. A survey conducted by the authors[1] in 2020 found that more than 50 percent of the interviewed executives felt that the gap between changes in the business environment, strategic choices and organization that should deliver on them – e.g., people strategy, incentive systems – was widening. To illustrate this point further, consider, for instance, a company which as part of its strategy targets a few market segments of several thousand customers each. Consider now the same company that under the effect of connectivity, AI and big data changes its strategy to offer as personalized a product as possible to thousands of segments of a few customers. Clearly the measures of success (and related risks) in the two cases are different and if monitoring systems do not adapt quickly enough the reporting will be biased, or even misleading.

**The Challenges to the Strategy Function**

The "blending" of the digital and physical world (e.g., World Economic Forum, 2016) triggers the need for a whole new set of resources and capabilities – e.g., information management, collaboration, orchestration – while reducing the value of many legacy resources and capabilities. Consider, for instance, the transformation in the automotive industry. It is predicted that within the next 10 years, 60 percent of the value of a car will reside in the electrical batteries and 30 percent in digital devices. What will be left of Mercedes', GE's and Ford's legacy resources and capabilities, such as engine assembly plants? Virtually all carmakers have their own versions of "connected cars" and "autonomous cars" initiatives that, for the survivors, will result in a completely different future organizational set-up and business model. Digital transformation challenges the very core of the "assets" of an organization and, as such, puts an ever-increasing pressure on corporate boards in terms of their involvement in strategy and strategizing.

Second, digital transformation brings forward a new innovation paradigm whereby innovation will come at the intersection of once disconnected knowledge domains (e.g., Kaplan and Vakili, 2015; Lanzolla et al., 2021). The emergence of popular acronyms such as fintech, agritech, etc., is associated with entrepreneurial ventures that are created at the intersection of

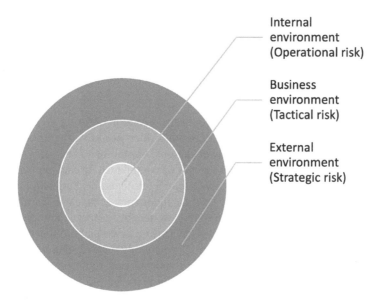

Internal
environment
(Operational risk)

Business
environment
(Tactical risk)

External
environment
(Strategic risk)

*Figure 17.1    Risks evolve at different pace*

once disconnected industries, with often "disruptive" outcomes. For instance, technology companies – e.g., Google, Apple, Amazon – are seeking to leverage their own acquired technological superiority to enter industries which were previously off-limits to them. Consider Google's
efforts in driverless cars, Apple Pay and Amazon's entry into the grocery market and, more
recently, into prescription medicines. As such, digital transformation increases the need for
knowledge diversity, both for "born digital" and traditional companies, as a core mechanism
for a company's sustainability. Therefore, corporate boards that traditionally involve members
with a high level of specialization in functional areas such as finance, accounting, marketing,
etc., may not have the right set of skills to respond to strategic challenges across the domains.

Finally, the abrupt pace of change enacted by digital technologies requires companies and
boards to adopt a culture of constant change and experimentation (e.g., Faraj et al., 2018;
Felin et al., 2017; Leonardi et al., 2012; Majchrzak et al., 2016; Orlikowski and Scott, 2014).
Consider the UK's national weather service, the Met Office, which since 2010 has already
entered the "hockey stick" (increasing returns) part of the technology performance curve.
The top management has embraced a state of constant organizational change, permanently
exploring new work practices and organizational forms. Or, consider Axel Springer, the
German publisher, which in order to deliver on the CEO's vision of becoming the "leading
digital publisher" over a period of seven years, from 2007 to 2013, completed 58 mergers
and acquisitions (M&As) in the digital space, out of a total of 63 M&As. In the same period,
Axel Springer disposed of, or wrote off, at least 20 percent of its new digital ventures. In
2003 digital business models accounted for virtually 0 percent of Axel Springer's results; in
2017, digital business models accounted for 72 percent of total revenues and 80 percent of
the group's earnings before interest, taxes, depreciation and amortization. As in any quoted
company, this successful transformation would have not been possible without the full support
of the company's board, but board members and investors need to have a thorough under-

standing of pros and cons associated with new technologies. As a result, the strategy function of the firm's corporate governance would be significantly undermined if board members did not possess knowledge, experience and skills that are increasingly required as an outcome of digital technological change.

## The Challenges to the Legitimacy Function

Corporate governance systems have also been instrumental in ensuring organizational legitimacy (Filatotchev et al., 2021), and this function has often been focused on compliance with national corporate governance codes and regulations. On the one hand, digital technologies can help with monitoring infringements/breaches of compliance. In fact, perhaps not surprisingly, companies in highly regulated sectors such as telecoms, banking and insurance show the greatest adoption of AI – which includes techniques such as machine learning – for monitoring regulatory compliance. For instance, an AI system at JPMorgan interprets 12,000 new commercial loan agreements a year, considerably cutting down on time spent by lawyers and loan officers. Many firms in Europe are using AI to comply with regulations such as the new General Data Protection Regulation (GDPR). AI is being used to detect the flow of personal data through a company's servers, and to make sure that data use is compliant with GDPR. However, as per the monitoring management function, digitizing compliance is subject to the same risks – see Table 17.1. Furthermore, as well as these challenges, the combined effect of pursuing business opportunities in a changing institutional environment presents unique challenges for the compliance-focused, legacy governance practices. In fact, traditionally, a key legitimacy role of governance functions was to ensure that the firm is in full compliance with rules and regulations presented by "soft" and "hard" laws in a particular country or sector. Digitalization presents three specific challenges to this governance function.

First, digital business models are often designed to operate across national jurisdictions and are exposed to what institutional theorists call "poly-centric institutional settings" (e.g., Zhu et al., 2017). What is considered legal in one institutional setting may be completely non-compliant in another. By moving their business into new institutional domains outside traditional regulation, firms take a huge gamble that their new business models will be unconditionally accepted by stakeholders. This gamble does not always pay off, and governance mechanisms do not always account for a potential loss of legitimacy even when strategic decisions are perfectly compliant with existing rules and regulations in a specific jurisdiction. In many instances, the law may impose sanctions, regardless of culpability, when breached (e.g., in the area of data protection). It is also the case that many of the legislative developments have extra-territorial application, whereby one country's law may have jurisdiction over individuals and corporations outside the country. Internet & Jurisdiction, a think-tank based in Paris, has documented dozens of cases of such extraterritoriality. Some are crude, such as when police in Brazil in March 2017 arrested a local Facebook executive because WhatsApp, the firm's messenger service, did not provide information requested for a criminal investigation (WhatsApp does not keep copies of messages).

Second, new strategies and business models are often deployed in a regulatory "vacuum" (e.g., Porter and Heppelmann, 2014; Zhu et al, 2017). Uber and Deliveroo are examples of how new forms of labor relations can emerge outside the existing regulations of work and employment. But a lack of regulation today does not mean that regulatory or law enforcement agencies will not interfere with an emerging industry tomorrow. This creates a significant challenge for governance legitimacy functions to be forward-looking in order to anticipate when and how a newly created market segment may be subject to a regulatory response. For instance, consider the evolving regulation around data privacy. In 2010 Facebook admitted that its then most popular applications, including *Farmville*, shared user data with advertisers, and it had to subsequently settle with the US Trade Commission regarding 20 years of third-party privacy audits. Google's StreetView has run into privacy battles with France, Germany and South Korea, to name a few. Other companies have been less fortunate, and data infringements have led to their demise either because of customer outrage or government intervention. Recently, Google has been fined by the European Union for infringing market dominance by manipulating search engine results (European Commission, 2017).

The ways companies handle data and data protection breaches also present a significant threat to organizational legitimacy. For example, in September 2017 hackers stole names, Social Security numbers, dates of birth and other critical personal information of 143 million Americans from Equifax. Ironically, this is one of three companies in the US – the other two are Experian and TransUnion – which dominate the business of gathering information on borrowing habits from banks and other sources and organize this data into scores used by lenders and other financial institutions to price credit. The fact that the company, which is supposedly an expert at protecting information, had not disclosed the breach, which allegedly happened over a period of 2.5 months, significantly undermined trust in its ability to store and handle personal data safely. Although the company made a statement that it went public after engaging an independent security expert to conduct a risk assessment, this loss of legitimacy may have significant governance implications. Analysts warned about an imminent regulatory probe, an investigation into possible insider share trading and an increase in proposals for class-action lawsuits against the company and its management (McLannahan, 2017).

The institutional "vacuum" challenge is augmented by another concurrent phenomenon: digital transformation is challenging even received legacy regulatory wisdom about what constitutes "market failure". As regulation normally targets areas where the government agencies perceive a "market failure", a growing ambiguity in terms of what these failures might be significantly affects the effectiveness of legitimacy functions of corporate governance. One example is the changing orientation of patents in the US, once the reference country for strict patent protection and patent enforcement law. Yet, this view is no longer fully shared by the US regulators and even by the US tech giants, who are pushing for the quasi abolition of patents (Foroohar, 2017). Increasingly, competition in the digital era is between tech company monopolies that have access to massive data sets and vast computing power, creating formidable barriers to entry. It is not yet clear whether the regulator(s) will take the view that in such environments competition is just a "click away" to disrupt any dominance or whether they will consider that the formidable economies of scale that protect winners will permanently distort economic efficiency and political and social dynamics. Depending on which orientation the regulator(s) will take, companies might find themselves grappling with completely different regulatory frameworks from what had been expected. In the UK, Google and Facebook have been increasingly seen as publishers and the chairman of the Office for Communications, the UK's media regulator, has recently raised the prospects of starting to regulate them accordingly. In Australia, the local competitive authority is suing Google for market dominance in the advertising market. Yet, on the other hand, in the US Google does not seem to be suffering from any regulatory setback.

## RESPONDING TO THE CHALLENGES: TOWARDS AN OPEN SOURCE CORPORATE GOVERNANCE

Given the new challenges described in Table 17.1, are "legacy models" of corporate governance still applicable in the new digital world? The "legacy model" of corporate governance is heavily reliant on financial controls to deal with governance problems. In this model, company shareholders are predominantly concerned with short-term profit maximization, and they would rely heavily on structural corporate governance mechanisms related to monitoring and oversight, as usually is the case when a company is controlled by dispersed owners or "transient" investors such as hedge funds. In this context, effective monitoring is associated with independent board members, information disclosure procedures, economic risk management, and internal and external audits. The firm's governance relies on a centralized, hierarchical system of accountability and reporting, and board monitoring and risk management extensively use financial performance indicators as key benchmarks. In terms of board member skills, financial literacy and experience with business strategies, such as divestment, M&As, re-financing, etc., are often regarded as paramount for effective board oversight. These systems of financial control are effective to the extent that they reduce agency costs and are hypothesized to result in positive efficiency outcomes and better financial performance. Equity-based remuneration linked to the overall financial performance provides another pillar of effective governance within the "legacy model". The second column in Table 17.2 summarizes the mechanisms through which "legacy governance" delivers on its functions.

Seeking to tackle the closed-system approach of legacy agency approaches, resource dependence (Pfeffer and Salancik, 1978) and comparative institutional theory (Aoki, 2004) have focused on how corporate governance relates to different organizational environments, and the limits and enablers of such systems. More recent research grounded in institutional theory and organizational sociology has largely advocated an "open systems" perspective, which suggests that different corporate governance practices may be more or less effective depending upon the contexts of different organizational environments (Aguilera et al., 2008). Within the field of corporate governance, this research comes closer to an "open systems" approach by recognizing that the effectiveness of corporate governance practices depends on a wider set of firm-related actors and institutional settings. This shifts attention from efficiency arguments (e.g., narrow definitions of financial performance) towards a broader understanding of effectiveness in terms of goal attainment in relation to the multiple objectives of different constituent stakeholders (i.e., employee satisfaction, supplier reciprocity, consumer loyalty, etc.).

Here we argue that to systemically address the challenges of the digital transformation (highlighted in Table 17.1) corporate governance should incorporate two new principles: (a) the need to systematically increase complementarities among internal and external stakeholders in both governance and strategy, and (b) the need to purposely balance short-term compliance and long-term legitimacy. These two principles are the foundations of what we call "open source" governance. Below we elaborate on the implications of the "open source" governance model for corporate governance practices and we contrast them with legacy governance's practices. Table 17.2 summarizes our key considerations.

Overall, open source governance shifts emphasis from the over-narrow agency perspective towards developing a system of interactions between the company and its ecosystem. A key part of open source governance is associated with transition to a reliance on "strategic" rather

*Table 17.2*     Legacy vs open source governance mechanisms and their underlying governance practices

| Governance factors | "Legacy governance" | "Open source" governance |
|---|---|---|
| Relationships with external stakeholders | "Shareholder supremacy" | Formal and systematic consideration of broader stakeholders' interests in setting goals and identifying risks |
| Shareholder objectives | • Short-term financial performance; <br> • Maximization of shareholder value | • Longer-term sustainability; <br> • Organizational legitimacy |
| Accountability and reporting | Centralized systems of accountability and communications | • Non-hierarchical systems of communications; <br> • Accountability to external constituencies; <br> • Breaking path dependency and black-boxing in decision-making |
| Board monitoring focus | • Financial performance of the firm (Return on Sales; Return on Assets) <br> • Digital strategy development is "out-sourced" to IT departments or external consultants | • Strategic objectives, including long-term sustainability of the firm; <br> • Business model transformation |
| Managerial incentives | • Executive share options; <br> • Incentive schemes linked to financial performance | Incentives include, alongside financial performance, broader indicators, such as social performance and cyber security |
| Risk management and control | Risks are mainly related to financial and economic factors | • Risks include a wide range of economic and social factors, including organizational legitimacy; <br> • Cyber risks and digital threats |
| External governance | Developed market for corporate control | Considerations of reputation and trust |

than "financial" controls within the firm's governance mechanism. These "strategic controls" are less concerned with short-term financial performance but may be focused instead on issues related to the organization's long-term sustainability and growth in market share, and stakeholder support. The "openness" of the firm's governance mechanisms ensures that stakeholder constituencies provide key inputs into the process of strategic control and provide context for the process of monitoring. Unlike formal, highly centralized systems of accountability and reporting based on financial indicators, "strategic controls" deploy more informal systems of communication between managers and stakeholders, as well as risk management systems focused on broader definitions of risk, including broader risks of de-legitimization. The latter includes a wide range of economic and social factors, such as organizational legitimacy vis-à-vis not only shareholders and customers but also broader social groups, such as user communities. In this type of governance, reputational and trust considerations, rather than the market for corporate control, underpin external governance pressures on managers.

The open source model of corporate governance imposes new demands on the structure and functioning of corporate boards. Improving board effectiveness in the context of digital transformation will entail a systematic redevelopment of governance policies associated with board mechanisms and director skills. In the short term, one of the most pressing issues is related to the new dimensions of board diversity, beyond gender, age and traditional legacy knowledge domains. For instance, while knowledge about cyber security has improved in many boards, even more "resident" cyber security knowledge – that is not outsourced to a consultant – is required. Crucially, boards should equip themselves with more knowledge integration skills. Perhaps here there is scope to redefine independent directors as boundary-spanners to share knowledge and experience between and across sectors. In the longer term, it will be important to recognize new types of strategic and organizational risks that should be considered and managed by the boards. These include risk of business disruption, risk of losing organizational legitimacy, business ecosystem risks and relational risks, among many others that the digital revolution may create in the near future.

Similarly, in terms of managerial incentives, new business models and technological changes in the market necessitate the incorporation of softer, intangible and behavioral-based performance measures within an objective setting and performance appraisal process. The performance management system combines the extent of achievement of individual performance objectives ("the what") and the values and behaviors required to deliver those results in a sustainable manner ("the how"). Again, the "open source" governance mechanism may provide a channel for stakeholder involvement in evaluating managerial performance in both individual targets and a complex context of digitalization, taking on board views of stakeholders in the firm's ecosystem.

Interestingly, some "profit-with-purpose" enterprises have opted for innovative forms of "open" governance to support their business models. For example, Cafédirect, an ethical grower and distributor of coffee based in the UK, decided to go public using an "ethical public offering" (EPO). In contrast to a conventional initial public offering on a stock exchange, Cafédirect issued its shares through the Ethical Exchange (Ethex) investment platform, a service offered by Triodos Bank. This funding mechanism provides access to shares to investors who support the firm's social purpose while limiting the degree to which shareholders could take control of the business. The largest shareholders include Oikocredit, Ecumenical Development Co-operative Society, Oxfam Activities Ltd, Cafédirect Producers Ltd and Rathbone Nominees Ltd. The company has one Guardians' share, held by the Guardian Share Company Ltd. In 2021, there were three members of the Guardian Share Company Ltd: Oxfam Activities Ltd, Cafédirect Producers Ltd and Oikocredit Ecumenical Development Co-Operative Society. The Guardians' share provides additional rights to ensure that Cafédirect follows its founding principles. More importantly, there is a direct stakeholders' representation on the Board. The eight-strong board reflects how seriously Cafédirect considers the interests of its stakeholders by maintaining representation on the board by two representatives of the growing community, a consumer and finance representative, a shareholder-nominated representative and a director nominated by the Guardian Share Company. Although these governance characteristics are in line with the UK's Companies Act, they represent an open governance system involving key stakeholders.

These considerations shift our view of corporate governance as an essentially internal, formal mechanism associated with monitoring and control towards an "open system" view of corporate governance that involves external, informal channels of influence. A key challenge for corporate boards is, therefore, to recognize these channels and integrate internal processes with these external factors, no small feat considering that corporate governance traditionally considered external factors exclusively in the context of regulation and compliance.

How can companies make open source governance happen? While digital transformation creates significant problems for legacy governance, digital technologies themselves can offer technological solutions to future governance models based on the open source governance framework. One possible design of open source governance includes "decision-rights partitioning" in the context of blockchain technology – i.e., how decision-making authority is split between the company's owners/shareholders and community members or, in other words, the degree of decentralization of the decision-making process. Another option might be leveraging decision support systems (DSS) designed to connect ever-growing numbers of firms in a market ecosystem, such as the Aladdin DSS developed by BlackRock in the investment management sector, or Bloomberg, among many others. Despite significant differences in their purpose and design, these DSS platforms typically include a learning interface where the participants in a network exchange information about successes and failures. This may be a template for future DSS platforms in the corporate governance field, connecting different stakeholders to the board. An aggregator functionality may help board members of a company in the center of this governance platform to recognize, interpret and act upon often very diverse aspirations of stakeholders. As with all stakeholder-centered governance mechanisms, this may be open to possible mismanagement and abuse. Therefore, the open source governance platform should limit access only to stakeholders in the firm's digital ecosystem. To avoid the pitfalls associated with using AI in decision-making systems that we discussed above, board members should have ultimate responsibility for information recognition, interpretation and usage.

## DISCUSSION AND FUTURE RESEARCH AGENDA

Digital transformation offers new possibilities for companies as well as new challenges (Lanzolla et al., 2021). Organizations are using digital technology to transform their products, processes and value chains, and to enter into new markets. It has enabled many companies to work with a wider range of "ecosystem" partners and offer their products and services to a wider/different range of clients. Digital technology has also significantly lowered the transaction and coordination costs that shaped the legacy organization and industry structures; the lowering of those costs has unleashed new possibilities for organizational forms, strategies and management processes. Still, digital transformation also has a dark side. For example, market concentration might increase because of digital incumbents' dominance, with dubious consequences for consumers; algorithms underpinning AI may amplify biases in decision-making (Lanzolla et al., 2021). Regulators (and the public) are still elaborating their responses to such structural changes. Yet, the current "regulatory vacuum" should not be considered as permanent, and history teaches that the drivers of legitimacy, and with them regulation, might suddenly change.

While grappling with these new possibilities and the associated challenges and trade-offs, managers must radically transform businesses and organizations, often far from their legacy resources, capabilities and business models. In this chapter we have argued that the challenges that digital transformation poses to corporate governance are daunting and cannot be fully addressed within the framework of legacy governance. Legacy corporate governance principles based on the agency perspective and focused on financial controls do not seem adequate to provide effective monitoring, strategy and legitimacy to organizations in the age of digital transformation. We have argued that corporate governance principles should embrace the new realities of openness, interdependencies, complexity, dynamism and fluidity, and corporate governance practices should change accordingly. Our discussion indicates that the notion of corporate governance effectiveness should be extended beyond the confines of manager–shareholder dichotomy, and the effectiveness of firm-level governance mechanisms should be assessed from a multi-stakeholder perspective. Complementing and building on the emergent "open system" approach to corporate governance theory (Filatotchev et al., 2021), our proposed open source corporate governance introduces new principles and highlights the importance of strategic controls (as opposed to financial controls) to provide effective governance to companies in the digital age.

This argumentation provides important opportunities for theory building. With respect to corporate governance, for example, digital business models lead to "open" firms with more permeable boundaries pursuing their strategic objectives with, within and across ecosystems (see discussion in Jacobides et al., 2018, about the difference of these new forms of organizing). Does this require that researchers also revisit theoretical principles around corporate governance, starting with its application – should it apply exclusively to the inner corporation or the "extended" organization (i.e., the ecosystem)? Further, open source governance would signify a more decentralized governance model where the firm "community" (key stakeholders and actors) have a say in the monitoring and other functions, which would invert the process, making it more participative and bottom-up. In this sense, some authors, when discussing new issues related to regulation of big tech companies designed to tame their activities and power, are proposing such forms of decentralized governance empowering third-party bodies to check continuously on the platform practices through "in situ" data access and algorithm scrutiny (see, for example, Cennamo et al., 2020). While we do not advocate for an introduction of new forms of "digital regulation", our proposed open source governance approach emphasizes the importance of the interfirm relationships that matter to the firm's organizing and functioning.

Further, an emergent socio-political perspective in the corporate governance field suggests that how markets react to a firm's actions is an outcome of stakeholders' perceptions of its legitimacy rather than rational, efficiency-centered optimization decisions (Filatotchev et al., 2021). Legitimacy is the "generalized perception or assumption that the actions of an entity are desirable, proper, or appropriate, within some socially constructed system of norms, values, beliefs, and definitions" (Suchman, 1995, p. 574). Various actors inside and outside the organization tend to focus on institutionalized rules (also called institutional logics) when evaluating management processes and their outcomes. Therefore, as Filatotchev et al. (2020) argue, we must also recognize how particular taken-for-granted ideas that underpin both scholars' research efforts and the *raison d'être* of organizations are also products of relations of dominance, particularly an institutional logic of "shareholder supremacy" that originated in the US/UK corporate concept, and how powerful institutional investors and their associations promote the ideas. Until recently, this logic underpinned fundamental approaches to the roles and objectives of firm-level governance and, according to some scholars, promoted ideas of shareholder value maximization, productivity and financial efficiency as if these were self-evidently desirable and in the interests of all.

Specifically, one of the core principles of traditional governance is focusing on clear priorities and serving the fiduciary role of shareholders. What does this mean in an open governance approach? Is this principle still standing, or is it challenged, and how? Given that innovation and the sources of advantage in the digital space are to a great extent unanticipated, should board members favor experimentation in grey areas or curtail activity in such domains to minimize risks? Today, scholars, business practitioners and societies in general are challenging the very foundations of the "shareholder supremacy" perspective of corporate governance and corporate social responsibility. Simultaneously, we are experiencing a resurgence of the concept of corporate purpose, along with the creation of a new category of corporations – "profit-with-purpose corporations". This new perspective, which in the past few years surfaced in the corporate law of several countries, including the US and France, adds to the traditional governance objectives related to the company's financial performance an explicit commitment towards a wider societal purpose within the bylaws. Filatotchev, Aguilera and Wright (2020) argue that corporate governance innovations accompany this shift in the dominant institutional logic towards a greater account of stakeholders' interests. Existing theories of corporate governance, such as agency and transaction cost economics, are limited in terms of explaining antecedents and outcomes of corporate governance innovations. Because of this, scholars and the academic disciplines within which they situate their questions require novel theoretical approaches to inform our understanding of contemporary governance in today's diverse institutional and technological settings.

## CONCLUDING REMARKS

The adoption of open source corporate governance very much depends on company exposures to digital transformation. For instance, sectors that are increasingly relying on the usage of digital platforms connecting various stakeholders may be more in need of introducing various elements of the open source governance outlined above. On the other hand, companies in more mature or regulated industries such as banking may focus on supporting governance mechanisms more focused on the traditional notions of monitoring and control. Overall, we maintain that legacy vs open source governance should be seen as two extremes or poles in a continuum instead of just two polarized discrete extremes with nothing in the middle. The openness of the firm's governance mechanism to external stakeholders may help to find a right balance and ensure the effectiveness of governance in handling various challenges associated with the "digital revolution".

## NOTE

1.  Unpublished manuscript. Please contact the authors for a copy.

## REFERENCES

Aguilera, R., Filatotchev, I., Jackson, G., and Gospel, H. 2008. An organizational approach to comparative corporate governance: Costs, contingencies, and complementarities. *Organization Science*, 19(3), 475–92.

Almirall, E., and Casadesus-Masanell, R. 2010. Open versus closed innovation: A model of discovery and divergence. *Academy of Management Review*, 35(1), 27–47.

Aoki, M. 2004. Comparative institutional analysis of corporate governance. In Grandori, A. (Ed.), *Corporate Governance and Firm Organization: Microfoundations and Structural Reforms*: 31–45. Oxford Academic.

Bailey, D.E., Leonardi, P.M., and Barley, S.R. 2012. The lure of the virtual. *Organization Science*, 23(5), 1485–504.

Brunswicker, S., Almirall, E., and Majchrzak, A. 2019. Optimizing and satisficing: The interplay between platform architecture and producers' design strategies for platform performance. *MIS Quarterly*, 43(4), 1249–77.

Casadesus-Masanell, R., and Zhu, F. 2013. Business model innovation and competitive imitation: The case of sponsor-based business models. *Strategic Management Journal*, 34(4), 464–82.

Cennamo, C. 2018. Building the value of next-generation platforms: The paradox of diminishing returns. *Journal of Management*, 44(8), 3038–69.

Cennamo, C., Dagnino, G.B., Di Minin, A., & Lanzolla, G. 2020. Managing digital transformation: Scope of transformation and modalities of value co-generation and delivery. *California Management Review*, 62(4), 5–16.

Cennamo, C., and Santaló, J. 2013. Platform competition: Strategic trade-offs in platform markets. *Strategic Management Journal*, 34(11), 1331–50.

Cennamo, C., and Santaló, J. 2019. Generativity tension and value creation in platform ecosystems. *Organization Science*, 30(3), 617–41.

Chatterjee, S., Harrison, J.S., and Bergh, D.D. 2003. Failed takeover attempts, corporate governance and refocusing. *Strategic Management Journal*, 24(1), 87–96.

Daily, C.M., Dalton, D.R., and Cannella, A.A., Jr. 2003. Corporate governance: Decades of dialogue and data. *Academy of Management Review*, 28(3), 371–82.

D'Aveni, R.A., Dagnino, G.B., and Smith, K.G. 2010. The age of temporary advantage. *Strategic Management Journal*, 31(13), 1371–85.

Eisenhardt, K.M. 1998. Agency theory: An assessment and review. *Academy of Management Review*, 14(1), 57–74.

Euromonitor. 2015. Half the world's population will be online by 2030. https://www.euromonitor.com/article/half-the-worlds-population-will-be-online-by-2030.

European Commission. 2017. Antitrust: Commission fines Google €2.42 billion for abusing dominance as search engine by giving illegal advantage to own comparison shopping service – Factsheet. https://ec.europa.eu/commission/presscorner/detail/es/MEMO_17_1785.

Fama, E.F., and Jensen, M.C. 1983. Separation of ownership and control. *Journal of Law and Economics*, 26(2), 301–25.

Faraj, S., Pachidi, S., and Sayegh, K. 2018. Working and organizing in the age of the learning algorithm. *Information and Organization*, 28(1), 62–70.

Felin, T., Lakhani, K.R., and Tushman, M.L. 2017. Firms, crowds, and innovation. *Strategic Organization*, 15(2), 119–40.

Filatotchev, I., Aguilera, R., and Wright, M. 2020. From governance of innovation to innovations in corporate governance. *Academy of Management Perspectives*, 34(2), 173–81.

Filatotchev, I., Ireland, D., and Stahl, G. 2021. Contextualizing management research: An open systems perspective. *Journal of Management Studies*, forthcoming.

Filatotchev, I., Wright, M., Uhlenbruck, K., Tihanyi, L., & Hoskisson, R.E. 2003. Governance, organizational capabilities, and restructuring in transition economies. *Journal of World Business*, 38(4), 331–47.

Foroohar, R. 2017. Big Tech vs Big Pharma: The battle over US patent protection. *Financial Times*, 16 October. https://www.ft.com/content/6c5b2cca-ae8b-11e7-beba-5521c713abf4.

Jacobides, M.G., Cennamo, C., and Gawer, A. 2018. Towards a theory of ecosystems. *Strategic Management Journal*, 39(8), 2255–76.

Kaplan, S., and Vakili, K. 2015. The double-edged sword of recombination in breakthrough innovation. *Strategic Management Journal*, 36(10), 1435–57.

Kellogg, K.C., Valentine, M.A., and Christin, A. 2020. Algorithms at work: The new contested terrain of control. *Academy of Management Annals*, 14(1), 366–410.

Lanzolla, G., Pesce, D., and Tucci, C.L. 2021. The digital transformation of search and recombination in the innovation function: Tensions and an integrative framework. *Journal of Product Innovation Management*, 38(1), 90–113.

Leonardi, P.M., Nardi, B.A., and Kallinikos, J. (Eds). 2012. *Materiality and Organizing: Social Interaction in a Technological World*. Oxford University Press on Demand.

Majchrzak, A., Markus, M.L., and Wareham, J. 2016. Designing for digital transformation: Lessons for information systems research from the study of ICT and societal challenges. *MIS Quarterly*, 40(2), 267–77.

McLannahan, B. 2017. Equifax flaws exposed by hack attack. *Financial Times*, 12 September. https://www.ft.com/content/2b8b769e-9754-11e7-b83c-9588e51488a0.

Orlikowski, W.J., and Scott, S.V. 2014. What happens when evaluation goes online? Exploring apparatuses of valuation in the travel sector. *Organization Science*, 25(3), 868–91.

Parker, G.G., Van Alstyne, M.W., and Choudary, S.P. 2016. *Platform Revolution: How Networked Markets Are Transforming the Economy and How to Make Them Work for You.* W.W. Norton & Company.

Pfeffer, J., and Salancik, G. 1978. *The External Control of Organizations.* Harper & Row.

Porter, M.E., and Heppelmann, J.E. 2014. How smart, connected products are transforming competition. *Harvard Business Review*, 92(11), 64–88.

Statista. 2023. Number of Internet of Things (IoT) connected devices worldwide from 2019 to 2021, with forecasts from 2022 to 2030. https://www.statista.com/statistics/1183457/iot-connected-devices -worldwide/.

Suchman, M.C. 1995. Managing legitimacy: Strategic and institutional approaches. *Academy of Management Review*, 20(3), 571–610.

Teece, D.J. 2010. Business models, business strategy and innovation. *Long Range Planning*, 43(2–3), 172–94.

Westphal, J.D. 1999. Collaboration in the boardroom: Behavioral and performance consequences of CEO-board social ties. *Academy of Management Journal*, 42(1), 7–24.

World Economic Forum. 2016. The Fourth Industrial Revolution: What it means, how to respond. https://www.weforum.org/agenda/2016/01/the-fourth-industrial-revolution-what-it-means-and-how -to-respond/.

Yoo, Y., Henfridsson, O., and Lyytinen, K. 2010. Research commentary: The new organizing logic of digital innovation – An agenda for information systems research. *Information Systems Research*, 21(4), 724–35.

Yoo, Y., et al. 2012. Organizing for innovation in the digitized world. *Organization Science*, 23(5), 1398–408.

Zhu, F., et al. 2017. *Ant Financial.* Harvard Business School Publishing.

Zhu, F., and Furr, N. 2016. Products to platforms: Making the leap. *Harvard Business Review*, 94(4), 72–8.

Zhu, F., and Iansiti, M. 2012. Entry into platform-based markets. *Strategic Management Journal*, 33(1), 88–106.

Zuboff, S. 2019. *The Age of Surveillance Capitalism: The Fight for a Human Future at the New Frontier of Power.* Profile Books.

# 18. The impact of artificial intelligence on management practice

*Sophia Shtepa, Yongjian Bao and Oleksiy Osiyevskyy*

## INTRODUCTION

The artificial intelligence (AI) winter is thawing, reviving humankind's aspirations for these computational agents. Though relatively recent (since the mid-2010s), marked advances in machines' ability to act appropriately, exhibit flexibility, and learn from experience follow a persistent, historical enhancement of computing power (Poole & Mackworth, 2010). As predicted by Moore's law, semiconductor performance doubled biennially over the past forty years (roughly corresponding to the number of transistors fitting per computer chip) (Moore, 1965). Additionally, power is now easily upped through distributed and scalable computing in the cloud; i.e., by drawing on the aggregated capacity of multiple machines, many of which one neither owns nor operates.

These refinements in computing power invigorated machine learning, a subfield of AI focalizing algorithms and systems capable of achieving cumulative performance improvements on specific tasks through repeated experience (Samuel, 1959). Surpassing earlier hopes to simply replicate human reasoning, machine learning technologies can generate statistical predictions from given data faster and more accurately than humans (Agrawal et al., 2018). Machines are especially advantaged when there are large volumes of unstructured data to learn from (i.e., big data), as greater learning exposure leads to prediction accuracy gains (McAfee et al., 2012). Resultantly, AI can take on the essential, cognitive tasks of management; i.e., defining agendas, setting goals, designing actions, and evaluating and choosing alternatives (Simon et al., 1987). Further, machines may outperform human managers at some decision-making activities, as they can quickly spot hidden, weak patterns and garner nuanced insights from big data. AI, therefore, portends a transformation of management practices across industries, ushering in the Fourth Industrial Revolution (Schwab, 2016).

Yet, despite becoming a hot topic among business practitioners and scholars, the potential of AI is still to be systemically linked with established theoretical perspectives in strategic management. For example, a seminal work of Agrawal et al. (2018) discusses the strategic implications of AI with a narrow view of the technologies as merely a means to reduce prediction costs. In contrast, we pose that AI improves predictions and the corresponding quality of managerial decision-making, while also enhancing the ability to transfer knowledge within an organization; all these mechanisms have strategic implications going far beyond prediction cost reduction. In particular, AI technologies help managers to minimize the bounded rationality problem, altering a crucial micro-foundation of management. Managers can then use AI to tackle cognitive tasks related to various decision problems and cultivate greater cognitive synergy throughout the organization. Consequently, AI could profoundly impact management practices with respect to micro-economic mechanisms of value creation and capture; that is, organizational business models (Biloshapka & Osiyevskyy, 2018).

In this chapter, we lay out and expand upon these premises. The proposed framework is summarized in Figure 18.1, outlining a set of general mechanisms through which AI technologies are affecting organizational business models. Elaborating the key links in this model, we introduce four distinct domains of decision problems tackled by AI (determination, design, deliberation, and discovery), outlining the conditions and effective ways of applying AI technologies in different situations. We finish by discussing the implications of AI for creating a sustainable competitive advantage, concentrating on contextual factors and boundary conditions that define the efficiency of digital AI strategies.

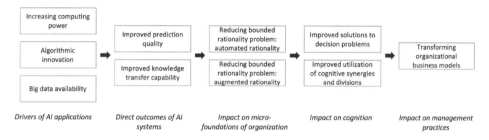

*Figure 18.1*     *The impact of AI technologies on management practices: general mechanisms*

## BEYOND BOUNDED RATIONALITY

Originated by Herbert Simon, the bounded rationality concept describes a fundamental assumption about humans' 'scarcity of mind' (e.g., Simon, 1955). The quality of managerial decision-making, in line with this view, is constrained both by insufficient knowledge of the future and imperfect processing of available information (e.g., Simon, 1955). While some cognitive skills can be improved with practice (e.g., systemically checking for alternatives to avoid tunnel vision), humans predominantly make 'satisficing' rather than 'optimizing' decisions. That is, managers seek solutions that are 'good enough' given the extent of humans' cognitive ability and a finite time for contemplation.

Given sufficient computing power and data to learn from, AI has no such limitations. Correspondingly, machines could supply organizations with 'automated rationality', characterized by a faster and less error-prone performance of cognitive tasks (especially when the job is predefined and repetitive). Particularly, AI is advantaged by an ability to analyze big volumes of real-time, unstructured, and diverse inputs. Moreover, big data boosts prediction accuracy for AI by serving as additional learning material. At the same time, humans find it extremely difficult and time-consuming (if not altogether impossible) to comprehend and generate meaningful insights from similarly large data. There are limits to the amount of data points humans can retain, leading them to categorize information (Migliore & Chinta, 2017). Though useful, this simplification incorporates biases into decisions and lowers accuracy (Migliore & Chinta, 2017). Furthermore, humans tend to rely on a recognition heuristic, selecting options that they are already familiar with (even when new knowledge is introduced) (Goldstein & Gigenzer, 2008). Therefore, humans' accuracy initially increases with additional data but eventually falls, undermined by an inability to process the new information (Goldstein

& Gigenzer, 2008). Resultantly, the quality of human solutions may decrease with additional inputs, even when provided with extra time; at best, decisions would be similar or improve marginally (Osiyevskyy et al., 2020).

Moreover, AI can attain 'augmented rationality'; that is, arrive at highly nuanced and unimagined conclusions. For example, AI can identify elusive, weak-signal patterns and conceive highly complex phenomena. This is possible because a robust, multi-dimensional architecture underlies the technologies' understanding of reality (sometimes with hundreds of millions of dimensions). Comparatively, the human brain employs categorization and framing to make sense of a problem, often liberally and without skepticism. Resultantly, humans tend to recognize only the strongest of patterns and have predetermined assumptions about the relevant and important facets of a decision (i.e., thinking in the box). Of course, AI-generated solutions are not perfect either, being contingent on algorithm and data quality. However, AI can arrive at the *next-best* decisions, ones that are not the best but are significantly better than those produced by humans. Therefore, while not quite optimal, AI solutions exceed the mere 'good enough' standard of 'satisficing' decision-making mode.

Admittedly, experienced managers do have a major advantage over AI systems when data is scarce. Over time, these decision-makers acquire 'tacit' knowledge, which guides their thinking about future decisions (Polanyi, 1958, 1966). Though a manager can apply this knowledge in many different situations, it is difficult or impossible to fully convey the experience to other managers or AI systems. Contrastingly, AI can (potentially) learn everything another system knows, thus possessing (a theoretically) unlimited knowledge-transfer capability. Information processing can therefore be standardized and leveled up across an organization or open innovation cohort. However, until sufficient data becomes available for the AI in a particular context, humans may be the firm's best bet. Yet, this advantage fades and disappears once data is abundant, as humans cannot keep up with AI's cognitive capacity (see Figure 18.2).

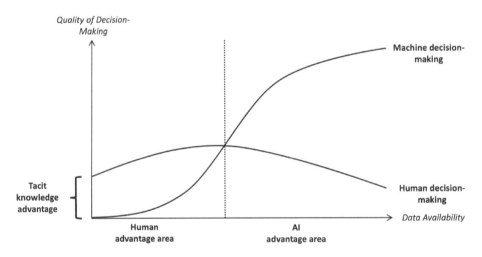

*Source:*   Adapted from: Osiyevskyy et al. (2020).

*Figure 18.2*   *The impact of data availability on the quality of machine and human decision-making*

## APPLICATIONS OF AI FOR DECISION PROBLEMS AND COGNITIVE SYNERGY

Through automating and augmenting rationality, AI can aid organizations with four types of decision problems: determination, design, deliberation, and discovery. The four domains (inspired by Frank Knight's (1921) seminal work) are differentiated by the levels of uncertainty surrounding a decision's goals, means, and implementation processes; that is, by the way in which knowledge is applied to cope with the uncertainty (see Figure 18.3).

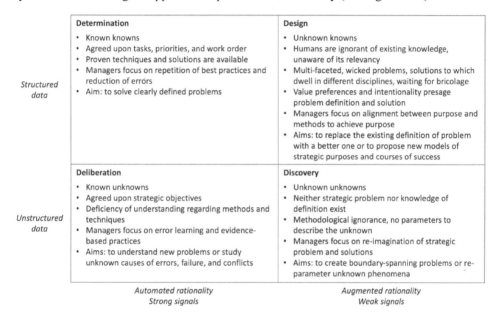

*Figure 18.3    AI decision problems: the four domains*

'Determination' refers to decisions with clear problem definitions and proven, best-practice solutions. They concern 'known knowns', matters wherein both the abstract question and the concrete answers are known to the decision-makers. Often, these tasks are repetitive, follow an 'if-then' logic, and require analysis of structured data. Accordingly, 'determination' is ideal for AI-enabled automation with associated rationality gains (e.g., speed and accuracy).

'Design', on the other hand, deals with 'unknown knowns': information is available, often in a structured form, but decision-makers have yet to identify its relevance or formulate strategic goals incorporating its insights. The goals of such decisions may be to redefine the problem, propose new strategic purposes, or ascertain new means for achieving existing aims. Importantly, ignorance of the information's relevance is not merely a matter of education, as in the case of knowledge outside one's discipline. Some ideas' invisibility may instead be ascribed to incongruence with decision-makers' cultural identity or individual intentions. For example, the association of schooling with physical campuses and sense-based, in-person lessons resulted in online education being previously deemed an inferior learning design. Widespread adoption during the COVID-19 pandemic, however, has redefined the perception and valuation of online learning as an alternative, additional, or augmented method of education. Using AI, organizations could minimize the effect of such cultural and individual biases, becoming innovators or at least early adopters of disruptive ideas. Hence, applying AI to 'design' problems constitutes rationality augmentation, with the technologies making connections unhindered by preconceptions of items' relevance or weight.

'Deliberation', the third decision problem, arises when one has an abstract question but limited awareness of potential answers (i.e., 'known unknowns'). In such instances, AI can search for strong, predefined signals among unstructured data, automating an otherwise lengthy and difficult cognitive process. Organizations face two types of 'deliberation' problems, scientific and value-directed. Scientific 'deliberation' refers to inquiries of abnormal results; e.g., errors during implementation, tactic failure, or variations in firm performance. Experts set out to diagnose the anomaly's cause, coming up with new methods to examine the premises and conditions of existing problems. Value-directed 'deliberation', contrastingly, is triggered by reflection upon moral and ethical concerns. For example, a firm aspiring to sustainability will likely learn that the concept is polysemic and elusive, without clear, universal standards or methods for 'being sustainable'. Subsequently, experts could direct AI to identify valuation and measurement mechanisms for sustainability within the unique context of their own organization.

Lastly, 'discovery' addresses decisions with meager information about both the problem and possible solutions (i.e., 'unknown unknowns'). Applying weak-learning AI to unstructured data, firms can utilize the machines' augmented rationality to identify unthought-of categories and connections. Resultantly, decision-makers can re-parameter obscure phenomena and re-imagine problem bounds and definitions. Often, such queries will be inspired by experts' imagination and curiosity, or encounters with new, abstract ideas (in both fiction and non-fiction). For example, attempt to imagine what the world will be like once the biological intelligence of humans is merged with the silicon intelligence of machines. Will humans possess the capacity for automated and augmented rationality within our own minds and what would that even look like? What would change about the ways in which we learn, socialize, and work? Would the increase in intelligence garner positive gains for individuals and societies as a whole? Or will super-powers exploit this new reality, leading to a confrontation that results in human society's devolution? Perhaps, the future holds something else entirely, which we have yet to imagine, let alone establish means for understanding and coping. With AI, exploration can begin in these uncharted waters, propelling the formation of new, innovative ideas.

Along with improving solutions to the four kinds of decision problems, the application of AI will allow firms to achieve greater cognitive synergy among the organization's members. In particular, for 'determination' and 'design' decisions as humans already possess potentially relevant knowledge about concrete practices. In 'determination' tasks, for example, the premises, causality, and performance measures related to a problem are known, just perhaps not extensively by the top management. Accordingly, sourcing and applying AI analysis to the insights of front-line staff would allow managers to incorporate a more detailed and direct understanding to big-picture problems. Further, employees may provide inputs for the AI's consideration to which designated decision-makers are culturally or individually ignorant; hence, strengthening 'design' solutions. Resultantly, organizations engaging in cognitive synergy may develop an edge over competitors.

Moreover, for the purpose of understanding organizational cognitive synergy one may regard AI systems as organizational 'members' based on their ability to complete cognitive assignments and provide intelligent suggestions. Subsequently, cognitive synergy gains can be found not only among humans but also between AI systems because of their (theoretically) unlimited and near-instantaneous knowledge transfer capability. One system, therefore, can communicate the results of its analysis to another system for use as inputs to improve performance upon a different cognitive task.

Importantly, corporations will continue to depend on expert, human knowledge for meaningful problems like 'deliberation' and 'discovery'. These require intentionality and judgment, like the need for predefined strategic objectives/abstract concepts when 'deliberating'. Organizations must, therefore, rely on humans' tacit knowledge and imagination which is difficult or impossible to transfer to other humans or machines. Correspondingly, accomplishing these tasks will require a division of cognition among members of the organization, with AI playing a supportive role to enhance experts' rationality (see Figure 18.4).

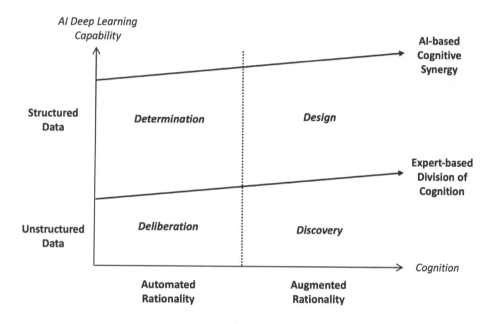

*Figure 18.4*    *Cognitive synergy and division of cognition*

## DEMONSTRATIVE CASES: APPLICATIONS OF AI FOR DECISION PROBLEMS ACROSS THE FOUR DOMAINS

**Determination**

1.  At the beginning of the COVID-19 pandemic, the Fourth Paradigm, a Chinese AI-focused unicorn company founded by veterans of Baidu (Google's Chinese equivalent), was commissioned to develop a model to understand potential responses and their impacts on the

spread of the disease. Though the starting data samples were small, the system was able to train with an automated machine learning (AutoML) tool. With additional data, the system has continued to optimize its predictions regarding possible response strategies and their effectiveness. For example, it deemed mass testing at the early stages of the virus' introduction to an area as the single most critical and promising course of action. Applying these findings, human decision-makers were able to increase control over the transmission of COVID-19.

2. A global chain store was plagued by warehouse logistics, and faced with a plethora of variables and their many dynamic interactions. Trying to plan an equipment arrangement, the firm had to consider factors like the size of the warehouse, the types of goods stored, and seasonal stock changes (to name a few). Previously, managers applied heuristic rules based on their experience and prepared to tolerate a wide range of errors. Warehouses would also keep many employees on stand-by, to intervene in case of a misjudgment.

   With AutoML, the firm built a virtual system to serve as a digital twin of the physical warehouse environment. The twin bore a high degree of similarity to the real working environment, allowing for authentic and useful simulation. Managers could then inquire to the AI for optimal equipment plans given any combination of variables, without being burdened by the physical cost of such experimentation. Accordingly, managers could visualize potential scenarios and select next-best, AI-recommended warehouse layouts.

3. A company selling chicken eggs faced a persistent problem: its product is perishable and unsuited for long-distance shipping, yet freshness is a key element of value. Previously, human managers applied tacit knowledge to make decisions about the firm's nation-wide production and distribution network. AI was applied to, firstly, map all variables and their dynamic interactions to optimize logistics scheduling. Then, using accumulated data, the system provided recommendations for improving the allocation of production plants. Correspondingly, the AI system minimized manager bias/error while capturing useful tacit knowledge.

## Design

1. One of the clients of the previously discussed Fourth Paradigm is a bank that services commercial customers with highly diverse needs. In the past, the marketing department could use at most 100 rules informed by historical experience to design and promote value propositions. The effectiveness of these efforts was questionable, at best. With the help of AI, however, the firm could generate suggestions for customers based on hundreds of thousands of rules and more than 20 million data clusters. Resultantly, predictions improved, and the marketing and sales staff were freed to socialize with customers and enhance the experiential value of the bank's services.

2. Diabetes is a chronic medical condition, coping with which involves a significant life-style component (cf. merely medication). Upon diagnosis, one may find support not only in their doctor but in relatives and community members, for example, to process feelings or learn sugar-free recipes. AI can be another support for people with diabetes, especially because each patient is unique. Additionally, treatment is documented but complex – involving observation, monitoring, diagnosis, recommendation, reminders, and feedback – going beyond the cognitive and administrative capacity of medical professionals. An AI-powered

app, therefore, could tailor treatment programs for individual patients and provide persons with relevant, customized help.

3. In partnership with International Business Machines' (IBM) Watson, EquBot manages an AI-directed exchange-traded fund: AI Powered Equity ETF (AIEQ). The machine deals with unknown knowns, combing through 'news, social media, industry and analyst reports, financial statements on over 6,000 U.S. companies, technical, macro, market data, and more' (ETF Managers Group, 2021). Resultantly, EquBot's understanding of markets incorporates information and relations that human decision-makers falsely deem irrelevant.

## Deliberation

1. Often, conflicts and controversy arise over AI's ability to tailor recommendations to individual preferences and needs in the financial and healthcare sectors. The underlying issues are more social, cultural, and political than technological, and emerge through practice rather than being identifiable a priori. One such controversy may revolve around privacy protection in an AI app, particularly if the system becomes very strong (i.e., provides accurate predictions about sensitive matters with minimal data). Problems like this cannot be automatically solved by AI and must instead be deliberated by human experts in the context of social value and cultural characteristics. Once the moral and ethical issues are clarified, AI could subsequently assist by providing technological solutions to the newly defined problem. Correspondingly, the firm benefits from a division of cognition, drawing on both human and AI strengths. Sticking with the previous example, privacy protection can be ensured by using sandbox technology. That is, processing of abstract, categorized data with no way to identify an individual user's identity.

2. In oil mining, each well has unique characteristics. If engineers tried to precisely label all potential variables, an AI model's reliability would increase but at great cost. Resultantly, AI systems are sometimes employed for analysis of oil wells, even with incomplete information. Using automatic and supervised learning, AI can produce models with acceptable levels of error. Human agents then review the machine's mistakes and make recommendations for the next round of AutoML training. Using both the experts' judgment and AI capacity for learning (i.e., having divisions of cognition), organizations can reduce the costs of data and incrementally improve the model's quality.

3. Movie distributors recently moved beyond simplistic, genre-based recommendations (e.g., action, romance, drama), and producers are next. In the current approach, production companies fail to recognize hundreds of vectors; that is, variables of audience appeal, such as stage design, costumes, music, and theme. Indeed, viewers themselves may be unaware of the effect that individual vectors or a combination thereof have on their interest. Using augmented learning, AI can experiment with novel vector mixes at a minimized cost and unearth the impact of known unknowns.

## Discovery

1. Tumor lysis syndrome (TLS) is a rare condition, characterized by a constellation of symptoms that can be misinterpreted as single issues. Problematically, misdiagnosis used to be common with attempts to develop a robust diagnostic criterion further complicated by the particularity of each patient and existing samples' one-directionality. That is, when

patients came to doctors, they already showed symptoms; the studied samples are all posi-tive, without negative samples to compare against. AI can provide a solution by generating a noisy, negative sample to compensate for the missing data. Further, once doctors apply their expertise and tacit knowledge to set up/validate potentially relevant parameters, AI can be engaged in supervised learning. The systems can then recommend novel com-binations, representations, and prototypes to stimulate human experts' imagination and accelerate the study of the condition. Applying this division of cognition – human experts proposing a broad, initial direction and AI following with unthought-of connections and categories – the diagnosis of TLS has been exponentially improved.

2. Provided with a broad direction by human experts, AI can create unlimited simulations of unexplored phenomena in a digital twin of the physical environment. This is particularly appealing, for example, to the electric car industry, where learning about the risk and consequences of design choices is very costly. Each test crash is an investment in mate-rials and assembly, with information about other electric cars' performance (as opposed to non-electric) on certain tests often unavailable. Physical testing can further be morally challenging, requiring managers to imagine all manner of possible tragedies (e.g., colli-sion impacts to pedestrians or malfunctions harming passengers). Accordingly, it may be advantageous to have AI on the job, self-generating all kinds of scenarios for virtual testing in a digital twin. From the results, human experts can then provide further directions for new rounds of testing. Correspondingly, the firm could use both a division of cognition (i.e., AI analysis guided by human judgment) and a cognitive synergy (i.e., AI results used as inputs for human judgment).

3. Automation Anywhere's Discovery Bot is a tool for automatic process discovery, begun by collecting data on employee interactions with enterprise solutions (e.g., customer relationship management) and applications like Microsoft Excel (Automation Anywhere, 2021). The system subsequently identifies processes that could be automated and recom-mends automation plans based on their business potential. Correspondingly, Automation Anywhere has innovated robotic process automation, drawing on a cognitive synergy beyond that offered by process mining.

## THE IMPACT OF AI ON ORGANIZATIONAL BUSINESS MODELS

AI-enabled improvements of rationality, decision problem solutions, and organizational cognitive synergy portend a transformation of value creation and capture mechanisms. To discuss this potential, we will be employing the four-dimensional theoretical lens developed by Osiyevskyy et al. (2018) based on a coherent summary of existing frameworks. Osiyevskyy et al. (2018) propose that organizational business models have four broad characteristics: the target industry, the stakeholder value proposition, the design of the activity system, and the resources for the business model.

Regarding the target industry, we first pose that AI allows for optimal market defini-tion; that is, identifying the firm's competitive arena. As data on products/services and consumers is often already available, this task requires determination and design decisions. Correspondingly, AI can be applied to sift through large volumes of data and produce detailed representations about competing value offerings and additive product features. The systems could identify elusive overlap between firms' propositions, including functional similarities that humans might overlook because of cultural or individual bias.

Further, with automated and augmented rationality, AI technologies can effectively segment the market, including to the scale of individual consumers. Firms, correspondingly, can take advantage of the 'microtargeting' phenomenon, offering products that meet individuals' needs, desires, and tastes (Murray & Scime, 2010). At the same time, managers can use AI to determine when the firm would be better off offering standardized products to larger market segments to benefit from economies of scale.

AI, therefore, can aid in identifying consumer segments that would be interested in the firm's value proposition (i.e., value targeting) (Osiyevskyy et al., 2020). With near-instantaneous data, value-targeting improvements could even occur in real time in both online and physical locations. For example, in a physical store, customers may be recommended additional, related products through the store app based on monitoring of what they have so far placed in their cart (e.g., in a store like Amazon Go Grocery). Moreover, AI can be used to predict the most effective way to communicate the value proposition to different market segments; for example, by analyzing reactions to targeted advertisements and specific phrasing (Osiyevskyy et al., 2020).

To exemplify, we refer to the case of a snack food company that struggled to discern whether its online promotions resulted in increased sales. Stumped, the firm employed an AI system to track users' behavior on the company's website and make informed, instant product recommendations to shoppers. Through targeted advertising, customers were persuaded to engage in cumulative purchasing and repeated visits. Resultantly, the program enabled an opportunity for long-term customer relationship management and the firm redefined its promotion problem to one of customer service and commitment.

AI could further aid managers by finding unoccupied niches and other unserved demand. Commonly, a solution to consumer needs already exists and is merely hidden, meaning that firms should approach this cognitive task as a design problem. AI systems, subsequently, can be used to search through diverse knowledge disciplines and fed inputs from all organizational members. However, sometimes the search for unserved demand may take the form of discovery decisions. In such cases, managers should point AI toward a broad, unexplored question to identify completely unknown consumer demand and solutions. Therefore, the firm can draw on both cognitive synergy and a division of cognition for improving its performance on these tasks.

For a specific example of AI application, consider the technology's power to indicate if demand for particular niche products potentially exceeds demand for those that are widely available and sold in large volumes (Anderson, 2004). Subsequently, the firm could fill the demand for less popular and common products, likely with decreased marketing and distribution costs (Anderson, 2004). AI, correspondingly, would allow firms to 'profit from the long tail' of demand, instead of competing for the small, known portion (Anderson, 2004).

As for the stakeholder value proposition, AI technologies, firstly, could allow managers to identify all organizational stakeholders and their interconnections. This is a deliberation problem, with predefined search criteria but imperfect a priori knowledge of the answers. Subsequently, the firm could take advantage of stakeholder interconnections to benefit itself; i.e., leverage network effects. For example, AI can be used to determine whether a connection exists between the number of women developers/project managers and the proportion of an app's clientele who are female. Such interaction may occur when companies seek to provide a service to the broad population, with success depending on the ability to recognize and meet the unique needs of women. An app meant to help persons monitor their health, for example, is more likely to be used by cisgender women if it includes a means for tracking one's menstrual and fertility cycles. Furthermore, as caregiver roles are still overwhelmingly performed by women, female users may appreciate the ability to create profiles for multiple people on one health app (e.g., for children or elders in their care). Similarly, women may have unique needs when it comes to ride-share apps; for example, the option to only be served by female drivers for one's comfort and feeling of safety. Consequently, a firm might benefit from having experienced women in decision-making roles on such projects, to perceive and come up with creative solutions for otherwise unknown or ignored consumers' desires. With AI, an organization could identify whether such an interconnection – between female decision-makers and the attractiveness of a firm's value proposition to female consumers – or similar relationships exist among its stakeholders. Then, the firm can leverage the interconnections to benefit itself; for example, by increasing the number of female decision-makers to maximize market share.

Additionally, AI can aid firms in offering individualized, optimal value propositions to each stakeholder, maximizing customers' Willingness to Pay (i.e., the monetary value one is willing to give up for a firm's product or service) (Biloshapka & Osiyevskyy, 2018). This may include individualized, customized offerings or a modularization of solution components, allowing customers to purchase individual parts or mix and match pieces of the product. Initially, decisions about optimal value propositions would fall into the category of deliberation, with an associated division of cognition. Managers would first decide the search direction; for example, by setting up a requirement for value propositions to be in line with the firm's brand or conducive to profit generation (otherwise, some stakeholders' desired product and pricing combination might put the firm out of business). Then, AI's augmented rationality can be applied to look for fitting propositions, unhindered by managers' preconceptions of what consumers want and how the firm should attempt to serve them. Later, when more is known about consumers' ideal value proposition, the firm can automate the process of generating customized offerings. Resultantly, AI could determine, in real time, promising suggestions to pitch to customers to improve the firm's overall performance.

Looking next at the activity system design, AI can be used, firstly, to optimize revenue models for maximizing value capture. For example, AI systems can be directed to deliberate upon pricing mechanisms, producing suggestions to boost consumers' Willingness to Pay (e.g., individualized pricing like with online airline bookings or temporally dependent pricing like for soon-to-perish goods at a grocery). Further, AI can search for existing yet untapped revenue streams, performing a design decision that may otherwise be influenced by human bias.

Secondly, AI could optimize research and development (R&D) processes, for example, by creating digital twins (i.e., virtual models representing real phenomena). Accordingly, firms can simulate experiments that would otherwise be far too difficult to perform (e.g., costly, impractical, or unethical) to narrow down the most promising experiments for further testing. Additionally, AI could aid researchers in reviewing literature and other text (e.g., announcements from competitors), keeping the firm on top of new opportunities and threats. Moreover, AI can be used in R&D processes for design and discovery tasks; for example, searching for hidden connections to known things among other disciplines or directing the system to search for weak signals in unexplored territory.

Thirdly, AI can be used to optimize production/service processes, provided operations have been formalized and codified. Unlike humans, AI systems can keep track of entire production/ service processes and communicate with other AI systems or Internet of Things (IoT)-imbued objects near-instantaneously. Correspondingly, the technologies can use automated rationality to complete determination tasks, making in-the-moment decisions with predefined rules.

Firms, therefore, are free to pursue mass customization with near-instantaneous response time to market demand, meaning fewer materials and man-hours wasted. Microtargeting based on AI segmentation of markets subsequently becomes a viable option, including for Go-To-Market strategies (i.e., for launching new products or entering new markets). Additionally, doing more with less allows firms to be more eco-friendly, providing a possibility to incorporate sustainable production/service as part of value propositions.

To exemplify AI applied in production, we look to a case of custom chip manufacturers. The process is complex, involving hundreds of machines and tens of hundreds of procedures; for a 7- to 8-hour production run, planning can take 4–5 hours with multiple-day breaks between different orders to retool and set up new production flows. Also, customers often keep some of the chip dimensions secret to protect their intellectual property rights, resulting in the manufacturer guessing about production requirements during the planning stage. Accordingly, the manufacturer can improve planning by using a digital twin, which allows for extensive testing and feedback time at a scale of seconds. AI can further aid in imagining the protected part of customers' orders, improving the efficiency of modeling. Moreover, the manufacturer can now provide feedback to customers on potential design improvements – a value-adding service.

Furthermore, AI can be used to improve humans' production/service delivery performance (even without formalizing and codifying operations). For example, AI can compare employees' motions and movements to identify whether some approaches are quicker, more accurate, less costly, etc. Additionally, AI can be used to process employees' inputs regarding these design problems, as front-line members may possess a detailed, direct knowledge unavailable to managers. Organizations could also analyze customer responses to specific phrases used by service staff, augmenting employees' ability to communicate the value proposition. Plus, AI could monitor humans to suggest timing and length of breaks required for their optimal performance.

Firms could further apply AI to conduct predictive maintenance, identifying potential equipment failure before it occurs. Initially, this may be a matter of deliberation as managers attempt to learn about breakdown conditions. Down the road, however, AI can be used to automate the screening process based on pre-set rules.

Finally, AI technologies redefine what resources an organization needs to outperform its competitors. Specifically, big data for machines to learn from becomes a key resource, in order to garner predictions beyond human ability. However, firms should be cautious investing in big data for big data's sake, as volume alone may not be enough to provide superior performance (Cappa et al., 2021; Ghasemaghaei & Calic, 2020). Indeed, data should be suitable to the task at hand (Farah, 2016); for example, having high velocity if the task requires near-instantaneous decisions. Principally, firms must have sufficient data to produce predictions accurate enough for minimizing the possibility of costly errors while simultaneously keeping the cost of data as low as possible.

Additionally, firms will require resources to support the functions of AI and its integration in the organization. For example, to take advantage of AI's enhanced knowledge transfer capability, firms must invest in middleware, allowing for data sharing between machines. Similarly, firms may invest in latency-reducing technologies, like dedicated fiber-optic connectivity between data centers and edge computing (i.e., processing data at proximate nodes, instead of centralized data centers, with 5G networks being the mobile version of this). Moreover, firms may need to invest in middleware that simply and coherently displays the results of AI analyses to managers and employees, for quick comprehension.

Furthermore, firms will need to reconfigure their existing resources, discarding or repurposing no-longer-useful assets (e.g., modifying a fleet of regular vehicles into self-driving ones). Regarding human resources, organizations will, firstly, need to identify roles to which current employee skills can be applied for superior performance. For example, humans may be particularly helpful in communicating AI recommendations to customers, because of an ability to inspire trust (Joshi et al., 2021). Indeed, value appropriation may depend on firms' ability to cultivate consumer confidence regarding AI abilities and recommendations (Kaplan & Haenlein, 2019). In particular, for systems that consumers directly interact with or ones that make sensitive decisions (e.g., AI determining interest rates for bank loans).

Firms may also need to upgrade their data science and analytics capabilities, by hiring new staff or training existing employees. The effort may particularly be directed toward upskilling experienced managers, to properly take advantage of both their tacit knowledge and AI-augmented rationality. Lastly, firms must establish practices for collecting and utilizing the knowledge of all the organization's members. Subsequently, the firm can begin to cultivate cognitive synergy for superior performance.

## DISCUSSION

### Digital AI Strategies and Sustainable Competitive Advantage

The essence of our argument is that the development of AI technologies has the potential to substantively change the established management practices and business models. This prediction is made on the premise that AI systems trained on big data can alleviate the managerial bounded rationality problem, moving from satisficing to optimizing mode in managerial decision-making. We discuss the micro-foundational impact of these technologies on the process of managerial decision-making, stressing their ability to enable automated and augmented rationality. Then, we present the exploration of the impact of AI in four distinct domains of decision problems: determination, design, deliberation, and discovery.

With burgeoning applications of AI from automated to augmented rationality, managers begin to sense the implications of how the virtual cognitive power precedes actual behavior and results. Reality is increasingly a fractal and factual representation of what has been decided. The recognition of four types of decision problems will help organizations to synergize the power of human cognition with the potentials of AI decision tools. To take advantage of AI beyond the reduction of prediction costs, we must develop new organizational routines and practices that promote opportunities for cognitive synergy between human agency and AI systems. When organizations learn to switch freely between the division of cognition and cognitive synergy, an AI-based organizational ambidexterity will finally be exhibited between the flow of decisions between the four domains discussed above. We hope our framework provides a good starting point.

Unraveling these micro-processes as a result of AI application to managerial decision-making forms the basis for understanding the micro-foundations of digital strategy. Yet, a crucial remaining question remains unanswered: can AI lead to transient or permanent competitive advantage for a company? Can the AI-enabled optimization of the business model and related decisions yield superior performance that can be eventually matched by other firms as they implement and optimize their AI-based processes, or whether a more sustainable advantage can be achieved?

To answer this fundamental strategic question, it is essential to get back to the foundational framework of the resource-based view of the firm, implying that competitive advantage stems from ownership or control of a valuable, rare, inimitable, and non-substitutable resource (Barney, 1991). The above-discussed bounded-rationality-alleviating benefits of AI technologies are obviously valuable to a firm, yet with respect to the other three characteristics, a more detailed analysis is needed. The three core drivers of business AI applications are (see Figure 18.1): (1) computing power, (2) algorithmic innovation, and (3) big data availability. The first two drivers are becoming increasingly available and commoditized, and hence can be purchased on the strategic factor market (Barney, 1986). In other words, organizations can barely draw on new algorithms or computing power for securing their competitive advantage, as these are getting competitively irrelevant, only able to level the playing field among firms. Exclusive access to large, unique datasets, however, could be a strategic asset that is rare, inimitable, and non-substitutable, generating abnormally high returns. Crucial here is the uniqueness of the big datasets, which must be accumulated by the individual firms and not tradeable on the strategic factors market (Barney, 1986; Dierickx & Cool, 1989). By this means, the established firms with exclusive access to big data may shield themselves from newcomers and smaller firms, resulting in maintaining superior performance in concentrated industries. All in all, data is becoming 'the new oil' (Agrawal et al., 2018), a crude resource that yields significant profits when refined (e.g., Bhageshpur, 2019). Not surprisingly, existing literature suggests that big data is becoming especially valuable, improving customer satisfaction, firm reputation, and financial performance (Grover et al., 2018; Raguseo & Vitari, 2018). Firms have found big data to aid in augmenting decision-making, reducing costs, boosting productivity and operations efficiency, and cultivating process and product innovation (Wamba et al., 2017; Wamba et al., 2019b). Therefore, our proposition that big data is crucial to secure a competitive advantage from digital AI strategies is corroborated by the insights of numerous prior studies (e.g., Ghasemaghaei et al., 2018; Wamba et al., 2019a), providing the evidence that it allows firms to grow market share and lessen threats from newcomers and small firms (Grover et al., 2018; Szczepański, 2020).

**Contextual Factors and Boundary Conditions**

The linear nature of our framework (see Figure 18.1) and the thesis that unique big data is the primary factor through which AI technologies are affecting organizational business models and creating sustainable competitive advantage should not create a misleading impression that there is one way to employ these technologies, or that they are effective in all industries and situations. Our theoretical framework reflects the 'converging mean' outlining general mechanisms; yet, as with any strategy (including focal digital AI strategy), specific contextual factors and boundary conditions determine its applicability and efficiency. Because of inevitable strategic trade-offs, in some contexts, the AI-enabled decision-making processes might destroy corporate value or be competitively irrelevant.

When evaluating the effectiveness of digital AI strategy, it is important first to identify the dominant focal AI decision problems (the four domains in Figure 18.3); that is: is one dealing with known knowns, unknown knowns, known unknowns, or unknown unknowns? Are there agreed-upon strategic objectives or a defined outcome that is crucial for the overall business strategy? Does the data (even that which is only slightly related to the focal decision domain) exist, and is it extensive, is it structured in a useful way? Notably, the decisions can involve more than one of these pairs – an organization may first need to approach a big, wicked problem as a 'design' problem, then once the overall solution is clear, will have to perform a 'deliberation' decision in determining the details of the method, and later codifying and formalizing the process as a repetitive 'determination' decision.

Once the domain of AI decision problems is identified, it is crucial to consider the time for making the decisions, the cost vs cost-savings of applying AI, the likely quality of manager vs AI decision-making, and the cost of errors. For example, in an immediate situation with little data, a knowledgeable manager is likely to make a better call than a new AI system (see Figure 18.2).

On a broader level, investments in big data that fuel the AI decision-making systems frequently result in disappointment (e.g., Ghasemaghaei et al., 2018; Grover et al., 2018). Commonly, scholars point out the importance of big data analytics capabilities (Gupta & George, 2016; Wamba et al., 2017) as well as data and/or information quality (e.g., minimal noise, accuracy, completeness) and system quality (e.g., security and adaptability of data handling) (Grover et al., 2018; Ren et al., 2017). Recent work, however, has questioned the assumption that 'bigger is always better', with scholars finding that volume has an insignificant or even negative effect on data value and firm performance (Cappa et al., 2021; Ghasemaghaei, 2021; Ghasemaghaei & Calic, 2020). We join the latter groups of scholars in doubting the universality of big data and AI decision-making, pointing out that strategic trade-offs ultimately determine the conditions when large quantities of data and AI technologies applied to them become a strategic asset, allowing a firm to secure a competitive advantage. The issue is that large data noticeably enhances decision accuracy only up to a certain point; after it, the data-accuracy curve plateaus, with additional inputs producing marginal accuracy improvements (see the 'Machine decision-making' curve in Figure 18.2). Given the exorbitant marginal costs of data acquisition, it might be sensible for firms to subsequently stick with small data (or the big data already in the firm's possession). Foregoing further data acquisition may be especially reasonable if the cost of errors is low; that is, if an inaccurate prediction results in a bearable loss (including opportunity costs). For example, the consequences of a mistake are likely less severe for AI applications directing targeted advertisements than for systems tasked with optimizing treatment for cancer patients. As such, the strategic value and competitive advantage of unique big data enabling a firm's digital AI strategy is determined by the interplay of contextual factors, most importantly the marginal prediction accuracy curve (see Figure 18.2), data acquisition cost, and cost of errors.

## A Way Ahead: Future Research Directions

The framework proposed in this study linking AI technologies with organizational business models and competitive advantage opens a fertile path for future research.

First, it is essential to elaborate theoretically and analyze empirically the conditions under which digital AI strategies become the best strategic responses for addressing specific business issues across different contexts (e.g., sectors, industries, institutional arrangements). How and when does AI help firms in creating and sustaining competitive advantage? The practical objective of this research agenda is to reduce the uncertainty of investing in big data and AI systems, allowing firms to allocate resources efficiently and achieve their strategic goals.

Second, the relationship between digital AI strategies and organizational business models has to be elaborated further. How does AI transform dominant industry business models? Which new business models become possible thanks to these technologies?

Third, what practices and organizational routines can firms use to promote cognitive synergy and ambidexterity? How do these settings change across the four domains of AI decision problems (determination, design, deliberation, and discovery)?

Finally, employing bounded rationality as this study's focal micro-foundation of management should be considered a first step in providing a holistic understanding of the impact of AI technologies on management practices. It is important to explain and analyze the role of other micro-foundations as links in this process. In particular, in addition to bounded rationality of managerial decision-makers, the second crucial micro-foundation of management practice is bounded reliability of humans (Kano & Verbeke, 2015; Verbeke & Greidanus, 2009). This concept emphasizes the existence of bounds of individuals' reliability in fulfilling commitments, reflecting the 'scarcity of making good on open-ended promises' (Verbeke & Greidanus, 2009, p. 1482) similarly to Simon's (1955) bounded rationality reflecting the scarcity of mind. While not denying malevolent, intentional opportunism as a premise for broken promises, bounded reliability stresses the fact that there could be other, benevolent causes occurring much more frequently than opportunism (Kano & Verbeke, 2015; Verbeke & Greidanus, 2009). The important common feature of non-opportunistic cases of bounded reliability is that all of them stem from psychological reasons, such as an inability to properly plan and impulsivity in making commitments (overcommitment), inability to concentrate on the task at hand (reprioritization), and inability to pursue an agreed-upon strategy when the implementation conflicts with the individual's view of oneself (identity-based discordance) (Kano & Verbeke, 2015; Verbeke & Greidanus, 2009). AI systems are invulnerable to these psychological limits, meaning that instances of bounded reliability will be reduced as more and more decisions are made by the technologies. With bounded rationality and bounded reliability thus mitigated, AI carries the potential to transform organizational forms and boundaries, beyond the impact on business models elaborated in the current study.

## CONCLUSION

In 1992, the US Olympic basketball team was considered the dream team, consisting of all inductees of the Basketball Hall of Fame except one. Before the team packed up and headed to Barcelona, they played with a group of college students in a scrimmage and lost. Lack of routinized collaboration in team play was a key factor, although individually each player was the best. Will AI-empowered advantage become transient or transformative? The conclusion is still in the making. But two things can be stated now: (1) we can leverage the cognitive synergy between human agency and AI into an integrated model of decision-making, and (2) we can extend the new cognitive capability into all four dimensions of the business model.

Once we routinize the collaboration between human agency and AI, the strategic competitive advantage will emerge and stay.

## REFERENCES

Agrawal, A., Gans, J., & Goldfarb, A. (2018). *Prediction Machines: The Simple Economics of Artificial Intelligence*. Harvard Business Review Press.
Anderson, C. (2004). The long tail. *Wired Magazine*, *12*, 170–77.
Automation Anywhere (2021). Discovery Bot: Uncovering all the inefficiencies you can't see. https://www.automationanywhere.com/products/discovery-bot.
Barney, J. (1991). Firm resources and sustained competitive advantage. *Journal of Management*, *17*(1), 99–120.
Barney, J.B. (1986). Strategic factor markets: Expectations, luck, and business strategy. *Management Science*, *32*(10), 1231–41.
Bhageshpur, K. (2019, November). Data is the new oil – And that's a good thing. *Forbes*. https://www.forbes.com/sites/forbestechcouncil/2019/11/15/data-is-the-new-oil-and-thats-a-good-thing/?sh=3ab5f4537304.
Biloshapka, V., & Osiyevskyy, O. (2018). Value creation mechanisms of business models: Proposition, targeting, appropriation, and delivery. *International Journal of Entrepreneurship and Innovation*, *19*(3), 166–76.
Cappa, F., Oriani, R., Peruffo, E., & McCarthy, I. (2021). Big data for creating and capturing value in the digitalized environment: Unpacking the effects of volume, variety, and veracity on firm performance. *Journal of Product Innovation Management*, *38*(1), 49–67.
Dierickx, I., & Cool, K. (1989). Asset stock accumulation and sustainability of competitive advantage. *Management Science*, *35*(12), 1504–11.
ETF Managers Group (2021). AI Powered Equity ETF. Etfmg. https://etfmg.com/funds/aieq/.
Farah, B.N. (2016). Big data: What data and why? *Journal of Management Policy and Practice*, *17*(1), 11–18.
Ghasemaghaei, M. (2021). Understanding the impact of big data on firm performance: The necessity of conceptually differentiating among big data characteristics. *International Journal of Information Management*, *57*(August 2019), 102055.
Ghasemaghaei, M., & Calic, G. (2020). Assessing the impact of big data on firm innovation performance: Big data is not always better data. *Journal of Business Research*, *108*(C), 147–62.
Ghasemaghaei, M., Ebrahimi, S., & Hassanein, K. (2018). Data analytics competency for improving firm decision making performance. *Journal of Strategic Information Systems*, *27*(1), 101–13.
Goldstein, D.G., & Gigerenzer, G. (2008). The Recognition Heuristic and the Less-Is-More Effect. In C.R. Plott & V.L. Smitt (Eds.), *Handbook of Experimental Economics Results* (Vol. 1, Issue C, pp. 987–92). Amsterdam: North Holland.
Grover, V., Chiang, R.H.L., Liang, T.P., & Zhang, D. (2018). Creating strategic business value from big data analytics: A research framework. *Journal of Management Information Systems*, *35*(2), 388–423.
Gupta, M., & George, J.F. (2016). Toward the development of a big data analytics capability. *Information and Management*, *53*(8), 1049–64.
Joshi, M.P., Su, N., Austin, R.D., & Sundaram, A.K. (2021). Why so many data science projects fail to deliver. *MIT Sloan Management Review*, *62*(3), 85–90.
Kano, L., & Verbeke, A. (2015). The three faces of bounded reliability: Alfred Chandler and the micro-foundations of management theory. *California Management Review*, *58*(1), 97–122.
Kaplan, A., & Haenlein, M. (2019). Siri, Siri, in my hand: Who's the fairest in the land? On the interpretations, illustrations, and implications of artificial intelligence. *Business Horizons*, *62*(1), 15–25.
Knight, F.H. (1921). *Risk, Uncertainty and Profit*. Dover 2006 unabridged republication of the edition published by Houghton Mifflin Company.
McAfee, A., Brynjolfsson, E., Davenport, T.H., Patil, D.J., & Barton, D. (2012). Big data: the management revolution. *Harvard Business Review*, *90*(10), 60–68.

Migliore, L.A., & Chinta, R. (2017). Demystifying the big data phenomenon for strategic leadership. *SAM Advanced Management Journal*, *82*(1), 48–58.

Moore, G.E. (1965). Cramming more components onto integrated circuits. *Electronics*, *38*(8), 114–17.

Murray, G.R., & Scime, A. (2010). Microtargeting and electorate segmentation: Data mining the American National Election Studies. *Journal of Political Marketing*, *9*(3), 143–66.

Osiyevskyy, O., Bao, Y., & DaSilva, C.M. (2020). Using AI to Improve Economic Productivity: A Business Model Perspective. In J.M. Munoz & A. Naqvi (Eds.), *Handbook of Artificial Intelligence and Robotic Process Automation: Policy and Government Application* (pp. 57–66). London: Anthem Press.

Osiyevskyy, O., Troshkova, M., & Bao, Y. (2018). What Makes a Global Business Model? In A. Presenza. & L.R. Sheehan (Eds.), *Geopolitics and Strategic Management in the Global Economy* (pp. 19–39). Pennsylvania: IGI Global.

Polanyi, M. (1958). *Personal Knowledge: Towards a Post-Critical Philosophy*. London: Routledge & Kegan Paul.

Polanyi, M. (1966). *The Tacit Dimension*. London: Routledge.

Poole, D.L., & Mackworth, A.K. (2010). *Artificial Intelligence: Foundations of Computational Agents*. Cambridge: Cambridge University Press.

Raguseo, E., & Vitari, C. (2018). Investments in big data analytics and firm performance: An empirical investigation of direct and mediating effects. *International Journal of Production Research*, *56*(15), 5206–21.

Ren, S.J., Fosso Wamba, S., Akter, S., Dubey, R., & Childe, S.J. (2017). Modelling quality dynamics, business value and firm performance in a big data analytics environment. *International Journal of Production Research*, *55*(17), 5011–26.

Samuel, A.L. (1959). Some studies in machine learning using the game of checkers. *IBM Journal of Research and Development*, *3*(3), 210–29.

Schwab, K. (2016). *The Fourth Industrial Revolution*. Geneva: World Economic Forum.

Simon, H. (1955). A behavioral model of rational choice. *Quarterly Journal of Economics*, *69*(1), 99. doi: 10.2307/1884852.

Simon, H.A., Dantzig, G.B., Hogarth, R., Plott, C.R., Raiffa, H., Schelling, T.C., … & Winter, S. (1987). Decision making and problem solving. *Interfaces*, *17*(5), 11–31.

Szczepański, M. (2020). *Is Data the New Oil? Competition Issues in the Digital Economy*. N.p.: European Parliamentary Research Service.

Verbeke, A., & Greidanus, N.S. (2009). The end of the opportunism vs trust debate: Bounded reliability as a new envelope concept in research on MNE governance. *Journal of International Business Studies*, *40*(9), 1471–95.

Wamba, S.F., Akter, S., & de Bourmont, M. (2019a). Quality dominant logic in big data analytics and firm performance. *Business Process Management Journal*, *25*(3), 512–32.

Wamba, S.F., Akter, S., Trinchera, L., & de Bourmont, M. (2019b). Turning information quality into firm performance in the big data economy. *Management Decision*, *57*(8), 1756–83.

Wamba, S.F., Gunasekaran, A., Akter, S., Ren, S.J.-f., Dubey, R., & Childe, S.J. (2017). Big data analytics and firm performance: Effects of dynamic capabilities. *Journal of Business Research*, *70*, 356–65.

# 19. The strategic use of big data analytics: applications in business practice and effects on firm performance

*Giovanni Battista Dagnino and Guglielmo La Bruna*

## 1.    INTRODUCTION

In the midst of the fourth industrial revolution, data are increasingly playing a fundamental role. The amount of data produced every day is really huge; actually, the so-called big data (BD) is radically changing the way firms operate and their organizational structures. However, simple data do not have great value per se: it is the information that can be extracted from them, by applying analytical methods, that is the real source of value for firms. For this reason, the implementation of data analysis technologies is today a significant factor for the success or failure of a firm. In fact, it is by capitalizing on data and managing to leverage the business analytics (BA) that firms are now able to extract value from data and increase their competitive advantage.

Recent research by Forbes Insight and Cisco shows that current data analysis techniques must be included virtually in all firms' new business initiatives. In addition, 51 per cent of C-suite executives in North America and Europe confirm that the importance of BA will continue to grow in the coming years as their market share will only increase (*Forbes*, 2018).

The BD phenomenon is clearly growing in a consistent manner; just think: 90 per cent of the existing data available has been generated in the last two years (*Forbes*, 2018). Around four billion people worldwide are active on the web, and about three billion of them use social media (Statista, 2022). Each day, a single user generates an average of 12 gigabytes of data that is monitored in real time (Domo, 2018). These numbers give an idea of the huge amount of data that is generated and that contains an element of great value: knowledge potential.

The ability to analyse large amounts of data allows firms to generate new knowledge helpful for taking more informed decisions in business and strategic activities. From customizing customer communication to increasing the efficiency of production processes, through flow and emergency management, analytics is having a huge impact on all business processes.

In this context, advanced analytics (AA) are considered innovative analytical platforms capable of generating advanced insights to support business decision-making processes. AA are in fact scalable and customizable platforms that can be effectively adapted to various sectors and firms to meet their needs, ranging from the financial and insurance sector to the manufacturing and distribution sector to healthcare and logistics. This is also possible because data-driven firms are typically characterized by a high information density, which deeply facilitates the use of AA and allows them to fully express their potential.

According to Polytechnic of Milan Digital Observatory (2017), an analytics platform is defined as "The integration of a set of complementary technologies in order to create a unified and collaborative system able to support the entire data life cycle within the organization in a scalable way" (Vercellis et al., 2019b).

Actually, "advanced analytics" is a general expression that simply means to apply various advanced analytic techniques to data so as to answer questions or solve problems. This is not a technology by itself, but rather a group of tools that are used in combination with one another to gain information, analyse that information, and predict outcomes of solutions to problems (Bose, 2009). AA go beyond traditional business intelligence (BI) solutions based on performance indicators, dashboards and the querying of data warehouses to incorporate algorithmic techniques from machine learning, artificial intelligence, natural language processing and other computer science disciplines (Rose et al., 2017). Gartner defined AA as:

> the autonomous or semi-autonomous examination of data or content using sophisticated techniques and tools, typically beyond those of traditional business intelligence (BI), to discover deeper insights, make predictions, or generate recommendations. AA techniques include those techniques such as data/text mining, machine learning, pattern matching, forecasting, visualization, semantic analysis, sentiment analysis, network and cluster analysis, multivariate statistics, graph analysis, simulation, complex event processing, neural networks. (Gartner, 2017)

It is therefore possible to say that AA represent a suite or cluster of analytical applications that helps measure, predict, and optimize organizational performance and customer relationships.

This definition provides a fairly complete idea of the platform and its potential within a firm. From such definition, it is clear that it is not enough to apply simple software or update the firm's existing hardware to achieve better capacity in data management and analysis, but a plurality of different technologies is needed, where individuals are dedicated to managing specific sources or a specific phase of data collection or manipulation. Such technology plurality, aimed at the implementation of state-of-the-art technological architecture, is necessary from a technical-structural point of view, due to the inner nature of the BD phenomenon, which leads to a higher degree of complexity in terms of volumes, variety and data speed. Specific technologies are thus required for managing such data flows. From a strategic point of view, it is also important that data have a central position within the firm for the multiple operations that are carried out based on them. Given the various functions that have to interact with data, the IT function, the various lines of business, data science and data governance teams, many actors ought to act on data and each of them is influenced by very different needs, objectives and skills. To be able to appreciate these digital technologies as well as their characteristics and potential, in the remainder of this chapter we analyse four types of AA and then extract the advantages that can be drawn from their implementation in some industrial sectors.

In particular, we can refer to four kinds of AA that are listed below:

1. Descriptive analytics. This type includes the mathematical-statistical models used to describe the current or past situation of business processes and/or different functional areas (Vercellis et al., 2019a);
2. Predictive analytics. This type of AA includes a number of mathematical-statistical models, machine learning algorithms and analysis of past data trends, in order to provide predictions about the probability of future scenarios (Kim and Dewi, 2019);
3. Prescriptive analytics. This is the step immediately following predictive analytics. Using machine learning algorithms and mathematical-statistical models, it provides the decision-maker with operational/strategic solutions based on the analyses carried out,

providing advice on possible effects and results of actions that could maximize the value of some firms' key performance indicators (KPIs) (Lepenioti et al., 2020);

4. Automated analytics. This type of analytics uses, like the previous ones, mathematical models and machine learning algorithms that allow one to automate a certain action or process, which has been identified as optimal in that given context, interacting with the related business systems (Cao and Wachowicz, 2019).

The remainder of this chapter is organized as follows. Section 2 looks closely at the four types of AA. Section 3 features the key factors driving the performance effects of AA. Section 4 discusses the strategic advantages and disadvantages arising from the adoption of AA. Section 5 argues about the application of AA in four relevant sectors: finance and insurance, manufacturing, healthcare, and logistics and supply chain. Section 6 will draw some conclusions and gather a few lines for future research in the expanding AA–performance relationship domain.

## 2.    KEY TYPES OF ADVANCED ANALYTICS

In more detail, the four types of analytics are discussed as follows.

### 2.1    Descriptive Analytics

Characterized by descriptive statistics, they help describe a phenomenon through different measures that can capture its relevant dimensions, thereby facilitating the interpretation of data and the identification of information for decision-making (Banerjee et al., 2013; Delen and Zolbanin, 2018). Descriptive analytics help look into the past in order to generate some inferences (Saggi and Jain, 2018) and to establish an understanding about "what happened" and about "what is happening" (Duan et al., 2020; Sivarajah et al., 2017).

They are the simplest type of analytics, allowing one to condense BD into smaller, more useful information packages. Most raw data, especially BD, cannot be used in the form in which they come, but must be processed to extract information from them. It is estimated that over 80 per cent of business analyses, especially social analytics, are mainly descriptive. Thanks to descriptive analytics it is possible, in essence, to describe a set of data (Medeiros and Maçada, 2022). This type of analysis is the initial one to be performed on a data set and is commonly applied to large volumes of data, such as census data.

Descriptive analysis begins by providing a static view of the past but, as more instances accumulate in data sources documenting past experience, assessment steps, classification and categorization can be performed repeatedly by fast and efficient algorithms, thereby equipping the overall work process with a measure of adaptability. When descriptive analysis reaches a point where it supports preventive action, predictive analytics comes into play, which applies advanced techniques to examine scenarios and helps detect hidden patterns in large amounts of data in order to project future events (Guess, 2014).

### 2.2    Predictive Analytics

As mentioned earlier, predictive analytics use past-understanding data to make "predictions" about the future. Predictive analytics are characterized by forecasting and probability models, statistical analysis and scoring models (Appelbaum et al., 2017; Saggi and Jain, 2018). They support the discovery of patterns and relationships in the data in order to answer the question of what may happen in the future, predict potential results and explain the drivers of what has been observed (Banerjee et al., 2013; Duan et al., 2020).

Predictive analysis is applied both in real time to provide instant information about the operating process (e.g., in real-time storage actions via chat messages or real-time identification of suspicious transactions) or in batch methodology (to target new customers on a website or direct mail to drive cross-selling/up-selling, expected churn rate,[1] etc.) (Medeiros and Maçada, 2022). These predictions are made by examining data from the past, by detecting patterns or relationships in these data and then extrapolating those relationships by projecting them over a later period of time. For example, a particular type of insurance credit that falls into a certain category that has proven problematic in the past could be reported for a more in-depth investigation (Baum et al., 2018).

Predictive modelling techniques can also be used to examine data to assess hypotheses. If each observation is composed of several attributes, it may be useful to understand if some combinations of a subset of attributes are predictive of a combination of other attributes. For example, claims can be examined in order to validate the assumption that age, gender and postal code can predict the likelihood of claims regarding car insurance.

Predictive modelling tools can help both validate and generate assumptions. This is especially useful when some of the attributes are actions determined by business decision-makers (Mujawar and Joshi, 2015).

### 2.3    Prescriptive Analytics

Prescriptive analytics are a kind of predictive analysis used mainly when it is essential to prescribe an action. It will be the firms' decision-maker who looks at this information and decides how to act, but a possible action or set of possible actions will be suggested by the system. They go beyond describing, explaining and forecasting to suggest "what courses of action can be taken" in the future, in order to optimize processes and achieve business objectives; that is, this analysis associates decision alternatives with forecasting results (Banerjee et al., 2013). Prescriptive analytics can be described as an optimization approach, aiming to answer what needs to be done, in addition to recommending courses of action or solutions, simulating probable results, which can improve the accuracy of predictions, simulations and decisions (Medeiros and Maçada, 2022).

Moreover, thanks to prescriptive analytics it is likely to predict more than one possible future. In essence, some object data are used to predict values for another object. Models are able to provide predictions, but accurate prediction depends heavily on measuring the right variables. Although there are better and worse prediction models, the best combination is a high number of data and the application of a simple model. Predictive analytics are the next step in data analytics. They use a variety of statistical modelling, data mining, artificial intelligence and machine learning techniques to study recent and historical data, allowing analysts to make predictions about the future. The aim, however, is to predict what might happen in the future, since all predictive analyses are probabilistic in nature (Song et al., 2013).

In addition, prescriptive analysis requires a predictive model with two additional components: actionable data and a feedback system that tracks the results of the action taken. Since a prescriptive model is able to predict the possible consequences on the basis of the different choices of action, it can also recommend the best course of action for any predetermined result (Bertsimas and Kallus, 2019).

### 2.4    Automated Analytics

In view of the results of descriptive and predictive analyses, automated analytics are in a position to activate actions defined on the basis of rules. Rules which may in turn be the result of an analytical process, such as the study of the behaviour of a given machine against certain conditions being analysed. The automated actions that it is able to perform are applicable to several sectors: you can automatically change an online price, automatically view the best landing page, determine which email to automatically send to a customer, even drive a car automatically.

Automated analytics are increasingly needed in a world where customers want real-time responses, where every marketing promotion needs to be tailored and customized, and where data are everywhere and need to be analysed to become usable (Davenport, 2015).

In addition, automated analyses are based on how the analyses are used. The term should not be confused with automated, or at least semi-automated, analysis creation using tools such as machine learning. Automated analysis, in order to work effectively, has to be incorporated into other systems that generate data for analysis and then act after the analytical result has been achieved. For example, when applied to a production plant, the software may be integrated with different sensors that can simultaneously control different parts of the production machinery with the aim of removing the time where a broken machine is waiting for repair by predicting and preventing the possible failures before their occurrence (Dreyfus and Kyritsis, 2018).

Thanks to automated analytics, it will be possible to read the information generated by the various sensors in real time, and to identify in advance the probability of a failure or the need to act on the machine with a preventive maintenance intervention. This integration implies that automated analysis must be closely linked to IT organizations and chief information officers and that this type of analysis cannot be carried out separately or ad hoc, but must be integrated into an analytics business platform (Chen and Sun, 2018).

Having analysed the four types of analytics, we are in the right place to understand their potential, how they are applied and what task they perform, and we can grasp the need for their integration. We have also seen that each kind of analytics carries out a specific task; therefore their integration in a single platform may allow a higher level of control of a firm's key variables to provide compelling support for business decisions.

## 3.    FACTORS DRIVING THE EFFECTS OF ADVANCED ANALYTICS: KEY CONTINGENCIES OF EFFECTIVE AA

As mentioned earlier, AA can be used in a very versatile way in various industrial sectors, thereby allowing firms to achieve higher levels of performance. In order to measure the effect of AA on the firms' economic and financial performance, a preliminary study was carried out on a sample of 50 Italian firms of various sizes, from small and medium-sized enterprises (SMEs) to larger and more structured ones, operating in various sectors (such as manufacturing, banking and insurance, utilities and logistics) in the period 2015–2019 (La Bruna et al.,

2021). The study has made it possible to empirically observe significant differences in the economic and financial performance of firms adopting AA in their operating processes vis-à-vis those which do not adopt them. The results obtained show that there is a direct correlation between the use of AA and an increase in firm turnover. Three other interesting results have been observed thanks to this study:

(a)   the first result shows that some sectors (i.e., the manufacturing sector followed by the banking and insurance sector and then the logistics sector) benefit more than others from the positive effects of the use of AA;

(b)   the second one shows that the information intensity of each sector is an additional variable capable of influencing the effect of AA on performance;[2]

(c)   the third one illustrates that large firms are usually the ones having direct access to AA advantages because SMEs generally struggle to evolve data analysis systems and usually take the follower role when compared to large firms. The reasons for this situation refer to the absence of financial resources to invest, as well as to the nonexistence of a technology-oriented mentality guiding SMEs' management towards the adoption of AA technologies.

On the basis of these initial results, we can posit that firms that are able to use AA in an accurate manner are also able to achieve a competitive advantage vis-à-vis other firms that are not able to do so. Competitive advantage emerges when firms are able to develop the capacity to analyse the data they can access and extract relevant information from them so as to convert them into knowledge. By optimizing the value added resulting from each decision, this idiosyncratic ability allows them to achieve more in-depth market knowledge, and to reveal a more fluid decision-making process, because it is based on the analysis of a larger number of variables and a larger number of different scenarios.

## 4.   STRATEGIC ADVANTAGES AND DISADVANTAGES OF FIRMS USING ADVANCED ANALYTICS

Thanks to digital disruptions, firms have acquired the option of collecting and storing large amounts of data that are the operational basis of AA, and that need to be exploited to create value. As we have seen, in fact AA are one of the main levers supporting firms' digital transformation. The ability to convert raw data into informed strategic decisions and to use them in new innovative and creative ways thus becomes an element of strategic differentiation for all firms operating in a highly dynamically competitive context.

Analytics can be helpful throughout the intervention of firm's top management (Havlena, 2013). For example, chief marketing managers can use analytics to win a better understanding of their customers and improve customer loyalty. The chief financial officer, on the other hand, can improve the financial performance management and pursue financial forecasts. Risk management managers can get a holistic view of risk, fraud and compliance information across the organization and take necessary actions in the light of this information. Last but not least, operations managers can gain a better understanding of supply chains and supply operations to improve their efficiency.

However, we acknowledge that many times it is anything but easy to convince firms' top managers to take the road of implementing analytics. One of the reasons for this is the difficulty for managers of visualizing in advance the real benefits in terms of performance improvement resulting from the implementation of AA. In this regard, a 2017 study on the retail sector in the UK shows that the managers interviewed argue that it is difficult to measure the positive effect that analytics may actually bring to the firm as a whole, while it is easier to identify the one made locally in the individual functions in which they are applied (Ramanathan et al., 2017).

## 4.1    Strategic Advantages from the Adoption of Advanced Analytics

Since the implementation of data analysis technologies might be a relevant factor leading to the success or failure of a firm, AA are nowadays adopted by an increasing number of firms, sometimes for targeting to gain a competitive advantage, at other times merely for fear of lagging behind their competitors.

In the previous part of this chapter, we have discussed how BD and AA work to pave the way to their areas of application. In this section, we explore the issue of the strategic advantage that firms can achieve by implementing an AA platform.

### Achieving competitive advantage and the rapid identification of new business opportunities

The first advantage that can be accessed from the use of AA is definitely the competitive advantage that a firm achieves when it has matured a certain ability to use these technologies. The combination of historical data and data collected in real time, in addition to the ability to combine and analyse the bulk of this information, gives firms a competitive advantage because interruptions or changes in service continue to affect almost all industries. For example, firms in highly competitive markets where customers are ready to switch suppliers when better offers arrive (for instance, telephone operators) can detect, thanks to AA, "abandonment" signals and send their client base customized offers designed to maintain the service and preserve profitability.

Second is the possibility AA offer to rapidly identify new business opportunities and gain an in-depth knowledge of emerging markets. This means that the firm is able to obtain a first-mover advantage (Chambers and Dinsmore, 2014) in new businesses, since it manages to turn into profit the opportunities that stem from them. These are the possibility of obtaining the right of pre-emption on some assets that are difficult to find and that are of key importance in the market, or the possibility of establishing partnerships with other firms at favourable conditions.

### Acquiring an in-depth knowledge of consumers

From a customer management viewpoint, AA bring a strategic advantage from gaining a deeper understanding of customers and of their needs. In fact, AA allow firms to gain a series of in-depth insights essential to marketing functions to help them understand how to interact better with customers. This condition is fulfilled since AA allow firms to analyse historical information to understand which past programs have been successful and then apply predictive algorithms to be more successful in the future. Firms' decision-makers are then able to study multiple factors, including wealth, different levels of price sensitivity, similarities with different brands and key characteristics of the behaviour of their potential customers.

**Reducing costs**
AA allow significant cost reduction thanks to the analysis of data developed at the firm level to identify opportunities for cost reduction and situations of money-wasting and inefficiencies. For example, insurance firms analyse large amounts of claims data for models that could be signs of possible fraud and that deserve a closer look from investigators, while manufacturing firms can manage to remap some of their production processes, thereby allowing them to increase the efficiency in their production chain or plants (Seddon et al., 2016).

**Near-real-time warnings and predictive maintenance**
Near-real-time data analysis can provide timely warnings about production and service problems, ultimately leading to superior products. Manufacturers can integrate their production lines with dozens of digital sensors to closely track and correct problems associated with out-of-range tolerances, production waste and other quality-control problems. Moreover, thanks to the implementation of AA, it is possible to obtain information on predictive maintenance, which enables maintenance operations on machinery before a problem develops, thus avoiding the need to stop the production chain in an unexpected way, and thereby allowing notable cost savings.

**Accelerating growth**
The implementation of AA in a firm may also lead to much faster business growth. An advanced ability to scan the environment, and the market positions the firm has, raises a robust strategic advantage compared to competitors. In fact, it gives the firm the opportunity to act within the new context developing in the reference market, taking into account many more variables, with a higher problem-solving ability and the ability to predict different scenarios. Being able to act first often gives firms the possibility of adapting better to the new business reality.

## 4.2 Strategic Disadvantages from the Adoption of Advanced Analytics

Having identified the most significant strategic advantages of introducing AA, we identify some disadvantages resulting from the use of this technology. We start by saying that identifying disadvantages resulting from the use of the AA is anything but simple since the evolution of data analysis methods and the ability to extract and exploit information (a specific characteristic of AA) usually do not bring real disadvantages to firms at the strategic level. To identify disadvantages, we therefore need to focus on the cases of mistaken use of AA or on implementation errors that may lead to failures in exploiting AA properly.

**No return on investment and firm reorganization**
It can happen that a firm decides to implement an AA platform without having developed in advance adequate skills in the field of data science. Assuming that there are few or no organizational and commitment problems during the implementation process, the firm would arrive at the end of the process with a very powerful platform available, which results in high investment costs that users are not able to govern. At this point, the return on investment resulting from the AA investment would be rather low, and the firm would find itself burning a part of the capital regarding an investment that it is not able to properly exploit. This would locate the firm in a position of strategic disadvantage compared to its competitors since it would have

less capital to invest in other endeavours and, at the same time, would find itself in a situation of compelled reorganization that could lead to efficiency loss and process slowdown.

### Implementation of innovative technology too early

Another situation that may arise is the development and implementation of an AA technology that is excessively advanced compared to its internal needs or compared to the external situation in the market. This situation occurs when a firm assumes the position of forerunner with respect to technology, thereby implementing in the analytics platform some tool that it is not able to make the best use of for a specific purpose or that requires a type of input data that cannot be found. While being able to implement a new technology before its competitors could bring in a competitive advantage, it may happen that the new AA technology has not developed at its best to fit firms' needs. This would lead to a waste of time as well as to investing capital without an effective monetary return. This situation would place a firm in a disadvantage position vis-à-vis its competitors.

### Lack of commitment and resulting organizational problems

A typical problem that may arise during the implementation of an AA platform is related to top management's or business units' commitment. Usually when such a situation occurs, the project implementation ends in advance and new AA technologies are not adopted. However, there might be situations in which, despite the lack of a strong commitment of the business units, the project is developed anyway and the AA technologies are implemented. In such instances, organizational problems could occur within some business units, resulting from the difficulty of managing the AA platform. Such problems would lead to a reduction in the efficiency of business lines and a consequent loss of competitive advantage compared to competitors.

It should be noted that situations of this kind are not particularly common in large firms, which usually thoroughly evaluate their investments before deciding to proceed with the implementation of such innovative tools, with a strong impact at the organizational level.

Moreover, most of the large firms that have implemented AA platforms have recorded an improvement of their competitive position in the market that has been alternatively strong, medium or mild. It is also possible to observe this condition in a research study Deloitte conducted in 2013 on senior business advisors of North America's service firms (Figure 19.1). Such a study clearly underscores that the share of respondents who claim not to have received any advantage from the implementation of AA tools reaches only 3 per cent of the total respondents.

This finding does nothing else than confirm that the increased ability to analyse data and draw useful information from it to buttress the decision-making processes usually leads to an effective improvement in firm performance. The performance increase may vary depending on the type of firm, the industry in which it operates, its information intensity, the type of technology implemented and the level of technical knowledge already present in the firm that is needed for an appropriate data science process governance.

DOES ANALYTICS IMPROVE COMPETITIVE POSITIONING?

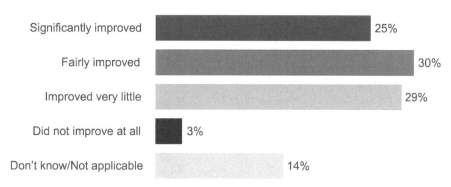

Significantly improved — 25%
Fairly improved — 30%
Improved very little — 29%
Did not improve at all — 3%
Don't know/Not applicable — 14%

*Source:*   *The Analytics Advantage: We're Just Getting Started.* Deloitte Analytics Advantage Survey 2013.

*Figure 19.1    Improvement from adoption of advanced analytics*

## 5.    THE USE OF ADVANCED ANALYTICS IN FOUR INDUSTRIAL SECTORS

### 5.1    Finance and Insurance

Since financial institutions manage large amounts of customer data and use data analysis in sub-sectors, such as capital market trading, the financial and insurance sector has been a data-driven sector for many years. The insurance business is also based on using data analysis to effectively understand and assess risk. Insurance firm officials and actuaries depend on data analysis to perform their roles. Therefore, data have traditionally played a central role in this sector. In addition, especially in recent years there has been a rapid prevalence of data that fall within the domain of BD; i.e., higher volume and speed of data, and a wider variety of information resources resulting from the increase in new customers, markets and regulatory data coming from multiple sources. For instance, a huge commercial value comes from large volumes of insurance claims documentation, which are mainly in text form and contain descriptions entered by call center operators, and notes associated with individual claims and specific cases.

By applying AA technologies, it is possible to extract value from BD more efficiently, faster and in more targeted fashion by also analysing unconstructed data. For these reasons, the introduction of AA in the financial and insurance sector brings numerous benefits to the firms operating in this area.

We can highlight some key points:

- Advanced levels of customer knowledge, engagement and experience. Thanks to the digitalization of financial products and services and the increasing number of customers interacting with businesses using digital channels, there is an opportunity for firms to improve the level of engagement of their customers and proactively increase their experience or user experience. To achieve this condition, AA facilitate the extraction of information from new sources and non-structured databases such as social media;

- Advanced fraud detection and prevention features. Financial services institutions have always been vulnerable to fraud. Criminal individuals and organizations are working to defraud financial institutions, and the sophistication and complexity of the models they adopt evolves quite hastily over time. In the past, banks were only able to analyse a small sample of transactions in an attempt to detect fraud. The advent of BD and AA has given banks the opportunity to use broader databases to identify guidelines for fraud and thus minimize their exposure to this risk;
- Advanced analysis of market trading. Driven by growing demand for faster execution, trading in financial markets began to digitalize several years ago. Thanks to BD and the use of AA-based analysis techniques, trading strategies using sophisticated algorithms to trade on financial markets much faster and more efficiently than in the past become conceivable.

## 5.2    Manufacturing

In the area of manufacturing, the challenge is to implement AA by applying these technologies to large databases so as to extract information helpful to the firm and take momentous decisions. The key benefits are increased efficiency in design and production activities, increased product quality and innovation, greater consumer satisfaction, more accurate demand forecasting, increased productivity and better management of the global value chain.

The data analysed come from numerous sources: production machinery, systems for supply chain management, systems monitoring the performance of products already sold, RFID (radio frequency identification), devices that track the product (for which an increase is expected from 12 million in 2011 to 209 billion in 2021), comments on social media and other systems including digital design, product engineering and computerized production systems (Manyika et al., 2011).

Several signals, such as the vibrations and pressure extracted from the sensors present in the machines and the historical data relating to these elements, are used by AA thanks to the help of cloud computing. This leads to the creation of an information system regarding the production chain equipment as a whole that is able to predict performance problems. The system becomes able to self-assess its current condition and the deterioration of the equipment in such a way as to allow decisions to be taken on the preventive maintenance interventions to be carried out. Such interventions will shun potential problems and prevent unexpected downtime or blockages in the production process (Lee, 2014).

There are several advantages of using AA in this area. Some of them are reported below to show the potential of these technologies in manufacturing production:

- Research, development and design. By leveraging input data and detailed customer information, it is possible to build products with features tailored to their needs, thereby reducing product development costs. It is also possible to receive user feedback faster, thereby improving existing products and developing new ones. The same process of development and engineering of new prototypes, which increases the degree of innovation, turns much faster using AA platforms;
- Supply chain. Using AA, it becomes easier to predict customer demand and improve planning across the supply chain, thus using resources more efficiently and increasing the

level of service. It is also possible to obtain a better response in time to optimize inventory management;

- Production in a strict sense. With a focus on production in a strict sense, we can observe various advantages deriving from the use of AA, which embrace the increase in the efficiency of production processes thanks to the use of simulation techniques applied to large volumes of data generated by the analysis of the characteristics of the products themselves. It is also possible to reduce the number of modifications to be made at the design stage, as well as the cost of the prototype manufacturing process and the time it takes to complete it, thus increasing its reliability.

In addition, the application of AA allows firms to control and optimize production and supply processes, thereby reducing waste and maximizing the efficiency of the entire production chain, thanks to the analysis of data from sensors placed on the equipment that, thanks to AA, can be analysed in real time.

## 5.3    Healthcare

The COVID-19 pandemic has put on the table the importance of analysing a large amount of data in a short time in the healthcare sector. Without using analytical technologies, it would have been much more difficult to produce a vaccine in such short time span (8–9 months). In addition, the healthcare industry is facing a kind of data tsunami, which is generated and accumulated continuously. This involves clinical data generated by decision support systems, such as:

- medical notes and prescriptions, medical images, and data from laboratories, pharmacies, insurance firms and other organizations;
- electronic health records (digital health archives, called EHR);
- data generated by machines and data sensors, such as those from vital signal monitoring and genomic data, including genotype and gene expression.

In particular, digital health records provide in-depth clinical knowledge and the patient's pathological picture: such data can be used to search for associations in medical diagnosis and to examine the temporal relationships between events to identify disease progression. The expected raw sequencing data from each person is approximately four terabytes of data (genomics-driven big data like genotyping, gene expression, sequencing data) and each payer-supplier could build an array with hundreds of thousands of patients with different information and parameters (e.g., demography, care, and results) collected over a long period of time.[3] In addition, incoming real-time applications, such as early detection of infections, will help identify infections much more quickly and indicate the right therapies, thus preventing infections and, more importantly, reducing mortality rates (Chen et al., 2012).[4]

The veracity of the data, subject to errors (especially non-structured ones characterized by great variability) is an important objective to pursue in the healthcare domain. In fact, the quality of health data is fundamental: medical decisions, which often affect the lives or deaths of individuals, depend to a large extent on information accuracy.

The main BD analytics applications used in healthcare are queries, reports, online analytical processing and data mining. These techniques are used to aggregate, manipulate, analyse and visualize all data. The use of AA in this field allows firms to obtain a number of benefits, such as:

- Cost reduction. Increasing efficiency is one of the most important benefits and is made possible by a number of practices. First, the comparative effectiveness research (CER) and the analysis of large databases concerning the characteristics of the patient, and the costs and results of therapies, make it possible to identify the most cost-effective treatments. Second, the creation of process maps and dashboards from the supplier database allows one to identify sources of variability and waste. Finally, the analysis of pathological images and trends to estimate future demand for drugs and the use of predictive models developed by pharmaceutical firms through the aggregation of research data promote a more advantageous allocation of R&D resources;
- Better results thanks to higher-quality decisions (higher quality of therapies and high patient satisfaction). CER and data transparency, ensured by the development of process maps and dashboards, also reduce the incidence of both harmful and prescribed therapies and improve the quality of care. Clinical decision support systems, in which doctors insert their therapies that are then compared with the guidelines, also warn against any prescription errors, such as those involving drugs that could have negative effects on patients. The same predictive models make drug R&D faster and more specific, thus encouraging much faster marketing of medicines and the production of specific compounds with a high success rate. Finally, the use of a database with data from all patients and therapies at a national level can ensure rapid detection of infectious diseases and control of possible global epidemics through a special programme, thus ensuring the monitoring of public health and an improvement in the quality of life itself;
- Customization of the care therapy. Huge databases are analyzed to verify the relationships between genetic variations, predisposition to specific diseases and individual responses to certain drugs. In such a way, it becomes possible to develop personalized drugs, ensuring more effective care therapies and early diagnosis;
- Prevention. The use of AA as predictive and patient segmentation models can allow the identification of individuals who can benefit from proactive care or lifestyle changes, thus supporting the prevention of any health problems;
- Development of new business models. Clinical patient data and aggregated and synthesized medical databases may be sold to third parties. These clinical databases make it possible to start new businesses, such as analysing clinical outcomes for payers who can make better operational decisions, or analysing databases to discover biomarkers that select therapies.

### 5.4  Logistics and Supply Chain

The analysis of BD in the logistics area and in the management of the supply chain (so-called logistics and supply chain management, or LSCM) has recently received increasing attention in the literature due to its complexity and the prominent role it has in improving firms' overall performance. In a survey conducted by Accenture in 2014, more than a third of respondents reported being involved in designing projects for the implementation of LSCM field analysis; and three out of ten confirmed that they already had an initiative in place to implement the analysis (Accenture, 2014).

In fact, firm logistics faces quite a significant challenge today, such as delays in shipments and delivery, rising fuel costs, rising costs in several raw materials and commodities (e.g., oil, gas, wheat, iron, steel, copper and others), inconsistent suppliers and constantly increasing customer expectations. These can cause inefficiencies and waste in the supply chain (Barnaghi et al., 2013). Therefore, firms tend to adopt AA in their logistics and supply chain operations to improve the visibility, flexibility and integration of global supply chains and logistics processes, as well as to effectively manage demand volatility and cost fluctuations. In the strategic phase of supply chain planning, AA play a crucial role. Firms use AA to make decisions about procurement and supply chain network design, as well as design, product development and demand planning. We examine three points in the following.

**Strategic procurement becomes collaborative**
It focuses on managing relations with suppliers by analysing the costs of organizing and acquiring raw materials and services more conveniently for all the actors involved. By using AA in the strategic procurement planning process, firms can optimize their financial performance, minimize operating costs and improve the performance of their suppliers. It is also possible for firms to analyse their spending profiles, procurement processes and future demand trends. Second, AA facilitate the development of optimal procurement strategies by assessing supply market trends and supplier inputs and outputs. Analysis and assessment tools are used to formulate these strategies, including, for example, cost modelling and risk assessment. These tools are also used to define appropriate bargaining terms and parameters, realize optimal processes and bidding parameters, and select suppliers based on their best value offers (Shen and Williams, 2012).

**Design of the supply chain network**
Supply network design studies how the supply chain can be configured from a physical and infrastructure perspective. This process includes decisions concerning the number, location and size of production facilities and distribution centres and/or warehouses acting as intermediate storage points and shipping points between existing plants and retailers. Supply network design problems can be classified into two categories in terms of information available on demand: those with known demand and those with fluctuations or uncertainties in demand. In particular, network design with uncertain demand is suitable for capturing changes in demand patterns, product mix, production processes, procurement strategies and operating costs (Soleimani et al., 2014). The amount of data involved in the design of the supply network is actually immense: from aggregated product requests in each retailer to plant capacity, to shipping costs per unit between each pair of locations and the fixed operating cost in each potential location. By using AA, it is possible to address supply network design issues in both situations, whether in designing a network with known demand or one with uncertain demand. The decision variables used in the analyses include continuous variables, which represent the quantities to be shipped between different locations, and binary variables, which indicate whether each structure should be opened or closed.

**Demand planning**
A key aspect of logistics management is process and operations management to meet demand and tackle its changes. However, process variation and demand variability can become an obstacle to achieving the correct alignment between process capacity and demand. Effective

operational management capacity planning requires accurate demand forecasting, the ability to translate forecasts into capacity requirements, and supply chain operations that meet expected demand. Therefore, demand planning is critical to planning the operations of the entire supply chain and requires the use of predictive analytics techniques, thanks to time series analysis. The time series analysis methodology includes "exponential damping", which is widely used both for short-term forecasts and for medium-term forecasts, since it can incorporate both trend and seasonality. Another interesting method is the self-regressive model, which offers demand forecasting over a given period using the weighted sum of demand values in previous periods. Using demand forecasting techniques, it is possible to optimize marketing, production and storage management processes and make logistics processes more efficient, thus ensuring regularity in customer and supplier satisfaction (Laurent Lim et al., 2014).

## 6.   CONCLUSION

The continuous evolution of markets compels firms to adopt the most AA technologies to keep pace with their competitors as well as to be able to respond adequately to the expanding needs of consumers. Actually, AA may help firms make their decision-making process smoother and reduce the risk of taking dire decisions. In this increasingly unstable context, several firms have started to experience the important value of data analysis, as well as the information that can be extracted with such powerful analytical tools. By examining their key features, potential, the operational contribution they can make and the strategic advantage that firms may win thanks to their use, this chapter has allowed us first to clarify some key issues related to AA adoption by firms. In particular, we deepened the analysis of the application of AA in four important economic sectors: finance and insurance, manufacturing, healthcare, and logistics and supply chain.

Second, we have also observed that AA advantages accrue to large firms in particular since SMEs generally struggle to keep up with the competitive race to evolve data analysis systems, thereby taking the follower role when compared to large firms. The reasons why this happens are tied to the SMEs' lack of financial resources to invest, as well as to the absence of a technology-oriented mentality that guides SMEs' management towards approaching and adopting AA-related technologies. The latter circumstance is to be considered even more relevant. Often, the "SME problem in AA adoption" is not merely related to the shortage in capital investment or to the complicated access to borrow it, but much more to the recurrent "entrepreneurial inability" or "inner resistance" to perceive and appropriate the need to innovate by using these advanced data-driven technologies. This condition in the medium term is likely to become a penalizing factor vis-à-vis bigger firms, since it risks eroding the SMEs' capacity to keep the levels of their sales and market shares.

Finally, we have underscored that it is not enough to adopt the most updated AA technologies to be successful and able to compete with the competition, since it is of fundamental importance for firms (of any size) to develop the know-how and acquire the right strategic, managerial and operations set-up allowing them to make the best use of the technologies adopted so as to optimize the generation of value deriving from them. We therefore acknowledge that sometimes firms need a change of course; this change of course could be facilitated, in the future, by the unremitting reduction in the costs of accessing AA technologies.

## 7.     LIMITATIONS AND AVENUES FOR FUTURE RESEARCH

Before ending the chapter, it seems helpful to present a research agenda on the main aspects we need to focus on and the knowledge gaps/limitations of the study performed to unveil the opportunities for future research in this direction. First, to have a more solid foundation on which to establish the strategic advantage that the use of AA may bring to firms, a larger database is certainly needed. This larger database would be able to ground adequately the significance of the correlation between the use of AA and an effective increase in the economic and financial performance of the firms studied. In fact, we are absolutely aware that the number of firms in the sample, although well mixed, is relatively small to symbolize the total population, and the grounding would possibly require data collected over a longer period of time and selected using statistical randomization methods.

Second, we acknowledge that there are differences in the impact of AA on business performance, and this also depends on the sector in which the firms operate. It would therefore be interesting to deepen this aspect by investigating the time needed for this effect to be visible, as well as if there are other analytical technologies that may lead to better results in terms of performance increase.

Third, it would also be interesting to verify whether the use of AA can be aimed not only at improving the economic and financial performance of firms, but also at improving their performance as concerns the issue of sustainability. It would in fact be of great importance for a firm to use the state-of-the-art data analysis technologies to reduce its social and environmental impact and its carbon footprint.

Last but not least, future research would be probably interested in taking into account the evolution over time of the impact of the use of AA on firms' performance, by expanding the analysis in other sectors that go beyond the four analyzed (i.e., finance and insurance, manufacturing, healthcare, and logistics and supply chain), such as tourism and hospitality, energy, electronics and semiconductors, and so on.

## NOTES

1.  Churn rate is the percentage of customers or subscribers who stop using the services offered by a firm for a period of time.
2.  Firm business processes are both facilitated by and embedded with IT. Business information intensity (BII) needs to acknowledge the pervasiveness of IT in contemporary business processes. Consistent with the extant literature (Chandra and Calderon, 2005), it is possible to use BII to indicate the content and the extent of IT usage in firms' products and value chain. A firm with high (low) IT content in its value chain, as well as in its products, would have high (low) BII. BII can be modelled at both the product and the business process levels (Chandra and Calderon, 2009). Industries where the highest supply of information is exhibited, or data-driven industries (i.e., manufacturing and financial-insurance), are usually able to make a better use of AA potential vis-à-vis other industries.
3.  Payers are insurance firms, healthcare firms, contractors and claims managers as part of state medical care programs, while providers are hospitals, clinics and health care providers.
4.  Variety is one of the characteristics of health data. In fact, there are structured data that can be easily stored, queried, analyzed and manipulated and that, together with semi-structured data, include tools for reading and converting paper documents into EHR. In addition to these, non-structured data include handwritten notes from doctors and nurses, paper prescriptions, X-rays, and medical imaging.

# REFERENCES

Accenture (2014). *Big Data Analytics in Supply Chain: Hype or Here to Stay?* Dublin: Accenture.

Appelbaum, D., Kogan, A., Vasarhelyi, M., and Yan, Z. (2017). Impact of business analytics and enterprise systems on managerial accounting. *International Journal of Accounting Information Systems*, 25(C), 29–44.

Banerjee, A., Bandyopadhyay, T., and Acharya, P. (2013). Data analytics: Hyped up aspirations or true potential? *Vikalpa*, 38(4), 1–12.

Barnaghi, P., Sheth, A., and Henson, C.A. (2013). From data to actionable knowledge: Big data challenges in the web of thing. *IEEE Intelligent Systems*, 28(6), 6–11.

Baum, J., Laroque, C., Oeser, B., Skoogh, A., and Subramaniyan, M. (2018). Applications of big data analytics and related technologies in maintenance: Literature-based research. *Machines*, 6(4), 54.

Bertsimas, D., and Kallus, N. (2019). From predictive to prescriptive analytics. *Management Science*, 66(3), 1025–44.

Bose, R. (2009). Advanced analytics: Opportunities and challenges. *Industrial Management & Data Systems*, 109(2), 155–79.

Cao, H., and Wachowicz, M. (2019). The design of an IoT-GIS platform for performing automated analytical tasks. *Computers, Environment and Urban Systems*, 74, 23–40.

Chambers, M., and Dinsmore, T.W. (2014). *Advanced Analytics Methodologies: Driving Business Value with Analytics*. Upper Saddle River, NJ: Pearson Education.

Chandra, A., and Calderon, T. (2005). Challenges and constraints to the diffusion of biometrics in information systems. *Communications of the ACM*, 48(12), 101–6.

Chandra, A., and Calderon, T. (2009). Information intensity, control deficiency risk, and materiality. *Managerial Auditing Journal*, 24(3), 220–32.

Chen, H., Chiang, R.H.L., and Storey, V.C. (2012). Business intelligence and analytics: From big data to big impact. *MIS Quarterly*, 36(4), 1165–88.

Chen, Y.-T., and Sun, E.W. (2018). Automated Business Analytics for Artificial Intelligence in Big Data @X4.0 Era. In: M. Dehmer and F. Emmert-Streib (Eds), *Frontiers in Data Science*. Boca Raton, FL: CRC Press, pp. 227–55.

Davenport, T.H. (2015, January 14). The rise of automated analytics. *Wall Street Journal*. https://www.wsj.com/articles/BL-CIOB-6061.

Delen, D., and Zolbanin, H.M. (2018). The analytics paradigm in business research. *Journal of Business Research*, 90, 186–95.

Domo (2018). Data Never Sleeps 6.0. https://www.domo.com/assets/downloads/18_domo_data-never-sleeps-6+verticals.pdf.

Dreyfus, P.-A., and Kyritsis, D.C. (2018). A Framework Based on Predictive Maintenance, Zero-Defect Manufacturing and Scheduling Under Uncertainty Tools, to Optimize Production Capacities of High-End Quality Products. In: I. Moon, G.M. Lee, J. Park, D. Kiritsis and G. von Cieminski (Eds), *Advances in Production Management Systems: Smart Manufacturing for Industry 4.0*. Cham: Springer, pp. 296–303.

Duan, Y., Cao, G., and Edwards, J.S. (2020). Understanding the impact of business analytics on innovation. *European Journal of Operational Research*, 281(3), 673–86.

*Forbes* (2018, August 15). 6 reasons why investment in analytics is essential. https://www.forbes.com/sites/insights-cisco/2018/08/15/6-reasons-why-investment-in-analytics-is-essential/?sh=36124bd15eff.

Gartner (2017). Gartner IT glossary. http://www.gartner.com/it-glossary/advanced-analytics.

Guess, A.R. (2014). 3 types of data analytics: Descriptive, predictive, and prescriptive. Dataversity. https://www.dataversity.net/3-types-data-analytics-descriptive-predictive-prescriptive/.

Havlena, M. (2013). What is business analytics. Personal blog. http://www.havlena.net/en/business-analytics-intelligence/big-data-analytics-part-1-what-is-business-analytics/.

Kim, C.F., and Dewi, D.A. (2019). A review of data analytics adoption in business industry. *INTI Journal*, 2019(034).

La Bruna, G., Dagnino, G.B., and Notarstefano, G. (2021). The effect of advanced analytics on firm performance: An empirical analysis of Italian firms. Working paper presented at Third Conference on

Digital Transformation: Competitive Renaissance through Digital Transformation. Italian Society of Management and University of Pavia (February 2021).

Laurent Lim, L., Alpan, G., and Penz, B. (2014). Reconciling sales and operations management with distant suppliers in the automotive industry: A simulation approach. *International Journal of Production Economics*, 151(C), 20–36.

Lee, J. (2014). Service, innovation and smart analytics for industry 4.0 and big data environment. *Procedia CIRP*, 16, 3–8.

Lepenioti, K., Bousdekis, A., Apostolou, D., and Mentzas, G. (2020). Prescriptive analytics: Literature review and research challenges. *International Journal of Information Management*, 50, 57–70.

Manyika, J., Chui, M., Brown, B., Bughin, J., Dobbs, R., Roxburgh, C., and Hung Byers, A. (2011). *Big Data: The Next Frontier for Innovation, Competition and Productivity*. N.p.: McKinsey Global Institute.

Medeiros, M.M.d., and Maçada, A.C.G. (2022). Competitive advantage of data-driven analytical capabilities: the role of big data visualization and of organizational agility. *Management Decision*, 60(4), 953–75.

Mujawar, S., and Joshi, A. (2015). Data analytics types, tools and their comparison. *International Journal of Advanced Research in Computer and Communication Engineering*, 4(2), 488–91.

Ramanathan, R., Philpott, E., Duan, Y., and Cao, G. (2017). Adoption of business analytics and impact on performance: A qualitative study in retail. *Production Planning & Control*, 28(11–12), 985–98.

Rose, J., Berndtsson, M., Mathiason, G., and Larsson, P. (2017). The advanced analytics jump-start: Definition, process model, best practices. *Journal of Information Systems and Technology Management*, 14(3), 339–60.

Saggi, M.K., and Jain, S. (2018). A survey towards an integration of big data analytics to big insights for value-creation. *Information Processing and Management*, 54, 758–90.

Seddon, P.B., Constantinidis, D., Tamm, T., and Dod, H. (2016). How does business analytics contribute to business value? *Information Systems Journal*, 27(3), 237–69.

Shen, Y., and Williams, S.P. (2012). Strategic sourcing for the short-lifecycle products. *International Journal of Production Economics*, 139(2), 575–85.

Sivarajah, U., Kamal, M.M., Irani, Z., and Weerakkody, V. (2017). Critical analysis of big data challenges and analytical methods. *Journal of Business Research*, 70, 263–86.

Soleimani, H., Seyyed-Esfahani, M., and Govindan, K. (2014). Incorporating risk measures in closed-loop supply chain network design. *International Journal of Production Research*, 52(6), 1843–67.

Song, S., Kim, D.J., Hwang, M., Kim, J., Jeong, D., Lee, S., Jung, H., & Sung, W. (2013). Prescriptive analytics system for improving research power. *2013 IEEE 16th International Conference on Computational Science and Engineering*, 1144–45.

Statista (2022, June). Number of social media users worldwide from 2017 to 2027. https://www.statista.com/statistics/278414/number-of-worldwide-social-network-users/.

Vercellis, C., Piva, A., Di Deo, I., and Leccardi, F. (2019a). *Il mercato analytics in Italia nel 2019*. Milan: Osservatorio.net.

Vercellis, C., Piva, A., Di Deo, I., and Leccardi, F. (2019b). *Le tecnologie di gestione e analisi dei dati: un modello di self-assessment*. Milan: Osservatorio.net.

# 20. Digital coopetition: creating and capturing value with rivals in the age of algorithms, big data, and platforms

*Georg Reischauer and Werner H. Hoffmann*

## 1. INTRODUCTION

Across industries, firms increasingly engage in coopetition and thus both compete and cooperate with rivals (Brandenburger & Nalebuff, 1996; Hoffmann et al., 2018; Minà et al., 2020). This is not surprising given "coopetition is a strategy that holds the greatest potential for firms' performance" (Le Roy & Czakon, 2016: 3). The decision to engage in an interplay of cooperative and competitive behavior is driven by the aim to enhance a firm's innovation performance (Chiambaretto et al., 2020; Pekovic et al., 2020; Ritala & Sainio, 2013) or financial performance (Gnyawali & Charleton, 2018; Ritala, 2012). It also a preferred strategy chosen in response to technological changes or as a proactive move to develop new technologies to create a competitive advantage (Ranganathan et al., 2018; Rusko, 2019).

Currently, we are witnessing the rise of a new generation of technologies that are digital (Adner et al., 2019; Cennamo et al., 2020; Lanzolla et al., 2018; Schildt, 2020; Teece, 2018). Important examples examined by strategy scholars include platforms (Cennamo, 2019), artificial intelligence (AI; Schildt, 2020), big data (Schildt, 2017), and cloud competing (Khanagha et al., 2021). More and more scholars suggest that these technologies not only change the fabrics of corporate strategy but require firms to develop and implement digital strategies (Menz et al., 2021) but also how firms engage in coopetition (Ansari et al., 2016; Gnyawali et al., 2010; Zhu et al., 2020). However, it is not yet clear how far coopetitive relationships that are embedded into digital technologies (Cepa & Schildt, 2019) differ from "traditional" coopetitive relationships, and what this means for future research. To address this issue, we will lay the grounds for and advance future research on digital coopetition, which we define as simultaneous and technologically embedded competition and cooperation amongst firms to create and capture value for each other.

In the remainder of this work, we take four steps. First, we outline the tenets of the coopetition perspective (Section 2). Second, we develop the concept of digital coopetition, which includes specifying the conditions that make digital coopetition the dominant coopetition form and elaborating on how digital coopetition differs from traditional coopetition. Third, we develop a preliminary research agenda on digital coopetition. Finally, we conclude why digital coopetition should be considered an important element of digital strategy.

## 2.    COOPETITION

"Coopetition" refers to the simultaneous competition and cooperation amongst firms to create and capture value for each other (Brandenburger & Nalebuff, 1996). Interfirm relationships are thus coopetitive when there is a simultaneous presence of cooperation and competition as well as when participating firms leverage these linkages to create and capture value (Czakon et al., forthcoming).

The ways firms engage in coopetition varies with respect to resource similarity and degree of market commonality (Minà et al., 2020). Specifically, Gnyawali and Charleton (2018) argue that there are four forms of coopetition. First, firms that engage in "mutual pursuits" aim for individual superiority in the face of simultaneous dependencies because of their cooperation. Second, when coopeting through "resource leverage," firms improve their individual competitive position while accessing a shared resource pool. Third, coopeting firms engaging in "safeguarded resources" both share and protect resources against third parties. "Relevant commitments," finally, is at hand when coopeting firms contribute a large number of resources towards their relationship.

Amongst the reasons why firms engage in coopetition are enhanced innovation performance (Chiambaretto et al., 2020; Pekovic et al., 2020; Ritala & Sainio, 2013) or financial performance (Gnyawali & Charleton, 2018; Ritala, 2012). Moreover, coopetition can increase the chances of survival in the face of technological changes (Ansari & Krop, 2012; Czakon et al., forthcoming; Gnyawali et al., 2006; Minà et al., 2020; Ranganathan et al., 2018; Ritala, 2012). In the words of Hamel et al. (1989: 134): "[u]sing an alliance with a competitor to acquire new technologies or skills is not devious. It reflects the commitment and capacity of each partner to absorb the skills of the other." For instance, the development and utilization of new technologies can be more efficient because coopeting firms are able to divide development tasks according to their capabilities (Gnyawali & Park, 2011; Gomes-Casseres et al., 2006).

## 3.    DIGITAL COOPETITION

A considerable amount of research on coopetition has been carried out in industries such as food, wine, or tourism where firms hardly use digital technologies as the basis of their value-creating and value-capturing operations (Gernsheimer et al., 2021; Gnyawali & Charleton, 2018). As we discuss next, this presents an issue as more and more firms redefine their operations in order to create and capture value with digital technologies, which requires us to rethink the tenets of coopetition. We do so by putting forward the notion of digital coopetition. Building on Brandenburger and Nalebuff (1996), we define digital coopetition as simultaneous and technologically embedded competition and cooperation amongst firms to create and capture value for each other. Thus, the key difference to traditional ways of coopetition is that value creation and value capture of firms is fundamentally embedded into digital technologies. "Technological embeddedness" refers to the "extent of monitoring, control and optimization of intra and inter-organizational tasks accomplished through technology at the interface of the inter-organizational relationship" (Cepa & Schildt, 2019: 93).

We use Apple and Facebook to exemplify the distinctiveness and relevance of digital coopetition. For years, both were key allies in the mobile revolution, providing the channel and its content. Both companies run platforms with growing ecosystems of other companies, large and small, around them. They are a "power couple" of the mobile internet that exemplifies well some of the key drivers of digital coopetition.

A competitive schism between Apple and Facebook has revolved around advertising, and specifically the advertising of mobile games. The developers of mobile games, a growing industry, can choose to advertise their games either on Facebook's news feed or on Apple's App Store. These firms effectively auction the attention of their customers to developers, who use real-time data to optimize their advertising. It makes little sense to advertise games to the kinds of users who only play the free version and never spend money in the game. In spring 2021, Apple struck at the heart of Facebook's advertising business by severing the data flows that link advertising on Facebook to the installation and spending within games. In a masterful public relations move, Apple claimed that the crippling blow against Facebook was all about consumer privacy. Unless users explicitly allow tracking across applications, developers can no longer make the necessary connection between advertising spending and subsequent revenue. That is, unless they advertise on Apple's App Store. In Facebook's quarterly earnings call on January 27, 2021, Mark Zuckerberg, the CEO of Facebook, gave the following statement:

> We are also seeing Apple's business depend more and more on gaining share in apps and services against us and other developers. So Apple has every incentive to use their dominant platform position to interfere with how our apps and other apps work, which they regularly do to preference their own.

As this example shows, digital coopetition brings forth new opportunities for collaboration, but at the same time creates incentives for opportunistic efforts to leverage control over data, customer relationships, or both, to gain advantage over the "coopetitor." In what follows, we outline the firm-level condition that gives rise to digital coopetition and provide a comparison between digital coopetition and traditional coopetition.

## 3.1    Enabler

Building on recent advances on the role of digital technologies for business and corporate strategy (Menz et al., 2021; Sebastian et al., 2017; Vial, 2019; Volberda et al., 2021), we argue that digital coopetition becomes the dominant coopetition form when firms use one or more of four sets of technologies to create and capture value.

The first set are "platform technologies," broadly defined as digital infrastructures that connect firms and/or individuals (Gawer, 2014). The range of platform types includes transaction platforms such as Uber or Airbnb that function as a matchmaker of supply and demand (Reischauer & Mair, 2018; Rochet & Tirole, 2003); platform ecosystems, in which one or few firms offer the infrastructure for other firms to innovate and provide offerings such as videogames or operating systems (Cennamo & Santaló, 2019; Jacobides et al., 2018; Wen & Zhu, 2019); and information platforms such as TripAdvisor or Craigslist that monetize information created by users in several ways, notably advertising (Seamans & Zhu, 2017).

The second set of digital technologies are "mobile technologies" that are used for the purpose of service initiation, agreement, or fulfillment. These technologies create and capture value by using related location or mobility information to enable, support, or conduct transactions (Pousttchi et al., 2015). Examples include payment apps (such as PayPal or Venmo) and navigation apps (such as Google Maps or Apple Maps).

A third set are "analysis technologies," including aspects such as big data and artificial intelligence. Analytics based on big data "promise to make managers more omniscient, equipping them with the capability to perceive the world in ever-greater detail and scope" (Schildt, 2020: 22). Schildt (2017) distinguishes between optimizing-oriented analytics and open-ended analytics. Several applications focus on optimization, meaning data is analyzed with the purpose to govern processes, sometimes also automatically, so as to maximize or minimize predefined outputs, such as costs or revenues. In contrast, open-ended analytics "distil useful insights from large volumes of data" (p. 25). Examples include Google Search and Affectiva, a firm that turns video feeds from cameras into quantitative measures of emotions, allowing users to better understand emotional responses to advertising and movie trailers (Schildt, 2020).

A fourth important group of digital technologies are "cloud computing and internet of things technologies." Cloud competing is about ways of "enabling ubiquitous, convenient, on-demand network access to a shared pool of configurable computing resources (e.g., networks, servers, storage, applications, and services) that can be rapidly provisioned and released with minimal management effort or service provider interaction" (Mell & Grance, 2011: 2), allowing firms to be flexible and agile. With the internet of things approach, devices connect themselves to others and can be remotely controlled (Khanagha et al., 2021).

Often, firms combine one or more of platform technologies, mobile technologies, analysis technologies, and cloud computing and internet of things technologies in their offerings. For instance, Hilti – a firm that makes tools and machinery for professional end-users in industrial markets with a rent-based business model – uses analytics to estimate the durability of its products and possible demands, as well as offering smartphone-based applications that allow instant interaction with customer service.

Defining the use of platform technologies, mobile technologies, analysis technologies, as well as cloud computing and internet of things technologies, as a firm-level condition enabling digital coopetition is important to move away from a more macro industry-based understanding of the impact of digital technologies on coopetition, as called upon by several scholars (Adner et al., 2019; Cennamo et al., 2020; Lanzolla et al., 2018). Accordingly, firms in the same industry that use these technologies to create and capture value may engage in digital coopetition, whereas firms that do not foresee more traditional ways of coopetition. Consider the example of tourism: while some hotels mainly attract customers and form relationships with other hotels via platforms, others do not have their operations deeply embedded with digital technologies.

## 3.2    Comparison with Traditional Coopetition

The embeddedness into digital technologies that is characteristic for digital coopetition has profound consequences for coopetitive relationships (Cepa & Schildt, 2019; Rusko, 2019). Thus, digital technologies do not just escalate the same coopetitive dynamics research has already observed for firms. In particular, as we elaborate in this section, the embeddedness of coopetitive relationships into digital technologies redefines the phases of managing coopetitive relationships, namely their initiation, execution, and termination (Dorn et al., 2016; Gernsheimer et al., 2021). Table 20.1 offers a summary of this discussion.

For the initiation of coopetition, two differences are at hand. First, scholars identified the rationale to engage in traditional coopetitive relationships as asking whether it is more effective to exchange within or without the "firm boundaries – with a bright-line distinction between

*Table 20.1*     *Differences between traditional coopetition and digital coopetition across phases*

| Coopetition phase | Traditional coopetition | Digital coopetition |
|---|---|---|
| Initiation | *Rationale*: whether exchanges are more effective within or outside firm boundaries | *Rationale*: how to bundle and/or facilitate exchanges to better create and capture value |
| | *Mode*: individualized | *Mode*: standardized |
| Execution | *Performance evaluation*: period-sensitive | *Performance evaluation*: ad hoc |
| Termination | *Triggers*: Negative outcomes (e.g., knowledge leakage) | *Triggers*: absence of temporary advantage |

those economic activities 'within' a firm's boundary, and those 'outside' a firm's boundary" (Alvarez et al., 2020: 711). In contrast, when deciding to initiate a digital coopetition, there is rising evidence that managers ask how to bundle and/or facilitate exchanges to create and capture value (Alvarez et al., 2020; Gawer, 2022). This presents a very different rationale. Second, modes to enter a traditional coopetition and a digital coopetition also differ. For traditional coopetition, the time to start tends to be longer as it involves both parties assessing the compatibility and relatedness of each other's resources (Hoffmann et al., 2018) and requires the establishment of trust between firms (Barretta, 2008). Put differently, entering a coopetitive relationship is typically a rather individualized matter. Moreover, often industry-wide events trigger traditional coopetition (Madhavan et al., 1998). In contrast, there is revising evidence of the quick start of digital coopetition. Especially when platform technologies are used, firms can engage with each other quicker because of higher standardization and higher transparency of interactions (Lanzolla & Frankort, 2016; Zhu et al., 2020). Moreover, entering a digital coopetition is faster because of lower switching costs (Basaure et al., 2020; Rietveld & Schilling, 2021). Overall, entering a coopetitive relationship is more standardized.

Also, the execution of traditional and digital coopetition differs, especially with regard to the evaluation of the performance of coopetitive relationships. For traditional forms, evaluation of the arrangements typically involves the assessment of performance over a longer period of time (Chiambaretto et al., 2020; Pekovic et al., 2020; Ritala & Sainio, 2013). However, in the case of digital coopetition, the new wave of metrics (e.g., usage numbers, access numbers) allow ad hoc evaluations of coopetitive relationships (Altman et al., 2021; Zhu et al., 2020).

Finally, the termination of coopetition also varies, especially when it comes to the triggers that end coopetition. When engaging in traditional coopetition, the main reasons to end coopetitive relationships were negative outcomes such as knowledge leakages (Khanna et al., 1998; Raza-Ullah, 2020; Raza-Ullah et al., 2014). In contrast, for digital coopetition we see the quest for temporary advantages (Dagnino et al., 2021; D'Aveni et al., 2010) as an important trigger that causes a firm to end its coopetitive relationships. Such can be the case when the entry of a platform in a new market is too slow (Stallkamp & Schotter, 2021).

## 4.     TOWARDS A RESEARCH AGENDA ON DIGITAL COOPETITION

Having specified the conditions that likely make digital coopetition the dominant coopetition form and how digital differs from traditional coopetition, we now provide a research agenda on digital coopetition. For this purpose, we draw upon the coopetition framework developed

*Table 20.2*     *Future research avenues on digital coopetition*

| Dimension | Open questions |
| --- | --- |
| Antecedents | *Environmental antecedents* |
| | • How do changes of (platform) ecosystems trigger digital coopetition within and across (platform) ecosystems? |
| | • Which types of industry events predict engagements in digital coopetition and how do firms categorize industry events as relevant for their coopetitive relationships? |
| | • How do firms in mature industries other than the focal industry or ecosystem start digital coopetition? |
| | • What is the role of public organizations in engaging in digital coopetition? |
| | *Firm antecedents* |
| | • What non-technological capabilities enable digital coopetition? |
| | • What is the role of access to rare information resources and under which conditions do rare information resources predict digital coopetition? |
| | • How do firms assess each other's capabilities and resources with respect to digital technologies *ex ante*? |
| | • Are firms more or less likely to engage in digital coopetition with firms that are similar in terms of using and adopting digital technologies? |
| Nature of the interplay | • Are firms specializing in competition when engaging in digital coopetition and under which conditions is this beneficial? |
| | • Are firms entering more and less exclusive coopetitive relationships when engaging in digital coopetition and under which conditions is this beneficial? |
| | • What is the role of rival type and power in how competition and cooperation reinforce each other? |
| | • Are multilateral coopetitive engagements more likely when engaging in digital coopetition and under which conditions is this beneficial? |
| | • Are indirect coopetitive engagements more likely when engaging in digital coopetition and under which conditions is this beneficial? |
| Tensions | • Which tensions identified for traditional coopetition are also tensions characteristic for digital coopetition? |
| | • Which tensions are distinct for digital coopetition (e.g., trade-off between "old" and "new" and digital offerings, optimal distinctiveness in multiple markets, digital coopetition between challengers and incumbents)? |
| Managing tensions | • How do firms pursue organizational separation and persuade stakeholders that the chosen organizational separation represents an adequate approach when engaging in digital coopetition? |
| | • How do firms put temporal separation for digital offerings into action when engaging in digital coopetition? |
| | • What are the drivers and different pathways of domain separation when engaging in digital coopetition? |
| | • What is the nature and structure of capabilities used to achieve a contextual integration when engaging in digital coopetition? |
| | • Which approaches to manage coopetition tensions are used together, what motivated their choice, and what are the performance implications? |

by Hoffmann et al. (2018) and focus on four dimensions: antecedents, the nature of interplay between digital competition and digital cooperation, tensions, and how tensions are managed. For each dimension, we discuss promising directions for future research.[1] Table 20.2 provides a summary.

## 4.1     Antecedents

### 4.1.1     Environmental antecedents

One important group of antecedents that trigger a start of coopetitive relationships are environmental antecedents (Bengtsson & Kock, 2014; Gernsheimer et al., 2021). But we need to know more about environmental factors that make digital coopetition likely.

The first open question pertains to the role of technological change. As Padula and Dagnino (2007) argued for traditional coopetition, in industries that are rapidly changing because of new technologies, firms are more likely to enter cooperative relationships. When it comes to digital technologies, there is growing evidence that the changes triggered by them will remain an important antecedent for digital coopetition (Ansari et al., 2016; Basaure et al., 2020; Schildt, 2020). However, a shift in level of analysis, from industry to ecosystem, seems important to mirror the cross-industry nature of ecosystems (Adner & Lieberman, 2021). For example, Hannah and Eisenhardt (2018) found that firms in the residential solar industry pursue different coopetition strategies depending on which sets of technologies they special-ize in. As industries are increasingly converging because of digital technologies (Kim et al., 2015), it will be important to study how changes not of entire industries but of ecosystems trigger coopetition, both within ecosystems and across ecosystems. This holds for both types of ecosystems, those coordinated by and based on a platform (such as Android) or ecosystems without such a platform (as characteristic in the automotive industry) (Jacobides et al., 2018).

Second, given the sharp rise of data that is challenging how firms sense information – making it likely that events are missed or are ignored because of the rapid pace induced by technologies (Teece, 2018) – it might be that industry events (Gnyawali et al., 2010; Madhavan et al., 1998) become less important to trigger coopetition. In particular, we need to know more about which types of industry events predict engagements in digital coopetition and how firms categorize industry events as relevant for their coopetitive relationships.

Third, it will be important to reassess the role of industry maturity (Hoffmann et al., 2018). For traditional coopetition, it was suggested that coopetitive engagements are more likely for mature industries, such as the airline industry or automotive industry. For future research it would be interesting to explore how firms in mature industries other than the focal industry or ecosystem start digital coopetition. Likewise, given the growth of public funding schemes and public organizations that aim to digitalize mature industries such as manufacturing (Reischauer, 2018), it will be important to study the role of public organizations in nurturing how firms enter digital coopetition.

### 4.1.2   Firm antecedents

Another important group of antecedents are firm antecedents (Hoffmann et al., 2018).

In particular, three fields of inquiry are important to revisit to advance our understanding of digital coopetition.

First, previous research identified the relevance of organizational capabilities and resources in starting traditional coopetition (Bengtsson et al., 2016; Lavie, 2006; Lorenzoni & Lipparini, 1999). Three aspects regarding organizational capabilities and resources are particularly promising for future research on digital coopetition. First, we know that interfirm complemen-tarities between capabilities and/or resources are an important trigger of entering a coopetitive relationship (Dyer et al., 2018). However, as recent studies suggest (Estrada & Dong, 2020; John & Ross, 2022), complementarities only with respect to technologies might not be a suf-ficient condition as digitally embedded coopetitive relationships are becoming less durable and stable. This opens up the important question for future research of what non-technological capabilities (e.g., human resources) enable firms to pursue digital coopetition. Second, scholars have identified the access to rare resources as an antecedent of traditional coopetition, as this allows firms to learn or utilize rare resources in their own offerings (Gnyawali & Park, 2011). Because of the drastic changes of digital technologies that come with a mass aggregation of information resources (Adner et al., 2019), it seems likely that the access to rare information resources (e.g., existing user base of a platform, unique datasets) will be a key antecedent to collaborate with competitors. Examining whether this holds true and under which conditions seems a highly promising road for future research. Third, managers need to assess the value of their firm's resources to determine complementarities between resources of rivals they consider competing with (Barney, 2002). However, it remains unclear how managers assess information resources that are particularly relevant when it comes to digital coopetition. It will thus be important to foster our understanding of how firms assess each other's capabilities and resources with respect to digital technologies *ex ante*.

A second important firm-level antecedent is the self-perception of a firm with respect to, for example, its strategic position and competitive pressure. Research on traditional coopetition suggested that perceived similarity amongst firms makes coopetition likely (Dorn et al., 2016). For instance, Ranganathan et al. (2018) found that rivals in the hardware industry who share many common technology interests are more likely to cooperate on a new related technology. Given that the imperative of becoming (more) "digital" also has strong symbolic character (Hanelt et al., 2021; Khanagha et al., 2021; Schildt, 2017), we can expect that firms seek to engage in digital coopetition with firms they consider to be similar in terms of using and adopting digital technologies. However, whether this holds true remains to be studied.

## 4.2    Nature of the Interplay

Five dimensions specify the nature of the interplay between competition and cooperation (Hoffmann et al., 2018). In this section, we outline basic insights on each and propose promising avenues for future research for each dimension.

First, while some coopetitive engagements are characterized by a balance of competitive and cooperative forces, others specialize in either one or the other. Because of the qualitative changes of digital technologies (Adner et al., 2019), the expansion potential of digital technologies (Müller et al., 2018), as well as the fragility of digital coopetitive relationships (see Section 3.2), we can expect a dominance of specializations in competitive engagements, while keeping cooperation at a minimum. Future research needs put this idea to the test.

The second dimension puts the spotlight on the temporality of competition and cooperation.

Traditional coopetitive relationships tend to be exclusive and restricted to a smaller number of firms involved in a relationship (Brandenburger & Nalebuff, 1996; Gnyawali & Charleton, 2018). In contrast, recent studies suggest that when firms create and capture value with digital technologies, they tend to coopete with more firms in a less exclusive way. A telling example is multi-homing, the decision of a product owner to offer them on multiple platforms simultaneously (Basaure et al., 2020; Cennamo et al., 2018; Park et al., 2021). Overall, because of lower transaction costs and lower entry barriers (Basaure et al., 2020), simultaneous engagements in digital coopetition seem more likely.

However, empirical research that provides evidence for this thought is needed.

A third important facet of the nature of coopetition is to whether competition and cooperation constrain (which is often assumed) or reinforce each other. For traditional coopetition, long-term alliances with rivals in particular can be reinforcing over time and altering in different periods (Hoffmann et al., 2018). Future research on digital coopetition should examine the role of rival type and power (such as a provider of a general-purpose technologies or a specialized start-up) in how competition and cooperation reinforce each other.

The fourth dimension centers on the number of involved actors and distinguishes between bilateral and multilateral coopetition. While bilateral coopetition involves two firms engaged in coopetition, the latter foresees at least three different firms. Turning to digital coopetition, we can expect that the ongoing standardization and increasing portability of data (Adner et al., 2019; Cennamo et al., 2020) will make multilateral coopetitive engagements more likely; future research should provide a clear picture of under which conditions multilateral coopetitive engagements are most beneficial.

A fifth facet that sheds light on the interplay between competition and cooperation is that between direct and indirect coopetition; the latter being at hand when a firm "compete[s] indirectly with another firm by virtue of their independent cooperation with the same alliance partners" (Hoffmann et al., 2018: 3040). Relating this distinction to digital coopetition, the increasing numbers of engagements suggest that firms end up with more indirect coopetitive engagements (Basaure et al., 2020; Cennamo et al., 2018; Park et al., 2021). To back this theoretically grounded observation, future research is warranted.

## 4.3    Tensions

Engaging in coopetition is challenging. Amongst the tensions identified for traditional coopetition are knowledge leakages, opportunistic behaviors, lack of commitment, and instability (Khanna et al., 1998; Raza-Ullah, 2020; Raza-Ullah et al., 2014). These tensions result from the fact that cooperation and competition each come with different corporate behaviors. While cooperation often entails sharing of resources, competition often means opportunistic behavior (Hoffmann et al., 2018). There are several promising routes for future research on tensions of digital coopetition.

First, future research could investigate which tensions identified for traditional coopetition are also tensions characteristic for digital coopetition. For example, leakages of non-rare knowledge might be less problematic given the increased availability of data (Adner et al., 2019; Schildt, 2020).

Second, future studies should explore which tensions are distinct for digital coopetition. Emerging research suggests several possible ones:

1.  For incumbents that digitalize their offerings, one tension may be related with the sources of value creation (Amit & Zott, 2001). When the share of value creation through digital offerings increases, this could threaten and damage the ways the same incumbent competes with and cooperates on less digital offerings. In other words, firms may face the tension resulting from the trade-off between "old" and "new" and digital offerings.
2.  Another tension resulting from the global scaling of operations (e.g., in the case of platforms, such as ride-sharing platforms as championed by Uber and Lyft; Jordan, 2017), will be to achieve optimal distinctiveness in different markets. Thus, incumbents may need to address the tension to balance opposing pressures for differentiation to gain competitive advantage and conformity to gain legitimacy across markets (Taeuscher et al., 2020; Taeuscher & Rothe, 2021; Zhao et al., 2017).
3.  Tensions could further result in the case of a digital coopetition between incumbents and challengers that are based on similar sources, as this allows challengers to capture value using the incumbent resources (Karhu & Ritala, 2021). This especially includes tensions related to data. Data drives collaboration, because it can be leveraged across settings (it is

fungible) and it is not spent when used (it is inexhaustible). Data thus creates collaborative relationships that risk turning competitive because data gives advantage. But customer relationships are also affected. As the customer relationships move from the analogue to digital world, access to customers becomes a valuable resource that can be leveraged over time through diverse business models. Digital customer relationships enable companies to address and "monetize" the needs and wants of their customers much more effectively. But opportunities to monetize customer attention create collaborative relationships that risk turning competitive. Future research should therefore advance our understanding of the conditions and specifics of a digital coopetition between incumbents and challengers.

## 4.4   Managing Tensions

Tensions resulting from engaging in coopetition require managerial attention. For traditional coopetition, four approaches to manage tensions have been put forward (Hoffmann et al., 2018). In this section, we outline each approach in promising ways for future research.

The first approach is an "organizational separation" of activities to compete and cooperate, often also referred to as "organizational ambidexterity" (Junni et al., 2013). While this approach can entail different units in larger multidivisional firms, for smaller firms this means to define clear rules of engagement for competitive and cooperative activities (Lavie & Singh, 2011). When pursuing this approach, tensions are managed by avoiding the internal processing of the (conflicting) demands of cooperation and coopetition at the same place. There is growing evidence that organizational separation remains a valid pathway when it comes to digital technologies (Kretschmer & Khashabi, 2020). However, our understanding is still limited when it comes to more insights on how incumbents organize to engage in digital coopetition. Also, how incumbents persuade stakeholders that their organizational separation represents an adequate approach to coopete remains under-studied.

The second approach to manage tensions of traditional coopetition is "temporal separation," an approach "whereby the firm oscillates between competition and cooperation over time, with the aim of restricting the time periods during which it competes and cooperates simultaneously with the same partner" (Hoffmann et al., 2018: 3043). Temporal separation is particularly effective when the shorter periods overlap and the longer the period is of either a pure competition or cooperation. Temporal separation comes with the challenge to manage the transitions between the different logics and demands of competition and cooperation (Hoffmann et al., 2018). Emerging research suggests that because of digital technologies, these challenges might be less severe. In particular, the multi-homing strategy where firms offer the same products and services on different platforms at the same time (Basaure et al., 2020; Cennamo et al., 2018; Park et al., 2021) and the growing data standardization (Koutroumpis et al., 2020) seem to enable a sustained temporal separation. Future research needs to verify this observation. Moreover, what remain unclear and a fruitful subject of future research are process models that specify how incumbents put temporal separation for digital offerings into action. Does this, for example, entail distinct capabilities, such as distinct digital capabilities? Likewise, how does sustained temporal separation differ when a firm engages in coopetitive relationships across multiple ecosystems?

The third approach to cope with the tension of coopetition identified by the literature is "domain separation." When following this approach, a firm simultaneously competes and cooperates simultaneously in different domains such as product lines, value chain parts, or countries. For traditional competition, domain separation was found to be beneficial under the condition that there is little interdependence between domains (Hoffmann et al., 2018). Recent studies suggest that domain separation is also a suitable approach for digital coopetition. For example, incumbent platforms like Google have spread into multiple domains at once (Müller et al., 2018). Moreover, the pivotal role of complements in platform ecosystems (e.g., apps in the Apple iOS ecosystem) increases the need for platform providers to diverge into multiple domains and form cooperation, while at the same time competing with other platform ecosystems (e.g., Apple iOS vs Google's Android) (Adner & Lieberman, 2021). Inspired by these advancements, future research could explore the drivers and different pathways of domain separation of digital technologies, especially alongside the life cycle. Moreover, it would be interesting to examine the performance implications of different pathways of domain separation. For instance, does it require a portfolio approach to balance these multiple engagements (Aversa et al., forthcoming; Hoffmann, 2007)?

The final approach to tackle the challenges of coopetition is "contextual integration." In contrast to the previous approaches, coopeting firms that pursue this approach aim to manage cooperative and competitive behavior simultaneously within the same organizational unit and thereby tackle tensions directly (Hoffmann et al., 2018). Contextual integration involves establishing a context that nurtures and sustains discipline (defined as having clear standards, fast-cycle feedback, and consistent sanctions), support (instilled by the access to resources outside of one's own unit and more help-oriented senior management), and trust (Ghoshal & Bartlett, 1994). Moreover, contextual integration also entails the development of capabilities that "support concurrent competition and cooperation with the same counterparts" (Hoffmann et al., 2018: 3043). More and more scholars observe that doing so will require capabilities in addition to established ones like alliance management (Altman & Tushman, 2017; Helfat & Raubitschek, 2018; Teece, 2017). However, research on the nature and outcomes of these capabilities characteristic for firms that embrace digital coopetition remains scarce.

Aside from the research avenues outlined for each approach, it seems highly important to examine which of the approaches to manage coopetition tensions are used together, what motivated the choice of that approach, and what outcomes are created.

## 5.    CONCLUSION

Since being put forward by Brandenburger and Nalebuff (1996), coopetition has become an important way to thrive in the face of technological changes and to develop technologies redefining industries (Ranganathan et al., 2018; Rusko, 2019). However, the current landscape of digital technologies redefines how firms enter, execute, and terminate coopetitive relationships (Adner et al., 2019; Cennamo et al., 2020; Lanzolla et al., 2018; Schildt, 2020; Teece, 2018). To address this issue, we in this chapter advance the concept of digital coopetition – which differs from "traditional coopetition" in that coopetitive relationships are deeply embedded into digital technologies (Cepa & Schildt, 2019) – and develop a preliminary research agenda on digital coopetition that covers antecedents, nature, tensions, and how to manage these tensions. In doing so, we follow Hoffmann et al. (2018: 3045), who suggested that the "the interplay of competition and cooperation can be studied using different lenses and analytical approaches, each providing a unique perspective on this interesting phenomenon."

We believe digital coopetition will become a crucial strategy to be considered as part of digital strategies for two main reasons (Menz et al., 2021). First, digitally enabled structures such as ecosystems, platforms, and AI-based applications often come with interdependencies (Jacobides et al., 2018), which will require firms to engage with rivals. Second, the several opportunities created by the various uses of digital technologies and thereby-triggered transformations (Björkdahl, 2020; Hanelt et al., 2021; Lanzolla et al., 2018) are redefining the boundaries of industries, making entries from and cooperation with larger firms that suddenly turn into a rival more likely. Consider the above example of Facebook and Google in the advertising domain. Another example are carmakers that are considering partnerships with retail platforms to gain a competitive edge over other carmakers.

The dynamics triggered by digital technologies nurture a promising ground for research on digital coopetition, as they enable scholars to study the "variation in intensity and balance of competition and cooperation, or how such variation may affect outcomes" (Gnyawali & Charleton, 2018: 2512). Given the increased proliferation of digital technologies in industries around the globe, exploring antecedents, natures, tensions, and how to manage tensions of digital coopetition will be a highly important field of inquiry for theory and practice alike.

## NOTE

1. We limit our discussion to the organizational and interfirm level and thus do not cover the individual level.

## REFERENCES

Adner, R., & Lieberman, M. (2021). Disruption through complements. *Strategy Science*, 6(1), 91–109.

Adner, R., Puranam, P., & Zhu, F. (2019). What is different about digital strategy? From quantitative to qualitative change. *Strategy Science*, 4(4), 253–61.

Altman, E.J., Nagle, F., & Tushman, M.L. (2021). The translucent hand of managed ecosystems: Engaging communities for value creation and capture. *Academy of Management Annals*, forthcoming.

Altman, E.J., & Tushman, M.L. (2017). Platforms, open/user innovation, and ecosystems: A strategic leadership perspective. *Advances in Strategic Management*, 37, 177–207.

Alvarez, S.A., Zander, U., Barney, J.B., & Afuah, A. (2020). Developing a theory of the firm for the 21st century. *Academy of Management Review*, 45(4), 711–6.

Amit, R., & Zott, C. (2001). Value creation in e-business. *Strategic Management Journal*, 22(6–7), 493–520.

Ansari, S., Garud, R., & Kumaraswamy, A. (2016). The disruptor's dilemma: Tivo and the U.S. television ecosystem. *Strategic Management Journal*, 37(9), 1829–53.

Ansari, S., & Krop, P. (2012). Incumbent performance in the face of a radical innovation: Towards a framework for incumbent challenger dynamics. *Research Policy*, 41(8), 1357–74.

Aversa, P., Haefliger, S., Hueller, F., & Reza, D.G. (forthcoming). Customer complementarity in the digital space: Exploring Amazon's business model diversification. *Long Range Planning*.

Barney, J. (2002). *Gaining and Sustaining Competitive Advantage* (2nd ed.). Upper Saddle River, NJ: Prentice Hall.

Barretta, A. (2008). The functioning of co-opetition in the health-care sector: An explorative analysis. *Scandinavian Journal of Management*, 24(3), 209–20.

Basaure, A., Vesselkov, A., & Töyli, J. (2020). Internet of things (IoT) platform competition: Consumer switching versus provider multihoming. *Technovation*, 90–91, 102101.

Bengtsson, M., & Kock, S. (2014). Coopetition – quo vadis? Past accomplishments and future challenges. *Industrial Marketing Management*, 43(2), 180–88.

Bengtsson, M., Raza-Ullah, T., & Vanyushyn, V. (2016). The coopetition paradox and tension: The moderating role of coopetition capability. *Industrial Marketing Management*, 53, 19–30.

Björkdahl, J. (2020). Strategies for digitalization in manufacturing firms. *California Management Review*, 62(4), 17–36.

Brandenburger, A., & Nalebuff, B. (1996). *Coopetition*. New York, NY: Currency Doubleday.

Cennamo, C. (2019). Competing in digital markets: A platform-based perspective. *Academy of Management Perspectives*, 35(2), 265–91.

Cennamo, C., Dagnino, G.B., Di Minin, A., & Lanzolla, G. (2020). Managing digital transformation: Scope of transformation and modalities of value co-generation and delivery. *California Management Review*, 62(4), 5–16.

Cennamo, C., Ozalp, H., & Kretschmer, T. (2018). Platform architecture and quality trade-offs of multi-homing complements. *Information Systems Research*, 29(2), 461–78.

Cennamo, C., & Santaló, J. (2019). Generativity tension and value creation in platform ecosystems. *Organization Science*, 30(3), 617–41.

Cepa, K., & Schildt, H. (2019). Technological embeddedness of inter-organizational collaboration processes. *Research in the Sociology of Organizations*, 64, 91–115.

Chiambaretto, P., Bengtsson, M., Fernandez, A.-S., & Näsholm, M.H. (2020). Small and large firms' trade-off between benefits and risks when choosing a coopetitor for innovation. *Long Range Planning*, 53(1), 101876.

Czakon, W., Srivastava, M.K., Le Roy, F., & Gnyawali, D. (forthcoming). Coopetition strategies: Critical issues and research directions. *Long Range Planning*.

D'Aveni, R.A., Dagnino, G.B., & Smith, K.G. (2010). The age of temporary advantage. *Strategic Management Journal*, 31(13), 1371–85.

Dagnino, G.B., Picone, P.M., & Ferrigno, G. (2021). Temporary competitive advantage: A state-of-the-art literature review and research directions. *International Journal of Management Reviews*, 23(1), 85–115.

Dorn, S., Schweiger, B., & Albers, S. (2016). Levels, phases and themes of coopetition: A systematic literature review and research agenda. *European Management Journal*, 34(5), 484–500.

Dyer, J.H., Singh, H., & Hesterly, W.S. (2018). The relational view revisited: A dynamic perspective on value creation and value capture. *Strategic Management Journal*, 39(12), 3140–62.

Estrada, I., & Dong, J.Q. (2020). Learning from experience? Technological investments and the impact of coopetition experience on firm profitability. *Long Range Planning*, 53(1), 101866.

Gawer, A. (2014). Bridging differing perspectives on technological platforms: Toward an integrative framework. *Research Policy*, 43(7), 1239–49.

Gawer, A. (2022). Digital platforms' boundaries: The interplay of firm scope, platform sides, and digital interfaces. *Long Range Planning*, forthcoming.

Gernsheimer, O., Kanbach, D.K., & Gast, J. (2021). Coopetition research: A systematic literature review on recent accomplishments and trajectories. *Industrial Marketing Management*, 96, 113–34.

Ghoshal, S., & Bartlett, C.A. (1994). Linking organizational context and managerial action: The dimensions of quality of management. *Strategic Management Journal*, 15(S2), 91–112.

Gnyawali, D.R., & Charleton, T.R. (2018). Nuances in the interplay of competition and cooperation: Towards a theory of coopetition. *Journal of Management*, 44(7), 2511–34.

Gnyawali, D.R., Fan, W., & Penner, J. (2010). Competitive actions and dynamics in the digital age: An empirical investigation of social networking firms. *Information Systems Research*, 21(3), 594–613.

Gnyawali, D.R., He, J., & Madhavan, R. (2006). Impact of co-opetition on firm competitive behavior: An empirical examination. *Journal of Management*, 32(4), 507–30.

Gnyawali, D.R., & Park, B.-J. (2011). Co-opetition between giants: Collaboration with competitors for technological innovation. *Research Policy*, 40(5), 650–63.

Gomes-Casseres, B., Hagedoorn, J., & Jaffe, A.B. (2006). Do alliances promote knowledge flows? *Journal of Financial Economics*, 80(1), 5–33.

Hamel, G., Doz, Y., & Prahalad, C.K. (1989). Collaborate with your competitors – and win. *Harvard Business Review*, 67(1), 133–9.

Hanelt, A., Bohnsack, R., Marz, D., & Antunes Marante, C. (2021). A systematic review of the literature on digital transformation: Insights and implications for strategy and organizational change. *Journal of Management Studies*, 58(5), 1159–97.

Hannah, D.P., & Eisenhardt, K.M. (2018). How firms navigate cooperation and competition in nascent ecosystems. *Strategic Management Journal*, 39(12), 3163–92.

Helfat, C.E., & Raubitschek, R.S. (2018). Dynamic and integrative capabilities for profiting from innovation in digital platform-based ecosystems. *Research Policy*, 47(8), 1391–9.

Hoffmann, W.H. (2007). Strategies for managing a portfolio of alliances. *Strategic Management Journal*, 28(8), 827–56.

Hoffmann, W.H., Lavie, D., Reuer, J.J., & Shipilov, A. (2018). The interplay of competition and cooperation. *Strategic Management Journal*, 39(12), 3033–52.

Jacobides, M.G., Cennamo, C., & Gawer, A. (2018). Towards a theory of ecosystems. *Strategic Management Journal*, 39(8), 2255–76.

John, K., & Ross, D. (2022). How a firm's value capture affects value creation in its ecosystem. *Academy of Management Review*, forthcoming.

Jordan, J.M. (2017). Challenges to large-scale digital organization: The case of Uber. *Journal of Organization Design*, 6(1), 11.

Junni, P., Sarala, R.M., Taras, V., & Tarba, S.Y. (2013). Organizational ambidexterity and performance: A meta-analysis. *Academy of Management Perspectives*, 27(4), 299–312.

Karhu, K., & Ritala, P. (2021). Slicing the cake without baking it: Opportunistic platform entry strategies in digital markets. *Long Range Planning*, 54(5).

Khanagha, S., Ansari, S., Paroutis, S., & Oviedo, L. (2021). Mutualism and the dynamics of new platform creation: A study of cisco and fog computing. *Strategic Management Journal*, forthcoming.

Khanna, T., Gulati, R., & Nohria, N. (1998). The dynamics of learning alliances: Competition, cooperation, and relative scope. *Strategic Management Journal*, 19(3), 193–210.

Kim, N., Lee, H., Kim, W., Lee, H., & Suh, J.H. (2015). Dynamic patterns of industry convergence: Evidence from a large amount of unstructured data. *Research Policy*, 44(9), 1734–48.

Koutroumpis, P., Leiponen, A., & Thomas, L.D.W. (2020). Markets for data. *Industrial and Corporate Change*, 29(3), 645–60.

Kretschmer, T., & Khashabi, P. (2020). Digital transformation and organization design: An integrated approach. *California Management Review*, 0008125620940296.

Lanzolla, G., & Frankort, H.T.W. (2016). The online shadow of offline signals: Which sellers get contacted in online B2B marketplaces? *Academy of Management Journal*, 59(1), 207–31.

Lanzolla, G., Lorenz, A., Miron-Spektor, E., Schilling, M., Solinas, G., & Tucci, C. (2018). Digital transformation: What is new if anything? *Academy of Management Discoveries*, 4(3).

Lavie, D. (2006). Capability reconfiguration: An analysis of incumbent responses to technological change. *Academy of Management Review*, 31(1), 153–74.

Lavie, D., & Singh, H. (2011). The evolution of alliance portfolios: The case of Unisys. *Industrial and Corporate Change*, 21(3), 763–809.

Le Roy, F., & Czakon, W. (2016). Managing coopetition: The missing link between strategy and performance. *Industrial Marketing Management*, 53, 3–6.

Lorenzoni, G., & Lipparini, A. (1999). The leveraging of interfirm relationships as a distinctive organizational capability: A longitudinal study. *Strategic Management Journal*, 20(4), 317–38.

Madhavan, R., Koka, B.R., & Prescott, J.E. (1998). Networks in transition: How industry events (re) shape interfirm relationships. *Strategic Management Journal*, 19(5), 439–59.

Mell, P., & Grance, T. (2011). *The NIST Definition of Cloud Computing*. Gaithersburg, MD: NIST. https://csrc.nist.gov/publications/detail/sp/800-145/final.

Menz, M., Kunisch, S., Birkinshaw, J., Collis, D.J., Foss, N.J., Hoskisson, R.E., & Prescott, J.E. (2021). Corporate strategy and the theory of the firm in the digital age. *Journal of Management Studies*, forthcoming.

Minà, A., Dagnino, G.B., & Vagnani, G. (2020). An interpretive framework of the interplay of competition and cooperation. *Journal of Management and Governance*, 24(1), 1–35.

Müller, C.N., Kijl, B., & Visnjic, I. (2018). Envelopment lessons to manage digital platforms: The cases of Google and Yahoo. *Strategic Change*, 27(2), 139–49.

Padula, G., & Dagnino, G.B. (2007). Untangling the rise of coopetition: The intrusion of competition in a cooperative game structure. *International Studies of Management & Organization*, 37(2), 32–52.

Park, K.F., Seamans, R., & Zhu, F. (2021). Homing and platform responses to entry: Historical evidence from the U.S. newspaper industry. *Strategic Management Journal*, 42(4), 684–709.

Pekovic, S., Grolleau, G., & Mzoughi, N. (2020). Coopetition in innovation activities and firms' economic performance: An empirical analysis. *Creativity and Innovation Management*, 29(1), 85–98.

Pousttchi, K., Tilson, D., Lyytinen, K., & Hufenbach, Y. (2015). Introduction to the special issue on mobile commerce: Mobile commerce research yesterday, today, tomorrow – What remains to be done? *International Journal of Electronic Commerce*, 19(4), 1–20.

Ranganathan, R., Ghosh, A., & Rosenkopf, L. (2018). Competition–cooperation interplay during multi-firm technology coordination: The effect of firm heterogeneity on conflict and consensus in a technology standards organization. *Strategic Management Journal*, 39(12), 3193–221.

Raza-Ullah, T. (2020). Experiencing the paradox of coopetition: A moderated mediation framework explaining the paradoxical tension–performance relationship. *Long Range Planning*, 53(1), 101863.

Raza-Ullah, T., Bengtsson, M., & Kock, S. (2014). The coopetition paradox and tension in coopetition at multiple levels. *Industrial Marketing Management*, 43(2), 189–98.

Reischauer, G. (2018). Industry 4.0 as policy-driven discourse to institutionalize innovation systems in manufacturing. *Technological Forecasting & Social Change*, 132, 26–33.

Reischauer, G., & Mair, J. (2018). How organizations strategically govern online communities: Lessons from the sharing economy. *Academy of Management Discoveries*, 4(3), 220–47.

Rietveld, J., & Schilling, M.A. (2021). Platform competition: A systematic and interdisciplinary review of the literature. *Journal of Management*, 47(6), 1528–63.

Ritala, P. (2012). Coopetition strategy – when is it successful? Empirical evidence on innovation and market performance. *British Journal of Management*, 23(3), 307–24.

Ritala, P., & Sainio, L.-M. (2013). Coopetition for radical innovation: Technology, market and business-model perspectives. *Technology Analysis & Strategic Management*, 26(2), 155–69.

Rochet, J.-C., & Tirole, J. (2003). Platform competition in two-sided markets. *Journal of the European Economic Association*, 1(4), 990–1029.

Rusko, R. (2019). Is coopetitive decision-making a black box? Technology and digitisation as decision-makers and drivers of coopetition. *Technology Analysis & Strategic Management*, 31(8), 888–901.

Schildt, H. (2017). Big data and organizational design: The brave new world of algorithmic management and computer augmented transparency. *Innovation: Organization & Management*, 19(1), 23–30.

Schildt, H. (2020). *The Data Imperative: How Digitalization Is Reshaping Management, Organizing, and Work.* Oxford: Oxford University Press.

Seamans, R., & Zhu, F. (2017). Repositioning and cost-cutting: The impact of competition on platform strategies. *Strategy Science*, 2(2), 83–99.

Sebastian, I.M., Ross, J.W., Beath, C., Mocker, M., Moloney, K.G., & Fonstad, N.O. (2017). How big old companies navigate digital transformation. *MIS Quarterly Executive*, 16(3), 197–213.

Stallkamp, M., & Schotter, A.P.J. (2021). Platforms without borders? The international strategies of digital platform firms. *Global Strategy Journal*, 11(1), 58–80.

Taeuscher, K., Bouncken, R.B., & Pesch, R. (2020). Gaining legitimacy by being different: Optimal distinctiveness in crowdfunding platforms. *Academy of Management Journal*, 64(1), 149–79.

Taeuscher, K., & Rothe, H. (2021). Optimal distinctiveness in platform markets: Leveraging complementors as legitimacy buffers. *Strategic Management Journal*, 42(2), 435–61.

Teece, D.J. (2017). Capabilities and (digital) platform lifecycles. *Advances in Strategic Management*, 37, 211–25.

Teece, D.J. (2018). Profiting from innovation in the digital economy: Enabling technologies, standards, and licensing models in the wireless world. *Research Policy*, 47(8), 1367–87.

Vial, G. (2019). Understanding digital transformation: A review and a research agenda. *Journal of Strategic Information Systems*, 28(2), 118–44.

Volberda, H.W., Khanagha, S., Baden-Fuller, C., Mihalache, O.R., & Birkinshaw, J. (2021). Strategizing in a digital world: Overcoming cognitive barriers, reconfiguring routines and introducing new organizational forms. *Long Range Planning*, 54(5), 102110.

Wen, W., & Zhu, F. (2019). Threat of platform-owner entry and complementor responses: Evidence from the mobile app market. *Strategic Management Journal*, 40(9), 1336–67.

Zhao, E.Y., Fisher, G., Lounsbury, M., & Miller, D. (2017). Optimal distinctiveness: Broadening the interface between institutional theory and strategic management. *Strategic Management Journal*, 38(1), 93–113.

Zhu, Y., Wang, V.L., Wang, Y.J., & Nastos, J. (2020). Business-to-business referral as digital coopetition strategy. *European Journal of Marketing*, 54(6), 1181–203.

# 21. Key open innovation issues in the digital age: a field-driven research agenda

*Giulio Ferrigno and Alberto Di Minin*

## 1.     INTRODUCTION

Digital technologies have become a key enabler of companies' innovation in today's business landscape (Urbinati et al., 2020). They are completely reshaping the business arena in which companies operate and provide many opportunities that could be explored (Bergamaschi et al., 2020). Nowadays, numerous companies have digitalized their innovation processes to be more competitive in the market and better equipped to deal with technological changes (Cennamo, 2021; Cennamo et al., 2020). At the same time, the companies' innovation processes have become more open and require greater resources in the different implementation phases to capture and transfer knowledge within and outside the firms' boundaries (Boudreau & Lakhani, 2009; Chesbrough, 2003; Chesbrough et al., 2014; West & Gallagher, 2006). Therefore, open innovation has become a key component of digital strategies (Urbinati et al., 2020). In fact, many scholars have pointed to the importance of open innovation for a firm's use of digital strategies. For example, Christensen et al. (2005) investigated how diverse open innovation strategies can be used by digital companies. Furthermore, Roberts et al. (2012) examined the role that absorptive capacity in the information system research might play in favoring the assimilation of complex IT innovation. Moreover, some recent contributions emphasized the role of a market for ideas as a virtual marketplace that operates at the intersection between digital technologies and open innovation (Natalicchio et al., 2014). Despite the proliferation of studies that tried to investigate open innovation in relation to the digital technologies concept, Dahlander et al. (2021) claimed that extant research could benefit from a comprehensive understanding of what aspects of open innovation strategies could be considered particularly critical for the design and implementation of digital strategies. To tackle this issue, in this chapter we review recent studies on open innovation to shed more light on the aspects of open innovation that should be considered in the design and implementation of digital strategies. More specifically, we submit three constructs of open innovation that should be considered by companies willing to design, develop, and implement digital strategies: (1) purposeful knowledge exchange (Taura & Radicic, 2019), (2) business model alignment (Cennamo et al., 2020), and (3) strategic management of intellectual property rights (Hagedoorn & Zobel, 2015; Miric et al., 2019). Afterwards, we validate the relevance of these constructs through three representative case studies of European companies that have opened up their innovation processes and benefited from the development of digital technologies (i.e., King of App, GoOpti, and Cynny). Drawing on a rich and detailed discussion of the selected cases, the chapter provides two significant contributions. First, it offers a more comprehensive understanding of open innovation in the digital age (Urbinati et al., 2020; Vial, 2019). More specifically, this study unveils three main aspects (purposeful knowledge exchange, business model alignment, and strategic management of intellectual property rights) that stem from open innovation literature and are relevant for the design, development, and implementation of digital strategies (Stefan et al., 2021). Second, it discusses empirical evidence about these three key issues through qualitative documentation of firms that have developed digital technologies in their open innovation processes (Waller et al., 2015).

## 2.   MANAGING OPEN INNOVATION IN A DIGITAL WORLD: KEY ISSUES

In the early 2000s, Henry Chesbrough used the term "open innovation" to indicate an approach to innovation that allowed companies to cope with some environmental, organizational, and technological changes that were affecting the future of companies operating in the high-tech sectors. In his 2003 essay "The Era of Open Innovation", the Berkeley professor highlighted how market globalization, the convergence of technologies on the market and the reduction of the life cycle of products posed important managerial challenges to the traditional model with which companies used to innovate. According to Chesbrough, the "closed innovation" paradigm – i.e., innovation originated within companies – was no longer a model of innovation sufficient to ensure their survival and prosperity (Chesbrough, 2003). In fact, companies had to rethink the ways in which they generated ideas and brought them to the market, trying to go beyond their business boundaries and drawing on ideas, resources and technological skills that came from outside (Boudreau & Lakhani, 2009), in particular from startups, universities, research organizations, suppliers, and business consultants. These actors represent sources of knowledge that, if not considered and valued, could jeopardize the future of the companies themselves. Therefore, Chesbrough (2003) proposed an approach based on open innovation, which valued the ways of interaction between companies and the outside world. Inter-company agreements, economic support for startups, hackathons, acquisitions of innovative startups by large companies, corporate accelerators, partnerships with universities, research centers, and innovation incubators represented the concrete ways through which companies can adopt an open innovation approach. Such an approach, since its introduction, has generated a lot of acclaim, both academic and managerial, thus developing the entrepreneurial contexts of many companies, from large to small companies, from any part of the world, from incumbent companies to newly established ones (Di Minin & Ferrigno, 2020). Almost two decades later, this approach still allows companies to innovate in the digital era (Urbinati et al., 2020). As a matter of fact, numerous studies have emphasized that open innovation allows companies to build an ecosystem where people, organizations, and sectors can foster co-creation (Adner & Kapoor, 2010; Gassmann et al., 2010; Jeppesen & Lakhani, 2010), thereby going beyond the organizational boundaries within companies' innovation ecosystem (Bogers et al., 2018). Moreover, some studies have pointed out that a more nuanced understanding of digital innovation can be achieved through an analysis of the interplay between individual-level factors and community- or collective-level factors (Acar, 2019; Shaikh & Levina, 2019; Verstegen et al., 2019). However, while many scholars have discussed the relevance of open innovation for a firm's use of digital strategies, Dahlander et al. (2021) advocated that ongoing research could benefit from an analysis of what aspects of open innovation strategies could be considered particularly challenging for the design and implementation of digital strategies. To contribute to this debate, the present study aims to explore open innovation in digital transformation and discloses three main features that should be considered in the design and implementation of digital strategies: (1) purposeful knowledge exchange (Taura & Radicic, 2019), (2) business model alignment (Cennamo et al., 2020), and (3) strategic management of intellectual property rights (Hagedoorn & Zobel, 2015; Miric et al., 2019). In the subsections that follow, each of these open innovation's features will be discussed.

## 2.1   Purposeful Knowledge Exchange

The first element of open innovation that, according to the literature, should be taken into account in the design and implementation of digital strategies is represented by the purposeful knowledge exchange that occurs among the actors involved in the open innovation processes (Taura & Radicic, 2019). "Knowledge exchange" refers to both inflows and outflows of knowledge that partners can access when they open up their processes (Cassiman & Veugeulars, 2006). It is well known in the literature that when companies open up their innovation processes, collaboration with people and organizations outside the company is inevitably promoted (Boudreau & Lakhani, 2009; Chesbrough, 2003). Therefore, companies must purposefully source, screen, evaluate, acquire, and leverage external knowledge resources for their innovation processes (Dahlander & Gann, 2010; Lanzolla et al., 2021). This key feature of open innovation is also vital for the design and implementation of digital strategies. In fact, complementary and diversified inter-partners knowledge exchange allows partners to remain competitive and economically resilient in a digital and globalized business environment (Cennamo, 2021). Moreover, because companies operate in an increasingly turbulent environment that is characterized by uncertainties (Dagnino et al., 2021), knowledge exchange represents a key strategic resource for organizations that are willing to create a competitive advantage in the digital world (Lanzolla et al., 2021). Last but not least, knowledge exchange influences a firm's propensity to innovate (Lasagni, 2012), and also its frequency (Taura & Radicic, 2019).

## 2.2   Business Model Alignment

The second feature of open innovation that, according to the literature, is relevant for the design and implementation of digital strategies is business model alignment (Cennamo et al., 2020). It is well known in the literature that partners should align their business models to accommodate their open innovation strategies and to subsequently enhance innovative performance. In fact, empirical evidence strongly suggests that companies willing to engage in open innovation must (at least partly) re-organize their business models to positively affect the sources of knowledge from external partners and their subsequent exploitation for innovation (Foss et al., 2011). Moreover, since companies involved in open innovation are strongly dependent on external sources of knowledge, the development of complementary internal networks that facilitate accessing and integrating the acquired knowledge into the company's innovation processes acquires pivotal importance (Hansen & Nohria, 2004). Extant literature highlights that this internal reorganization concerns realigning the organizational structure as well as developing knowledge capabilities and new organizational practices that positively affect the external source of knowledge and its subsequent exploitation for innovation (Saebi & Foss, 2015). This element of open innovation is also essential for the design and implementation of digital strategies. To better meet the needs of the targeted customers, companies must continuously align their technologies with the ones that are required by the market in which they operate (Remane et al., 2017). This alignment implies that companies invest in developing as well as evolving business-enabling technologies to satisfy market needs (Saebi & Foss, 2015). Moreover, business models in the digital world are different from traditional ones because value is determined in use (Vargo & Lusch, 2008) and digital products and services become increasingly more valuable as more users join (Gambardella et al., 2017; Shapiro & Varian, 1999). In addition, digital business models may be different from traditional ones due to the firm's use of digital technology on one hand, the use of platforms on the other hand (allowing for network effects), and also due to the enhanced digital consumer behavior (e.g., Cozzolino et al., 2021; El Sawy & Pereira, 2013). Therefore, aligning business models becomes even more important for the design and implementation of digital strategies (Remane et al., 2017). Lastly, in a digital and hyper-connected world companies need to balance benefits among an ecosystem with multiple organizations and individuals involved (Iansiti & Levien, 2004). Consequently, integrating and orchestrating a complex ecosystem of multiple actors in the firm's business models allows companies to sufficiently account for these new logics.

## 2.3    Strategic Management of Intellectual Property Rights

The third element of open innovation that, according to the literature, is relevant for the design and implementation of digital strategies relates to the strategic management of intellectual property rights (Hagedoorn & Zobel, 2015; Stefan et al., 2021). A relatively small body of literature has paid considerable attention to the strategic management of intellectual property rights (i.e., patents, trademarks, copyrights, design rights, and trade secrets in terms of technical or commercial information) in open innovation processes. We observe a dichotomy in the strategic management of intellectual property rights in open innovation literature. On the one hand, many authors have emphasized the advantages of intellectual property rights protection for companies conducting open innovation (Chesbrough, 2006; Miric et al., 2019; Sandulli & Chesbrough, 2009). For instance, Sandulli and Chesbrough (2009) have shown that strong intellectual property rights may enable companies to capture value from their innovation activities (Hurmelinna-Laukkanen & Ritala, 2015). Similarly, Pisano and Teece (2007) have claimed that a strong regime of appropriability facilitates the exchange of knowledge between companies when they realize that their intangible assets are difficult to imitate or appropriate. On the other, scholars have stressed that strong intellectual property rights may threaten open innovation. For instance, Pènin et al. (2011) have advocated that intellectual property rights protection may damage broad accessibility of knowledge, resources, and technology, a pivotal element of open innovation. Laursen and Salter (2014) have recognized that intellectual property rights protection may hinder partners from sharing information that would otherwise cost. This key aspect of open innovation is even more relevant for the design and implementation of digital strategies (Nambisan et al., 2019). In fact, in the digital age, anyone with access to a computer and the Internet can use copyrighted content almost instantaneously, with astonishing ease, thereby bypassing many types of intellectual property rights protection (Miric et al., 2019; Vial, 2019). This, in turn, implies that managing copyrights has evolved as a distant legal notion regarding confronting the concept in a number of common online activities (Miric et al., 2019; Palfrey et al., 2009). Moreover, the potential of customers as contributors of value-creating resources (e.g., data) has been powered by many digitally enabled devices (including mobile phones and the Internet of Things) and technologies (e.g., big data analytics, image recognition, machine learning, and artificial intelligence). These developments, in turn, have enhanced the scope and type of resources that a firm can access and utilize, which, in turn, can lead to different configurations of intellectual property rights in open innovation collaborations (Afuah & Tucci, 2000; Amit & Han, 2017).

## 3.    METHODOLOGY

### 3.1    Research Setting and Corporates' Background

To investigate the relevance of these three main open innovation features – i.e., (1) purposeful knowledge exchange, (2) business model alignment, and (3) strategic management of intellectual property rights – that we have extracted from the literature, we performed a multiple case study analysis (Eisenhardt & Graebner, 2007; Siggelkow, 2007, Yin, 2009). Three reasons led us to make this choice. First, multiple case studies allow researchers to understand the similarities and differences between the cases and therefore contribute to the literature with important implications from their differences and similarities (Eisenhardt & Graebner, 2007). Second, the evidence generated from a multiple case study is stronger and more reliable than a single case study and permits a wider discovering of theoretical evolution (Yin, 2009). Third, when the analysis is more intensely grounded in different empirical evidence, this research setting allows one to create a more convincing theory (Siggelkow, 2007). Hence, it seems that a multiple case study analysis may be considered as an appropriate research approach to explore the relevance of key open innovation issues in the digital era.

### 3.2    Theoretical Sampling

The selection of the three case studies relies on the basic principles of theoretical sampling (Glaser & Strauss, 1967; Mason, 1996; Pettigrew, 1990). Several reasons have led us to investigate King of App, GoOpti, and Cynny as representative case studies of European companies adopting open innovation in the digital age. First, the three companies are among the small and medium-sized enterprises (SMEs) that benefited from SME Instrument, public funding distributed by the Horizon 2020 programme. These companies won this public competition because they were considered the "European Innovation Champions"; i.e., SMEs with high ambition for growth and internationalization, proposing innovative entrepreneurial projects. For these reasons, we considered the three companies as an interesting and relevant dataset of representative case studies of European companies adopting open innovation in the digital age (Vial, 2019). Second, the selection of the three cases results from the combination of ongoing research activities and theoretical interest (Dell'Era et al., 2020; Dubois & Gadde, 2002; Siggelkow, 2007). The analysis of the three cases is indeed part of a broader Joint Research Centre research project aimed at exploring how new and original business strategies were emerging among European SMEs that applied to the SMEi funding program and operating through digital platforms and markets (De Marco et al., 2019). Third, we selected the three cases because of data access. The existence of significant amounts of information provides an important opportunity to dig deeper in the understanding of the three key issues for open innovation in the digital age (Vial, 2019). Below we report a description of the three case studies. Further information about the companies is reported in Table 21.1.

*Table 21.1    A descriptive comparison of the three companies studied*

| Case study | Industry | Foundation year | Size (employees) | Total funding raised (million $) | Headquarters |
|---|---|---|---|---|---|
| King of App | Apps, mobile advertising, software | 2014 | 1–10 | 1.5 | Lleida, Spain |
| GoOpti | Transportation, travel, travel agency | 2011 | 51–100 | 4.99 | Ljubljana, Slovenia |
| Cynny | Artificial intelligence, blockchain, digital marketing, video advertising | 2015 | 11–50 | 13.62 | Florence, Italy |

### 3.2.1    King of App

King of App is a startup that offers digital tools to support the creation of other platforms, a phenomenon that is becoming more and more common in the web environment. This startup has developed and launched the first open-source CMS (mobile content management system), an online tool that allows developers, designers, and even inexperienced users to program and create mobile apps faster and cheaper than usual approaches used in the traditional advertising market.

### 3.2.2    GoOpti

GoOpti is a company that has set up a digital platform that intends to transform the service industries. The GoOpti platform addresses a segment of the demand transport market (shared and private transfers) to replace traditional public and private transport and the use of a personal car. More specifically, the innovations of this platform are initially aimed at small market segments (which are typically unattractive to traditional service companies) and, through the development of a different value proposition, which relies on new features offered at a lower price, are able to scale up by offering the performance required by traditional customers.

### 3.2.3    Cynny

Cynny S.p.A. operates as a platform that favors the interaction between machines and man. It represents the heart of a group of four companies, namely Cynny Inc., established in 2012 in California (100 percent stake); in 2013 the group also acquired a 2 percent stake in a hardware engineering company, Ambedded Technologies Co. Ltd, based in Taiwan, and in November 2015 it established Cynny Space S.r.l. in Florence, Italy (with a 72 percent share). The Cynny group currently employs a team composed of more than 35 highly experienced people, 17 of whom develop special artificial intelligence algorithms. In 2017, the company had a turnover of approximately 1.4 million euros and filed seven patents. Cynny has developed MorphCast, technology based on blockchain systems and artificial intelligence. This technology allows the use of images stored online that change according to the user's emotional reactions. After developing this technology, the company's CEO, Stefano Bargagni, realized that the best way to facilitate the adoption of this digital technology was through its integration into existing platforms and apps to allow the MorphCast player to function as a commercial for partner platforms. The company is still conducting research and development and is also exploring the idea to add other opportunities to expand its business.

### 3.3    Data Collection

The data collection process relied on multiple sources to exploit the synergistic effects of triangulation (Eisenhardt, 1989; Jick, 1979). First, we collected secondary data sources, including web interviews, speeches, press releases, newspapers, specialized websites, and various other web sources. Second, we contacted the three companies (i.e., King of App, GoOpti, and Cynny) through email and phone calls, providing an overview of our research and its purposes, to gather their preliminary consent to participate in the study. After confirming their interest in the research study, we conducted three interviews with founders or key managers of the three companies (one per company). The interviews took place from February to March 2018, lasted between 30 and 60 minutes, and revolved around the three key issues – i.e., (1) purposeful knowledge exchange, (2) business model alignment, and (3) strategic management of intellectual property rights – we have extracted from open innovation literature. Finally, in September 2018 we re-contacted the companies' managers to share our notes. This approach enabled us to ensure we gained a full understanding of the open innovation issues that were relevant for the digitalization processes of the three companies. In some cases, brief follow-up telephone interviews with managers were conducted.

### 3.4    Data Analysis

The considerable amount of data collected about the three companies was then analyzed using an inductive and confirmatory approach in our empirical analysis (Lee et al., 1999). Confirmatory approaches are likely to confirm a researcher's preconceived notions and they are well recognized in the literature (Ruddin, 2006; Yin, 2009). In this chapter, we used an approach similar to previous literature (Ferrigno & Cucino, 2021). First, we conducted a within-case analysis of each company. Second, we performed a cross-case analysis among the three companies. In particular, we followed Eisenhardt (1989) to examine themes, similarities, and differences across cases as well as to dissect a trend that characterizes each firm. In both analyses, each source was analyzed separately by each author and the technique of brainstorming was used to interpret the different sources. We completed this iterative process when we achieved theoretical saturation (Eisenhardt & Graebner, 2007).

## 4.    DISCUSSION OF THE CASE STUDIES

The inductive case-based approach allows us to offer an empirical analysis of open innovation in the digital era. More specifically, in the subsections that follow we shall present empirical evidence of the three elements of open innovation that, according to the literature, should be considered by companies willing to design, develop and implement digital strategies: (1) purposeful knowledge exchange (Taura & Radicic, 2019), (2) business model alignment (Cennamo et al., 2020), and (3) strategic management of intellectual property rights (Hagedoorn & Zobel, 2015).

## 4.1    Purposeful Knowledge Exchange

As earlier discussed, the first element of open innovation that, according to the literature, becomes relevant for the design and implementation of digital strategies relates to the knowledge exchange that is purposefully created by the firm involved in open innovation activities. In this chapter, we find that GoOpti has purposefully favored knowledge exchange by shifting from a traditional business to a digital marketplace in which the company operates as mediator between the actors involved in the platform of long-distance shuttle services. On the demand side, the platform combines passengers with similar travel time limitations on the same vehicle and allows them to benefit from the lowest price possible (demand aggregator). On the supply side, the platform supports contractual relationships with local franchisees (i.e., transportation companies) in the different countries in which it operates. The platform also supports suppliers with risk management, routing, and payment transaction services.

> GoOpti made a shift from a traditional business to a digital marketplace for shared transfer. The ecosystem created by the platform allowed developing a new value proposition based on convenience and affordability of long-distance shuttle services, as two performance dimensions meeting the low-end travel needs in this segment. (Marko Guček, Founder of GoOpti)

The knowledge exchange between passengers and suppliers of the GoOpti platform has enabled the company to create a competitive advantage in the digital world. In fact, from being a typical transportation company owning the vehicles and allowing other transportation companies to join towards a franchising business model, the company has based its value proposition on a business model of a multi-sided platform in some cities which, although it proved to be extremely challenging and resources-intensive, has enabled the company to achieve a competitive advantage.

> We started GoOpti with the mission to create new opportunities. At first, we were interested in how to create a reliable and low-cost personalized service that could be profitable on long-distance routes. As avid travelers ourselves, we knew that we need to find an ideal option that can be a bit more expensive than a regular public transfer (e.g., bus or train), but still more affordable than a taxi. So, we came up with the idea to form a company that would help travelers get to the airport at an optimal time, for an affordable price, any day of the year. Our mission today is much bigger – we create opportunities and provide reliability to travelers and drivers (transport companies) by organizing dynamic shuttles on routes that aren't directly connected by public transportation, while helping reduce the number of personal vehicles on the road. (Marko Guček)

However, geography remained a barrier affecting the knowledge exchange between the actors involved in the GoOpti digital platform. Cultural, logistic, and administrative distances persist across diversified national contexts, making it difficult to propose, extend, and validate a value proposition beyond the Italian target market. Such limitations raised actual difficulties and increased the costs of the scale-up phase. Moreover, the company faced many difficulties during the pandemic, and this enabled it to re-focus its digitalization strategies again.

> As a company focused exclusively on airport transfers, we were hit hard by the pandemic. We sadly had to let go of a big part of our team, quickly adapt to the situation, redirect our skills, and find new financing opportunities. The first thing we did was developing a grocery delivery service, which still successfully operates today and is generating some additional revenue for our franchisees. But most importantly, we have been working on new sustainable mobility solutions which enable us to use our

know-how and implement it on intra- and intercity connections. We are looking at local routes in the cities where we have already established a presence, which are not covered with direct public transport and where most of the population still uses their car. With our personalized services, we want to offer them a new traveling experience that still gives them the same commodity as a personal car, but much more freedom and the option to move more sustainably. (Marko Guček)

## 4.2    Business Model Alignment

As indicated earlier, a second feature of open innovation that, according to the literature, is relevant for the design and implementation of digital strategies is business model alignment (Cennamo et al., 2020). The literature suggests that companies should align their business models to accommodate their open innovation strategies and to subsequently enhance innovative performance. More specifically, companies must continuously align their technologies with the ones that are required by the market in which they operate (Remane et al., 2017). This alignment implies that companies invest in developing as well as evolving business-enabling technologies to satisfy market needs (Saebi & Foss, 2015). We found that Cynny has aligned its technologies with the ones required by the market. In fact, at the beginning of the venture, Cynny developed a purely technological approach that was then shaped by a market strategy based on the needs and market expertise of potential customers.

To better satisfy the needs of the targeted customers, Cynny benefited from the strong entrepreneurial expertise and technical background of its founder and CEO, Stefano Bargagni.

> Innovation comes from inventing in isolation but, at one point or another, it is necessary to relate to the market and listening to the customer is a must. (Stefano Bargagni)

Bargagni is indeed a businessman but also an inventor gaining the trust of more than 600 stakeholders and investors. Investors' trust was gained thanks to strong corporate governance and the experience of the founder, but also a high-level managerial and technical team, and large R&D investments (80 percent of the capital).

Moreover, in a digital and hyper-connected world, scaling the platform requires business model evolution.

> Running a startup is like driving a sailboat. You have to follow the directions of the wind and learn to change route and strategy when it is necessary. (Stefano Bargagni)

In other words, companies need to integrate and orchestrate a complex ecosystem of multiple actors in their business models to allow companies to sufficiently account for these new logics (Iansiti & Levien, 2004). In the case of Cynny, the company integrated external innovations or products on top of its platform technology, but closely monitored the activities of external contributors to innovation and/or customers. The brands involved in Cynny's platform are the content sources for advertising videos distributed to viewers; however, Cynny does not leave the brands any space in the use of viewers' data or its protected technology, which is only applied to the content provided by the brands. We found that Cynny has evolved its business model from business-to-consumer (B2C) to business-to-business (B2B), becoming an integrator platform. The company wanted to integrate its technology with partners' platforms, and to achieve this aim it has connected the dots of the entire advertising value chain and orchestrated the interests of involved stakeholders.

We are implementing bots that integrate with all platforms, Facebook, WeChat, Telegram, Slack, Twitter, in order to spread the use of MorphCast quickly and make it attractive to advertising companies. (Stefano Bargagni)

Therefore, Cynny showed the ambition of further developing its platform to target different markets, potentially becoming a platform mediating work and offering its technology for the recognition of micro-facial expression to the development of tailored learning experiences.

## 4.3    Strategic Management of Intellectual Property Rights

As previously argued, a third feature of open innovation that, according to the literature, is relevant for the design and implementation of digital strategies refers to the strategic management of intellectual property rights (i.e., patents, trademarks, copyrights, design rights, and trade secrets in terms of technical or commercial information) (Hagedoorn & Zobel, 2015).

In the digital age, copyrighted content can be used almost instantaneously through a computer connected to the Internet. Therefore, issues related to intellectual property rights protection are bypassed (Miric et al., 2019; Vial, 2019). King of App developed a platform for platform technology, offering a space where all the tools to build other platforms and apps can be found in the same place and with different templates available. To scale up, King of App has developed its business through application programming interface integration with other platforms, facilitating the connection with the tools on which other platforms are built and engaging the developers' community.

The company, which has gone from having three people in its beginnings to about 30 employees today, is also seeking to get closer to companies not only that want to create their own apps but also those that can develop their business by creating apps for third parties; such as advertising, communication or web development agencies. To do this, the 'startup' is initiating actions such as face-to-face events of direct interrelation, such as workshops, 'meetups' or hackathons to publicize its technology. (Sabrina Boado, Head of Marketing at King of App)

Moreover, managing intellectual property rights implies that companies strategically find a balance between value creation and value capture dynamics that inevitably come out in the adoption of their digitally enabled devices and developed technologies. To engage the developers' community and create value, the company has leveraged on indirect network effects through an academy programme (online training) aiming at shifting customers from the user side to the developers' side of the platform (Gambardella et al., 2017). The platform developed by King of App creates value in the marketing, advertising, and design industries, resulting in a dramatic lowering of the price and the time to develop mobile applications for small companies. The platform disintermediates traditional actors, shifting the focus from the B2C segment to a new B2B market where developers can build, programme, and share modules. In this perspective, this type of platform has reduced the transaction costs (e.g., search efforts, customer lock-in) of the mobile app market and has an integrator platform business model. At the same time, acting as a two-sided digital platform wedged between two sides of the market, King of App was also able to capture value from its technologies. On one side, it provides the developers' community (external innovators developing their own items using the free platform features) with additional paid services, such as professional technical support, training, and form filling. On the other side, it maintains an online store allowing companies to create their own projects and build communities (Miric et al., 2019).

> King of App does not seek to be a proprietary technology but has the same vision as WordPress, not only in terms of modular architecture and open source, but in simply being 'an arbiter of an ecosystem' in which third parties can create plug-in modules for new functionalities, appearance themes or transversal services that help improve the apps and their monetization. (Xavier Barata, Founder of King of App)

## 5.    CONCLUSION

In this section, we discuss how this chapter advances both theoretical and practical contributions to, respectively, open innovation and digital transformation, and practitioners. Afterwards, we highlight its limitations and suggest a few intriguing directions for future research.

### 5.1    Theoretical Contributions

This chapter proffers two theoretical contributions to both open innovation and digital transformation research. First, it is one of the initial few empirical studies that tries to shed more light on the elements of open innovation that should be considered in the design and implementation of digital strategies. Digital technologies are considered a key asset of companies' innovation (Nambisan et al., 2019) and more frequently these technologies are developed by opening up firms' innovation processes (Urbinati et al., 2020). However, while many scholars have started to analyze open innovation in the digital age, few contributions have tried to understand what open innovation issues could be considered critical in the digital transformation. In this chapter, we attempt to provide a more comprehensive understanding of open innovation in the digital age (Dahlander et al., 2021; Vial, 2019). Drawing on open innovation literature in the digital era, we found three constructs of open innovation that should be considered by companies willing to design, develop, and implement digital strategies: (1) purposeful knowledge exchange (Taura & Radicic, 2019), (2) business model alignment (Cennamo et al., 2020), and (3) strategic management of intellectual property rights (Hagedoorn & Zobel, 2015). Second, we document the empirical relevance of these three elements of open innovation issues in a business context (Halinen & Törnroos, 2005). By drawing on a qualitative analysis of three companies that opened up their innovation processes and benefited from the development of digital technologies (King of App, Cynny, and GoOpti), the study shows that purposeful knowledge exchange, business model alignment, and strategic management of intellectual property rights are relevant for the innovation processes of these companies (Miric et al., 2019). In doing so, the study enriches the array of qualitative studies on the use of open innovation for the design and implementation of digital technologies (Waller et al., 2015).

### 5.2    Managerial Implications

This study also provides some useful guidelines that could guide managers willing to open up companies' innovation processes to be more competitive in today's digital arena. They should pay attention to the critical issues of open innovation we found relevant for the design and implementation of digital technologies. More specifically, in this chapter, we highlight three elements of open innovation (i.e., purposeful knowledge exchange, business model alignment, and strategic management of intellectual property rights) whose importance cannot be ignored by executives. Therefore, managers willing to develop digital technologies should start to open up the innovation processes of their companies and pay attention to the three elements of open innovation. As a matter of fact, the exchange of information and knowledge is the basis of every approach regarding how to innovate today. It is anachronistic to think that innovation can be done without involving other partners in the innovation processes. The arena is too competitive today and the environment is very volatile and dynamic. To keep up with these dynamics, managers must get out of the perspective of closed innovation. Moreover, competing in the digital world also means being able to align, in the shortest possible time, your business model with what is required by the market today. Not embracing this philosophy means leaving the market. Furthermore, innovating inevitably involves questions about the slice of value that can be appropriate for the company. Making open innovation in the digital world also means that managers must be able to strategically defend the intellectual property rights on the innovation that is created. Intellectual property rights that are too rigid inevitably damage the collaboration. Too-soft intellectual property rights, on the other hand, can erode the company's future competitive advantage. The right balance clearly depends on the partners, the market, and the technologies that are developed. More importantly, from the analysis of the three case studies we distill five pieces of advice for managers willing to adopt an open innovation approach and design a digital strategy: (1) managing frictions is a balancing act, (2) scaling the platform requires business model evolution, (3) previous experience matters, (4) greater engagement with your customers is invaluable, and (5) building an ecosystem may amplify the sharing effect.

### 5.2.1  Managing frictions is a balancing act

We observe that the cases we analyzed actually applied different mechanisms of focusing on customer retention (King of Apps) or friction creation (Cynny) even before developing and experimenting on specific business models. Drawing on this evidence, we therefore invite managers to find ways to make friction as productive as possible and eliminate unproductive friction. A productive friction may be purposefully created when diverse actors are engaged towards an outcome they feel as important. Unproductive friction can instead arise from miscommunication, interpersonal conflict, competition for resources, political behavior, different mindsets, etc.

Differently from a traditional world, where the interests of the actors involved in a company's business are separately considered, the core business of digital platform companies is to align the interests of different communities converging on the platform. While value creation and experimentation are supported by the development of infrastructures based on digital technologies, value capture mechanisms require the trigger of direct and indirect network effects. Creating productive elements of friction and eliminating the unproductive ones is a balancing act of a digital world.

### 5.2.2  Scaling the platform requires business model evolution

Cynny has evolved its business model from B2C to B2B, becoming an integrator platform. The company wanted to integrate its technology with partners' platforms, and in order to do that it is connecting the dots of the entire advertising value chain and orchestrating the interests of involved stakeholders. Therefore, companies willing to scale up their platform should be aware that their business model might change over time. Being adaptive and responsive to what the market and customers need may offer a series of temporary competitive advantages that find a harmony in the long-term vision of the entrepreneur.

Differently from a traditional world, in which the managers have to put in place activities that are functional to the achievement of a long-term planned strategy, in a digital world managers should not be stuck to their entrepreneurial ideas and the value proposition of their business models. Adopting an open innovation approach and designing a digital strategy imply that managers should be open to new changes in the market and adjust the key elements characterizing the essence of their business models in a certain time window of their strategy journey.

### 5.2.3   Previous experience matters

As most of our cases showed, past experiences of the entrepreneur are powerful sources of inspiration, since they enable the recognition or discovery of opportunities in the pre-startup phase. The experience of every entrepreneur, even the greatest and those who have achieved the most, is marked by some failures and shortcomings. However, it is from failing that an entrepreneur may learn and accrue his or her consolidated knowledge.

Differently from a traditional world, an entrepreneur with previous digital experience is the right one to helm any digital company. Customers should be guided in using the digital tools and therefore experience is fundamental when new ideas are tested; knowledge from past experience also helps in focusing on the development of effective value propositions in digital markets, as the cases of King of Apps and Cynny show.

### 5.2.4   Greater engagement with your customers

We noted that in the case of GoOpti, the company encouraged people to rethink mobility and provide more practical and sustainable ways to move around. The company's goal is still to expand its airport shuttle services in new cities in Italy and beyond, but also to start building a shared mobility ecosystem and extend its offerings with new inter- and intracity services for daily commuters and occasional travelers. In five years GoOpti services will hopefully be available in ten more countries. But to achieve this aim, the company made its clients think differently, unconventionally, or from a new mobility perspective.

Differently from a traditional world, where this type of engagement with the customer may occur rarely, in a digital world this type of engagement occurs more often. In a digital world, customers may be engaged continuously through many different digital media channels and in different ways. Blog posts, newsletters, PR campaigns, promotions, or even special offers are just some examples of how it is possible to address customer questions, decrease misconceptions, and generate sales. Clients are more digital-oriented and creative, and thus more likely to welcome and be part of unconventional solutions to their problems. Therefore, in a digital world, customers are more engaged.

### 5.2.5   Building an ecosystem may amplify the sharing effect

We observed in the case of King of App, for example, that the company has increasingly involved its customers through a series of digital activities that were meant to build a developers' ecosystem. To involve the developers' community the company has launched an online training academy programme. This initiative allowed the firm to move customers to the developers' side of the platform. Accessing the ecosystem resources had a big impact and helped King of App with the new venture.

Differently from a traditional world, where the content may be shared only physically and thus limited to certain circumstances, in a digital world the content is easily shareable. Most digital channels feature sharing capabilities that allow campaigns and articles to be shared with multiple followers. This helps to create an amplifying effect and can directly impact sales results. Therefore, managers should be aware that when they create a content, they should think what could make it shareable. Building an ecosystem of digital channels may amplify this effect.

## 5.3    Limitations

Since it explores a new subfield of study (open innovation and digital transformation), this chapter has also some limitations that may be fertile ground for future research. First, we studied three key elements of open innovation (i.e., purposeful knowledge exchange, business model alignment, and strategic management of intellectual property rights) that are relevant for the design and implementation of digital strategies. Second, we found evidence of the above-mentioned elements of open innovation in three digital companies. Moreover, we are aware that other types of elements of open innovation can be considered of pivotal importance for the design and implementation of digital strategies.

Third, additional cases might complement and build upon the findings of this study by exploring other important issues of open innovation that should be taken into consideration by companies willing to achieve a competitive advantage through the development of digital technologies. Fourth, our qualitative analysis is based on three paradigmatic examples of SMEs that benefited from the SME Instrument funding scheme and opened up their innovation processes to develop digital strategies. Since open innovation research has shown that SMEs' open innovation processes can be different from large companies' (Spithoven et al., 2013), it would be interesting to investigate whether additional features might emerge from an in-depth analysis of large companies' open innovation processes.

# REFERENCES

Acar, O.A. (2019). Motivations and solution appropriateness in crowdsourcing challenges for innovation. *Research Policy*, 48(8), 103716.

Adner, R., & Kapoor, R. (2010). Value creation in innovation ecosystems: How the structure of technological interdependence affects firm performance in new technology generations. *Strategic Management Journal*, 31(3), 306–33.

Afuah, A., & Tucci, C.L. (2000). *Internet Business Models and Strategies: Text and Cases*. New York, NY: McGraw-Hill Higher Education.

Amit, R., & Han, X. (2017). Value creation through novel resource configurations in a digitally enabled world. *Strategic Entrepreneurship Journal*, 11(3), 228–42.

Bergamaschi, M., Bettinelli, C., Lissana, E., & Picone, P.M. (2020). Past, ongoing, and future debate on the interplay between internationalization and digitalization. *Journal of Management and Governance*, 25, 983–1032.

Bogers, M., Chesbrough, H., & Moedas, C. (2018). Open innovation: Research, practices, and policies. *California Management Review*, 60(2), 5–16.

Boudreau, K.J., & Lakhani, K.R. (2009). How to manage outside innovation. *MIT Sloan Management Review*, 50(4), 69–76.

Cassiman, B., & Veugelers, R. (2006). In search of complementarity in innovation strategy: Internal R&D and external knowledge acquisition. *Management Science*, 52(1), 68–82.

Cennamo, C. (2021). Competing in digital markets: A platform-based perspective. *Academy of Management Perspectives*, 35(2), 265–91.

Cennamo, C., Dagnino, G.B., Di Minin, A., & Lanzolla, G. (2020). Managing digital transformation: Scope of transformation and modalities of value co-generation and delivery. *California Management Review*, 62(4), 5–16.

Chesbrough, H. (2006). *Open Business Models: How to Thrive in the New Innovation Landscape.* Boston, MA: Harvard Business School Press.

Chesbrough, H., Kim, S., & Agogino, A. (2014). Chez Panisse: Building an open innovation ecosystem. *California Management Review*, 56(4), 144–71.

Chesbrough, H.W. (2003). *Open Innovation: The New Imperative for Creating and Profiting from Technology.* Boston, MA: Harvard Business Press.

Christensen, J.F., Olesen, M.H., & Kjær, J.S. (2005). The industrial dynamics of open innovation: Evidence from the transformation of consumer electronics. *Research Policy*, 34(10), 1533–49.

Cozzolino, A., Corbo, L., & Aversa, P. (2021). Digital platform-based ecosystems: The evolution of collaboration and competition between incumbent producers and entrant platforms. *Journal of Business Research*, 126, 385–400.

Dagnino, G.B., Picone, P.M., & Ferrigno, G. (2021). Temporary competitive advantage: A state-of-the-art literature review and research directions. *International Journal of Management Reviews*, 23(1), 85–115.

Dahlander, L., & Gann, D.M. (2010). How open is innovation? *Research Policy*, 39(6), 699–709.

Dahlander, L., Gann, D.M., & Wallin, M.W. (2021). How open is innovation? A retrospective and ideas forward. *Research Policy*, 50(4), 104218.

De Marco, C.E., Di Minin, A., Marullo, C., & Nepelski, D. (2019). *An Analysis of SME Instrument Business Proposals and Case Studies.* Luxembourg: Publications Office of the European Union.

Dell'Era, C., Di Minin, A., Ferrigno, G., Frattini, F., Landoni, P., & Verganti, R. (2020). Value capture in open innovation processes with radical circles: A qualitative analysis of companies' collaborations with Slow Food, Memphis, and Free Software Foundation. *Technological Forecasting and Social Change*, 158, 120128.

Di Minin, A., & Ferrigno, G. (2020). Il paradigma open innovation per i contesti imprenditoriali: il caso del Competence Center Artes 4.0. In Lazzeroni, M., and Morazzoni, M. (eds), *Interpretare la quarta rivoluzione industriale. La geografia in dialogo con le altre discipline.* Rome: Carocci Editore.

Dubois, A., & Gadde, L.E. (2002). Systematic combining: An abductive approach to case research. *Journal of Business Research*, 55(7), 553–60.

Eisenhardt, K.M. (1989). Building theories from case study research. *Academy of Management Review*, 14(4), 532–50.

Eisenhardt, K., & Graebner, M. (2007). Theory building from cases: Opportunities and challenges. *Academy of Management Journal*, 50(1), 25–32.

El Sawy, O.A., & Pereira, F. (2013). *Business Modelling in the Dynamic Digital Space: An Ecosystem Approach.* Heidelberg: Springer.

Ferrigno, G., & Cucino, V. (2021). Innovating and transforming during COVID-19: Insights from Italian firms. *R&D Management*, 51(4), 325–38.

Foss, N.J., Laursen, K., & Pedersen, T. (2011). Linking customer interaction and innovation: The mediating role of new organizational practices. *Organization Science*, 22(4), 980–99.

Gambardella, A., Raasch, C., & Von Hippel, E. (2017). The user innovation paradigm: Impacts on markets and welfare. *Management Science*, 63(5), 1450–68.

Gassmann, O., Enkel, E., & Chesbrough, H. (2010). The future of open innovation. *R&D Management*, 40(3), 213–21.

Glaser, B.G., & Strauss, A.L. (1967). *The Discovery of Grounded Theory: Strategies for Qualitative Research.* Chicago, IL: Aldine.

Hagedoorn, J., and Zobel, A.-K. (2015). The role of contracts and intellectual property rights in open innovation. *Technology Analysis & Strategic Management*, 27(9), 1050–67.

Halinen, A., & Törnroos, J.Å. (2005). Using case methods in the study of contemporary business networks. *Journal of Business Research*, 58(9), 1285–97.

Hansen, M.T., & Nohria, N. (2004). How to build collaborative advantage. *MIT Sloan Management Review*, 46(1), 22.

Hurmelinna-Laukkanen, P., & Ritala, P. (2015). Revisiting innovation appropriability: Means, processes, strategies and boundary conditions. In *Academy of Management Proceedings* (Vol. 2015, No. 1, p. 14725). Briarcliff Manor, NY: Academy of Management.

Iansiti, M., & Levien, R. (2004). Creating value in your business ecosystem. *Harvard Business Review*, March 2004.

Jeppesen, L.B., & Lakhani, K.R. (2010). Marginality and problem-solving effectiveness in broadcast search. *Organization Science*, 21(5), 1016–33.

Jick, T.D. (1979). Mixing qualitative and quantitative methods: Triangulation in action. *Administrative Science Quarterly*, 24(4), 602–11.

Lanzolla, G., Pesce, D., & Tucci, C.L. (2021). The digital transformation of search and recombination in the innovation function: Tensions and an integrative framework. *Journal of Product Innovation Management*, 38(1), 90–113.

Lasagni, A. (2012). How can external relationships enhance innovation in SMEs? New evidence for Europe. *Journal of Small Business Management*, 50(2), 310–39.

Laursen, K., & Salter, A. (2014). The paradox of openness: Appropriability, external search and collaboration. *Research Policy*. Published online ahead of print: doi:10.1016/j.respol.2013.10004.

Lee, T.W., Mitchell, T.R., & Sablynski, C.J. (1999). Qualitative research in organizational and vocational psychology, 1979–1999. *Journal of Vocational Behavior*, 55(2), 161–87.

Mason, J. (1996). *Qualitative Researching*. Newbury Park, CA: SAGE.

Miric, M., Boudreau, K.J., & Jeppesen, L.B. (2019). Protecting their digital assets: The use of formal & informal appropriability strategies by app developers. *Research Policy*, 48(8), 103738.

Nambisan, S., Wright, M., & Feldman, M. (2019). The digital transformation of innovation and entrepreneurship: Progress, challenges and key themes. *Research Policy*, 48(8), 103773.

Natalicchio, A., Messeni Petruzzelli, A., & Garavelli, A.C. (2014) Markets for ideas: Literature review and unanswered questions. *Technovation*, 34, 65–76.

Palfrey, J., Gasser, U., Simun, M., & Barnes, R.F. (2009). Youth, creativity, and copyright in the digital age. *International Journal of Learning and Media*, 1(2), 79–97.

Pènin, J., Hussler, C., & Burger-Helmchen, T. (2011). New shapes and new stakes: A portrait of open innovation as a promising phenomenon. *Journal of Innovation Economics Management*, 1(7), 11–29.

Pettigrew, A.M. (1990). Longitudinal field research on change: Theory and practice. *Organization Science*, 1(3), 267–92.

Pisano, G.P., & Teece, D.J. (2007). How to capture value from innovation: Shaping intellectual property and industry architecture. *California Management Review*, 50(1), 278–96.

Remane, G., Hanelt, A., Nickerson, R.C., & Kolbe, L.M. (2017). Discovering digital business models in traditional industries. *Journal of Business Strategy*, 38(2), 41–51.

Roberts, N., Galluch, P.S., Dinger, M., and Grover, V. (2012) Absorptive capacity and information systems research: Review, synthesis, and directions for future research. *MIS Quarterly*, 36, 625–48.

Ruddin, L.P. (2006). You can generalize stupid! Social scientists, Bent Flyvbjerg, and case study methodology. *Qualitative Inquiry*, 12(4), 797–812.

Saebi, T., & Foss, N.J. (2015). Business models for open innovation: Matching heterogeneous open innovation strategies with business model dimensions. *European Management Journal*, 33(3), 201–13.

Sandulli, F., & Chesbrough, H. (2009). The two faces of open business models. Working Paper.

Shaikh, M., & Levina, N. (2019). Selecting an open innovation community as an alliance partner: Looking for healthy communities and ecosystems. *Research Policy*, 48(8), 103766.

Shapiro, C., & Varian, H.R. (1999). The art of standards wars. *California Management Review*, 41(2), 8–32.

Siggelkow, N. (2007). Persuasion with case studies. *Academy of Management Journal*, 50(1), 20–24.

Spithoven, A., Vanhaverbeke, W., & Roijakkers, N. (2013). Open innovation practices in SMEs and large enterprises. *Small Business Economics*, 41(3), 537–62.

Stefan, I., Hurmelinna-Laukkanen, P., & Vanhaverbeke, W. (2021). Trajectories towards balancing value creation and capture: Resolution paths and tension loops in open innovation projects. *International Journal of Project Management*, 39(2), 139–53.

Taura, N., & Radicic, D. (2019). Intra-cluster knowledge exchange and frequency of product innovation in a digital cluster. *Journal of Small Business Management*, 57, 350–73.

Urbinati, A., Chiaroni, D., Chiesa, V., & Frattini, F. (2020). The role of digital technologies in open innovation processes: An exploratory multiple case study analysis. *R&D Management*, 50(1), 136–60.

Vargo, S.L., & Lusch, R.F. (2008). Service-dominant logic: Continuing the evolution. *Journal of the Academy of Marketing Science*, 36(1), 1–10.

Verstegen, L., Houkes, W., & Reymen, I. (2019). Configuring collective digital-technology usage in dynamic and complex design practices. *Research Policy*, 48(8), 103696.

Vial, G. (2019). Understanding digital transformation: A review and a research agenda. *Journal of Strategic Information Systems*, 28(2), 118–44.

Waller, V., Farquharson, K., & Dempsey, D. (2015). *Qualitative Social Research: Contemporary Methods for the Digital Age*. Los Angeles, CA: SAGE.

West, J., & Gallagher, S. (2006). Challenges of open innovation: The paradox of firm investment in open-source software. *R&D Management*, 36(3), 319–31.

Yin, R.K. (2009). *Case Study Research: Design and Methods* (4th ed.). Newbury Park, CA: SAGE.

# 22. What is digital strategy and does it really matter?

*Feng Li*

## INTRODUCTION

The notion of digital strategy has evolved considerably over the past 30 years, from the strategy for the IT department (i.e., the IT strategy), and the digitization, digitalization and digital transformation strategy for different functions (e.g., accounting, operations, marketing) and business processes, to, more recently, the business strategy for the organization facilitated, supported, or enabled by growing digital capabilities (Bharadwaj et al., 2013; Westerman, 2017). The underpinning digital technologies, infrastructures and services have also evolved, from the centralized private corporate networks based on mainframe computers and distributed computing based on the client–server architecture to ubiquitous computing based on affordable mobile devices, pervasive mobile networks, accessible cloud services and the extensive Internet of Things (IoT) (or Internet in Everything [IET], including wearable technologies, autonomous vehicles, smart homes, and Industry 4.0). Other emerging technologies and applications are constantly bringing additional digital capabilities to the mix, from a multi-cloud environment, edge computing, big data analytics, machine learning and artificial intelligence (AI), and robotics, to a range of other emerging technologies including VR/AR/XR (virtual reality/augmented reality/mixed reality), blockchain, additive manufacturing and 3D printing, and quantum computing, to name a few.

However, such rapid developments have added considerable confusion to our understanding of what digital strategy is, why it is necessary for most (if not all) organizations, and how it manifests in different types of organizations. The literature often fails to specify explicitly the type of digital strategy and the underpinning digital technologies in question, which is particularly problematic given the rapid pace of change in both the notion of digital strategy itself and the underpinning digital technologies. The slow and prolonged academic publication cycles typical of most leading peer-reviewed journals in business management have further exacerbated the problem, as the same terminologies are often used to illustrate rapidly evolving phenomena at different levels of analysis, from different perspectives and during different stages of technological and business evolution, to mean subtly or significantly different things – a form of unconscious or even deliberate "concept creeping". This raises both theoretical challenges to understanding the phenomena, and practical challenges in using past experience and insight to inform strategic planning and future actions.

In this chapter, the evolving notion of digital strategy and the underpinning digital technologies are discussed. Then an overarching framework is outlined to explain the fundamental reasons why every organization needs a digital strategy. The framework is based on two fundamental changes in the business environment – the changing nature of the economy (the knowledge or information economy) and the continuous rapid development of digital technologies, infrastructure and services; the latter is often referred to as the IT Revolution, the ICTs (information and communications technologies) Revolution, the Digital Technology Revolution, or the Fourth Industrial Revolution/Industry 4.0. These changes together are rede-fining the "rules of the game", forcing all organizations to evaluate and re-invent their strate-gies and business models by innovatively exploiting the rapidly expanding digital capabilities. Following this, the business implications for incumbents and digital native firms are explored, and three emerging approaches that some leading organizations have successfully deployed to manage the transition to new technologies, new strategies and business models, and new organizational designs in their digital transformation journeys, are discussed. Finally, the theoretical implications are summarized, and three new areas for future research – particularly the need for new theoretical framing and new methodological approaches – are highlighted.

## WHAT IS A DIGITAL STRATEGY?

The notion of digital strategy has been evolving rapidly. It has been used as an umbrella concept to refer to the IT strategy for an organization; the digitization, digitalization, and digital transformation strategy for different functions and business processes; the digital trans-formation strategy for an organization as a whole; and more recently, the business strategy facilitated, supported or enabled by digital technologies. Today, "digital strategy" is increas-ingly used to refer to the strategic plan formulated in an organization to achieve long-term business objectives by exploiting existing and emerging digital capabilities. In other words, "digital strategy" refers to the business strategy for an organization underpinned by digital technologies in the digital economy (Westerman, 2017).

However, in many organizations, and in the literature studying such organizations, the concept of digital strategy has been used "flexibly" to illustrate a range of phenomena, often with different starting points, from different perspectives and at different levels of analysis to serve many different objectives. As an analytical concept, it lacks clarity and rigour, which has been made worse by the erratic pace of change and the growing number of studies and publications. Today, digital strategy has been approached from many different perspectives, in disciplines ranging from information systems and innovation management to strategic management, to serve a variety of objectives at multiple levels of the organization. This often causes confusion for academics and business leaders alike, undermines cumulative learning efforts and diminishes our ability to draw effectively on the work of one another.

Over the past decade, significant progress has been made in our understanding of the "how" – and to a less extent, the "why" – of digital strategy, including the scope, process and per-spective for digital strategy making and execution, and the associated theoretical and practical developments around digitization, digitalization and digital transformation at different levels and functions of organizations. Importantly, several conceptual frameworks have emerged in different disciplines, including both cognitive tools for understanding digital strategy and digital transformation efforts, and planning tools to guide practice and actions. In this section, some of the most influential perspectives are reviewed briefly (Table 22.1).

### The Information Systems Perspective

Much of the early work on digital strategy was from the information systems (IS) perspective, as "digital strategy" was initially used to refer to the IT strategy in organizations and how it

*Table 22.1*    *Different perspectives on digital strategy*

| Perspectives | Focuses | Challenges and opportunities | Exemplary studies |
|---|---|---|---|
| The information systems perspective | IT strategy for business functions IT strategy for the organization as a whole | How to align IT and business strategy at the functional and organizational levels<br><br>How to use digital capabilities for value creation and sustainable competitive advantages | Bakos & Treacy, 1986; Rockart & Scott Morton, 1984; Hagel & Seely Brown, 2001; Yoo, Henfridsson & Lyytinen 2010; Bharadwaj et al., 2013 |
| The innovation perspective | Adoption of digital technologies in different types of organizations<br>Products, processes, and business models innovations through digitization | How to frame, understand, and explain the new context of innovation brought about by pervasive digitalization | Yoo, Henfridsson & Lyytinen 2010; Lyytinen, 2021; Lanzolla, Pesce & Tucci, 2021 |
| The information economics perspective | The transition from the industrial to the information economy<br>The changing costs of economic activities in relation to digitization (e.g., search, replication cost, transportation, tracking, and verification) | How the rapid reduction in the cost of storage, computation, and transmission of data translates into reduction in economic costs associated with digital economic activity<br>How the reduction in economic costs leads to fundamental changes in economic activity at different levels | Bell, 1973; Porat, 1977; OECD, 1986; Hepworth, 1990; Li, 1995; Dawson, Hirt & Scanlan, 2016; Goldfarb & Tucker, 2019 |
| The strategic management perspective | Functional strategy for the IT department<br>Using digital capabilities to underpin and enable new strategy and business model for the organization | How to frame the shift of digital capabilities from *quantitative* advances to *qualitative* changes<br>How to use emerging digital capabilities to reshape the functional and corporate strategies | Jacobides, Cennamo & Gawer, 2018; Adner, Puranam & Zhu, 2019; Cennamo et al., 2020; Iansiti & Lakhani, 2020; Li, 2022 |
| Other perspectives | Effective new approaches for developing digital strategies and executing digital transformation | How to develop effective approaches to ensure successful digital transformation | Ross, Sebastian & Beath, 2017; Sebastian et al., 2017; Ross, Beath & Mocker, 2019; Siebel, 2019; Saldanha, 2019; Li, 2020 |

can be aligned with, and support, the business strategy. A significant number of studies have been published since the 1980s. Before the turn of the century, most studies focused on how proprietary IT systems can (and should) be developed and used in organizations and their various functions and processes, with a particular focus on using IT assets to support business strategy and improve business performance (e.g., Bakos & Treacy, 1986); and understanding the implications of changes in IT for corporate strategy (Rockart & Scott Morton, 1984).

Since the mid-1990s, the commercialization of the internet and the rapid development of e-commerce and e-business have given rise to a new approach to corporate IT, when big providers of IT hardware, software and services actively promoted "IT as a service" via the internet – from SaaS (software as a service) and PaaS (platform as a service) to IaaS (infrastructure as a service) – rather than supporting organizations owning and maintaining their own hardware and software (Hagel & Seely Brown, 2001). Organizations are increasingly nudged to shift their focuses from ensuring service availability at minimum costs to improving business performance through IT, by reducing costs and improving efficiency, enabling corporate restructuring and business process reengineering, and aligning corporate IT development with business strategy. This trend has accelerated considerably since the early 2000s – especially after the dotcom crash – when major technology providers invested heavily in digital infrastructure and services to operationalize the new approach to corporate IT. The trend in IT outsourcing and offshoring, together with the increasing consumerization of IT, also served to accelerate this process (Li, 2007, 2020).

Most studies of digital strategy in IS focused on the IT strategy for the organization and its various business functions, which is primarily viewed as a functional-level strategy that must be aligned with the firm's chosen business strategy. Under the alignment view, business strategy directed IT strategy. Over the last decade, as the business infrastructure has been digitized with increased interconnections amongst products, processes and services, the critical role of digital technologies in transforming strategies, business processes, capabilities, products and services, and interfirm relationships, is increasingly recognized. As a result, it has been argued that the role of IT strategy should be shifted from that of a functional-level strategy aligned but subordinate to business strategy to one that reflects a fusion between IT strategy and business strategy (Bharadwaj et al., 2013).

Today, as digital technologies continue to evolve rapidly, advanced digital services have become increasingly affordable and accessible to a growing range of business functions and professions with different levels of technical skills and competences. The consumerization of IT has further undermined the role and credibility of the corporate IT departments in many organizations, and some business functions have increasingly hired their own IT staff, or brought in external consultants, to assist them with their IT requirements in response to a rapidly changing business environment. In addition, the high cost and high failure rate of large corporate IT projects have served to erode the credibility of IT functions – and chief information officers (CIOs) or chief technology officers (CTOs) – amongst senior business leaders. As a consequence, the role of the IT function in many organizations, and the IS perspective that studies such practice, has lost considerable influence. Researchers from other disciplines, from innovation, marketing and operations to strategy, are increasingly exploring innovation and business transformation enabled by digital capabilities, which served to further undermine the influence of IS research in corporate strategic thinking.

Despite such problems, however, some frameworks have emerged which can be used to explain the fundamental changes that IT is enabling. Yoo, Henfridsson and Lyytinen (2010) argue that pervasive digitization has given birth to a new product architecture in organizations, which extends the modular architecture of physical products by incorporating four loosely coupled layers of devices, networks, services and content created by digital technologies. The new architecture transforms the way firms organize for innovation in the digital age. The framework provides a useful tool to systematically understand the impacts of digital technology on firms' strategies, structures and processes, particularly the role of digital technology in creating business values and building sustainable competitive advantages. Using the examples of Amazon's Kindle and Apple's iPhone, they highlighted the transformative impact of digital technologies on industrial-age products, and how the digitization of well-established products (such as books and telephones) sparks profound changes in the industrial structure and competitive landscape, blurring industry boundaries and creating new threats and opportunities.

Similarly, Bharadwaj et al. (2013) argue that the time is right to rethink the role of IT strategy, from that of a functional-level strategy to one that reflects a fusion between IT strategy and business strategy. They outline a framework to call for new research to explore how external digital trends and key organizational shifts will influence the scope, scale and speed of digital business strategy and the sources of business value creation and capture, and how such changes affect performance.

Going forward, new effort is needed to revitalize the influence of IS research in corporate strategic thinking. Leading digital transformation requires a broad and unique mix of capabilities and knowledge. Successful leaders are expected to establish a continuous programme of transformation, improve their organization's digital maturity and find innovative ways to extract business value from their data. This requires technological expertise, business acumen and the ability to manage a complex network of stakeholders both within and outside the organization. The CIO is ideally positioned to take on such a role, but unfortunately, as a recent study of UK job adverts suggests, employers are not looking to CIOs to lead their digital strategy and business transformation (Harding, 2021). A fundamental rethink of digital strategy research from the IS perspective is still needed.

**The Innovation Perspective**

From the innovation perspective, many studies have examined how digital technologies are adopted in different types of organizations, and how digitization is leading to innovations in products, processes and business models. Indeed, the continuous rapid development of digital technologies is leading to changes in the dominant technological and economic paradigms, resulting in systemic failures of a growing number of companies across different sectors. The failures of many iconic companies – from JC Penney and Kodak to GE – are not because these companies are not innovative, but rather many such companies "could not ultimately innovate how they should innovate as dictated by the emerging digital innovation regime … and they are innovating in wrong places, at wrong time[s], and in a wrong way" (Lyytinen, 2021). New research is needed to explore how to frame, understand and explain the new context of innovation that has been brought about by pervasive digitalization, which permeates all industries and their business models.

Many previous studies examined the proliferation of digital technologies from the perspectives of technology adoption and the diffusion of technological innovations across different industries and countries; and a large number of critical success factors (CSFs) have been identified and validated as contributing to or inhibiting technological adoption and its effective use in different contexts. More recently, Lyytinen (2021) examined how digital innovation differs from earlier forms of industrial innovation by identifying the foundations of digital innovation logics. He argued that the difference is more significant than replacing analogue information with digital information across industrial organizations. By reviewing the specific ontological status of digital material in industrial operations and related conditions for innovation, he went on to argue that digital innovation advances through three processes of embedding – which is defined as "a process of interlacing elements of one innovation domain to that of another". The three types of embedding necessary for digital innovation are operational embedding (code-computer), virtual embedding (real world phenomena-code) and contextual embedding (use of code-social setting). Each embedding operates relatively autonomously and its conditions for success and goals are separate; each embedding constitutes a unique leverage point for further expansion of digital innovation; and the phases and processes that underlie innovation in the two regimes differ and follow differential logics. However, more research is needed to understand the mechanisms and nuances of such processes; and in particular, how such processes can be incorporated into innovation strategies and new business strategies for organizations in the digital age.

## The Information Economics Perspective

Research on information economics examines whether and how digital technology changes economic activity. A large number of studies have been published over the last half a century. Back in 1962, it was argued that the American economy had become a knowledge or information economy, because nearly half of the American workforce could be regarded as information workers; and nearly half of the value added in all products and production processes was made up of informational content (Machlup, 1962). This was followed by a series of comprehensive studies of the post-industrial, knowledge or information economy around the world during the 1970s, 1980s and 1990s (Bell, 1973; Porat, 1977; OECD, 1986; Hepworth, 1990; Li, 1995).

In the 1990s, a "Revolution in Interaction" was predicted in the context of the information economy, as the rapid development of ICTs would fundamentally redefine transaction costs, which from the institutional economics perspective would radically alter the boundaries between firms and markets, leading to significant changes in organizational forms, inter-organizational relations and consumer behaviour (Li, 1995, 2007; Butler et al., 1997; Johnson, Manyika & Yee, 2005). More recently, Goldfarb and Tucker (2019) argue that digital technology has reduced the cost of storage, computation and transmission of data, which translates into reductions in five distinct economic costs associated with digital economic activity – search costs, replication costs, transportation costs, tracking costs and verification cost. These reductions in economic costs are leading to fundamental changes in economic activity at different levels. These themes inform our understanding of the nature of digital economic activity, and the interaction between digital and non-digital settings.

The information economics perspective is particularly useful in shifting the focus of researchers and business leaders from identifying which player might emerge to disrupt a particular industry, to the nature of the change and disruption that can be expected in an industry and in the economy as a whole (Dawson, Hirt & Scanlan, 2016). In other words, it is particularly helpful in understanding the "why" of digital strategy.

## The Strategic Management Perspective

Strategic management has traditionally treated digital technologies as one of many – however important – inputs to an organization's strategy; and digital strategy is seen as a functional strategy for the IT department that supports the business strategy. However, more recently a radical change has occurred as the fundamental role of digital technologies in underpinning and enabling new strategy and business models is increasingly emphasized.

Adner, Puranam and Zhu (2019) argued the recent attention paid to the challenge of digital transformation signals an inflection point in the impact of digital technology on the competitive landscape. This transition can be understood as a shift from the *quantitative* advances that have historically characterized digital progress (e.g., Moore's law, Metcalf's law) to *qualitative* changes embodied in three core processes underlying modern digital transformation: representation, connectivity and aggregation, with profound implications for firms' strategy. In other words, from the strategic management perspective, the nature of digital transformation – and the strategic and organizational impact of digital technologies – is shifting from a change in *degree* to a change in *kind*.

Today, an increasing number of companies – both incumbents and digital native firms from different industries – are (re-)positioning themselves as (digital) technology-driven organizations, built on the rapidly growing digital capabilities to capture and analyse vast lakes of data from external and internal sources. Such growing capabilities have been deployed by different organizations to support new business models based on new ways of value creation and capture. In particular, as digital technologies become more pervasive, and companies move further up the maturity stages in their digital transformation journey, digital strategy and business strategy have increasingly meshed into one. This raises fundamental questions about the continued validity and effectiveness of the established strategy literature that has largely emerged during the industrial age – be it the industry-based view (Porter, 1980), the resource-based view (Barney, 1991; Teece, Pisano & Shuen, 1997), or the institution-based view (Peng, 2002); and it calls for the development of robust new tools and frameworks to help senior business leaders develop and implement new strategies and business models in the digital age (Li, 2022).

**Other Perspectives**

Many other studies have also investigated new approaches for developing digital strategies and executing digital transformation from different perspectives (e.g., Ross, Sebastian & Beath, 2017; Sebastian et al., 2017; Ross, Beath & Mocker, 2019; Saldanha, 2019; Siebel, 2019; Li, 2020). However, despite significant progress, an overarching framework that coherently integrates different perspectives and explains the *fundamental* reasons why every organization needs a digital strategy is still lacking. When asked, management scholars, organizational leaders, and business consultants alike invariably give varied, eclectic and often idiosyncratic answers. An overarching framework incorporating different perspectives and levels of analysis will improve consistency and provide a solid foundation for systematically developing, executing and evaluating digital strategy in the rapidly evolving digital economy.

## DOES IT REALLY MATTER?

The question is, therefore, not so much "does it matter" as "why it matters and how". Despite significant theoretical progress and practical development over the past 30 years, the fundamental reasons why a digital strategy is necessary for most organizations remain poorly articulated. From the contingency perspective, strategy must evolve in response to changes in the business environment, and a major focus of strategic decision-making is how best to ensure strong alignment, or fit, between an organization's strategy (and structure) and its environment (Sarta, Durand & Vergn, 2021). Since digital strategy for the information age represents a fundamental departure from the traditional business strategy for the industrial age, what fundamental changes have happened in the business environment that call for a radical change in the business strategy to become digitally driven?

A wide range of incremental and radical changes can be identified in the business environment, from the changing global geopolitical and economic order, the growing environmental challenges and unsustainable development, to social exclusion and the increasingly ageing population in a significant number of countries. However, two intertwined, irreversible changes have emerged and become firmly established (not just in developed countries but also in many developing countries), which fundamentally transform the global business environment. These two fundamental changes are calling for new digital strategies in all organizations.

**The Digital Technology Revolution**

Digital technologies have been developing rapidly and exponentially for well over half a century. This has been illustrated as the IT Revolution, ICTs Revolution, Digital (Technology) Revolution, or the Fourth Industrial Revolution (or Industry 4.0), amongst others. The revolution is not just about the rapid development of digital technologies per se, but also the infrastructure and services that made new digital capabilities based on such technologies increasingly affordable, accessible and ubiquitous to a growing proportion of organizations and individuals (workers and consumers). As Adner, Puranam and Zhu (2019) argued, the nature of the change has shifted from a change in *degree* to a change in *kind*.

The Digital Technology Revolution is based on the technological convergence between computing and telecommunications, which began to develop rapidly at large scale from the 1980s, enabling computing resources to be remotely accessible at low costs (Li, 1995). This growing capability enables organizations from different sectors to radically reorganize what is located where, and how people and activities are administered, relationships coordinated and controlled, and products and services produced, delivered and consumed, particularly in terms of who does what, with whom, where, when, how and how much (Li, 1995). Such new flexibility is increasingly incorporated into emerging strategies and business models for organizations, and more recently has become fundamental to the new strategies in nearly all organizations. The rapid development of AI and data analytics (including data mining and machine learning) is further expanding our digital capabilities from data capture, transmission and storage to complex data manipulation and analysis, generating new intelligence and supporting decision-making in ways that were inconceivable only a few years ago.

The Technological Revolution has evolved over multiple stages, and every time the development seemed to have stagnated, a plethora of new technologies, infrastructures and services emerged to further accelerate the development, expanding the digital capabilities for organizations and individuals. The current explosive growth in a range of emerging technologies, from mobile communications based on 5G, cloud and edge computing, big data analytics and machine learning, AI, and the IoT and its application across different sectors and domains, to augmented reality, virtual reality, 3D printing, blockchain and quantum computing, as well as advanced infrastructures and services to make such emerging technologies affordable and accessible to all, are further accelerating the technological developments. The Digital Technology Revolution is still continuing and accelerating, often exponentially.

**The Digital Economy**

The Digital Technology Revolution would not have been so significant if the nature of the economy had not changed in tandem. Different from the industrial economy, the information (intangible) content in all products and production processes represents a significant and steadily growing proportion of economic activities in all sectors (including primary and secondary industries); and information labour represents an increasingly larger proportion of the workforce, well over 50 percent since the 1980s in all Organisation for Economic Co-operation and Development (OECD) countries. "Information", and the associated data, knowledge, insight and intelligence, has become the most significant resource – and commodity – in the world (Hepworth, 1990; Li, 1995, 2007).

The concept of the digital economy has gained popularity in recent years. It is different from the information economy, as the digital economy focuses primarily on the part of the information economy that can be digitally captured, manipulated and represented. Since a significant amount of information is still locked up in people's heads, and a large proportion of information in our economic activities and everyday lives remains in non-digital form or still not digitally captured, it indicates that there is still significant scope for the further development of the digital economy. The rapid proliferation of the IoT and wearable technologies, smart homes, autonomous vehicles and Industry 4.0 systems are capturing and converting vast amounts of previously analogue information into digital forms. This will open up significant new opportunities for a new round of innovations in strategies and business models, as well as products, services and business processes.

Today, digital native organizations are competing simultaneously in multiple sectors and geographies, disrupting a host of industries via their rapidly expanding ecosystems, particularly via the platform strategy and business model (Ozalp, Cennamo & Gawer, 2018; Cennamo, 2019). Incumbents are using new digital capabilities to transform strategies and business models to address the existential threats posed by digital natives (Li, 2018, 2020). Despite the ubiquity and profound impact of digitization, however, industries are on average less than 40 percent digitized (Bughin, LaBerge & Mellbye, 2017). As digitization continues to gather pace and deepens across different sectors and domains, more pervasive and radical disruptions are inevitable. There will be big winners – and many losers.

**The Emerging Cyber-Physical Environment**

With the rapid development of digital infrastructure and digital economy since the 1990s, a new digital space has emerged which coexists, and often intertwines, with the physical space and place of our world. This has greatly increased the complexity and flexibility of the new space economy for organizations and individuals (Li, 1995; Li, Whalley & Williams, 2001). The rapid development of synthetic, virtual spaces and the metaverse, including spaces based on massively multiplayer online role-playing games (MMORPGs), VR and AR, is creating new virtual worlds that significantly extend our socio-economic environment (Papagiannidis, Bourlakis & Li, 2008; Bourlakis, Papagiannidis & Li, 2009). Organizations and individuals increasingly live in multiple spaces incorporating the physical, digital and virtual spaces, which are creating new business and social opportunities and challenges (Li, Papagiannidis & Bourlakis, 2010).

Furthermore, with the rapid proliferation of the IoT, the internet is increasingly transformed from a communication network between people to a control network directly embedded in the physical world, which is seen as even more consequential than the shift from the industrial to a digital information economy (DeNardis, 2020). Today the internet has become "a control system connecting vehicles, wearable devices, home appliances, drones, medical equipment, currency, and every conceivable industrial sector. Cyberspace now completely and often imperceptibly permeates offline spaces, blurring boundaries between material and virtual worlds" (DeNardis, 2020: p. 1). The renewed enthusiasm for the metaverse (perhaps symbolized by Facebook's name change to Meta in 2021) underpinned by AR/VR, blockchain, cryptocurrencies, decentralized finance, NFTs (non-fungible tokens) and the decentralized Web 3.0 environment more generally, is stimulating a new round of rapid expansion of the virtual spaces for organizations and individuals. These developments have significant implications for economic growth, business models, individual rights and governance – and the digital strategies for organizations.

## Platform Ecosystems

One of the most significant manifestations of the Digital Technology Revolution and the digital economy thus far is perhaps the rapid rise of digital platforms and their wider ecosystems. Platforms are firms "that facilitate transactions and govern interactions between two or more distinct user groups who are connected via an indirect network" (Rietveld & Schilling, 2020). Their wider ecosystems have been conceptualized as meta-organizations "with less formal and less hierarchical structures than firms, but more closely coupled than traditional markets" (Kretschmer et al., 2021). The emergence of platform ecosystems is redefining the rules of competition in a growing number of sectors and domains, and indeed, platforms have already become the dominant business models in a number of industries.

A plethora of digital platforms have emerged around the world using data-driven business models, disrupting a growing number of industries (Shi, Li & Chumnumpan, 2021). The power of platforms is reflected in the fact that seven of the world's top eight companies by market capitalization use platform-based business models. The emergence of digital platforms has been viewed as a paradigm shift in the way businesses are organized, as the traditional model of the integrated firm with its hierarchical supply chain is increasingly replaced by dynamic groups of largely independent partners working together to deliver integrated products and services (Kapoor, 2018; Shipilov & Gawer, 2020). These features raise complex strategic challenges and opportunities on how firms compete and collaborate with one another within a platform ecosystem, and how digital platforms disrupt incumbents and compete with other digital platforms (Jacobides, Cennamo & Gawer, 2018; Cusumano, Yoffie & Gawer, 2019; Li, 2022).

Different from traditional organizations, most digital platforms do not take ownership of products and production processes but rather depend primarily on resources and activities provided by independent firms in their ecosystems. Compared to traditional firms and non-digital intermediaries, digital platforms can introduce new transaction mechanisms more rapidly and at much lower cost, quickly provide access to capabilities that may be too expensive or time-consuming to build within a firm, scale much faster than an individual business, and enable both high variety and a high capacity to evolve (Kapoor, 2018; Zhao et al., 2020; Kretschmer et al., 2021; Li, 2022).

However, digital platforms are unevenly distributed around the world. Of the 70 largest digital platforms, 90 percent originated from the US and China (UNCTAD, 2019). Surprisingly, Europe's share is only 4 percent, and less than 1 percent originated from Africa and Latin America combined. The seven "super platforms" – Microsoft, Apple, Amazon, Google, Facebook, Tencent, and Alibaba – account for two-thirds of the total market value. The substantial lead held by the US and China in a range of promising emerging technologies (e.g., cloud, AI, the IoT and blockchain) will have significant implications for the future development of the digital economy (UNCTAD, 2019; Li, 2022). It will be interesting to see how the geography of the global platform economy evolves in the next phase of the digital economy.

**A New Framework: The Reasons Why Every Organization Needs a Digital Strategy**

The nature of our economy has changed from that of an industrial economy to an information economy in which data (information) has become the most crucial and valuable resource and commodity for all organizations. At the same time, digital technologies, infrastructure, and services continue to develop rapidly and exponentially, giving all organizations and individuals growing digital capabilities at affordable prices. The combination of these two intertwined developments has given rise to a new digital business environment that is fundamentally different from the business environment of the industrial economy, with its own "new rules of the game". The new rules of the digital economy require all organizations to develop and execute strategies by innovatively exploiting our growing digital capabilities.

The new business environment has given rise to the emergence of a series of digital platforms and ecosystems, which fundamentally redefine how firms compete within platform ecosystems, and how digital platforms disrupt incumbents and compete with other platforms in a growing number of industries. It is also facilitating the emergence of a complex, rapidly evolving cyber-physical environment for all organizations and individuals; and the rapid expansion of the metaverse and virtual spaces is adding an important new dimension to our space economy. Within such a radically different, and rapidly evolving, business environment, all organizations need to evaluate and re-invent the way their business is organized and conducted. In other words, all organizations need a new digitally driven strategy to guide their development and survival in the new business environment (Figure 22.1).

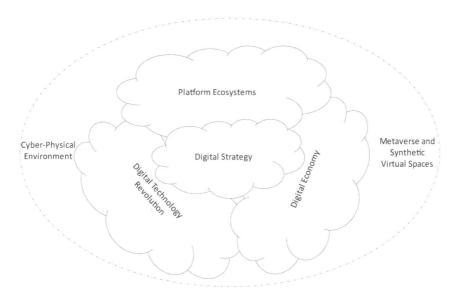

*Figure 22.1    The reasons why a digital strategy is necessary*

## MANAGING THE TRANSITION: THREE EMERGING APPROACHES

Ever since Marc Andreessen's opinion piece in the *Wall Street Journal*, "Why Software Is Eating The World", in 2011, numerous commentators have argued that every business is a tech business or digital business. By extension, every business strategy needs to be a digital strategy. Examples such as Kodak, Walmart, Amazon, and Alibaba are often used to illustrate the existential threat and fundamental changes facing all organizations.

Indeed, as the digital and the analogue worlds are increasingly meshing into one cyber-physical space (DeNardis, 2020), the digital infrastructure is transforming the way all organizations operate and compete (Iansiti & Lakhani, 2020). The focus today is not just about new technologies, deployed by new digital native companies, disrupting incumbents across different industries. The transformation is more fundamental, which redefines how every organization in the economy senses, creates, delivers and captures value, across all sectors, in both developed and developing countries (Zeng, 2018; Li, 2020).

As Iansiti and Lakhani (2020) argued, the failure of Kodak, for example, was not the result of increasing competition from its arch-rival Fuji or from new digital photography start-ups. Instead, the rapid proliferation of smartphones, together with the rise of a range of social media companies from Facebook to Instagram, created a set of value propositions for consumers that Kodak found impossible to compete with. Despite its various efforts, Kodak simply became collateral damage from the meteoric rise of social media companies.

Similarly, Amazon and Alibaba are often touted as the posterchildren that embody the way digital business transforms traditional industries. One consequence is that numerous retailers have failed to survive the relentless onslaught. Even the mighty Walmart, one of the most efficient and innovative retailers built on a data-rich supply chain, struggled to protect its core markets. Without radical transformation of its strategy to fully capitalize on current and emerging digital capabilities, Walmart will continue to struggle in the face of the onslaught from Amazon and a number of other e-commerce companies. Similar trends have been observed in China and Europe, as well as several other emerging economies (e.g., India, Brazil, and African, Middle Eastern, and ASEAN [Association of Southeast Asian Nations] countries).

Further, some disruptions from digital native firms may come from radical changes in consumer behaviours and new market creation nudged by digital firms. For example, Deliveroo, the food delivery platform for restaurants and takeaways, and Gopuff, the ultrafast grocery delivery company, are more than just local delivery service providers. Their business models are not only dependent on the network effect of the platform business model and data-driven operations, but also on nudging gradual changes in consumer behaviour so as to create new markets. Since the COVID-19 lockdown in March 2020, investors have ploughed billions of dollars into ultrafast on-demand grocery delivery services such as Instacart, Glovo, Getir, and Gopuff. Some of these apps use "dark stores" – little local warehouses designed to serve people within a small radius – to stock a few thousand popular items which can then be delivered via electric bike in as little as 10 minutes. This trend initially started in some large cities in China, but such ultrafast delivery services are now proliferating rapidly in cities from London and New York to Istanbul, and they could potentially revolutionize everyday shopping around the world. In the US, at least a dozen such start-ups – with names such as Buyk and 1520 – promise to deliver everything from a single pint of milk to a full grocery basket to your door in 15 minutes or less without extra fees. Different from grocery shopping based on the online supermarket business models, which are usually built around one large weekly shop, ultrafast delivery enables *on-demand* grocery shopping, which competes directly with corner shops and convenience stores. Developments such as these are increasingly making every business a digital business or data-driven business, and every business strategy a digital strategy. All organizations need to step back to evaluate and re-conceive the way their business is organized and conducted, from internal systems and supplier relations to consumer interactions.

However, my research shows that the leadership challenge is often not in coming up with more new ideas to develop new strategies and business models enabled by digital technologies (most senior business leaders I worked with have more new ideas than they could deploy), but rather in successfully managing the transition from where the organization is toward a desired future state in the rapidly evolving business environment. This can only be achieved by frequently evaluating and re-calibrating both the path and the destination for the organization in the rapidly evolving new business environment, informed by emerging intelligence from internal and external sources. This perhaps explains why digital strategies and digital transformation initiatives are notoriously difficult to get right (Reeves et al., 2018). My research with some leading global digital firms (e.g., Amazon, Alibaba, Baidu, Google, VMWare and Slack) has found that at least three new approaches are emerging, which enable them to effectively manage the transition while mitigating the huge risks involved (for more details please see Li, 2020 and 2022). It should be emphasized that the list is not exhaustive, and other new approaches are also being developed in these and other organizations.

**Innovating by Experimenting**

Despite the growing uncertainty in the business environment, the traditional annual or multiyear cycles of strategy making and execution have persisted in many organizations. There is nothing wrong with periodic strategic retreat by senior business leaders to take stock and envision the future, but traditional linear approaches of strategy making and execution are no longer fit for purpose. They are rooted in a level of certainty and predefined paths and outcomes for the organization that no longer exist. When the future is uncertain and the destination and path are frequently shifting, it is essential for business leaders to use emerging intelligence to inform, evaluate and update – and recalibrate – strategic plans on a regular or even continuous basis. This calls for an iterative, learning process where strategy is increasingly made, refined and recalibrated through execution.

One popular approach is innovating by experimenting, which enables businesses to try out many new ideas inexpensively (Li, 2018). Emerging intelligence from internal and external sources can be used to evaluate them. As a senior executive from Alibaba remarked: "If an idea works, then scale it up rapidly; if not, move on to other ideas and you have not lost much" (interview with author; see also Li, 2022). This approach gives business leaders the opportunities to test and learn, which has been proven far more effective than traditional linear approaches. The bottom line is that in today's unpredictable digital environment, it is no longer viable to develop a new strategy and then execute it over many years. Instead, strategy is increasingly defined as an overall direction, and the broad path and final destination are frequently re-evaluated and recalibrated through execution and informed by emerging intelligence.

Furthermore, innovating by experimenting is not just about being tolerant of failures, but more importantly, about developing the capacity for error recognition and correction, a point that has been repeatedly emphasized in companies from Alibaba to Amazon. This approach significantly increases the odds of delivering great results through new strategies and business models enabled by digital technologies.

**Radical Transformation through Incremental Approaches**

In many ways, the digital economy is fundamentally different from the industrial or the service economies. The rules (economics) of the game and the key players in the market are changing, so the mismatch between traditional business models and the digital future is often too great to bridge in many organizations. However, a radical transformation does not have to be planned and implemented in one big step. Rather, radical changes can be achieved through a series of incremental steps (Li, 2022).

For example, some leading businesses use an outcome-driven approach to ensure digital transformation initiatives are delivering the expected results at each stage. By breaking up large-scale, radical digital transformation into smaller, more manageable strategic investments, organizations are able to experiment with many new ideas based on rapid piloting and scaling (Li, 2019). This approach enables organizations to nurture and test an evolving portfolio of innovations and constantly move forward while avoiding the high risks of one big bet. Ineffective ideas can be killed off before they cause real, irreversible damage. Different from the "big bang" approach, this approach asks business leaders to decide whether the initial up-front investment is worth making in the light of potential returns, and if the balance changes, they can stop investing. In doing so, radical transformation is achieved through a series of incremental steps, while the high risks associated with radical transformation are effectively mitigated and managed.

**Dynamic Sustainable Advantages through an Evolving Portfolio of Temporary Advantages**

One of the main objectives of a digital strategy – indeed, any strategy – is to deliver sustainable competitive advantages (SCAs), but in the digital economy few competitive advantages are genuinely sustainable for a prolonged period. Most competitive advantages are temporary, or transient, in nature, and can be eroded rapidly or suddenly, often as a result of innovation or imitation by competitors (D'Aveni et al., 2010; Li, 2022). However, one key new feature of the digital economy is the network effect and the "winner-takes-all" market dynamic, where only one or two key players can eventually thrive and become dominant in each market niche. When sustainable advantages are rare and difficult to come by, successive temporary advantages can snowball with the dynamic of increasing return to scale and the network effect. It follows that instead of obsessing with the elusive SCAs, some senior business leaders are increasingly pursuing temporary advantages successively by experimenting with an evolving portfolio of incremental – and sometimes radical – innovations. The gains from each temporary advantage are often small or even trivial, but the cumulative effect can be significant over time, and any one such temporary advantage can become "the last straw" to tip the balance of competition. In so doing, SCAs are achieved dynamically through an evolving portfolio of temporary advantages, when successive new temporary advantages are introduced before the old ones are eroded by competitors. This is clearly reflected in the competition between American and Chinese digital firms in China – for example, Alibaba vs Amazon and Uber vs Didi Chuxing.

A further benefit of this approach is that instead of treating strategy as a predefined plan, it allows companies to treat strategy as a direction for action. It encourages business leaders to focus on short-term decisions and execution, but with the long-term strategy and destination in mind. It also enables business leaders to explore alternative routes frequently rather than presuming there is only one path or one best way. In some cases, it even allows business leaders to change destination as the market changes and as new intelligence emerges. In so doing, strategy and execution are intertwined, and emerging intelligence from execution and other sources is used to inform the evaluation and recalibration of the strategic direction. As Rosabeth Moss Kanter argued: "A strategy is never excellent in and of itself; it is shaped, enhanced, or limited by implementation. Top leaders can provide the framework and tools for a team, but the game is won on the playing field" (Kanter, 2017). The power of this approach cannot be over-emphasized in today's volatile business environment. The result is that (digital) strategy is increasingly made and recalibrated through execution.

## CONTRIBUTIONS AND FUTURE RESEARCH

This chapter discussed the evolving notion of digital strategy and the underpinning digital technologies, developed an overarching framework for the fundamental reasons why every organization needs a digital strategy, and explored the management implications for digital native firms and incumbents alike operating and competing in the digital age. The framework is based on two fundamental changes in the business environment: the changing nature of the economy and the continuous rapid development of digital technologies. These changes together redefine the "rules of the game" and enable the emergence of new platform ecosystems across industries, forcing all organizations to re-invent their business strategy by exploiting the rapidly expanding digital capabilities. As the digital and physical worlds are increasingly meshed into one, a new cyber-physical environment is emerging which has profound implications for how digital strategy is developed, executed and evaluated in the next phase of the digital economy. The rapid development of synthetic virtual worlds and the metaverse (based on VR/AR, blockchain, cryptocurrencies, and Web3.0 technologies) may add a significant new dimension to the new business environment. Effectively managing the transition to new technologies, new strategies and business models, and new organizational designs, has become a significant challenge for researchers, business leaders, consultants and policy makers. Three emerging approaches that have been successfully deployed in some of the most successful organizations in the world are discussed.

More systematic research is clearly needed to define key concepts, conceptualize emerging approaches and develop robust theoretical frameworks to facilitate understanding, guide practice and maximize impact. Three types of new research are particularly needed.

Firstly, qualitative research based on (longitudinal) case studies and ethnographic approaches is needed to identify and illustrate emerging international best practice in both developed and emerging economies. We need to explore the complex new relations between strategy and execution and conceptualize effective approaches to manage the transition to new strategies, new business models and new organizational designs. In particular, our research context needs to expand well beyond traditional centres of innovations in North America, Europe and Japan, as exciting new approaches are emerging in newly industrialized economies such as South Korea and Singapore, and in emerging economies such as China, India, the Middle East, the ASEAN economies, Brazil and Africa.

Secondly, through large-scale quantitative research, new studies are needed to identify, measure, validate and compare the complex relations between the key factors, triggers, drivers, processes, mechanisms and contexts for digital strategy and digital transformation. New insights from such studies can inform the development and validation of new theories and be used to guide practice and policy making.

Thirdly, the rapid pace of change calls for the development of new research methods, as our existing methods, perspectives and approaches are often too slow and too rigid and take too long to make sense of emerging phenomena and offer practical guidance in a robust and timely fashion. Technologies continue to develop extremely rapidly and exponentially, and when published studies in mainstream academic journals are often based on data that are 5–10 years old, the "new insights" are essentially derived from technologies and management thinking that are two or even three generations old. New research methods are urgently needed to identify, conceptualize and validate emerging phenomena as and when they emerge, long before they become quantitatively significant in the real world. In particular, emerging approaches that take advantage of new digital tools – such as topic modelling, sentiment analysis and bibliometric analysis – allow us to make sense of a vast quantity of structured and unstructured data in ways that were inconceivable in the past.

## REFERENCES

Adner, R., Puranam, P., & Zhu, F. (2019). What is different about digital strategy? From quantitative to qualitative change. *Strategy Science, 4*(4), 253–61.
Bakos, Y., & Treacy, M. (1986). Information technology and corporate strategy: A research perspective. *MIS Quarterly*, June, 107–19.
Barney, J. (1991). Firm resources and sustained competitive advantage. *Journal of Management, 17*(1), 99–120.
Bell, D. (1973). *The Coming of the Post-Industrial Society.* New York, NY: Basic Books.
Bharadwaj, A., El Sawy, O.A., Pavlou, P.A., & Venkatraman, N. (2013). Digital business strategy: Toward a next generation of insights. *MIS Quarterly, 37*(2), 471–82.
Bourlakis, M., Papagiannidis, S., & Li, F. (2009). Retail spatial evolution: Paving the way from traditional to metaverse retailing. *Electronic Commerce Research, 9*(1–2), 135–48.
Bughin, J., LaBerge, L., & Mellbye, A. (2017). The case for digital reinvention. *McKinsey Quarterly*, February 17. https://www.mckinsey.com/business-functions/mckinsey-digital/our-insights/the-case -for-digital-reinvention.
Butler, P., Hall, T.W., Hanna, A.M., Mendonca, L., Auguste, B., & Manyika, J. (1997). A revolution in interaction. *McKinsey Quarterly, 1997*(1), 4–23.
Cennamo, C. (2019). Competing in digital markets: A platform-based perspective. *Academy of Management Perspectives, 35*(2). doi.org/10.5465/amp.2016.0048.
Cennamo, C., Dagnino, G., Di Minin, R., & Lanzolla, G. (2020). Managing digital transformation: Scope of transformation and modalities of value co-generation and delivery. *California Management Review, 62*(4), 5–16.
Cusumano, M.A., Yoffie, D.B., & Gawer, A. (2019). *The Business of Platforms: Strategy in the Age of Digital Competition, Innovation, and Power.* New York, NY: HarperCollins.
D'Aveni, R.A., Dagnino, G.B., & Smith, K.G. (2010). The age of temporary advantage. *Strategic Management Journal, 31*, 1371–85.

Dawson, A., Hirt, M., & Scanlan, J. (2016). The economic essentials of digital strategy. *McKinsey Quarterly*. https://www.mckinsey.com/capabilities/strategy-and-corporate-finance/our-insights/the-economic-essentials-of-digital-strategy.

DeNardis, L. (2020). *The Internet in Everything: Freedom and Security in a World with No Off Switch*. New Haven, CT: Yale University Press.

Goldfarb, A., & Tucker, C. (2019). Digital economics. *Journal of Economic Literature*, *57*(1), 3–43.

Hagel, J., III, & Seely Brown, J. (2001). Your next IT strategy. *Harvard Business Review*. https://hbr.org/2001/10/your-next-it-strategy.

Harding, D.J. (2021). Who is leading digital transformation? Not CIOs, job ads suggest. *Tech Monitor*, May 3. https://techmonitor.ai/leadership/digital-transformation/who-leading-digital-transformation-not-cios-job-ads-suggest.

Hepworth, M. (1990). *Geography of the Information Economy*. London: Belhaven.

Iansiti, M., & Lakhani, K.R. (2020). *Competing in the Age of AI: Strategy and Leadership When Algorithms and Networks Run the World*. Boston, MA: Harvard Business School Publishing.

Jacobides, M., Cennamo, C., & Gawer, A (2018). Towards a theory of ecosystems. *Strategic Management Journal*, *39*(8), 2255–76.

Johnson, B.C., Manyika, J.M., & Yee, L.A. (2005). The next revolution in interaction. *McKinsey Quarterly*, *2005*(4), 21–2.

Kanter, R.M. (2017). Smart leaders focus on execution first and strategy second. *Harvard Business Review*, November.

Kapoor, R. (2018). Ecosystems: Broadening the locus of value creation. *Journal of Organization Design*, *7*(1), 12.

Kretschmer, T., Leiponen, A., Schilling, M., & Vasudeva, G. (2021). Platform ecosystems as meta-organizations: Implications for platform strategies. *Strategic Management Journal*, *43*(3), 405–24.

Lanzolla, G., Pesce, D., & Tucci, C. (2021). The digital transformation of search and recombination in the innovation function: Tensions and an integrative framework. *Journal of Product Innovation Management* (forthcoming).

Li, F. (1995). *The Geography of Business Information: Corporate Networks and the Spatial and Functional Corporate Restructuring*. Chichester: John Wiley & Son.

Li, F. (2007). *What is eBusiness? How the Internet Transforms Organizations*. Oxford: Blackwell.

Li, F. (2018). *Innovating in the Exponential Economy: Digital Disruption and Bridging the New Innovation-Execution Gap*. Palo Alto, CA: VMWare Technologies.

Li, F. (2019). Why have all Western internet firms (WIFs) failed in China? A phenomenon-based study. *Academy of Management Discoveries*, *5*(1), 13–37.

Li, F. (2020). Leading digital transformation: Three emerging approaches for managing the transition. *International Journal of Operations & Production Management*, *40*(6), 809–17.

Li, F. (2022). Sustainable competitive advantages via temporary advantages: Insights from the competition between American and Chinese digital platforms in China. *British Journal of Management*, 33(4), 2009–32.

Li, F., Papagiannidis, S., & Boulakis, M. (2010). Living in 'multiple spaces': Extending our socio-economic environment through virtual worlds. *Environment and Planning D: Society and Space*, *28*(3), 425–46.

Li, F., Whalley, J., & Williams, H. (2001). Between the electronic and physical spaces: Implications for organizations in the networked economy. *Environment and Planning A*, *33*, 699–716.

Lyytinen, K. (2021). Innovation logics in the digital era: A systemic review of the emerging digital innovation regime. *Organization & Management*, Special Issue on Digital Innovation (forthcoming).

Machlup, F. (1962). *The Production and Distribution of Knowledge in the United States*. Princeton, NJ: Princeton University Press.

OECD (1986). *Trends in the Information Economy*. Paris: OECD.

Ozalp, H., Cennamo, C., & Gawer, A. (2018). Disruption in platform-based ecosystems. *Journal of Management Studies*, 55, 1203–41.

Papagiannidis, S., Bourlakis, M., & Li, F. (2008). Making real money in virtual worlds: MMORPGs and emerging business opportunities, challenges and ethical implications in metaverses. *Technological Forecasting and Social Change*, *75*(5), 610–22.

Peng, M.W. (2002). Towards an institution-based view of business strategy. *Asia Pacific Journal of Management*, *19*, 251–67.

Porat, M.U. (1977). *The Information Economy: Definition and Measurement*. Washington, DC: US Department of Commerce. OCLC 5184933.

Porter, M.E. (1980). *Competitive Strategy: Techniques for Analyzing Industries and Competitors*. New York, NY: Free Press.

Reeves, M., Fæste, L., Hassan, F., Parikh, H., & Whitaker, K. (2018). Preemptive transformation: Fix it before it breaks. BCG. https://www.bcg.com/publications/2018/preemptive-transformation-fix-it -before-it-breaks.

Rietveld, J., & Schilling, M. (2020). Platform competition: A systematic and interdisciplinary review of the literature. *Journal of Management*. doi:10.1177/0149206320969791.

Rockart, J.F., & Scott Morton, M.S. (1984). Implications of changes in information technology for corporate strategy. *Interfaces*, *14*(1), 84–95. doi:10.1287/inte.14.1.84.

Ross, J.W., Beath, C.M., & Mocker, M. (2019). *Designed for Digital: How to Architect Your Business for Sustained Success*. Cambridge, MA: MIT Press.

Ross, J.W., Sebastian, I.M., & Beath, C.M. (2017). How to develop a great digital strategy. *MIT Sloan Management Review*, *58*(2), 7–9. http://mitsmr.com/2fAqNTk

Saldanha, T. (2019). *Why Digital Transformations Fail: The Surprising Disciplines of How to Take off and Stay Ahead*. Oakland, NJ: Berrett-Koehler.

Sarta, A., Durand, R., & Vergn, J.P. (2021). Organizational adaptation. *Journal of Management*, *47*(1). https://doi.org/10.1177/0149206320929088.

Sebastian, I.M., Ross, J.W., Beath, C., Mocker, M., Moloney, K., & Fonstad, N. (2017). How big old companies navigate digital transformation. *MIS Quarterly Executive*, *16*(3), 197–213.

Shi, X., Li, F., & Chumnumpan, P. (2021). Platform development: Emerging insights from a nascent industry. *Journal of Management*, *47*(8), 2037–73.

Shipilov, A., & Gawer, A. (2020). Integrating research on inter-organizational networks and ecosystems. *Academy of Management Annals*, *14*, 92–121.

Siebel, T.M. (2019). *Digital Transformation: Survive and Thrive in an Era of Mass Extinction*. New York, NY: Rosetta Books.

Teece, D.J., Pisano, G., & Shuen, A. (1997). Dynamic capabilities and strategic management. *Strategic Management Journal*, *18*(7), 509–33.

UNCTAD (2019). *The Digital Economy Report 2019*. New York, NY: United Nations Publications.

Westerman, G. (2017). Your company doesn't need a digital strategy. *MIT Sloan Management Review*. http://mitsmr.com/2Gk4a0h.

Yoo, Y., Henfridsson, O., & Lyytinen, K. (2010). The new organizing logic of digital innovation: An agenda for information systems research. *Information Systems Research*, *21*(4), 724–35.

Zeng, M. (2018). *Smart Business: What Alibaba's Success Reveals about the Future of Strategy*. Boston, MA: Harvard Business Review Press.

Zhao, Y., Von Delft, S., Morgan-Thomas, A., & Buck, T. (2020). The evolution of platform business models: Exploring competitive battles in the world of platforms. *Long Range Planning*, *53*(4), 101892.

# Index

academic literature on freemium strategies 128–33, 136
accessibility/transferability, digitization 87
activity system design of business models 334–6
adapter strategy 70–72, 75
adaptive ecosystem 163–6
    *vs.* centralized ecosystem 167, 170–71
    *see also* centralized ecosystem; decentralized ecosystem
Adner, R. 3, 66, 152, 398, 400
advance analytics (AA) *see* big data analytics
Aggarwal, V.A. 62
agility 43, 45–6
Agrawal, A. 324
Aguilera, R. 321
AI *see* artificial intelligence (AI)
Airbnb 24, 26–7, 73, 174, 185–8
Alaimo, C. 274
Alemdar, H. 87
algorithms 256–7, 311–12
Alibaba 404
alliances 161
Amazon 29, 30, 33, 64, 162, 163, 167, 204, 404
Amazon Prime 29, 32
American economy 398
America Online (AOL) 105–6, 109, 126
Amit, R. 63, 77
analysis technologies 363
Animesh, A. 133
anti-competitive practices 300
AOL *see* America Online (AOL)
API *see* Application Program Interfaces (API)
Appel, G. 129
Apple 60–61, 162, 163, 167, 361–2
    App Store 224–5, 227
        governance 228–34
        monetization rules 229–32
        review process 228–9, 232
        social movements against 224–5, 228–34
    iOS 232
Application Program Interfaces (API) 160, 186–7
AR *see* augmented reality (AR)
Aral, S. 134
architect strategy 66–8, 75
Arnosti, N. 188
artificial intelligence (AI) 314, 324, 325
    applications for decision problems 327
    deliberation 328, 331, 333

design 327–8, 330–31
determination 327–30
discovery 328, 331–2
augmented rationality 326–8, 333, 334, 336
automated rationality 327, 328, 333, 335, 336
cognitive synergy 329
contextual factors and boundary conditions 337–8
digital strategies 336–9
future research 338–9
for humans' production/service delivery performance 335
impact on organizational business models 332–6
optimization of production/service processes 335
in R&D processes 334
ArtistShare 63
Aspara, J. 103
audience measurement 247
augmented rationality 326–8, 333, 334, 336
augmented reality (AR) 89
automated analytics 344, 346
automated machine learning (AutoML) 330
automated monitoring systems 311
automated rationality 327, 328, 333, 335, 336
automation 310–11
AutoML *see* automated machine learning (AutoML)
Au, Y.A. 132

BA *see* business analytics (BA)
Baden-Fuller, C. 103
Bailey, D.E. 88
balance of compliance and legitimacy 310, 316
Balis, J. 90
Bapna, R. 132
Basecamp 232
BASF 65
Baskerville, R.L., ontological reversal 88–9
Baum, J.R. 121
behavioral engagement of user 212–13, 215–17, 220
Benbasat, I. 132
Bezos napkin 194, 199, 201, 204
Bharadwaj, A. 396
big bang approach 406
big data 202, 203, 325, 335, 337–9, 342–3, 363